International Economics

International Economics
THE THEORY OF POLICY

GERALD M. MEIER

New York Oxford
OXFORD UNIVERSITY PRESS
1980

Library of Congress Cataloging in Publication Data

Meier, Gerald M
    International economics.

    Bibliography: p.
    Includes index.
    1.   International economic relations.
    2.   Economic development.   I.   Title
    HF1411.M439   382.1   79-18710
    ISBN 0-19-502757-4

Printed in the United States of America

The author gratefully acknowledges permission to reprint selections from the following:

Development Planning by Jan Tinbergen. Copyright ©, 1967, by Jan Tinbergen. Used
    with permission of McGraw-Hill Book Company
Protective Tariffs by Frank Graham (1934). Princeton University Press
Trade and Welfare by J. E. Meade (1955), by permission of Oxford University Press
Essays in the Theory of Unemployment by Joan Robinson (1947), by permission of Basil
    Blackwell Publisher
"The Diffusion of Development" by W. Arthur Lewis, in T. Wilson and A. S. Skinner,
    eds., *The Market and the State*, by permission of Oxford University Press
Norman S. Buchanan and Howard S. Ellis, *Approaches to Economic Development*. Copy-
    right © 1955 by the Twentieth Century Fund, Inc. Reprinted by permission

To

A. L.

G. H.

H. M.

J. R. H.

a teacher's teachers

Preface

As economics books go, this one does not even look difficult. It is not intended to be. I simply want to set forth as directly and succinctly as possible some central normative principles of international economics.

Economists have long debated the issues of trade policy, balance of payments policy, and development policy — the three parts of this text. But in our time, economic models have become ever more complex, and technique is frequently practiced for its own sake. Students naturally become dismayed when they cannot discover the basic relationships because they are covered over by elaborate filigree. Unfortunately, students also often become too enmeshed in the curiosa and arcania of "high theory" to comprehend the wider questions that must absorb economists when they move from being model builders to policy-makers. I have tried therefore to write in a large way about the fundamental normative principles that underlie commercial policy, international payments policy, and international development policy. I hope that this return to the first principles of international economic policy will have more meaning for students than yet another book on theoretical refinements, or one that is empirical, institutional, or descriptive.

During the period of classical political economy in the eighteenth and nineteenth centuries, the English classical economists "shared a common interest in economic reform, which manifested itself, not so much in common support of specific measures though there was much of that — as in a commonly held belief that the application of certain methods of approach and analysis, the recently discovered science of Political Economy, offered superior hopes for what they would have called improvement" (Lionel Robbins, *The Theory of Economic Policy in English Classical Political Economy,* 1952, p. 4). Today we must again become absorbed with these profound questions of "improvement." But we must now do so using modern analysis that is more rigorous, and yet not so technically complex that it has only a tenuous, if any, connection with our ultimate objective — the pursuit of more effective policies for social betterment.

Ever since Adam Smith's criticism of Mercantilism, successive generations have argued the merits of free trade versus protection. In Part I, therefore, the case for free trade, the conditions of optimal governmental interventions, and the different effects of various trade policies are appraised.

During the past half-century, problems of maintaining simultaneously domestic economic stability and balance in international payments have become ever more perplexing. Keynesian analysis has been extended to the open economy; monetary and fiscal policies have been related to the balance of payments; the search for international monetary order is still with us. These problems of international monetary economics are analyzed in Part II.

During the past three decades, there has been a concerted effort to accelerate the development of poor countries. The future of these countries depends in large part on the course of their trade and access to external resources. In Part III, the problems of national development are interpreted in an international context.

Our discussion will be mainly verbal: mathematics is absent, and the diagrams have been kept to a bare minimum. The more extensive geometrical expositions are reserved for optional Appendices that can be omitted with no loss of the central argument.

If I slight the mathematics and the geometry, I give more attention than is usual to the history of thought. Economics does not advance in the same way as do the natural sciences; the insights of an earlier-day economist might still be valuable. And, after all, international trade is the oldest branch of economics as a disciplined subject. The history of economic thought is too rich to be neglected. I have therefore tried to relate some thought of the past to policy dilemmas that did not appear just today. If these problems have continued to be perplexing for so long a time, they must surely be "real" problems worthy also of this generation's concern.

I have benefited from all the authors of international textbooks who have preceded me. Special thanks are due W.M. Corden, John Cuddington, James S. Hanson, Robert Stern and T.N. Srinivasan for their criticisms and perceptive suggestions on parts of the manuscript. Pamela Adler has steadily, but cheerfully transformed a mass of handwritten scrawls into a proper typescript. Paul Brophy kindly provided general research assistance. Above all, I am indebted to several generations of students who have helped me distill the essentials of this subject and have inspired whatever merit this book might have.

Pedagogical Note: This book is for a one-semester or a one-quarter undergraduate course in international economics in which policy-oriented theory is emphasized. Only an introductory economics course is a prerequisite. But even without such a course, a student could easily remove any initial deficiency by some elementary background reading as needed.

For students who wish supplementary readings, an annotated list is provided at the end of each chapter. These offer more detailed exposition, analysis of select topics, or more advanced theoretical treatment.

Empirical studies or policy materials can also readily supplement this book. To aid in this, I have prepared a trilogy on policy problems in international political economy that could be parallel reading with this text: *Problems of Trade Policy, Problems of a World Monetary Order*, and *Problems of Cooperation for Development*.

G. M. M.

Stanford
April 1979

Contents

III THEORY OF INTERNATIONAL DEVELOPMENT POLICY

International Economics

Prologue: Toward an International Public Order

Now, more than ever, we need to try to understand what international economic policy is all about. The consequences of a greater degree of "internationalization" are upon us. But there is no authoritative international normative process to bring order to international economic affairs. The result is that each nation practices suboptimal policies, and nations compete among themselves in policy-making. We shall therefore try to clarify the principles of international economic action, in the hope that the quality of public decisions in the international economy might be improved both in the choice of objectives and the use of policy instruments.

"Internationalization" of the Economic System

It is fashionable to characterize our age in terms of interdependence. This is not a new phenomenon: for centuries the world economy has become ever more integrated. In the past quarter-century, however, the pace of integration has accelerated. And the implications of interdependence have become more pronounced, as measured by the duration of international economic conflicts, the extent of the economic gains and losses to the parties affected, and the inadequacy of policy instruments to resolve the conflicts.

An outstanding feature of the internationalization of the economic system has been the **increase in the flows** of commodities, factors of production, management, technology, and financial capital across national borders. Not only have the movements of these goods, services, and factors increased, but they have also become more responsive, or more **elastic**, to differences between domestic and foreign variables. The **stocks** of factors of foreign origin are now also much larger within a country. We refer to these three phenomena—flows, elasticity, and stocks—as the "**internationalization of markets.**"[1]

This internationalization process is reflected in statistics that indicate that during the last two decades, while world output has been growing about 4% per year, world trade has been growing about 8% and production by foreign subsidiaries has been growing by some 10%. Export and import shares of output have increased considerably in practically all industrial sectors. A growing percentage of world trade is becoming intra-industry trade (reflecting economies of scale and increased demand for differentiated products) and even intra-firm trade by transnational firms (reflecting decomposition of production activities around the world).

Another side of the internationalization process has been the internationalization of **institutions.** Beyond the nation state, a number of intergovernmental institutions have arisen—ranging from international organizations, such as the General Agreement on Tariffs and Trade (GATT), the World Bank, the International Monetary Fund (IMF), and the United Nations Conference on Trade and Development (UNCTAD), to regional groups, such as the European Economic Community (EEC), Latin American Free Trade Area (LAFTA), the Andean Group, Association of Southeast Asian Nations (ASEAN), or the Organization for Economic Cooperation and Development (OECD). Interest groups, such as labor unions, employer associations, and foundations, have also expanded across national borders. Above all, the population of multinational corporations has increased remarkably, and many more large firms operate an expanding number of foreign subsidiaries in a number of countries.

As a result of the internationalization of the economic system, we must incorporate other units of analysis than the nation state (or a variety of "actors," as the political scientist would say). We must also consider policy issues that are not delimited by national territorial boundaries. Important decision-making units are not only national governments, but also international organizations, regional organizations, transnational interest groups, and multinational corporations. These

---

[1]This process is elaborated by Assar Lindbeck in "The Changing Role of the National State," *Kyklos,* 28 (1975), 23–46.

nonterritorial participants in the transnational economy shape decisions and events that transcend national frontiers.

Each unit has a different decision domain, characterized by different objectives, responsibilities, constituencies, time concern, and power. And yet, they all interact within a transnational economy that is essentially decentralized. The operational domain of transnational economic transactions extends beyond the jurisdictional domain of independent nations. Each decision-making unit is actually part of a larger decision process. But there is no central decision unit in the system. The relationships and interactions among different decision-making units therefore demand more analysis and evaluation.

International Economic Conflicts

To an economist, the internationalization of markets has the virtue of promoting efficiency, specialization, and competition. To the national policy-maker, however, internationalization has a negative side, heightening the sensitivity and increasing the vulnerability of the nation to external events and developments. International economics confronts national politics. If the objectives of two or more actors in the transnational economy become incompatible, international economic tensions and conflicts result. This is especially likely when there are changes in world production, and the distribution of the world product alters over time, with resultant benefits and detriments to different nations and to various groups within each nation.

The conflicts can be grouped into three general categories: (i) those that arise because a nation **seeks to acquire a larger share of the gains** from trade or foreign investment; (ii) those that arise when a country **tries to avoid being damaged or injured** by developments in another country; and (iii) those that arise because a country wants to **maintain its domestic autonomy in policy-making** when confronted with an international event.

More specifically, the major conflicts tend to be over the following issues:

i. **Markets:** The attempt of each nation to have greater access for its exports in the markets of other countries and to have ready access to imports of needed resources from the markets of other countries.
ii. **Terms of trade:** The attempt of each country to improve its terms of trade by raising export prices relative to import prices.

iii. **Terms of foreign investment:** The attempt by host governments to raise the benefit-cost ratio of foreign capital inflows.

iv. **Externalities:** The attempt to avoid the impact of detrimental spillovers or to capture more of the external benefits of a production activity.

v. **Adjustment costs to imports:** The attempt of each nation to minimize the "market disruption" or the "domestic injury" caused by greater imports.

vi. **Costs of balance of payments adjustment:** The attempt of each nation to minimize the cost of adjusting to a disequilibrium in its balance of payments by avoiding remedial policies or by trying to place some of the burden of adjustment on other countries.

vii. **Stabilization policies:** The attempt of each nation to exercise national economic autonomy in stabilizing its own economy, without subjecting its policies to external conditions.

Recognizing the stresses that are inherent in the internationalization process, we must ask by what means are the conflicts resolved or at least mitigated? There is no well-defined international normative process to keep pace with other features of the internationalization process. We therefore must search for a normative order that will accommodate conflicts, make "better" choices, and control change. Is it possible to establish more effective management of the internationalization process, so that there will be an economic order with less discord? Can nations improve the quality of their own policy-making, without injuring other nations? What rules, norms, or standards can be invoked to control the behavior of nations in the transnational economy?

The driving technological, economic, and political forces behind the internationalization process will not wane, but as internationalization proceeds, we shall have to seek policy solutions for future conflicts. The challenge is to improve these policy solutions. This is difficult because the outlines of decision-making processes in the world community remain vague, supranational institutions are few, and their power to pursue international public policy-making is limited. The internationalization of institutions has not kept pace with the internationalization of markets. International economics, in the sense of the internationalization of markets, will continue to be opposed by national politics, since governments desire to retain autonomy over economic policies. Nations will only too readily tend to compete among themselves in policy-making, which coordination of

Nobel Laureate JAN TINBERGEN, *Development Planning* (1967), 189–190

We are becoming increasingly conscious of the fact that the well-being of each separate country does not depend simply on the government of that country alone, but to a great extent on what happens in other countries. We also know that there are often conflicts of interest between different countries. If our aim is to promote the well-being of every nation as much as possible, then we must ask ourselves how we can best organise economic and social policy for the world as a whole. Even though it is not yet possible to establish a world government, we must force ourselves to be guided by the question, what would a world government do, if we are to see what the best policy is. We must make the interests of the world as a whole the basis of our own policy.

This immediately confronts us with the question as to which affairs can be left to the national authorities or to various other authorities at a lower level, and which affairs must be dealt with at a higher than national level. It has long been recognised that the supranational level is the only possible level for a number of means of economic policy. Yet, even though we have in certain cases accepted a higher authority than that of the national governments, we have certainly not yet reached the point where the two authorities are perfectly balanced. On the contrary, the world is still groaning under far too heavy a weight of traditional and emotional nationalism, which again and again plunges entire communities into disaster.

national policies remains an ideal. Nonetheless, if progress is to be made, it will necessarily depend first on understanding the basic principles of international economic policy.

The Three Problem Areas

To analyze and evaluate international economic conduct, we shall find it useful to have a conceptual framework within which we might systematize what would otherwise appear as an incomprehensibly wide array of diverse topics. Fortunately, the current concerns of the subject, as well as its intellectual history, can be considered under three major problem areas that have long been—and give promise of continuing to be—of central importance in the study of international economic relations. We can subject each of these three problem areas, in turn, to three levels of analysis.

Although international economic relations are wide-ranging, most of the important policy issues fall into place within three major problem areas: (i) **trade and welfare**, (ii) **trade and stability**, and (iii) **trade and development**. Each of these problem areas lends itself to three types of analysis: (i) **theoretical**, (ii) **empirical**, and (iii) **normative**.

The problems of international resource allocation, the determinants of the pattern of world trade, the gains from trade, the relative merits of free trade and protection—all these problems relate to trade and welfare. The central issue is economic efficiency in the international economy, and this becomes, in large part, an application of international welfare economics.

The body of theory corresponding to this first problem area is that of classical and neoclassical trade theory. It begins with Adam Smith's refutation of mercantilist regulations (1776), proceeds to David Ricardo's celebrated exposition of the doctrine of comparative advantage (1817), and continues through John Stuart Mill, Alfred Marshall, and more modern economists, such as Jacob Viner and Gottfried Haberler.

This theory is labeled "pure" in the sense of being the non-monetary theory of international trade in equilibrium. In determining relative prices and real incomes in international trade, it concentrates on the "real" non-monetary forces of trade, such as factor supply, productivity, and technology, and establishes whether an equilibrium solution exists. In recent years, this theory has been extended and refined through the infusion of the more systematic elements of the "new welfare economics."

Some of the more prominent manifestations of this trade and welfare problem appear in the operation of the General Agreement on Tariffs and Trade (GATT), the European Economic Community (EEC), the United States' Trade Acts, and the proliferation of non-tariff distortions of trade. Policy problems in this area have become more complex as an earlier generation's concern with "freer trade" has had to accommodate to recent demands for 'fairer trade" and "orderly trade."

The second problem area—trade and stability—involves the interrelationships between international trade and national income. What are the relationships between internal balance and external balance? What are the causes of balance of payments disequilibrium? How may the disequilibrium be corrected? This branch of trade theory is usually termed the "monetary theory" of trade. It is now in an active state of revision and extension to incorporate problems of unemployment and inflation not previously experienced. Economists have also had to rethink many of their preconceptions in this area as a result of the recent phenomenon of "managed floating" in the international monetary system.

In the interwar period (1918–1939), international currency order aroused widespread concern as the relative international economic harmony of the pre-1914 era disappeared with the sufferance of mass unemployment, abandonment of the gold bullion standard, spread of tariffs, quantitative restrictions, exchange controls, and competitive currency devaluations. Since World War II, this problem area has appeared most prominently in the context of the operations of the IMF, the series of international monetary crises in the 1960s, and the efforts at international monetary reform since 1971. Policy issues in this area have also become increasingly complex as nations strive to achieve both internal and external balance.

The third problem area—trade and development—poses many vital policy issues. The debate over the connections between foreign trade and the economic development of poor nations has become increasingly lively. Unlike the other two problem areas, a distinct and substantial body of theory has not yet emerged to make analysis of this problem area feasible. From post-Keynesian growth models, however, a number of theoretical insights may be gained—even though we still await the dynamic theory of trade needed to analyze this problem.

Particular examples of the problems of trade and development are to be seen in national development plans of poor countries, foreign aid programs, policies with respect to transnational enterprises, the operation of the World Bank, and the demands of the United Nations and UNCTAD for a "New International Economic Order."

The Three Levels of Analysis

As with economic problems generally, the particular problems of international economics can be analyzed at three different levels.

The first is **theoretical**. At this level, statements are made of the "if . . . then" kind: "If conditions x and y exist, then the result is z." These are logically necessary statements of what might be. The behavior is **hypothetical**. In theoretical analysis there is some abstraction from all the elements of the problem, logical concepts are used, and the reasoning is deductive. This type of analysis culminates in a theory, a schema, or a model—the purpose of which is to have explanatory value by allowing the analyst to draw correct inferences. This explanatory value is relevant for predicting future results or "retrodicting" the past.

The second level of analysis is **empirical**. Here statements are of the "is" kind. Instead of being concerned with hypothetical behavior, the economist focuses on **actual** behavior, and the statements are descriptive about behavioral relations and institutional arrangements. The analysis is directed toward a given state of affairs or involves measurement of the outcomes of particular changes in the economy.

The third level is **normative**. Here the statements are about what "ought" to be or should not be. The language is evaluative and prescriptive. The concern is with **optimal** behavior, in contrast with actual behavior or hypothetical behavior. This is the level of analysis at which alternative objectives are evaluated, and policy strategies and procedures designated to attain specified goals.

Toward Normative Principles

Although we have distinguished three levels of analysis, it would be a false issue to confront theory *versus* practice or theory *versus* policy. These are not dichotomies, but they are interrelated. Theory, practice, and policy all contribute to each other. We need theory to understand what **is**, and to go on to what **ought** to be. This is understandable because the theory of international economics has mainly developed from an inquiry into actual problems and policies. The best of theory is not merely internally consistent, it is also externally relevant. Long ago, the theory of comparative advantage was promulgated out of Ricardo's desire to repeal the Corn Laws (Britain's duties on grain imports). The modern theory of balance of payments adjustment and the relationships between international trade and economic stability essentially were also developed from the Keynesian concern with the Great Depression of the 1930s. Study of the relationships between international trade and development has been stimulated by the practical challenges of the poverty of nations and the policy objectives of accelerating the development of less developed countries. Economics has always been devoted to the possibility of social betterment. It is therefore not surprising to find new theory being offered in response to current economic problems and policy issues. An initial study of what-might-be is undertaken in order to have eventually a fuller appreciation and deeper understanding of applied problems and policy issues.

Nobel Laureate MILTON FRIEDMAN, "Nobel Lecture: Inflation and Unemployment," *Journal of Political Economy*, 85 (June 1977), 453

In order to recommend a course of action to achieve an objective, we must first know whether that course of action will in fact promote the objective. Positive scientific knowledge that enables us to predict the consequences of a possible course of action is clearly a prerequisite for the normative judgment whether that course of action is desirable. The Road to Hell is paved with good intentions, precisely because of the neglect of this rather obvious point.

Beyond the choice of problems to be analyzed, theory has other policy implications. The **purpose** of policy-making is to reduce the divergence between a preferred situation and the actual situation. But before remedial policy can be initiated, theory is first necessary to determine what the actual situation is. The "facts" do not speak for themselves; one has to integrate them logically. We must be able to ask questions of the facts, give meaning to the facts, and avoid the superficiality of measurement without theory. Although theory is most usefully viewed as the handmaiden of applied economics, a competent applied economist needs sound grounding in theory. And without the capacity to apply economic analysis, it is impossible to make the first necessary step toward policy prescription.

After diagnosing the actual situation, the economist, as a policy advisor, must go on to elucidate for the "decision-maker" the alternative courses of action available to remedy the actual situation and approach the preferred situation. The presentation of a theory can be compared to the construction of a map.[2] Even if we were to deny the economist the right to select a destination, leaving goal determination to only the "political" policy-maker, nonetheless the economist is still needed to "read" the map' and draw inferences that would otherwise not be apparent to the policy-maker.

First, the economist can help the policy-maker avoid inconsistent destinations, i.e., a clash of objectives, by pointing out a possible conflict. For example, the economist might indicate the inconsistency between domestic farm price supports and the maintenance of free trade

[2] For a full elaboration of the analogy between theories and maps, see Stephen Toulmin, *The Philosophy of Science* (1953), Chap. IV.

in agricultural products. Or the economist might demonstrate that a policy of import substitution constitutes an implicit tax on exports and that the sought-after improvement in the balance of payments through import substitution is offset by losses on the side of export revenue.

The economist can also reveal alternative routes to a destination, i.e., alternative policy instruments to achieve the target objective. For example, a balance of payments deficit might be reduced through a policy of deflation or devaluation or direct controls on imports. Unknown routes might also be disclosed. For instance, it may be shown that devaluation is identical to an *ad valorem* subsidy on all exports and an *ad valorem* tax on all imports.

Finally, shortcuts can be indicated, i.e., the best feasible routes might be determined. As we shall discuss later, the ideal method of solving a problem—"the first best optimum"—may not be attainable in a situation. Policy then may have to be directed toward a "second-best" solution. But the policy-maker may want to be **sure of at least achieving the second-best solution and not the third, fourth, or "nth best."** In this regard, theory can aid in ranking a **hierarchy of policies.** For instance, if it is desired to shelter a domestic industry from foreign competition, the theory of trade policy might demonstrate that a subsidy is preferable to a tariff and that a tariff, in turn, is preferable to a quota on imports.

More directly, the theory of trade policy itself or theory of balance of payments policy or theory of development policy can indicate what will happen in the economy if no change is made, or what can be made to happen by policy measures that control certain strategic variables. The **theory of policy**—with which we shall be mainly concerned—states that "if conditions a and b exist, then policy measure x will result in y and z." It is obviously useful to be able to elucidate the consequences of alternative policy decisions and to indicate, in the sense of a conditional prediction, what will be the benefits and costs of alternative policy measures before the policy is taken instead of having to await the actual results on a trial and error basis.

For these reasons, theory is indispensable for policy.

I

Theory of Trade Policy

1

International Specialization

No economic policy issue has an older intellectual history of disputation than free trade versus protection. Underlying the debate is the long evolution of the "pure" or non-monetary theory of trade. This has been concerned with three central questions:

i. **What commodities will a country export and import under free trade?**
ii. **What determines the terms of trade** (ratio of export prices to import prices)?
iii. **What are the gains from trade?**

The third question is clearly policy-relevant, but so are the other two. All three questions are interrelated, and their answers quickly slide over from positive theory to normative theory—from explaining what would be the pattern of trade under free trade to prescribing a free trade regime as "optimal" because it maximizes the "gains from trade." The normative conclusions, however, have not gone unchallenged, and we shall later consider whether, under certain conditions, some form of policy intervention might not be superior to free trade.

We begin this chapter with the first question and consider the determinants of the composition and direction of trade under free trade. We shall then investigate the various sources of trade: absolute advantage, comparative advantage based on comparative labor productivity, comparative advantage based on differential endowments of productive factors, and other sources of comparative advantage that are related to technological differences, economies of scale, and other dynamic phenomena.

THOMAS MUN, *England's Treasure by Forraign Trade* (1664), (Basil Blackwell, 1949), 5

Although a Kingdom may be enriched by gifts received, or by purchase taken from some other Nations, yet these are things uncertain and of small consideration when they happen. The ordinary means therefore to encrease our wealth and treasure is by *Forraign Trade,* wherein wee must ever observe this rule; to sell more to strangers yearly than wee consume of theirs in value. For suppose that when this Kingdom is plentifully served with the Cloth, Lead, Tinn, Iron, Fish and other native commodities, we doe yearly export the overplus to forraign Countries to the value of twenty two hundred thousand pounds; by which means we are enabled beyond the Seas to buy and bring in forraign wares for our use and Consumptions, to the value of twenty hundred thousand pounds; By this order duly kept in our trading, we may rest assured that the Kingdom shall be enriched yearly two hundred thousand pounds, which must be brought to us in so much Treasure; because that part of our stock which is not returned to us in wares must necessarily be brought home in treasure.

Absolute Advantage

Adam Smith examined the sources of trade when he condemned the "Mercantile System" for inhibiting economic growth by misallocating resources and being in conflict with "the obvious and simple system of natural liberty," which was Smith's ideal. Attacking "the mean and malignant expedients of the mercantile system" that controlled imports and exports (through import prohibitions, duties, bounties on exports, and monopolistic trading companies), Smith argued that "Britain should by all means be made a free port . . . that there should be no interruptions of any kind to free trade . . . and that free commerce and liberty of exchange should be allowed with all nations and for all things."[1] This policy conclusion rested upon some theory of what would determine the pattern of trade if there were no mercantilist restrictions. Trade would then be based on **absolute advantage**—the capacity of a country to produce its export commodities at absolutely lower cost in terms of real resources used at home than abroad and to import those commodities

[1]Adam Smith, *An Inquiry into the Nature and Causes of the Wealth of Nations* (1776; Glasgow edition, 1976), Book IV, Chap. III, 488–98.

that another country can produce at absolutely lower real cost than at home.

In Smith's words,[2]

It is the maxim of every prudent master of a family, never to attempt to make at home what it will cost him more to make than to buy. The tailor does not attempt to make his own shoes, but buys them of the shoemaker. The shoemaker does not attempt to make his own clothes, but employs a tailor. The farmer attempts to make neither the one nor the other, but employs those different artificers. All of them find it for their interest to employ their whole industry in a way in which they have some advantage over their neighbours, and to purchase with a part of its produce, or what is the same thing, with the price of a part of it, whatever else they have occasion for.

What is prudence in the conduct of every private family, can scarce be folly in that of a great kingdom. If a foreign country can supply us with a commodity cheaper than we ourselves can make it, better buy it of them with some part of the produce of our own industry, employed in a way in which we have some advantage. The general industry of the country, being always in proportion to the capital which employs it, will not thereby be diminished . . . ; but only left to find out the way in which it can be employed with the greatest advantage. It is certainly not employed to the greatest advantage, when it is thus directed towards an object which it can buy cheaper than it can make. . . .

The natural advantages which one country has over another in producing particular commodities are sometimes so great, that it is acknowledged by all the world to be in vain to struggle with them. By means of glasses, hotbeds and hotwalls, very good grapes can be raised in Scotland, and very good wine too can be made of them at about thirty times the expense for which at least equally good can be brought from foreign countries. Would it be a reasonable law to prohibit the importation of all foreign wines, merely to encourage the making of claret and burgundy in Scotland? But if there would be a manifest absurdity in turning towards any employment, thirty times more of the capital and industry of the country, than would be necessary to purchase from foreign countries an equal quantity of the commodities wanted, there must be an absurdity, though not altogether so glaring, yet exactly of the same kind, in turning towards any such employment a thirtieth, or even a three hundredth part more of either. Whether the advantages which one country has over another, be natural or acquired, is in this respect of no consequence. As long the one country has these advantages, and the other wants them, it will always be more advantageous for the latter,

[2] Smith, *op cit.*, Book IV, Chap. II, 456–59.

rather to buy of the former than to make. It is an acquired advantage only, which one artificer has over his neighbour, who exercises another trade; and yet they both find it more advantageous to buy of one another, than to make what does not belong to their particular trades.

Thus, just as the division of labor increases output in domestic trade, so too would the international division of labor, based on absolute advantage, augment the "value of annual produce." To Smith, international trade was simply a specific manifestation of the **general principle of exchange,** and international specialization followed the dominant principle of the division of labor. Promoting this specialization were differences in climate, qualities of soil, and other natural or acquired advantages, which resulted in absolute differences in real costs of production. As the cost of growing grapes in Scotland illustrates, a country does not import because it is physically impossible to produce the importable commodity, but rather because the real cost of doing so would exceed what it would cost **to specialize on its low-cost export commodity and exchange it for the import.**

Besides absolute differences in real cost, Smith has another explanation, which refers to trade as an exchange of "surpluses" of commodities above their domestic consumption. Smith states,[3]

Between whatever places foreign trade is carried on, they all of them derive two distinct benefits from it. It carries out that surplus part of the produce of their land and labour for which there is no demand among them, and brings back in return for it something else for which there is a demand. It gives a value to their superfluities, by exchanging them for something else, which may satisfy a part of their wants, and increase their enjoyments. By means of it, the narrowness of the home market does not hinder the division of labour in any particular branch of an art or manufacture from being carried to the highest perfection. By opening a more extensive market for whatever part of the produce of their labour may exceed the home consumption, it encourages them to improve its productive powers, and to augment its annual produce to the utmost, and thereby to increase the real revenue and wealth of the society. These great and important services foreign trade is continually occupied in performing, to all the different countries between which it is carried on.

In this passage, Smith emphasizes that foreign trade, by widening the extent of the market, improves the division of labor and thereby

[3]Smith, *op cit.,* Book IV, Chap. I, 446–47.

JOSEPH A. SCHUMPETER, *History of Economic Analysis* (1954), 473

In all the questions he [Ricardo] touched, he was on the side that would have won out anyhow, but to the victory of which he contributed usable argument, earning corresponding applause. Though others did the same, his advocacy was more brilliant, more arresting, than was theirs: there is no superflous sentence in his pages; no qualification, *however necessary,* weakens his argument; and there is just enough genuine analysis about it to convince practically and, at the same time, to *satisfy high intellectual standards* but not enough to deter. . . . It is neither his advocacy of winning policies per se, nor his theory per se, that, to this day, makes of him, in the eyes of some, the first economist of all times, but a felicitous combination of both.

raises productivity within the trading country. Moreover, foreign trade provides an outlet for surpluses of particular commodities above their home requirements. Myint terms these two theories the **"productivity" theory** and the **"vent for surplus" theory**, respectively.[4] Long neglected, these theories have recently been revived to explain the trade of less developed countries. (We return to this in Part III.)

Comparative Advantage

But what if a country is able to produce every commodity at an absolutely lower real cost than another country (instead of just one or two commodities, as in Smith's example)? Would there then still be a basis for trade? The answer is "yes"—according to David Ricardo's celebrated principle of **comparative** advantage. Under conditions of free trade, a country will specialize in the production and export of those commodities it can produce with greatest comparative advantage, i.e., those commodities for which its costs are **comparatively lowest,** and will import commodities in which it has a comparative disadvantage, i.e., those commodities it can produce only at high relative cost.

In his short chapter on comparative advantage, Ricardo provided the

[4]Hla Myint, "The 'Classical Theory' of International Trade and the Underdeveloped Countries," *Economic Journal,* 68 (June 1958), 317–37; Myint, "Adam Smith's Theory of International Trade in the Perspective of Economic Development," *Economica,* 44 (Aug. 1977), 231–48.

Table 1.1

Country	Amount of Labor Required for Producing 1 Unit of	
	wine	cloth
Portugal	80	90
England	120	100

Table 1.2

Country	$1w$	$1c$
Portugal	100	200
England	120	100

Table 1.3

Country	$1w$	$1c$
Portugal	60	50
England	120	100

intellectual foundations for the eventual repeal in 1846 of the Corn Laws.

To illustrate the meaning of comparative costs, Ricardo focused on a simple example of two countries, two commodities, and one factor of production, labor—a $2 \times 2 \times 1$ model. Consider this example in Table 1.1. In Portugal (P), 1 unit of wine ($1w$) costs 80 units of labor and 1 unit of cloth ($1c$) costs 90 units of labor, while in England (E), $1w$ costs 120 units of labor and $1c$ costs 100 units of labor.

In contrast, Smith's case of absolute advantage would be represented by figures such as those shown in Table 1.2. This table represents "**absolute differences in cost,**" with P having an absolute advantage in w, and E having an absolute advantage in c.

Another possible case is shown in Table 1.3. In this special case, P has an absolute advantage in both commodities, but by the same amount: it is twice as productive in both w and c. This is a condition of "**equal differences in cost,**" and there would be no basis for foreign trade. For in each country, $1.2c$ could be produced by sacrificing the production of 1*w*, and there could be no international exchange ratio established between the domestic cost ratios such that benefit would ensue to each country from trading. (This will become clear after the next case of "comparative differences in cost.")

It is, however, scarcely conceivable that a country would be equally inefficient (or equally efficient) in all activities. Instead it is likely that there will be a difference between the ratios of the costs in the different countries. It will then be cheaper to acquire goods through trade than to produce them at home when the terms of international exchange are more favorable than the ratio of costs at which they could be produced at home.

This returns us to Ricardo's example: the interesting question is whether P would export one commodity and import another commodity even though it could produce both commodities at absolutely lower costs than E. Ricardo[5] answered that

> It would be . . . advantageous for her (Portugal) to export wine in exchange for cloth. This exchange might even take place, notwithstanding that the commodity imported by Portugal could be produced there with less labour than in England. Though she could make the cloth with the labour of 90 men, she would import it from a country where it required the labour of 100 men to produce it, because it would be advantageous to her rather to employ her capital in the production of wine, for which *she would obtain more cloth from England, than she could produce by diverting a portion of her capital from the cultivation of vines to the manufacture of cloth.* [Italics added.]

In drawing this conclusion, Ricardo assumes domestic mobility of resources, but international immobility (so that labor does not migrate to the higher productivity country), production subject to constant returns to scale (constant costs in each activity), and perfectly competitive markets. To emphasize the "real" theory of international trade equilibrium, Ricardo abstracts from any monetary imbalance and assumes that exports must equal imports, with no capital flows.

The Ricardian example (Table 1.1) shows that P has an absolute advantage in both *w* and *c*, but a **comparatively greater advantage** in *w*, since $80/120 < 90/100$; P is superior to E in the production of both commodities, but "more superior" in *w* than in *c*. (It does not matter whether the cost ratios we compare are $80/120: 90/100$ or $80/90$:

[5]David Ricardo, *On the Principles of Political Economy and Taxation* (1817), Chap. VII [Sraffa edition, Cambridge (1951), 135].

Figure 1.1

Pre-trade and Post-trade Positions for England

MD: production-possibility frontier. Slope is the domestic exchange ratio or marginal rate of domestic transformation, MRT_d.

MF: availability frontier or consumption-possibility frontier. Slope is the international exchange ratio or marginal rate of foreign transformation, MRT_f.

B: pre-trade equilibrium position.

T: post-trade equilibrium position. *MC* exported in exchange for imports *CT*.

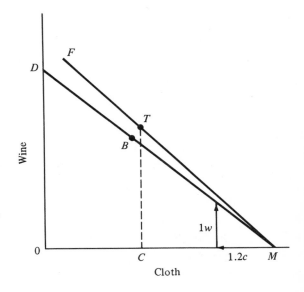

120/100.) In both commodities E has an absolute disadvantage, but a **lesser disadvantage** in *c*. If labor is perfectly mobile within each country and prices equal labor costs, then in the pre-trade situation, the domestic exchange ratio between the two commodities would be 1*w:* .88*c* in P, and 1*w:* 1.2*c* in E. (The exchange ratio in physical units is the reciprocal of the price ratio.) Thus, *w* is comparatively cheap in P, whereas *c* is comparatively cheap in E.

This can be represented diagrammatically in Figure 1.1, in which the production-possibility frontier for E is denoted by *MD.* The location of *M* and *D* are determined by the total supply of labor in E. The points along *MD* indicate maximum possible combinations of *w* and *c* that could be produced in E with the existing labor supply. The slope of *MD* shows the rate at which the resources embodied in the production of one commodity can be transformed into the production of another commodity. In this case, the labor that produces 1.2*c* can be transformed into the production of 1*w* by sacrificing the production of 1.2*c*. The condition of constant costs in each activity makes *MD* a straight line. The slope of the production frontier is termed the "**marginal rate of domestic transformation**" (**MRT_d**) because it shows the rate at which one commodity can be "transformed" into another in the production process.

We can also view the slope, or MRT_d as identifying the **marginal cost** of one commodity in terms of the other or as denoting the **opportunity cost** of one commodity in terms of the other. If product markets

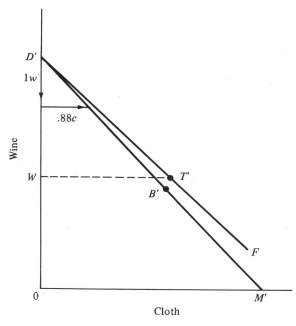

Figure 1.2
Pre-trade and Post-trade Positions for Portugal

$D'M'$: production-possibility frontier, MRT_d.

$D'F$: availability frontier or consumption-possibility frontier, MRT_f (slope of $D'F$ = slope of MF in Figure 1.1).

B': pre-trade equilibrium position.

T': post-trade equilibrium position— $D'W$ exported in exchange for WT' imports.

are perfectly competitive, prices must equal marginal costs. Therefore, the slope of the production possibility curve also indicates the ratio of marginal costs of the two commodities. The marginal cost, or opportunity cost of producing one more unit of w, is the forgone production of 1.2 units of c.

The slope of E's production-possibility frontier represents its comparative cost ratio; P will have a different production-possibility frontier, determined by its total supply of labor and ratio of marginal costs, such as that in Figure 1.2. Given different production frontiers in the two countries, a basis for international trade arises from these **relative productivity differentials** or differences in the countries' comparative cost ratios. After opening E and P to foreign trade, some exchange ratio on world markets will be established. This **international exchange ratio must lie within the range of the domestic exchange ratios,** between Portugal's $1w$: $.88c$ ratio and England's $1w$: $1.2c$ (ignoring transportation costs). Otherwise one country would not trade. If, for example, the international exchange ratio were $1w$: $1.5c$, E would not trade c for w at this international rate when it could produce $1w$ by forgoing the production of only $1.2c$ at home. Even though P would have a high demand for c at this rate, a supply of c would not be forthcoming from E until the rate became more favorable than $1w$: $1.2c$ for E. Exactly where the rate will be established between the domestic exchange ratios will depend on world demand and supply conditions. It was left to J.S. Mill (1848) to determine the "equilibrium terms of trade."

Mill noted that although both countries might benefit from trade on any terms within the range set by the comparative cost ratios, only one of these terms would also result in a balanced trade in which exports pay for imports. For a balanced trade, the terms must be such that the amount of w that E would purchase with c, at those terms, would cost the same amount of c that P would want to buy with w. The exact position of these equilibrium terms of international exchange will depend on the intensity and elasticity of E's demand for w and P's demand for c. (This is illustrated diagrammatically in the Appendix, p. 00).

In Mill's words,[6]

> The produce of a country exchanges for the produce of other countries, at such values as are required in order that the whole of her exports may exactly pay for the whole of her imports. This law of International Values is but an extension of the more general law of Value, which we called the Equation of Supply and Demand. We have seen that the value of a commodity always so adjusts itself as to bring the demand to the exact level of the supply. But all trade, either between nations or individuals, is an interchange of commodities, in which the things that they respectively have to sell, constitute also their means of purchase: the supply brought by the one constitutes his demand for what is brought by the other. So that supply and demand are but another expression for reciprocal demand: and to say that value will adjust itself so as to equalize demand with supply, is in fact to say that it will adjust itself so as to equalize the demand on one side with the demand on the other.

Of all the possible international exchange ratios between P's and E's comparative cost ratios, we have taken MF in Figure 1.1 and $D'F$ in Figure 1.2 as the equilibrium terms (MF and $D'F$ have the same slope). At these terms of trade, the value of exports equals the value of imports for E and P.

Let us say that demand and supply conditions determine the equilibrium international ratio as $1w:1c$. Then E would specialize in the production of c, its comparative advantage commodity (lesser disadvantage), and export $1c$ for $1w$, thereby **gaining** .17 unit of wine for each unit of cloth exported (the pre-trade exchange ratio is $1c:.83w$). Alternatively, E would acquire $1w$ at a lower real cost than in the pre-trade

[6]John Stuart Mill, *Principles of Political Economy* (1848), Book III.

GOTTFRIED HABERLER, "The Future of World Trade" in *Readings in the Theory of International Trade* (1949), 539–40

Even in the land of Adam Smith, Ricardo, J.S. Mill, and Marshall it is not only necessary to explain again and again to laymen and politicians but also to remind certain economists that trade is governed by comparative not by absolute advantage and cost.

situation (a saving of .2 unit of c because the pre-trade exchange ratio is $1w$: $1.2c$). And P would specialize in w, its comparative advantage commodity (greater advantage), thereby **gaining** .12 unit of cloth for each unit of wine exported (the pre-trade exchange ratio is $1w$: .88c). Alternatively, P would acquire the same quantity of w and c as produced before trade at a lower total real cost after trade.

Note that in this example specialization will be complete: each country concentrates its entire production on one commodity because, as long as constant costs of production prevail, the country's comparative advantage does not narrow as the country produces more. (The production frontier is characterized by a constant rate of transformation, so that comparative advantage does not run out by encountering increasing costs of production with larger outputs.) Therefore P allocates all its labor to w, whereas E allocates all its labor to c; and both then trade at the international exchange ratio. This is illustrated for E in Figure 1.1, in which the slope of MF is now the international exchange ratio or the **marginal rate of foreign transformation (MRT_f)**, indicating the "availability" of w and c on international markets. Exactly where the **equilibrium trading position T will be on this availability line** (or consumption possibility line) depends on the equilibrium conditions $D_c = S_c$ and $D_w = S_w$. At T, the amount of c exported by E (MC) must equal the amount of c imported by P (WT' in Figure 1.2), and the amount of w exported by P ($D'W$ in Figure 1.2) must equal the amount of w imported by E (CT in Figure 1.1).

It is clear from Figure 1.1 that MF, the availability frontier with international trade (MRT_f), lies beyond MD, the production frontier (MRT_d); or $MRT_d < MRT_f$. This means that the cost of w in terms of c is greater on E's domestic markets than on international markets. **The cost of "indirectly producing" the importable commodity w**

through specialization in the export commodity c is less than if E produced the importable w directly at home.

Before trade, E would have produced and consumed the combination of w and c given at point B. The combination of outputs at B would be determined by demand conditions and the price of c in terms of w. After being opened to trade, the new international exchange ratio (slope of MF) would be established, and both P and E would trade at this ratio. Thus E transfers resources to c, produces OM of c, consumes OC at home, and exports MC to P in exchange for CT of w from P.

A similar analysis holds for P in Figure 1.2. After obtaining access to world markets, P shifts resources from the production of w and c represented by B' to the production of OD' of w, consumes OW of w, exports WD' of w (equal to CT in Figure 1.1), and imports WT' of c (equal to MC in Figure 1.1).

To summarize: The Ricardian explanation of the pattern of international specialization rests on the principle of comparative advantage. Differences between countries in the **comparative productivity of labor** (technological differences in the production functions) give rise to comparative differences in real costs and to differences in the countries' pre-trade commodity price ratios. When the countries are opened to foreign trade, a common international price ratio can then be established between the domestic price ratios. At home, the cost of one commodity in terms of another is greater than on world markets, and the country therefore specializes in producing the commodity that uses fewer resources than would be needed to produce domestically the commodity it imports. It exports the commodity in which it has a comparative advantage and imports the commodity in which it has a comparative disadvantage. Thus, **the cost of "indirectly producing" imports through specialization on exports is less than if the country produced the imports directly at home.**

Exports can be viewed as the intermediate goods used for the "production" of imports. Foreign trade is like an industry that uses exports as inputs to produce imports as output. Indeed, in a centrally planned economy, in which the foreign trade sector is treated as an industry, the principle of comparative advantage should be adopted as the efficiency rule for determining what to export and what to import. In following its comparative advantage, each country maximizes output (imports) per unit of input (exports).

If the number of commodities and number of countries are increased, the model becomes more complicated, but the logic of the analysis remains the same.[7] Commodities will be ranked by their comparative factor-productivity ratios such that each of a country's exports will have a higher factor-productivity ratio than each of its imports. Any number of commodities in any number of countries can be arranged in a chain of declining comparative advantage. In this chain, the position of the dividing line beteen exports and imports will depend on demand conditions for each country's products and on the equilibrium conditions that world demand equals world supply and that value of exports equals value of imports for each country.[8]

Although the Ricardian analysis establishes a basis for international specialization according to comparative differences in real cost, it is, of course, necessary to **translate the comparative differences in real cost into absolute differences in money prices.** Obviously, any buyer of imports will only purchase imports if its absolute money price is less than the price of a domestic substitute good. This translation into absolute differences in money price will follow, provided the **relative wage differentials are within the relative productivity differentials.** If, for example, labor is three times more productive in country *I* than in country *II*, the absolute money price of the exports from *I* will be less than the absolute money price of the substitute commodity in *II*, provided the money wage rate is not more than three times higher in *I* than in *II*. This can be illustrated by comparing the results in Table 1.4 (a) and (b).

Under competitive conditions, the wage differences must be within the productivity differences (real cost), or else only one country would be able to export, and its wage rates would be bid up to compensate for this. Or the exchange rate would have to be altered to preserve the condition of balanced trade. (We shall have more to say about the balance of payments adjustment process in Part II.)

We can more readily understand how comparative differences in real costs become translated into differences in absolute money prices if we appreciate the relationships between productivity, wage rates, foreign currency exchange rates, and the resultant changes in absolute prices. Suppose country *I* is more productive than country *II* in every commodity, and that *I* can therefore readily export to *II*, but *II* cannot export to

---

[7] Ricardian trade theory has been refined continually and generalized down to the present day. For a recent (advanced) discussion, see R. Dornbusch, S. Fischer, and P. A. Samuelson, "Comparative Advantage, Trade, and Payments in a Ricardian Model with a Continuum of Goods," *American Economic Review*, 67 (Dec. 1977), 823–39.

[8] See J. Bhagwati, "The Pure Theory of International Trade: A Survey," *Economic Journal*, 74 (March 1964), 5–6, and Ronald Findlay, *Trade and Specialization* (1970), 62–69.

Table 1.4

		Amount of Labor Required for Producing 1 Unit of		Wage Rate per Labor Unit at Existing Foreign Currency Exchange Rate	Money Price of X	Money Price of Y
Country		X	Y			
	(a)					
I		5	10	$2	$10	$20
II		6	30	$1	$ 6	$30
	(b)					
I		5	10	$3	$15	$30
II		6	30	$1	$ 6	$30

I. But when the demand increases for I's exports, its wage rates will also increase, thereby raising its absolute prices and reducing its competitive advantage. The fall in demand in II may also lower wage rates and absolute prices in II, thereby allowing II to acquire a comparative advantage in another commodity. Or as the demand rises for I's currency on foreign exchange markets, the price of I's currency in terms of II's currency will rise (I's currency will appreciate), and this will cause the demand for I's exports to decline and will raise I's demand for imports. Thus, through wage changes or foreign exchange rate movements, the goods of country I will rise in price and those of country II will fall.

Similarly, even if one industry in I is so competitive that it dominates the world export market (say, Japanese electronics), the resulting exchange rate appreciation (say, a change from ¥ 200: $1 to ¥ 150: $1) will make other export industries in I less competitive. Because of variations in wage rates and exchange rates the underlying differences in comparative real costs are reflected in differences in absolute prices.

Aside from explaining the pattern of international specialization, the Ricardian model—despite its highly simplified statement—allows us to draw a number of policy conclusions. We can, for instance, immediately think of several policy decisions that could increase a country's exports. Recognizing that another country will import if the money price of imports is absolutely lower than the price of domestic substitutes, we can summarize the foregoing analysis in the relationship below.

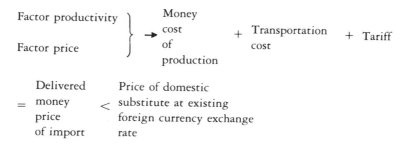

Exports of the first country could be increased if the second country lowered its tariffs (the free-trade assumption), transportation costs fell (the no transportation cost assumption), or the money cost of producing the first country's exports declined because of an increase in factor productivity or a lower factor price (the basis for translating comparative differences in labor costs into absolute differences in money costs and money prices). Alternatively, the country could allow its currency to depreciate on the foreign exchange markets so that the prices of its exports would be lowered in terms of foreign currency. (More on this in Part II.)

In explaining the basis of trade, the theory of comparative costs has a remarkably high degree of generality. It can be applied widely to problems of resource allocation—whether for an individual, for a country or for several countries or within a multi-product enterprise. Its logic is institution-free and applicable to any decision mechanism that must exercise the logic of choice. As Lord Robbins[9] concludes,

This analysis must surely be regarded as one of the main triumphs of abstract economic thought, far transcending in importance the problems of international trade to which it was first applied; it ultimately explains, not only the advantages arising here, but also any advantages arising from specialization anywhere where there are unequal differences in potentialities. It establishes, too, principles of action, not only for market economies, but also for any economic organization which aspires to rational allocation of resources. Other things being equal, a purely Collectivist economy should organize its resources so as to minimize the comparative opportunity costs of achieving any particular goal.

[9]Lionel Robbins, *Political Economy: Past and Present* (1976), 154. Fritz Machlup also concludes that "the invention of the law of comparative advantage may be regarded as one of the greatest achievements of economic theory." Machlup, *A History of Thought on Economic Integration* (1977), 42.

Nobel Laureate PAUL A. SAMUELSON, Presidential Address, *International Economic Relations* (1969), 9

[Economics] puts its best foot forward when it speaks out on international trade. This was brought home to me years ago when I was in the Society of Fellows at Harvard along with the mathematician Stanislaw Ulam. Ulam, who was to become an originator of the Monte Carlo method and co-discoverer of the hydrogen bomb, was already at a tender age a world famous topologist. And he was a delightful conversationalist, wandering lazily over all domains of knowledge. He used to tease me by saying, "Name me one proposition in all of the social sciences which is both true and non-trivial." This was a test that I always failed. But now, some thirty years later, on the staircase so to speak, an appropriate answer occurs to me: The Ricardian theory of comparative advantage: the demonstration that trade is mutually profitable even when one country is absolutely more—or less—productive in terms of every commodity. That it is logically true need not be argued before a mathematician; that it is not trivial is attested by the thousands of important and intelligent men who have never been able to grasp the doctrine for themselves or to believe it after it was explained to them. (Just to give one instance: "Boss" Kettering was a famous inventor of the recent epoch, having developed the self-starting auto and many other important devices. Yet this founder of General Motors and pioneer in cancer research never could understand why it might pay to send American cotton to Japan to be spun into cloth and then sent back to the United States.)

Although Ricardo's logic is powerful, his technical analysis leaves much to be desired by modern standards. Ricardo simply assumes at the outset differences in labor productivity in order to represent the comparative cost situation, but he does not explain the determinants of the comparative cost situation. He also restricts his analysis to one factor of production and a labor theory of value. Subsequent developments in the pure theory of trade have focused on relative factor endowments, technology, and demand conditions as the determinants of comparative cost ratios. The models have also been generalized to incorporate increasing costs or decreasing costs. Further, the static analysis has been extended to comparative statics and some attempt at dynamic analysis.

Factor Proportions Model

Many of the deficiencies in the Ricardian model are remedied in the more modern factor proportions model developed by Heckscher (1919), Ohlin (1933), and more recently by Samuelson (1948 and since)—the H-O-S model. The starting point for this model is the very opposite of Ricardo's. Instead of one factor being assumed, it is recognized that countries are endowed with many factors, but in different proportions. As long as there are international differences in relative factor endowments, this alone suffices to explain differences in comparative cost and the basis for international specialization.

Assume identity of factor qualities and production functions among all countries (each country would produce with the same techniques of production if confronted with identical factor prices); no economies to scale (a uniform increase in all inputs will increase output in the same proportion); and the same pattern of demand in every country (all goods are consumed in the same proportion at different levels of real income per head in each country). Even with the strong assumptions that all these variables are identical in every country, there is still a **sufficient source of trade as long as the relative factor endowments differ among the countries.** Relative factor abundance accounts for comparative advantage: **a country will export commodities that use intensively in their production the country's relatively abundant factor.**

Consider the quantities of two factors, Labor (L) and Capital (K). If the ratio of L/K in country I is greater than the ratio of L/K in country II, country I is abundant in L and II in K. The relatively abundant factor will also have the relatively lower factor price (wages will be relatively low in I, and the return of K relatively low in II). Commodities embodying intensively the relatively abundant factor will therefore have a relatively low marginal cost and, in turn, a relatively low money price. The labor-abundant country will be able to sell on world markets labor-intensive commodities at a low price, whereas the capital-abundant country will export capital-intensive commodities. Thus, **the minimum difference between countries which is a sufficient condition to explain the pattern of trade is national differences in relative factor endowments.**

We can readily think of simple illustrations of the factor proportions theory. If the factor endowment of the U.S. economy is relatively abundant in capital, technology, or skilled labor, then we could expect manufactured exports from the United States to be capital-intensive, technology-intensive, or skilled labor-intensive (aircraft, scientific equipment, pharmaceuticals, office machinery). If, however, an economy's factor endowment is relatively abundant in unskilled labor, then it should tend to specialize in exports using comparatively large amounts of unskilled labor (lower grade textiles, apparel, and semi-manufactures from Hong Kong, Korea, Taiwan). Or if an economy's relatively abundant factor is land, we would expect land-intensive exports (sugar from Jamaica, wheat and wool from Australia, coffee from Brazil). The more broadly we define the concept of a "factor"—so that we extend beyond the narrow sets of homogeneous factors, capital and labor—the more adequately the factor-proportions theorem explains trade patterns. We can also appreciate that a country's factor endowment changes over time, so that its composition of exports will also change (the United States, for example, has evolved historically from specializing in land-intensive and other natural resource-intensive exports to export industries that are now intensive in technology, high skill, and research).

The H-O-S analysis can be summarized in a series of diagrams, as follows:

> Consider two countries, I and II;
>
> two commodities, w and c;
>
> two factors, L and K.
>
> Let the production of w be L-intensive, and the production of c be K-intensive.
>
> Let the factor endowment in I be relatively L-abundant,
>
> and in II relatively-K-abundant.

With this $2 \times 2 \times 2$ model, (2 countries, 2 commodities, 2 factors) we can illustrate diagrammatically the basis for international trade and the equilibrium conditions of trade. The logic of the analysis would be the same for a multi-country, multi-commodity, multi-factor model; but for simplicity we draw only two-dimensional diagrams.

We can first recognize the generality of production conditions, as in Figure 1.3. For country I, three alternative production-possibility frontiers are represented: MBD, MD, and MRD. MD represents the Ricardian case of constant costs, previously considered. MBD denotes increasing costs (the production frontier is concave to the origin). There are diminishing returns to the variable input in the production of each product. As I produces more c, it must sacrifice production of more w (the slope of MBD becomes steeper as production moves from M toward

Figure 1.3

Production-Possibility Frontiers

The slope of the production-possibility frontier, or product transformation curve, represents the opportunity cost of producing *c* in terms of *w*. This is equivalent to the marginal rate of domestic transformation (MRT_d) of *w* for *c*. *MBD* represents increasing opportunity costs or diminishing marginal rate of transformation of *w* for *c* (as more *c* is produced, greater amounts of *w* must be sacrificed to produce one additional unit of *c*). *MD* represents constant opportunity costs, or constant marginal rate of transformation of *w* for *c*. *MRD* represents decreasing opportunity costs, or increasing marginal rate of transformation of *w* for *c*.

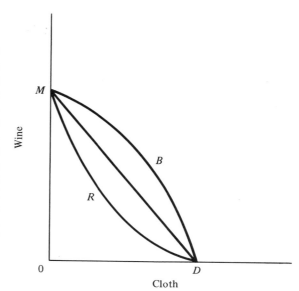

D). **Cost is a sacrificed benefit,** and thus, this is a case of **increasing opportunity costs.** As more *c* is produced, the marginal opportunity cost of producing *c* rises, and the price of *c* in terms of *w* rises (the absolute slope of *MBD* becomes greater).

In contrast, *MRD* represents decreasing opportunity costs (the production frontier is convex to the origin). As *I* produces more *c*, it need sacrifice less *w* because of increasing returns to scale.

We may next establish the **pre-trade equilibrium position.** In Figure 1.4, the area *OMBD* represents *I*'s production-possibility set, and the curve *MBD* its production-possibility frontier. In order for production to be in equilibrium in perfectly competitive markets, the price of *w* (P_w) must equal the marginal cost of *w* (MC_w), and price of *c* (P_c) must equal the marginal cost of *c* (MC_c). Let the line P_1, tangent to *MD* at *B*, represent the domestic price line. The slope of this line is the commodity exchange ratio of *w* for *c* before international trade. This slope shows the relative price of *c*, that is, the amount of *w* that must be sacrificed for 1 unit of *c*. The relative price of *c*, or the commodity exchange ratio of *w* for *c*, is equal to the inverse of the ratio of the absolute money prices. For example, if P_w is $20 and P_c is $10, the ratio of the absolute prices of *w* to *c* is 2/1. The relative price of *c* is the inverse of this ratio, or 1/2, indicating 1 unit of *w* has to be sacrificed for 2 units of *c*. The domestic price line P_1 has a slope of 1 unit *w* downward and 2 units of *c* to the right.

Figure 1.4

Country *I:*

Pre-trade Position

P_1: domestic price line (slope is commodity exchange ratio).

B: home production and consumption point: $P_c/P_w = MRT_d = MRS$.

OH: home production and consumption of *c.*

OX: home production and consumption of *w.*

Post-trade Position:

P_2: international price line (common to P'_2 for Country *II*).

B': equilibrium production point.

B'N: exports of *w* in exchange for *NT* = imports of *c.*

T: equilibrium consumption point (OX' of *w* and OD' of *c*): $MRT_d = MRT_f = MRS$.

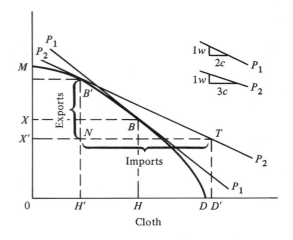

At *B*, the commodity exchange ratio (slope of the domestic price line) equals the marginal cost ratio (slope of the production frontier), which is the MRT_d (marginal rate of transformation in domestic production). At this production point, the marginal cost of each commodity equals its price. Producers would therefore be in equilibrium producing the combination of *w* and *c* represented at *B.*

If *B* is the pre-trade equilibrium position, then consumers must also be in equilibrium at this production point. This means that consumers are willing to substitute *w* for *c* in their consumption pattern—call this the **marginal rate of substitution** of *w* for *c* in consumption, or **MRS**—at the same rate as the domestic commodity exchange ratio of 1*w* for 2*c*. Each consumer would be at a consumption point where the individual's $MRS = P_c/P_w$, and this would be the same for all consumers consuming both goods.[10]

[10] Each consumer's *MRS* (the absolute slope $-\Delta w/\Delta c$ along the individual consumer's indifference curve between *w* and *c*) must equal the price ratio P_c/P_w (the absolute slope of the consumer's budget line). These equilibrium conditions are developed fully in any of a number of elementary texts. See, for example, Robert Dorfman, *The Price System* (1964), 105–25; and Jack Hirshleifer, *Price Theory and Application* (1976), 443–46. A "community indifference

Therefore, at B, we arrive at the following set of **pre-trade equilibrium conditions:**

$$\frac{P_c}{P_w} = MRT_d = MRS, \qquad (1.1)$$

where P_c/P_w is the slope of the domestic price line; MRT_d, the slope of the domestic production frontier; and MRS, the ratio of substitution in consumption. This means that **the rate at which commodities exchange on domestic markets, the rate of their transformation in domestic production, and the rate of their substitution in consumption are all equivalent.** Producers are maximizing profits while consumers maximize their "satisfaction" ("utility," or reach their maximum indifference curves). Production is on the frontier (full employment and efficient resource allocation), the relative valuation of products by consumers (MRS) is equal to the relative costs of production (MRT_d), and the MRS and MRT_d are equal to the relative prices of the commodities.

Now consider country II. A similar analysis can be applied, but the production possibility set for II is now given as the area $ORES$ in Figure 1.5. The production-possibility frontier RES is biased toward the production of c, and w is more expensive to produce in II. In contrast, the production frontier in country I is biased toward the production of w, and c is more expensive to produce in I. The different shapes of the production frontiers reflect different relative factor endowments. **The slope of a country's production-possibility frontier (MC ratio) is its comparative cost ratio. Therefore, as long as the slopes of the production-possibility frontiers differ at the points of pre-trade equilibrium (B and E), there is a basis for trade between I and II.**

Suppose in II, before trade, the domestic commodity exchange ratio was $1w:5c$. At this ratio, the equilibrium pre-trade production and consumption point would be at E. In each country, $P_c/P_w = MRT_d = MRS$. But the MRT_d in I at B differs from that in II at E. If the countries are opened to trade, some commodity price ratio could be established on world markets between $(MRT_d)_I$ and $(MRT_d)_{II}$. Assume

---

curve" could be drawn at B, tangent to the production frontier and price line. But such a curve indicating *community* preferences is only the product of the economist's geometrical skill, not an empirical construct. For the limitations on resorting to a community preference map, see the Appendix to Chap. 2. Instead of retreating to this facile geometrical escape, it is better to understand the meaning of consumer equilibrium and recognize that its conditions must hold for each consumer.

Figure 1.5

Country *II:*

Pre-trade Position:

P'_1: domestic price line.

E: equilibrium production and consumption point: $P_c/P_w = MRT_d = MRS$.

OM: home production and consumption of c.

ON: home production and consumption of w.

Post-trade Position:

P'_2: international price line (common to P_2 for country I).

E': equilibrium production point.

$E'F'$: exports of c in exchange for $F'T'$ = imports of w.

T': equilibrium consumption point: (ON' of w and OF of c): $MRT_d = MRT_f$ = MRS.

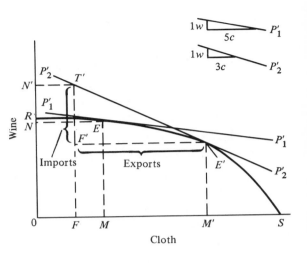

that equilibrium conditions of demand and supply set this international commodity exchange ratio at $1w:3c$. (For the mechanics of exactly determining the equilibrium international price ratio, see the Appendix at the end of this chapter.) The international exchange ratio can be termed the **marginal rate of transformation through foreign trade (MRT$_f$)**; this shows the rate at which one commodity can be transformed (exchanged) into another on world markets. This trade in effect introduces another **"technological" process of transforming domestic resources (exports) into foreign resources (imports).** This foreign rate of transformation is the slope of the international price line P_2 (Figure 1.4) or P'_2 (Figure 1.5). In response to the additional possibilities for transforming w into c on world markets, country I will reallocate resources away from c into w, the labor-intensive commodity that has a relatively low cost of production because I's factor endowment is relatively labor-abundant. Resources will be reallocated toward w, which has a relatively higher price on world markets, until finally the equilibrium allocation is reached at production point B' (Figure 1.4), where the MC ratio or MRT_d is now equal to the international exchange ratio or the marginal rate of transformation through foreign trade (MRT_f). Then I will consume OH' of c and $H'N$ of w at home and will export $B'N$ of w in exchange for NT of c, consuming the bundle of w and c at T after trade ($D'T$ of w and OD' of c).

We know that the post-trade consumption position must lie on the international price line (consumption frontier), but its exact position at T is determined by the equilibrium condition that the international exchange ratio equals the MRS in consumption. Therefore, **in equilibrium after trade (at T), the following equilibrium marginal conditions hold:**

$$MRT_d = MRT_f = MRS, \tag{1.2}$$

where MRT_d is the slope of the production-possibility frontier; MRT_f, the slope of the international price line; and MRS, the ratio of substitution in consumption.

A similar analysis applies to country II (Figure 1.5), which will also trade along the international price line P'_2 (P'_2 has the same slope as P_2 for I). Resources will therefore be reallocated from E to E', into the capital-intensive commodity c because this is the relatively inexpensive commodity in II. Total home production will be OM' of c and $M'E'$ of w. Out of this home production, OF of c and FF' of w will be consumed domestically. The difference of $M'F = E'F'$ of c will be exported in exchange for $F'T'$ imports of w. Country II's exports equal country I's imports, and II's imports equal I's exports. The final equilibrium consumption point after trade will be T' at which point the same type of marginal conditions as expressed in equation (1.2) will also hold for II.

We can note that, after trade, each country continues to produce some w and some c: **specialization is incomplete** in this model, unlike the complete specialization of the Ricardian model. There is incomplete specialization because the model allows for increasing costs, as reflected by the concave production frontiers. Each country has a comparative advantage in the product intensive in its abundant factor over a certain range of production. At a certain output (B' and E'), the relative costs of producing c and w are equal in I and II, and the specialization does not proceed beyond this output.

If, however, each country had decreasing costs, as indicated by a production frontier convex from the origin (as MRD in Figure 1.3), then a country would never lose its comparative advantage as it produced more of its comparative advantage commodity. Indeed, the range of comparative advantage would widen, and the country would continue producing the commodity until specialization became **complete.**

The factor proportions model also illustrates the important principle that when factors are not freely mobile between countries, **the factors in effect move in the guise of the commodities traded** if trade is unrestricted. Although labor does not physically move from *I* to *II,* it does so indirectly by being embodied in the labor-intensive commodity from *I.* **Commodity trade therefore tends to be a substitute for international factor movements.** If the exchange of commodities is restricted, there will be larger discrepancies in factor prices, which will increase factor movements or create differences in factor returns if factors are not mobile internationally.

If there were free trade in commodities, there would be a tendency toward partial factor price equalization. When the demand for the abundant factor increases in the exportable commodity, and the demand for the scarce factor falls, there will be a rise in the price of the abundant factor relative to the price of the scarce factor.[11]

Other Sources of Trade

The previous theories of international trade have depended on the assumption of purely competitive product and factor markets. This has allowed the development of general equilibrium analysis and emphasis on normative implications. Other sources of trade, however, can be recognized once we depart from the purely competitive assumption, and allow monopolistic competition and especially the existence of multinational corporations—and when we depart from the assumption of international immobility of factors, and allow international capital movements and technology diffusion.[12] If we now relax the "givens" in the

[11] Under highly restrictive assumptions, it has been demonstrated that free trade will result in complete equalization of the factor prices, both absolute and relative. See Paul A. Samuelson, "International Trade and the Equalization of Factor Prices," *Economic Journal,* 58 (June 1948), 163; "International Factor-Price Equalization Once Again," *Economic Journal,* 59 (June 1949), 181. The deviations in the real world from the extreme conditions postulated in the factor price equalization theorem can readily account for the actual inequalities in factor prices.

[12] These additional considerations do not destroy the relevance of traditional trade theory; but they do add some supplementary considerations that were ignored in the H-O-S model. See H.G. Johnson, "International Trade Theory and Monopolistic Competition Theory," in R. Kuenne (ed.), *Monopolistic Competition Theory: Studies in Impact* (1967), 203–18; Thomas D. Willett, "International Trade Theory is Still Relevant," *Banca Nazionale del Lavoro,* 24 (Sept. 1971), 276–92; Richard E. Caves, *International Trade, International Investment, and Imperfect Markets* (1974); and W.M. Corden, "Multinational Corporations and Trade Theory," in John H. Dunning (ed.), *Economic Analysis and the Multinational Enterprise* (1974).

factor proportions model, we can readily identify additional sources of trade. **When production functions are not identical** in each country, a country may import a commodity because it simply does not not have the technical knowledge or skills to produce it. **If economies of scale are realized** in the production of a commodity, this commodity may at some scale of output become lower in price than in other countries and become exportable. **When consumption patterns differ,** a country may export a commodity for which it has relatively low demand, whereas the importing country has a relatively high demand for the product.

The Ricardian model tends to emphasize trade as an exchange of primary products (wine) for manufactures (cloth), whereas the factor proportions model, or H-O-S model, tends to emphasize the "historical" factor endowments and the localization of natural resources in relatively different amounts in different countries. The major share of the composition of world trade and the most rapidly growing type of trade, however, is the exchange of manufactures for manufactures—both intermediate and finished industrial products. Although the H-O-S model is at its best in establishing the reasons for trade in natural resource intensive products, additional forces should be recognized to explain trade in manufactures. This can be readily done by allowing the 'givens" of the H-O-S analysis to become variables. Once this is done, **differences in the production functions, presence of economies of scale, and different demand patterns can then account for much of the trade in manufactures.** In addition, we should recognize how differences in the availability of skilled labor (human capital), Research and Development (R & D) expenditure, technological change, and the "product cycle" contribute to trade promotion.

The factor proportions model can be extended and more broadly applied to incorporate human capital and R & D as **"research endowments."** These endowments may differ among countries, but even if they were the same, it would be most unlikely that each country's endowment would be used to develop and produce the same "research-intensive" products at the same time. The extensive range of **product differentiation** within industry provides a strong source of international trade, and a country's export industries may well show higher rates of technical progress through "research effort" (either in product innovations or process innovations) than the same industries in its trading partners.[13] It might

[13] W. Gruber, D. Mehta, and R. Vernon, "The R & D Factor in International Trade and International Investment of United States Industries," *Journal of Political Economy*, 75 (Feb.

also explain intraindustry trade, in which one product variety is exchanged for another product variety within the same general industrial category.[14] In an industrial export industry of an advanced economy, the characteristics of high skill-intensity, high research-intensity, technical change, economies of scale, and innovations are all likely to be strongly inter-related.[15]

When we include **technology as a factor of production,** we must place more emphasis on returns to scale, product differentiation, and product age—elements of the **technological gap** theory of trade. This theory stresses that technology is not a free good and that the transmission of knowledge from one country to another occurs only after some time lag. When information does not flow freely across national boundaries, three important conclusions can be drawn: (i) innovation of new products and processes is more likely to occur near a market where there is a strong demand for them than in a country with little demand; (ii) the producing firm is more likely to supply risk capital for the production of the new product if demand exists in its home market than if it has to go to a foreign market; and (iii) a producer located close to a market has a lower cost in transferring market knowledge into product design changes than one located far from the market.[16]

These conclusions support the "**product life cycle model**" as a useful explanation of trade in manufactures. In this model the focus is on the production and marketing characteristics of a product as a function of time, and the emphasis is on the technical capabilities of the supplier as a determinant of trade flows.[17] As the intensities of different inputs change over the product's life cycle, so too does the comparative advantage of producing the product in one country or another. By dealing with innovations and product differentiation, this model necessarily involves monopolistically competitive firms—increasingly, trans-

---

1967), 20–37, and M.V. Posner, "International Trade and Technical Change," *Oxford Economic Papers*, 13 (Oct. 1961), 323–41.

[14] H.G. Grubel and P.J. Lloyd, *Intra-Industry Trade* (1975).

[15] Donald Keesing, "Labor Skills and Comparative Advantage," *American Economic Review*, 56 (May 1966), 549–81; Keesing, "The Impact of Research and Development on United States Trade," *Journal of Political Economy*, 75 (Feb. 1967), 45; Robert Baldwin, "Determinants of the Commodity Structure of U.S. Trade," *American Economic Review*, 61 (March 1971), 126–46; and Richard Cooper, "Growth and Trade: Some Hypotheses about Long-Term Trends," *Journal of Economic History*, 24 (Dec. 1964), 609–28.

[16] Louis T. Wells, Jr. (ed.), *The Product Life Cycle and International Trade* (1972), 6.

[17] Raymond Vernon, "International Investment and International Trade in the Product Cycle," *Quarterly Journal of Economics*, 80 (May 1966), 190–207. Also, Harry G. Johnson, *Comparative Cost and Commercial Policy Theory for a Developing World Economy* (Wicksell Lectures 1968), 32–39.

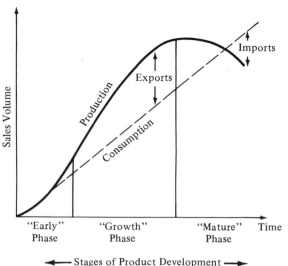

Figure 1.6
Product Cycle and Trade

A country may initially be an exporter of a new product, then lose its comparative advantage when the product becomes "mature," and finally become an importer of the product.

national or multinational corporations—and also foreign investments and their effect on trade patterns.

Figure 1.6 helps explain the product life cycle model. The sales volume of a product is plotted over time. Three phases are delimited. In the "early" phase, a new product that is research- and high skill-intensive is introduced. Product design is still being adapted, costs are high, and sales are low. The suppliers therefore concentrate on the home market where any technical difficulties in production can be most readily solved and where demand is less elastic. In the second "growth" phase, mass production and distribution become possible. Costs and price fall, and the product become exportable (in the amount given by the difference between the sales curve and domestic consumption line in Figure 1.6). In this phase of the product life cycle, suppliers may deem it a strategic competitive advantage to establish foreign subsidiaries to produce overseas. In the third "mature" phase, the product and manufacturing operations have become standardized and routine, sales then level off, price-elasticity of demand is high, and exports diminish. Whereas in the first two phases, the innovating country had advantages from introducing and producing the newest products, these advantages are lost by the third phase. The trading partner, which formerly imported the product, may now be able to duplicate its routine type of production. The technology may now be licensed to foreign producers, or the technology may have become publicly available. Overseas producers may now gain a comparative advantage in the "old" product and actually begin to export it to third countries and to the first country, which has lost its initial comparative advantage. As the technological gap and imitation gap narrow, so does the product gap. As the comparative advantage in input requirements changes over the product's life cycle, so does the comparative advantage of producing the product in one country rather than another. **Through technical change, there is a continually changing international division of labor.**

As a limiting case, the determinants of the trade structure may change so much over time that a country that initially imported a product begins to substitute for the import with home-competing production, becomes more efficient in its import-substitution production, and eventually acquires a comparative advantage for the mature product and is then able to export it. This is the other side of the product cycle and can be termed the "catching-up product cycle."[18] The product cycle explains from the viewpoint of an advanced country how comparative advantage of a new product is first acquired in the advanced economy and then transmitted to less developed economies through trade and investment. The catching-up process in the less developed countries describes the sequence from imports to eventual exportation of the standardized product as domestic costs reach the international competitive cost threshold. For the history of Japan's development this has been called the "wild geese-flying pattern of industrial development,"[19] as depicted in Figure 1.7. As one country acquires new comparative advantages in products with different input requirements, other countries "in the queue" move into a comparative advantage position in the earlier products (for example, South Korea and Taiwan become more competitive with Japan in the more labor-intensive products, while Japan moves on to the more skill- and knowledge-intensive products).

Although most explanations of international trade are based on supply-oriented theories of comparative advantage, **demand conditions** should not be overlooked. Some theorists note that the range of exports is determined by internal demand. Countries first produce goods designed for the tastes of their home markets because of the need for close contact between producers and consumers in the early stages of development of a market. Countries first become efficient in the manufacture of goods that fit into the economic structure of their domestic

---

[18]Kiyoshi Kojima, *Japan and a New World Economic Order* (1977), 150–52.

[19]Kaname Akamatsu, "A Historical Pattern of Economic Growth in Developing Countries," *The Developing Economies* (March–Aug. 1962), and Miyohei Shinohara, *Growth and Cycles in the Japanese Economy* (1962), 58.

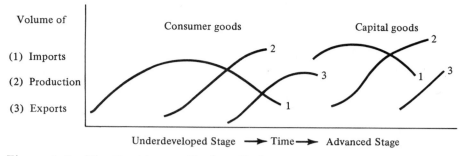

Figure 1.7   The Catching-up Product Cycle

The developing country proceeds over time from imports of a particular product to its import-substitution production and eventual export of the commodity. The catching-up process may begin with simple consumer goods; at a more advanced stage of development, the pattern may be repeated for capital goods.

markets. After that, if scale economies arise from specialization in the home market, the goods will be exported to foreign markets with similar demands. Under this theory, it is hypothesized that trade is likely to be greater between countries with similar per capita incomes, and hence, similar tastes.[20]

Also emphasizing the demand side, the **variety hypothesis,** as an explanation of international trade, states that as real income increases, purchasers tend to buy more varieties of a product, and since a greater number of these extra varieties come from abroad than from home sources, the share of imports in demand tends to increase. For imports as a whole, the quantity of imports tends to increase more than proportionally with real income per capita.[21]

This is a simple recognition that trade takes place because the wider market offers more choice, since the number of different goods available from abroad will be much greater than the number available from home producers. Three specific hypotheses follow: (i) the income-elasticity of demand for imports is greater, the greater the opportunities for variety in international trade; (ii) growth in international trade resulting from growth in real income is biased toward commodities that have the greatest opportunities for variety; (iii) imports spread more widely over their sources as incomes and imports increase. These hypotheses predict that international trade becomes increasingly biased in favor of commodities that offer the most scope for variation.

[20] Staffan Burenstam-Lindner, *An Essay on Trade and Transformation* (1961). But empirical evidence is weak; see review by Harry G. Johnson, *Economica,* 31 (Feb. 1964), 89–90.

[21] T. Barker, "International Trade and Economic Growth: An Alternative to the Neo-classical Approach," *Cambridge Journal of Economics,* 1 (June 1977), 153–72.

The Scope for International Specialization

When we recognize the dynamic quality of comparative advantage and the continually changing character of the international division of labor, we may naturally wonder about the prospects for international trade. As national economies grow, it is to be expected that the volume of trade will increase from forces on the demand side. But at a given level of income, the volume of trade will also depend on the structure of comparative costs. The scope for international specialization will be wider, and the trade potential greater, the wider the gaps in the comparative advantages of different countries. Further, as national output grows, the composition of that output might be **pro-trade biased,** in the sense that exports increase in greater proportion than import-competing commodities. Or national growth might be **anti-trade biased,** in the sense that import substitutes increase in greater proportion than exports.

Since World War II, the volume of international trade has grown not only absolutely but also as a percentage of world output. Can we expect that international trade will continue to acquire greater relative importance? The answer will depend on changes in the pattern of demand, the differences in production conditions among countries, and the course of technical change. (We ignore government imposed restrictions on the free flow of goods and capital.)

It could be inferred from the factor proportions theory that the gap of comparative advantage will narrow as national relative demand patterns become more similar, as technology is more rapidly diffused internationally, and as technological change provides synthetics that can replace natural resources. But even if a larger number of countries become technically capable of producing a wider range of commodities, it does not follow, of course, that they could all produce at anything near the level of comparable real costs. The issue remains whether differences of "efficiency" between countries will narrow or widen.

There are strong forces that tend to widen the gap of comparative advantage and expand the scope for international specialization and trade. Technological change, both rapid in pace and extensive in range, keeps production functions different in various countries. Technical advances in transportation and communication also promote specialization. Economies of scale in the production of exportables widen comparative advantage. As income rises, the income-elasticity of demand also tends to increase, and this creates a greater demand for more differentiated products—and hence more specialization. Finally, two other developments in recent years have had a significant effect on widening comparative advantage. One is the increased skewness in the geographical location of consumption and production of raw materials. The second is the growth of the multinational corporation. This intensifies international specialization by allowing a potential comparative advantage in an overseas country to become effective through the receipt of capital and technology. For example, natural resources or labor, which had not been utilized for lack of capital or technology, may now become economically productive. By bringing into existence these resources that earlier were essentially non-existent economically, the migration of capital and technology actually increases differences in factor endowments. The multinational corporation is also often an agent that introduces the production of a new product in another country, thereby "short circuiting" some of the stages of the product cycle.[22]

It is therefore not surprising that the forces that have accelerated the process of internationalization of markets (discussed in the Prologue) should also be the forces that will increase the scope for international specialization. The international transmission of real forces affecting productivity over the longer run deserves as much attention as the shorter period transmission of monetary forces (to be examined in Part II).

If this chapter began by indicating the major determinants of the structure of international trade, it must end by emphasizing that these determinants are not immutable, but are continually changing. **And as comparative advantage changes, the gains from trade will change**—creating significant problems of trade policy. We turn to these problems in the next three chapters.

Supplementary Readings

Several excellent surveys of trade theory can be useful supplements to this book. Although listed here, they will be relevant throughout Part I. They also contain extensive bibliographies that can be consulted for subsequent chapters.

J. Bhagwati, "The Pure Theory of International Trade," *Economic Journal,* 74 (March 1964), 1–84;

Richard E. Caves, *Trade and Economic Structure* (1960);

John S. Chipman, "A Survey of the Theory of International Trade: Part 1, The Classical Theory," *Econometrica,* 33 (July 1965), 477–519; "Part 2, The Neo-Classical

[22]Raymond Vernon and Louis T. Wells, Jr., *Economic Environment of International Business* (1976), 196–97.

Theory," *Econometrica,* 33 (Oct. 1965), 685–760; "Part 3, The Modern Theory," *Econometrica,* 34 (Jan. 1966), 18–76;

W. M. Corden, *Recent Developments in the Theory of International Trade,* Princeton Special Papers in International Economics, No. 7 (March 1965);

Gottfried Haberler, *A Survey of International Trade Theory,* Princeton Special Papers in International Economics, No. 1 (July 1961);

Harry G. Johnson, "International Trade: Theory," *International Encyclopedia of Social Sciences* (1968), vol. 8, 83–96.

For the development of classical international trade theory from Smith's absolute advantage approach through the comparative cost developments of Torrens and Ricardo to the formulation of reciprocal demand by Torrens and J.S. Mill, see D.P. O'Brien, *The Classical Economists* (1975), especially Chap. 7 (with bibliography). Still unrivaled for its scholarly treatment of the history of doctrine and for its statement of the classical theory of comparative costs and international values is Jacob Viner's *Studies in the Theory of International Trade* (1937).

A comprehensive survey of major recent developments in the empirical testing of trade theories is presented by Robert M. Stern, "Testing Trade Theories," in Peter B. Kenen (ed.), *International Trade and Finance: Frontiers for Research* (1975), 3–49, with extensive bibliography.

Also noteworthy are R. E. Baldwin, "Determinants of the Commodity Structure of U.S Trade," *American Economic Review,* 61 (March 1971), 126–46; Seev Hirsch, *Location of Industry and International Competitiveness* (1967); R. Vernon (ed.), *The Technology Factor in International Trade* (1970); and E. E. Leamer, "The Commodity Composition of International Trade in Manufactures: An Empirical Analysis," *Oxford Economic Papers,* 26 (Nov. 1974), 350–74.

APPENDIX

General Equilibrium Analysis

This Appendix extends the geometrical analysis of the comparative cost doctrine. It does so in four directions: (i) it derives the production-possibility frontier from the underlying production functions; (ii) it derives the equilibrium international exchange ratio (MRT_f) from the supply and demand conditions of each country; (iii) it denotes the general equilibrium conditions of the post-trade position; and (iv) it illustrates the effects of growth on trade.

This extension indicates that international trade theory is very much a matter of general equilibrium analysis and emphasizes that this analysis can be used—at least in comparative statics form—to demonstrate how comparative advantage is constantly changing and a new international division of labor is continually emerging.

Derivation of the Production-Possibility Frontier

Consider a $2 \times 2 \times 2$ model. Let the countries be I and II, the commodities w and c, and the factors "labor" (L) and "capital" (K). We assume (i) purely competitive conditions prevail in product and factor markets; (ii) the production functions of w and c are subject to constant returns to scale, but to diminishing returns to the variable input; (iii) w is the more "labor-intensive" industry, in the sense that, at the same relative prices for L and K in both industries, L/K is greater in the production of w than the corresponding ratio in c; (iv) w is always labor-intensive and c is always capital-intensive, whatever the relative supply of factors and the ratio of factor prices (there is no "factor reversal"); and (v) in each country L and K are fixed in total amount, and technical knowledge, consumer tastes, and the distribution of income between factors are all held constant. (We shall remove the fifth assumption below.)

Examine first the **derivation of the production-possibility frontier for country** I. There will be a **production technology** for w, as illustrated in Figure 1.8 (a) and another production technology for c, as illustrated in Figure 1.8 (b), indicating the isoquants (constant product curves) for various combinations of L and K.

We now ask: What allocation of L and K between w and c will be **technically efficient**, in the sense of maximizing the possible combinations of w and c that I could produce? To discover the efficient points that will be production-maximizing, we construct an Edgeworth-Bowley type of production box diagram, as in Figure 1.9. The dimensions of the box are fixed by the given amounts of L ($O_wL_w = O_cL_c$) and K ($O_wK_w = O_cK_c$) in I. The isoquants for w are drawn from the origin O_w, whereas those for c are inverted from Figure 1.8 (b) and drawn from the origin O_c on Figure 1.9.

Corresponding to any production point in the box will be four co-ordinates

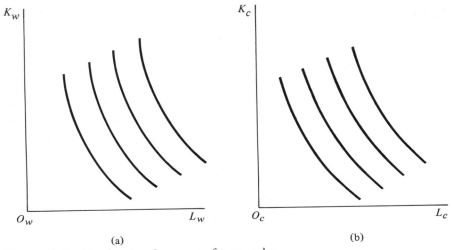

Figure 1.8   Production Isoquants for w and c

Various combinations of capital and labor will produce different outputs of w and of c. The production technology for w is illustrated in Figure 1.8 (a), and another production technology for c, in Figure 1.8 (b). The isoquants (constant product curves) increase in value to the northeast.

showing the amount of labor and capital used for the production of w and c, the total L and K used for w and c always being equal to the fixed supplies available. At point e, the ratio of $L{:}K$ in w is greater than the ratio of $L{:}K$ in c; the total amounts of L and K are fully utilized by assumption; and most significantly, e lies on an isoquant for w and an isoquant for c simultaneously. This latter condition makes e an efficient point of production. This can be recognized by considering the alternative point i, which is a feasible combination of production for w and c, just as every point in the box is. But this feasible point is not an efficient point. At i, the marginal rates of substitution of K for L or the ratios of marginal product of $K{:}$ marginal product of L differ. Labor and capital could be reallocated from point i to reach e, where more c is produced without any less w being produced, or to reach e', where more w could be produced without any less c being produced. Point e is therefore an **efficient point,** in the sense of maximizing the output of w given that a specified amount of c is produced. So too is e' an efficient point. All points of tangency along $O_w O_c$ are therefore efficient, and the locus of the points of tangency of the two sets of isoquants forms what can be termed an "**efficiency locus**" $O_w O_c$ in capital-labor space. Along this locus, the allocation of L and K is production-maximizing: at each point, for a given level of production of one of the commodities, there is also the maximum possible production of the other commodity. This logical ordering condition is met at each point of tangency, the ratio between the marginal productivities of the factors (given by the slope of the isoquants) in the production of one commodity is equal to

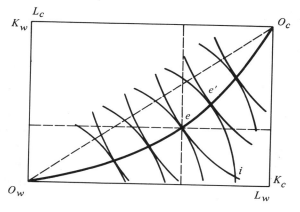

Figure 1.9
Production Box Diagram

i: a feasible point, but not an efficient point.

e,e': efficient points.

O_wO_c: efficiency locus.

the ratio between their marginal productivities in the production of the other commodity. It is then impossible to produce more of one commodity without reducing the output of the other.

The output levels of the two commodities corresponding to each point on the efficiency locus can be shown on a separate diagram. Thus, by simply reading off the amounts of w and c along O_wO_c and translating these amounts to a plane such as in Figure 1.3, (p. 31), we derive the **"production-possibility frontier"** *MBD* in product space. The slope of *MBD* at any point denotes the ratio of the marginal opportunity costs of w in terms of c, the marginal opportunity cost of producing an additional unit of one commodity being measured by the necessary reduction of the output of the other. In Figure 1.3, the production frontier is concave to the origin, indicating that the marginal opportunity cost of transforming one commodity, c, into the other, w, is increasing as more of the commodity c is produced. This concavity property is related to the law of diminishing marginal productivity when the commodities are produced with different factor intensities and we assume constant returns to scale for both production functions. The different factor intensities mean that the ratio of marginal physical product of L to the marginal physical product of K is always equalized between the two industries w and c by using a higher ratio of $L{:}K$ in w (the L-intensive industry) and a lower ratio of $L{:}K$ in c (the K-intensive industry). Therefore, when the production of one commodity is expanded, it must use factors in a more costly combination, as factors are not released from the declining industry in proportions that are optimal for the expanding industry. With constant returns to scale in the production functions, the production-possibility frontier is concave to a degree depending on the elasticities of substitution between the inputs. The concavity would be even more pronounced if there were diminishing returns to scale.[1]

---

[1]See also, W.F. Stolper and P.A. Samuelson, "Protection and Real Wages," *Review of Economic Studies*, 9 (Nov. 1941), 58–73; R.E. Caves, *Trade and Economic Structure* (1960), 30–35; Samuelson, "International Factor-Price Equalization Once Again," *Economic Journal*, 59 (June 1949), 184–87; and Ronald Findlay, *Trade and Specialization* (1970), 22–29.

A linear production-possibility frontier results only if the efficiency locus in Figure 1.9 corresponds to the diagonal of the box, indicating that the labor: capital ratio is the same for both commodities, and there are constant returns to scale. This would be a special case of constant opportunity costs. So too would the Ricardian production-possibility frontier, based on a one factor model.

Finally, if we depart from the assumption of constant returns to scale and instead allow for increasing returns to scale, then there can be decreasing marginal (opportunity) costs as one product expands—provided that the increasing returns are strong enough to overpower the effect of diminishing returns to a factor along an isoquant. The frontier is then convex to the origin (such as MRD in Figure 1.3).

Derivation of International Exchange Ratio

Assume that the two countries I and II have been opened to trade. Let us now determine how the equilibrium international price ratio (such as P_2 in Figure 1.4, p. 32) will be established. If we consider varying terms of trade, we can derive a schedule of how much each country would be willing to export in exchange for imports at different international exchange ratios. This schedule can be represented by a Marshallian **reciprocal demand curve** (the supply of exports is the demand for imports) or a **foreign offer curve**. Once we derive each country's offer curve, we can determine the equilibrium terms of trade and the equilibrium volume of exports and imports for each country.

To derive the offer curve for country I, we assume alternative international price ratios for the commodities and consider how, as the international price ratio changes, country I will export and import different amounts according to its production possibilities and preference pattern. If the international exchange ratio were identical with the domestic exchange ratio in I, namely slope of P_1 in Figure 1.4, I would continue to produce and consume the combination of w and c indicated at B in Figure 1.4. This would be equivalent to having the international exchange ratio coincide with the domestic exchange ratio in Figure 1.10, and there would be no basis for trade by I. If, however, the international exchange ratio diverges from the initial domestic exchange ratio, production and consumption will change, and the domestic production and consumption of each commodity will no longer be equal. The direction and degree of alteration will depend on the extent of the difference between the international price ratio and the domestic price ratio, the shape of the production-possibility frontier, and the preference pattern.

If in Figure 1.4, the international price line (P_2) becomes steeper than the domestic price line, a unit of c will exchange for more units of w on the world market than on the home market; the country will accordingly specialize in the production of c. In contrast, if the international price line (P_2) becomes less steep than the domestic price line (P_1), a unit of w will exchange for more

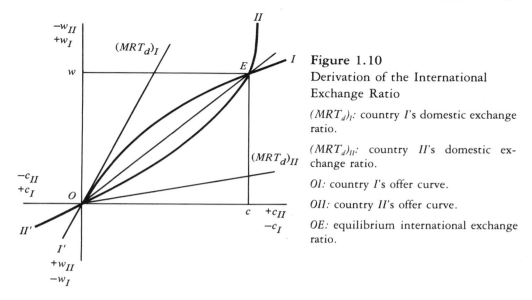

Figure 1.10

Derivation of the International
Exchange Ratio

$(MRT_d)_I$: country I's domestic exchange
ratio.

$(MRT_d)_{II}$: country II's domestic exchange ratio.

OI: country I's offer curve.

OII: country II's offer curve.

OE: equilibrium international exchange
ratio.

units of c on the world market than on the home market, and the country will tend to specialize in w. In Figure 1.10, this would be represented by an international price line to the right of I's domestic exchange ratio.

We may now derive I's offer curve, OI in Figure 1.10, by plotting in the first quadrant I's offers of w for c at the various international price lines less steep than P_1, and by plotting in the third quadrant I's offers of c for w at the international price lines steeper than P_1. In Figure 1.10, $+w_I$ and $-w_{II}$ denote exports of w from I and imports of w into II, respectively, $+c_{II}$ and $-c_I$ represent exports of c from II and imports of c into I, respectively. Thus, I's offer curve, OI, signifies that for a certain quantity Ow of I's exports, the quantity wE ($= Oc$) of II's product is demanded as imports into I.

Country II's offer curve can be derived in a similar fashion. It is represented by the curve OII in Figure 1.10. Only the first quandrant in which the offer curves intersect is of practical interest. If there is free trade, no transport costs, and no surplus or deficit in the balance of trade, then the position of trade equilibrium will be at E, the point of intersection of the offer curves; OE is the equilibrium international exchange ratio.

To recognize that E is a position of stable equilibrium, consider in Figure 1.11 international price lines that differ from the international price line OE. To the right of OE, along the international price line OMM', there is an excess demand for II's exports of c. (II would be willing to export OX of c in exchange for $XM = ON$ of w, but I would be willing to export OX' of w in exchange for $X'M' = OD$ of c). The relative price of II's exports must then rise. If, however, the international price line were to the left of OE, say at ON, there would be an excess supply of II's exports of c at this higher price, and the relative price of II's exports must then fall. Only at an international

Figure 1.11
The Equilibrium International Price Line

OMM': not an equilibrium international price line—excess demand for *II*'s exports, and price would rise to *OE*.

ON: not an equilibrium international price line—excess supply of *II*'s exports, and price would fall to *OE*.

OE: equilibrium international price line.

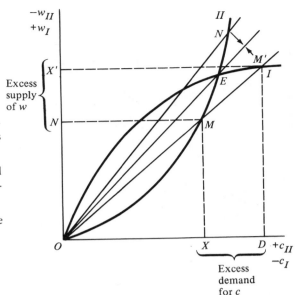

exchange ratio represented by OE do $D_c = S_c$ and $D_w = S_w$ and the value of exports = value of imports for each country.

If in Figure 1.4, the trading point T is an equilibrium trading position for country I, the point T must then lie on II's offer curve at E in Figure 1.10, and $B'X'$ of w exports in Figure 1.4 equals Ow of exports of w in Figure 1.10, whereas $X'T$ of imports of c in Figure 1.4 equals Oc imports of c in Figure 1.10. A similar analysis would apply to the trading position of T' for country II in Figure 1.5 (p. 00).

Equilibrium Conditions

The equilibrium conditions at the post-trade equilibrium position can be spelled out more thoroughly. Corresponding to the derivation of the equilibrium trading position are a number of adjustments in domestic production and consumption. As Edgeworth observed: "A movement along a supply-and-demand curve of international trade should be considered as attended with rearrangements of internal trade; as the movement of the hand of a clock corresponds to considerable unseen movements of the machinery."[2]

To determine the post-trade equilibrium position, we successively derived the following: the isoquants for each commodity, the box diagram and the efficiency locus, the production-possibility frontier, the domestic pre-trade equilibrium position, the offer curves and the international exchange ratio, and finally the post-trade equilibrium position.

At the trading equilibrium position, a number of marginal conditions hold:

[2]F.Y. Edgeworth, *Papers Relating to Political Economy*, II (1925), 32.

i. Marginal rates of substitution between any pair of factors are the same in all industries in which they are used (the efficiency locus).

ii. Price of a factor equals the value of its marginal product, and this is equal in all industries (perfectly competitive factor markets).

iii. Marginal rates of transformation in production of different commodities equal the rates at which they exchange on international markets (perfectly competitive product markets) and the rates of substitution in consumption ($MRT_d = MRT_f = MRS$).

iv. Marginal rates of substitution of any pair of commodities are the same for all consumers consuming both goods (tangency of budget line with indifference curve on each individual's preference map).

v. No excess demand or excess supply for any commodity (intersection of offer curves), and value of exports equals value of imports (balance of payments equilibrium).

vi. Finally, the factor price equalization theorem can also be derived if the following conditions prevail: the production functions for each commodity are identical between countries, the production functions show constant returns to scale in each product, the law of diminishing marginal productivity holds, there are different factor intensities for different products at all factor prices (factor-intensity rankings never reverse at different factor prices), there is free trade with no transport costs, factor and product markets are perfectly competitive, and incomplete specialization characterizes trade (some of each commodity is produced in each country). In equilibrium, real factor prices must then be exactly the same in each trading country.

The proof of this conclusion can be formulated rigorously.[3] Its validity can be recognized intuitively, however, by realizing that when a country exports a commodity there is an increase in the demand for its relatively abundant factor that is used intensively in the expanding exportable commodity, and therefore the real price of this factor rises, while the real price falls for the scarce factor used intensively in the contracting importable commodity. An increase in the ratio of the return to the abundant factor to the return to the scarce factor must, in a competitive market, push up the price of the commodity that is intensive in the abundant factor relative to the commodity that is intensive in the scarce factor. Since under free trade each country trades at the same international exchange ratio, the same commodity-price ratio must entail the same factor-price ratio in each country—so long as some of each commodity is produced in each country and is priced at marginal cost.[4]

[3] See P.A. Samuelson, "International Factor-Price Equalization Once Again," *Economic Journal*, 59 (June 1949), 181–97.
[4] This will hold so long as the number of commodities is greater than the number of factors, provided the countries produce at least r goods in common, where r is the number of factors.

Figure 1.12

Changes in Factor Supplies

Five different types of factor accumulation can occur:

  (i) movement of O_c to the northeast along $O_w O_c$;

  (ii) movement of O_c into region β;

  (iii) movement of O_c into region α;

  (iv) movement of O_c along $O_c L'$;

  (v) movement of O_c along $O_c K'$.

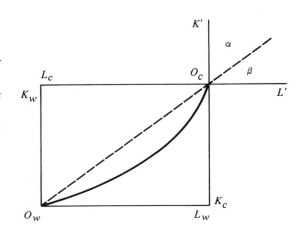

Effects of Growth on Trade

We have already stressed that comparative costs and the international division of labor are continually changing. To analyze this more thoroughly, we must depart from the static analysis we have so far followed. A truly dynamic analysis of the changing determinants of trade is too complex to be presented here; an analysis simply in terms of comparative statics will be thorough enough.

We shall first systematize the changes that may occur in the determinants of trade, then consider the pro-trade or anti-trade "biases" these changes create, and finally, translate these biases into shifts in the offer curves, with resultant changes in the terms of trade, volume, and composition of trade.

Changes in the determinants of trade can occur on both the production and consumption sides. In production, there can be variations in factor endowments and technology. Introducing various types of **changes in factor supplies** will mean that the dimensions of the box diagram in Figure 1.9 (p. 00), will expand or contract according to whether the factors increase or decrease in supply. Different production effects can be illustrated by movements of the O_c origin into the quadrant northeast of O_c, as indicated in Figure 1.12.

(i) A movement along $O_w O_c$—that is, the absolute amounts of L and K increase proportionately so that the relative factor endowment remains the same, but becomes larger in amount. The production-possibility frontier would then retain the same shape, but would shift out proportionately for both exportables and importables. This can be classified as a "neutral" production effect.[5]

(ii) A movement into region β—that is, labor increases proportionately more than does capital. The family of c-isoquants that originated previously at O_c must now be shifted northeastwards to the new origin in region β. This

---

[5]For a more detailed analysis, and references to original sources, see G.M. Meier, *International Trade and Development* (1963), Chap. 2.

will bring into tangency isoquants that originally neither touched nor intersected, thereby forming a new efficiency locus. The production-possibility frontier derived from this new efficiency locus will then lie beyond the initial frontier at all points, and the outward shift of the frontier will be proportionately greater in the direction of the labor-intensive commodity w at constant prices. A proportionately greater increase in the factor that is embodied most intensively in the exportable good will thus result in the supply of exports (w) increasing in greater proportion than the supply of importables (c), at constant output prices. This type of output expansion can be termed "export-biased," or "pro-trade-biased."

(iii) A movement into region α—that is, capital increases proportionately more than labor. The origin O_c will shift into this region, and a new efficiency locus will be formed. The new production-possibility frontier will then lie beyond the initial frontier at all points; but at constant prices, the outward shift of the frontier will be proportionately greater in the direction of the capital-intensive commodity, which is, in this case, the importable commodity. This type of output expansion can be classified as "import-biased' or "anti-trade-biased."

(iv) A movement along O_cL'—that is, there is an increase in the labor supply without any increase in the quantity of capital. The production effect will be to expand the supply of exportables (c) and reduce the domestic supply of importables (w) at constant prices. In order to absorb the augmented factor it is necessary to secure more of the factor as well; this can be achieved only by freeing the other factor from the industry in which it is used intensively, resulting in a contraction of that industry.[6] The new point on the production frontier (corresponding to the initial prices) will entail an absolute increase in the output of the exportable commodity and an absolute reduction in the output of the importable commodity. This is an "ultra-export-biased" or "ultra-pro-trade-bias" production effect.

(v) A movement along O_cK'—that is, the quantity of capital increases without any increase in the labor supply. By reasoning similar to that above, the production effect will be an increase in the supply of the capital-intensive importable (c) and a reduction in the supply of the labor-intensive exportable (w). This type of output expansion that reduces the domestic production of exportables can be classified as "ultra-import-biased" or "ultra-anti-trade-biased."

The five types of **production effects** due to the different types of factor accumulation can be summarized in simple geometrical terms as in Figure 1.13. Let the international price line P_2' be drawn parallel to and to the right of P_2, indicating constant relative prices, but expanded production. If the path of output expansion from B' is along the straight line $B'N$, the production effect is neutral: the supply of exportables and the supply of importables

[6] For a rigorous statement, see T.M. Rybczynski, "Factor Endowment and Relative Commodity Prices," *Economica*, 22 (Nov. 1955), 336–41.

Figure 1.13

Production Effects

(i) Neutral: expansion along $B'N$;

(ii) Export-bias: expansion along $B'X$;

(iii) Import-bias: expansion along $B'A$;

(iv) Ultra-export-bias: expansion along $B'U$;

(v) Ultra-import-bias: expansion along $B'U'$.

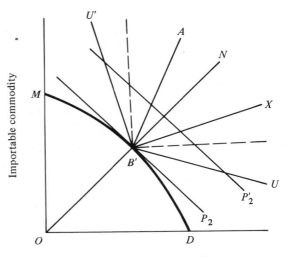

Exportable commodity

increase in the same proportion. If the output expansion line rises to the right of $B'N$, such as $B'X$, the production effect is export-biased: the supply of exportables increases in greater proportion than the supply of importables. If the line rises to the left of $B'N$, as $B'A$, the production effect is import-biased: the supply of importables increases in greater proportion than the supply of exportables. If it slopes negatively, such as $B'U$, the effect is ultra-export-biased: the domestic production of import-competing goods is reduced. And if it slopes negatively in the other direction, such as $B'U'$, the production effect is ultra-import-biased: the supply of exportables is reduced.

Technological progress will also alter the structure of comparative costs. Different types of bias in production will depend on what type of technical change occurs in the exportable or importable industries. A technical innovation may be "labor-saving" in the sense that, at constant factor prices, it lowers the optimal ratio of labor to capital; at the initial factor prices, the cost of producing a given output is then reduced, and the supply of the "saved" factor labor is in effect increased. Or the innovation may be "capital-saving" in the sense that the optimal ratio of capital to labor is lowered at the original relative factor prices; the cost of production is again lowered, and a quantity of the "saved" factor capital is set free. Finally, the innovation may be "neutral," inasmuch as it is neither labor-saving nor capital-saving, but allows a reduction by the same proportion in the amounts of the two factors required to produce a given quantity of output; the optimal factor ratio is unaltered, but the output obtainable from a given combination of factors is increased. The analysis of the production effects of technological change is similar to the previous analysis for changes in factor supply.[7]

[7] For a more detailed analysis, see references in book cited in note 5, above.

Turning from production, we should also recognize that there will be similar biases on the side of **consumption** as income changes. If, at constant relative prices, an expansion of income raises the demand for importables in the same proportion as it increases the demand for exportables, the consumption effect can be termed neutral. If the growth of income raises the demand for importables in greater proportion than it increases the demand for exportables, the consumption effect can be termed export-biased (pro-trade-biased)—that is, home demand is biased **against** exportables, and thus relatively more of the exportable commodity is available for export. If the growth of income raises the demand for importables in lesser proportion than it increases the demand for exportables, the consumption effect is import-biased—that is, home demand is biased **against** imports.[8]

Beyond changes in income, the pattern of demand might, of course, also change because the preference system will be modified as tastes change or income is redistributed. The analysis is similar. If, for example, tastes change in favor of the exportable, or there is a redistribution of income in favor of the factor that has higher average and marginal propensities to consume the exportable, the consumption effect is import-biased (anti-trade-biased).

We can now combine the various production and consumption effects to determine the overall effect or "**country bias.**" The country bias will show the total effect on the country's demand for imports. To determine this total effect, we must weigh the change in the domestic supply of importables, as given by the production effect, against the change in demand for importables, as given by the consumption effect. According to the type and degree of country bias, there will be a **shift in the country's offer curve,** and a **new international trade equilibrium** will tend to result. The type of country bias will determine the direction of the movement of the offer curve, whereas the extent of the shift in the offer curve will depend on the degree of the overall bias and on the rate of growth in total production.

If the production and consumption effects are both in the same direction or if one is neutral, the country bias is export- or import-biased. If, however, the production and consumption effects are in opposite directions, the country bias will depend on the degrees of bias in production and consumption. Table 1.5 summarizes the variety of country biases that may result from different combinations of production and consumption effects.[9]

The different types of country bias can be translated into different shifts of

---

[8] The remaining possible consumption effects are ultra-export-biased when the demand for exportables falls absolutely as income rises and ultra-import-biased when the demand for importables falls absolutely as income rises. These are, however, exceptional cases involving inferior goods, lower per capita income with population growth as aggregate income rises, or the possible effects of income redistribution. We ignore these complications.

[9] Cf. J. Black and P.P. Streeten, "La Balance Commerciale les termes de l'échange et la croissance économique," *Économie Appliquée,* 10 (April–Sept. 1957), 308.

Table 1.5

Type of Consumption Effect	Type of Production Effect				
	N	*X*	*M*	*UM*	*UX*
N	*N*	*X*	*M* or *UM*	*UM*	*X* or *UX*
X	*X*	*X*	Not *UX*	*UM*	*X* or *UX*
M	*M* or *UM*	Not *UX*	*M* or *UM*	*UM*	Not *UM*

Key
  N: neutral   *M:* import-bias   *UX:* ultra-export-bias
  X: export-bias   *UM:* ultra-import-bias

the offer curve, as in figure 1.14.[10] Country *II*'s offer curve originally intersects country *I*'s offer curve at *E*. Let *II* now experience changes in production
and consumption as growth occurs. The various possible shifts in the offer
curve can then be represented by II_N, a neutral country bias; II_X, an overall
export-bias; II_M, an overall import-bias; or II_{UM}, an overall ultra-import bias.
It is clear that with the shift in the offer curve there will be a change in the
terms of trade, the volume of trade, and the composition of trade.

A similar analysis could be applied to country *I* to complete the analysis of
how comparative advantage might change for both trading countries as a
consequence of changes in factor supply, technology, and demand conditions.

[10]A rigorous geometrical proof of the position of the new offer curve, under various cases of
growth, is presented by F.L. Pryor, "Economic Growth and the Terms of Trade," *Oxford
Economic Papers*, 18 (March 1966), 45–57.

Figure 1.14
Shifts in Offer Curves

The shifts in the offer curves result in
changes in the volume of trade, composition of trade, and terms of trade.

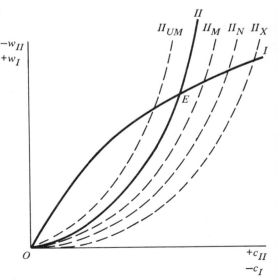

2

The Gains from Trade

We now come to the welfare implications of trade that are so essential for evaluating trade policy. In Chapter 1, it was implied that there are gains from trade based on a rational pattern of international specialization; it was also indicated what the trade structure would be under free trade, with the further implication that free trade should be pursued because the resulting specialization and voluntary exchange can raise the real income of each trading nation. Except under special conditions, to be examined in Chapters 3 and 4, the gains from trade constitute the case for **the optimality of free trade.** We shall now concentrate on the advantages of international specialization.

Ricardo indicated the gains from trade in terms of the greater consumption available to a country for the same input of labor. To Ricardo, "the extension of foreign trade . . . will very powerfully contribute to increase the mass of commodities, and therefore, the sum of enjoyments."[1] And this will be true for each trading nation. In modern terminology, **trade is a positive sum game.**

Since Ricardo's day, the concepts of the "mass of commodities" and the "sum of enjoyments" have been extensively refined by each succeeding generation of economists. Ricardo's insights on the merits of free trade can now be stated precisely in terms of an increase in real national income attained by an optimal allocation of resources on a worldwide basis: conditions of "Pareto international efficiency" can be expressed in general equilibrium terms, as we shall soon see below.

[1]David Ricardo, *Principles of Political Economy and Taxation* (1817), 107.

Figure 2.1

Free Trade is Superior to No Trade

SS' is the domestic supply curve. The home price with no trade is P_h. A prohibitive tariff would be at the specific rate $P_f P_h$, or at the *ad valorem* rate $P_f P_h / O P_f$.

When trade policy changes from prohibitive protection at P_h to free trade at P_f, the excess of the gain in consumers' surplus over loss in producers' surplus is $EE'H$, OH' is produced at home, and $H'M'$ is imported at P_f.

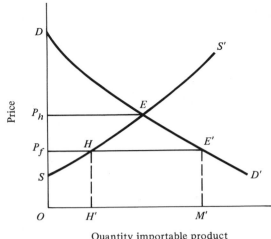

Quantity importable product

Optimality of Free Trade

Before turning to the modern general equilibrium analysis, however, we shall first note how the case for free trade can be argued in terms of partial welfare economics analysis. Partial welfare analysis does not consider all hypothetical welfare distributions, but merely those that exist before and after the contemplated policy change in one industry. A convenient approach to this type of analysis is to consider what happens to consumers' surplus and producers' surplus after there is a policy change that affects an industry.

Marshall (1890) defined consumer's surplus or rent as "the excess of the price which he [a consumer] would be willing to pay rather than go without the thing, over that which he actually does pay." The economic measure of this "surplus satisfaction" is the area between the demand curve and price line[2] (such as DP_hE in Figure 2.1, when the market price is P_h).

On the side of supply, "the price required to call forth the exertion necessary for producing any given amount of a commodity may be

---

[2] When the demand curve is for total market demand, the demand curves of many individual consumers have been aggregated, and it then becomes a question whether the apostrophe is rightly placed before or after the "s." If we refer to consumers' surplus, then we must assume that the marginal utility of money is constant for the poor man and the rich man, and we use a constant utility demand curve. Marshall placed the apostrophe after the "s" by appealing to the fact that "by far the greater number of the events with which economics deals, affect in about equal proportions all the different classes of society."

For extensive refinement of consumers' surplus, see J.R. Hicks, "The Rehabilitation of Consumers' Surplus," *Review of Economic Studies*, 8 (Feb. 1941), 108–16.

called the **supply price** for that amount during the same time." But producers will have "differential advantages," resulting in different levels of their cost curves. Thus, the supply curve SS' slopes upwards to the right, with a higher price being needed to bring forth a supply from the higher-cost firms. The difference between the price line and the supply curve is producer's surplus or rent—a surplus remuneration that is greater than the amount necessary to call forth the supply from the lower cost firms.[3] Producers' surplus under prohibitive protection, with the domestic price at P_b, would amount to P_bES in Figure 2.1.

Consider now **a change from no trade to free trade.** In Figure 2.1, let P_b represent the domestic price before trade, and assume that there is a prohibitive tariff—say, at the specific rate of P_fP_b per unit of import, or the *ad valorem* rate P_fP_b/OP_f—sufficiently high to prevent any imports, so that all the demand is filled from home supply. Under free trade the price would be P_f, the border price that includes transportation costs to the importing country. The country would then produce OH' at home and import $H'M'$. For simplicity we assume that the import supply curve is infinitely elastic at P_f (the importing country can demand all the commodity desired at a constant price). When the country moves from no trade to free trade, consumers' surplus increases from DEP_b to $DE'P_f$, a gain to consumers of $P_bEE'P_f$. Producers' surplus decreases from P_bES to P_fHS, a loss to producers of P_bEHP_f. But the gain to consumers is greater than the loss to producers by the amount $EE'H$. It would therefore be **possible for the gainers (the consumers) to compensate the losers (producers) and still be better off in the free-trade situation than in the no-trade situation.** Conversely, it would be impossible for the future losers (producers) to bribe the future gainers (consumers) not to "vote" for free trade. If it were politically desired, the government could tax consumers an amount equivalent to P_bEHP_f, and taxes could be remitted by this amount for producers. Since potential economic welfare (real income) has increased, the producers could be brought back to their initial income level, while consumers could be left better off after the policy change.

Consider next **a change from protection to free trade.** In Figure 2.2, the price with tariff (P_t) falls to the free-trade price P_f. Home production would then decline from OH' to OH'', while imports would increase from $H'M'$ to $H''M''$. The effects would be

[3] For difficulties associated with the use of producers' surplus, see E.J. Mishan, "What is Producers' Surplus?" *American Economic Review*, 58 (Dec. 1968), 1269–82.

Figure 2.2

Free Trade is Superior to Restricted Trade

If the tariff $P_f P_t$ or $P_f P_t / OP_f$ is eliminated, the effects are:

increase in consumers' surplus: $P_t M C P_f$;

decrease in producers' surplus: $P_t H E P_f$;

loss in government tariff revenue: $HMNT$;

net gain: HTE (production gain) and MNC (consumption gain).

An increase in price from the free trade P_f to price with tariff P_t would result in the production and consumption "deadweight losses," HTE and MNC, respectively.

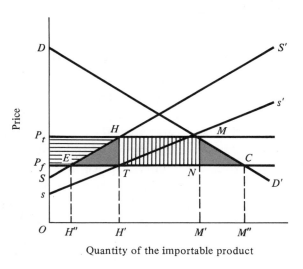

Quantity of the importable product

an increase in consumers' surplus: $P_t M C P_f$

a decrease in producers' surplus: $P_t H E P_f$

a loss in government tariff revenue: $HMNT$.

Gains to consumers exceed losses to producers and the government by the amount of the two shaded triangles HTE and MNC.

Alternatively, we can note that the value of output produced elsewhere in the economy after the tariff is reduced is $H''EHH'$ (the area under the supply curve represents the opportunity cost of factors that can be used elsewhere in the economy). But the imports equivalent to the domestic goods that these resources produced under the tariff now cost only $H''ETH'$. The **net production gain** to the economy is therefore HTE. And the **net consumption gain** to the economy is MNC. **Potential welfare** has increased. It would be possible, if politically desired, to tax consumers an amount equivalent to the loss in producers' surplus and government revenue, remit taxes to producers so that they are no worse off than before the policy change to free trade, and still leave consumers better off under free trade by the amount of the shaded triangles.

This gain from free trade will, however, be overstated if the resources displaced from domestic production are not absorbed in alternative employment. The value of the released resources that were previously involved in the sheltered domestic production are represented by

$H''EHH'$ in Figure 2.2. If these resources are not immediately absorbed elsewhere at earnings rates equal to their marginal productivity, then the relevant part of the area $H''EHH'$ that remains idle should be deducted from the two triangles HTE and MNC. To be precise, the net direct gain or loss of welfare from reducing the tariff is the present value of the two shaded triangles—determined by discounting the sum over the appropriate time period and at some appropriate interest rate— minus the present value of the loss of productive output during the transitional period when displaced resources are idle.[4]

Finally, consider the reverse **movement from free trade (P_f) to protection (P_t).** We assume that the tariff does not cause the foreign suppliers to lower their export price—that is, the tariff-imposing country is a small country that cannot affect its terms of trade. Home production would then expand from OH'' to OH', while imports would fall from $H''M''$ to $H'M'$. The effects would be

a decrease in consumers' surplus: P_tMCP_f

an increase in producers' surpus: P_tHEP_f

an increase in government tariff revenue: $HMNT$.

The decrease in consumers' surplus is offset in part by the gains to the producers and government. **But consumers still lose more than the producers and the government gain.** There remain the two shaded triangles HTE and MNC, representing the **production and consumption "deadweight losses,"** respectively.

The production deadweight loss is transferred from consumers to inefficient domestic producers. The consumption deadweight loss means less is consumed at a higher price. It would be impossible for the gainers under protection (producers and government) to compensate the losers (consumers) sufficiently to leave consumers as well off as they were under free trade. If, however, there were a "vote" for protection or free trade, it would "pay" the consumers to bribe producers not to vote for protection (a tariff). Or under free trade, taxes could be imposed on consumers in an amount sufficient to compensate producers and government for lost tariff revenue, while still leaving consumers better off under free trade than protection.

The **cost of protection** therefore consists of a **production cost** and a **consumption cost.** The production cost is the excess real cost of secur-

[4] R.E. Baldwin and J. Mutti, "Policy Issues in Adjustment Assistance: The United States," in Helen Hughes (ed.), *Prospects for Partnership* (1973), 153.

ing $H''H'$ from inefficient home producers instead of from imports. This can be calculated as the "cash cost" or **"subsidy-equivalent"**—the cash cost to the Treasury of a production subsidy to the protected industry that would have the same protective effect as the tariff.[5] The subsidy-equivalent of the tariff in Figure 2.2 is $P_f P_t HT$. If there were a production subsidy (a negative tariff), designed to obtain the same amount of protection for home industry, the *ad valorem* subsidy would shift the domestic supply curve down to the new position ss'. This subsidy would raise home output to OH', with a protection effect identical with that of the tariff-equivalent. But there would be no consumption effect because P_f does not rise. And, although there will be a redistribution to producers, the increased revenue to home suppliers comes not from consumers, as in the case of a tariff, but from the Treasury.

The consumption cost under a tariff can be calculated by a compensating variation in income—that is, by the amount consumers' money income would have to increase to leave them as well off after protection as they were in the free-trade situation before prices rose.

From a consideration of the gains and losses in this type of partial analysis, we can conclude that

free trade is superior to no trade,[6] and

free trade is superior to a tariff.

In each case, the gains from trade are composed of a **consumption gain** and a **production gain**. Whether expressed as an increase in the "mass of commodities and sum of enjoyments," an increase in consumers' surplus, or an increase in real income, the consumption gain amounts to the substitution of lower-cost imports for higher-cost domestic goods. The production gain arises from the allocation of resources away from the direct production of importables in higher-cost home production to the specialization in the lower-cost production of exportables. The export sector indirectly "produces" the importables on the world market, and this conversion of domestic resources into foreign resources will raise the trading country's real income if the alternative domestic employment of resources used in the export sector would

---

[5] For a review of empirical measures, see W.M. Corden, "The Costs and Consequences of Protection: A Survey of Empirical Work," in P.B. Kenen (ed.), *International Trade and Finance* (1975), 51–60.

[6] It can also be demonstrated that restricted trade (by tariffs, quotas, or exchange restrictions) is superior to no trade. See M.C. Kemp, "The Gain from International Trade," *Economic Journal*, 72 (Dec. 1962), 803–19. We are concentrating here, however, on a comparison of free trade and protection.

FRANK GRAHAM, *Protective Tariffs* (1934), 58–59

Whether a country is rich or poor, big or little, new or old, with or without high standards of living, agricultural, industrial, or mixed, makes no difference. It is a matter of mathematics, quite independent of environment, that there is an inherent gain in the specialization along the lines of comparative competence which unshackled trade tends to develop.

There is no possible refutation of this analysis. Advocates of a restrictive commercial policy must, in logic, accept it as a fact and attempt to show that the gain may be outweighed by economic or other considerations of superior importance. . . . The presumption is always in favor of free trade, since the gain therefrom is certain, and the loss, if any, dependent upon incidental circumstance. This presumption is rebuttable but it is ever present; and, in this sense, the classical economists were right in insisting that free trade is a ubiquitous and timeless principle. Other things being equal, it will enable people to have more goods of every kind than would otherwise be possible.

---

have lower productivity. Moreover, the gains from trade are **mutual gains**: every trading nation enjoys a consumption gain and a production gain.

Pareto International Efficiency

Free trade is also optimal in the sense of representing a **Pareto-efficient situation** in which no one can be made better off without someone else being made worse off. Recalling the analysis of the last chapter, we know that—given a country's production possibility set—any position on the country's production-possibility frontier is **production-maximizing**. This represents **technical efficiency**,[7] and each point on the production frontier qualifies for the decisive round of determining the position of **economic efficiency** or the position that is **production-**

---

[7] We saw that under a competitive price system, free trade will in fact establish a production point on the production frontier. Under a different institutional system—for instance, central planning—the efficiency rule would still be the same: planners would follow the rule of equating *foreign* prices with the marginal rate of transformation in domestic production. Cf. J. Bhagwati, "The Gains from Trade Once Again," *Oxford Economic Papers*, 20 (July 1968), 139–40.

Figure 2.3

World Production-Possibility
Frontier

The world production-possibility frontier is determined by the condition that
under free trade the marginal rate of
domestic transformation must be the
same in countries *I* and *II*. Any point
on the world production-possibility
frontier denotes efficient production in
the world economy.

O_I: origin of country *I*'s production-
possibility frontier.

O_{II}: origin of country *II*'s production-
possibility frontier.

PF: world production-possibility frontier.

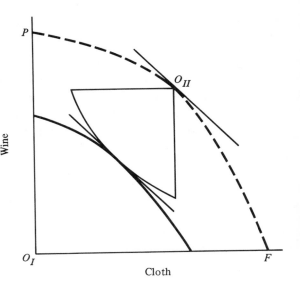

optimizing. But which is the best among the feasible alternatives?
Where is the "winner" among points that have qualified as technically
efficient? We have already seen that in a competitive price system the
production-optimizing situation in the closed economy is represented
by the point on the production frontier at which the price ratio, marginal rate of domestic transformation, and marginal rate of substitution in
consumption are all equal [see Figure 1.4 and equation (1.1)]. This was
a point of Pareto national efficiency, denoting both technical efficiency
and exchange efficiency.

If the economy now moves from no trade to free trade, the free-trade
trading point will represent a situation of **Pareto international efficiency.** We can first recognize that production under free trade will
take place on the boundary of the **world** production-possibility frontier. This can be seen if we aggregate the two countries' production-
possibility frontiers into a world production frontier, as in Figure 2.3.
Under free trade, the two countries will trade at the same international
price ratio. Therefore, in each country, the marginal rate of domestic
transformation (slope of the country's production frontier) is equal to
the price ratio. Given that the free-trade price ratio is the same for both
countries, the marginal rate of domestic transformation must also be
the same in both countries. This can be illustrated in Figure 2.3 by
revolving the production frontier diagram for country *II*, keeping the
axes parallel to that of country *I*, and determining the points of tan-

gency of the two production frontiers where both countries are producing at the same marginal rate of transformation. The origin of II's production frontier will then trace out the world production-possibility frontier. Any point on the world production frontier denotes efficient production in the world economy: given the level of world output for w, the level of c is maximized under the constraints of given techniques of production, factor supply, and factor location.

The virtue of free trade is not only that it makes **world production efficient in the technical sense.** It also leads to **economic efficiency in the Pareto-efficiency sense of achieving a situation in which it is impossible to make someone better off without making anyone worse off.** This follows from the fact that, under free trade, consumers face the same prices in both countries; they equate the price ratio to their marginal rates of substitution; and the common marginal rate of domestic transformation in production is equal to the common marginal rate of substitution in consumption. Again, both technical efficiency and exchange efficiency are achieved. Producers are in equilibrium, consumers are in equilibrium, and it would be impossible to make anyone better off without making someone else worse off.

The international price line (or the availability frontier or consumption frontier, the slope of which is the marginal rate of foreign transformation) lies beyond each country's production frontier, indicating the larger combinations of the products available to the country through free trade (see Figure 2.4). On this international price line, the free-trade position is the Pareto-dominant position (represented by T in Figure 2.4). At this position, free trade makes available a larger bundle of goods than could be produced on the country's own production-possibility frontier. The result is as if the production frontier had shifted outwards (now going through T). And as a result of free trade, real national income has increased. If we were to measure the post-trade output (q_2) against the pre-trade output (q_1), both valued at post-trade prices (p_2), then the index numbers would show $\Sigma p_2 q_2 > \Sigma p_2 q_1$, and $q_2 > q_1$.[8] Given the constraints of the production frontier and national prices, no other level of real income would make the community better off in the sense of allowing someone to be better off without making someone worse off. At the free-trade position, there is no scope for any further voluntary exchange or recontracting that would make someone

---

[8] This also implies $\Sigma p_1 q_1 < \Sigma p_1 q_2$, where p_1 are pre-trade prices. If, however, we introduce considerations of income distributions in the two situations, the index numbers may give an ambiguous result. The problem is examined in the Appendix.

Figure 2.4

Effects of a Tariff

P_1: international price line under free trade.

P_2: domestic price line with tariff on w.

P_3: parallel to P_1, and shows combinations of w and c that have same value at world prices as does the home production point H. National income in w units at world prices is reduced by the tariff on w from OF to OM.

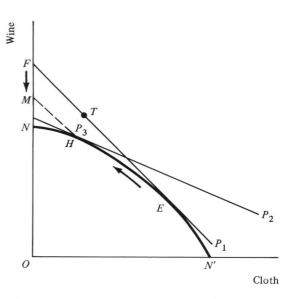

better off and no one worse off. **The perfectly competitive equilibrium situation, the free-trade situation, and the situation of Pareto international efficiency are all equivalent.**

If, however, there were an import duty, then the international price line, allowing for the tariff, would cut the production-possibility frontier instead of being tangent to it. The tariff acts as a wedge between domestic prices and world prices, raising the domestic relative price of the protected commodity. Resources are then shifted into the protected import-competing industry, but national income at world prices is reduced. This is illustrated in Figure 2.4,[9] where a tariff on w raises the relative domestic price of w (indicated by line P_2) and induces a movement of resources from the free-trade production point of E to the tariff production point of H. Under free trade, the value of production is OF, measured in units of w. After the tariff is imposed, the value of production at world prices is indicated by the restricted consumption-possibility line P_3, drawn parallel to the free-trade international price line at the domestic production point H. The tariff-imposing country's consumption after the tariff must lie somewhere along P_3, where the domestic price ratio is equal to the marginal rate of substitution in consumption. But it is clear that the consumption possibilities along P_3 are all inferior to the consumption possibilities available along P_1 with free trade. The value of aggregate production at world prices, measured in units of w, is reduced to OM after the tariff. And the

[9]See R.E. Caves and R.W. Jones, *World Trade and Payments* (2nd ed.) (1977), 180.

equivalency between the marginal rate of domestic transformation (slope of the production frontier) and the marginal rate of foreign transformation (slope of the international price line) has been destroyed. The cost to the tariff-imposing country of obtaining another unit of w, as measured by the marginal rate of foreign transformation, is less than the value to the consumers of having another unit of w, as measured by the domestic price of w. This discrepancy between value and cost indicates that the importation of another unit of w, at world prices, would yield more in consumer satisfaction than would be sacrificed in cost.[10] But the tariff actually reduces imports and lowers real income.

We have assumed that the tariff-imposing country is too small a country to affect its terms of trade (we return to this possibility in Chapter 3). In this situation, our analysis indicates that a tariff destroys the conditions of Pareto international efficiency and that **the allocation under free trade is Pareto dominant to that of restricted trade.**

Distribution of the Gains

If the free-trade situation is Pareto dominant to no trade and to restricted trade, then all the trading nations gain under free trade. But how are the gains divided among the nations?

This will depend on both the volume of trade and the terms of trade. The greater the volume of trade, the greater the gains from trade, "on the average," for each country through international specialization. And the more favorable the terms of trade for a country, the more that country gains "at the margin." When a country's terms of trade improve, it can export less for the same volume of imports, or it can import more for the same volume of exports. Therefore, **its real income from a given output rises as its terms of trade improve.**

We have previously noted (Appendix, Chapter 1) that the terms of trade are determined by the intensity and elasticity of each country's demand for imports, within a region of potential gain between the trading countries' domestic exchange ratios (see Figure 1.10). Considering two countries I and II, we can say that within the region of gain, the closer the terms of trade to I's domestic exchange ratio, the more II

---

[10]For a more detailed exposition, see R.E. Caves and R.W. Jones, *World Trade and Payments* (1977), 179–85. Even if the tariff revenue is redistributed to consumers, so that disposable personal income is greater than the value of domestic production, the tariff still harms consumers by forcing them to lower indifference curves; *op. cit.*, pp. 181–83.

gains from trade. If the terms of trade are just short of I's cost ratio, II obtains practically all the benefit from trade. Although both countries are better off under trade than in autarky, the division of the gain is determined by the location of the equilibrium international price line relative to each country's domestic exchange ratio. The country with the less intense and more elastic demand for imports will enjoy the more favorable terms of trade as the international price line approaches the other country's domestic cost ratio.

The terms of trade, however, relate to a **unit** of trade, and the trend of the terms of trade can be an index for only the trend of gain from trade per unit of trade. For an index of the **total** amount of gain from trade, we should multiply the terms of trade index by a physical index of the volume of trade. It is then possible to see that the **total** gain index might increase at the same time as the **unit** gain index became unfavorable, if the latter was associated with an increase in the volume of trade.[11]

Terms of Trade

More ambiguities, however, surround the terms of trade than we have so far admitted. We should first distinguish **several different concepts of the terms of trade:** commodity, income, single-factoral, double-factoral, real cost, and utility terms of trade. These several concepts fall into three categories: (i) those that relate to the **ratio of exchange between commodities**—the commodity and income terms of trade; (ii) those that relate to the **interchange between productive resources**—the single-factoral and double-factoral terms of trade; and (iii) those that interpret the gains from trade **in terms of utility analysis**—the real cost and utility terms of trade.

The **commodity terms of trade** (T) are calculated by dividing an index of prices of the country's commodity exports (P_x) during a specified period of time, or at a point in time, by an index of the country's import prices (P_m).[12] An increase in $T = (P_x/P_m)$ indicates that a larger volume of imports could be enjoyed, on the basis of price relations only, in exchange for a given volume of exports. Or the country could now export less to receive the same amount of imports. The country's

[11] Jacob Viner, *Studies in the Theory of International Trade* (1937), 563–64.
[12] We could extend the concept to include services (insurance, banking, transportation, etc.) and compute the terms of trade on current account.

real income rises faster than output because the purchasing power of its exports rises.

The **income terms of trade** (I) adjusts the movements in the commodity terms of trade for changes in export volume. It is expressed as $I = T \cdot Q_x$, where Q_x is the export volume index for a specified period of time. A rise in I indicates that the country can obtain a larger volume of imports from the sale of its exports: its "capacity to import," based on exports, has increased.

According to the direction and magnitude of the changes in P_x and Q_x the changes in T and I can be in opposite directions. If, for example, with unchanged import prices, export prices have fallen, but export quantities (Q_x) have increased by a greater percentage than the decrease in P_x, the income terms of trade will have improved despite a deterioration in the commodity terms of trade.

The **single-factoral terms of trade** (S) adjusts the commodity terms of trade for changes in productivity in producing exports. It can be expresed as $S = T \cdot Z_x$, where Z_x is an export productivity index during a period of time. A rise in S is a favorable movement in the sense that a greater quantity of imports can be obtained per unit of factor-input used in the production of exportables.

If T is corrected for changes in productivity in producing imports as well as exports, the result is the **double-factoral terms of trade** (D), expressed as $D = T \cdot Z_x/Z_m$, where Z_m is an import productivity index. A rise in D shows that one unit of home factors embodied in exports now exchanges for more units of the foreign factors embodied in imports. When there is a change in the factor cost of producing imports, D will diverge from S.

To distinguish these concepts, consider these simple examples: Assume that P_x is 1.10 (the average price of exports has risen by 10% from the base year); Z_x is 1.05 (output per unit of input has increased by 5% in the production of exportables); P_m is 1.00 (import prices have remained unchanged); Z_m is 1.10 (output per unit of input has increased by 10% in the production of imports).

The various measures of the terms of trade will then be:

$T = (P_x/P_m) = 1.10/1.00 = 1.10$. One unit of exports now buys 10% more imports.

$S = T \cdot Z_x = 1.10 \times 1.05 = 1.15$. One unit of resources in the country's exports now buys 15% more imports.

$D = T \cdot Z_x / Z_m = 1.10 \times 1.05 / 1.10 = 1.05$. One unit of resources in the country's exports now buys 5% more foreign resources than in the base period.[13]

It would be wonderfully simple for welfare analysis if we could proceed directly to define in utility terms the total amount of gain from trade. This would measure the excess of the total utility accruing from imports over the total sacrifice of utility involved in the production of exports.[14] This would be indicated by a measure of the real cost terms of trade and the utility terms of trade. But to do this, we would have to calculate the disutility involved in export production and the relative average utility derived from various commodities. Recognizing that the production of exports involves disutility (subjective costs of production), we would correct the single-factoral terms of trade index by multiplying S by the reciprocal of an index of the amount of disutility per unit of factor inputs used in producing exports.[15] This would give a real cost terms of trade index (R). If R rises, this would indicate that the amount of imports obtained per unit of real cost (unit of disutility) has risen.

Such a measure would be in the tradition of the classical economists who, when dealing with questions of public policy, were concerned with subjective costs or "disutilities."[16] When Ricardo resorted to a pain cost theory of value, he was conveying the feeling that "toil and sweat" were involved in production and that it is desirable to minimize the real cost of labor per unit of output. The art of persuasion in policy-making often depends on emotive language, interlaced with technical analysis.

On the side of demand, we would also want to allow for changes in the relative desirability of the imports and the domestic commodities whose home consumption is sacrificed because of the use of resources in export production. We would therefore want to incorporate into R an index of the relative average utility per unit of imports and of forgone domestic commodities. The resultant index would be the utility terms of trade (U), equal to R multiplied by an index of the relative utility of imports and forgone commodities.[17]

[13]Cf. Haberler, *op. cit.*, 24–25. The measurements of Z_x and Z_m raise complex statistical problems that we blithely and conveniently ignore.

[14]Viner, *op. cit.*, 557.

[15]*Ibid.*, 559.

[16]*Ibid.*, 492.

[17]*Ibid.*, 560–61.

Unfortunately, however, we cannot calculate a "disutility coefficient" for the factors embodied in exports. Nor can we place a cardinal measurement on the relative average utility of imports and the sacrificed domestic commodities. Moreover, a change in the terms of trade is merely a summary index of underlying forces—such as changes in productivity, factor prices, and demand conditions (see Appendix, p. 56). For any welfare measurement, we must evaluate the causes that are behind the changes in the terms of trade. If, for instance, the commodity terms deteriorate because productivity in export production increases and export prices fall, this would not necessarily have any adverse welfare effects. In this case, the single-factoral terms improve, and the deterioration in the commodity terms reflects only the increased productivity in the country's export sector. As long as productivity in the export sector is rising faster than the prices of its exports are falling, the country's real income rises despite the deterioration in its commodity terms of trade. If the prices of exports in terms of imports fall by a smaller percentage than the percentage increase in productivity, the country clearly benefits from its ability to obtain a greater quantity of imports per unit of factors embodied in its exports.

Even if the prices of imports rise, the deterioration in the commodity terms of trade does not necessarily indicate adverse welfare effects, for consumers' preferences may have changed in favor of imports. This could result from a change in tastes, a redistribution of income, or technological progress that leads to importing goods of much greater quality, albeit at slightly higher prices. The intervening change in the preference system or quality makes it impossible to conclude that the subsequent trading pattern is inferior to the previous situation merely because the commodity terms have worsened. If the terms deteriorate because demand increases for imports, it may not be true that from the criterion of "utility" a loss is incurred. We would want to consider not only the utility of the import alone, but also its utility relative to that of the domestic commodities that can no longer be consumed when resources must be allocated to the export sector. We would then be back to the utility terms of trade index—if it were only measurable.

We have also already noted that a country's income terms of trade can improve at the same time its commodity terms worsen. Indeed, the income terms might improve because of a deterioration in the commodity terms: as export prices decline, the country's exports may increase sufficiently to improve the income terms of trade. The country's capacity to import is then greater. (It would, of course, be even better for the country if this new greater volume of exports could be traded at unchanged export prices. But this would be a completely hypothetical situation, whereas the relevant consideration is the effect of the actual price change between the base period and the present.)

We must avoid the fallacy of equating a change in any of the various terms of trade with a variation in the amount or even the direction of change in the gains from trade. We could not do this until we determined the underlying forces causing the change in the terms of trade and connected the terms of trade—relating to a unit of trade—with the volume of trade. Even though policy debates commonly refer to the "terms of trade," the economist cannot accept any one of the measures of the terms of trade as a reliable indicator of changes in economic welfare. Any index of the terms of trade remains only a summary index of changes in other variables that have welfare significance in their own right and require independent assessment.

Dynamic Gains from Trade

We have so far emphasized the static gains from trade—the increase in each country's real income based on efficient international resource allocation. But the **dynamic aspects of trade** are of equal importance. Although dynamic elements were not central in classical and neoclassical thought, they were not ignored. John Stuart Mill, for one, was particularly clear on the dynamic gains. Trade, according to comparative advantage, results in a "more efficient employment of the productive forces of the world," and this Mill considered to be the "direct economical advantage of foreign trade." But, emphasized Mill, "there are, besides, indirect effects, which must be counted as benefits of a high order." One of the most significant "indirect" dynamic benefits, according to Mill,[18] is

the tendency of every extension of the market to improve the processes of production. A country which produces for a larger market than its own, can introduce a more extended division of labour, can make greater

[18]John Stuart Mill, *Principles of Political Economy* (1848), vol. II, Book III, Chap. XVII, Sec. 5. See also Smith's earlier statement on the benefits of trade by widening the extent of the market: Smith, *Wealth of Nations* (1776), Book IV, Chap. 1, par. 31.

use of machinery, and is more likely to make inventions and improvements in the processes of production.

More generally, Hla Myint has emphasized the dynamic "productivity" theory of international trade that was part of classical thought. The "productivity" theory links growth of the domestic economy to a country's foreign trade by interpreting trade as a dynamic force: trade widens the extent of the market and the scope of the division of labor, permits a greater use of machinery, stimulates innovations, overcomes technical indivisibilities, raises the productivity of labor, and generally enables the trading country to enjoy increasing returns and further growth.[19]

In more modern terminology, free trade may also promote what Leibenstein has called "X-efficiency."[20] By X-efficiency is meant the presence of some forces that cause the firm to purchase and utilize all of its inputs "efficiently," so as to reduce real costs per unit of output. Motivational elements contribute to an increase in productivity and make the firm produce closer to its minimal cost equilibrium. X-efficiency improves allocation within the firm, as distinct from the orthodox allocative efficiency among firms or industries.

Trade, with the exposure that it brings to the competition of world markets, can stimulate greater managerial effort and hence improve X-efficiency. Free trade makes it impossible for management to enjoy the quiet life of a monopolist in a sheltered industry. In defensive response to the greater competitive pressures from overseas, import-competing firms will have to reduce their managerial slack and pursue cost-reducing methods of production through greater effort, more intensive search for best methods of production, or the utilization of new information.

This view of the impact of trade emphasizes the supply side of a country's growth—the opportunity trade provides a country for removing its domestic shortages and overcoming the diseconomies of the small size of its domestic market. This advantage is especially important for small developing countries. Also significant is the opportunity

[19] Hla Myint, "The 'Classical Theory' of International Trade and the Underdeveloped Countries," *Economic Journal,* 68 (June 1958), 318–19, and Myint, "Adam Smith's Theory of International Trade in the Perspective of Economic Development," *Economica,* 44 (Aug. 1977), 231–48.

[20] H. Leibenstein, "Allocative Efficiency versus 'X-Efficiency,' " *American Economic Review,* 56 (June 1966), 392–415, and Leibenstein, *General X-Efficiency Theory and Economic Development* (1978). Also, cf. W.M. Corden, *Trade Policy and Economic Welfare* (1974), 224–31.

trade offers for the exchange of goods with less growth potential for goods with more growth potential, thereby quickening the progress that results from a given effort on the savings side.[21] An obvious example is the opportunity to import capital goods and materials required for development projects. (We shall discuss more thoroughly the particular problems of "development through trade" as related to poor countries in Part III.)

Classical economists also noted the effects of trade on the domestic factor supply, especially on capital accumulation. Real income rises through the more efficient resource allocation associated with international trade, and the capacity to save, in turn, increases. The stimulus to investment is also strengthened by the realization of increasing returns in the wider markets overseas trade provides. There are also some benefits from foreign investment attracted to the export sector.

Of increasing significance in a rapidly changing technological world is technological diffusion and adaption, the transfer of skills, and know-how—all the elements that might contribute to accelerating the country's "learning rate." Theories of the determinants of a **country's "learning rate"** are not yet formalized.[22] But foreign trade has to be allotted a substantial role in these theories via the competitive stimuli it creates, its "cost reduction" effects through the realization of economies of scale, and its contribution to increasing productivity and developing new skills. Dynamic learning scale economies are important consequences of international specialization.

The dynamic gains from trade can be summarized as a movement along the production frontier in accordance with the pre-existing comparative cost situation, which then tends to push the production frontier upward and outward.[23] Above and beyond the static gains that result from the more efficient resource allocation with given production functions, international trade also **transforms production functions** and **induces outward shifts in the production frontier.**

The limited space devoted to the dynamic gains from trade, as compared with our lengthier discussion of the static gains, should not be taken as an indication that the dynamic gains are less important. On the contrary, their quantitative significance far surpasses that of the

[21]J.R. Hicks, *Essays in World Economics* (1959), 132.

[22]Elements of such a theory might be found in the writings on "learning by doing" and "X-efficiency." Cf. Kenneth Arrow, "The Economic Implications of Learning by Doing," *Review of Economic Studies,* 29 (June 1962), 155–73; Leibenstein, *op. cit;* and Allyn Young, "Increasing Returns and Economic Progress," *Economic Journal,* 38 (Dec. 1928), 527–42.

[23]Gottfried Haberler, *International Trade and Economic Development* (1959), 14.

static welfare gains.[24] We say less about the dynamic gains only because the economist cannot analyze dynamic gains as rigorously as the static gains. Moreover, in determining the gains, it is easier to estimate the static welfare gain of the lower prices of imports after liberalization than it is to estimate such dynamic effects as economies of scale, X-efficiency, stimulus to investment, and creation of knowledge. Regardless of the brevity of our discussion, we must emphasize that **the gains from trade do not result merely from a once-over change toward efficient resource allocation among industries, but are being continually augmented by the dynamic gains.**

Unequal Exchange

In the classical and neoclassical tradition, we have so far viewed the gains from trade from a cosmopolitan perspective, considering the mutual gains from trade and the "natural harmony of interests" that orthodox theory believed existed in the international economy. But the descendants of Ricardo have always been opposed by the descendants of Lenin, who emphasize the political, social, and historical forces of imperialism instead of market forces. More recently, the French economist Emmanuel propounded the theory of "unequal exchange" for trade between a low-wage country and high-wage country. Using Marxian reproduction schemes, Emmanuel argues that with different techniques of production, the equilibrium rate of profit—and hence, growth of the economy—is higher with trade for the high-wage country, but lower for the low-wage country.[25] There is allegedly a transfer of "surplus value" from the low-wage to the high-wage country via the terms of trade. Other critics of traditional trade theory (particularly in Latin America) subscribe to the theory of "dependency."[26] They view the world economy as being polarized, with poor peripheral countries being

[24] See William R. Cline et al., *Trade Negotiations in the Tokyo Round, a Quantitative Assessment* (1978), 78–80. This study of the effects of future trade liberalization estimates that the annual total welfare gains including dynamic effects would be about five times as large as the static welfare gains. Also see R.J. Wonnacott and P. Wonnacott, *Free Trade Between the United States and Canada: The Potential Economic Effects* (1967); R.J. Wonnacott, *Canada's Trade Option,* (1975); and Bela Belassa (ed.), *European Economic Integration* (1975), 79–118.

[25] A. Emmanuel, *Unequal Exchange: A Study of the Imperialism of Trade* (1972), Chap. 3; G. Pilling, "Imperialism, Trade and 'Unequal Exchange': The Work of Arghir Emmanuel," *Economy and Society,* 2 (1973); and Jan Otto Anderson, *Studies in the Theory of Unequal Exchange Between Nations* (1976).

[26] See pp. 330, below.

dependent upon rich center countries, to the detriment of the development of the periphery.

In their broadest implications, all the views that oppose traditional theory are raising the question whether international trade operates as a mechanism of international inequality to widen the gap between rich and poor countries. Is there a conflict of interests instead of a harmony of interests in the international marketplace? Can countries develop through trade, or does trade actually inhibit their development? We shall return to these controversial questions in Chapters 11 through 13.

Supplementary Readings

Outstanding articles on the gains from trade are Paul A. Samuelson, "The Gains from International Trade," *Canadian Journal of Economics and Political Science*, 5 (May 1939), 195–205; Samuelson, "The Gains from International Trade Once Again,"*Economic Journal*, 72 (Dec. 1962), 820–29; R.E. Baldwin, "The New Welfare Economics and Gains in International Trade," *Quarterly Journal of Economics*, 66 (Feb. 1952), 91–101; and Jagdish Bhagwati, "The Gains From Trade Once Again," *Oxford Economic Papers*, 20 (July 1968), 137–48.

Also of interest are H.G. Johnson, "The Standard Theory of Tariffs," *Canadian Journal of Economics and Political Science* (Aug. 1969), 333–52; Tibor Scitovsky, 'A Reconsideration of the Theory of Tariffs," *Review of Economic Studies*, 9 (1942), 89–110; and Martin J. Bailey, "The Interpretation and Application of the Compensation Principle," *Economic Journal*, 64 (March 1954), 39–52.

On the cost of protection, an excellent survey article is W.M. Corden, "The Costs and Consequences of Protection: A Survey of Empirical Work," in Peter B. Kenen (ed.), *International Trade and Finance* (1975), 51–92, with extensive bibliography.

APPENDIX
Welfare Criteria

Welfare economics seeks to establish optimum criteria that will allow economists to judge alternative policies or particular forms of economic organization. In assessing whether a particular policy enhances "economic welfare," we normally have to consider the gains and losses that accrue to the individuals composing the economy. We have to weight the gains to some against the losses to others by some means. The economist usually expresses approval of a reorganization or policy by saying that the new situation is Pareto-superior to the previous situation or policy.

This does not mean that welfare economics is "value free." Rather it means that the Pareto principle is the mildest of the mild value premises to which most people would subscribe. The search for a value-free welfare economics is misguided because policy-making necessarily involves the production and distribution of values. What welfare economics can do is make the value judgments explicit and determine if they are "warranted" in terms of some axiological system.[1]

We stated in this chapter that free trade is superior to no trade and that free trade is superior to a tariff. And we demonstrated this from the viewpoint of technical efficiency, in which technical efficiency is defined in the sense that it is possible to get more of one good and no less of the other when the opportunity to trade is available.

But what of the demand side? What of Ricardo's increase in the "sum of enjoyments?" Will free trade enable the economy to maximize total well-being or welfare? Can we also say that free trade Pareto-dominates the no trade situation or the tariff situation, in the sense that it makes at least someone better off and no one worse off than the no trade or tariff situation?[2]

In asking this question we immediately confront the problem of the incomparability of different persons' utilities, for it is a rare policy measure that will make everyone better off. Instead some are made better off, while others are made worse off. How then can we make any interpersonal comparisons when individuals' utility levels are not cardinally measurable or additive? How can we avoid distributional value judgments?

When repealing the Corn Laws, for example, Ricardo would undoubtedly have concluded that the gains to consumers (through lower prices) and capitalists (through higher profits because of lower wages when the price of wheat fell) were greater than the losses to the landlords (through loss of rent). For Ricardo considered the interest of the landlords as being "always opposed" to those of the rest of society, and their rent was simply a surplus, which could

[1] See Amartya K. Sen, *Collective Choice and Social Welfare* (1970), Chap. 5.
[2] In Pareto's terminology, is it possible to increase the *ophélimité* of some individuals without that of any others being decreased? Vilfredo Pareto, *Cours d'Économie Politique* (1897) I, 20 ff.

not lead to a greater supply of the "original and indestructible powers of the soil." Therefore, Ricardo did not hesitate to make the explicit value judgment that the resultant distribution of income under free trade was desirable.

The modern day economist, however, is not so bold. How can the economist weight the gain in income—or more broadly, utility—to one group while another group loses income or utility? A resort to community indifference curves does not avoid the difficulty. For, unlike the preference map of indifference curves for an individual, the community indifference curves on the prefernce map for a community can intersect and give inconsistent results. This is because the same bundle of goods can have a different value according to how it is distributed. It is possible that, given one income distribution, a pattern of consumption would be superior to a second pattern; but given a different initial distribution of income, the second would be superior to the first. Inconsistency or intransitivity in the social ordering can result—and this would be reflected in intersecting community indifference curves that make it impossible to conclude that one position is superior to another.[3] A consistent set of community indifference curves that have the same properties as an individual preference map (downward sloping indifference curves, convex to the origin, and non-intersecting) requires at least two of the following conditions: (i) identical incomes of all individuals in the community, (ii) identical tastes of all individuals, and (iii) indifference curves for all individuals such that the proportions in which commodities are consumed depend only on relative commodity prices.[4] But, delightfully expeditious as community indifference curves are for a diagrammatic "solution," it is obviously unrealistic to assume either identical incomes or identical tastes for all individuals in the community. Community indifference curves lack necessary empirical content.

If we refrain from using community indifference curves, we are left with the need to find some way of avoiding interpersonal comparisons while resorting to some principle of social choice that selects among the various members of the Pareto-efficient subset. The following approaches are possible:

(i) Appeal to a social welfare function (social utility index, social decision function, constitution). It is conceivable that a well-ordered function is definable that would include among its arguments a particular distribution of income that is considered desirable.[5] One could write the social welfare function in the form $W = W(z_1, z_2 \ldots)$, where the zs represent all possible variables, including non-economic variables. A particular W function may

---

[3] For the classic statement of the impossibility of passing from individual preferences (orderings) to social preference (ordering) under certain "reasonable" conditions, see K.J. Arrow, *Social Choice and Individual Values* (2nd ed., 1963).

[4] See P.A. Samuelson, "Social Indifference Curves," *Quarterly Journal of Economics*, 70 (Feb. 1956), 1–22.

[5] A. Bergson, "A Reformulation of Certain Aspects of Welfare Economics," *Quarterly Journal of Economics*, 52 (Feb. 1938), 310–34, and P.A. Samuelson, *Foundations of Economic Analysis* (1947), Chap. 8.

take the form $W[u_1(x_1), u_2(x_2) \ldots, u_n(x_n)]$, where u_n is the utility function of the nth individual, and x_n is a description of the real income, labor, and leisure time of the nth individual, and the functional form of W implicitly takes care of the weighting. If we are willing to accept the determination by some authority (a dictator, a central planning agency, an ethical observer) as to what the W function is, and how the utility indices of the different individuals should be weighted, then we can compare the pre- and post-policy situations and determine if W has increased in terms of the resultant income distribution. This is tantamount to an explicit weighting system for income distributions,[6] and the contours of the social welfare function would then be a set of community indifference curves. But though W is definable, the real question is just who is to be the social decision-maker to define it? And who is to accept it?

(ii) An alternative approach would be to establish a Pareto-efficient allocation for a **given** income distribution. We can keep conditions of technical efficiency completely separate from issues of equity, and simply determine the Pareto-efficient allocation of resources for a given income distribution—without inquiring into the merits of the income distribution. We establish the conditions of technical efficiency (production-maximizing) and exchange efficiency (production-optimizing) with a given distribution of income. There would then be a different Pareto-efficient allocation for each different income distribution, and the economist would remain non-judgmental as among them.

(iii) Another possibility is to use the **compensation test**. We can demonstrate a **potential** Pareto improvement by showing that out of the higher real income achieved by a policy, it would be possible for the gainers to compensate the losers, so that the losers would be restored to the same income they enjoyed before the policy change, while the gainers would still retain some gain. In the new situation, the redistribution could be brought about by lump sum taxes (income or inheritance taxes) on the gainers and transfers to the losers. Such a distribution of income—in which no one is left is worse off and some one is better off—can be termed a **Pareto-efficient distribution**.

The compensation test would consist of a double criterion: first, that the gainers can compensate the losers and still be left with some gain; and second, that the prospective losers could not compensate the prospective gainers for non-implementation of the proposed policy change.[7] (Or, those hurt by a

---

[6]Cf. Meade's proposal for the use of explicit welfare or distributional weights: J.E. Meade, *Trade and Welfare, Mathematical Supplement* (1955), Chap. II. If the political authority used, for instance, a distributional weight of 1 for individual *1* and 0.75 for individual *2*, then the political authority would be indifferent between giving an additional $0.75 to individual *1* or $1 to individual *2*.

[7]The first test is usually called the Kaldor-Hicks compensation criterion, and the second the Scitovsky-reversal criterion. See N. Kaldor, "Welfare Propositions in Economics and Interpersonal Comparisons of Utility," *Economic Journal*, 49 (Sept. 1939), 549–52; J.R. Hicks, "The

change to free trade from a tariff situation would not be able to bribe those who gain from free trade to go back to protection.)

The second step is a reversal test that is required to assure that the first situation (before the policy) is not preferred to the second situation (after the policy) if the income of the first situation were distributed as it was in the second. It must be impossible to make everyone as well off in the first situation by any redistribution of the actual quantities acquired in the second situation. If this reversal test is not fulfilled, it is possible that simultaneously situation I should be preferred to situation II and situation II be preferred to situation I.

The diagrams in Figure 2.5 illustrate the compensation tests. The axes in the figure represent the utility levels of the two individuals 1 and 2.[8] The utility levels are represented only ordinally. Let Q_I denote the utility levels before a policy change, and let other points along $Q_I H$ in Figure 2.5(a) represent alternate income distributions with the existing policy. Then $Q_I H$ is a utility-possibility function for situation I; $Q_{II} J$ is another utility-possibility function for situation II.

Now consider a policy change, and let Q_{II} represent the position that would be reached after the policy change, and other points along $Q_{II} J$ represent alternate distributions after the policy change. A change from Q_I to Q_{II} would make individual 1 worse off and individual 2 better off. But disagreement over Q_{II} could be resolved by redistribution. In Figure 2.5(a), redistribution from Q_{II} to J, after the policy change, would represent compensation of the loser by the gainer. Since at J both individuals are better off than the initial point Q_I, it follows that II is Pareto-superior to I.

Consider, however, Figure 2.5(b). If the policy change now results in movement from Q_I to Q_{II}, the gainer could not compensate the loser and still remain a gainer. But if the policy were repealed, with compensation for repeal, the point H, which lies northeast of Q_{II}, could be reached. The net movement from Q_{II} to H would then be a Paretian improvement. Thus, in this case, the double criterion is not fulfilled when moving from Q_I to Q_{II}. In

---

Foundations of Welfare Economics," *Economic Journal* (Dec. 1939), 696–712; and T. Scitovsky, "A Note on Welfare Propositions in Economics," *Review of Economic Studies*, 9 (Nov. 1941), 77–88. According to Scitovsky, "We must first see whether it is possible in the new situation so to redistribute income as to make everybody better off than he [*sic*] was in the initial situation; secondly, we must see whether starting from the initial situation it is not possible by a mere redistribution of income to reach a position superior to the new situation, again from everybody's point of view. If the first is possible and the second impossible, we shall say that the new situation is better than the old was. If the first is impossible but the second possible, we shall say that the new situation is worse; whereas if both are possible or both are impossible, we shall refrain from making a welfare proposition."

[8] Cf. the diagrams in D.M. Winch, *Analytical Welfare Economics* (1971), 145; Ronald Findlay, *Trade and Specialization* (1970), 113–18; and P.A. Samuelson, "Evaluation of Real National Income," *Oxford Economic Papers*, 2 (Jan. 1950), 1–29.

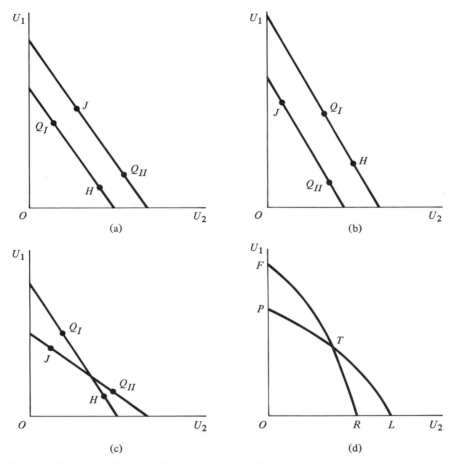

Figure 2.5   Utility-Possibility Curves and Compensation Tests

fact, Q_I is preferred to Q_{II}. The double-bribe criterion unambiguously ranks Q_I over Q_{II}.

Now consider Figure 2.5(c). Assume that the initial utility level enjoyed by the two individuals is H. Suppose a policy change now occurs and moves the welfare point to J. Individual 1 is then better off, but individual 2 is worse off. It would, however, be possible to move by compensation from J to Q_{II}, where both would be better off than in the original situation H. But, with the original collection of goods, it is possible to move from H to Q_I where both 1 and 2 are better off than at J. The reversal test is therefore not fulfilled. Both the new situation *and* the new distribution are not superior to the old situation.

To have situation II Pareto-superior to situation I, the double criterion of the compensation test requires that the utility-possibility curve of II be outside the utility-possibility curve of I in the neighborhood of the two points (before and after the policy). If, for example, in Figure 2.5(d), FTL represents the utility-possibility function corresponding to the free-trade situation, and *PTR* represents the utility-possibility function corresponding to protection (or the no-trade situation), then *FTL* lies uniformly outside *PTR* (though touching it at *T*), indicating that the free-trade situation is superior (or, at a minimum, equivalent) to the tariff (or no-trade) situation.[9] If the utility-possibility function of *II* lies everywhere beyond that of *I*, then the superior-for-all-income distribution criterion will be fulfilled.

More generally, each point on the production-possibility frontier yields a point utility-possibility curve. The outer envelope of the set of utility-possibility curves represents the alternate maximum pairs of utility levels that could be achieved by varying the combination of goods produced on the production frontier as well as their distribution. This envelope can be termed the situation utility-possibility frontier, and the welfare optimum must be at some point on this frontier. This is true for an individualistic welfare function that respects the Pareto criterion, i.e., Social Welfare $= W \{u_1, \ldots u_n\}$ and W is increasing in each of its arguments.

Although the compensation test might appear to free us from interpersonal comparisons, we should note two special features of the test. First, the test has a conservative bias toward the *status quo ante:* it is "good" to bring losers back to their original position. In terms of a social welfare function or welfare weights, this might be suboptimal income distribution. It is, however, probably the least controversial designation of a desirable income distribution and is commonly used by welfare economists. Second, the compensation test indicates only potential Pareto improvement—that the indicated income distribution could be achieved. Whether it actually is achieved, however, is an additional political choice. If compensation is not actually paid, welfare need not have improved. If the government does actually choose to impose the necessary lump sum taxes and transfers, it is further assumed that the redistribution is costless, that there are no adverse effects on incentives, and that no distortions are created elsewhere in the system to diminish welfare.

Considering the mixture of efficiency and equity considerations we inevitably encounter when evaluating trade policies, we might usefully make a clearer distinction between conditions of "Pareto efficiency" and "social optimality."[10]

In discussing the free-trade situation, we referred to "Pareto international efficiency" (Chapter 2, pp. 63–67). Such a situation is commonly termed a Pareto optimal situation for the **given** distribution of income. But in this sense, there will be any number of Pareto optimal situations—one for each

[9]Cf. J. Bhagwati, "The Gains from Trade Once Again," *Oxford Economic Papers,* 20 (July 1968), 141–42.

[10]What we term technical efficiency is sometimes called the physical optimum, and what we term exchange efficiency is sometimes called the subjective optimum. A situation that fulfills the conditions of both the physical optimum and subjective optimum is then called the general optimum or Top-Level Optimum. See Hla Myint, *Theories of Welfare Economics* (1948), Chap. 8; E.J. Mishan, *Welfare Economics* (1964), 17–36.

distribution of income postulated. **The** Pareto optimal situation is then taken to be the *optimum optimorum* (the best of the best)—the Pareto-efficient situation with **the** socially desirable income distribution. This is termed the social welfare optimum.

By Pareto efficient we mean a situation of economic efficiency, i.e., the attainment of the conditions of technical efficiency (production-maximizing, pp. 45–48) plus exchange efficiency (production-optimizing, pp. 50–51), with a **given** distribution of income.[11] By social optimality we mean that the conditions of Pareto efficiency are fulfilled for a **socially desirable** distribution of income.[12] Pareto efficiency is thus a necessary, but not sufficient condition of overall social optimality.

Because the distribution effects are inherent in any policy problem, it is misleading to refer to policy-making as "social engineering," as is sometimes done. Policy-making is necessarily more than a matter of establishing conditions of mechanical efficiency. Economists may choose to be oblivious to income distribution—but it is still intrinsic to the problem, even if unrecognized.

Recently, however, more attention has been given to the issue of distribution in terms of distributive justice or distributional equity. A situation of Pareto efficiency can be quite different from a situation with a "just" distribution. If economists have in the past given so much consideration to specifying the conditions of Pareto efficiency, it may not be amiss to hope that in the future they might begin to say more on matters of distributional equity as well as efficiency.[13]

---

[11]Many writers call "Pareto optimality" what we call "Pareto efficiency." Corden, however, distinguishes between Pareto efficiency and Pareto optimality: the latter refers to Pareto efficiency combined with the socially desired income distribution [W.M. Corden, *Trade Policy and Economic Welfare* (1974), 104–9]. Corden's Pareto optimality is therefore similar to our social optimality.

[12]It is conceivable that a socially desirable distribution could be that of Pareto efficiency, with *actual* redistribution made to compensate the losers.

[13]See John Rawls, *A Theory of Justice* (1971), and Sen, *op. cit.*, Chap. 9. For an interesting tentative beginning, see Hal R. Varian, "Distributive Justice, Welfare Economics, and the Theory of Fairness," *Philosophy and Public Affairs,* 4 (Spring 1975), 223–47; Lester Thurow, "Toward a Definition of Economic Justice," *Public Interest* (Spring 1973), 56 ff.; Arthur M. Okun, *Equality and Efficiency: The Big Tradeoff* (1975); and J.E. Meade, *The Just Economy* (1977).

3

Optimal Trade Interventions

It is now time to temper some of our conclusions from the preceding chapters. Are there any exceptions to the conclusions that free trade is Pareto-superior to no trade, and free trade is Pareto-superior to restricted trade? If the logic of our previous analysis is correct, then exceptions can arise only if we make one or more of the following modifications to our earlier analysis: (i) we no longer adopt the cosmopolitan viewpoint, but instead consider only that of national advantage; (ii) some of the postulated conditions of a perfectly competitive economy do not exist; and (iii) we change the goal from that of Pareto efficiency to some other social objective with non-economic elements.

Any of these changes expands the context of the free-trade versus protection debate. And in this wider context, some of our prior conclusions have to be modified.

The Welfare Economist's Conclusions

We know that in practice governments resort to a number of policy instruments to restrict trade for various objectives. Tariffs, quotas, voluntary export restraints, taxes, subsidies, exchange rate restrictions—all these, and more, appear in a country's foreign trade regime. In most cases, these trade restrictions are imposed to stimulate exports or restrict imports in order to protect particular interests,[1] promote

---

[1]These interests can be to protect the status of specific industries confronting foreign competition, the income distribution for a certain group, or to protect against "low-wage" foreign labor.

employment, ease a balance of payments problem, foster industrialization, or to retaliate against a foreign country.

But which of the various policy instruments is optimal or "first best" to achieve the desired objective? The actual practice of protection is likely to deviate enormously from what the welfare economist would specify as optimal policy interventions. In practice, the policy measures undertaken are likely to be second best, third best, or nth best. Moreover, the arguments on behalf of the policy interventions are likely to be non-economic. And frequently what purports to be an "argument" for protection is really a "non-argument" for protection, but rather an argument for some other type of policy.

What, then, would be the optimal trade interventions? To answer this, we shall now adopt the perspective of the welfare economist. After summarizing the welfare economist's conclusions, we shall explain how these conclusions were reached.[2]

Summary of the welfare economist's analysis:

Free trade is Pareto-superior to no trade.

Restricted trade is Pareto-superior to no trade.

Free trade is Pareto-superior to restricted trade.

Except: An "Optimum tariff" is Pareto-superior to free trade when there are international market distortions and the criterion is only "welfare" of nationals.

And: An "Optimum subsidy" is Pareto-superior to a tariff when there are domestic market distortions.

Stated succinctly, the welfare economist would argue that "the only **first-best economic argument** for protection is the optimum tariff. All other arguments for protection should really be arguments for some form of government intervention in the domestic economy, and the use of tariffs in these cases would be sub-optimal policy."[3]

[2]In elaborating these conclusions, the following sections draw on H.G. Johnson, "Optimal Trade Intervention in the Presence of Domestic Distortions," in R.E. Caves et al. (eds.), *Trade, Growth and the Balance of Payments: Essays in Honor of Gottfried Haberler* (1965), 3–34; Jagdish Bhagwati and V.K. Ramaswami, "Domestic Distortions, Tariffs and the Theory of Optimum Subsidy," *Journal of Political Economy*, 71 (Feb. 1963), 44–50; Bhagwati, "The Generalized Theory of Distortions and Welfare," in Bhagwati et al. (ed.), *Trade, Balance of Payments and Growth: Essays in Honor of C.P. Kindleberger*, (1971), 69–90; and Bhagwati, *The Theory and Practice of Commercial Policy: Departures from Unified Exchange Rates*, Princeton Special Papers in International Economics No. 8 (Jan. 1968).

[3]J. Bhagwati and T.N. Srinivasan, "Optimal Intervention to Achieve Non-economic Objectives," *Review of Economic Studies*, 36 (Jan. 1969), 27; Bhagwati, "Non-economic Objectives and

Non-economic Arguments and Non-arguments

To begin explaining how these conclusions were reached, let us first cut through the non-economic arguments and the non-arguments for protection.

If, by an economic argument for protection, we mean one that leads to an increase in real national income or, more precisely, to a tariff situation that Pareto-dominates free trade, then several arguments can be ruled out as being non-economic in character because they do not fulfill the economic welfare criteria. The non-economic arguments for protection recommend protection as a means of achieving objectives with respect to the structure and composition of output that are desired for their own sake rather than as a means of increasing real income.

"Protection for national security" is one such non-economic argument. Even Adam Smith favored "defence before opulence," and the national security argument has persisted in various forms. But the criterion is not an economic one.

Similarly, "protection for the modern values of industrialization (or the simple virtues of agriculture) as a superior way of life" is for non-economic objectives that are not consistent with an increase in real income over the free-trade situation. So too is self-sufficiency (independence from the foreigner) for purposes of nationalism. (The case for import substitution in developing countries will be evaluated in detail in Chapter 12.)

We could interpret these non-economic desires as demands for collective consumption goods—"goods" that are valued by the society as a whole, even though their attainment may mean sacrificing some potential real income. Although they are not economic goods in the strict sense, the economist might still offer advice on how to achieve these collective consumption goods at the least cost. Even though fulfillment of the objective cannot be tested by a Pareto criterion, it may still be of value to meet the objective in the least costly fashion. For example, if the country's objective is increased domestic industrial production, a tariff will be more costly (through the loss of consumers' surplus) than would a subsidy to promote domestic production.

Non-arguments for protection purport to, but in logical examination

the Efficiency Properties of Trade," *Journal of Political Economy*, 75 (Oct. 1968), 738; Bhagwati, *The Theory and Practice of Commercial Policy: Departures from Unified Exchange Rates, op. cit.*, 31–47; and H.G. Johnson, "The Cost of Protection and the Scientific Tariff," *Journal of Political Economy*, 68 (Aug. 1960), 327–45.

do not lead to the recommendation of tariffs. A favorite is protection to stimulate employment. Even Keynes, in 1931 during the Great Depression, advocated a tariff to stimulate employment in Britain. But this was before he wrote *The General Theory of Employment, Interest, and Money,* which was to show that the appropriate remedial policies for unemployment are fiscal policy and monetary policy. To export unemployment through protection is a beggar-thy-neighbor policy. Moreover, it cannot be as effective in increasing employment as can the public management of aggregate demand combined with exchange rate variations.

Similarly, balance of payments difficulties do not constitute a true argument for protection. Instead of trying to restrict imports, it would be preferable to remove the underlying causes of the balance of payments pressure—normally domestic inflation or the maintenance of an overvalued exchange rate. Deflation or depreciation of the home currency in terms of foreign currency is therefore in order. (More on this in Part II.)

Ranking of Alternative Policies

If trade intervention is to be justified economically, it must be because conditions depart from the marginal equivalencies established earlier for the optimality of free trade. We saw that free trade fulfills the following (first-order) marginal conditions of Pareto efficiency:

(i) Marginal rates of substitution of factors are equal among all producers (absence of factor market distortions).

(ii) Marginal rates of transformation of goods in domestic production (MRT_d) are equal among all producers (absence of differential producer taxation, or absence of distortion in producer prices).

(iii) Marginal rates of substitution of goods in consumption (MRS) are equal among all consumers (absence of differential consumer taxation, or absence of distortion in consumer prices).

(iv) Marginal rates of transformation in production are equal to marginal rates of substitution in consumption (absence of commodity taxation).

(v) Marginal rates of transformation are equal in domestic production and in foreign trade (MRT_f) (non-intervention in foreign trade).

Either **externalities or absence of perfect competition** in any of the commodity or factor markets can lead to violations of these conditions. **The equivalence is then destroyed between MRS, MRT_d, and MRT_f.** If there is a divergence between marginal social costs and marginal private costs or between private and social benefits or between revenue or marginal cost and price in the country's international trade, then trade interventions may be called for to correct the divergences. If divergences cannot be removed directly, as they usually cannot, then they must be offset or neutralized by some trade intervention. But which of the alternative trade interventions should be adopted?

To determine the optimal type of trade intervention, we shall obviously have to be able to **rank alternative policies** that correct the divergences. The prevalent policy choices of an international character are trade tariffs, subsidies, and quantitative restrictions.[4] The most common domestic policies that affect a country's pattern of foreign trade are taxes and subsidies on production and consumption and taxes and subsidies on factor use.

Ranking alternative policies involves the "theory of the second best."[5] In a world in which the first-best conditions of Pareto optimality do not actually exist throughout the entire system, we have to use the second-best criterion. We have to ask: Given a policy constraint that does not allow the removal of some other distortion in the general system, what is the optimum policy for the remaining part of the system? The optimum policy will be second best in comparison with the standard first-best conditions of the entire system. For example, if free trade cannot be achieved throughout the world, will free trade within a customs union or a free-trade area for a limited number of countries still be desirable? It does not follow that the removal of tariffs in part of the world **necessarily** leads to an increase in economic welfare as long as another part of the world maintains tariffs.[6] But the economist might show what policy leads toward or away from the second-best welfare maximum. In this sense, the economist recognizes that the actual economy is inferior to the ideal, first-best optimum conditions, but the economist as policy adviser then seeks to establish policies that are second best instead of third best or fourth best or *n*th best. The

---

[4] Voluntary Export Restraints and Orderly Marketing Agreements are variants of quantitative restrictions and will be considered in Chap. 4. Foreign exchange restrictions can also be used for trade intervention purposes, but we reserve their treatment for Part II.

[5] J.E. Meade, *Trade and Welfare* (1955), Chap. VII, and R.G. Lipsey and K. Lancaster, "The General Theory of Second Best," *Review of Economic Studies,* 24 (1956), 11–32.

[6] The reduction in tariffs to zero within the customs union may cause trade diversion, and a superior policy might be to reduce tariffs within the customs union to a level below the external tariff maintained by the union, but greater than zero. See Lipsey and Lancaster, *op. cit.;* Chap. 4, this volume.

degrees of inferiority away from the ideal are minimized, so that the result is quasi-optimal (a constrained optimum). If the economy must have distortions, the best set of distortions is established (the second-best solution is found instead of the third-best).

More directly, economists evaluate the optimal way of offsetting the distortions that cannot be removed. "Optimal" in this context means that the **policy intervention should be directed specifically to the point at which the divergence occurs** and should correct the source of the divergence itself without creating any other by-product distortion elsewhere in the system. For any given marginal divergence, or set of divergences, there is then a first-best optimal policy or set of policies.[7] This is, in simplest language, the "first-best partial policy in a second-best world"—the best policy in a suboptimal world where general first-best conditions cannot be established uniformly.[8] Inferior to the first-best policy will be other policies that create by-product distortions as they attempt to correct the initial distortion. These policies can then be ranked as second best, third best, fourth best, etc., according to the number of additional by-product distortions the successive policies impose. We shall adopt this practice of **establishing a hierarchy of policies that correct a given distortion, ranging from the first-best downward.**

The number of alternative policies considered will, of course, depend on the policy adviser's interpretation of what is technically feasible and politically conceivable.

Because they are secondary issues that do not affect the central logic of the analysis, we normally make the following assumptions:[9] (i) Subsidies can be financed by "non-distortionary" taxes, such as lump sum taxes that do not affect incentives. Financing can also be realized not by raising taxes, but by forgoing other governmental expenditure. The equivalence of a subsidy on one product can also be achieved by taxing other products or by remitting taxes on the product that is to be subsidized. (ii) Taxation involves no collection costs. (iii) There are no costs of disbursement of subsidies. (iv) The income distribution effects of various policies can be neglected, or else they are evaluated by one of the methods discussed in Chapter 2 (Appendix).

[7] W.M. Corden, *Trade Policy and Economic Welfare* (1974), 28–31; also, references in note 2, above.

[8] For a more elegant (but more complex) statement that clarifies the different meanings of "second best," see J. Bhagwati, "The Pure Theory of International Trade: A Survey," *Economic Journal*, 74 (March 1964), 56–57, n 1.

[9] These assumptions are analyzed fully by Corden, *op. cit*, Chap. 3.

If, in contrast to these assumptions, there actually are costs to financing a subsidy, then we should seek the minimum-cost package of taxes, that is, a policy that minimizes the by-product distortion costs of financing and disbursing the subsidy.

It is an empirical question whether departure from these assumptions will change the ranking of policies in any particular situation. For example, if the collection costs of financing a subsidy through taxes were so much larger than those of a tariff, it is conceivable that the tariff would then become superior to the subsidy, even though on other grounds we had originally established that a subsidy was a first-best way and a tariff a second-best way of correcting the distortion. The subsidy would then have to be just high enough for the marginal gain from partially correcting the distortion to be equal to the marginal by-product costs.[10]

It is reasonable, however, to argue that in practice the ranking of policies is unlikely to be affected by the existence of collection and distortion costs because the first-best policy is initially selected by the criterion that it be directed precisely to the point of the divergence.

Optimum Tariff

A long-standing argument for protection has been the "terms of trade" argument. From the viewpoint of national advantage, a country with monopoly power or monopsony power in its foreign trade can improve its terms of trade by taxing its exports (if it has monopoly power) or taxing its imports (if it has monopsony power). A tax on exports can be passed on to the foreign buyer, whereas a tariff on imports can result in a lowering of the price of the imports—calculated before the duty—in order to retain the market of the tariff-imposing country. In either case, the commodity terms of trade would improve.

The "terms of trade argument" was well known to classical economists, who recognized it as an exception to free trade.[11] But they noted that the gain to one country was a loss to another: the cosmopolitan viewpoint of mutual gains had changed to the national viewpoint in a zero-sum game. Moreover, they were cautious about the application of

---

[10] Corden, *op. cit.*, 47.

[11] J.S. Mill, *Essays on Some Unsettled Questions of Political Economy* (1844), 24–36; F.Y. Edgeworth, "Appreciation of Mathematical Theories," *Economic Journal*, 18 (1908), 392–403, 541–56; and Alfred Marshall, "Memorandum on the Fiscal Policy of International Trade," in Marshall, *Official Papers* (1926), 36–42.

this argument: they thought that a government could readily overdo its application to the detriment of even the tariff-imposing country. As Edgeworth warned, "the direct use of the theory is likely to be small. But it is to be feared that its abuse will be considerable. Let us admire the skill of the analyst, but label the subject of his investigation *Poison.*"[12]

The essence of the terms of trade argument is that "the foreigner pays the duty." By taxing its exports, the monopolist country raises its export price. By taxing its imports, the monopsonist country causes the foreign country to reduce its export price. The tax is thereby absorbed by the foreigner.

Our previous analysis of a tariff in Chapter 2 was based on the small country assumption—that is, the country could not influence the terms of trade and, as a price-taker, it accepted a perfectly elastic supply of imports at the world price (see Figure 2.2, p. 60). If now, however, the tariff-imposing country is sufficiently large to affect the world price, the world price (P_f) may fall when the tariff is imposed, and demand falls. To the extent that the export price declines, the production loss (*HTE* in Figure 2.2) and the consumption loss (*MNC*) of the tariff will be less, at the limit zero, if the exporter lowers the foreign price by the full amount of the tariff. The more elastic the import demand of the tariff-imposing country and the less elastic the export supply of the exporting country, the more will the export price be reduced and the terms of trade improve for the tariff-imposing country.

While the terms of trade improve, however, the volume of trade decreases. Gains at the margin in the terms of trade are being offset by losses "on the average" in the gains from trade through the reduced volume of trade. An optimal degree of taxation should therefore be sought. The **optimum tariff** will be one that improves the country's terms of trade just up to the point where the marginal gain from the improved terms of trade is equal to the marginal loss from a reduced volume of trade.

The conditions for an optimum have been spelled out with considerable refinement.[13] The case for a tariff arises initially because of the existence of a **distortion in international markets**—there is a divergence between marginal revenue or marginal cost and market price in

---

[12] Edgeworth, *op. cit.,* 556.

[13] For derivation of the formula for the optimal tariff rate, and refinements, see H.G. Johnson, "Optimum Welfare and Maximum Revenue Tariffs," *Review of Economic Studies,* XIX(1) (1950), 28–35; Johnson, "Alternative Optimum Tariff Formulae," in Johnson, *International Trade and Economic Growth* (1958); and Corden, *op. cit.,* 187–200.

international trade. Just as a monopolistic firm equates marginal revenue and marginal cost instead of price and marginal cost, so too should a country with national monopoly power. This market imperfection means that world market prices diverge from the MRT_f. There is an **international distortion** so that $MRT_f \neq MRT_d = MRS$. Free trade makes the price ratio or average terms of trade equal to the marginal cost ratio (MRT_d). But the average terms of trade equal the marginal terms of trade only if national monopoly power does not exist. The existence of national monopoly power means that the exporting country can gain more by equating its marginal terms of trade MRT_f (i.e., its marginal revenue or marginal receipts from exports) to its MRT_d (i.e., its marginal opportunity cost in domestic production). This can be done through a tariff that corrects the divergence in international markets. Because the distortion relates to foreign transactions, the intervention in trade will be the first-best remedial policy: it will achieve equality between MRT_d and MRT_f without destroying the domestic equality between MRS and MRT_d. (A second-best policy would be either a tax-cum-subsidy on production or on factor use.)

But what is the optimum degree of trade restriction? The objective is not to maximize, but to optimize, the terms of trade. The optimum degree of trade restriction equates the marginal gain from improved terms of trade to the marginal loss from the contraction of the international division of labor. Just as a monopolist does not charge the highest possible unit price, but instead maximizes total profit by equating marginal revenue and marginal cost, so too a country with monopoly power should not try to maximize the terms of trade, but should make the marginal receipts from exports equal to its marginal cost ratio (MRT_d). As long as the foreigner's demand is not perfectly elastic, the terms of trade can be improved by the exercise of monopoly power. If the foreigner has a very inelastic demand for imports from the exporting country, a tax on exports may even allow the country to obtain more imports for fewer exports. In the normal case, the terms of trade would improve, but the volume of trade would also decrease. The optimum tariff rate would then be a rate that would improve the terms of trade just up **to the point where the gain from improved terms of trade begins to be offset by a loss from the smaller volume of trade:** the marginal value of exports would equal the marginal value of imports. The lower the elasticity of foreign supply to the tariff-imposing country, or the more inelastic the demand for the country's exports, the higher is the optimal tariff rate.

Although there is a symmetry between export taxes and import duties,[14] more countries tend to have monopoly power than monoposony power and to seek an improvement in their terms of trade through export taxes. The effectiveness of this policy, however, will depend on the inelasticity of the foreigner's demand for imports, the bargaining power of the respective countries, and the capacity for retaliation by the importing country.[15] It also depends on whether the government spends the revenue on imports or on the country's exportables or whether it increases the government's surplus or reduces other taxes. It must also be remembered that the optimum tariff situation represents only a potential optimum: the distribution of income issue still has to be settled by some welfare criterion.

Optimum Subsidy

If an **international** distortion calls for an optimum tariff, a **domestic** distortion requires an **optimum subsidy** as the first-best remedial policy. Just as there exists an optimum tariff policy for a divergence between foreign prices and MRT_f, so too does there exist an optimum subsidy policy for a divergence between domestic prices and MRT_d.[16] Domestic distortions commonly take the form of a divergence between private cost and social cost within the country because of externalities in production or imperfections in a factor market. Domestic prices will then not measure social opportunity costs as indicated by the MRT_d. The **domestic distortion** will mean that $MRT_d \neq MRS = MRT_f$. The **first-best policy** to bring the MRT_d into equality with the MRS will involve a **domestic tax-cum-subsidy policy**, aimed specifically at the source of the divergence between market prices and social opportunity costs.

External economies in product markets can occur when expansion in industry *1* confers a side-effect benefit on industry *2*, but industry *1* cannot appropriate the whole of the social return. If fewer units of

[14]A.P. Lerner, "The Symmetry between Import and Export Taxes," *Economica*, 3 (Aug. 1936), 306–13.

[15]Both countries are normally worse off when the new tariff-ridden equilibrium is at a lower volume of trade. Under special conditions, however, the country imposing the initial optimum tariff may be better off than under free trade, even if retaliation occurs; see H.G. Johnson, "Optimum Tariffs and Retaliation," *Review of Economic Studies*, 21 (1954), 142–53.

[16]See J. Bhagwati and V.K. Ramaswami, "Dometic Distortions, Tariffs, and the Theory of Optimum Subsidy," *Journal of Political Economy*, 71 (Feb. 1963), 44–50; also, references in note 2, above.

inputs are required to produce a unit of output in industry *2* as a result of the expansion of industry *1*, there is an external economy from *1*'s expansion; but the price system does not register this benefit, and industry is not paid for this external benefit. This may occur when industry *1* trains labor that becomes freely available to industry *2* or when the expansion of industry *1* creates and diffuses knowledge that becomes freely available to industry *2*. The output of industry *1* will therefore be less than it should be if its private costs were lowered to the true social cost or if the value of its output were raised to its true social benefit. When domestic prices do not reflect the true social marginal cost or social benefit, the true $MRT_d < MRT_f$.

If in Figure 1.5, p. 34, there was an externality in the production of *c*, such that the market does not remunerate *c*-firms for the increment that *c* creates in *w*-output, the production externality would result in non-tangency between the MRT_f and the production-possibility frontier. A production subsidy on *c*, equal to the degree of external economies, would then bring about the tangency of MRT_f and MRT_d at a greater output of *c*.

If the external economies arise in an import-competing industry, then the first-best policy would be a subsidy on production in that industry. If the external economies stem from expansion of an export industry, the first-best policy is subsidization of that industry.

A tariff would correct the distortion of domestic prices from opportunity costs, but it would achieve this production gain at the expense of introducing a consumption-distortion cost through the rise in prices. In other words, a tariff could equalize MRT_d and MRT_f, but at the same time it would cause a by-product distortion of destroying the equality between MRS and MRT_f. A tariff would therefore be a second-best policy in comparison with the subsidy. A quota on imports would create even more by-product distortions, as will be explained in the next chapter, and would therefore be a third-best policy.

A diagrammatic analysis of the optimum subsidy argument is presented in Figure 3.1.[17] Let there be external economies created in the import-competing industry. There is then a marginal divergence between private and social cost. This is represented in Figure 3.1 by noting that SS', the private money cost, exceeds ss', the social cost, by the proportion *d* of SS'. Under free trade, P_1 is the price, OQ_1 is home output, and Q_1Q_4 are imports. When $ss' < SS'$, this import-competing

[17]See Corden, *op. cit.*, 9–12; H.G. Johnson, "Tariffs and Economic Development," *Journal of Development Studies*, 1 (Oct. 1964), 3–30.

Figure 3.1

Optimum Subsidy

Pre-subsidy:

P_1 = free trade price;

OQ_1 = home output;

Q_1Q_4 = imports.

Post-subsidy:

Subsidy = P_1P_2 per unit, or *ad valorem* rate (d) of P_1P_2/OP_1;

P_2 = $(1 + d) P_1$ = price for producers;

P_1 = price for consumers;

OQ_2 = optimum home output because at OQ_2 the marginal social cost of home output = marginal cost of imports (P_1);

Q_1Q_2 = increase in home output;

Q_1KLQ_2 = social cost of Q_1Q_2;

$Q_1K'LQ_2$ = cost of imports replaced;

$KK'L$ = social gain from subsidy.

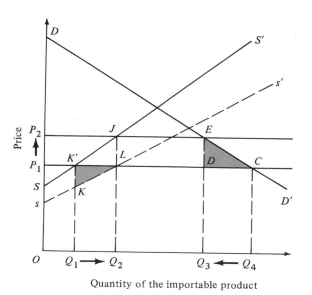

Quantity of the importable product

If the country had imposed a tariff at rate d, instead of an equivalent subsidy, the price would have risen from P_1 to P_2; imports would have decreased from Q_2Q_4 to Q_2Q_3; and the consumption loss would have been EDC as the result of the tariff.

industry ideally should produce OQ_2, because at this output the marginal social cost of production would equal the marginal cost of imports. Therefore, there should be a subsidy on production at the rate d per unit, where d is the proportional excess of private over social cost. This raises P_1 to P_2 = $(1 + d) P_1$ for producers, and stimulates home output to OQ_2. The subsidy increases domestic output by Q_1Q_2, but consumers still pay P_1.

The social gain brought about by the subsidy can be calculated as follows. The **social cost of the protected output** is the area under the social marginal cost curve Q_1KLQ_2. The **value of the imports that are replaced** is $Q_1Q_2 \cdot P_1$ or $Q_1K'LQ_2$. **The import replacement cost is** therefore less than the value of the imports by the shaded triangle *KK'L*.

The subsidy at the rate of P_1P_2 per unit, or alternatively, the *ad valorem* rate P_1P_2/OP_1, is the optimal rate because a higher subsidy would reduce this total gain by stimulating home output to a point where the marginal social cost of production exceeds the marginal cost of imports (to the right of OQ_2), whereas a lower subsidy would cause home output to be at a point where the marginal social cost of import replacement is still less than the marginal cost of imports (to the left of OQ_2).

If the subsidy is financed by taxation, the redistributive effects of the subsidy are as follows: the taxpayers lose P_2JLP_1; home producers gain $P_2JK'P_1$; and the beneficiaries of the external economies created by the extra output gain $K'JLK$. There is a net gain to the country of the amount $KK'L$.

If the trade intervention had taken the form of a tariff, instead of a subsidy, the same production effect could have been realized, but a by-product distortion would be created in the form of a consumption loss. Thus, if the government had intervened with a tariff at the rate d (P_1P_2/OP_1), the consumption loss would have been an increase in price to consumers from P_1 to P_2, a reduction in quantity demanded by Q_4Q_3, and a loss in consumers' surplus by the shaded triangle *CED*.

The **infant industry argument** for intervention can be expressed best in terms of external economies, and hence, as a case of a domestic divergence justifying an optimum subsidy. The essential argument is that when an infant industry expands, it yields external economies over time by creating and diffusing knowledge or training labor that becomes freely available to other firms. The infant industry creates an asset from which other firms freely benefit. The social returns on the creation of long-term learning capital are then greater than the private returns, and the market would not provide enough of the activity that creates the external economy.

Sometimes the argument is mistakenly based on the premise that an industry suffers losses on an investment for a certain period and then realizes profits, at a later date, after the industry grows and overcomes the initial production difficulties. But this delay in the realization of profit does not in itself justify government protection. The initial investment will have private profitability if the future output allows the interest to be earned on the initial investment. The costs of growth, which are later recovered, can form part of normal market calculations and require no special subsidization. If, however, the capital market is imperfect and the social rate of discount is less than the current market rate of interest, then we have a situation that may justify a subsidy on the creation of long-term learning capital.[18]

If, for example, a pioneer firm incurs expenses on acquiring knowledge, which is then available free to later entrants, there is a case for an optimal subsidy to the learning process. Similarly, one firm's investment can give rise to an externality if, in accordance with "learning by doing," productivity in the capital goods industry is a function of cumulative gross investment, so that if a firm invests more today, the return on any given level of investment undertaken by **any** firm tomorrow will be higher. An optimal subsidy on investment would then be justified. These cases indicate that the private market may underestimate the future benefits of an investment in the acquisition of knowledge. It is also possible that the private capital market overestimates the time preference for returns, with private firms desiring returns within a shorter period of time than would society, which may have greater concern for the future than has the firm. The social rate of discount is then less than the current market rate of interest, and the investment may be socially profitable even though privately unprofitable. Again, subsidization of investment would be appropriate.

In factor markets there is also a case for an optimum subsidy policy whenever there is a divergence between social and private marginal costs in factor use. A factor market imperfection will again cause $MRT_d \neq MRS = MRT_f$. A distortionary wage differential between activities for the same factor is a common instance of this, especially in less developed countries. The market wage in the advanced manufacturing sector of the economy tends to be greater than the alternative opportunity cost of labor in agriculture. When labor migrates from the rural to the urban sector, the sacrifice in agricultural output is less than the value of the manufacturing wage. The market price of the factor does not reflect the social cost of the input: a true accounting or shadow wage would be less than the actual wage facing the manufacturing sector. The result is that the price ratio understates the profitability of transforming agriculture into manufactures. The manufacturing sector, which is an import-competing sector, employs less labor than would be

---

[18]For an incisive discussion of capital market imperfections, see Corden, *op. cit.*, 253–55.

JOHN STUART MILL, *Principles of Political Economy* (1848), Book V., Chap. 10

> The only case in which, on mere principles of political economy, protecting duties can be defensible, is when they are imposed temporarily (especially in a young and rising nation) in hopes of naturalizing a foreign industry, in itself perfectly suitable to the circumstances of the country. The superiority of one country over another in a branch of production often arises only from having begun it sooner. . . . But it cannot be expected that individuals should, at their own risk, or rather to their certain loss, introduce a new manufacture, and bear the burden of carrying it on until the producers have been educated up to the level of those with whom the processes are traditional. A protecting duty, continued, for a reasonable time, might sometimes be the least inconvenient mode in which the nation can tax itself for the support of such an experiment.

socially desirable.[19] To offset the distortionary wage differential, the first-best policy would be a factor subsidy geared directly to the amount of labor employment provided by the import-competing firms. Second-best policy would be a subsidy on manufacturing production, and third-best a tariff to protect import-competing manufacturing firms. The production subsidy and tariff would shift production toward more manufacturing output, but it would not remove the wage differential, and therefore the economy would still operate on an inefficient production-possibility frontier. Moreover, the tariff would create an added consumption cost. A quota to protect the import-competing manufacturing firms would be fourth-best policy because of its additional consumption cost and physical limitation on imports.

In each of these cases, it is most desirable that the subsidy be directed as specifically as possible to the exact source of the externality. The optimal subsidy is geared to labor training or to investment in creation of knowledge or to labor employment—not simply a general subsidy to the firm. A general subsidy would not distinguish among production activities or type of factor inputs and hence would lead to some by-product distortion.

[19] The economy will not operate on its efficient production-possibility frontier because the two sectors will have, in equilibrium, unequal rates of substitution between factors. The argument for tax-cum-subsidy measures on factor use is elaborated more fully by Bhagwati, *The Theory and Practice of Commercial Policy, op. cit.*, 17–22.

The Optimal and the Actual

The welfare economist's canons may be honored more in the breach than in the observance. But if the quality of policy-making is to be improved, it is first necessary to identify the deviation between the ideal 'first-best" policy and the actual practice.

In practice, the optimum tariff argument is only too likely to degenerate into retaliatory rounds of tariff increases. The process is harmful to all concerned. But as long as it remains in the individual interest of each country separately to raise tariffs, a collective attempt to arrest the process is ineffectual if not backed by international sanctions.[20] Free trade is not a natural state for the world economy; it must be enforced by some international code of conduct.

There are also practical limits to the optimum subsidy argument. The calculation of external economies is obviously difficult. Furthermore, it is unlikely that in practice the subsidy can be financed by non-distortive, lump sum taxes and disbursed in a costless manner. If the act of financing the subsidy is likely to impose inevitable distortion and collection costs, then in practice it is not optimal to correct the original distortion completely or to use only a subsidy and not a tariff.[21] A first-best policy must in practice also entail a first-best financing package. These costs in financing may weaken the case for a subsidy over a tariff. So too will subsidy-disbursement costs. But the size of these costs is really an empirical issue, requiring comparison of the collection and distortion costs for alternative financing packages.[22] The subsidy can be provided directly from general tax revenue or by a decrease in government expenditure elsewhere or by a tax exemption, or

---

[20]Cf. T. Scitovsky, "A Reconsideration of the Theory of Tariffs,' *Review of Economic Studies,* 9 (1942), 89–110.
[21]Meade, *Trade and Welfare* (1955), 237–38.
[22]See Corden, *op. cit.,* Chap. 3.

F. Y. EDGEWORTH, "Theory of International Values," *Economic Journal,* 4 (March 1894), 48

(P)rotection might procure economic advantage in certain cases, if there was a government wise enough to discriminate those cases, and strong enough to confine itself to them; but this condition is very unlikely to be fulfilled.

H.G. JOHNSON, "Optimal Trade Intervention in the Presence of Domestic Distortions," in R.E. Caves et al. (eds.), *Trade, Growth and the Balance of Payments* (1965), 8

Finally, something should be said about the bearing of theoretical analysis of the arguments for protection on practical policy-making and the assessment of actual tariff systems. The demonstration that in certain carefully defined circumstances a tariff levied at a theoretically specified rate would make a country better off than it would be under free trade is not—contrary to the implication of many economic writings on protection—equivalent to a demonstration that past or present tariffs have in fact made the nations imposing them better off than they would have been under free trade, or a justification of whatever tariffs legislators might choose to adopt. Modern economic analysis of the cases in which a tariff or other governmental intervention in the price system would improve economic welfare, in other words, does not constitute a defense of indiscriminate protectionism and a rejection of the market mechanism; rather, it points to a number of respects in which the market mechanism fails to work as it should, and indicates remedies designed to make the market function properly. The usefulness of the exercise depends precisely on the assumption that legislators do not normally know what makes for improvement of economic welfare, and would be prepared to act on better information if it could be provided. If economists did not customarily accept this assumption, their work on economic policy would have to be oriented entirely differently; in particular, research on commercial policy would—depending on the theory of government adopted—be concerned with inferring from actual tariff structures either the divergences between social and private costs and benefits discovered by the collective wisdom of the legislators to exist in the economy, or the political power of various economic groups in the community, as measured by their capacity to extort transfers of income from their fellow-citizens.

a rebate of another tax for the industry to be subsidized, or by an increased tax on a competitive industry.

Without the empirical studies, there is, however, an initial popular bias in favor of a tariff over a subsidy. For a tariff taxes consumers and refunds part or all of the revenue to subsidize producers—thereby bringing about the collection and simultaneous disbursement in a less costly way than the financing of a subsidy. Moreover, the tariff subsidizes producers in a covert fashion. The protected industry tends to prefer this to a subsidy, which is explicit and therefore subject to continual budgetary review. For these reasons, the tariff, rather than the subsidy, is the prevalent form of trade intervention in practice.

The infant industry argument is most likely to be misdirected in practice. Again the problem of estimating the magnitude of external economies and forecasting changes in cost conditions is formidable. And what is termed an infant industry in practice is not restricted to the demonstration of external economies, as it should be. Nor is the temporary condition of the protection respected: instead, the industry is likely to acquire a vested interest to be sheltered far into adulthood. Indeed, protection of senescent industries becomes even more widespread than protection of infant industries.

Finally, the welfare economist's canons are completely ignored when trade interventions are used for balance of payments purposes, employment creation, or non-economic objectives.

Not surprisingly, the gap between the ideal "first-best" policy and actual practice is indeed wide. But we must first understand the ideal and recognize the gap before there can be improvement.

Supplementary Readings

For the seminal discussion of the theory of domestic divergences, ses J.E. Meade, *Trade and Welfare* (1955), Chap. XIV. Two comprehensive survey articles are Stephen P. Magee's "Factor Market Distortions, Production and Trade: A Survey," *Oxford Economic Papers*, 25 (March 1973), 1–43, and R.M. Stern's "Tariffs and Other Measures of Trade Control: A Survey of Recent Developments," *Journal of Economic Literature*, 11 (Sept. 1973), 857–88. Also outstanding are W.M. Corden's *Trade Policy and Economic Welfare* (1974) and M. Michaely's *Theory of Commercial Policy* (1977).

Several articles have become classic in this subject: J. Bhagwati and V.K. Ramaswami, "Domestic Distortions, Tariffs and the Theory of Optimum Subsidy," *Journal of Political Economy*, 71 (Feb. 1963), 44–50; J. Bhagwati, V.K. Ramaswami, and T.N. Srinivasan, "Domestic Distortions, Tariffs, and the Theory of Optimum Subsidy: Some Further Results," *Journal of Political Economy*, 77 (Nov.–Dec. 1969), 1005–10; J. Bhagwati, "The Generalized Theory of Distortions and Welfare," in Bhagwati et al. (eds.), *Trade, Balance of Payments and Growth* (1971), 69–90; and H.G. Johnson, "Optimal Trade Intervention in the Presence of Domestic Distortions," in R.E. Caves et al. (eds.), *Trade, Growth and the Balance of Payments* (1965), 3–34.

4

Fair Trade

Of all the policy objectives for protection in practice, that of "fair trade" has become increasingly pronounced. Appeals to "fairness"—whatever that may mean—have been voiced to justify quantitative restrictions (QRs), voluntary export restraints (VERs) or orderly marketing agreements (OMAs), anti-dumping measures, and countervailing duties on subsidized exports. The resort to these trade restrictions reveals a growing trend to regulate trade in order to avoid "market disruption" or to ensure an "orderly market." In this chapter we analyze a number of protective devices other than tariffs and some additional arguments for intervention—all related to the conflict between trade liberalization and measures of trade intervention to protect fair competition.

In essence, the pro-restriction argument is that a country does not have a right to trade freely with another country when that trade inflicts "material injury" on the importing country. This immediately raises problems of determining "material injury" and of devising optimal remedial policies. The problems become more intense as the structure of comparative costs changes, and a different distribution of benefits and detriments ensues. Those who have suffered a detriment have become more influential in seeking to overrule the dictates of the market. The increasing resort to market safeguards reflects these factors. But in protecting home markets, countries have adopted policies that are third-best, fourth-best, or nth-best policies. The resulting costs to their domestic economies, as well as the international market, have as a result been unnecessarily high.

The Cost of Market Disruption

Strong as is the free-trade case, it fails to consider the costs of the transition period from protection to free trade, or it assumes that the benefits in the free-trade situation more than compensate for any costs endured during the transition period.

Although free trade is optimal under the conditions we have previously specified, the path to free trade is not without its costs: the "invisible hand" can strangle as it achieves an efficient allocation of resources. Even though Ricardo advocated repeal of the Corn Laws, he stated that "the best policy of the State would be, to lay a tax, decreasing in amount from time to time, on the importation of foreign corn, for a limited number of years, in order to afford to the home-grower an opportunity to withdraw his capital gradually from the land." Ricardo proposed only a gradual reduction of the duty of twenty shillings by one shilling every year until it reached ten shillings. To "at once drive capital from the land" would "be rash and hazardous" and there should be "a due regard to temporary interests."[1] When a tariff is reduced, the losses tend to be immediate and concentrated in the domestic import-competing industry; but in contrast, the benefits to consumers and export industries accrue over a longer period of time and are dispersed throughout the economy. A sharp increase in imports, whether it is induced by a tariff reduction or whether it simply occurs autonomously, will evoke requests by domestic producers of import-competing products for some form of market safeguard to limit imports. Complaints of "domestic injury" are frequent. When the costs are more visible to a government than the benefits, the policy reaction is frequently to raise a previously lowered tariff, impose quantitative restrictions on imports, or apply countervailing duties or anti-dumping restrictions. These actions are increasingly being justified in the interests of "fair trade"—in some sense of not having the domestic market disrupted by too high a share of imports, produced abroad under conditions that are "unfair" in comparison with domestic competitors.

When imports cause "injury," they are akin to pollution, accidents, or nuisance—an aspect of the general problem of devising remedial

---

[1]P. Sraffa (ed.), *The Works and Correspondence of David Ricardo,* Vol. I, 266–68; Vol. IV, 264, 266. When the Corn Laws were actually repealed, a fund of £ 2 million was established to extend the draining techniques of high farming among the landowners in England, and another fund of £ 1 million was established for Ireland. See C.P. Kindleberger, *Government and International Trade* (Princeton Essays in International Finance, July 1978), 4–5.

ADAM SMITH, *An Inquiry into the Nature and Causes of the Wealth of Nations* (1776; Glasgow edition, 1976), 471–72

> The undertaker of a great manufacture who, by the home markets being suddenly laid open to the competition of foreigners, should be obliged to abandon his trade, would no doubt suffer very considerably. That part of his capital which had usually been employed in purchasing materials and in paying his workmen, might, without much difficulty, perhaps, find another employment. But that part of it which was fixed in workhouses, and in the instruments of trade, could scarce be disposed of without considerable loss. The equitable regard, therefore, to his interest requires that changes of this kind should never be introduced suddenly, but slowly, gradually, and after a very long warning. The legislature, were it possible that its deliberations could be always directed, not by the clamorous importunity of partial interests, but by an extensive view of the general good, ought upon this very account, perhaps, to be particularly careful neither to establish any new monopolies of this kind, nor to extend further those which are already established. Every such regulation introduces some degree of real disorder into the constitution of the state, which it will be difficult afterwards to cure without occasioning another disorder.

---

policies for externalities. The critical question is who shall bear the "burden" or the cost of market readjustment when trade barriers are reduced? Should the burden or costs be left where they fall because of market forces?

Before evaluating the various policies that have been adopted to safeguard domestic industry, we should first conceptualize the "ideal" approach to the problem. Considering the problem of imports and market disruption, an economist would state that the decision to permit imports should be decided by the market—unless the market is flawed, and the marginal social damage from imports exceeds their marginal social benefit. The "marginal social damage" from imports is not, however, self-defining. Rather the term is as narrow or as broad as some social decision-maker cares to make it. The terms "market disruption" and "domestic injury" are attempts to define the social damage. The terms can be interpreted to refer to dislocation costs that result from imports that are not fully calculated by the market—namely, the cost of unemployment, the cost of transferring the displaced resources to new activities, and the value of the output forgone until resources move to new productive activities.

In decreasing its imports to reduce the dislocation costs, however, a country also suffers a loss of the gains from trade—both static efficiency gains and the dynamic gains of competition from imports. The "marginal cost of import restriction" includes the loss of these efficiency and dynamic gains.

The objective, therefore, is to reduce the sum of the dislocation costs and the costs of avoiding dislocation. This is equivalent to determining **an optimal level of imports at which the marginal social damage from imports equals the marginal cost of import restriction.** At any volume of imports that is less than the optimal, the marginal cost of import-restriction would exceed the marginal social damage from imports, and imports should not be so severely restricted. Conversely, at any volume of imports that is greater than the optimal, the marginal social damage from imports will exceed the marginal cost of import-restriction, and imports should be restricted.

The objective will therefore be fulfilled along a scale of importation between zero restriction of imports-with-maximum disruption and total restriction with zero disruption. The location of the optimal level of imports can be indicated using Figure. 4.1.[2] Suppose that in the absence of any control over imports, the increasing marginal social damage from imports was measured by the line OC, increasing as imports increase. But restrictions on imports also have their costs: the lower the imports, the higher the marginal cost of import restriction, as represented by line DD'. The amount of imports represented by OM, determined by the intersection of these two lines, is the optimal amount of imports. Any amount less than OM would entail an additional excess of costs of import restriction over the value of the reduction of the damage to society. If the amount imported were larger than OM, there would be an excess of the value of the increased damage to society over the saving in costs of import restriction. If the administrative process is costless to restrict imports to OM, then OM is the optimal quantity of imports.

Various policy instruments are available to restrict imports to the optimal level: subsidies, tariff quotas, tariffs, voluntary export restraints or orderly marketing agreements, and quantitative restrictions. As in Chapter 3, we may rank the alternative policy measures in a hierarchy.

---

[2]A similar analysis for pollution abatement is used by J. Meade, *Theory of Economic Externalities* (1973), 58.

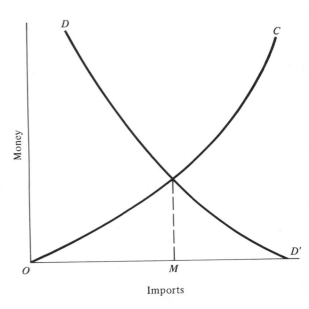

Figure 4.1
Locating the Optimal Quantity of Imports

OC: marginal social damage from imports.

DD': marginal cost of import restriction.

OM: optimal quantity of imports.

Import Quotas

A quota specifies that so many units of imports, or a certain value of imports, will be allowed during a certain time period from specified sources. A quota might also be combined with a tariff by having the tariff rate increase as imports reach higher levels. A quota can also apply to either imports or exports. The essential feature of quotas is some direct and specific physical control on import or export volume, regardless of the price relationship between countries.

Let us now compare the effect of an import quota with a tariff. In Figure 4.2, a tariff would cause imports to be reduced from $H''M''$ to $H'M'$ when the tariff raises the price of imports from the world free-trade price of P_f to the price of imports with tariff of P_t. The direct imposition of a quota in the amount of HM (= $H'M'$) units will produce the same effects. In Figure 4.2, a total supply curve for domestic supply of the importable plus imports is to the right of SS'_d by the amount of the quota HM at every price above P_f. The import quota of HM leads to the same equilibrium as would the tariff at rate P_fP_t/OP_f, except that P_fP_t/OP_f would now be the import premium rate on the free-trade import price. There is thus an **equivalence between a tariff and a quota.** In particular, **corresponding to every tariff rate, there is a quota that will produce equivalent results in protecting domestic production of the importable product, raising domestic price, reducing domestic consumption, and restricting import**

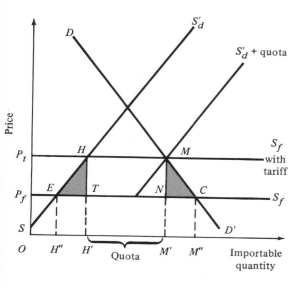

Figure 4.2

The Equivalence of Tariffs and Quotas under Competitive Conditions

The domestic demand and supply curves for a product are DD' and SS'_d. The world price is OP_f, and S_f is the foreign supply curve under free trade. A tariff at the rate P_fP_t/OP_f shifts the S_f curve upward and raises the price to OP_t. Imports are reduced from $H''M''$ to $H'M'$, and domestic output expands from OH'' to OH'. As with a tariff, the quota creates the deadweight losses of HTE in production and MNC in consumption. The import premium $HMNT$ can accrue to holders of import licenses.

volume. But this equivalence holds only under perfectly competitive conditions in the import-competing industry. If, for example, there is any monopoly power in domestic production, an import quota would reinforce the monopoly position. A tariff, however, would allow imports freely at the tariff-inclusion price, and as long as the foreign exporter can sell under the tariff, the domestic monopoly will confront foreign competition. When intercountry price relationships are severed completely, as under a quota, the resultant market structures will be less competitive. By being isolated from market forces, completely avoiding the dictates of the price system and resorting to specific physical controls, **quantitative restrictions are inferior to a tariff.** Though a quota may achieve some of the same objectives as a tariff, it does so at added cost.

Moreover, the tariff and a quota have **different redistributive effects.** The limited supply of imports creates some quota profit instead of tariff revenue. This can be distributed in various ways—either to the importers of the limited supply or to the exporters or to the government by charging a license fee for imports, or by auctioning off the import licenses to the highest competitive bidders. Under a quota, the difference between OP_t and OP_f (Figure 4.2) is the amount of profit per unit that the importer with a license to import can obtain on the home market. If licenses are auctioned, importers would be willing to pay up to P_fP_t per unit of import for the privilege of importing. Depending on the alternative ways by which the permissible quota is allocated among the various claimants for imports, there will be different gains to different domestic importers. If, for example, the government simply allocates import licenses freely on a "first come, first served" basis, the domestic importers will capture the scarcity rent. But if the government requires competitive bidding by would-be importers, the quota profit can be transferred into government revenue. Or if the government awards the licenses to foreign exporters, or if the exporters have sufficient market power, they might capture the surplus from higher export prices instead of allowing quota holders to profit.

Orderly Marketing Agreements

Countries have increasingly resorted to bilaterally negotiated restraints, such as voluntary export restraints (VERs) or orderly marketing agreements (OMAs). (The difference between VERs and OMAs is a technical legal one: OMAs are agreements between two governments, whereas the VER is negotiated directly with the foreign export industry.) Instead of the importing country imposing a quota or raising tariffs, an exporting country "voluntarily" agrees to restrict its exports to a certain amount or to a maximum rate of growth. The VER, or OMA, has certain features of expediency. It first bypasses the General Agreement on Tariffs and Trade (GATT) and avoids the conditions specified by GATT for using a quota or increasing a previously reduced tariff (Article XIX). The GATT conditions are more restrictive—namely, the imports must be due to a prior tariff reduction, the country that imposes a market safeguard must do so on a most-favored-nation basis, and it must offer in return some compensation in another tariff reduction or else face retaliation.

Similarly, an OMA avoids the restrictions on import relief contained in any domestic legislation (such as the U.S. Trade Act of 1979, Section 101). Instead of following most-favored-nation treatment, the OMA can be applied in a discriminatory fashion to a specific country. And, as with any quantitative restriction, there is none of the unpredictability that characterizes a tariff: regardless of the differential between domestic and foreign prices, imports are restricted to a definite quantity. For the exporting country, the OMA can forestall the more restrictive effects of a unilateral imposition of a quota. Finally, there need not be any public disclosure of a VER that is arranged by private industries.

The effects on domestic production and consumption in the importing country will be similar under a quota and an OMA. But the distribution of the **scarcity premia** created by the import restraints may more readily go to the exporting country under the OMA. The division of the difference between the free-trade price and the higher price after imports are restrained is more likely to be in favor of the exporting country when it administers the controls. Under a quota, the importing country can allocate the limited imports among importers who can capture the scarcity premia. But under OMAs or VERs, an oligopolistic group of exporters can organize a cartel and earn the monopoly rents from the export restriction. Indeed, if the VER were truly voluntary, it would be nothing less than an export cartel that controlled supply to maximize profits from the trade restraint (compare OPEC).[3] If, however, an oligopsonistic set of importers buy from competitive exporters, the importers may capture most of the scarcity premia on imports.

In resorting to OMAs, the determination of "serious injury" is too often based on national political pressures instead of economic analysis. It would be desirable if bilaterally negotiated agreements could be brought under multilateral surveillance by some international review body. Although it may initially be difficult for nations to agree on a standard of "serious injury," the international review body would serve a useful function in attempting to harmonize national procedures, providing an international forum for additional consultation, and eventually establishing more definitive criteria for the use of market safeguards. Moreover, in the event a national finding of injury was not found acceptable internationally, the safeguard-invoking country might then be made to offer equivalent compensation to, or suffer corresponding retaliation by, its trading partners. If, however, the finding is accepted, then trading partners could be asked to waive their right to compensation or retaliation.

Further, it would be desirable if countries could be given an effective assurance of a continually growing access to the protected market and of a foreseeable removal of the market safeguard. This is especially vital for newly industrializing countries who are entering export markets. To this end, the right to invoke GATT's Article XIX might be conditioned by requirements that (i) the protection afforded by the safeguard measure be degressive over a certain number of years and terminal within some designated time period; (ii) the invoking country is obli-

---

[3]Cf. Carl van Duyne, "Commodity Cartels and the Theory of Derived Demand," *Kyklos*, 28 (1975), 597–611.

gated to promote adjustments that will reduce the dislocation costs; and (iii) the use of the safeguard measures and the adjustment efforts must be open to multilateral surveillance.

If the situation of "serious injury" is to be ameliorated, and dislocation costs reduced, governments must pursue adjustment policies. Otherwise industries that prefer protection to adjustment will continue the pressure for retention of the market safeguard. The international review body should therefore insist that the market safeguard mechanism be coupled with appropriate policies of adjustment assistance. In various ways, efforts could be made to limit the use of safeguards and promote adjustment measures. For example, the incentives of adjustment assistance would be intensified if retaliation were permitted or if additional and proportionately larger concessions were required whenever the safeguards are not removed or reduced after a designated time period. Any protective measure could also be required to be sharply degressive over a fairly short time span. If countries would agree to use production subsidies, rather than tariffs or quotas, the fiscal cost might also induce speedier adjustment policies. At the least, methods of international surveillance could be instituted to disclose the types of adjustment policies being used and to monitor their progress.

Export Subsidies

Another practice of exporting countries that meets with the disfavor of importing countries is the use of export subsidies. Although quotas and OMAs violate the dictates of market efficiency—in the interest of maintaining a condition the importing country likes to call "fair trade"—the opposition to export subsidies can actually be justified on efficiency criteria. For, in terms of the allocation of world resources, export subsidies encourage too many resources into foreign-traded commodities unless there are production externalities. The export subsidy makes private cost less than social cost, thereby inducing exporters to produce a greater output at which the marginal social cost in the subsidizing country exceeds the free international prices of exports. The exporter acquires an artificially larger share of world markets. (We exclude the exceptional and rare case in which an export subsidy may be used as an optimum subsidy.)

The range of export subsidies can be extensive and subtle. Because tariffs and subsidies are policy substitutes, the resort to subsidies as instruments of industrial policy has become much more extensive with the reduction of tariffs. The disguised quality of a subsidy also makes it more appealing than the explicit protection of a tariff. And as governments have become increasingly concerned with the status of particular industries, sections, and groups within the nation, the practice of subsidization has spread. Export subsidies are most common in agriculture, usually to reinforce domestic price supports above world market prices. But subsidies have also assumed other forms—especially special government-supported financing facilities at below private market rates for exporters, favorable export-credit insurance and guarantee arrangements, R & D support from the government, investment grants, training and education programs, rebates of direct taxes, over-rebates of indirect taxes, income tax deferrals, and other tax advantages. If domestic industries face stricter environmental standards or higher effluent fees than industries overseas, they are also likely to seek protection against the "unfair" use of "cheap" foreign environmental resources in other countries.[4]

The range of subsidies is thus wide, often being only implicit or indirect. Moreover, when the subsidy is paid on the use of a particular input, the effect on unit costs of production is difficult to determine. So too is it complicated to assess by how much a subsidy results in a fall in price.

To neutralize an export subsidy, importing countries commonly impose countervailing duties. The GATT (Article VI) allows a country to levy a countervailing duty if it determines that the effect of a domestic subsidy by another country is such as to cause or threaten to cause material injury to one of its industries. American trade legislation also directs the U.S. Treasury to impose a countervailing duty when an industry in the United States is materially injured, or is threatened with material injury, or the establishment of an industry in the United States is materially retarded by reason of subsidized imports. In more general language the Treaty establishing the European Economic Community states that "any aid . . . which distorts or threatens to distort competition by favoring certain enterprises or certain productions shall, to the extent to which it adversely affects trade between Member States, be deemed to be incompatible with the Common Market" (Article 92). The legal interpretations raise questions of what is a "subsidy" or a

---

[4] For a more complete analysis, see H. Peter Gray, "Commercial Policy Implications of Environmental Controls," in Ingo Walter (ed.), *Studies in International Environmental Economics* (1976), Chap. 7.

"material injury," and whether differential treatment should be allowed for developing countries.

The right to retaliate with countervailing duties rests, of course, on the premise that subsidies are "bad." But some subsidies might correct market distortions and actually raise world income when properly used. We should, therefore, **differentiate between the justifiable and un-justifiable type of subsidy,** according to the effects on the benefits of trade and world income that result from an efficient use of each country's resources. In no other class of nontariff trade distortions is the need more apparent for a set of general rules and an institutional arrangement, utilizing GATT, for judging specific cases by these guidelines.[5] Regarding the application of U.S countervailing duties, it has been suggested that subsidy practices be grouped into three categories as to whether they are prohibited, conditional, or permitted. Countries would then be allowed to take countervailing action against prohibited practices without any conditions; the injury test would be applied in the second category; and permissible subsidies would be exempt from countervailing duties.[6]

As with the various nontariff barriers generally, a more reasoned approach to the problem of export subsidies is difficult not only because it requires new international action, but also because a subsidy is normally coupled to some particular domestic policy at the macroeconomic level, and hence its modification depends upon a prior change in domestic policy.

Anti-dumping Action

Also of increasing importance are anti-dumping regulations. The charge that foreigners are "dumping" their exports is frequently heard. American trade legislation has long required the imposition of anti-dumping duties when dumping is found to result in domestic injury. The GATT has established an anti-dumping code implementing GATT Article VI, which allows anti-dumping duties if it is established that the imports taxed have been dumped and if the importing country "determines that the effect of dumping . . . is such as to cause or threaten an injury to an established domestic industry, or is such as to retard materially the establishment of a domestic industry."

[5] See Robert E. Baldwin, *Non-tariff Distortions of International Trade* (1970), 130–31.
[6] Bela Balassa and Michael Sharpston, *Export Subsidies by Developing Countries* (1977), 24.

But how is "dumping" to be defined? The GATT code and most national anti-dumping regulations define dumping as the sale of a product abroad at a lower price than is charged domestically. This becomes ambiguous when the several possible dimensions of "price" and "product" are considered. It is also a wider definition than the alternative one of defining dumping as the sale of the product abroad at below cost.

The sale of a product at two different prices in two different markets is simply the practice of price discrimination. This is realizable when producers possess some monopolistic power in their home market, confront different demand elasticities in the two markets, and when their exports cannot be resold in the home market. Demand is generally more elastic abroad than at home because of the greater number of competing suppliers in export markets[7] or because domestic oligopolists expect domestic rivals to follow price cuts, whereas sellers in foreign markets are less likely to react. To maximize profits, a price discriminator then lowers the price in the more elastic foreign market and raises the price in the home market. More will be sold abroad, and less at home, until the marginal revenue from each separate market equals the marginal cost of the total output.

But why should an importing country consider this "unfair trade" and undesirable? After all, the consumer does enjoy lower-priced imports. In answer, the criticism of dumping is usually that it may be **predatory**—once the exporter has acquired a large share of the market, the price will be raised to the detriment of the consumer. This, however, depends upon the dumper acquiring a monopoly in the importing market over all other potential world suppliers—a rare case. Or the dumping may be **sporadic**, causing uncertainty concerning future prices and creating periods of unemployment and adjustment problems whenever the foreigner chooses to dump surplus stocks. The criterion of "material injury," however, reflects neither of these considerations, but refers again simply to the effect of the domestic import-competing industry. The costs and benefits have different time profiles; discounting the future social losses against present gains will reduce the net loss to the economy from predatory or sporadic dumping. As long as dumping occurs, the gains go to the importing country (gains to consumers are greater than losses to import-competing producers). If only the practice were permanent, it would not be objectionable! Countries who

---

[7]This is not universally true. Consider the international cartel among exporters of oil and the case of "reverse dumping"—lower prices at home and higher abroad.

take anti-dumping action harm only themselves[8]—unless the dumping is predatory or sporadic, domestic producers are not in fact compensated, and adjustment costs are weighted heavily.

Adjustment Assistance

As indicated in our discussion of OMAs, the problem of market safeguards should be analyzed in conjunction with measures of adjustment assistance. Indeed, one may even prefer to define market disruption as simply the inability or unwillingness to make adequate adjustments to imports. Adjustment assistance has taken various forms: direct compensation to workers and firms in industries suffering "serious injury" from imports, retraining and relocation allowances for displaced workers, employment and marketing information, technical assistance, financial assistance and tax relief to firms. The objective of these measures, however, should be to provide **transformation** assistance—that is, promote the movement of resources out of the industry that is losing its comparative advantage—not to perpetuate the retention of inefficient resources in the depressed industry. No matter what their particular form, adjustment measures must avoid trade-distorting effects: an inefficient adjustment assistance measure has no more merit than does an inefficient VER or tariff or QR.

Adjustment assistance and market safeguards are not substitute policies, but complementary. Whereas market safeguards slow down the speed of the change that has to be absorbed, the adjustment assistance should be designed to increase the speed with which change can be absorbed. Optimum policy with respect to change associated with the dynamic sequence of comparative advantage requires **joint optimization** with respect to both types of policy, not prior choice of one line or other of policy and subsequent optimization with respect to it alone.[9] The case for market safeguards must be that the adjustment cost can be reduced by extending the transformation process in time. The justification of adjustment assistance is that it hastens the removal of trade restrictions. Otherwise, the case for assistance to an import-competing industry has no more merit than assistance to exporters "injured" by competition from other exporting countries or assistance to any domes-

[8] Peter Lloyd, *Anti-dumping Actions and the GATT System* (1977), 12–14.
[9] H.G. Johnson, "Technological Change and Comparative Advantage: An Advanced Country's Viewpoint," *Journal World Trade Law*, 9 (Jan.–Feb. 1975), 13.

tic firm "injured" by economic changes. The removal of trade distortions must be the ultimate purpose of adjustment assistance. From the viewpoint of the U.S. economy as a whole, empirical studies have shown that the cost of adjustment assistance to affected workers and firms is much smaller than the benefits of reduced prices for consumers, of a more efficient allocation of domestic resources, and of the avoidance of retaliatory protectionist action by other countries that would adversely affect American exports.[10]

Neither market safeguards nor adjustment assistance should be protectionist by opposing the dictates of comparative advantage, but instead should be devoted to providing transformation assistance along a socially optimal time path. The specification of such a time path would require the complex application of optimal control theory. The general objective, however, can be simply stated as trying to maximize the time-separated benefits from imports minus the costs of reallocation. Not the prevention of change, but the optimal pacing of change is the objective.

To make the transformation assistance more effective, the conversion of resources to higher productivity uses should be promoted as early as possible. Instead of delaying an investigation and an adjustment assistance program until "serious injury" has been determined, it may be more sensible to shift to an "early warning' approach that makes it possible both to anticipate probable difficulties and to deal with these at an early stage. In essence, the problem is to devise an anticipatory, comprehensive approach that will reflect the changing character of the international division of labor and facilitate the movement of resources in the direction of more efficient international resource allocation. This problem of dislocation will become more acute—and the time for adjustment shorter—as technology is diffused more rapidly to the LDCs, transnational corporations expand, and the developing countries accelerate their industrialization process. As these countries acquire a wider comparative advantage in the well-standardized, labor-intensive manufacturing industries, they will become increasingly competitive with the older, labor-intensive, import-sensitive industries of the more developed countries. To facilitate this change, incentives are needed for speedier adjustment policies, at the same time as the protectionist

---

[10] Stephen P. Magee, "The Welfare Effects of Restriction on U.S. Trade," *Brookings Papers on Economic Activity* (1972), 645–708; Ilse Mintz, *U.S. Import Quotas: Costs and Consequences* (1973); and Thomas B. Birnberg, *Economic Effects of Changes in Trade Relations between Developed and Less Developed Countries* (1978).

effects of market safeguards are continually reduced and ultimately eliminated.

Tariff Discrimination

All the questions of fair trade we have so far considered relate to alleged injury in the importing country. There can, however, also be **injury to an exporting country** through the trade practices of importing countries. This can arise not simply through tariffs as such, but through the special ways in which tariffs are imposed in **preferential trading arrangements** and in **tariff structures.**

A preferential trading arrangement, such as a customs union or free-trade area, is of special interest because it combines some effects of free trade and protection. A customs union maintains a common external tariff, but free trade among its members. A free-trade area allows each member to maintain its own external tariff, while having free trade among the members.[11] Both the customs union and the free-trade area practice non-discrimination among members, but discriminate against outside countries by providing preferences to members (100% preferences). Although non-discrimination is a basic principle of GATT (Article I), an exception is allowed for a customs union or free-trade area (Article XXIV).

Because it combines elements of free trade and protection, the formation of a customs union raises the interesting question whether it is beneficial for both its members and the rest of the world. Since the free trade is not universal, does optimizing a part of the system improve economic welfare for the entire system when another part of the system still has a distortion? This question again leads us to the **"theory of the second best."** This theory, it will be recalled, states that if an economy cannot attain all the optimum conditions (the problem is one of a constrained optimum), then the fulfillment of one of these conditions will not necesarily make the economy "better off" than would its non-fulfillment.[12] If it is impossible to satisfy **all** the optimum conditions

---

[11] A third form of regional integration, a common market, adopts free trade and the free movement of capital and labor among member countries. A fourth form, an economic union, has not only complete free trade among members, and free migration of factors, but also a common currency and common policies.

[12] See R.G. Lipsey and K. Lancaster, "The Genral Theory of Second Best," *Review of Economic Studies,* 24 (1956), 11–32. Lipsey and Lancaster stated that "given that one of the Paretian optimum conditions cannot be fulfilled, then an optimum situation can be achieved only by

(in this case, to make all relative prices equal to all rates of transformation in production), then a change that satisfies **some** of the optimum conditions (in this case making some relative prices equal to some rates of transformation in production) may make things better or worse. This result follows because the removal of one distortion can intensify another distortion elsewhere.

Whether world welfare increases or not under a preferential trading arrangement depends on the trade-creating versus the trade-diverting effects of the discriminatory elimination of tariffs exclusively on member countries of the preferential trading group. "**Trade creation**" occurs when high-cost domestic output of one member country is replaced with lower-cost production from another member. This improves the resource allocation and is consistent with free trade. "**Trade diversion**," however, means that because of the external tariff, there is a diversion of output from a low-cost outside source of supply to a high-cost source within the union.[13] The higher-cost exporter within the union can sell to another member because it does not face the external tariff. This reduces the efficiency of world production and is a movement away from free trade. The tariff revenue that formerly went to the tariff-imposing country's government now goes to the higher-cost producers in the other member country.

Trade creation will be more likely under the following conditions: the higher the initial tariff rates between members; the greater the degree of overlapping among member countries between the class of commodities produced under tariff protection before the union; the higher the elasticity of demand for imports on which duties are reduced; the higher the elasticity of supply of exports from members; the lower the external tariff on products for which members reduce tariffs;

---

departing from all the other Paretian conditions. . . . The optimum situation finally attained may be termed a second-best optimum because it is achieved subject to a constraint which, by definition, prevents the attainment of a Paretian optimum."

[13] Viner developed the concepts of trade creation and trade diversion; and he demonstrated that trade creation will increase and trade diversion will decrease welfare for the world—based on the assumptions of fixed coefficients in consumption, constant costs in production, and absence of distortions in the economy. See Jacob Viner, *The Customs Union Issue* (1950). It has however, been claimed that trade diversion is not necessarily detrimental if there are variable coefficients in consumption, or increasing returns to scale in production. See R.G. Lipsey, "The Theory of Customs Union: A General Survey," *Economic Journal,* 70 (Sept. 1960), 496–513, and Jagdish Bhagwati, "Customs Union and Welfare Improvement," *Economic Journal,* 81 (Sept. 1971), 580–87. But see H.G. Johnson, "Trade-Diverting Customs Unions: A Comment," *Economic Journal,* 84 (Sept. 1974), 618–21.

and the larger the preferential area. (At the extreme, if the union included all countries, there could be no trade diversion.)

If trade diversion occurs, welfare would have been improved if the preferences among members had not been 100%, but something less. Up to a point, some discrimination in favor of members of a customs union or free-trade area could be trade-creating, but becomes trade-diverting beyond that point. Again, this is a problem of optimization in a sub-system, and does not necessarily call for free trade as in the entire system. Tariffs that discriminate 100% in favor of member countries against the rest of the world may be third best compared with a second-best policy of having some tariffs on members, but less than the tariffs on non-members.

Nations that are discriminated against by the preferences are naturally inclined to complain that the preferences are a form of "unfair trade," excluding them from the union's markets. If only they were beneficiaries of the preferences, they too could trade in the union. Non-members are therefore anxious to have the external tariff of the union as low as possible.

Effective Protection

So far we have considered tariffs as if they were levied only on the final products being traded. But tariffs are also imposed on **intermediate goods** that are used as inputs into final products. In processing, domestic industry adds value to the intermediate imports (yarn to clothing, cocoa powder to chocolate, leather to shoes). We must therefore examine the **entire tariff structure** to determine the degree of protection. When we do this, we are likely to find that tariffs are imposed at differential rates on intermediate goods and final products, with the rates rising as the imports change from crude raw materials and foodstuffs to semi-manufactures to the more finished capital goods and consumer goods. When the tariff rates cascade or escalate according to the degree of processing or stage of production, the **"effective" rate of protection is higher than the nominal rate.** The effective rate of protection indicates the extent to which the tariff structure enables the domestic value of the factors used in a stage of domestic productive activity to exceed their value at world market prices under free trade. The effect of protection on domestic value added will affect international resource allocation.

To illustrate the effective rate of protection, let us consider a final product Y and an imported intermediate good X that is an input in the production of Y. Let the world price per unit of Y be \$100, the world price of X be \$80, and the value added by domestic labor and capital in the processing stage of X into Y be \$20. If the nominal tariff on Y is 10%, the domestic price of Y rises to \$110. The domestic processing stage of X into Y can now absorb \$30 per unit of Y-output for domestic labor and capital, compared with \$20 under free trade. The effective protection on the domestic processing stage is therefore 50% = (\$30-\$20)/\$20, compared with the nominal tariff of 10%. With effective protection amounting to 50%, the domestic producer can be much less efficient than the foreign producer and still retain the home market. The foreign producer faces the additional handicap of having to be all the more efficient than the domestic producer to compete in the domestic producer's market.

More generally, if there is a tariff on only the end product, the effective tariff rate (e) for the industry is $e = t/v$, where t is the tariff rate on the end product, and v is the percentage of domestic-value-added in producing the final product. If there are also tariffs on imported inputs, $e = (t - t_m s_m)/v$, where t_m is the weighted average rate of nominal tariffs on the imported inputs, and s_m is the percentage of imported inputs in the total output.

The effective rate of protection will exceed the nominal tariff rate so long as the nominal rate exceeds the weighted average tariff on inputs. And the protection to domestic value added will be greater the larger the share of imported inputs used (i.e., the smaller the proportion of value added per unit contributed by the protected domestic factors of production).[14]

Although any tariff on the final product acts as if it were a subsidy to domestic production, a tariff on an intermediate good acts as an added cost, or a tax, on the final product. A reduction in tariffs on intermediate inputs will therefore give greater protection to, or act as a subsidy for, the domestic stage of processing. In this sense, a country can become more protective by lowering tariffs, provided the tariffs are on intermediate goods. The effective protection on value added will be higher the greater the difference between the nominal tariff rates on the finished products and imported inputs, and the less the proportion of domestic value added in the final price.

[14] For the derivation of the formula by which to calculate the effective rate of protection, see W.M. Corden, *The Theory of Protection* (1971), 35–39.

Other countries that want to export the processed product confront higher effective rates of protection than the nominal rates. Exporters therefore object to the escalation of the tariff rates. As less developed countries want to export manufactures, they are especially critical of effective rates of protection, claiming that the tariff structures of the developed countries bias their imports from less developed countries toward unprocessed primary products. The poor country is forced to remain a "hewer of wood and drawer of water." All countries, however, now realize that trade liberalization is to be sought not only in lowering nominal tariff rates, but also through the reduction of rate differentials within a country's tariff structure in order to reduce the effective rates of protection.

Export Controls

Finally, the use of export controls also raises issues of "fair trade." Governments have increasingly limited their exports by taxing exports or, at their own initiative, imposing quantitative restrictions on exports. If import controls question the right of access to markets, the export controls question the right of access to supplies.

Governments impose export controls for various reasons.[15] "National security" has been a favorite rationale, as exemplified in the retention of strategic materials for domestic use, in export controls as a bargaining instrument in foreign policy, in embargoes, and in "trading with the enemy" provisions. More purely economic are the objectives of avoiding physical shortages, of reinforcing domestic price controls, of stimulating domestic processing activities, and of improving the terms of trade. Export controls have been imposed on resources or commodities in short supply within the country both to avoid unemployment and to restrain inflation. If the shortage of an input acts as a constraint on employment, its export might be controlled. If during an inflationary period, domestic supplies become short, a country may also try to "export its inflation" by limiting sales overseas of its scarce products. And if domestic price controls are imposed to repress inflation, export licensing may be used to reinforce the domestic price controls. Instead of export-

[15]For a summary of the purposes and methods of government export controls in recent years, see C. Fred Bergsten, *Completing the GATT: Toward New International Rules to Govern Export Controls* (1974), 5–14.

ing raw materials, a country may try to stimulate domestic processing industries that utilize the raw materials by assuring access of domestic producers to the raw material inputs or by reducing the costs of these inputs to domestic producers by restraining the export of the raw materials. This objective can be couched in "infant industry" language. To improve the terms of trade of the producing country, or at least to forestall their decline, is another reason for export controls that force up world prices of its exports. (The particular use of international commodity agreements will be considered in Part III.)

Of special interest is the question whether export controls will succeed in raising export prices. This ability to increase price requires sufficient market power, indicated essentially by three conditions: (i) a dominant position by the country in the export market or the capacity for effective collusion by a group of the producer nations (ii) an inelastic demand for the product in consumer countries, and (iii) a low elasticity of supply of alternative materials for consumer countries. If the price elasticity of foreign demand for the restricted commodity is sufficiently low, the value of export receipts for the commodity may rise.

To the extent that measures to control export prices succeed, however, they impose real costs on the international community. These costs arise when export controls induce the production of costlier sources of supply, aggravate inflationary pressures in consuming countries, slow down the rate of growth in consuming countries, and provoke retaliatory measures.

Just as import controls should be limited to conditions that are "justifiable," so too should an international code of conduct **distinguish the permissible conditions for export controls** (perhaps through the amendment of the GATT). The "national security" and "infant processing industry" arguments are most persuasive. Like the escape clause for import controls, a test for "domestic injury" might also be applied to the use of export controls. But as with import controls, there should be a coupling of adjustment assistance with some time limit to the use of export controls to ensure that the controls do not substitute for other necessary remedial policies. If exports are to be limited, it is also less burdensome to do so by taxes than by quotas; taxes do not sever connection with market conditions as do quantitative restrictions, and the proceeds of export taxes accrue to the government instead of having private firms or government monopolies receive a windfall, as usually occurs with quantitative controls.

Nobel Laureate J. E. MEADE, *Trade and Welfare* (1955), 571

[I]n modern conditions it is really not possible to achieve a liberal international economic order merely by free trade between sovereign nations; something more positive in the way of international economic institutions (if not of supranational economic authorities) is required for this purpose. . . . The mere negative act of outlawing or limiting the use of protective devices in the modern world requires the international supervision, if not the supranational policing, of a number of economic arrangements which are primarily of domestic concern. Moreover, if it be true that a liberal economic order in the modern world can be built successfully only if national governments will avoid certain types of domestic policy, the need for some degree of continuing intergovern-mental discussion or supra-governmental control of domestic policies is obvious.

Toward a Public Order

Export controls and the other policies related to "fair trade," as well as all the other trade policies we have discussed, re-emphasize the need for a normative order in trading arrangements. The normative principles we have examined need to be embodied in **justifiable international economic conduct.** While the welfare economist argues the optimality of free trade, national governments are only too prone to embrace protectionist policies. Protection—rather than free trade—is the natural state in the world economy, and nationally competitive trade policies displace the mutual gains from trade. **Free trade must, therefore, be enforced by some authoritative policy formation process,** with an international mechanism for resolving conflicts over market access and access to supplies. The central problem is how to devise **institutional devices that will establish these normative principles** in practice. At a procedural level, this control may range from international notifi-cation and consultation about a proposed trade policy to the formation of an international code of conduct with binding limitations on the use of specific trade policies except under specified conditions.

Non-discrimination or most-favored-nation treatment has been a basic principle of trade negotiations. But this principle has been eroded by regional blocs and by preferential trading arrangements. Reciprocity has been another principle of trade negotiations, but this stems more from a protectionist psychology than a free-trade rationale: if the gains from trade are on the import side, then trade liberalization is to the benefit of the tariff-reducing country even if other countries do not reduce their tariffs. To emphasize exports rather than imports is to return to a mercantilist philosophy. If, however, a country raises tariffs, it has been required to offer some compensation in the form of a tariff reduction on another commodity or else face retaliation. The principle of compensation has also been diluted by escape clauses that allow protection, without compensation, under conditions of market disruption or material injury. The problem of compensation merges into the wider problem of more favorable treatment for developing countries. Although the equality of nations is propounded politically and legally, the economic reality is that of inequality. Trading relationshps have become more complicated by this fact, as we shall again see in Part III.

Non-tariff distortions have also moved the debate into a wider context than simply the old-fashioned tariff debate. The non-tariff distortions are closely linked to issues of "fair trade," which are as ambiguous as they are controversial.

Especially needed now is clarification of international rules that will "draw the line" between legitimate actions to protect fair competition and abuse of these actions for protectionist purposes.

Finally, it is apparent that it is even more difficult for a country to institute efficient trade policies when it has a balance of payments problem. Trade protection is often balance of payments protection in the absence of an effective adjustment mechanism. The management of international trading arrangements therefore requires, in turn, the management of international payments problems—our next topic.

Supplementary Readings

On the general problem of non-tariff barriers, see R.E. Baldwin, *Non-tariff Distortions of International Trade* (1970); G. Curzon and V. Curzon, *Hidden Barriers to International Trade* (1970).

The classic work on dumping is Jacob Viner, *Dumping: A Problem in International Trade* (1923). A recent analysis is by Peter Lloyd, *Anti-Dumping Actions and the GATT System* (1977).

An excellent exposition of effective protection is presented in W.M. Corden, *The Theory of Protection* (1971). Also, H.G. Grubel and H.G. Johnson (eds.), *Effective Tariff Protection* (1971). A comparison of tariffs, quotas, and VERs is available from

C. Fred Bergsten, "On the Non-Equivalence of Import Quotas and 'Voluntary' Export Restraints," in C. Fred Bergsten (ed.), *Toward a New World Trade Policy: The Maidenhead Papers* (1975), 239–71; Hirofumi Shibata, "A Note on the Equivalence of Tariffs and Quotas," *American Economic Review,* 58 (March 1968), 137–42; and Richard J. Sweeney, Edward Tower, and Thomas D. Willett, "The Ranking of Alternative Tariff and Quota Policies in the Presence of Domestic Monopoly," *Journal of International Economics,* 7 (1977), 349–62.

Issues of adjustment assistance are analyzed by R.E. Baldwin and J.H. Mutti, "Policy Issues in Adjustment Assistance," in Helen Hughes (ed.), *Prospects for Partnership* (1973), 149–86; Goran Ohlin (OECD Development Centre), *Adjustment for Trade* (1975).

Two survey articles of preferential trading arrangements are Melvyn Krauss, "Recent Developments in Customs Union Theory: An Interpretative Survey," *Journal of Economic Literature,* 10 (June 1972), 424–30 and R.G. Lipsey, "The Theory of Customs Unions: A General Survey," *Economic Journal,* 70 (September 1960), 496–513. More recent analyses are in Melvyn Krauss (ed.), *The Economics of Integration* (1973) and R.G. Lipsey, *The Theory of Customs Unions: A General Equilibrium Analysis* (1970).

For additional readings related to topics covered in Part I, consult the extensive bibliography in M. Michaely, *Theory of Commercial Policy* (1977), 231–39.

II

Theory of Balance
of Payments Policy

5

Balance of Payments Problems

We have so far avoided worrying about the balance of payments by assuming an automatic mechanism of balance of payments adjustment through internal price and wage changes or exchange rate adjustments that are sufficiently effective to keep the value of a country's exports equal to its imports. That assumption allowed us to focus exclusively on the non-monetary aspects of international trade—to pierce what classical economists called the "monetary veil" and to concentrate on the longer-run "real" forces determining the pattern of trade.

We must now remove that convenient assumption and become familiar with some fundamental principles of international monetary economics. This will equip us to analyze balance of payments problems, which are now a major preoccupation of many countries. If the international economic community is ever to achieve the full potential of the gains from liberalized trade (as discussed in Part I), and if there is to be the power to meet the challenging problems of world poverty (which we shall discuss in Part III), then it is essential that balance of payments problems be overcome.

In recent years, however, the monetary complications of trade have confronted policy-makers with severe problems. Since 1973, the international monetary system (some critics might say "non-system") has become one of floating exchange rates, but with discretionary official intervention to manage the float (again, some critics might say a "dirty float"). The managed floating regime contrasts with the previous system of pegged-but-adjustable exchange rates established at the Bretton Woods conference at the end of World War II, and enduring until 1971. Since the collapse of the Bretton Woods system, there have been any number of proposals for international monetary reform. But at the same time, the foreign exchange markets have necessarily had to continue functioning in some manner.

Countries have responded to the departure from the old system in a variety of ways: some peg their currencies to a single currency, some to the Special Drawing Right (SDR), some to other baskets of currencies, some have joined in a currency area with limited margins of fluctuations in the exchange rates between partner countries (European Monetary System), and some float independently. Generalization is impossible. Experience with floating rates has still been too brief to allow definitive assessment of the efficacy of the newer regime. Moreover, a number of monetary officials and some quarters of the international financial community still yearn for a return to some features of the pre-1971 regime. Some IMF statements also refer to the objective of returning to "stable but adjustable rates" (whatever that might mean).

All this ambiguity makes it impossible to predict what type of international monetary system will prevail in the years ahead. Instead of assuming any one definite type of regime, we might be better advised to approach the problems of international monetary economics with more perspective—emphasizing some principles that are relevant regardless of type of regime, recalling some essential features of the Bretton Woods system, and then moving on to some present-day realities. For the past does inform, and recognition of the persistent normative principles can be of greater value than overconcern with current institutional details.

This chapter serves as an introduction to some normative principles of balance of payments policy that will be relevant in a variety of international monetary regimes.

An Uneasy Triangle

The overriding international economic policy question is whether a country can attain simultaneously **the multiple objectives of internal balance, trade liberalization, and external balance.** Until the recent years of stagflation—that is, unemployment together with inflation—the objective of "internal balance" was full employment. The influence of Keynesian economics had made full employment an unquestioned objective. And in the Keynesian system, prices were assumed constant until full employment was reached. But the experience of stagflation has led governments to consider the content of internal balance more broadly—as the maximum level of unemployment and level of inflation that can be tolerated.[1]

"Trade liberalization"—the attempt to reduce restrictions on foreign trade and on international capital movements—has also been a professed goal of nations adhering to the General Agreement on Tariffs and Trade (GATT) and the International Monetary Fund (IMF). And GATT's emphasis on non-discrimination and reciprocity in tariff concessions and its eschewal of non-tariff barriers (except the allowance of quantitative restrictions for balance of payments reasons) have been basic to postwar efforts to achieve freer multilateral trade. Convertibility between national currencies, a unified exchange rate for all types of transactions (in contrast to multiple rates for different types of transactions), and removal of restrictions on capital movements are recognized obligations of the member nations of the IMF. The allowance by GATT of QRs for balance of payments reasons is inconsistent with the goals of the IMF.

External balance is equivalent to balance of payments equilibrium. The analysis in this and the next four chapters is essential to our understanding of the implications of "balance of payments equilibrium." Insofar as a government may not want its exchange rate to vary, and therefore intervenes in foreign exchange markets to hold its rate fixed, the objective of external balance may mean balance of payments equilibrium with fixed rates.

To the extent that the policy objectives conflict, there will have to be some policy trade-offs. The trade-offs occur because the objectives are incompatible, the country does not have sufficient policy instruments to achieve all targets, or the policies of other countries prevent their achievement. This can be represented in Figure 5.1 by the uneasy triangle that has one of the policy objectives at each of three vertices. We are asking: Can an economy be at vertices 1, 2, 3 simultaneously? Or must it move away from one vertex to reach another? In their efforts to achieve internal balance, countries have often moved away from "trade liberalization" by resorting to import restrictions. Even though, in our reasoning in Chapter 3, we labeled the advocacy of trade restrictions in order to promote full employment a "non-argument" or an "nth-best" policy measure, nonetheless in reality, governmental policies have often had this neo-mercantilistic purpose.

Another conflict may arise when the pursuit of internal balance en-

[1] See James Meade, "The Meaning of 'Internal Balance,' " *Economic Journl*, 88 (Sept. 1978), 423–36.

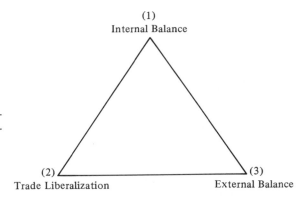

Figure 5.1

An Uneasy Triangle of Policy Objectives

Can a country achieve all these objectives simultaneously? Or is there a conflict among the multiple objectives?

(1) Internal Balance

(2) Trade Liberalization

(3) External Balance

tails "balance of payments disequilibrium" (the meaning of which we shall soon explore) or the departure from the existing exchange rate. As the country undertakes expansionary domestic measures to achieve full employment, it is possible that imports increase or exports fall so much that a balance of payments deficit arises. Some trade-off must then occur between internal balance and external balance or between internal balance and trade liberalization.

Finally, if the balance of payments should be disturbed, causing a deficit to arise, the country may attempt to return to "balance of payments equilibrium" by departing from internal balance through measures that restrict employment and contract income, in order to reduce imports and stimulate exports, or by moving away from trade liberalization though the imposition of trade restrictions.[2]

When confronted by these policy conflicts, most governments have opted for internal balance, even if this has meant a retreat from trade liberalization or pressure on their balance of payments. **The central problem of the international monetary system has therefore been how to allow nations to pursue their domestic economic objectives without having to forgo the gains from trade or suffer balance of payments disequilibrium.**[3]

Interestingly enough, this problem was anticipated at the Bretton Woods Conference that established the IMF. It was then believed that

[2] The remaining possibility is unlikely in practice—namely, that concentration on "trade liberalization" is pursued to such an extent that it causes departure from internal balance or external balance.

[3] In his study of *The Economics of Interdependence: Economic Policy in the Atlantic Community* (1968), Richard N. Cooper states that the central problem of international economic cooperation is "how to keep the manifold benefits of extensive international economic intercourse free of crippling restrictions while at the same time preserving a maximum degree of freedom for each nation to pursue its legitimate economic objectives" (p. 5).

the Fund would allow nations to give primacy to their domestic employment policies over balance of payments adjustment. In his explanation of the IMF proposals to the House of Lords, Keynes[4] looked forward to the Fund as providing "an international setting within which the new domestic policies [of full employment] can occupy a comfortable place." And again,[5]

We are determined that, in future, the external value of sterling shall conform to its internal value as set by our own domestic policies, and not the other way round. Secondly, we intend to retain control of our domestic rate of interest, so that we can keep it as low as suits our own purposes, without interference from the ebb and flow of international capital movements or flights of hot money. Thirdly, whilst we intend to prevent inflation at home, we will not accept deflation at the dictate of influences from outside. In other words, we abjure the instruments of bank rate and credit contraction operating through the increase of unemployment as a means of forcing our domestic economy into line with external factors.

As we shall see, it is ironical that the breakdown of the Bretton Woods system now makes Keynes's statement more consistent with a system of flexible exchange rates than with the older, pegged-but-adjustable system. For the Bretton Woods system, however, Keynes's belief that national policies for full employment could be given priority rested on three assumptions:

First, the IMF would be a source of international liquidity in a sufficient amount to give a deficit country time for the adjustment mechanism to operate on its balance of payments without having to resort to deflationary measures or trade restrictions.

Second, although exchange rates were to remain fixed in the short run, they would have some flexibility in the long run insofar as the Fund would approve an alteration of exchange rates when a country experienced "fundamental disequilibrium."

Third, deficit countries would not alone have to bear all the responsibility for re-equilibrating their balance of payments, but that surplus countries would share the responsibility. If a surplus country took no remedial action, and its currency remained in short supply on foreign exchange markets, then the IMF's "scarce-currency" clause could become operative permitting the Fund to proceed to ration its supply of

---

[4]John Maynard Keynes, "The International Monetary Fund," in Seymour E. Harris (ed.), *The New Economics: Keynes' Influence on Theory and Public Policy* (1947), 377.

[5]*Ibid.*, 374.

the scarce currency, and allowing member countries to discriminate against imports from the surplus country.

Each of these presumptions is now being strongly questioned as a result of the postwar series of crises in the international payments system. How the international monetary system is to be reformed remains a major international economic policy controversy. Many economists would contend that the world economy still confronts the same central problem that it did at the Bretton Woods Conference. They would also argue that international monetary conditions inhibit trade liberalization, higher rates of growth in the major industrial nations, and a higher rate of development in the poor nations.

If we are to evaluate these contentions and assess the need for international monetary reform, we shall have to gain some understanding in the next two chapters of how the mechanism of balance of payments adjustment operates and what the instruments of balance of payments policy are. But before doing that, we must begin at the beginning with some review of balance of payments accounting and gain a clearer view of the meaning of "balance of payments equilibrium."

Balance of Payments Accounting

As with most statistics, those of a country's balance of payments do not in themselves provide answers to analytical questions. A country's balance of payments is simply a systematic summary record of all the economic transactions during a given period between its residents and residents of the rest of the world. As such, it records the sources and applications of funds for a country's external transactions. All entries in the balance of payments represent flows.

There is no one "correct" way to present the balance of payments. The desired format depends on the type of international monetary system that prevails and the analytical problems that one wants to consider in the light of the country's international transactions. We shall later discuss various types of international monetary regimes in considerable detail. Now we need only distinguish among monetary systems that maintain fixed exchange rates, that allow freely floating rates, or that maintain "managed floating" of rates. If rates are to be maintained within specified margins around fixed par values (say, ± 1% of par as was true from 1946 to 1971), then official monetary authorities must

C.P. KINDLEBERGER, "Measuring Equilibrium in the Balance of Payments," *Journal of Political Economy,* 77 (Nov. 1969), 873

It is tempting to suggest that we should abolish balance-of-payments statistics. Two of the world's strongest currencies—the pound sterling prior to 1913 and the Swiss franc today—lacked a complete statement of the position. New York as a financial center has only a limited idea of the network of its financial flows vis-à-vis the rest of the country. Textbooks insist that governmental authorities need balance-of-payments data to guide changes in monetary, fiscal, exchange, commercial, and other policies, although journalists and speculators seem to react to the data more sensitively than do governments. Realpolitik makes clear, however, that balance-of-payments figures are collected and published, and that it is impossible to discontinue the process. The question then is how to present them.

intervene on foreign exchange markets, buying or selling foreign currencies, in order to close gaps between the amounts of their currencies demanded and supplied at exchange rates within the permissible margins. If in private transactions there is an excess supply of the foreign currency, so that the home currency would appreciate, the monetary authority must supply more home currency (demand more foreign currency) to hold the exchange rate. (If the dollar flows to Germany, the Bundesbank has to buy the dollars with deutsche marks to stop appreciation of the mark.) Or if there is an excess demand for the foreign currency, the monetary authority must supply more of the foreign currency out of its international reserves to prevent the home currency from depreciating. (If the dollar demand for marks increases, the Federal Reserve has to supply marks on the foreign exchange market to hold the dollar:mark rate.) These interventions on the foreign exchange market will be reflected in the country's holdings of international reserve assets. A "balance of official reserve transactions" has therefore been used to indicate the net change in the country's international reserves as a result of exchange-market intervention.

If, however, rates are freely floating, there will be no need for international reserves, and all the balancing will be accomplished through exchange rate movements until supply equals demand on the foreign exchange markets. But if countries intervene to manage the float—that is, to prevent their exchange rates from moving beyond a limited range—the monetary authority will again need internationally acceptable monetary assets with which to intervene on the exchange market to hold the rate within the desired range.

We need not become enmeshed here in the details of balance of payments accounting. We should, however, understand the fundamental accounting proposition that **"the balance of payments always balances but this is no sign of balance of payments equilibrium."**

In simple accounting terms, the balance of payments will always balance because it is based on a double-entry bookkeeping principle in which the two sides of every transaction are recorded with a "credit" or "plus" ($+$) entry and a "debit" or "minus" ($-$) entry. A credit is an entry for a transaction that reduces assets within a country or increases the liabilities of a country. A debit is an entry for a transaction that increases assets within the country or reduces liabilities of the country. **Credit** items arise from **sales** of goods, claims, or reserve assets and are matched by **debit** items that arise from **purchases** of good, claims or reserve assets.

To illustrate how the two sides of a transaction might be recorded, consider the export of goods from the United States to England. In the United States balance of payments, the sale of an export is recorded as a credit item. The export might be paid for by English importers drawing down their deposits in American banks (a decrease in a United States liability)—a debit item of "short term capital outflow." Or the American exporter might acquire deposits in English banks (an increase in United States assets)—a debit item. Or the exporter might accept a certificate of indebtedness from the importer, and the debit item would be short-term capital (an import of a trade credit bill). If the export is simply a gift, the debit item would be a "unilateral transfer to foreigners." Or if the exports were bartered for imports, the import would be the counterpart debit item.

More generally, the balance of payments is a form of flow of funds statement that shows changes in assets, liabilities, and net worth over time. The **sources** of funds are exports, investment income, transfer payments received, and long-term and short-term borrowing. The **uses** of funds are imports, investment income paid abroad, transfer payments abroad, long-term and short-term lending and investing abroad, and increases in official reserve assets.[6]

[6]Accounting details may be gleaned from an elementary accounting text. Students of accounting will recognize that the balance of payments is neither a balance sheet nor an income

Considering foreign exchange markets, we should note that the credit entries reflect the sources, whereas the debit entries indicate the uses of foreign exchange. The credit entries are therefore equivalent to the **actual** sales of foreign exchange (supply of foreign exchange), whereas the debit items reflect the **actual** purchases of foreign exchange (demand for foreign exchange).

The treatment of capital and gold flows requires special notice. A **capital inflow** is a **credit** item (think of the **sale** or export of the corresponding security). A long-term capital inflow in the United States results from foreigners buying long-term securities from Americans (that is, portfolio investment in credit instruments with a maturity greater than one year) or engaging in private direct foreign investment in the United States (that is, establishing a foreign branch or acquiring a controlling equity interest in an enterprise in the United States).

A short-term capital inflow into the United States results from foreigners buying short-term government and corporate securities (maturity of one year or less), from foreigners increasing their holdings of commercial claims, from foreigners increasing their balances in American banks, or from withdrawing American deposits in foreign banks. When there is a short-term capital inflow to a country, the country's liabilities to foreigners increase, or the country's claims on foreigners decrease. The foreign holders of short-term assets may be foreign official monetary authorities or private foreign holders (persons, corporations, banks).

A **capital outflow** would be a **debit** entry (think of the **purchase** or import of the corresponding security). A short-term capital outflow from the United States would consist of an increase in American deposits in foreign banks, an increase in U.S. holdings of foreign short-term government and corporate securities or commercial claims, or a withdrawal of foreign deposits from U.S. banks.

A **gold outflow** is a **credit** entry (think of the **sale** or export of gold). This can occur if the U.S. Treasury sold gold to foreign official holders of dollar assets, as the Treasury did until August 15, 1971 when the dollar was declared no longer convertible into gold.

All the transactions entering the balance of payments can be grouped into three broad accounts within the balance of payments: the **current account,** which records transactions in goods and services and transfer

---

statement, but a form of flow of funds statement. For more details, see Charles N. Henning et al., *International Financial Management* (1978), Chap. 2.

payments;[7] the **capital account,** which represents a change in a country's foreign assets and liabilities; and the **official international reserve account,** which records transactions in monetary gold and other reserve assets (notably convertible currencies, the country's "reserve tranche" at the IMF, and SDRs).[8]

A consolidated balance of payments table can be constructed from the following illustrative transactions:

	Debits (−)	Credits (+)
Current Account		
A. Goods and Services		
1. Merchandise exports		+
2. Merchandise imports	−	
3. Shipping payments	−	
4. Tourist expenditures	−	
5. Interest and dividends received		+
B. Unilateral Transfers		
6. Private remittances received		+
7. Government transfers abroad	−	
Capital Account		
8. Long-term capital inflow (net)		+
9. Repayment on loans	−	
10. Short-term capital outflow (net)	−	
Official Reserves		
11. Official purchases of foreign currencies	−	
12. Allocation of SDRs received		+

[7]Within the current account, the "balance of trade" account refers to the balance of "visible" current transactions—the sales and purchases of merchandise. Other items in the current account are "invisibles", such as freight, insurance, travel, investment income (interest, dividends, branch profits).

[8]The U.S. dollar has acquired the role of being the primary reserve currency in the sense that it is used as an international asset by central banks. Most foreign governments keep a portion of their foreign exchange reserves in the form of dollar deposits at the Federal Reserve Bank of New York. Provisions of the IMF will be discussed in Chap. 9. At this point, we need only note that when a country joined the IMF, it deposited with the IMF its subscription, of which 25% was paid in gold and 75% in its own currency. The former "gold tranche" of 25% is now the "reserve tranche," and countries may pay this with SDRs. On the basis of its subscription, the country has "drawing rights" with the Fund by which it can draw other convertible currencies. A country's drawings from the IMF enter as a credit item in its balance of payments.

The transactions in the current account affect national income and, in terms of income analysis, the level of output and employment. Transactions in the capital account affect the international debtor or creditor position of the country and the distribution of wealth and debt. Transactions in the international reserve account determine the stock of foreign reserves available to the country for purposes of settling any "deficit" in the current account or capital account.

To say that the "balance of payments always balances" is to say that a net credit balance in one of these accounts must have a counterpart net debit balance in one of the other accounts or in a combination of the two other accounts. The algebraic sum of the net credit and debit balances of the three accounts must equal zero. Thus, a net credit balance on current account of say, $+\$1$ billion, may have a counterpart net debit balance on capital account of $-\$1$ billion (that is, an outflow of capital), a net inflow of gold by $\$1$ billion, or a combination of capital outflow and gold inflow equal to the $\$1$ billion surplus on current account.

The "balance" in the balance of payments will have its equivalent "balance" in the foreign exchange markets. But the question remains: How is this balance achieved? What are the settlement items in the balance of payments that are "settling" the balance? And what are the transactions in foreign exchange markets that are making actual demand for foreign exchange equal to actual supply of foreign exchange?

Although we have divided all balance of payments items into the current, capital and international reserve accounts, other groupings are possible. Regardless of what type of groupings is adopted, however, it is important to realize that the act of classifying the transactions does not in itself imply any cause-effect relationships among the groupings. **The discovery of the interrelationships among the various items is a matter of analytical judgment, requiring interpretation and economic analysis of the data.** And for this, we need additional principles of balance of payments analysis.

Concept of a "Deficit"

If the balance of payments always balances, how then can there ever be a "deficit" or "surplus" in the balance of payments"? When all the items in the balance of payments are included, it is true that an overall deficit or surplus is not possible. If, however, we exclude from consideration some transactions—namely, those that act as "settlement" transactions—then **the balance of the remaining "ordinary" transactions can be in deficit or surplus.** The items that we include are placed "above the line" that separates ordinary from settlement transactions; the items we exclude as settlement items are placed "below the line" in the sense that they accomplish the financing of any deficit in the ordinary items above the line.

The measurement of a deficit in the balance of payments will therefore depend on where we draw the line. The difficult question is: **What items should be placed below the line as settlement items?** Where should we draw the line through the accounts and place below the line the settlement (or balancing or residual) items that "finance" the items above the line? There is no single definite answer to this question. Since our interest in determining the deficit is to be able to consider the need for remedial policy action, and since the interpretation of the country's need for corrective policies may differ, so too may the interpretation of what is the deficit in the country's balance of payments.

Sometimes items below the line are referred to as "accommodating" or "compensatory" items in contrast to the "autonomous" items above the line. This simplifies the problem by implying that the items below the line are "induced" by the sum of the autonomous transactions and occur as the result of the need for residual "financing" to cover a surplus or deficit in the autonomous transactions. This simple distinction is, however, illusory. It is extremely difficult operationally to determine which transactions are truly compensatory and which are not: this is essentially a question of the ultimate motives of the monetary authorities as well as the private sector, and this judgment must be inevitably subjective.[9]

When gold acts as a monetary reserve (not as a simple commodity), the changes in gold reserves act to balance international payments. Monetary gold flows should therefore be placed below the line, and a gold outflow (a credit item) would indicate the size of the deficit or the negative balance above the line.

When, however, we consider capital items, differences of judgment vary greatly over which capital transactions should be placed above the line and which should be regarded as settlement items to be placed

[9]Cf. Richard N. Cooper, "The Balance of Payments in Review," *Journal of Political Economy*, 74 (Aug. 1966), 384.

below the line. The differences revolve about the question of how to treat short-term, private capital movements.

Should an inflow of foreign, short-term private capital—for example, the increase in holdings of U.S. bank deposits by foreign individuals, foreign firms, or foreign commercial banks—be treated as a settlement item, in the same way as a gold outflow or inflow of official short-term capital? Or should it be treated as an autonomous transaction, primarily in response to market forces, and placed above the line? The argument for placing it below the line as a balancing item rests on the possibility that a foreign private holder of short-term dollars can sell his dollars to his own central bank: the changes in liquid liabilities to private foreigners can thus always be transferred to foreign central banks and thereby become a claim on the gold reserves, if the dollar is convertible into gold. In contrast, the inflow of foreign, short-term private capital might have been motivated by an increased foreign demand for dollars for investment purposes and for working balances; to this extent, the changes in short-term claims of foreign commercial banks should be viewed as capital movements of a market-oriented, business type rather than as settlement items. It is inherently impossible to resolve this conceptual argument one way or the other in all circumstances, for all time. To do so, it would be necessary to determine exactly the motivations of the foreign private holders.

Depending on how this question of motivation is answered, and hence whether foreign, private short-term capital is placed above or below the line, there can be different measures of the balance of payments position. Until 1976, the balance of payments data of the United States were presented in a format that emphasized three different balances.

One interpretation of the overall balance of payments position was based on the "**basic transactions**" concept. According to this concept, the balance on goods, services, transfers, and long-term capital transactions are considered as "basic." They are recorded above the line, leaving a balance on these transactions to be offset by the following items placed below the line: U.S. and foreign short-term capital movements, both private and official; gold movements; and net errors and omissions (since changes in this item are believed to consist mainly of changes in unrecorded flows of short-term capital). The rationale offered for the "basic balance" concept is that it attempts to measure underlying long-term trends in the economy by abstracting from such "volatile" items as short-term capital flows. Another reason offered is that the items placed below the line are those that are most sensitive to changes in government policy, particularly monetary policy. But the "volatility" and "policy-sensitivity" of different transactions are not that clear cut, especially over time.

A second measure was labeled the **"liquidity"** concept of a deficit or surplus. And a third measurement was based on the "official settlements" or **"official reserve transactions"** concept of a deficit or surplus.

The liquidity and official settlements measures agree on a minimum list of transactions that belong above the line as contributing to the overall balance—viz., transactions in goods and services, remittances and pensions, U.S. government grants and capital movements, and movements of private U.S. and foreign long-term capital (except for changes in foreign holdings of U.S. Government bonds and notes). Both measures also agree on a minimum list of transactions that belong below the line as financing or settling the overall balance—viz., changes in U.S. monetary reserves and the IMF position and changes in assets held in the United States by foreign official monetary institutions. The difference between the two measures, therefore, involves the treatment of changes in short-term capital. The "net liquidity" concept places foreign private short-term capital and foreign holdings of U.S. government bonds and notes below the line.

In contrast, the official reserve transactions balance focuses on type of transactor—specifically, between the monetary authorities and all other transactors—and therefore places above the line those movements of foreign short-term capital and changes in foreign holdings of U.S. government bonds and notes that do not represent changes in the assets of foreign official monetary institutions. The official settlements concept thus leaves below the line as settlement items only reserve transactions—viz., changes in the reserve assets of U.S. monetary authorities (gold and convertible currencies and IMF position) and of foreign official monetary institutions (holdings of U.S. government securities and short-term capital).[10]

[10]All official transactions cannot, however, be considered as accommodating. The accumulation of reserves by official agencies of the OPEC members during the 1970s are included in the official settlements balance, but these OPEC reserves are largely the result of investment decisions by OPEC members and really represent a capital inflow, not official action by OPEC members to sustain the dollar exchange rate. These balances can just as reasonably be considered as autonomous transactions above the line. Further, many foreign official institutions invest their dollar balances in the Eurodollar market. This increases private Eurodollar bank claims on

There are inherent difficulties in singling out one concept for defining a country's payments surplus or deficit because any accounting framework of measurement is essentially classificatory, not analytical. It represents an *ex post* grouping of international transactions by type or by transactor, but does not indicate the gaps to be filled, in an *ex ante* sense, which is the relevant sense for the notion of disequilibrium. Nor does the accounting indicate the motivation for the transaction.[11]

Further, the format for presenting balance of payments statistics should change as the international monetary system changes. Accordingly, whereas overall balances (basic, net liquidity, and official reserve transactions balances) had formerly been shown in the United States balance of payments statistics, a **revised format** was introduced in 1976 to reflect the **new regime of managed floating** instead of fixed exchange rates. Under freely floating rates, there can in principle be no imbalance of payments, and the overall balances are no longer of concern. The revised format therefore shifts attention to the international transactions giving rise to demand and supply conditions in the foreign exchange market. Instead of concentrating on an overall deficit or surplus, **the emphasis is now on analyzing the relationship between changes in international transactions and changes in the exchange rate.** The revised format is indicated in the Appendix (Tables 5.2 and 5.3).

The data on international transactions can be arranged in two columns, one showing an increase in the amounts of dollars offered to be sold (an increase in debits), and the other an increase in the amounts offered to be purchased in the exchange market (an increase in credits). *Ex ante,* these pressures on the exchange rate are unlikely to be equal. But the statistics record transactions that also occurred after upward or downward pressures on the exchange rate, and *ex post* the supply and demand for dollars will be equalized. The other transactions, **including official exchange-market transactions,** undertaken to prevent or to reduce a change in the exchange rates, will make the totals of the two columns equal *ex post*.

Balances are not presented in Table 5.2 and 5.3, but only in memorandum items: the balance on goods and services, the balance on cur-

---

the United States and reduces official claims. But in reality, since the foreign official institution still maintains ownership and control of a claim against the United States, there has been no reduction in official claims against it. See Donald S. Kemp, "Balance of Payments Concepts—What Do They Really Mean?," *Federal Reserve Bank of St. Louis Review,* 57 (July 1975), 14–23.

[11]Cooper, "The Balance of Payments in Review," *op. cit.,* 388–89.

rent account, and the two summary items that comprise the financing of the balance on official reserve transactions (net changes in U.S. official reserve assets and in U.S. liabilities to foreign official agencies).

Although the United States has changed its balance of payments presentation, other countries may still report the several other balances. The IMF reporting is also closer to the earlier format of the United States. Table 5.4 in the Appendix shows the standard components in the IMF's balance of payments manual. Considering the present regime of managed floating, the fact that official intervention is now discretionary instead of mandatory has reduced the significance of the balance on official reserve transactions as a measure of exchange-market pressure. But the large amount of official intervention under managed floating has not destroyed its significance, and this measure may still usefully serve as a starting point for analysis. Although the elimination of the net liquidity balance and basic balance may be more attuned to the new regime of managed floating, many economists may still prefer to consider the official reserve transactions balance, or some "overall" balance, as a stable point of reference for analysis of the balance of payments and policy advice.[12] Fluctuations in foreign official dollar holdings are still largely influenced by interventions in the exchange market, and the amount of these interventions can be large. When rates are allowed to float, the buildup in foreign dollar holdings may be viewed as indicative of a future depreciation of the dollar vis-à-vis other major currencies.

In the pre-1971 system, the concern was to determine a "fundamental disequilibrium" in the balance of payments as justification for changing the pegged rates. With managed floating, the concern is now with pressures on the exchange rate and the degree of official intervention that might be needed to manage the exchange rate within a certain margin. Even under managed floating, the accommodating transactions give some measure of the imbalance in the exchange market, and fluctuations in reserves are still largely influenced by interventions in the exchange market.

At the same time, however, it is true that the dollar's strength or weakness may be reflected in exchange rate fluctuations that are actually occurring as a partial substitute for net reserve changes. Supplementary data are therefore now wanted to indicate exchange rate changes and the extent and impact of exchange-market intervention.

[12] See, e.g., Robert Triffin's comments in Robert M. Stern et al., *The Presentation of the U.S. Balance of Payments: A Symposium* (Aug. 1977), 24–28.

Balance of Payments Disequilibrium

Utilizing the official reserve transactions concept and assuming a fixed exchange rate regime, we may say that a country has a balance of payments deficit if its reserve assets are declining or if the claims of foreign monetary authorities on the country are rising. To the extent that this deficit cannot be continued indefinitely, but must be corrected, we may also conclude that the country is suffering from balance of payments disequilibrium. There is pressure on the balance of payments, and sooner or later some remedial policy measures will have to be undertaken to re-equilibrate the country's balance of payments. Sooner, if there is an outright balance of payments crisis; later, if the country is allowed a longer breathing period by being able to draw upon a sufficient cushion of gold reserves, convertible foreign currencies, and its creditor position in the IMF.

We focus on the deficit country as being in disequilibrium. It is, however, just as true to say that equilibrium in a country's balance of payments is the absence of a surplus, rather than the absence of a deficit. A country has a balance of payments surplus, according to the official settlements concept, if its reserve assets are increasing or if the claims of foreign monetary authorities on the country are decreasing. Although the balance of payments of the surplus country is also in disequilibrium, the surplus country is not compelled to take corrective action—as the deficit country must sooner or later do.[13]

If we were to avoid any policy judgment, and employ only a strictly positivistic criterion of balance of payments disequilibrium, we would look at only items in the balance of payments accounts to determine whether or not equilibrium exists. By the liquidity concept of the deficit, disequilibrium would be indicated by an outflow of monetary gold reserves and convertible currencies, drawings at the IMF, or an inflow of private or official short-term capital. By the official settlements concept, disequilibrium would be indicated by these same items except that an inflow of private short-term capital would not be indicative of disequilibrium.

The liquidity concept thus exaggerates the degree of balance of payments disequilibrium if the inflow of private short-term capital is for ordinary personal and business reasons. Private holders of dollars cannot

---

[13] To facilitate the adjustment mechanism, it would, of course, be desirable for the surplus country to take appropriate policy action that would complement—rather than compete with—action by the deficit country. For a discussion of this, see Chap. 10, this volume.

directly sell their dollar holdings to the U.S. Treasury for gold, but they can sell their dollars for other currencies on the foreign exchange market. In their efforts to maintain fixed exchange rates (and thus stop their own currencies from appreciating against the dollar), foreign monetary authorities would absorb the increased supply of dollars. As official holders of dollars, the foreign monetary authorities were in a position to redeem the dollars in gold at the U.S. Treasury until August 15, 1971, when the dollar was declared inconvertible into gold. If the private foreign holdings of dollars are not going to be sold on the foreign exchange market, but are kept for investment and working balances purposes, then the United States need not take corrective action because of this private short-term capital inflow, and the liquidity concept of the deficit would exaggerate the degree of disequilibrium in the U.S. balance of payments.

Suppose, however, that no deficit is indicated in a country's balance of payments on either the liquidity or official settlements concepts. Can it then be said that the country has no balance of payments problems? On the narrow balance of payments accounting criterion, this would be true. But what if the country has imposed high tariffs and import quotas to prevent a greater demand for imports from being realized? If the country removed its trade restrictions, there would be a deficit on current account, and the country would then encounter a balance of payments disequilibrium by the balance of payments criterion. Only the trade restrictions prevent the balance of payments disequilibrium; if trade is liberalized, the disequilibrium will be apparent. In this situation, to say that the country does have a balance of payments problem, even though there is no deficit, is to move to a normative level of analysis and make some judgment on desirable policy objectives. If the avoidance of direct controls on trade and capital movements is a policy objective, the sacrifice of this objective to avoid an international payments deficit might be interpreted, in effect, as a balance of payments problem. Some remedial policy measures need to be undertaken so that the country might enjoy both liberalized trade and no balance of payments deficit.

Another situation might be that a country has no balance of payments deficit (by any concept), but the country is suffering a level of unemployment greater than that in other countries. If the country were to undertake policies that brought the economy to full employment, then the demand for imports would also increase, and the country's balance of payments might then show a deficit. In this case, it is only because the country is foresaking a desirable policy target—namely, full employment—that it is able to avoid an international payments deficit, which would then appear as balance of payments disequilibrium. Again, the open appearance of a potential balance of payments problem is being avoided by sacrificing another policy objective. The high level of unemployment is acting, in effect, as a substitute for a reserve outflow or short-term capital inflow. Some other remedial policy measures would be necessary to achieve both full employment and the avoidance of a balance of payments deficit.

We may thus conclude that a country's balance of payments can be considered in equilibrium if there is an absence of changes in items below the line—provided that the country is not suffering excessive unemployment or imposing controls over current and capital transactions to avoid the appearance of these settlement items. This conclusion reiterates the point that **the analysis of balance of payments equilibrium necessarily has a normative dimension** insofar as it prescribes what policies (in our discussion, internal balance and freer trade) should obtain before any imbalance in payments is measured. Proceeding beyond the positivistic balance of payments accounting criterion, we have added additional criteria and now refer to a standard of performance: when this standard is not met, the balance of payments is in disequilibrium. Recognizing that what matters are the determinant forces that underlie the various transactions in the balance of payments and the country's various policy targets, we must realize that **instead of trying to measure a country's balance of payments disequilibrium, we must concentrate on analyzing its various components and composition.**

What we say about a balance of payments deficit under fixed exchange rates would also apply under flexible rates, provided the government wants to avoid the pressure of depreciation on is currency in terms of foreign currency. Official intervention on the exchange market to maintain an overvalued rate is indicative of an underlying "deficit."

The Range of Remedial Policy Instruments

Given a situation of disequilibrium in its balance of payments, a government must take remedial action if it cannot look forward to having an actual deficit in its balance of payments supported through "accommodating" capital imports and depletion of international reserve assets or is unwilling to endure excessive unemployment or direct controls to avoid a deficit. By what means can balance of payments equilibrium then be restored? How rapidly? And with what repercussions to the domestic economy? These questions are still at the center of international monetary problems when central banks and monetary authorities exercise discretion in their interventions on exchange markets. As long as governments do not allow fully flexible rates—but manage the rates—these questions will persist.

The next four chapters should help provide some answers by considering alternative processes of adjustment to disequilibrium. Our underlying schema will embody the usual method of comparative statics— that is, a comparison of the "old" and 'new" states of equilibrium. We shall begin with the initial position of balance of payments equilibrium. We shall then allow for some disequilibrating change—a "disturbance" to the balance of payments. Some process of adjustment must then be set in motion, and we shall want to focus on the various re-equilibrating measures involved in the alternative adjustment processes. Finally, we shall note the new position of equilibrium that will be reached after the adjustment process has worked itself out.

In examining alternative adjustment processes, we shall want to interpret the various possible remedial policy measures. The boundary conditions on the range of policy instruments available to a country depend in part on the type of international monetary system that exists. According to whether a country is on a pure gold standard, gold-exchange standard, or inconvertible paper currency standard, its capacity to alter exchange rates will differ. These alternative international monetary systems are considered in some detail in Chapter 9, with special attention to the hybrid "managed floating" regime. Policy measures will clearly be affected by how a government decides to cope with floating rates. The country's choice of policy measures will also be affected by whether the country's currency is a reserve currency. Also significant are the policies being followed by other countries: there are many instruments of economic policy for which it is the **relative** differences among countries (relative price levels or relative interest rate differentials) that affect international trade flows or international capital movements and, hence, the exchange rate.

The type of international monetary system and the policies of other countries will condition which policies a country with a balance of payments problem **can** pursue. Additional considerations will enter into its choice of which policies it **wants** to pursue. Foremost among these are a judgment on the source of the disturbance to the country's balance of payments and a due regard for other domestic policy objectives that might be affected by the instruments selected to remedy the balance of payments problem.

Subsequent chapters will emphasize that different policy instruments will be appropriate, according to the different sources of disequilibria and the different domestic economic conditions of the country. Regardless, however, of the various policy instruments and alternative adjustment processes, it will be important to note the extent to which the adjustment process involves **"price effects"** or **"expenditure-switching"** and **"income effects"** or **"expenditure-reducing."**

The "price effects" in the adjustment process refer to changes in the relative price structure within the country—that is, the relative prices of importables, exportables, and home goods—together with a consideration of the relevant price-elasticities of demand for the tradables and non-tradables. Tradables are composed of exportables and importables. Exportables are the actual exports and the close substitutes for exports sold domestically. Importables are the actual imports as well as import-competing goods produced and sold domestically. The domestic prices of tradables are determined mainly by forces in the world market, among which the exchange rate is highly significant. The prices of non-tradables are determined by domestic supply and demand condition.

An **expenditure-switching policy,** such as a devaluation of the home currency, will raise the domestic price of tradables relative to the price of non-tradables and, thereby, cause a switch in the pattern of production and the pattern of expenditure. The allocation of home resources will switch out of the production of non-tradables to the production of tradables. And the pattern of expenditure will switch away from tradables, to non-tradables. Based on these price effects, one type of analysis of devaluation is the **elasticities approach** (Chapter 6).

The "income effects" refer to changes in national income, associated with changes in total output and the level of employment. **"Expenditure-reducing"** policies are composed of tight monetary and fiscal policies that contract the economy. Since the "absorption" of goods and services is equivalent to the aggregate demand generated by consumption, investment, and government expenditures, the **absorption approach** to the adjustment mechanism emphasizes disabsorption or expenditure reduction to lower the domestic demand for tradables in order to improve the country's balance of payments position (Chapter 7).

Another approach to the adjustment mechanism is the monetarist. In the **monetary approach,** money is a stock whose optimal level is related to current output and whose actual level can be adjusted through balance of payments surpluses or deficits. If the actual stock of money is not equal to the desired stock, the stock disequilibrium will be removed through reserve flows in the balance of payments. Remedial policies must therefore concentrate on the change in domestic credit creation relative to the demand for money (Chapter 8).

Although the "monetary approach" to the balance of payments is based on the premise of fixed-but-adjustable exchange rates, it has recently become more common to adopt an **asset-market approach** to the exchange rate. This focuses more broadly on changes in asset portfolios as the proximate cause of exchange-rate variations in the short run. The capital flows associated with international trade in financial assets can be a part of the adjustment process, as well as a source of pressure on the exchange rate (Chapter 8).

Regardless of the policy instruments used to re-equilibrate the balance of payments, **no adjustment process is economically painless or costless.** When we consider in Chapters 9 and 10 the adjustment processes under different international monetary systems, we shall want to consider the "cost" of the different adjustment processes according to the degree of change needed in income and price levels and the distribution of the adjustment cost between countries and within a country.

In order to distinguish the price effects and income effects that result from expenditure-switching or expenditure-reducing policies, we now turn to some background analysis of the foreign exchange market and the relationship between trade and national income.

Supplementary Readings

Different views on the "best" format for the presentation of balance of payments statistics are presented in *Report by the Office of Management and Budget, Advisory Committee on the Presentation of Balance of Payments Statistics,* reprinted in *Survey of Current Business,* 56 (June 1976), 18–27; R.M. Stern et al., *The Presentation of the U.S. Balance of Payments: A Symposium,* Princeton Essays in International Finance, No. 123 (Aug. 1977); U.S Bureau of the Budget, Review Committee for Balance of Payments Statistics, *The Balance of Payments Statistics of the United States: A Review and Appraisal* (1965).

Questions of measuring and analyzing balance of payments equilibrium are considered by C.P. Kindleberger, "Measuring Equilibrium in the Balance of Payments," *Journal of Political Economy,* 77 (Nov./Dec. 1969), 873–91; R.N. Cooper, "The Balance of Payments in Review," *Journal of Political Economy,* 75 (Aug. 1966), 379–95; R. Mundell, "The Balance of Payments," *International Encyclopedia of the Social Sciences,* 8 (1968), 1–11; J.E. Meade, *The Balance of Payments* (1951), Chaps. 1–3.

APPENDIX

Balance of Payments Accounting

Table 5.1.[1]

UNITED STATES BALANCE OF PAYMENTS, 1971–74

In millions of dollars; + denotes increase in claims on, or
reduction in liabilities to, foreigners

Type of Balance	1971	1972	1973	1974
Exports of goods	+43,311	+49,388	+71,379	+ 98,268
Imports of goods	−45,579	−55,797	−70,424	−103,796
Merchandise trade balance	− 2,268	− 6,409	+ 995	− 5,528
Services, net	+ 2,031	+ 479	+ 3,222	+ 9,102
Balance of goods and services	− 237	− 5,930	+ 4,177	+ 3,574
Unilateral transfers, net	− 3,642	− 3,780	− 3,842	− 7,182
Balance on current account	− 3,879	− 9,710	+ 335	− 3,608
United States Government capital flows, net (excluding reserve transactions)	− 2,376	− 1,335	− 1,490	+ 1,118
United States direct investment abroad	− 4,738	− 3,530	− 4,968	− 7,268
Foreign direct investment in the United States	− 175	+ 380	+ 2,656	+ 2,224
United States purchases of foreign securities, net	− 1,113	− 618	− 759	− 1,990
Foreign purchases of United States securities (excluding Treasury issues), net	+ 2,289	+ 4,507	+ 4,055	+ 672
Net change in long-term claims on foreigners	− 780	− 1,550	−1,366	− 1,560
Net change in long-term liabilities to foreigners	+ 134	+ 743	+ 559	− 515
Balance on current account and long-term capital (basic balance)	−10,637	−11,113	− 977	− 10,927
Net change in nonliquid short-term claims on foreigners	− 2,332	− 1,763	− 5,069	− 14,789
Net change in nonliquid short-term liabilities to foreigners	− 15	+ 221	+ 831	+ 1,840
Errors and omissions	− 9,698	− 1,884	− 2,436	+ 4,834
Net liquidity balance (excluding allocations of SDRs)*	−22,682	−14,539	− 7,651	− 19,043
Net change in liquid claims on foreigners	− 1,097	− 1,247	− 1,951	− 6,113
Gross liquidity balance (excluding allocations of SDRs)*	−23,779	−15,786	− 9,602	− 25,156

---

[1] This is the old format of the U.S. balance of payments. It last appeared in the *Survey of Current Business* (March 1976).

Table 5.1. continued

UNITED STATES BALANCE OF PAYMENTS, 1971–74

In millions of dollars; + denotes increase in claims on, or
reduction in liabilities to, foreigners

Type of Balance	1971	1972	1973	1974
Net change in liquid liabilities to private foreign accounts	− 6,691	+ 4,722	+ 4,294	+ 16,782
Allocation of SDRs*	+ 717	+ 710	0	0
Official reserve transactions balance	−29,753	−10,354	− 5,308	− 8,374
Net change in primary reserve assets†	+ 998	− 121	+ 242	− 169
Net change in reserve position in the IMF (Secondary reserve assets)†	+ 1,350	+ 153	− 33	− 1,265
Net change in liabilities to official foreign accounts	+27,405	+10,322	+5,099	+ 9,808
Balance on all accounts	0	0	0	0

Note: Because of rounding, figures do not necessarily add to totals.
*SDRs, Special drawing rights.
†Excludes revaluations of assets to reflect changes in the par value of the dollar or in market exchange rates.

Table 5.2. Revised Format Summary of U.S. International Transactions for 1975 (Billions of dollars)[1]

New Format Line		Credits (+)	Debits (−)
1	**Exports of goods and services**	148.4	
2	Merchandise, excluding military	107.1	
3–13	Services and other, including military	41.3	
14	**Transfers under U.S. military grant programs**	1.7	
15	**Imports of goods and services**		−132.1
16	Merchandise, excluding military		−98.2
17–27	Services and other, including military		−33.9
28	**Transfers under U.S. military grant programs**		−1.7
29	**Unilateral transfers (excluding military)**		−4.6
30	U.S. Government grants		−2.9
31	U.S. Government pensions and other transfers		−0.8
32	Private remittances and other transfers		−0.9
33	**U.S. assets abroad, net (increase/capital outflow (−))**		−31.1
34–38	U.S. official reserve assets, net		−0.6
39–42	U.S. Government assets, other, net		−3.5
43	U.S. private assets, net		−27.1
44	Direct investment abroad		−6.3
45	Foreign securities		−6.2
	Nonbank claims		
46	Long-term		−0.4
47	Short-term		−0.9
	Bank claims		
48	Long-term		−2.4
49	Short-term		−10.9
50	**Foreign assets in the U.S., net (increase/capital inflow (+))**	14.9	
51–57	Foreign official assets in the U.S., net	6.3	
58	Other foreign assets in the U.S., net	8.5	
59	Direct investments in the U.S.	2.4	
60–61	U.S. Treasury and other U.S. securities	5.4	
	Nonbank liabilities		
62	Long-term	0.3	
63	Short-term		−0.2
	Bank liabilities		
64	Long-term		−0.4
65	Short-term	1.0	
66	**Allocation of special drawing rights**		

[1]Historical series have been revised according to this format back to 1960 on an annual basis and on a quarterly basis back to 1966.

Table 5.2. continued

New Format Line		Credits (+)	Debits (−)
67	Statistical discrepancy	4.6	
	Memoranda:		
68	Balance on merchandise trade (lines 2 and 16)		8.9
69	Balance on goods and services (lines 1 and 15)		16.3
70	Balance on goods, services, and remittances (lines 69, 31, and 32)		14.6
71	Balance on current account (lines 69 and 29)		11.7
	Transactions in official reserve assets:		
72	Increase (−) in U.S. official reserve assets (line 34)		−0.6
73	Increase (+) in foreign official assets in U.S. (line 51 less line 55)		4.6

Source: Adapted from "Table 1—U.S. International Transactions," *Survey of Current Business*, 56 (June 1976), 32–33.

Table 5.3

U.S. International Transactions*		1975	1976	1977
Exports of goods and services (excl. transfers under military grants)	mil. $	155,656	171,274	183,214
Merchandise, adjusted, excl. military	do	107,088	114,694	120,585
Transfers under U.S. military agency sales contracts	mil. $	3,919	5,213	7,079
Receipts of income on U.S. assets abroad	do	25,359	29,244	32,100
Other services	do	19,290	22,124	23,452
Imports of goods and services	do	−132,595	−161,913	−193,727
Merchandise, adjusted, excl. military		−98,041	−124,047	−151,644
Direct defense expenditures	do	−4,795	−4,901	−5,745
Payments of income on foreign assets in the U.S.	mil. $	−12,564	−13,311	−14,593
Other services	do	−17,194	−19,655	−21,746
Unilateral transfers (excl. military grants), net	mil. $	−4,615	−5,022	−4,708
U.S. Government grants (excl. military)	do	−2,894	−3,145	−2,776
Other	do	−1,721	−1,878	−1,932
U.S. assets abroad, net	do	−39,444	−50,608	−34,650
U.S. official reserve, net	do	−607	−2,530	−231
U.S. Gov't, other than official reserve, net		−3,470	−4,213	−3,679
U.S. private, net	do	−35,368	−43,865	−30,740
Direct investment abroad	do	−14,244	−11,614	−12,215
Foreign assets in the U.S., net	do	15,550	36,969	50,869
Foreign official, net	do	6,907	18,073	37,124
Other foreign, net	do	8,643	18,897	13,746
Direct investment in the U.S.	do	2,603	4,347	3,338
Allocations of special drawing rights	do	—	—	—
Statistical discrepancy	do	5,449	9,300	−998
Memoranda:				
Balance on merchandise trade	do	9,047	−9,353	−31,059
Balance on goods and services	do	23,060	9,361	−10,514
Balance on goods, services and remittances	do	21,339	7,483	−12,545
Balance on current account	do	18,445	4,339	−15,221

*Credits, +; debits, −.
Source: *Survey of Current Business* (June 1978).

Table 5.4. Standard Components of the Balance of Payments[1]

1. **CURRENT ACCOUNT**
   A. **Goods, Services, and Income**
      Merchandise
      Shipment
      Other Transportation
         Passenger services
         Port services, etc.
      Travel
      Investment Income
         Direct investment income
            Reinvested earnings
            Distributed earnings
         Other
            Resident official, including interofficial
            Foreign official, excluding interofficial
            Private
      Other Goods, Services, and Income
      Official
         Interofficial
         Other, resident official
         Other, foreign official
      Private
         Labor income, n.i.e.
         Other

   B. **Unrequited Transfers**
      Private
         Migrants' transfers
         Workers' remittances
         Other
      Official
         Interofficial
         Other, resident official
         Other, foreign official

II. **CAPITAL ACCOUNT**
   A. **Capital, excluding reserves**
      Direct Investment
         Abroad
            Equity capital
            Reinvestment of earnings
            Other long-term capital
            Short-term capital
         In reporting economy
            Equity capital
            Reinvestment of earnings
            Other long-term capital
            Short-term capital
      Portfolio Investment
         Public sector bonds
            Assets
            Liabilities constituting foreign authorities' reserves
            Other liabilities
         Other bonds
            Assets
            Liabilities constituting foreign authorities' reserves
            Other liabilities
         Corporate equities
            Assets
            Liabilities constituting foreign authorities' reserves
            Other liabilities
      Other Capital
         Long-term capital
            Resident official sector
               Drawings and repayments on loans extended
               Other assets
               Liabilities constituting foriegn authorities' reserves
               Drawings and repayments on other loans received
               Other liabilities

[1]This manual helps member countries of the IMF compile and report their balance of payments data in a uniform manner. No preference is expressed in the manual, however, for any one method of appraising balance of payments developments.

Table 5.4. continued

Deposit money banks	Short-term capital	**B. Reserves**
Drawings and repayments on loans extended	Resident official sector	Monetary Gold
	Loans extended	Total change in holdings
Other assets	Other assets	Counterpart to monetization/ demonetization
Liabilities constituting foreign authorities' reserves: denominated in national currency	Liabilities constituting foreign authorities' reserves	Counterpart to valuation change
	Other loans received	Special Drawing Rights
	Other liabilities	Total change in holdings
Liabilities constituting foreign authorities' reserves: denominated in foreign currency	Deposit money banks	Counterpart to allocation/ cancellation
	Assets	
	Liabilities constituting foreign authorities' reserves: denominated in national currency	Counterpart to valuation change
Drawings and repayments on loans received		Reserve Position in the Fund
		Total change in holdings
Other liabilities	Liabilities constituting foreign authorities' reserves: denominated in foreign currency	Counterpart to valuation change
Other sectors		Foreign Exchange Assets
Drawings and repayments on loans extended		Total change in holdings
Other assets	Other liabilities	Counterpart to valuation change
Liabilities constituting foreign authorities' reserves	Other sectors	Other Claims
	Loans extended	Total change in holdings
	Other assets	Counterpart to valuation change
Drawings and repayments on other loans received	Liabilities constituting foreign authorities' reserves	Use of Fund Credit
		Total change in holdings
	Other loans received	Counterpart to valuation change
Other liabilities	Other liabilities	

Source: IMF, *Balance of Payments Manual* (4th ed., 1978).

6

The Adjustment Process: Elasticities Approach

We want to concentrate now on the "price effects" in the mechanism of adjustment. To do so, we consider how the adjustment mechanism would operate if foreign exchange rates were freely fluctuating. We shall assume that each country has its own independent money, with no officially fixed tie to gold or any foreign currency, and that the government adopts no active policy explicitly designed to influence the exchange rate, but instead allows it to be determined by the unrestricted interplay of demand and supply conditions. We shall later (Chapter 9) examine the alternative sytems of having exchange rates determined by each country pegging its currency in terms of gold (such as under a pure gold standard), having the rate influenced by an international institution (such as the International Monetary Fund) that determines the initial par values of its members' currencies and then exercises some control over an "adjustable peg" in its rates, or having, as at present, a regime of "managed floating," under which rates are flexible, but not fully so, because governments intervene in the foreign exchange market to offset the direction and extent of the movement in rates. For now, however, we focus on a system of freely fluctuating exchange rates based on inconvertible paper currencies to see the full force of changes in the foreign exchange rate, their repercussions, and how these repercussions relate to the adjustment process in the balance of payments.

Adjustment through the Foreign Exchanges

Of strategic importance in the adjustment process are relative price changes—how the prices of importables, exportables, and domestic (non-traded) goods change relative to one another. The "elasticities approach" to balance of payments analysis emphasizes these price changes and their effects on the value of exports and value of imports. Assuming no capital movements, so that the balance of payments (B) is the same as the balance of trade, the adjustment mechanism works directly on the balance of payments equation:

$$B = X - M, \tag{6.1}$$

where X is the value of exports and M is the value of imports.

If we assume full employment and abstract from income changes, X and M are a function of their price levels and the prices of substitutes.

Unless demand and supply functions are perfectly inelastic, a change in price will alter the quantity demanded and quantity supplied. This will then change the country's international payments situation. It is conceivable that if prices are sufficiently flexible and if the deficit country's price-elasticity of demand for imports and the price-elasticity of demand for the deficit country's exports are sufficiently high, the deficit can be corrected by domestic price changes only, without a change in total production and employment.

Given, however, the usual conditions of monopoly power and other market imperfections in product and factor markets, we cannot expect that whenever a modern-day economy experiences balance of payments disequilibrium, its domestic price will change sufficiently rapidly and fully to remove the disequilibrium. Factor and commodity prices are likely to be inflexible downward. A change in the country's foreign exchange rate, therefore, becomes important as an alternative way to adjust the prices of importables and exportables. Since the foreign exchange rate links the price levels of different countries, these prices of internationally traded goods relative to prices of non-traded goods can be altered by a variation in the foreign exchange rate.

The foreign exchange rate expresses the price of foreign currency (say, pound sterling) in terms of home currency (say, U.S. dollar), for example, $2.00:£1.00. By a "fall" in the price of foreign currency, we shall mean that "our" country pays fewer units of its home currency per unit of foreign currency. This is equivalent to an **appreciation** or **upward revaluation** of "our" currency. By a "rise" in the price of foreign currency, we shall mean that "our" country pays more units of its home currency per unit of foreign currency. This is equivalent to a **depreciation** or **devaluation** of "our" currency.[1]

If, say, the $:£ rate should change from $2.00:£1.00 to $1.80:£1.00, the dollar appreciates and the pound sterling depreciates. Consider now the price changes that ensue, from the standpoint of the United Kingdom, when the pound sterling depreciates. The export prices of British goods fall in terms of the dollar if the pound prices of British goods are not changed (a commodity that is priced at £10.00 formerly cost an American buyer $20.00 and now costs the buyer $18.00). At the same time, the import prices of American goods rise in terms of the pound sterling (a commodity that is priced at $200.00 formerly cost a British importer £100.00, but now costs the buyer £111.11). Thus, if domestic supply is perfectly elastic (constant costs of production) and if world prices of the international traded goods remain unchanged, depreciation of a country's currency lowers the prices of the country's exports in terms of foreign currency and raises the prices of the country's imports in terms of home currency. The effect of, say, a 10% rise in the price of foreign currency in terms of home currency is to raise the domestic price of imports in the depreciating country by 10%, while leaving the domestic prices of exports and domestic goods unchanged. In the foreign country, the prices of imports from the depreciating country will be lowered by 10% (still assuming perfectly elastic supply conditions). In contrast, appreciation of a country's currency lowers the prices of the country's imports in terms of home currency and raises the prices of the country's exports in terms of foreign currency.

If a flexible exchange rate system exists, a country that tends to have a balance of payments deficit will experience a depreciation of its currency on the foreign exchange market. We shall focus on the price mechanism of adjustment that ensues through a change in exchange rates by first assuming that national income remains constant (we remove this assumption in the next chapter when we consider "income effects" in the adjustment mechanism). We shall also assume that the government remains passive and adopts no policy measures expressly designed to correct the balance of payments. This neutral governmental

---

[1]"Appreciation" and "depreciation" refer to exchange rate movements on a freely fluctuating foreign exchange market, whereby the value of a currency changes with respect to other currencies. "Upward revaluation" and "devaluation" refer to deliberate changes of the exhange rate by a monetary authority's action in changing the value of the currency with respect to the price of gold or another primary reserve asset.

policy is assumed in order to concentrate on the "automatic" aspects of the adjustment mechanism. (We shall have much to say about active governmental policies in Chapters 9 and 10.)

The Market for Foreign Exchange

There is nothing unusual about the foreign exchange market except the novelty that the price being quoted is a price of money. If a country's currency is fully convertible, it can be freely exchanged into any other currency: a holder of dollars, for example, can freely transfer dollars into pounds sterling or French francs at a quoted rate. The quotation may be for the "spot rate," the current price, or the "forward rate," the rate at which foreign exchange may now be purchased for delivery three months or six months hence. The market is quite sophisticated institutionally, being elaborately linked on a worldwide basis through the selling and buying operations of brokers and bankers specializing in foreign exchange transactions. Three functions of the foreign exchange market are commonly emphasized: to transfer the purchasing power of one national currency into another; to provide short- and medium-term credit for foreign trade; and to provide, through the forward exchange market, facilities for hedging against losses from changes in the rate of exchange.

In an uncontrolled foreign exchange market, the $:£ rate as quoted in New York must be equivalent to the $:£ rate as quoted in London. Otherwise, "arbitrage"—the simultaneous buying of foreign exchanges in the cheap market and selling in the dear market—would occur and ensure a single rate for the $:£ exchange. If the rate were quoted as $2.00:£1.00 in New York, but $1.95:£1.00 in London, "two-point arbitrage" would occur, with arbitrageurs increasing the demand for pounds and supply of dollars in London and thereby raising the quotation in London; and the supply of pounds would increase in New York, thereby lowering the quotation until the discrepancy in the price of pounds is removed.

The "cross rates"—that is, the ratio between the exchange rates of two foreign currencies in terms of a third currency—must also be orderly. If, say, the $:£, £:Fr., and $:Fr. rates were not consistent, then again arbitrage would occur until the rates become orderly and left no latitude for realizing profits from discrepancies among exchange rates.

Figure 6.1

Normal Case of Adjustment
through Depreciation

Equilibrium exchange rate (r_o) is initially $2.00: £ 1.00.

Demand for £ then rises from D to
D', and a foreign exchange gap of GP
appears. This gap can be "filled" by an
outflow of foreign reserves (1); or "suppressed" by imposing direct controls on
imports (2); or "removed" by reducing
demand through deflation (3).

With freely fluctuating exchange
rates, the $ depreciates and the £ appre-
ciates to the new equilibrum exchange
rate of $2.50: £1.00. The quantity of
foreign exchange supplied will then increase (4a), and the quantity of foreign
exchange demanded will decrease (4b).

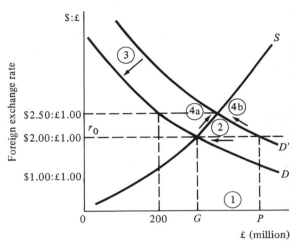

Volume of sterling traded for dollars

Our interest in the foreign exchange market centers upon the forces
of demand and supply in the spot market and the establishment of the
spot exchange rate.

The Demand for Foreign Exchange

The demand for another country's currency depends on the value of
payments to that country. Consider the American demand for British
pounds, as depicted in Figure 6.1. As the price of the £ falls in terms of
$ (the $ appreciates—say, from $2.50:£1.00 to $2.00:£1.00) the quantity of £ demanded increases. The value of all the payments from the
United States to the United Kingdom—all the debit items "above the
line" in the American balance of payments vis-à-vis the United Kingdom—will be equivalent to the American demand for £. Because the
amount imported from the United Kingdom will depend on the level of
national income in the United States, tastes of American consumers,
and prices of substitute commodities, the demand for £ will also depend on the same variables. The position of the U.S. demand curve for
£ will thus be higher (farther to the right in Figure 6.1) at each and
every possible exchange rate, the higher American national income, the
stronger the American tastes for British goods, and the higher the
prices of competitive goods. The demand curve may thus shift from D
to D' if national income rises in the United States or tastes shift in

favor of British imports or the prices of British imports fall relative to import-competing goods in the United States and relative to imports from other countries. (We ignore here the other possible sources of demand for foreign exchange by speculators and hedgers.)

The American demand for £ can also be viewed as the supply of $. Payments to the United Kingdom are made by converting $ into £: the demand for £ is the supply of $ on the $:£ foreign exchange market. This interpretation is analogous to the "reciprocal demand" analysis of Chapter 2. At a given exchange rate, the area under the demand curve denotes the supply of $ that Americans will pay for the quantity of £ represented on the horizontal axis. In Figure 6.1, for example, at the rate of $2.50:£1.00, the supply of $ would be $500 million (£200 million at $2.50:£1.00).

The price-elasticity of the demand for foreign exchange is derived from the price-elasticities of the demand for imports. If imports are commodities for which the demand is highly elastic, so too will the demand for the foreign exchange be highly elastic. A depreciation of the dollar will then result in a proportionately large decrease in the quantity of pounds demanded and a decrease in the total amount of dollars spent on pounds. If, however, the debit item is perfectly price-inelastic—for example, a fixed interest payment that must be paid in the foreign currency—then the demand for the foreign currency will also be perfectly inelastic. A depreciation of the dollar would then not reduce the quantity of pounds demanded and would only increase the quantity of dollars that would have to be supplied for the same number of pounds. Normally the demand curve for foreign currency will have some elasticity; and the elasticity will become greater, the longer the period considered, because adjustments in tastes and sources of supply are more apt to occur over the longer period.

The Supply of Foreign Exchange

We have already noted that the supply of a country's currency on the foreign exchange market is in essence its reciprocal demand. The supply of £ on the $:£ market, as viewed from the United States, is equivalent to the United Kingdom's demand for $. In other words, the supply of £ represents the credit items in the U.S. balance of payments with the United Kingdom—the receipts from the United Kingdom.

In Figure 6.1, the supply of £ slopes up to the right, indicating that a greater quantity of £ would be supplied as the $ depreciates and the £ appreciates. The elasticity of the supply again depends on the price-elasticities of the British demand for imports from the United States and the U.S. export supply: the more elastic the demand for these imports, the more elastic the supply of pounds. The position of the curve will depend on the United Kingdom's national income, the tastes of British consumers for American imports, and the prices of substitutes. The entire schedule will shift to the right, indicating a greater quantity of £ supplied at each and every exchange rate, if British national income rises, tastes change in favor of American goods, or prices of import-competing goods increase.

The "Foreign Exchange Gap"

Again consider Figure 6.1. If the demand schedule is initially at the level D, and the supply schedule is at the level S, then the exchange rate established by the free play of demand and supply conditions would be $2.00:£1.00. With given income and world prices, this is an "equilibrium exchange rate" in the sense that at this rate there is no excess demand for or excess supply of foreign exchange: the amount of £ that Americans would be willing to buy at $2.00:£1.00 is equal to the amount of £ that the British would be willing to sell at that exchange rate.

If, however, the demand schedule should now increase to D' (say, because of a change in tastes, income, or prices of substitutes), then at the old exchange rate of $2.00:£1.00, there would be an excess demand for £. At $2.00:£1.00, the quantity of £ Americans would be willing to buy would exceed the quantity of £ the British would be willing to supply by the amount GP of £. There is thus a **foreign exchange gap.**

Assume for the moment that the exchange rate is not free to move, either because countries adhere to a gold standard or because of some international agreement that requires the national monetary authority to intervene on the foreign exchange market to hold the rate fixed. The foreign exchange gap must then be filled—the excess demand covered—by an outflow of international reserves from the United States that can be converted to a supply of £ in the United Kingdom or by an inflow of short-term capital from the United Kingdom, indicating that the British are willing to hold short-term dollar assets instead of receiving payment in pounds. The reserve outflow and capital inflow "**fill the** gap" and are equivalent to the "below the line" settlement items in the balance of payments we discussed in Chapter 5.

But what if the American government wants to avoid an outflow of international reserves or a capital inflow? It must then either **suppress the foreign exchange gap** or remove the gap by some remedial measure. The gap can be suppressed by direct restrictions on imports—say, quantitative restrictions that would not allow imports greater than the amount OG of £. This would, in effect, prevent demand from rising from D to D'. But once the import controls were relaxed, demand would rise unless some underlying corrective action had been pursued.

If the government wishes not merely to suppress, but to **remove the gap** (but still abides by the rule of a fixed exchange rate), then it must resort to deflationary policy measures. Policies that will lower national income and prices in the United States will *pari passu* lower the demand for imports and possibly increase the demand for American exports, and hence the supply of £, thereby removing the excess demand for foreign exchange.

In short, if there is excess demand for foreign exchange, but a fixed exchange rate is to be maintained, then the deficit country must be prepared either to fill the gap, suppress the gap, or remove the gap by enduring deflation. These policies are depicted as 1, 2, and 3, respectively, in Figure 6.1.

The merit of a freely fluctuating exchange rate now becomes obvious. Instead of having to rely on the use of international reserve assets or the imposition of restrictive controls on trade or capital movements or the sufferance of deflation or unemployment, the deficit country can simply let the exchange rate go to its new level, which will constitute a **depreciation of the deficit country's currency.** Thus, the price of foreign currency will rise in Figure 6.1 from $2.00:£1.00 to $2.50:£1.00; the dollar depreciates, and the pound appreciates because of the increased demand for pounds. The export prices of American goods will now fall in terms of other currencies, and this should increase the quantity of exports. At the same time, the price of American exports may rise in terms of dollars, causing a reduction in domestic consumption and an increase in the amount available for exports from the United States. The prices of goods imported by the United States would tend to rise in terms of dollars, but to fall in foreign currency. The increase in the dollar price of imported goods would reduce the amount imported and increase the amount of import-competing goods produced at home. The depreciation of the dollar causes American products to displace British products in the domestic markets of both countries and in the markets of third countries to which both countries export. If the price-elasticities of demand are sufficiently high, the exports of the depreciating country will rise relative to its imports, and **the disequilibrium in the balance of payments will be corrected via price effects.**

Note, however, that although the United States has not had to impose direct controls or deflate, it has sacrificed a fixed exchange rate. If instead of moving away from fixed exchange rates, the government had been willing to trade off some unemployment (through deflationary policy measures) or some protectionism (through direct trade controls) for the maintenance of a fixed exchange rate, then we could not determine *ex ante* what the equilibrium exchange rate would be. When these other policies are possible variables, we cannot denote one exchange rate as **the** equilibrium exchange rate: the "equilibrium exchange rate" is then interdependent with the extent to which the government is willing to fill the foreign exchange gap, suppress the gap, or remove the gap by deflation. Our inability to determine an equilibrium exchange rate *ex ante* is simply another manifestation of **the possible policy trade-offs among depreciation, deflation, and direct controls.** The equilibrium rate is then relative to the degree of deflation or restriction the country is also willing to endure.

Efficacy of Exchange Depreciation

We have now seen that if a country simply lets its exchange rate go, it may prevent the intensification of an incipient deficit in its balance of payments without sacrificing full employment or liberal trade policies. That is certainly a substantial accomplishment. But the story may be somewhat more complicated. Depreciation may not operate so rapidly and effectively as implied above. Moreover, even if effective, depreciation will entail certain costs in the deficit country. There are also other disadvantages connected with a regime of freely fluctuating rates. We shall wait to summarize the advantages and disadvantages of freely fluctuating rates until Chapter 9. We now want to focus on exchange depreciation as a means of re-equilibrating the balance of payments.

Let us first examine the question whether exchange depreciation will always be effective in removing a balance of payments deficit. To be so, it must increase the value of exports or decrease the value of imports in

JOAN ROBINSON, *Essays in the Theory of Employment* (1947), 154

There is no one rate of exchange which is the equilibrium rate corresponding to a given state of world demands and techniques. In any given situation there is an equilibrium rate corresponding to each rate of interest and level of effective demand, and any rate of exchange, within very wide limits, can be turned into the equilibrium rate by altering the rate of interest appropriately. Moreover, any rate of exchange can be made comparable with any rate of interest provided that money wages can be sufficiently altered. The notion of *the* equilibrium exchange rate is a chimera.

terms of **foreign** currency by an amount sufficient to remove the excess demand for foreign currency.

As already noted in the preceding section, the initial "price effects" of depreciation will be

to raise, in terms of home currency, the price of importables into the deficit country relative to prices of its home goods;

to decrease, in terms of foreign currency, the prices of exportables from the depreciating country relative to the prices of home goods abroad;

to decrease, in terms of foreign currency, the prices of exportables from the depreciating country relative to the prices of exportables from third countries.

In the extreme case, the country with a depreciating currency may have a perfectly inelastic demand for imports ($\eta = 0$). The same quantity of imports would then be bought at the same foreign currency price. The country would pay more of its home currency for the same foreign exchange value of imports. More generally, the demand for imports will have some elasticity, and as the price of imports rises in terms of home currency, the foreign exchange value of imports will decrease.

The value of exports, however, poses more of a problem. As the price of exportables decreases in terms of foreign currency, the quantity of exports will increase unless foreign demand is perfectly inelastic. But what about the value of exports? If the foreign elasticity of demand is greater than unity (relatively elastic), the value of exports in terms of

JOAN ROBINSON, "The Foreign Exchanges" in *Essays in the Theory of Employment* (2nd ed., 1947), Part III, Chap. 1

The theory of the exchanges may be regarded as the analysis of the manner in which movements of the balance of trade and the balance of lending are equated to each other.

A change in the desire to lend abroad will tend to alter the exchange rate. The reaction upon the balance of trade of an alteration in the exchange rate must be examined at some length. Suppose that, after a certain exchange rate has been in force for some time, the amount which the inhabitants of the home country desire to lend abroad increases. At the ruling exchange rate the demand for foreign currency exceeds the supply and the exchange rate consequently falls. This has the effect of making home-produced goods appear cheaper to foreigners and so increasing the volume of exports. If the physical volume of exports increases their home price cannot fall, therefore the value of exports in terms of home currency must increase. But the effect on imports is more complicated. Foreign goods are now dearer at home, and while the physical volume of imports purchased out of a given income will decline, total expenditure upon them may increase. Thus a decline in the exchange rate will not necessarily increase the balance of trade. If the value of imports (reckoned in home currency) increases by more than the value of exports, then a fall in the exchange rate will reduce the balance of trade.

The argument may be treated in terms of four elasticities: the foreign elasticity of demand for exports, and the home elasticity of supply (which is influenced by the home elasticity of demand for exportable goods), the foreign elasticity of supply of imports and the home elasticity of demand for imports (which is influenced by the home elasticity of supply of rival commodities).

foreign currency will increase: an increase in the volume of exports leads to a greater amount of foreign currency being expended upon them, and the value of exports increases in greater proportion than the depreciation. If, however, the foreign elasticity of demand is less than unity (relatively inelastic), then the foreign currency value of exports will decrease.

The crucial question, therefore, is: If the foreign currency value of a country's exports decreases when the country's currency depreciates, will the decrease in the foreign currency value of the country's imports be more or less than the decrease in the foreign currency value of its exports? If the decrease in the foreign currency value of its exports is more than the decrease in the foreign currency value of its imports, then the country's deficit is worsened—not improved!

In **the normal case,** with a time period sufficiently long to overcome lags, the elasticities of demand for importables and exportables will be high enough to give the normal demand and supply curves for foreign exchange, as depicted in Figure 6.1. When the dollar depreciates from $2.00:£1.00 to $2.50:£1.00, the value of exports rises (indicated by the increasing quantity of pounds supplied) and the value of imports falls (indicated by the decreasing quantity of pounds demanded). The excess demand for pounds is removed through price changes. The foreign exchange market is characterized by **stable equilibrium:** a rise in price of the foreign currency tends to increase the quantity supplied relative to the quantity demanded.

The efficacy of exchange depreciation is often discussed in terms of the **"Marshall-Lerner condition,"** which states that depreciation will worsen a country's balance of payments if the sum of the absolute value of the demand elasticities for the country's exports and imports is not greater than unity. In other words, a country's balance of trade will improve or worsen as the deficiency below unity of home or foreign demand is more or less offset by the excess above zero of the other.[2]

Remember we are abstracting from changes in the level of national income. In actuality, when exports rise or imports fall, there would be secondary repercussions as the country's national income would increase, and the demand curve for foreign currency would shift upwards somewhat as the demand for imports rose with greater income. But we are considering for the moment only the initial impact of price changes. We shall allow for the secondary consequences when we combine price effects with income effects in Chapter 8.

Consider now, however, two other possibilities. Suppose first that the value of exports falls when the dollar depreciates (the supply curve of pounds is backward-bending because the British demand for imports

[2] This condition is not, however, a necessary condition if supply elasticities are low (so that costs of production and prices of goods change in domestic currency) or if there is initially an export surplus. If the balance of trade is initially in deficit, however, the sum of the two demand elasticities must exceed unity to reduce the deficit. For a discussion of the Marshall-Lerner condition, see A. Marshall, *Money, Credit and Commerce* (1924), Appendix J; A.P. Lerner, *The Economics of Control* (1944), 377–79; and Joan Robinson, *Essays in the Theory of Employment* (1947), 138–46.

from the United States is relatively inelastic). But the value of imports falls even more. The excess demand for pounds is therefore eliminated as the dollar depreciates. In this case, the elasticity of demand for foreign currency is greater than the elasticity of supply of foreign currency. In other words, the foreigner's elasticity of demand for American exports is less than unity, but the American elasticity of demand for imports is sufficiently greater than zero, so that the sum of the elasticities is greater than unity.

In the second case, suppose the value of exports falls as the dollar depreciates, but now the decrease in the value of exports is greater than the decrease in the value of imports. In this case, the percentage increase in quantity exported after depreciation is less than the percentage reduction in price of exports in foreign currency. The total quantity of foreign exchange supplied is then reduced after depreciation of the home currency. At the same time, imports are not reduced in quantity by a sufficient amount to reduce the foreign exchange value of imports by more than the fall in the foreign exchange value of exports. The excess demand for foreign exchange is therefore not eliminated: as the home currency depreciates, the excess demand for foreign currency becomes even greater, and the home currency depreciates all the more.

This is the "perverse case" of depreciation—a case of unstable equilibrium in the foreign exchange market. In this case, the supply curve slopes down from left to right (is backward-bending) and is flatter than the demand curve (cuts the demand curve from below). The elasticity of supply for foreign currency is greater than the elasticity of demand for foreign currency, so that depreciation of the dollar would move the exchange rate even farther from equilibrium. In terms of the Marshall-Lerner condition, the foreigner's elasticity of demand for American exports is less than unity, but the American elasticity of demand for imports is not sufficiently greater than zero, so that the sum of the elasticities is less than unity.

The perverse case is, however, unlikely to occur in reality—especially over the longer run after a depreciation occurs. The elasticities of demand are likely to be more elastic, the greater the degree of change in the exchange rate and the longer the change lasts. Once depreciation occurs, the price-elasticity of demand for imports would increase over time as the domestic import-competing industries produce more, and new sources of supply of imports are utilized. Unless money incomes and money wealth increased, the rise in prices of imports would also eventually affect the quantity of imports demanded. The price-elasticity of demand for the country's exports also tends to increase as potential exports enter foreign trade, and the range of exports widens. The longer the run, the more elastic the supply of exportables and the more elastic the foreign demand for exports. Although the possibility of the perverse case of depreciation was at one time of great interest to economists (and its analysis is still a good exercise for students), few economists now subscribe to "elasticity pessimism"—except possibly for primary producing countries with low capacity to transform during depression periods.[3]

For a short or intermediate period after a devaluation, however, it is possible for the devaluing country's exports to decline in terms of foreign currency. This is because the domestic-currency price of exports might be fixed in the short period, according to contracts already made or practices of administered pricing. Until domestic prices rise, the foreign currency value of exports may fall. There are also lags between changes in relative prices and actual increases in exports or decreases in imports traded. In the interim period, until the full price effects of the devaluation can be realized, the so-called **"J-curve effect"** can occur. In the short run following an exchange-rate change, the terms of trade may worsen for a depreciating country and improve for an appreciating country, and this may more than offset the volume effect of an exchange-rate change on the balance of trade. Subsequently the balance of trade may improve over the longer period. The letter J traces the initial deterioration and subsequent improvement in the balance of payments.

Cost of Adjustment through Price Changes

Even if conditions for the normal case of devaluation prevail, the adjustment mechanism will still have some side effects that impose **costs on the deficit country.** As we shall repeatedly see, no mechanism of adjustment is without its burden. **The central policy problem is to determine which of the alternative adjustment processes is least burdensome and how the burden of international adjustment is to be shared among deficit and surplus countries.**

In assessing the burden or costs of adjustment through depreciation, we should note the following consequences. Depreciation will have a

[3]It is generally believed that statisticl estimates of the price-elasticities of demand have been biased downward, and that the true elasticities justify more optimism. See the pioneering article by Guy H. Orcutt, "Measurement of Price Elasticities in International Trade," *Review of Economics and Statistics,* 32 (May 1950), 117–32. Also, Edward E. Leamer and Robert M. Stern, *Quantitative International Economics* (1970), Chap. 2.

ABBA P. LERNER, *The Economics of Control* (1944), 379–80

These possibilities [of low elasticities] are usually ignored or else pointed out as queer but practically unimportant cases. This is due in part to the tendency in economic writings to assume elasticities to be high because that would fit in better with the ideas of perfect competition on which, until recently, economic analysis was based, and partly to the related habit of assuming a world with many small countries, none of them large enough to influence prices appreciably. If this were true, such low elasticities as those here discussed, where the sum of two of them is less than unity, could be relegated to the realm of *curiosa*. But there are now large economic empires with tremendous control over the price at which they will buy, especially in the short period; and more important still is the proliferation of tariffs and quotas and exchange clearing schemes that are used as "defenses" against a country which reduces its costs or the value of its currency, or which tries to reduce its import balance by subsidizing exports. These have the effect of reducing the elasticity of demand for its exports. Indeed where the exports are fixed by quotas the demand is exactly zero. When such a country has cut its imports to the very minimum in its efforts to correct its balance of payments, the demand for the remaining imports will be very inelastic too. We then have the phenomenon just analyzed, which is not at all uncommon in times of international depression. One country after another is forced off the gold standard, finds its currency depreciating without this affording much relief, and is able to find a stable position only after a long fall in the value of its currency and the introduction of special restrictions on trade have so altered the situation that the elasticities are no longer so low.

general effect on all prices in the foreign trade sector, acting as an *ad valorem* subsidy on all exports and as an *ad valorem* tax on all imports. A 10% depreciation of a country's currency is equivalent to a 10% uniform import duty and a 10% uniform export subsidy. Instead, however, a government may want to be selective and alter only some prices of selective exports (such as non-traditional new exports) and selective imports (such as luxuries, but not necessities). Depreciation may then be costly in not being selective and in being **overly general in its impact.**

Depreciation will also require a shift in resources as the demand for exports increases, the demand for imports falls, and the demand for import-substitutes rises. Resources must then be transferred into the export and the import-competing sectors unless excess capacity already exists in these sectors. These **readjustments in resource allocation** are not frictionless or timeless: they involve costs of transfer. If the country's capacity to transform is low, the costs can be substantial.

Further, depreciation entails a change in the **distribution of income**. Those who consume importables suffer a rise in their cost of living and a fall in their real incomes. Exporters, on the other hand, reap a windfall because a unit of foreign currency is now worth more in terms of home currency. Factors employed in export and import-competing sectors are also likely to benefit as demand shifts toward these sectors.

From the viewpoint of a debtor country, debt-servicing payments fixed in terms of the creditor's currency are equivalent to an import that rises in value in proportion to the country's exchange depreciation. If **debt servicing** is considerable, depreciation will make it all the more burdensome.

Unless other countervailing policies are taken, depreciation will also generate **inflationary forces** that exacerbate the resource allocation and distribution of income effects. The increase in exports and decrease in imports will have an inflationary impact through the effect on aggregate demand, as will be seen in Chapter 7. In addition, there may be a cost-push type of inflation to the extent that imports rise in price, they are inputs, and firms have sufficient market power to raise commodity prices when their costs rise. Wages will also rise as the cost of living increases, and labor seeks to maintain real wages. If such price increases in the products and labor markets are allowed, the depreciation may become abortive as prices rise to offset the depreciation. If this is to be prevented, the country may have to impose contractionary monetary and fiscal policies, and possibly wage-price controls or some type of "social contract" to restrain increases in factor payments.

Another consequence of depreciation can be a deterioration in the country's commodity terms of trade. This depends on how export prices change relative to import prices when expressed in the same currency. Export prices decline in terms of the foreign currency, and import prices rise in terms of the home currency. But when export and import prices are both expressed in terms of one currency, the terms of trade might improve or deteriorate. In the perverse case, the terms of trade must worsen when the balance of payments worsens. But even in the normal case, the **terms of trade may worsen.** Whether the terms of trade turn against the depreciating country depends upon the relative size of the demand elasticities of the trading countries and their supply elasticities. The terms of trade are more likely to deteriorate under the following conditions: the less the demand shifts away from importables to exportables; the more elastic the supply of exports, so that export prices do not rise; and the more elastic the supply of imports, so that import prices do not fall.[4] In general, depreciation tends to worsen a country's terms of trade, the less elastic are demands relative to supplies. If the terms of trade do deteriorate, then even though the country's balance of payments improves, each unit of the country's exports would buy fewer imports. The rise in import prices relative to export prices would thus reduce real income per unit of output in the depreciating country.

Finally, if depreciation is effective in correcting the balance of payments deficit through price changes, it will *ipso facto* do so by increasing the volume of exports or reducing the volume of imports, thereby reducing the total amount of resources available for home consumption and investment. The "rest of the world" gains greater command over the depreciating country's resources, or the depreciating country has less command over foreign resources. The ultimate consequence of depreciation is that the deficit country's **real expenditure must decline.** Even though the mechanism of adjustment operates through price changes, its ultimate impact is on real income. When the value of a country's imports is initially greater than the value of its exports, then the removal of this deficit—by increasing exports or decreasing imports—must result in fewer resources being available to fulfill aggregate home demand.

Although depreciation has these undesirable side effects, the deficit country still is spared the alternative burden of a more general and deeper deflation in employment and income or the costs of direct controls on trade and capital movements. The prices of exportables and importables rise as compared with prices of domestic goods, and this shifts the demand from internationally traded to domestic goods, while stimulating foreign demand for and domestic production of exports. By operating directly on the value of exports and the value of imports through the effects of price changes, depreciation still allows the price mechanism to

---

[4] See G. Haberler, *A Survey of International Trade Theory*, (1961), 39–41; J.E. Meade, *The Balance of Payments* (1951), 235–47; and F. Machlup, "The Terms-of-Trade Effects of Devaluation upon Real Income and the Balance of Trade,"*Kyklos* (1956), 417–50.

guide the allocation of resources. Finally, depreciation does not restrict the volume of trade to the extent that the deficit country's exports increase even if its imports decline. In this way, the international division of labor and mutual gains from trade are maintained.

Supplementary Readings

For a discussion of foreign exchange markets, see L.B. Yeager, *International Monetary Relations* (1966), Chaps. 5–7; R.M. Stern, *The Balance of Payments* (1973), Chap. 3. The adjustment mechanism under flexible rates is analyzed in Joan Robinson, "The Foreign Exchanges," in H.S. Ellis and L.A. Metzler (eds.), *Readings in the Theory of International Trade* (1950), Chap. 4; E. Sohmen, 'Exchange Rates," *International Encyclopedia of the Social Sciences,* vol. 8 (1967), 11–16; S.A. Alexander, "Effects of Devaluation on a Trade Balance," in R.E. Caves and H.G. Johnson (eds.), *Readings in International Economics* (1968), Chap. 22; A.C. Harberger, "Currency Depreciation, Income, and the Balance of Trade," in Caves and Johnson, *op. cit.,* Chap. 21; Milton Friedman, "The Case for Flexible Exchange Rates," in Friedman, *Essays in Positive Economics* (1953), 157–203; R.E. Caves, "Flexible Exchange Rates," *American Economic Review, Papers and Proceedings,* 53 (May 1963), 120–29; G. Haberler, "The Market for Foreign Exchange and the Stability of the Balance of Payments: A Theoretical Analysis," *Kyklos,* 3 (1949), 193–218; R.N. Cooper, *Currency Devaluation in Developing Countries,* Princeton Essays in International Finance No. 86 (June 1971).

7

The Adjustment Process:
Absorption Approach

We now turn to other features of the adjustment process that involve
income changes. Until the advent of Keynesian economics, the traditional analysis of a country's adjustment to disequilibrium in its balance
of payments concentrated on the price and exchange-rate changes that
we discussed in the preceeding chapter. With the new perspective
provided by macroeconomics, economists soon realized that variations
in the level of national ouput, income, and expenditure also had considerable influence on the adjustment process. Indeed, at one extreme,
income analysis assumes constant prices and examines how variations in
only real ouput and income and expenditure affect the balance of payments. In this chapter we shall also begin with this assumption. In the
next chapter we shall extend our analysis until we finally allow for price
changes together with income changes and offer a synthesis of the price
and income effects of the adjustment process.

The Absorption Approach

When we focus on income changes we are emphasizing the "absorption
approach" to balance of trade problems. This approach simply recognizes that the values of exports and imports are a function of national
income and expenditure in the trading countries. Domestic absorption
is the national expenditure on both home-produced goods and imports.

The absorption approach specifically focuses on the accounting identity that a country's trade deficit or surplus is expressed as

$$B \equiv X - M \equiv (X + H) - (M + H) \equiv Y - E, \qquad (7.1)$$

where B is the balance of trade (identical with the balance of payments if there are no capital movements); X, the value of exports; H, home expenditure on home goods, equivalent to private consumption expenditure (C) plus private investment expenditure (I) plus governmental expenditure on goods and services (G) **net of imports**; M, the value of imports; Y, the real national income or domestic ouput; and E, the **national expenditure or real national "absorption"** of goods and services. The total absorption, or E, is composed of consumption, investment, and government expenditures (equivalent to $C + I + G$ **gross of imports**). The fundamental principle of the absorption approach is that the **balance of trade is improved** (the positive value of B is increased) if **aggregate real income (Y) is increased by more than domestic absorption (E).** The mechanism of adjustment to a trade imbalance must therefore involve effects on income and expenditure. Before we can trace through these effects, we must first understand in greater detail how the balance of trade fits into national income analysis.

The Balance of Trade and National Income

Consider first the simplest possible type of economy composed of households that consume (C), business firms that invest (I), no government sector, and no foreign trade. The value of this economy's national income (Y) will then be identically equal to the value of its domestic output (O) and to the value of its national expenditure (E); or

$$Y \equiv O \equiv E \equiv C + I \qquad (7.2)$$

Since actual or realized (*ex post*) "saving" (S) is defined as "not consuming," it follows, according to national income accounting, that in each period of time (t),

$$S_t \equiv Y_t - C_t \equiv I_t \qquad (7.3)$$

In behavioral terms, however, the level of consumption is a function of the level of income. There is a lag between the receipt of income and the expenditure of income on consumption. More specifically, an in-

SIDNEY S. ALEXANDER, "Effects of a Devaluation on a Trade Balance," *IMF Staff Papers* II (April 1952), 264

It is generally recognized that a country's net foreign trade balance is equal to the difference between the total goods and services produced in that country and the total goods and services taken off the market domestically. For brevity, the taking of goods and services off the market will be referred to here as absorption. Absorption then equals the sum of consumption plus investment as usually defined (including in investment any change in the holding of inventories). If a devaluation is to affect the foreign balance, it can do so in only two ways: (1) It can lead to a change in the production of goods and services in the country; this change will have associated with it an induced change in the absorption of goods and services so that the foreign balance will be altered by the difference between the change in income and the income-induced change in absorption. (2) The devaluation may change the amount of real absorption associated with any given level of real income.

---

crease in consumption "today" (t) (ΔC_t) is related by the marginal propensity to consume (c) to an increase in income "yesterday" (ΔY_{t-1}) or

$$\Delta C_t = c \, (\Delta Y_{t-1}) \tag{7.4}$$

"Intended" or "desired" (*ex ante*) saving (S^*) is then also a function of income, and

$$\Delta S_t^* = s \, (\Delta Y_{t-1}), \tag{7.5}$$

where ΔS_t^* is the increment of desired saving in the present period and s is the marginal propensity to save. In a closed economy with no government, $c + s = 1$.

Reconsidering equation (7.2), we can note that

$$\Delta Y_t \equiv \Delta C_t + \Delta I_t, \tag{7.6}$$

and since $\Delta C_t = c \, (\Delta Y_{t-1})$, it follows that, as $t \to \infty$, $\Delta Y = 1/(1-c)$ (ΔI) or $\Delta Y = (1/s) \, (\Delta I)$, where $1/(1-c)$ or $1/s$ is the "multiplier." The ΔY is the increment in income, to be added to the initial level of Y, after the multiplier has worked itself out over time. This chapter's

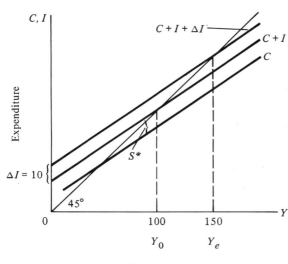

Figure 7.1
The Closed-Economy Multiplier

The initial equilibrium level of income is $Y_0 = C + I$. An increase in investment $(+\Delta I = 10)$ is then "multiplied," and income rises from Y_0 to the new equilibrium level Y_e where $I = S = S^*$. The increase in income is $\Delta Y = 50 = \Delta I + \Delta C = 10 + 40$.

Income, output

Appendix illustrates a dynamic sequence analysis of the multiplier working over time.

Following the simple Keynesian model of national income determination, we shall assume that an expansion of national income is the result of a change in **real** output. Only after "full employment" is reached will the price level rise. By assuming that prices are constant as output changes, we focus on real forces and ignore for the present the influence of monetary factors and changes in prices (to be considered in Chapter 8).

Consider changes in national income in more detail. If Y is initially at an equilibrium level of 100 ($Y_0 = 100$), and then I rises by $+ \Delta I = 10$ and stays at this new higher level, and $c = .8$, the level of Y will rise until it reaches a new higher equilibrium level (Y_e) of 150 [$Y_e = Y_0 + (1/.2) (10) = 100 + 50$]. At this new higher level of income, the ΔS^* will be $\Delta S^* = s (\Delta Y)$, or $.2(50) = 10$. After income has risen by the amount of 50 (composed of $\Delta I = 10$ and $\Delta C = 40$), the ΔS^* is exactly equal to the ΔI, and income can rise no higher: at this new level of Y, the "leakages" of saving from the income stream are exactly offsetting the "injections" of investment into the income stream. Below the new equilibrium level of Y, however, $I > S^*$, and Y rises. Levels of Y higher than the new equilibrium level could not be supported because at higher levels of income the situation would be $S^* > I$, and Y would fall.

Graphically this is summarized in the familiar $45°$ diagram of aggregate demand and supply as in Figure 7.1 or Figure 7.2.

Figure 7.2

Closed-Economy Multiplier with Increase in Investment

The saving schedule (S^*) is derived from the difference between income measured along the 45° guide line (Y) and the consumption function (C) in Figure 7.1 (not drawn to scale). I is assumed not to vary with Y. The initial level of income is Y_o, where $I = S = S^*$. Assume now an autonomous increase in investment from I to $I + \Delta I$. After income has increased by $+ \Delta Y = 50$, as a result of the $+\Delta I = 10$, the new higher equilibrium level of income will be Y_e, where investment equals saving.

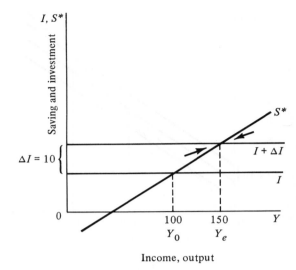

If we now introduce a governmental sector, equation (7.2) will become

$$Y \equiv 0 \equiv E \equiv C + I + G \tag{7.7}$$

Letting Y now represent disposable income (income after taxes), equation (7.6) becomes

$$\Delta Y = \frac{1}{1 - c}(\Delta I + \Delta G) \tag{7.8}$$

where $1/(1-c)$ or $1/s$ is again the "multiplier," but $c + s = 1$ is now the marginal propensity to consume and marginal propensity to save out of disposable income.

It also follows that if there is a positive ΔI or ΔG, then income will rise to a new higher equilibrium level (Y_e), and at this level the $\Delta S^* + \Delta T = \Delta I + \Delta G$, where ΔT is the increase in taxes. Being a form of "forced saving," taxes act as a leakage from the income stream analogous to saving. At levels of $Y > Y_e$, $I + G > S^* + T$, and Y increases. At levels of $Y > Y_e$, $S^* + T > I + G$, and Y decreases.

Finally, we may now open the economy to foreign trade. The value of domestic ouput (0) is then

$$0 = C + I + G + X - M, \tag{7.9}$$

where C, I, G, and X (exports) are now gross of any import content (for example, a final consumer good—say, a shirt—may contain imported intermediate inputs—say, cotton); and M represents imports that are subtracted from $(C + I + G + X)$ to obtain the value of domestic output, or the income produced by resources within the country.

National income is now, however,

$$Y = 0 \pm (D+U), \tag{7.10}$$

where $\pm D$ represents receipts (+) or payments (−) of dividends and interest, and $\pm U$ represents unilateral transfers (gifts and grants) received (+) or given abroad (−). Unlike a closed economy, the national income of an open economy can exceed the value of domestic output if net income payments are being received from abroad.

In an open economy, national expenditure (E), or the rate of total absorption of goods and services, can also exceed the value of domestic output by having imports exceed the country's exports. National expenditure is now

$$E = C + I + G = 0 - (X - M) \tag{7.11}$$

or

$$X - M = 0 - E \tag{7.12}$$

If $(D + U)$ are assumed to be zero, then $Y = 0$, and

$$X - M = Y - E \tag{7.13}$$

And since (*ex post*) $X - M = B$, we return to the basic eqution (7.1) with which we began: $B = Y - E$.

A central proposition that can be deduced from this analysis is that a "domestic imbalance" between investment and saving and an "international imbalance" between exports and imports are not too different kinds of disequilibria, but are the mirror images of each other: **the external imbalance reflects internal imbalance.**[1]

From equation (7.13), it is clear that if at full employment real E is greater than the country's real Y, then the excess absorption by consumption, investment, and government expenditures can only be made possible by an excess of imports over exports. The external deficit reflects an excess of spending over income at home. And this deficit in the balance of trade must be financed by an induced capital inflow or loss of foreign reserve assets.

We may note that at an equilibrium level of Y, it must be true (*ex post*) that $I + X + G = S^* + M + T$. We may say that "full

[1] See R.F. Harrod, *International Economics* (1957), 143.

equilibrium" would mean the simultaneous achievement of "internal balance," in the sense that $I + G = S* + T$, and "external balance" in the sense that $X = M$.

But is it possible that Y is at an equilibrium level, although there is not both "internal balance" and "external balance"? Indeed, the absence of "external balance" is a reflection of the absence of "internal balance"; without the external disequilibrium, the equilibrium level of Y could not be supported. If, for example, at a full employment equilibrium level of national income, $I + X + G = S* + M + T$, but $I > S*$ and $G > T$, then it must be true that $M > X$. This is equivalent to $E > Y$. In this situation, the trade imbalance is a direct manifestation of internal disequilibrium, and we may as readily speak of excess spending as of a balance of payments deficit, or as easily of "overabsorption" as of "overimporting." Under fixed rates, the excess absorption must be supported by an induced capital inflow or loss of foreign reserve assets. A country borrows from abroad—that is, utilizes foreign saving—to the extent that its current account is in deficit. Under flexible rates, the home currency will depreciate when $E > Y$.

If, in contrast, $S* > I$ and $T > G$, then it must be true that $X > M$. This is equivalent to $Y > E$. In this case, with fixed rates, the excess savings will flow overseas in the form of foreign investment (a capital outflow) or there will be an inflow of foreign reserves. A country saves and invests abroad to the extent that it has a surplus on current account (equal to a deficit on capital account). With flexible rates, the home currency would appreciate when $Y > E$.

It should be emphasized that a country that is engaged in net foreign borrowing will have an import surplus on current account, and a country engaged in foreign investment will have an export surplus on current account. The **real** transfer of capital is effected through the export surplus. Thus, if we abstract from the government sector,[2] $I_d + X = S + M$, where I_d represents domestic investment. Rewriting the equation, $S = I_d + X - M$. And $(X - M) = I_f$, where I_f represents net foreign investment, equivalent to the increase in the country's net official and private sector claims on foreigners. It follows that $S = I_d + I_f$. The nation's net savings are equal to total investment—that is, net domestic investment *plus* net foreign investment (or the balance of current foreign transactions).

[2]We could include $(G-T)$ as "loan expenditure" in I_d if the government runs a deficit, or in S if $T > G$. For the moment, we ignore G and T, or else we assume $G = T$.

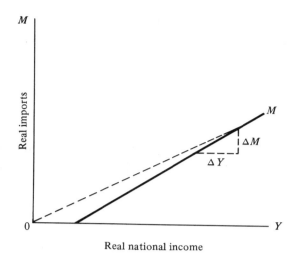

Figure 7.3

The Import Function

The import function shows how expenditure on imports (at constant prices) varies with changes in real national income. The slope of the import schedule ($\Delta M/\Delta Y$) is the marginal propensity to import (m). The average propensity to import (a) is the slope of the line from the origin (M/Y). The income elasticity of demand for imports η_m is m/a. In this figure, $a < m$.

The forgoing accounting relationships between national income and the balance of payments can be summarized as follows:

$$Y - E = S - I_d = X - M = I_f \tag{7.14}$$

The Import Function

The relationship between imports and national income should now be spelled out more fully. Analysis of the import function (M) is much like that of the consumption function. A change in imports (ΔM_t) is related to the change in real income from the previous period (ΔY_{t-1}) by the coefficient of the marginal propensity to import (m), so that

$$\Delta M_t = m\,(\Delta Y_{t-1}) \tag{7.15}$$

The functional relationship between imports and income can be depicted as in Figure 7.3. Whereas $m = \Delta M/\Delta Y$ (the slope of the M function in Figure 7.3), the average propensity to import (a) is M/Y (the slope of a line from the origin to the M function in Figure 7.3). The marginal propensity to import is assumed to be constant at all levels of income, but the average propensity varies according to the level of income.

The income-elasticity of demand for imports (η_y) is measured by the proportional change in imports over the proportional change in income, or

$$\eta_y = \frac{\Delta M / M}{\Delta Y / Y}$$

which is equivalent to m/a.

A country's income-elasticity of demand for imports may be greater than unity, even if it has a low m, provided that its a is even lower than its m. Empirical studies of the U.S. demand for imports conclude that the income-elasticity of demand for imports by the United States is greater than unity for this reason.[3] If Y falls by 5% in the United States, then the American demand for imports falls by more than 5%. To the rest of the world that exports to the United States, it is therefore all-important that the American economy stabilize its income at a high level. Otherwise the impact of a recession in national income in the United States is magnified on the exports of other countries.

Because countries have different income-elasticities of demand for imports, their trade balances will have different proportionate changes as their incomes vary over the business cycle, even if the income variations are proportionately the same. A country that has a higher income-elasticity of demand for imports than its trading partners will experience a deficit, even if all the countries were growing at the same rate. In contrast, if the country's income-elasticity of demand for imports is low relative to the income-elasticities of the countries to which it exports, the country would run a surplus if all incomes expanded at the same rate. If countries had the same income-elasticities, but one country's income grew more rapidly than incomes of the other countries, then that country would tend toward a deficit. The mechanism by which business fluctuations are propagated internationally is explained more fully in the Appendix to this chapter.

The Foreign Trade Multiplier

If we now rewrite the equation (7.7) for an open economy, it becomes

$$Y = C + I + G + X - M \pm (D + U) \qquad (7.16)$$

To consolidate, let C, I, G, and X now be net of any import content, and let X include $+D$ and $+U$. We may then write equation (7.16) as

$$Y = C + I + G + X \qquad (7.17)$$

[3]H.S. Houthakker and S.P. Magee, "Income and Price Elasticities in World Trade," *Review of Economics and Statistics*, 51 (May 1969), 111–25.

Equation (7.8) then becomes

$$\Delta Y = \frac{1}{1 - c} \ (\Delta I + \Delta G + \Delta X), \tag{7.18}$$

where $1/(1-c) = 1/(s + m)$, since now $c + s + m = 1$ (out of every dollar of disposable income, the only possible allocations are to consumption, savings, or imports).

It also follows that if there is now a positive ΔI or ΔG or ΔX, then income will rise to a new higher equilibrium level (Y_e), and at this level, $\Delta S^* + \Delta T + \Delta M = \Delta I + \Delta G + \Delta X$. At levels of $Y < Y_e$, $I + G + X > S^* + T + M$, and Y rises. At levels of $Y > Y_e$, $S^* + T + M > I + G + X$, and Y falls.

It will be noted that in the operation of the foreign trade multiplier, X acts as "injections" in the income stream, analogous to I and G. Imports, however, act as "leakages" from the income stream, analogous to S^* and T. The basic principle underlying the working-out of the foreign trade multiplier is that if the injections of $I + G + X$ initially are greater than the leakages $S^* + T + M$, then Y will rise; but as it rises, the higher level of Y induces more saving, tax revenue, and imports—until finally Y has risen to such a high level that the amount of $S^* + T + M$ now equals the amount of $I + G + X$, and Y is then at its new higher equilibrium level of Y_e.

If initially $S^* + T + M > I + G + X$, the process operates in reverse, with Y falling, and the value of $S^* + T + M$ becoming lower as Y falls until the leakages are no longer excessive, and the new lower Y_e is reached.

The working-out of the multiplier over time can be seen in detail in the Appendix to this chapter. A dynamic sequence analysis is presented there, but within the text we shall simply reason as if the multiplier acted instantaneously and calculate via equation (7.18) the final equilibrium level of income.[4]

Alternatively, we may consider the foreign trade multiplier in diagrammatic terms as in Figure 7.4. This Figure amends Figure 7.2 by including an import function (M) and exports (X). Exports are assumed to be independent of the level of Y, but imports are a function of Y, and the propensity to import behaves as in Figure 7.3. If initially the

---

[4]This is what Keynes referred to as the "logical theory of the multiplier." It is all we need for present purposes. To avoid, however, simply treating the multiplier as an algebraic formula and to understand instead the economic reasoning underlying it, the reader is referred to the Appendix to this chapter.

Figure 7.4

The Foreign Trade Multiplier with Increase in Exports

The initial equilibrium level of income is Y_o, where $I + X = S^* + M$. Given an increase in exports ($+\Delta X$), and given the M and S^* functions, the $+\Delta X$ is multiplied, and Y rises from Y_o to Y_e. At the new higher Y_e, the higher levels of $I + X$ equal the higher levels of $S^* + M$. But $S^* > I$, and $X > M$ by the amount $\overline{ab}$. The country has a trade surplus equal to $X - M = I_f$.

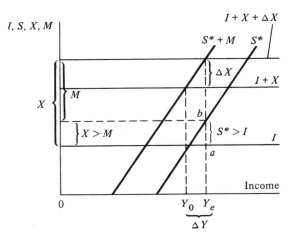

equilibrium level of income is at Y_o, with $I + X = S^* + M$, and now we allow for an increase in X of $+\Delta X$, then Y rises to the new equilibrium level of income at Y_e. At Y_e, $I + X + \Delta X$ are again equal to the higher level of $S^* + M$ that has been induced by the rise in income as a result of the initial increase in exports.

Adjustment through Income Changes

Let us now ask whether changes in a country's level of national income can alone restore equilibrium in its balance of trade. Assume a private economy with no G or T, and suppose that the value of exports initially equals the value of imports. But now the value of exports rises by 100 and remains at this new higher level (for some autonomous reason such as a change in foreign tastes or income in foreign countries). Let $m = 0.4$ and $s = 0.0$. What then will be the final balance of payments result?

We know that the $+\Delta X$ will raise Y, and we also know that imports will increase as income rises. But will the ΔM be sufficient through changes in only income to offset the ΔX and re-equilibrate the balance of payments without the need for price changes?

In this case, the $\Delta Y = (1/0.4)(100) = 250$. And with a $+\Delta Y$ of 250, there is an increase of imports of 100 [$\Delta M = m(\Delta Y) = 0.4(250)$], which exactly offsets the initial ΔX of 100. The rise in income, inducing M, has alone been sufficient to restore balance of trade equilibrium. But note the special condition that $s = 0.0$. In this case, it is

FRITZ MACHLUP, *International Trade and the National Income Multiplier* (1943), 214

If people insist on "deriving" positive policy recommendations from economic theories however incomplete—a practice which this writer has no wish to encourge—they might at least be sensible enough to turn from destructive commercial policy to more constructive "applications" of multiplier theory in international trade matters. For example, the case of parallel expansion in the major countries of the world may, under certain circumstances, have much to be said for it. I believe, however, that it is the case of capital export from countries with abundant capital supply to countries with meagre capital supply which is probably the most significant "lesson" from our analysis. . . .

An autonomous capital export . . . need not cause a reduction of primary disbursements in the lending country if the supply of capital in the country is large and if its money market is in a liquid position. An autonomous capital import, on the other hand, in a country with scarce supply and urgent demand for funds, is very likely to produce there a brisk expansion of disbursements. As a result, both nations will have their incomes increased, the borrowing country in consequence of the increased investment activity, the lending country in consequence of the increased export business.

---

because the only leakage in the system is imports that Y is allowed to rise sufficiently to induce enough M to cover the initial rise in X.

If there had been in addition a saving leakage ($s > 0.0$), then Y would not have risen by as much as 250, and the $+ \Delta M$ would be less than the initial $+ \Delta X$, and a balance of payments surplus woul' remain.

This is the result in Figure 7.4 when there is an increase in exports, but the saving function is positive. At the new Y_e, there is an excess of planned saving over planned investment ($S^* > I$) in the amount $\overline{ab}$, and exports exceed imports by the same amount $\overline{ab}$. The country is then engaged in foreign investing, so that saving equals total investment (domestic plus foreign investment).

This second case, allowing for a positive propensity to save, can be illustrated as follows: Let $\Delta X = 100$, $m = 0.3$, and $s = 0.2$. The ΔY is then $\Delta Y = (1/0.5)(100) = 200$. But the $\Delta M = 0.3 (200) = 60$. The increase in exports exceeds the increase in imports by 40. At the same time, the $\Delta S^* = s (\Delta Y) = 0.2 (200) = 40$. In the equation

$\Delta S^* + \Delta M = \Delta I + \Delta X$ (we have abstracted from the government sector in this case), the values at the new higher Y_e are $40 + 60 = 0 + 100$. A new equilibrium level of national income is reached, but the balance of payments cannot be re-equilibrated by only income changes. Some additional price changes would be necessary to increase imports further. The leakage of ΔS^* has prevented Y from rising sufficiently to induce an increase in imports equal to the initial increase in exports. Income changes have been sufficiently strong to remove only part of the initial balance of payments surplus. To remove the surplus completely, relative price changes are also needed (a rise in prices of exports and domestic import-competing goods relative to import prices).

The last case is of interest in indicating again that national income may be in equilibrium without the balance of payments being in equilibrium. At the new Y_e, it is significant that $S^* > I$ and $X > M$. This represents the case of a country engaged in foreign investment: **the excess of domestic saving over domestic investment is in effect being made available to foreigners through the export surplus in the balance of payments. The capital is being transferred in real terms in the form of the export surplus, and the export surplus is financed by a capital outflow.**

Consider yet another case. Let Y initially be in equilibrium with $I = S$ and $X = M$. But then allow the country's level of domestic investment to increase by $\Delta I = 100$. Assume $s = 0.1$ and $m = 0.4$. The $\Delta Y = (1/0.5)(100) = 200$. The new $Y_e = Y_o + 200$. At the new Y_e, $\Delta S^* = 0.1(200) = 20$, and $\Delta M = 0.4(200) = 80$. Again, Y_e will be an equilibrium level of national income because $\Delta I + \Delta X = \Delta S^* + \Delta M$ or $100 + 0 = 20 + 80$. But in this case, **planned investment exceeds savings** by 80, and **imports exceed exports** by the same amount. The country is engaged **in foreign borrowing** to support the balance of payments deficit or else is losing reserves in order to finance the deficit.

Cost of Adjustment through Income Changes

If a country has a deficit in its balance of payments and relies on a decline in income as a corrective process, the cost can be sizable. The decline in income is itself a cost that governments will want to avoid, unless the prior situation is one of inflation, and only disinflation— short of deflation—ensues. If, for example, there should be an autonomous fall in exports by say $-\Delta X = 100$ and $m = 0.4$ and $s = 0.1$, then the reduction in income will be $-\Delta Y = (1/0.5)(100) = 200$. As income falls, so too will imports. But the decline in imports is only $\Delta M = 0.4\ (200) = 80$. In this case, imports remain greater than exports by 20 even after the fall in national income. To restore balance of payments equilibrium through only income changes, another round of deflation would then be necessary. The country would then have to endure the costs of a tight money policy or an increase in taxes or decrease in government expenditure in order to reduce income and imports further.

Beyond the decline in income itself, the cost of adjustment through income changes may be aggravated if wages, costs, and prices are rigid downward, so that the deflation produces unemployment. The effects on employment and output are especially deleterious. Except in the inflationary situation, the removal of a balance of payments deficit through monetary and fiscal restraints will force the country to depart from the objective of internal balance. The country's domestic economic autonomy will have to be sacrificed.

The cost of adjustment via changes in aggregate demand will tend to be greater, the larger the economic size of the country. For in a larger country, foreign trade is likely to be a smaller part of national income, and it is therefore likely to require a larger absolute decline in aggregate demand to achieve a given absolute change in imports.

Beyond the cost to the deficit country, adjustment through deflation will reduce the exports of other countries to the deflating country, and this spreads the deflationary process overseas. The volume of world trade is thus contracted, and a deflationary bias is imparted to the world economy when deficit countries must deflate, and surplus countries avoid inflation by sterilization policies.

Although adjustment through income changes will have its costs, so too will any other remedial policy. A choice among alternative policies must therefore be undertaken according to their respective welfare costs. And the proper mix of policies must also be determined. To approach a more general theory of balance of payments policy, we should now allow for some other forces that we have not yet considered—namely, the role of monetary factors and capital flows. This consideration will extend our analysis from this chapter's emphasis on real factors under simple Keynesian assumptions to the recognition, in Chapter 8, of capital movements and monetary-portfolio factors. We can then undertake a synthesis of real and monetary factors in the adjustment process.

Supplementary Readings

The following articles are useful and contain numerous references to the literature: S.S. Alexander, "Effects of a Devaluation on a Trade Balance," *IMF Staff Papers*, 2 (April 1952), 263–78; F. Machlup, "Relative Prices and Aggregate Spending in the Analysis of Devaluation," *American Economic Review*, 45 (June 1955), 255–78; S.S. Alexander, "Effects of a Devaluation: A Simplified Synthesis of Elasticities and Absorption Approaches," *American Economic Review*, 49 (March 1959), 22–42; T.C. Tsiang, "The Role of Money in Trade-Balance Stability: Synthesis of the Elasticity and Absorption Approaches," *American Economic Review*, 51 (Dec. 1961), 912–36; and L.B. Yeager, "Absorption and Elasticity: A Fuller Reconsideration," *Economica*, 37 (Feb. 1970), 68–77.

Classic references are: F. Machlup, *International Trade and the National Income Multiplier* (1943); J.E. Meade, *The Theory of International Economic Policy, vol. I. The Balance of Payments* (1951).

APPENDIX
Foreign Trade Multiplier Analysis

This Appendix extends the simple (instantaneous) multiplier analysis to incorporate a dynamic sequence process of change over time, foreign repercussions, and the international transmission of economic fluctuations.[1]

The Dynamic Multiplier Process

A sequence analysis can trace the changes in the determinants of national income over time. To do this, we recognize that expenditures lag behind the receipt of income. The length of the lag is an empirical question: for profit recipients, the lag may be over a year, whereas for wage earners it may be a short period of weeks, with perhaps an average for the economy of three months.

Let the consumption function be expressed as

$$C_t = C_o + cY_{t-1}, \tag{7.19}$$

where c_o and c are constants with $0 < c < 1$.

The import function may be expressed as

$$M_t = M_0 + mY_{t-1}, \tag{7.20}$$

where M_0 and m are constants with $0 < m < 1$.

Further, the marginal propensities to consume domestic goods (c), save (s), and import (m) must equal unity:

$$c + s + m = 1 \tag{7.21}$$

Therefore,

$$c = 1 - (s + m) \tag{7.22}$$

We may now note how the level of national income (Y) will change in response to an autonomous disturbance—for example, an increase in exports (X). Let $+ \Delta X = 100$, and assume X remains at this new higher level. Let $s = 0.2$ and $m = 0.3$. As a result of the $+ \Delta X$, income will rise to a new higher level of Y. Using the formula for the foreign trade multiplier, $\Delta Y = [1/(s + m)] (\Delta X) = [1/(0.2 + 0.3)] (100) = 200$. This is the final result of the multiplier "working itself out." This, however, will take time—the length of time being dependent on the income-expenditure lag. Table 7.1 illustrates the sequence of income change over time. At time t, $+ \Delta X = 100$. As a result $\Delta C_{t+1} = 50$ and $\Delta Y_{t+1} = 150$. In period $t + 2$, $\Delta C = 75$ and $\Delta Y = 175$. Note that in each period of time the $+\Delta Y = [(\Delta X + \Delta I) -$

[1]For a pioneering and detailed study of the foreign trade multiplier, see Fritz Machlup, *International Trade and the National Income Multiplier* (1943).

Table 7.1. The Dynamic Multiplier Process Effects Over Time of an Autonomous Increase in Exports

If $s = 0.2$; $m = 0.3$; $+ \Delta X = 100$; $\Delta Y = ?$; and $\Delta M = ?$

			Period			
Variable	t	$t + 1$	$t + 2$	$t + 3$	. . . Limit	
ΔC	0	50	75	87.5	100	100
$+ \Delta I$	0	0	0	0	0	0
$+ \Delta X$	100	100	100	100	100	100
$= \Delta Y$	100	150	175	187.5	200	200

Derivations						
$\Delta C_t = C \Delta Y_{t-1}$		50	75	87.5	100	100
$\Delta M_t = m \Delta Y_{t-1}$		30	45	52.5	60	60
$\Delta S^*_t = \Delta Y_{t-1} - (\Delta C_t + \Delta M_t)$						
$= s\,(\Delta Y_{t-1})$		20	30	35	40	40
$\Delta S_t = \Delta Y_t - (\Delta C_t + \Delta M_t)$		70	55	47.5	40	40
$\Delta X_t - \Delta M_t$		70	55	47.5	40	40

$(\Delta S^* + \Delta M)$]. Thus, in period $t + 1$, $\Delta X + \Delta I = 100$, $\Delta M + \Delta S^* = 30 + 20 = 50$, and the ΔY between t and $t + 1$ is $150 - 100 = 50$.

The actual savings $\Delta S_t = \Delta Y_t - (\Delta C_t + \Delta M_t)$. Recall the equilibrium condition: $X + I = M + S$. It follows that $X - M = S - I$, and $\Delta X - \Delta M = \Delta S - \Delta I$. Thus, in period $t + 1$, $\Delta X - \Delta M = 70$ and $\Delta S - \Delta I = 70$. But actual saving is greater than intended saving ($\Delta S > \Delta S^*$) by 50, and the $+ \Delta C = 50$, resulting in $+ \Delta Y = 150$ in $t + 1$. In period $t + 2$, $+ \Delta S^*$ rises to 30, but ΔS is still greater than ΔS^* by 25, and the ΔC between $t + 1$ and $t + 2$ is $75 - 50 = 25$. As Y rises in each period, so too do the leakages S^* and M. Finally, at the limit, the $\Delta M + \Delta S^* = 60 + 40 = \Delta X + \Delta I = 100$.

Note the extent to which the multiplier has "worked itself out" by period $t + 3$. If the income-expenditure lag is three months, then most of the multiplier effect will be realized in nine months. But Y will still continue to increase as long as the injection of ΔX exceeds the leakages $\Delta S^* + \Delta M$.

At the final equilibrium level of Y, $\Delta S > \Delta I = \Delta X > \Delta M$ ($40 > 0 = 100 > 60$). The country has a trade surplus equal to its foreign investment ($\Delta X - \Delta M = \Delta I_f$).

The Complete Multiplier: Foreign Repercussions

The simple multiplier should also be extended to allow for foreign repercussions—that is, the change in income in one country is transmitted abroad through the induced change in its imports (the exports of the second country), and this will have, in turn, an effect on the first country.

Let the exports of country A be a function of income of country B, and the exports of country B be a function of income of country A. If exports of A increase, the income of B decreases as its imports increase, and the induced exports of A then fall. (This assumes that A's exports are at the expense of B's consumption of its domestic ouput—that is, the increase in B's import demand is not financed by credit expansion). The multiplier for country A (k_A) is then

$$k_A = \frac{1}{s_A + m_A + m_B (s_A/s_B)} \tag{7.23}$$

where s_A is the marginal propensity to save in country A, m_A, the marginal propensity to import in A, and $m_B (s_A/s_B)$,[2] the foreign repercussion. The multiplier will therefore be larger, the smaller the leakages s_A and m_A, the lower m_B, and the higher s_B. In contrast, the larger m_B, the greater will be the fall in B's imports following the reduction in B's income as a result of the increase in exports from A (increase in imports into B), and the smaller the foreign trade multiplier for A as a result of the greater foreign repercussions leakage to A.

International Transmission of Economic Fluctuations

The process by which a change in income in one country is tramsmitted to another country can be illustrated in a variety of cases. If country A is initially at a full employment level of income, with balance of payments equilibrium, and then investment decreases, the sequence is as depicted in Table 7.2.

The initial fall in investment in country A leads to a decline in income and a fall in imports in A. This results, in turn, in a decrease in exports from country B, and a decline in income and imports in B. After the transmission process is completed, world income (the combined incomes of A and B) will have declined by 200. The greater decline in income will be in A because the initial decline in investment in A is greater than the initial decline in exports in B. Each country is in balance of payments disequilibrium at the new equilibrium level of income. In country A, the decline in $I + X$ is $40 + 13\frac{1}{3}$, which equals the decline in $S + M$, which is $26\frac{2}{3} + 26\frac{2}{3}$. In country A, saving exceeds investment, and exports are greater than imports. In country B, investment exceeds saving, and imports are greater than exports.

Consider a second case with different marginal propensities to save and import, as in Table 7.3. The decline in world income is now the same as in the first case, but the fall in income of country A is greater than in the first case, whereas the decline in income of country B is less. At the new equilib-

[2] For derivation of the foreign trade multiplier with foreign repercussion, see Robert M. Stern, *The Balance of Payments* (1973), 175–85.

Table 7.2

Let ↓I = 40 in country A; s_A = 0.2; m_A = 0.2; s_B = 0.2; and m_B = 0.2

Period	↓I	Country A			Country B		
		↓X	↓Y	↓M	↓X	↓Y	↓M
1	40		100	20	20	50	10
2		10	25	5	5	$12\frac{1}{2}$	$2\frac{1}{2}$
3		$2\frac{1}{2}$	$6\frac{1}{4}$	$1\frac{1}{4}$	$1\frac{1}{4}$	$3\frac{1}{8}$	$\frac{5}{8}$
⋮		⋮	⋮	⋮	⋮	⋮	⋮
Limit		$13\frac{1}{3}$	$133\frac{1}{3}$	$26\frac{2}{3}$	$26\frac{2}{3}$	$66\frac{2}{3}$	$13\frac{1}{3}$

Table 7.3

Let ↓I = 40 in A; s_A = 0.2; m_A = 0.1; s_B = 0.2; and m_B = 0.3

Period	↓I	Country A			Country B		
		↓X	↓Y	↓M	↓X	↓Y	↓M
1	40		$133\frac{1}{3}$	$13\frac{1}{3}$	$13\frac{1}{3}$	$26\frac{2}{3}$	8
2		8	$26\frac{2}{3}$	$2\frac{2}{3}$	$2\frac{2}{3}$	$5\frac{1}{3}$	$1\frac{3}{5}$
3		$1\frac{3}{5}$	$5\frac{1}{3}$	$\frac{8}{15}$	$\frac{8}{15}$	$1\frac{1}{15}$	$\frac{1}{5}$
Limit		10	$166\frac{2}{3}$	$16\frac{2}{3}$	$16\frac{2}{3}$	$33\frac{1}{3}$	10

rium level of income, there is again a balance of payments disequilibrium in each country, but the size of the disequilibrium is less.

If other cases were considered, it would be seen that the multiplier is lower and hence the decline in income is less, the greater the marginal propensities to save and import. The larger the marginal propensity to import in the country with the initial fall in income, the greater the decline in income abroad.

8

Money and Asset Markets

More economists are now incorporating monetary considerations in their analysis of the determinants of the exchange rate. This represents a revival of a monetary view, or more generally an asset view, of the role of exchange rates. The monetary approach to the exchange rate is related to the monetary approach to the balance of payments. These approaches emphasize the **role of money and other assets** in determining the balance of payments under pegged exchange rates and in determining the exchange rate under freely flexible rates.[1]

The first section outlines the monetary approach to the balance of payments under fixed exchange rates. Now that exchange rates are floating, and financial capital movements are of large volume, an asset-market or portfolio-balance approach to exchange-rate determination has become more popular, as the second section indicates. A variety of forces that determine income in an open economy are combined in the third section, which presents an "*IS-LM-BP*" model. Finally, the last section synthesizes price and income effects and shows the complementarity of the elasticities, absorption, and monetary approaches.

The Monetary Approach

The monetary approach has recently been formulated—or more precisely, rediscovered from classical writers—as another interpretation of balance of payments adjustment, with policy implications that are both

[1] See, for instance, Jacob A. Frenkel and Harry G. Johnson (eds.), *The Economics of Exchange Rates* (1978); studies by other proponents are included in the Supplementary Readings.

similar to and distinct from the elasticities and multiplier approaches we have examined. The classical explanation of the adjustment mechanism was based long ago (1752) on David Hume's "price-specie-flow mechanism." According to this theory, an increase in the quantity of money in a country would raise domestic prices, thereby causing exports to fall and imports to rise. An expansion of issue of paper-currency substitutes for precious metals would lead merely to an outflow of precious metals. This would then cause the money supply and domestic prices to fall. In the surplus country, the gold inflow would cause an expansion in the money supply and a rise in prices. Equilibrium would then be restored through the price changes. The stock of international money would tend automatically to be so distributed among nations that each would have the quantity it demanded, consistent with international equilibrium. A corollary of Hume's analysis is the assertion that there is a "natural distribution" of the world money or reserve stock among the member countries of the world system toward which the actual distribution will gravitate.[2]

In propounding the modern monetarist approach to balance of payments theory, Johnson has observed how Hume's account is unsatisfactory in two respects. First, it fails to bring out clearly that it is the expenditure of **unwanted cash balances** (currency plus bank deposits) that leads to the import surplus and the corresponding gold flow and that it is the **adjustment of actual to desired cash balances,** through the combination of international redistribution of money and reduction of its purchasing power by rising prices, that eventually restores equilibrium. Second, in deducing the movement of prices involved in the adjustment process from a mechanical application of the quantity theory of money, Hume concentrated on the trade account as the locus of adjustment to international monetary disturbances to the neglect of financial capital movements (securities), and the analysis exaggerated the necessity of international money flows in the adjustment process.

The new monetary approach is a restatement of this classical tradition of international monetary theory, but is improved by the incorporation of modern concepts of **stock-flow adjustments** in monetary equilibrium processes. The emphasis is now not on relative price changes, but on the direct influence of excess demand for or supply of money on the balance between income and expenditure or more generally through

---

[2]Cf. Harry G. Johnson, "International Trade: Theory," *International Encyclopedia of the Social Sciences,* 8 (1968), 91–92, and Johnson, *Money, Balance of Payments Theory, and the International Monetary Problem,* Princeton Essays in International Finance, No. 124 (Nov. 1977), 3–5.

DAVID HUME, "Of the Balance of Trade" in *Political Discourses* (1752) in *Essays, Moral, Political and Literary* (1875 ed., I), 333–34

Suppose four-fifths of all the money in Great Britain to be annihilated in one night, and the nation reduced to the same condition, with regard to specie, as in the reigns of the Harrys and Edwards, what would be the consequence? Must not the price of all labour and commodities sink in proportion, and everything be sold as cheap as they were in those ages? What nation could then dispute with us in any foreign market, or pretend to navigate or to sell manufactures at the same price, which to us would afford sufficient profit? In how little time, therefore, must this bring back the money which we had lost, and raise us to the level of all the neighboring nations? Where, after we have arrived, we immediately lose the advantage of the cheapness of labour and commodities; and the farther flowing in of money is stopped by our fulness and repletion.

Again, suppose, that all the money of Great Britain were multiplied fivefold in a night, must not the contrary effect follow? Must not all labour and commodities rise to such an exorbitant height, that no neighboring nations could afford to buy from us; while their commodities, on the other hand, became comparatively so cheap, that, in spite of all the laws which could be formed, they would be run in upon us, and our money flow out; till we fall to a level with foreigners, and lose that great superiority of riches, which had laid us under such disadvantages?

Now, it is evident, that the same causes, which would correct these exorbitant inequalities, were they to happen miraculously, must prevent their happening in the common course of nature, and must for ever, in all neighboring nations, preserve money nearly proportionable to the art and industry of each nation.

---

production and consumption of goods or through borrowing and lending of assets. The emphasis is thereby on the **overall balance of payments,** not merely the balance of trade. It is also argued that the impact of the balance of payments on the domestic economy is via the **impact on the money supply.**

Proponents of the monetary approach view the balance of payments as in essence a **monetary phenomenon.**[3] The analysis is founded on

[3]This section relies on Johnson, *ibid.;* Johnson, "The Monetary Approach to Balance of Payments Theory and Policy," *Economica,* 44 (Aug. 1977), 217–30; and W.M. Corden, *Inflation, Exchange Rates and the World Economy* (1977).

Report of the Bullion Committee of 1810, in E. CANNAN, *The Paper Pound of 1797–1821,*
A Reprint of the Bullion Report (2nd ed., 1925), 17

> . . . in the event of the prices of commodities being raised in one
> country by an augmentation of its circulating medium, while no similar
> augmentation in the circulating medium of a neighbouring country has
> led to a similar rise in prices, the currencies of those two countries will
> no longer continue to bear the same relative value to each other as
> before. The intrinsic value of . . . the one currency being lessened,
> while that of the other remains unaltered, the Exchange will be . . . to
> the disadvantage of the former.

two fundamental points: (i) the tautology that changes in the domestic
money supply may be brought about either through changes in the
volume of domestic credit or through international exchanges of international reserve money for goods or securities; and (ii) the proposition
that a balance of payments deficit or surplus is a monetary phenomenon
representing a process of adjustment of actual to desired **stocks** of
money. The adjustment process cannot therefore be appropriately
treated as a permanent flow phenomenon representable as the residual of
inflows and outflows of expenditure on goods governed by relative
prices and incomes, as in the elasticities and absorption approaches.
Instead, contemporary theories of short-run equilibrium in exchange
markets and money markets determine interest rates and exchange rates
from conditions of **stock equilibrium**: the rates must move to levels
that will induce holders of domestic and foreign securities and of foreign and domestic currency to be willing to hold the existing stocks of
these various assets.[4]

Monetarists define a balance of payments deficit as being equal to an
excess-flow supply of money: the deficit is equal to the **excess of
domestic credit creation** (extra supply) over the increased demand for
cash balances (extra demand). The behavioral relationships involve the
stock demand for money as a stable function of income and the rate of
interest and wealth, such that the demand for money (cash balances)
increases as income rises and falls as the rate of interest rises (individuals

[4]This analysis underlies a study of recent policies in several countries: Stanley W. Black,
Floating Exchange Rates and National Economic Policy (1977).

change the composition of their portfolios from holding cash balances to purchase of securities).

When individuals believe that their cash balances are too large relative to their holdings of real goods and services, they will spend their **excessive money holdings** on goods, services, and securities—foreign and domestic. This leads to an **outflow of funds,** or adjustments in domestic rates, prices, and GNP. The difference between the demand for and supply of money of domestic origin is reflected in the "money account" of the balance of payments—that is, the change in international reserves or settlement items below the line. If excess supply of money is the proximate cause of the balance of payments problem, then the supply of money is the strategic policy variable that should be regulated.

In a fixed exchange-rate system, an excess demand for money can be supplied either by the acquisition of international reserve assets through a balance of payments surplus or through the domestic credit creation by the domestic central bank. The policy implication is that no policy for improving the balance of payments can be successful unless supported by an appropriate **restriction of dometic credit,** or by a policy that changes money demand (through a change in interest or income) so that people willingly hold the additional money supply.

Further, the balance of payments deficit or surplus represents a transient stock-adjustment process evoked by an initial inequality of desired and actual money stocks. In the language of the absorption approach, an excess of absorption over income now means either that cash balances are being run down or that new credit is being created to the extent of the balance of trade deficit. When cash balances are being run down, the public is making a portfolio adjustment: they are reducing their stock of money and increasing their stocks of goods and services or asset holdings. The rundown in domestic deposits causes an equivalent rundown in foreign exchange. An expenditure of unwanted cash balances leads to the import surplus. The adjustment of actual to desired cash balances, through the combination of **international redistribution of money** and reduction of its purchasing power by rising prices, eventually completes the **portfolio adjustment** and restores equilibrium.

In this explanation of the adjustment process, the monetary approach to balance of payments theory emphasizes that the demand for money is a **stock demand,** that stock disequilibria will be transient and remedied by accumulation or decumulation of stocks, and that the transient flows of international money to which they give rise will be re-

HARRY G. JOHNSON, *Money, Balance-of-Payments Theory, and the International Monetary Problem,* Princeton Essays in International Finance, No. 124 (Nov. 1977), 2–3, 6

Why do policy-makers and their professional economic advisors, who should know better, consistently retreat into "real" analyses of and solutions for monetary problems? I can offer only a brief sketch of an answer here: The "real" world is familiar, and identical with the "monetary" world as long as the price level is reasonably stable; everyone lives his normal life in a partial-equilibrium context in which money price changes are also real price changes. The "money" world of monetary macro-equilibrium and disequilibrium is by contrast unfamiliar and strange. Few people indeed possess either a systematic concept of the economy as a whole, as distinct from their own small corner of it, or the imagination to recognize what seem like "real" changes with "real" causes as being in reality monetary changes with monetary causes. . . .

Hence it requires a great deal of sophistication to treat money as a stock requiring application of stock-flow adjustment mechanisms. It is not surprising that even great monetary theorists like Wicksell and Keynes have found it more congenial to treat monetary adjustments proximately in terms of income-expenditure flow relationships motivated by the fixing of a disequilibrium relative price (the interest rate) through monetary policy, while politicians and the public prefer to attribute balance-of-payments deficits to prices being too high, businessmen and workers too lazy, or governments too spendthrift with the taxpayers' money.

placed by alterations in international flows of goods or securities. The stock-flow problems are analyzed in terms of portfolio choice theory, with **portfolio equilibrium** requiring that all stocks of money, securities, and goods are willingly held at the prevailing prices, incomes, and level of wealth.

A deficit or surplus therefore represents a reserve flow, and the only solutions to these reserve flows are processes that bring actual money balances to their desired levels. This adjustment can be accomplished automatically through the impact of reserve flows on portfolio changes or through appropriate monetary policies by the domestic monetary authorities.

A balance of payments deficit reflects a condition of excessive domestic money in circulation. Domestic firms and individuals are exchanging their excess holdings of money for foreign goods or securities. If the exchange rate is to be maintained, the central banks will then have to eliminate this excess supply of domestic currency by selling exchange reserves and buying the domestic currency, thereby withdrawing domestic currency from circulation.

In contrast, if the domestic money supply is not growing sufficiently rapidly to satisfy the existing demand for domestic money at the given exchange rate, the balance of payments will go into surplus. Individuals and firms will acquire the domestic currency by becoming net sellers of goods and securities to foreigners. The government can prevent its currency from appreciating by having an official exchange stabilization fund purchase the excess foreign currency from domestic nationals in return for domestic currency—thereby relieving the shortage of domestic currency while preventing appreciation. A domestic money supply operation is therefore always the dual of a purchase or sale of foreign exchange.

Under a system of freely floating exchange rates, depreciation can reequilibrate the balance of payments by reducing the real stock of money if fiscal and monetary policies maintain constancy in the level of money expenditure while the average domestic price level rises as a result of depreciation. When there is a disparity between the supply of and demand for money, the correction under floating exchange rates will be through depreciation of the country's currency, just as money account deficits occur with fixed exchange rates. The excess supply of money will result in an increase in the demand for domestically supplied real and financial assets as well as for foreign exchange in order to buy foreign supplies of real and financial assets. All prices, including the price of foreign exchange, will therefore rise. As depreciation lowers the real value of money and financial assets denominated in local currency, it will remove the excessive liquidity in individuals' asset portfolios. Individuals will increase their demand for money as they attempt to maintain the real value of that proportion of their wealth that they want to hold in the form of money balances.

Under freely floating rates, there are no intercountry movements of international reserves; but the required adjustments in actual money balances to their desired levels is accomplished by the changes in domestic prices and exchange rates. Thus, the original disparity between the demand for and supply of money will be corrected via a rise in domestic prices and a depreciation of the domestic currency that raises import-goods prices. This fits with the absorption approach insofar as absorption in real terms will fall as individuals—when faced with a lower real money supply (money supply corrected for price increase)—try to reconstitute their cash balances, and their expenditures will run below their incomes. A depreciation of the country's currency is therefore the equivalent of a reduction in the volume of domestic credit.

Financial Capital Movements

An essential feature of the monetary approach is its recognition that adjustment of desired stocks to actual stocks of international money may occur through either the trade account or the capital account or both. A current account deficit may reflect the community's desire to shift out of cash balances into stocks of goods, whereas a capital account deficit may reflect a decision to shift out of domestic money into securities. Instead of concentrating only on the adjustment mechanism through changes in the trade balance, the monetary approach emphasizes the role of private capital flows, especially the securities-portfolio stock adjustments that occur in response to international interest-rate differentials. If, for example, domestic credit expansion leads to excessive cash balances and hence to an increase in absorption, the rate of interest will fall. The increase in absorption will lead to a current account deficit. But now, with the lower rate of interest, some of the extra cash balances may also be transformed into foreign claims—securities, bonds, and bills—in an attempt to maintain a portfolio balance between cash and claims. Wealth holders will change their desired asset holdings according to the levels of interest rates and exchange rates and size of portfolio. Individuals and institutional investors will balance their portfolio holdings according to their estimates of expected rates of return on various assets and their degree of aversion to risk. The changes in portfolio balance will lead to financial capital movements. The import of claims, or export of capital, will also lead to a deficit on capital account. To stop the resultant outflow of foreign exchange reserves under fixed exchange rates, or a depreciation of the home currency under flexible rates, the domestic credit creation has to cease. In conformity with the monetary approach, the balance of payments is thus a monetary and not a real phenomenon, and a deficit can be corrected by only monetary means.

Financial or portfolio capital flows are sensitive to both the interest

EDWIN CANNAN, "The Application of the Theoretical Apparatus of Supply and Demand to Units of Currency," *Economic Journal,* 31 (1921), 453–54

> We may consequently think of the supply [of currency] as we think of the supply of houses, as being a stock rather than the annual produce . . . [and] of the demand for currency as being furnished by the ability and willingness of persons to hold currency.

rate and the exchange rate.[5] The foreign demand for assets denominated in the currency of a given country will be determined by the expected yield on that country's assets relative to the expected yield on assets denominated in other currencies. This expected relative yield reflects the interest-rate differential between the home country and the foreign country and the expected movement in the exchange rate. Exchange rate risks and the risk preferences of speculators will determine the degree of substitutability between assets denominated in domestic currency and assets denominated in foreign currencies. The degree of substitutability will determine, in turn, the elasticity of demand for domestic-currency assets with respect to their expected relative yield.

The change in the demand for foreign assets during a given time period will depend on changes in the interest-rate differential and in the expected exchange-rate depreciation or appreciation. In determining his portfolio balance, a prospective lender of financial capital (purchaser of a foreign security) will estimate the range of possible yields on a foreign security after converting the payments of interest into his domestic currency, allowing for the possibility of depreciation in the foreign currency during the period until maturity of the security. To hedge against the risk of depreciation, the lender can buy forward "**cover**" on the **forward exchange market** against the risk that a future change in the exchange rate might affect the capital value of the investor's holdings of foreign assets. The forward market provides contracts of varying maturities for the future delivery of a currency. By selling his expected foreign exchange forward, the lender can be assured of the amount of domestic currency that will be received 30 or 90 or 180 days hence.

Considering the relative returns from a domestic security and a for-

[5]This section is based on Jacques R. Artus and Andrew D. Crockett, *Floating Exchange Rates and the Need for Surveillance,* Princeton Essays in International Finance, No. 127 (May 1978), 5–10.

eign security, an investor would find covered interest arbitrage profitable if the proportionally higher interest yield on a foreign security exceeds the proportional discount on the foreign currency in the forward exchange market. If the foreign currency on the forward exchange market is trading at a sufficiently high forward premium, it may still be profitable to invest in foreign securities even though the foreign rate of interest is below the domestic rate. Interest arbitrageurs and currency arbitrageurs operate on the differentials, engaging in transactions from a cheap market to a dear one. Besides arbitrageurs, there may be speculators on the forward markets, and these may drive the forward rate to a margin that is considerably different from what would have been determined by only the arbitrageurs.[6]

Based on the forgoing considerations, an increasing number of economists have recently propounded an **asset-market theory of exchange-rate determination.** This approach views the exchange rate as an asset price—the relative price at which the stock of money, bonds, and other financial and real assets of a country will be willingly held by domestic and foreign asset holders. Variability in the factors that influence expected rates of return or relative risk will therefore tend to result in variability of exchange rates in a regime of floating rates. Only when the actual stocks of domestic and foreign assets that are held are equal to the desired stocks will the current demand for and current supply of a currency establish a flow equilibrium. In a short period of time, the potential demand for a currency resulting from changes in desired stocks of financial assets can be large relative to the flow demand that arises from current account transactions. This is because prices in goods markets normally change more gradually, there are longer lags in the adjustment of commodity trade to price changes, and the expectational factors are not as prominent as they are for financial transactions.

Although the asset-market theory is primarily directed to the short-run determinants of the exchange rate, other forces operate to determine the longer-run equilibrium rate. Shifts in interest differentials and changes in risk preferences of participants in the foreign exchange markets can therefore lead to sizable movements in short-run exchange rates that are inconsistent with effective adjustment in the longer run. Perhaps the major value of recognizing the influence of financial capital flows and

[6]For an elaboration, see S.C. Tsiang, "The Theory of Forward Exhange and Effects of Government Intervention on the Forward Market," *IMF Staff Papers* (April 1959), 75–106, and Herbert G. Grubel, *Forward Exchange, Speculation, and the International Flow of Capital* (1966), Chap. 10.

portfolio changes is in devising policies of exchange-rate management to reduce the instability arising from the short-run asset-market-disturbances and to indicate policy action that can reduce the short-run variability from the appropriate level for longer-run equilibrium.

The asset-market approach is also mainly relevant for countries that have financially deep capital and money markets and an absence of exchange controls so as to permit substantial arbitrage between domestic and foreign assets. In countries with thin financial markets, or limited possibilities for arbitrage, the exchange rate will be determined slightly by financial capital flows, but mainly by supply and demand in goods markets (under freely floating rates) and the amount of official intervention in currency markets (under managed floating).

Money and Income in an Open Economy

Earlier parts of our analysis have established some relationships between saving, investment, interest, money, and national income, and also the balance of payments. As a summary device, we can incorporate all these relationships in a single diagram, commonly referred to as the **IS-LM-BP diagram.**[7] In Figure 8.1, the IS curve shows the various combinations of the interest rate and income levels that will make investment equal to saving. Investment will be greater with a lower rate of interest, and saving will increase with a higher level of income. The IS curve therefore slopes down to the right. The IS curve is drawn for a given level of exports and imports. "Investment" is therefore to be considered more generally as **injections** into the income stream—that is, domestic investment, exports, and government expenditure. 'Savings" are to be considered more generally as **leakages** from income—that is, savings, imports, and taxes. The IS curve is also drawn initially under the assumption of a given exchange rate.

The LM curve shows combinations of the interest rate and income levels that will make the demand for money or liquidity preference (L) equal to the supply of money (M). The real money supply is constant along a given LM curve, and it is assumed that the money supply is completely controlled by the central bank's monetary policy. (A net international flow of money can be "sterilized" and not allowed to affect the domestic money through open market operations and changes in

---

[7]The IS-LM analysis is explained in detail in macroeconomics texts: for example, Rudiger Dornbusch and Stanley Fischer, *Macro-Economics* (1978), Chaps. 4, 18, 19.

Figure 8.1

Income Determination in the Open Economy

Given the schedules that equate injections and leakages in the income stream at different levels of interest rates and income levels (*IS*), and the demand for and stock of money (*LM*) and the demand and supply of foreign exchange (*BP*), the equilibrium position of the economy is determined at *E*. At *E*, the interest rate is i_o and the level of income is Y_o. There is equilibrium in all three markets—domestic goods, assets, and foreign exchange.

If *I* then falls to the level *IS'*, a new equilibrium is established at *E'*. But *E'* is now to the left of *BP* = 0, indicating that there is a balance of payments surplus.

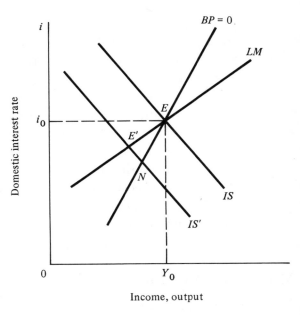

reserve requirements.) The *LM* curve is also drawn initially under the assumption that the exchange rate is given. The real demand for money to hold as cash balances depends on the transactions motive and the speculative motive. Transactions balances are related to the level of income, rising as income rises. Speculative balances are a function of the interest rate, falling when the rate of interest rises (the higher the interest rate, the more willing are investors to forgo a position of liquidity in favor of holding securities with higher yields). The *LM* curve slopes up to the right, indicating that financial markets are in equilibrium at lower levels of interest and income and at higher levels of interest and income. At lower levels of income, transactions demand is lower, leaving more of the given money supply available to satisfy the higher speculative demand at low interest rates. At higher income levels, transactions demand is higher, leaving less of the given money supply available to satisfy a smaller speculative demand at the higher interest rate. The more responsive the demand for money to a change in the interest rate, the flatter the *LM* curve. The *LM* curve would be vertical if the demand for money did not depend at all on the interest rate, but only on the level of income. And an increase in the real money supply will shift the *LM* schedule down and to the right, whereas a monetary contraction has the opposite effect of shifting *LM* up and to the left.

Now consider the balance of payments. The trade balance is a function of income, and the capital account is a function of the domestic interest rate. An increase in income will cause imports to rise, thereby worsening the balance of payments. But an increase in the interest rate will induce more short-term capital inflows, which could offset the trade deficit and leave the balance of payments in equilibrium. In Figure 8.1, the schedule $BP = 0$ represents combinations of interest rate and income that provide balance of payments equilibrium. The schedule is drawn for given exports (a country's exports are not a function of its own income level) and a given foreign interest rate. The BP curve will be flatter, the higher the degree of capital mobility with respect to the differential between domestic and foreign interest rates. The lower the marginal propensity to import, the flatter also the BP schedule. (A low marginal propensity to import means that the trade deficit does not increase so much when income rises, and therefore the interest rate need not rise so much to offset the rise in imports by a capital inflow.) The schedule is upward sloping, indicating that when income expands, interest rates must also be higher to attract the capital flows that finance the trade deficit. Thus, BP schedules above and to the left of $BP = 0$ would indicate a balance of payments surplus, whereas BP schedules below and to the right of $BP = 0$ would indicate a deficit.

The full equilibrium level in the economy can now be represented by E in Figure 8.1. Injections into the income stream equal leakages (IS); international receipts equal international payments ($BP = 0$); the money supply is therefore unchanging, and the demand for money equals the actual stock of it (LM). There is equilibrium in the domestic goods market, the assets market, and the foreign exchange market.

Departures from full equilibrium can be introduced by considering changes in any of the variables. Suppose, for instance, that I falls. The IS curve then shifts down to the left to IS' in Figure 8.1. The equilibrium level changes from E to E', where $IS' = LM$. But E' is now off the BP schedule, indicating by its position to the left of BP that there is a balance of payments surplus. The equality $I + X + G = S + M + T$ holds, but $(S + T) - (I + G)$ is positive and equals the balance of payments surplus $(X - M)$. International receipts exceed international payments, and the central bank purchases foreign exchange (with unchanged exchange rate), thereby increasing the money supply. The given interest rate i is then consistent with a higher level of income, meaning that the LM curve now shifts down to the right until it passes through N where a new full equilibrium is established.

As expected from our earlier analysis, a decline in investment reduces income (via the multiplier effect); a surplus appears in the balance of payments as imports decline; the interest rate falls as the money suppy expands; and investment and income then rise until the balance of payments surplus is removed.

In contrast, an increase in domestic investment will shift the *IS* curve to the right. Income will then rise. And so will imports. At the new equilibrium income level, the central bank will have to finance the trade deficit by selling foreign exchange if the exchange rate is to be maintained.

Depreciation of the domestic currency will shift the *LM* curve upward and to the left. This is because the depreciation will cause a rise in the domestic price level through higher prices of tradable goods, and at the higher price level, the public will demand more money for transactions purposes. The higher demand for money can be fulfilled from the speculative money balances only if the interest rate rises. After the depreciation, the demand for money and supply of money become equal only if at any given income level the interest rate is higher than it was before the depreciation.

In the case of a depreciation, the *BP* schedule also shifts downward and to the right. This is because imports fall and exports increase, thereby improving the trade balance. Equilibrium in the balance of payments would then require a lower interest rate to induce a greater outflow of capital if the balance of trade is in surplus.

Monetary policy can also shift the *LM* curve, and fiscal policy shifts the *IS* curve. We shall consider the various shifts in the *IS, LM,* and *BP* schedules when we analyze balance of payments policy in Chapter 10.

Synthesis of Price and Income Adjustments

The international economy is clearly not composed of countries with constant real income, and to the extent that a country's income is variable, its balance of payments will also change. It is also obvious that prices are not constant, and exports and imports are responsive to price variations. In reality, the adjustment process operates through both "price effects" and "income effects." Although we have so far considered each set of forces only separately, we must now attempt to synthesize the two approaches.

We have already seen that when a country's exports fall, imports are not likely to decline by the same amount—and the country is left with a deficit if only "automatic" income adjustments are considered. To complete fully the adjustment process, we must then remove the assumption of neutral government policy and allow the government to pursue active policies that will deflate national income further. As noted, a tight money policy, for example, may then be necessary to raise interest rates and thereby to cause a reduction in domestic investment in order to depress national income further.

In reality, however, some prices are also likely to occur to support the adjustment process. The reduction in the home demand for exportables will result in a fall in export prices unless supply is perfectly elastic. If the demand for exports is relatively elastic, then the initial price reduction will result in an increase in exports, so that the initial reduction in exports is offset, and the deficit is not so large. With the decline in domestic expenditure, the domestic price level may also fall. If the prices of inputs used in import-competing goods decline, and the prices of import-competing goods also fall, then there may be a "switching" in demand from imports to import-competing goods. And this increased demand for import-competing goods need not again raise import-competing prices if the elasticity of supply of import substitutes is sufficiently high. The result of this type of price change would also ease the adjustment process by supporting the income change with a price change that reduced imports.

Although it is a longer-run phenomenon, labor productivity might also increase in the export sector and in the import-competing sector. If wage rates can be held constant, or do not rise so much as to offset the entire increase in labor productivity, then "efficiency wages" and prices may decline in the deficit country and lessen the need for income changes to re-equilibrate the deficit country's balance of payments.

The interactions of income and price changes can also be recognized in the case of the depreciation of a country's currency. The depreciation will change not only price relationships; it will also have an impact, via the multiplier, on domestic income, output, and employment. Instead of considering only the partial-equilibrium analysis of the elasticities approach, we should recognize that changes in production and expenditure in one sector will have repercussions on the equilibrium of the rest of the economy. Ideally we would want to know the value of the "total" elasticities—that is, the value of the elasticities after allowing for all the changes involved in a depreciation.

In the first place, assuming that the partial elasticities are sufficiently high so that the country's exports increase or its imports decrease, there will then also be a stimulating effect on the country's national income via the foreign trade multiplier. As its income increases, its demand for foreign exchange shifts upward, and this has to be "automatically" offset or the country has to restrain deliberately this increase by appropriate "expenditure-changing" policies that limit the level of expenditure or income. The effect on prices may be interpreted as the "impact effect," the stimulus to exports and check to imports caused by the rise in the price of foreign exchange. The induced changes in income accompanying the rise in exports and decline of imports may then be interpreted as the "reversal effect," since they tend to counteract the initial impact effect of the depreciation.[8]

The essence of the absorption approach then becomes relevant: only if the depreciation leads, directly or indirectly, to a smaller increase in E than in Y can there by an improvement in B (see equation 7.1 p. 175). The balance of trade will improve only if the multiplier effect of higher output on total absorption is less than the increase in output itself. How far a country will have to allow depreciation of its currency in order to re-equilibrate its balance of payments will therefore depend not merely on the potential price-elasticities of demand for its imports and exports, but also on the income effects and the country's general policies directed to restraining inflation. If, prior to the depreciation, the economy is less than fully employed, then the income effect will not be so strong and will not be so significant in offsetting the initial impact effect of price changes. Expenditure-switching policies can succeed without any expenditure reduction only if the domestic economy has the capacity to increase output. If, however, the economy is already fully employed, then as exports increase and imports decrease with the impact effect, money income, but not real income, will increase; domestic prices will rise; and expenditure will be diverted to importables and exportables, thereby having a strong "reversal effect" that may swamp the initial price effects.

When a country is initially in an inflationary situation, and it then allows its currency to depreciate, the depreciation will be abortive unless the country also undertakes policies to deflate and offset the inflationary forces of the depreciation itself. Depreciation is inflationary

---

[8] See S. Alexander, "Effects of a Devaluation: A Simplified Synthesis of Elasticities and Absorption Approaches," *American Economic Review*, 49 (March 1959), 22–42. The "reversal coefficient" can be expressed in terms of the marginal propensities to save and to import of the relevant countries.

insofar as domestic prices for imports rise, domestic resources are transferred from the production of nontradable goods to tradables, and an increase in exports, or a decrease in imports, results in positive income effects via the multiplier. For this reason, depreciation is considered an inappropriate policy as long as inflation is allowed to persist. If a country allows its exchange rate to fluctuate freely, and it continues to tolerate domestic inflationary forces, its currency will continue to depreciate in terms of foreign currencies until the initial inflationary forces and the inflationary impact of the depreciation are offset.

This is merely to reiterate the fundamental principle that if depreciation is effective through the elasticity approach, it will then increase home income in the deficit country and have an income effect that makes the absorption approach relevant. To correct the balance of payments through depreciation, there must be an increase in the country's real output relative to its national expenditure. At less than full employment, the balance of payments improvement can be realized by increasing national output more than "absorption." After full employment, however, as inelastic supplies are encountered and prices increase, the level of money income, but not real income rises, and correction of the balance of payments then depends on whether absorption can be reduced. If there is to be "disabsorption" in the private sector, this will have to be equivalent to an increase in savings. This might happen even under inflationary conditions if individual savers are subject to money illusion (that is, savings increase with rising money rather than real income), if there is income redistribution from lower to higher marginal savings rate groups, or if there is income redistribution from the private to the government sector through progressive income taxation.

According to the absorption approach, it can also happen if the "real balance effect" is strong (the real value of cash holdings declines when prices rise, and the holders of cash want to restore their real holdings) so that a depreciation leads to a reduction in real expenditure if the money supply is kept constant. This agrees with the monetary approach. We have seen that the crux of the monetarists' analysis is the real balance effect and the associated stock-adjustment behavior by which actual real balances are adjusted to desired levels by international reserve flows in an open economy.

According to the monetarists, depreciation operates on the volume of real balances, and a depreciation is therefore equivalent to domestic credit contraction and works by deflating domestic real balances through a rise in the domestic price level. As the depreciation gives rise to an overall payments surplus, it will cause a net inflow (or slow down a net outflow) of money. To a monetarist, the depreciation improves the balance of payments by raising the money supply to meet demand. Or savings may respond to a rise in interest rates,[9] or may increase in the foreign trade sector as profits rise in the export and import-competing industries at the expense of the real wages of those who import at a higher price.[10] If monetary authorities would resist expansion of the money supply, deflation would balance trade following depreciation. These results, however, are unlikely to occur automatically in sufficient magnitude in many cases. Disabsorption will then have to be sought by active governmental policies that reduce $C + I + G$. Monetary policy becomes necessary to sterilize (that is, to offset through open market sales and credit contraction) the growth of domestic credit.

Nonetheless, it may be simplistic to contend that real income will not increase after full employment and, hence, that the balance of payments remedial measures can operate only on the side of cutting absorption instead of increasing real income. Even at full employment, depreciation may still effect an increase in real income through changes in resource allocation that will result from the change in the exchange rate. As the overvaluation of the domestic currency is reduced, resources will now be reallocated from domestic uses to the export and import-competing sectors where their contribution to real income is greater.

If the elasticities and absorption approaches emphasize that the adjustment mechanism must operate through both price effects and income effects, the monetary approach stresses that all balance of payments disequilibria could be handled by the use of domestic monetary policy. Thus, depreciation is only a substitute for domestic credit contraction, operating by reducing the world value of a country's money supply. According to the monetary approach, the preference for depreciation as a means of avoiding the equivalent domestic monetary contraction must be because of price and wage rigidity and money illusion.

[9] The impact of depreciation in terms of some significant relationships to money prices, interest rates, and the money supply is examined more fully by S.D. Tsiang, "The Role of Money in Trade-Balance Stability: Synthesis of the Elasticity and Absorption Approaches," *American Economic Review,* 51 (Dec. 1961), 912–36.

[10] This redistribution of income is significant, because if the real wages of those who import were not reduced, but instead their money wages were allowed to rise as import prices rose, then there would be no decrease in consumption by this group and no disabsorption in the entire economy even if profits rose in the foreign trade sector and were either saved or taxed away. But this kind of redistribution of income calls for a strong government taking unpopular measures. It is a difficult route for making depreciation effective.

Further, the depreciation will be ineffective if an expansion of domestic credit offsets the exchange-rate change. And the depreciation will have to continue unless the initial exchange-rate change is supported by slower domestic credit expansion.

We can now offer a summary comparison of the different approaches to the adjustment mechanism. The elasticities approach has been the traditional theory in which the demand for foreign exchange is determined by the demand for imports, measured as a **flow** of foreign money, and the supply of foreign exchange is determined by the amount foreigners spend on domestic exports, measured as a **flow** of foreign money. The elasticities are therefore significant in determining whether a devaluation or depreciation will re-equilibrate the balance of payments.

In contrast, the monetary approach views the exchange rate as the relative price of national monies instead of as the relative price of national outputs. The monetary approach also interprets the exchange rate as being determined by the conditions for equilibrium in the market for stocks of assets instead of by the conditions for equilibrium in the markets for flows of funds, as in the absorption approach. Although the monetary approach does not deny that changes in the exchange rate can have significant effects on relative commodity prices and that these price changes affect the balance of payments, it is contended that these effects must come through the impact of the relative price changes on the demand for money. A depreciation therefore operates through a rise in the demand for domestic money and a fall in the demand for foreign money, associated with the expansion of domestic output and the contraction of foreign output. To be in harmony with the elasticities approach, the monetarist approach would contend that price changes are merely the indirect means by which the national money demand and supply are equated.

The monetary approach also emphasizes the markets for stocks of assets instead of the markets for flows of funds. The effects of asset flows on asset stocks are usually not considered in the elasticities, absorption, or income-multiplier approaches. The monetary approach recognizes that although flows of funds occur to correct monetary disequilibrium, the demands and supplies of flows of funds are themselves a reflection of the requirement for asset-market equilibrium.

Because the monetary approach maintains that a balance of payments deficit reflects excess supply of money as a stock, the deficit represents only a phase of stock adjustment and is thus temporary and self-correcting. Provided that the monetary authorities do not create new domestic credit, the excess supply of money will be removed by an increase in purchases of foreign goods and foreign assets. When stock equilibrium is restored in the goods and assets markets, the deficit will have been removed. Being concerned with long-run equilibrium, the monetary approach views the effect of depreciation (or appreciation) as only transitory and maintains that in the long run, depreciation (or appreciation) will have raised (or lowered) only the domestic price level and not affected real variables. Being concerned with the long run, the monetarist model assumes that output and employment tend to full employment levels, with reactions to changes taking the form of price and wage adjustments. In contrast, the Keynesian income-multiplier model assumes that employment and output are variable at constant prices and wages. But in agreement with the absorption approach, the monetary approach recognizes that depreciation can reduce real money balances and thereby reduce absorption (E) out of a given real income (Y).

Because of the large number of solutions that are possible for any given disturbance to the balance of payments, we shall not specify theoretically the respective roles of price and income effects. It is difficult to offer one model that will synthesize both types of effects. Instead there are *a priori* any number of possible outcomes, depending on the relevant elasticities of demand and supply, price effects, income effects, changes in terms of trade, and effects on resource allocation. We can only reiterate the need to consider both price and income effects in the operation of the adjustment mechanism, and to undertake in each case a more general analysis that takes account of changes in relative prices and changes in income.[11] In effect, we have to synthesize the post-Keynesian monetary-income theory with general equilibrium price theory. The machinery behind the hands of Edgeworth's clock (recall the offer curve analysis of Part I) is now seen to be even more complex—including not only the non-monetary micro forces of international trade, but also the monetary-income macro forces.[12]

The emphasis on both price effects and income effects implies that the correction of the balance of payments will depend on decisions

[11] For an excellent brief summary of the differences and similarities in the successive balance of payments "approaches," see Harry G. Johnson, "Elasticity, Absorption, Keynesian Multiplier, Keynesian Policy, and Monetary Approaches to Devaluation Theory: A Simple Geometric Exposition," *American Economic Review*, 66 (June 1976), 448–52.

[12] For more advanced analysis in this direction, see R.W. Jones, "Stability Conditions in International Trade: A General Equilibrium Analysis," *International Economic Review*, 2 (May 1961), 199–209, and M.C. Kemp, *The Pure Theory of International Trade* (1969), 235 ff.

taken throughout the economy (as emphasized by the absorption approach) and not merely in the foreign trade sector (though this sector will ultimately be affected by decisions taken elsewhere). This double emphasis on both price and income effects is reflected in policy measures that may be "expenditure-switching" or "expenditure-reducing." **Expenditure-switching policies** divert spending on foreign-produced goods to home-produced goods. Among such policies are depreciation and the various forms of direct controls on imports. **Expenditure-reducing policies** reduce $C + I + G$ directly and through multiplier effects indirectly—policies such as higher taxes or tight monetary policies.

Some of these price and income effects may be automatically instituted, but some need to be realized through adjustment policies that are deliberately pursued. The nature of the existing international monetary system and the initial state of a country's domestic economy will determine which effects are automatically brought about—and the degree of their automaticity. Whether price effects or income effects play the dominant role in the adjustment process, the way in which price and income effects are interrelated, and the policy choices open to a country, will depend on whether the international monetary system is based on fixed exchange rates, freely floating rates, or "managed floating." The sources of international liquidity will also matter. So too will the state of the domestic economy—whether the economy is in recession or in an inflationary situation, for example. The next two chapters focus on these issues by concentrating on the nature of the different international monetary arrangements that are possible and the policies of balance of payments adjustment.

Supplementary Readings

The monetary approach to the balance of payments is presented in the following: R.A. Mundell, *International Economics* (1968); Mundell, *Monetary Theory* (1971); Marina V.N. Whitman, "Global Monetarism and the Monetary Approach to the Balance of Payments," *Brookings Papers in Economic Activity*, (March 1975), 491–555; Donald S. Kemp, "A Monetary View of the Balance of Payments," *Federal Reserve Bank of St. Louis* (April 1975), 14–22; H.G. Johnson, "The Monetary Approach: Balance of Payments Theory and Policy," *Economica*, 44 (Aug. 1977), 217–30; J.A. Frenkel and H.G. Johnson (eds.), *The Monetary Approach to the Balance of Payments* (1976); Stephen P. Magee, "The Empirical Evidence on the Monetary Approach to the Balance of Payments and Exchange Rates," *American Economic Review, Papers and Proceedings*, 66

(May 1976), 163–70; I.M.F., *The Monetary Approach to the Balance of Payments* (1977); John F.O. Bilson, "The Current Experience with Floating Exchange Rates: An Appraisal of the Monetary Approach," *American Economic Review, Papers & Proceedings,* 68 (May 1978), 392–97; and R.I. McKinnon, *Money in International Exchange* (1979).

A critical analysis of the monetary approach is presented by S.C. Tsiang, "The Monetary Theoretic Foundation of the Modern Monetary Approach to the Balance of Payments," *Oxford Economic Papers,* 29 (Nov. 1977), 319–38.

For extended treatment of portfolio theory, see J. Frenkel and C. Rodriguez, "Portfolio Equilibrium and the Balance of Payments: A Monetary Approach," *American Economic Review,* 65 (Sept. 1975), 674–88; R.I. McKinnon, "Portfolio Balance and International Payments Adjustment," in R. Mundell and A. Swoboda (eds.), *Monetary Problems of the International Economy* (1969), 199–234; Dale W. Henderson, "Modeling the Interdependence of National Money and Capital Markets," *American Economic Review,* 67 (Feb. 1977), 190–99; E. Classen and P. Salin (eds.), *Recent Issues in International Monetary Economics* (1975); and Peter Isard, *Exchange Rate Determination: A Survey of Popular Views and Recent Models,* Princeton Studies in International Finance, No. 42 (1978).

9

International Monetary Systems

We shall now focus on the theory of balance of payments policy in the context of different international monetary regimes. This chapter outlines international monetary arrangements that have existed in the past—the pure gold standard, an inconvertible paper standard, the gold exchange standard—and the present system of "managed floating." After examining how the different monetary systems operate, we shall establish in Chapter 10 some normative principles of balance of payments policy.

Although we shall have to consider some details of the operation of these different international monetary standards, we do not want to lose sight of the main features of the adjustment process. We should keep in mind the overriding question with which we began: Can nations achieve at one and the same time the policy objectives of internal stability (full employment and stable price levels) and external stability (balance of payments equilibrium), while liberalizing commercial policy? As we explore this central question in more specific terms, we shall want to **consider how the various international monetary systems provide different remedial measures for removing balance of payments disequilibrium, and how the burden or cost of adjustment is distributed among the various countries.**

Types of International Monetary Systems

The main features of an international monetary system are its type of exchange-rate regime, provisions of international official liquidity, and

Table 9.1. Possible International Monetary Systems

Exchange-rate Regime	Reserve Asset	Degree of Market Convertibility for Capital Movements
I. Fixed exchange rate	A. Gold	1. Full
II. Adjustable parities	B. Special Drawing Rights	2. Dual market
III. Gliding parities	C. U.S. dollars and other national currencies	3. Controlled
IV. Managed float		
V. Free float		

Source: Richard N. Cooper, "Prolegomena to the Choice of an International Monetary System," *International Organization,* 29 (Winter 1975), 67.
  I.A.1 represents the pure gold standard
  II.A.3 represents the original Bretton Woods system
    V.1 represents an inconvertible paper standard (no reserve asset)

its degree of convertibility for different transactions. Some of the various possible combinations of these elements can be noted from Table 9.1. There can be a large array of possible international monetary systems, drawing one element from each of the columns.

In the second column, the reserve assets provide international official liquidity—that is, the ultimate means of making international payments and the means by which a national monetary authority can intervene in the foreign exchange market to maintain a desired exchange rate. The extent of restrictions on international capital movements is shown in the third column (a dual market refers to full convertibility for current account transactions, but some control over the convertibility on capital account).

Pure Gold Standard: Fixed Exchange Rates

The essential characteristics of a pure gold standard (or gold bullion standard) are that national currencies are convertible into gold at fixed parities, gold is a means of settling international accounts, and **exchange rates are fixed** because every currency has a fixed gold value. Under the pure gold standard—as it existed during its hey-day from the 1870s to World War I, and again for the few years between Britain's return to the gold standard in 1925 and its departure during the Great Depression in 1931—each national monetary authority issued gold coins and paper money fully backed by gold (gold certificates); defined its national currency in terms of ounces of gold; and then stood ready to maintain convertibility between its currency and gold by buying and selling gold to individuals and other national monetary authorities. Thus, the U.S. Treasury bought and sold gold at $10.67 per Troy ounce of gold, whereas the Bank of England bought and sold gold at £4-4-11 per ounce. A $:£ exchange rate was therefore established at $4.86:£1. This rate was termed the "**mint parity**" rate, and actual exchange rates would be within the "gold points," which could depart only slightly from mint parity according to the commission charges by governments and the cost of shipping gold as a means of international payment. The upper limit of this departure from mint parity was the "**gold export point.**" If, for instance, these commissions and costs amounted to .02 cents per ounce of gold, then an American importer would never pay more than $4.88 per £1. Instead of paying more than the gold export point, the American importer would convert dollars into gold, ship gold, and convert gold into pounds—all of which could be done at a price of $4.88 per £1. At the gold export point, the supply of pounds was therefore in effect perfectly elastic. At the other extreme, in this example, the "**gold import point**" would never be below $4.84 per £1; instead of accepting less than this, the exporter would collect in pounds, convert the pounds into gold, ship the gold, and convert gold into dollars, thereby realizing at least $4.84:£1. At the gold import point, the demand for pounds would therefore be perfectly elastic.

Assume that demand and supply conditions in the $:£ foreign exchange market are initially such that the rate is at mint parity. If now the demand for imports from Britain should rise, the gold export point will be reached, and gold will flow from the United States to Britain. The gold outflow would keep the exchange rate from rising beyond the gold export point, since the gold outflow would be bought for pounds by the Bank of England, thereby removing the excess demand for pounds (or the reciprocal, the excess supply of dollars) in the foreign exchange market.

The gold outflow (a credit item) serves as a settlement item in the United States' balance of payments. But how is balance of payments equilibrium restored? How is the gold outflow stopped? To end the gold outflow from the United States and restore equilibrium, there must be forces that decrease the demand for pounds or increase the supply of pounds (that is, decrease imports from Britain or increase exports to Britain).

Under the pure gold standard, these forces were believed to operate according to Hume's **"price-specie-flow mechanism,"** as already noted in Chapter 8. Writing in the mid-eighteenth century, Hume wanted to expose the fallacy of the mercantilist view that a country should seek a "favorable" surplus on the balance of trade in order to augment the country's stock of gold and thereby its wealth and power. Hume argued that governmental efforts to increase exports above imports would be self-defeating, since the self-regulating price-specie-flow mechanism would determine the international distribution of specie. Governmental intervention of the mercantilist type would therefore be futile in trying to maintain a "level of money" above what would occur "in the common course of nature."

The central feature of the mechanism was the automatic self-adjustment of the balance of payments through price changes brought about by a change in the money supply. In the deficit country, when imports exceeded exports on current and "autonomous" capital accounts, there would be an excess demand for foreign currency; the gold export point would be reached; gold would flow out; the money supply would then have to contract; prices would fall; and the demand for exports would then increase, and the demand for imports would fall until equilibrium was restored and gold ceased flowing out.

In the surplus country, the effects would supposedly be the opposite: with an excess supply of foreign currency in the market (exports greater than imports), the gold import point would be reached, gold would flow into the surplus country, the quantity of money would increase, and prices would then rise, so that the demand for exports would fall, and the demand for imports would rise, thereby stopping the gold inflow and restoring equilibrium in the balance of payments.

Such is the usual "textbook version" of the adjustment mechanism under the pure gold standard. The monetary system plays the central role, prices vary inversely with the supply of money (as in the quantity theory of money $MV = PQ$),[1] and the re-equilibration in the balance of

---

[1]M denotes the quantity of money; V, the transactions velocity of circulation of money; P, the price level; and Q, an index of the volume of physical transactions in goods and services. In the simplest version of the quantity theory, V and Q are assumed constant at a full employment level of output, so that P varies directly with M.

payments comes through price changes (a worsening in the terms of trade of the deficit country and an improvement in the terms of trade of the surplus country). In reality, however, the actual operation was neither as smooth nor as painless as the price-specie-flow mechanism would imply. It is doubtful that conditions actually allowed the adjustment mechanism to operate rapidly and effectively through only relative price changes. Banks were not always fully loaned up, so that a gold outflow did not always require monetary contraction. Even if the money supply did decrease, it did not necessarily follow that money expenditures *(MV)* would also decline. But even if *MV* did decline, the prices in the deficit country would not necessarily fall proportionately: prices might be sticky downwards, and before a price decline could be effected, it may often have been necessary to effect a reduction in wages.

Furthermore, the "rules of the game" were not always followed by the surplus country. Instead of inflating, a surplus country could sterilize the gold inflow (not allow the inflow to affect the domestic money supply) or offset the inflow with open market sales of government bonds to the banking system. But if the surplus country did allow inflation to ensue, there was also a possibility that capital movements would be perverse in the sense of flowing from the deficit country to the surplus country where prices rose and profits were greater. Price stickiness, the discretionary power of the surplus country, and the perversity of capital movements all combined to make the adjustment mechanism of the pure gold standard not as smoothly operating as Hume's simple statement asserted.

In fact, the mechanism operated through **not only price changes, but also income changes.** In the deficit country, when the gold outflow caused a monetary contraction, this would, in turn, cause a rise in interest rates through tight monetary policies. Domestic investment would then fall, and via the multiplier process, national output, income, and employment would all decline. The deficit country would suffer **deflation**—and a deflation not only in prices, but also output and employment. Indeed, unemployment was often the most potent means of reducing money wage rates and thereby prices. Moreover, this deflation would have to be suffered by the deficit country regardless of the causes of the disequilibrium in its balance of payments and the appropriateness of deflating to correct the disequilibrium. Even worse, the deflation occurred regardless of the domestic state of the economy: even though there was already domestic imbalance—less than full employment—the dictates of external balance would nonetheless require a

RAGNAR NURKSE, *International Currency Experience* (1944), 229–30

In general, the need for exchange adjustments or exchange controls will tend to be the less frequent (a) the greater the total amount of international monetary reserves; (b) the greater and steadier the flow of international investment; and (c) the closer the correspondence or coordination between national policies affecting income, employment and prices, particularly in the leading industrial states. . . .

Maintenance of adequate employment and avoidance of price inflation are both essential elements of domestic stability. . . .

There was a growing tendency during the inter-war period to make international monetary policy conform to domestic social and economic policy and not the other way round. Yet the world was still economically interdependent; and an international currency mechanism for the multilateral exchange of goods and services, instead of primitive bilateral barter, was still a fundamental necessity for the great majority of countries. The problem was to find a system of international currency relations compatible with the requirements of domestic stability.

still greater departure from full employment. No wonder that in 1931, when Britain already had an unemployment rate of 12%, Britain chose to leave the pure gold standard rather than endure additional unemployment for the sake of maintaining a fixed exchange rate of $4.86:£1. Full employment finally became recognized as more important than fixed exchange rates. Instead of increasing unemployment, Britain let the exchange rate rise above the gold export point (between September and December 1931, the pound depreciated by 30%). In 1934, the United States also chose to stop converting its currency into gold for private individuals, and the U.S. Treasury devalued the dollar by raising the buying price of gold from $20.67 to $35 per ounce of gold.

With the emphasis on domestic full employment policies, governments found the constraints of the pure gold standard intolerable. As an international monetary system, it was **biased against the deficit country**. The deficit country was labeled the "guilty party" for spending too much, without any recognition that a surplus country could be spending too little—that is, could be tolerating a higher level of unemployment than the deficit country was willing to endure. The deficit country was also forced to take corrective action when gold flowed out, but the surplus country could exercise its own discretion with respect to the effects of the gold inflow on its domestic economy. International liquidity was limited in amount to gold reserves. Unless a country happened to possess such a large supply of gold reserves that it did not need to deflate when gold flowed out, or unless the adjustment process operated so rapidly and effectively that it did not have to lose much gold, the condition of the balance of payments exercised too much discipline over the country's domestic policies. Under the pure gold standard, the deficit country's autonomy in the pursuit of national economic objectives was severely limited. No nation's rate of inflation or deflation could deviate much from every other nation's. The time finally arrived during the Great Depression of the 1930s when countries chose to give priority to the attainment of full employment and domestic stability, even if it meant abandonment of the fair weather craft of the gold standard with its fixed exchange rates and its semblance of an automatic system of international monetary government.

Inconvertible Paper Standard: Freely Flexible Exchange Rates

At the other end of the spectrum from a pure gold standard is an inconvertible paper standard (such as existed in the period 1919–1925). Under a paper standard, gold plays no role in the monetary system: a nation's domestic currency is not expressed in terms of gold, and there is no convertibility between national currency and gold. Instead, exchange rates are **freely flexible** according to demand and supply conditions, and **no reserve asset** is required. We already discussed in Chapter 6 the mechanism of adjustment under freely flexible rates. It may now, however, be useful to bring together the various advantages claimed for flexible rates, and also to present the case against flexible rates.

The **simplicity** of its operative mechanism is an attractive feature of a fully flexible exchange rate system: all that is necessary is to let the rate go in the foreign exchange market. The adjustment is also **continual**. It begins when needed, and does not allow a deficit to build up and delay action with the result that more severe policies become necessary later, as can happen with fixed rates or an adjustable peg (periodic changes of par values). Flexible rates avoid the intensification of pressures on the balance of payments and the periodic crises that can occur when national policies are not coordinated while the exchange rates are fixed.

Especially appealing is the preservation of domestic economic autonomy: a deficit country need not sacrifice full employment policies or liberal trade policies in order to remove balance of payments disequilibrium. At the same time as domestic governments have **one less policy target** to worry about (fixed rates), they acquire **one more policy instrument** (exchange-rate adjustment)—another degree of freedom—which **allows them to disengage their monetary and fiscal policies from those of other countries.** When countries pursue divergent inflation rates, flexible rates allow an independent monetary policy and permit "disintegration" of the international economy on the financial level. But this financial insulation is not as disruptive of the internationalization of markets as would be the alternative of pegged rates and controls over trade and capital movements. Finally, if rates are allowed to float freely, there is **no need for international reserves:** instead of intervening with reserves to hold the rate, a deficit country will simply let its currency depreciate in terms of foreign currency.

The case against freely fluctuating rates rests on several charges. A government may think that price-elasticities of demand are so low that depreciation of the weak currency will only worsen its payments imbalance (the perverse case of depreciation, discussed in Chapter 6). But even if we rule this out, and assume depreciation would be effective in removing the payments imbalance, nonetheless it may have disadvantageous effects. The **uncertainty** about the future level of exchange rates can depress the volume of foreign trade and international investment. But the adherents of freely fluctuating rates claim that uncertainty over the rates is no greater than the alternative uncertainty over other corrective governmental policies or trade restrictions. Moreover, it is possible to spread the risks of exchange-rate movements through a forward exchange market. Exporters who expect to receive foreign exchange in the future can now sell the exchange receipts forward at a known price, while importers who will need foreign exchange in the future can now buy forward. It is, however, difficult to have a forward exchange market to cover capital transactions of a long-term character. And some countries, notably the less developed countries (LDCs), may have only thin forward markets.

Another argument against fluctuating exchange rates is that speculation on the future course of exchange rates may be of a **destabilizing character,** aggravating movements in rates and imposing losses in economic efficiency. If, for instance, speculators expect a further depreciation of a currency and therefore sell that currency, the depreciation will be brought about. Or if foreigners expect a further depreciation of another country's currency and therefore hold off importing from that country, the decreased demand for the country's currency may aggravate the depreciation of the currency. Capital flights away from the currency that is expected to soften will also reinforce the tendency for the currency to depreciate.

Again, adherents of freely fluctuating rates have some ready replies to this charge of destabilizing speculation. Speculation may actually be stabilizing: if the parties in the foreign exchange market have some notion of a "normal" rate, then they may buy when a currency weakens and sell when it strengthens, thereby stabilizing the market.[2] Even if it should be destabilizing, this could be offset by official counter-speculation through some governmental Exchange Equalization Fund that would conteract private speculators by officially demanding foreign exchange if the private demand became too weak or by officially supplying foreign exchange if the private demand became too strong. If, however, the Exchange Equalization Fund acts to hold the exchange rates within definite limits, and private speculation would be destabilizing, then the Exchange Equalization Fund may need even more foreign exchange reserves to hold the rates within the desired limits than would be needed under a fixed exchange-rate system (in which speculation is impossible).

Perhaps the major disadvantage of a freely fluctuating exchange-rate system may be its **inflationary bias**. Under fixed exchange rates, inflation is transferred across the rates. Suppose that a country inflates and experiences a balance of payments deficit, and its currency then flows out to another country with a stronger currency. The monetary authority of the country into which foreign currency is flowing enters the foreign exchange market and buys the foreign currency to stop the domestic currency from appreciating (thereby preventing the country's exports from becoming less competitive, as they would if the currency appreciated). When the monetary authority intervenes to hold the rate fixed, it increases the domestic money supply, and inflation is transmitted to the country with the stronger currency.

This would not happen under freely fluctuating rates. Some argue,

[2] For additional theoretical analysis of whether speculation may be stabilizing or destabilizing under floating exchange rates, see Milton Friedman, *Essays in Positive Economics* (1953), 157–203; Jerome Stein, "Destabilizing Speculative Activity Can Be Profitable," *Review of Economic Studies,* 43 (1961), 301–2; W.J. Baumol, "Speculation, Profitability, and Stability," *Review of Economics and Statistics,* 39 (1957), 263–71; and Egon Sohmen, *Flexible Exchange Rates* (rev. ed., 1969), 59–74.

however, that a fluctuating rate regime more readily allows the **generation of inflation** and that it also exacerbates inflation within the country, since a country with a freely fluctuating exchange rate could undergo inflation without having to worry about the loss of international reserves. The country would be subject to no balance of payments discipline, only a depreciation of its currency. True, the depreciation will raise prices, and this may be more evident to the public than a loss of reserves. But depletion of reserves may invoke stronger anti-inflationary policies than currency depreciation invokes because the reserves are limited in amount and because depreciation may gain some supporters within the community even though at the same time it adversely affects others.

Flexible rates may also permit a vicious circle of inflation, depreciation, and additional inflation. A rise in import prices fuels a "cost-push" inflation. If the depreciation then leads to a rise in money wages, as is likely when the cost of living rises, the depreciation becomes self-justifying. Destabilizing speculation or other shifts in capital flows may also exaggerate the depreciation and cause additional inflationary pressures. Once inflation is allowed to continue, there will be a steady depreciation in the country's currency, but there is nothing in the process of depreciation that operates to eliminate the inflationary cause of the country's balance of payments disequilibrium. On the contrary, the depreciation, if effective, would intensify the inflation by increasing exports and decreasing imports and raising the price level. Through both "demand-pull" and cost-push forces, the inflation would likely intensify.

Further, there is an **asymmetrical effect** between countries with depreciating and appreciating currencies. Prices and wages rise in the deficit country with a depreciating currency. In the surplus country, however, appreciation is unlikely to lead to a reduction in wages and prices when import prices fall. Instead there may simply be an increase in factor returns with sticky wages and prices. This ratchet effect imparts an **inflationary bias to the entire system.**

Against this criticism of flexible rates as being inflationary, defenders of flexibility emphasize that in the absence of at least accommodating monetary expansion, exchange-rate depreciation could not by itself set off a process of cumulative inflation and self-justifying depreciation. Moreover, as compared with the alternative exchange-rate regimes of the adjustable peg or a heavily managed exchange rate system, proponents of full flexibility argue that freely floating rates on balance give countries greater incentives to reduce inflation and greater ability to do so themselves when other countries do not reduce it.[3]

In assessing the case for or against flexible rates, we must also recall all the **costs of adjustment** through price changes. As we saw in Chapter 6, the burden or costs of freely fluctuating rates could be suboptimal by being over-general in having an impact on all prices in the foreign trade sector, requiring domestic mobility of resources, and possibly resulting in a deterioration of the country's commodity terms of trade, a change in the distribution of income, the imposition of anti-inflationary monetary and fiscal policies, and a reduction in the total amount of resources available to fulfill domestic aggregate demand.

The LDCs have little enthusiasm for freely fluctuating rates. These countries are mainly small open economies, generally under inflationary pressures and subject to balance of payments deficits. They would have to endure continually the costs of depreciation. Their burden in servicing foreign debt would also increase when the debt is denominated in an appreciating currency. Depreciation might also be ineffective when an LDC is in a situation of structural imbalance—that is, when the price-elasticity for exports of the developing country is low, imports are a fixed ratio of output and not readily compressible, and the marginal propensity to save is a constant that cannot be varied by relative price changes. Because the LDCs tend to experience greater export fluctuations and are more vulnerable to changes in their foreign trade sectors, the swings associated with pure floating would also tend to be more adverse for the LDCs than for developed countries.

As always, however, the crucial issue is **What is the better alternative policy?** A clear argument in favor of fluctuating rates is that it avoids the disadvantages of maintaining disequilibrium exchange rates supported by restrictions on imports, which are the alternative policies most readily adopted by developing countries. It also depoliticizes an alteration in the exchange rate, allowing governments to move away from an overvalued currency without the political repercussions that tend to occur in other monetary regimes. By avoiding unwanted changes in the domestic money supply, flexible rates may also allow a country to insulate itself from disturbances arising in other countries. Further, of prime importance is the beneficial effect on a developing country when fluctuating rates allow developed countries to be free of restrictive trade and exchange controls and to experience higher rates of

[3] See, for example, Thomas D. Willett, *Floating Exchange Rates and International Monetary Reform* (1977), Chap. 2.

growth, with a resultant increase in their demand for imports from developing countries.

Because the case for freely fluctuating rates is mixed, we might more appropriately say that the proponents of flexible rates are not so much in favor of flexibility as they are opposed to fixity in exchange rates. And proponents of fixed rates are not so much in favor of fixity as they are against flexibility.

Gold Exchange Standard: Adjustable Peg

Toward the end of World War II, a United Nations conference at Bretton Woods created the International Monetary Fund (IMF) as the central institution in the international monetary system. The operation of the IMF and the role played by the reserve currencies of the pound and especially the dollar endowed the international monetary system with its essential characteristics from 1946 to 1971. This system was the gold exchange standard, or more accurately the gold exchange and reserve currency standard, a mixture of commodity money (gold as a reserve asset) and credit money based on a commodity money reserve.

We could interpret much of the thinking at the Bretton Woods conference in terms of the uneasy triangle of how to allow nations to pursue their domestic economic goals without being required to forgo the gains from trade liberalization or suffer the costs of correcting a balance of payments disequilibrium. In the interests of the pledge to full employment after the war, nations would no longer tolerate, as they did under the pure gold standard, deflation in order to remove a balance of payments deficit. Nor did they want to endure again the successive rounds of competitive currency depreciations that had characterized the pre-war period. To provide domestic autonomy for the pursuit of full employment, nations wanted to be able to draw upon sources of international liquidity other than the limited amount of gold—hence, the provision for each member country's quota of **drawing rights** at the IMF. To avoid the extremes of a freely fluctuating rate, or a fixed rate, there must be initially some fixity of exchange rates, as designated by the IMF, but subsequently some provision for adjustments in the value of a country's currency, again as determined by the IMF, to correct a "**fundamental disequilibrium.**"

More specifically, the Fund established a rather detailed code of international economic conduct based on the following principles:

JOHN MAYNARD KEYNES, *Proposals for an International Clearing Union* (April 1943), in J. Keith Horsefield (ed.), *International Monetary Fund, 1945–1965*, vol. III: Documents (1969), 20

> We need a quantum of international currency, which is neither determined in an unpredictable and irrelevant manner as, for example, by the technical progress of the gold industry, nor subject to large variations depending on the gold reserve policies of individual countries; but is governed by the actual current requirements of world commerce, and is also capable of deliberate expansion and contraction to offset deflationary and inflationary tendencies in effective world demand.

(i) That a country's foreign exchange rate is a matter of international concern and that a par value system should be the subject of international scrutiny and endorsement. All member countries of the Fund must establish par values for their currencies, expressed in terms of gold or of the U.S. dollar of specified gold content, and may not change them without international permission. Exchange rates should therefore be fixed, with permitted fluctuations not exceeding 1% on either side of the fixed parities. To maintain the stability of its exchange rate, the official monetary authority of a member country should act as the residual buyer or seller on foreign exchange markets, intervening in the market as required to keep the currency from falling or rising.

The exchange rate may be subject to only periodic change—the "adjustable peg" feature of the Fund. But this variation in the exchange rate is to be allowed by the Fund only to correct a fundamental disequilibrium in the member's balance of payments. The criterion of fundamental disequilibrium was originally left unspecified, but it came to be interpreted by the Fund as meaning a persistent chronic deficit that could be corrected by devaluation.

(ii) That exchange controls on current international payments should be prohibited, except temporarily under certain conditions. Exchange controls on capital movements may be permitted, however, in order to ease balance of payments pressures.

Multiple exchange rates (that is, different rates according to type of transaction) are also not generally permitted. Instead, a unitary exchange rate should be established in order that international trade and capital flows not be regulated through the implicit taxation and subsidization effects of a multiple exchange-rate system.

(iii) That there must be some augmentation of national gold and currency reserves in order that countries are not forced to meet short-run balance of payments deficits by suffering domestic deflation of income and unemployment. This should be in the form of prescribed "drawing rights" by a member country on its "quota" at the Fund. The financial resources subscribed to the Fund constitute an international reserve pool of currencies against which members can draw for short-term financial assistance. The quotas have been periodically increased.

A member exercises its drawing rights by purchasing other currencies from the Fund with its own currency, subject to various rules. A member's drawing rights are equal to 125% of its quota, and are divided into five tranches (each equal to 25% of the country's quota). Only the first tranche (originally called the gold tranche and now the reserve tranche) can be drawn upon automatically and is considered to be an unconditional access to international liquidity. Beyond the first tranche, discretionary factors enter into the Fund's conditional decision on whether the member country can exercise its drawing rights and under what conditions, with respect to the drawing country's economic policies. A drawing country must repurchase within three to five years its own currency from the Fund by payment to the Fund in the foreign currency previously acquired or in any other currency acceptable to the Fund. Outstanding drawings are subject to interest charges that increase with the number of credit tranches used and with the time for which the drawing has been outstanding. This temporary access to the Fund's financial assistance is designed to offer only short-term financing to help ease the adjustment process for short-term balance of payments problems.

A new Special Drawing Rights (SDRs) facility was added to the Fund in 1969. This facility provides for the creation and distribution of reserve certificates (SDRs) as the result of deliberate and concerted decision by the members of the Fund participating in the SDRs facility (an 85% majority vote of Fund members is required to create SDRs). The SDRs constitute a major supplement to existing reserve assets on a permanent basis, backed simply by the obligation of Fund members to accept these new reserve certificates and pay a convertible currency in return. It is their acceptability, not any intrinsic worth, that bestows the function of reserve assets on SDRs. This mechanism of reserve creation merits special attention as being the first time in monetary history that the control of the volume of reserves was governed by international law and determined by the exercise of reason within the framework of law, instead of, as previously, by such random and uncoordinated influences as the deficits of the reserve currency countries, the volume of gold production, the pattern of its absorption, or conversions of reserve currencies into gold.

Each Fund member received SDRs in proportion to its IMF quota. Once created, SDRs are transferred by debiting the SDR account of the user and crediting the SDR account of the receiver, with the user country acquiring convertible currency from the receiving member—provided that the member drawing upon other members shall not make use of its SDRs in excess of 70% of its average cumulative allocation over a 5-year average period, and a member's obligation to provide currency will not extend beyond the point at which its holdings of the SDRs exceed twice its cumulative allocations.

Beyond the temporary use of the secondary source of reserves provided by the Fund, and short of altering the exchange rate to correct a fundamental disequilibrium, a deficit country was expected to undertake remedial measures to correct its balance of payments disequilibrium.

(iv) That a balance of payments is necessarily two sided between deficit countries and surplus countries, and the adjustment obligations are therefore the joint responsibility of these countries. Recognizing the principle that the surplus country should also undertake remedial action, the Fund Agreement permitted the Fund to declare that a particular currency suffers from a "general scarcity." If this "scarce currency" clause is invoked, members may impose a temporary limitation on exchange of the scarce currency and can practice discriminatory exchange restrictions against the scarce currency of a country that runs a large and persistent surplus in its balance of payments.

Although Keynes had earlier called gold a "barbaric relic" and now said that the IMF had "dethroned" gold, there was still some role left for gold—a role that was later to become controversial as the international monetary system came to be dominated by two reserve assets: gold and the dollar. At the outset, par values of currencies were expressed in terms of gold (or the dollar, the value of which was, in turn, expressed in terms of gold). Gold was also to serve as an international reserve asset, providing a means of international settlement through purchases and sales by official monetary authorities. By being left with these functions, gold was not demonetized under the IMF even if it was claimed that it had been dethroned from the central position it had previously occupied under the pure gold standard. During the Bretton Woods era, however, the contribution of gold to international liquidity was limited. During the 1950s and 1960s, the accumulation of dollar reserve assets became of far greater importance as a source of international liquidity.

The special position acquired by the dollar deserves emphasis. Under the gold exchange standard, the dollar acquired several functions more effectively than any other currency, becoming essentially a world currency. The dollar is widely used as a "vehicle" currency for transactions. The greatest part of world trade is transacted in dollars as the unit of account, medium of exchange, and standard of deferred payments. It was also the "key currency" behind the IMF system: the United States was the sole country to tie its currency to gold, and other countries pegged their currencies in relation to the gold value of the dollar. Consequently the dollar was also the primary "intervention currency" used to maintain exchange rates within the parity band. Most important, the dollar is also the primary "reserve currency" insofar as the dollar is an acceptable store of value, and countries accept dollars in settlement for international imbalances. Convertible currencies, under the Fund Agreement, were convertible into dollars; and dollars held by official monetary authorities were convertible into gold at a known price until 1971. The U.S. Treasury stood ready to buy gold from official foreign monetary authorities, and until August 15, 1971, it also stood ready to sell gold to these authorities at the par value of $35 per one ounce of gold. The official holdings of dollar balances become a major source of international liquidity—of greater importance than gold reserves, the unconditional drawing rights at the IMF, or SDRs. This, in turn, was the result of a deficit in the United States balance of payments.

It was, however, the irony of the gold exchange standard that the very means of creating international liquidity—namely, through the deficit in the American balance of payments—was contradictory to maintaining confidence in the principal reserve currency that was providing a larger increment to world monetary reserves than was gold or the IMF. The viability of the gold exchange standard, with its fixity of exchange rates and high dependence on the dollar, rested on the United States being able to cope with its international payments imbalance without devaluing the dollar. While the United States was investing long (through government and private capital outflows), it was borrowing short (through the willingness of foreigners to increase their holdings of dollar assets). As the U.S. gold stock diminished, foreign holders of dollars became less confident that the Treasury would continue to be able to convert the short-term liabilities into gold. Finally, in 1971, the Treasury closed the gold window and made the dollar inconvertible.

Over the next few years the Bretton Woods system collapsed. What were originally considered the very virtues of the system had now come to be considered by many as its vices. The IMF had increased liquidity, but only to a limited extent. The Fund also escaped from the extremes of the fixed exchange-rate system of the pure gold standard and the freely fluctuating rates of a paper standard. But its provision for an "adjustable peg" came to be viewed as a compromise that now embodied the worst, rather than the best, features of both the fixed and floating exchange-rate systems. There was neither the certainty of a truly permanently fixed rate nor the flexibility of a floating rate. Finally, the Fund dethroned gold, but did not demonetize it. The reliance on a national currency to provide international reserves exposed the reserve currency country to the risk of sudden and severe balance of payments deficits through short-term capital outflows induced by interest rate differentials or loss in confidence and speculative outflows. The co-existence of two reserve assets—the dollar and gold—proved impossible as long as asset holders could shift between them. The time came when the dollar had to be devalued or gold demonetized. The Bretton Woods system finally disintegrated from its lack of an adequate adjustment mechanism and its failure to provide for effective control of international liquidity.

Managed Floating

Following the suspension of gold convertibility by the United States, the Bretton Woods system gave way to a hybrid exchange-rate regime of nationally managed floating, joint floats, and pegged exchange rates. The margin of fluctuation widened considerably from the original ±1% of parity—first to 2.25% above and below the new "central rates" established by Agreement in 1971, and then to wider fluctuations in 1973. Only a relatively few major currencies (such as the U.S. and Canadian dollars, the pound sterling, the Japanese yen, and the Italian lira) have actually been allowed to float independently.

In mid-1979, 92 members of the IMF pegged their currencies—either to another currency, to the SDR, or to some other composite of currencies. Some European countries also float jointly in the newly formed (1979) European Monetary System, which establishes central rates and intervention limits within a narrow range of fluctuation among member currencies (all the members of the European Community except the United Kingdom).

Revealing that they desire the flexibility to be less than full flexibility, governments commonly have intervened in foreign exchange markets, buying or selling foreign exchange to manage the range of floating: hence the term **"managed"** or **"dirty" float.** The permissible fluctuation has at times been wide with substantial short-term fluctuations, but still considerably within the range that would have occurred if there had been no market intervention. Figure 9.1 indicates the degree of movement in exchange rates for selected industrial countries in recent years.

According to the portfolio balance theory we examined previously, a **stable equilibrium exchange rate** should exist. Suppose that households and firms have a stable demand for **real** cash balances as measured by the nominal stock of domestic money divided by the domestic price level. Portfolio balance is achieved as people adjust their real cash balance holdings to their unchanging real income. Let the exchange rate be initially at an equilibrium rate, such as r_0 in Figure 6.1 (p. 160). At r_0, the flow of foreign exchange earned by exporters equals the flow demanded by importers. But this is also an exchange rate that will equate the **stock** of real domestic money available to hold to the aggregate (domestic and foreign) demand for real domestic cash balances. If now there is for some reason a depreciation of the domestic currency in terms of foreign currency, the domestic price level will rise. For a given supply of domestic money, firms and households now find their real cash balances have fallen below the desired level. They will then try to reconstitute their cash balance holdings by selling other financial assets or more goods—including exportables—and demanding fewer importables. An excess supply of foreign exchange would result at this disequilibrium exchange rate, and the domestic currency would appreciate to its former level. Thus, if the supply of money is held constant, and the demand for money is stable, a stable equilibrium exchange rate does exist. Any incipient deficit or surplus on current account that would cause a movement in the exchange rate implies that individuals are trying either to build up their real cash balances or run them down. No

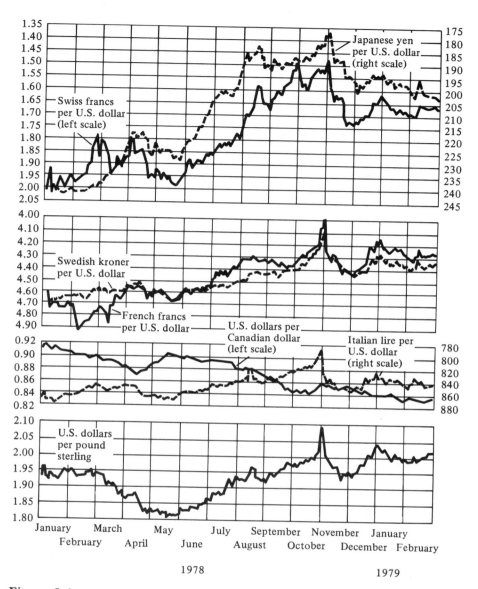

Figure 9.1

Movements in Exchange Rates. Spot exchange rates (based on noon quotations in New York). Data: IMF Treasurer's Department.

such deficit or surplus can therefore be sustained in the "long run" if the domestic supply of money is constant. Then a stable exchange rate that will equate the value of exports and imports can always be found.[4]

In practice, of course, domestic monetary authorities often lose control over the money supply for many reasons. A fiscal deficit in the government's budget is a common source of credit expansion. The depreciation may then continue to persist until the credit expansion is reversed and real cash balances fall below the desired level.

Exchange rates are now actually responding to various forces that may cause considerable fluctuation. Beyond the demand and supply of foreign exchange for current account transactions, conditions in the financial markets may now be more important for determining short-run exchange movements. Interest rate differentials induce large movements in short-term capital. Current rates of return, risk factors, and expected future rates of return are significant in determining the prices of foreign currencies. When these returns and risks change substantially, so too will exchange rates—unless governments intervene to manage the fluctuations in exchange rates. And this they have done.

Official intervention takes the form of selling a foreign currency when there is an excess demand for it and when the government does not want the domestic currency to depreciate in terms of the foreign currency. Or the central bank buys a foreign currency when there is an excess supply of the foreign currency in the foreign exchange market, and the government does not want the domestic currency to appreciate in terms of the foreign currency. The ability to manage the rate will therefore depend on the government's supply of foreign currency and on its ability to distinguish reversible short-run influences from those reflecting more fundamental changes in underlying conditions of national economic stability. Governments have been attempting to put upward or downward pressures on their currencies not only by direct intervention in the exchange markets, but also indirectly, by influencing foreign borrowing, imposing capital controls, and pursuing monetary policies. In view of competitive non-revaluations and "dirty floats," the essential question in practice has been what degree of flexibility is feasible—What is the acceptable and desirable range of limited flexibility?

Expectations and **speculation** can also have a significant effect on the exchange rate. The monetary approach, outlined in Chapter 8,

---

[4] This analysis follows that of R.I. McKinnon, *Money in International Exchange* (1979), Chap. 1.

identified the exchange rate as the relative price of national monies and emphasized asset-market equilibrium. If the relative prices of national monies are determined by forces that are similar to those that operate in any asset market, it is understandable why large, short-term fluctuations of exchange rates will result when the forces that lie behind exchange-market equilibrium are themselves subject to substantial short-term fluctuations.

In recent years movements in exchange rates have been too large to be explained by only changes in the relative prices of different national outputs. More important may be the role of changing expectations in determining exchange rates. Asset demands and supplies will be affected by changes in the expectations of asset holders concerning the returns on various assets. Nations' currencies are just one kind of asset investors may hold. If holders of a currency expect it to appreciate, the increase in demand to hold that currency will bring about its appreciation, and expectations will be self-fulfilling unless the monetary authorities allow the money supply to expand to meet the increase in demand. According to the monetary approach, one of the critical determinants of the equilibrium value of any national money is the supply of that money available to be held. Also important are the expectations about money demand. Expectations of the future supplies of and demands for various national monies will therefore influence, in turn, asset holders' expectations of future exchange rates.

If individuals, banks, and multinational corporations are well informed and well endowed with financial resources, they may intervene on the foreign exchange markets to prevent the rate from departing too far from what is believed to be its medium-term equilibrium level. If, however, there is insufficient private intervention through private capital flows, or if the monetary authorities believe that they have a better idea of what is the appropriate exchange rate than results from freely operating market forces, there may then be official intervention. The official intervention can be non-speculative—in the sense that the exchange-rate target can be realizable without having to impose exchange controls or without risking "giving up" so as to allow a discrete depreciation or appreciation to occur.[5] An excess demand for foreign currency must reflect an excess supply of domestic currency at the existing exchange rate. If the central bank can retire domestic money from circulation so as to eliminate the excess supply, the rate can be main-

[5]*Ibid.*, 170.

H. G. JOHNSON, *Balance-of-Payments Theory and the International Monetary Problem*, Princeton Essays in International Finance, No. 124 (Nov. 1977), 24

> I have said that, in my judgment, the regime of floating exchange rates is going to be with us for a long time. This raises the obvious question of whether eventually the world monetary system will return to a regime of fixed rates—or, more likely, "flexible" or "adjustably pegged" rates. My own hunch is that it will. One reason is historical: Britain after the Napoleonic War, the European countries after each of the two world wars, the United States after its period of floating (1860–79), not to speak of lesser countries practicing currency flotation for shorter or longer periods, all returned sooner or later to fixed exchange rates.

tained. This is a sufficient condition for official intervention to be non-speculative.

The total stock of **international liquidity** has also become highly responsive to the volume and incidence of official intervention in the foreign exchange markets and to the amount of borrowing by governments and government agencies in private international financial markets. An expansion of IMF quotas and an increase in SDR allocations have also increased official international liquidity. For some countries with managed floating rates, however, we must remember that the accumulation of the foreign exchange reserves is largely a result of payments imbalances and exchange-market policies, with official intervention in the foreign exchange market reflecting the desire of the authorities to prevent an unduly rapid or excessive movement of the exchange rate. This is particularly apt to occur when short-term capital flows are interpreted as excessively large and potentially reversible.

The IMF has attempted to enhance the position of the SDR and reduce the reserve role of gold. The official price of gold has been abolished; countries cannot peg their currencies to gold; and the first 25% of a country's IMF quota that used to be paid in gold is now payable in SDRs or in currencies. The SDR is increasingly used as a unit of account, and the interest paid on SDR holdings has been raised. Gold reserves, however, may be revalued at market prices, and this can increase their value, whereas SDRs still remain only a small proportion of total reserves. It remains to be seen whether gold will be completely demonetized or phased back into the international monetary system.

Outside the regulation of the IMF or any national monetary authority, the **Eurocurrency market** has also grown markedly. This market deals mainly in time deposits denominated in U.S. dollars on deposit with banks, so-called Eurobanks, outside the United States. (The term Eurocurrency can apply to any foreign-currency deposit denominated in a currency other than that of the host country. But the dollar is the most widely traded of all Eurocurrencies, and it dominates the international market for short-term capital as well as an increasing amount of intermediate-term credits of three to seven years' maturity.) The dollars may be transferred by American residents or foreigners from U.S. banks to offshore centers. Because Eurodollar reserves take the form of demand deposits with U.S. commercial banks, Eurodollar loans can be made as an addition to the credit provided by the U.S. monetary system.

The Euromarket began in the 1950s when East European governments decided to transfer their dollar accounts from American to European banks for fear that their deposits might be blocked by the U.S. government. The massive buildup in the Euromarket came during the 1960s, when the United States imposed controls on the outflow of dollars, thereby intensifying the demand for dollars through the Eurodollar market. Some central banks have also held part of their external reserves in the form of Eurodollars. In addition, Eurobanks have been able to offer higher interest rates on deposits, or make loans at lower rates than domestic banks, because there are no reserve requirements on Euromarket transactions. The expansion of the Eurocurrency market has greatly increased the international mobility of short-term capital and has been a major force integrating international capital markets. International capital markets can play an effective role in recycling funds from countries with balance of payments surpluses to countries in deficit. At the same time, the Eurocurrency market has aroused concern over whether it feeds inflation and is a source of instability on exchange markets.

Given the developments since 1971, the Governors of the IMF proposed, in their Jamaica Agreement of 1976, that the IMF Articles be amended to permit exchange-rate flexibility, thereby legitimizing the recent changes in the international monetary system. To many observers, however, the new Amendment to the IMF is "nothing less than an abandonment of a specified monetary order."[6] And some would say

[6] Fred Hirsch et al., *Alternatives to Monetary Disorder* (1977), 44. See also, E.M. Bernstein et al., *Reflections on Jamaica*, Princeton Essays in International Finance, No. 115 (April 1976).

that the Jamaica Agreement simply validated a non-system: it legalized the exchange-rate regime, which it could characterize no more clearly than "the one in force at January 1, 1976."

Others, however, interpret the Jamaica Agreement as recognizing the loose type of international monetary system based on exchange-rate flexibility that is now needed. It is commended for focusing primarily on the major principles of acceptable monetary behavior—leaving specific procedures to evolve over time within this basic framework.[7] But few would contend that the Jamaican Agreement gave definitive answers to questions of international monetary reform, and few expect it to guide future developments in the international monetary system. There is still a need to resolve the major problem areas of an international monetary system—liquidity, adjustment, and confidence. The control over the creation and distribution of international official liquidity is still subject to contending views. So too is the interpretation of the benefits and costs of various adjustment mechanisms. And attention must still be given to the question of confidence in reserve assets, with its correlative issue of official convertibility. We shall return to these unsettled issues of international monetary reform at the end of the next chapter. But first we need a better understanding of balance of payments policy before we can assess the present system of managed floating and its implications for the future.

Supplementary Readings

A number of biographies and autobiographies can be consulted for some lively accounts of policy-making under different international monetary systems:

Andrew Boyle, *Montagu Norman: A Biography* (1967);
Lester Chandler, *Benjamin Strong, Central Banker* (1958);
R.F. Harrod, *The Life of John Maynard Keynes* (1951);
David Rees, *Harry Dexter White: A Study in Paradox* (1973);
Charles Coombs, *The Arena of International Finance* (1976).

The history of the IMF is recorded in Margaret De Vries, *The International Monetary Fund, 1966–1971* (1976), and J. Keith Horsefield (ed.), *The International Monetary Fund, 1945–1965* (1969). For an account of the interwar period, see Ragnar Nurkse, *International Currency Experience* (1944).

On the gold standard, see Arthur Bloomfield, *Monetary Policy Under the International Gold Standard, 1880–1914* (1959).

[7]Willett, *op. cit.*, Chap. 3.

For an excellent interpretation of the period 1959–1971, see Susan Strange, *International Economic Relations of the Western World* (1976).

International liquidity is discussed by J.H. Williamson, "Surveys in Applied Economics: International Liquidity," *Economic Journal,* 83 (Sept., 1973), 685–746, and B.J. Cohen, "International Reserves and Liquidity," in P.B. Kenen (ed.), *International Trade and Finance* (1975), 411–52, with bibliography.

The relation between international liquidity and inflation is examined by David L. Fand, "World Reserves and World Inflation," *Banca Nazionale del Lavoro Quarterly Review,* No. 115 (Dec. 1975), 347–69, and H. Robert Heller, "International Reserves and World-Wide Inflation," *IMF Staff Papers,* 23 (March 1976), 61–87.

Two perceptive studies of the Eurocurrency market are by Paul Einzig, *The Euro-Dollar System* (2nd ed., 1973), and R.I. McKinnon, *The Eurocurrency Market,* Princeton Essays in International Finance, No. 125 (Dec. 1977).

10

Balance of Payments Policy

When a country has a balance of payments problem, the remedial policies it adopts will depend, of course, on its choice of policy targets and the range of feasible policy instruments. More specifically, the remedial policies will be conditioned by the cause of the disequilibrium, the state of the domestic economy, the type of international monetary system extant, and the policies being undertaken by other countries. What the country *wants* to do will depend on its analysis of the causes of its disequilibrium and the state of its own economy—for the country wants to achieve internal balance and external balance. What the country *can* do will depend on the policy options allowed by the type of international monetary system that exists and on the policies of foreign countries insofar as the policies undertaken by one country to affect its balance of payments might be neutralized or reinforced by the policies of other countries.

To elaborate on this problem, we shall now consider the different sources of balance of payments disequilibrium, the choice of remedial policies, and the distribution of adjustment costs.

The Feasible Policy-Space

We began our study of balance of payments problems by first recognizing the uneasy triangle confronting any country that attempts to pursue the policy objectives of achieving domestic economic stability while liberalizing trade and maintaining balance of payments equilibrium. The uneasy triangle symbolizes the effort to **attain internal balance and exter-**

nal balance without resorting to trade restrictions. Having surveyed alternative international monetary arrangements, we can now recognize that the present-day international economy cannot enforce the balance of payments discipline that should be imposed by a regime of fixed rates, nor can it manage the harmonization of national policies that is needed to maintain fixed rates. At the same time as nations are unwilling to forgo domestic balance for the sake of maintaining external balance, they frequently engage in a clash of national economic policies that make it extremely difficult to reduce trade restrictions or improve international monetary cooperation. If anything, the "uneasiness" of the triangle has intensified in recent years as countries have experienced balance of payments crises, and the commercial policies and international payments restrictions have become increasingly neo-mercantilistic. More and more countries have attempted to build up or husband their international reserves, to restrict their imports, and promote their exports—often with beggar-my-neighbor consequences.

If we recall the range of policy instruments available to a country that is seeking to adjust its balance of payments, we can recognize three broad ways for coping with imbalances. First, the country may pursue **"internal measures."** If it is a deficit country, it can deflate or disinflate its economy by an appropriately restrictive fiscal policy (increase taxes and decrease government expenditure) and a tight money policy (reduce money supply and raise interest rates). Second, the deficit country may resort to **"external measures"** and restrict its trade (increase tariffs and impose quantitative restrictions), limit capital outflows (impose exchange restrictions), or allow its currency to depreciate (practice non-intervention in the exchange market). Third, if the country has access to sufficient international liquidity it may be able to eschew both internal and external measures and simply cover its imbalance by **drawing upon its international reserve assets.**

The three vertices of the triangle in Figure 10.1 depict the exclusive use of each of these three broad ways in coping with international imbalances. If a country has to remove a balance of payments deficit, it must now select some set of policies within the triangle. The country need not proceed to one vertex or rely exclusively on one type of measure. But the feasible area of the triangle within which the country can operate will be bounded by certain constraints on the country's policy choices.[1] A country will want to retain a certain degree of

[1] The following analysis is adopted from R.N. Cooper, "The Relevance of International Liquidity to Developed Countries," *American Economic Review*, LVIII (May 1968), 627.

Figure 10.1

The Feasible Policy-Space for Coping with International Imbalance

I: Internal measures (expenditure-reducing policies).

E: External measures (expenditure-switching policies).

L: International official liquidity (expenditure-sustaining policies).

EL: Size of *ex ante* deficit.

Shaded triangle represents boundaries of the feasible policy-space.

At *A*, *EF* of the deficit is financed by international liquidity, *LC* of the deficit is removed by external measues, *FC* of the deficit is removed by internal measures.

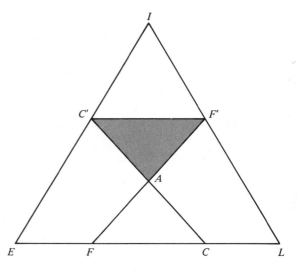

domestic autonomy in its policy-making and may therefore refuse to endure "internal measures" beyond the boundary line *C'F'*. It may also be unwilling to resort to "external measures" beyond the boundary line *CC'*. And the country's access to international official liquidity confines it to the left of the boundary *FF'*. The shaded area therefore represents the boundaries of the feasible policy-space. These boundaries will be determined by the nature of the international monetary system and the state of the domestic economy.

Suppose that the country selects within the policy-space (the shaded area in Figure 10.1) a particular policy position at *A*. If the triangle is an equilateral triangle, the size of the *ex ante* deficit will be denoted by the length of a side of the triangle. The deficit is *EL*. Of this total deficit, the portion *CL* is removed by external measures (expenditure-switching policies). Another portion of the deficit, represented by *EF*, is financed by international liquidity. The remaining portion *FC* is removed by internal measures (expenditure-reducing policies).

The shaded policy-space (Figure 10.1) contrasts with the pure gold standard, which operated at the vertex of "internal measures," an international paper standard, which would operate at the vertex of "external measures," of the international payments policies pursued during the 1930s and World War II, when countries again relied on "external measures." With the establishment of the IMF and the reliance on reserve currencies for additional liquidity after World War II, the area representing effective policy-making was able to move from the external measures vertex closer to the center of the triangle. Now the essential question is whether the feasible area of policy-making provides sufficient scope for the adjustment process to operate without requiring a country to remove its balance of payments deficit by sacrificing its domestic stability or its gains from trade. Can a government achieve both internal balance and external balance without imposing trade restrictions? The crucial issues confronting the international monetary system are whether the system requires fundamental modification so as to create more liquidity and allow the deficit country to move to the right of the boundary FF', whether the country will be forced to give up more domestic autonomy and endure policies beyond $C'F'$, whether the country will retreat farther from the objective of trade liberalization and undertake policies to the left of CC', or whether the country will not intervene in the exchange market and let its currency depreciate.

Stated somewhat differently, the essential international monetary problem now is that of payments adjustment—how to render the adjustment less burdensome without forsaking completely some balance of payments discipline.

Sources of Balance of Payments Disequilibrium

The sources of disturbance to a country's balance of payments are many—any change that increases the demand for foreign exchange or decreases the supply of foreign exchange. The disturbance to a pre-existing equilibrium may be as varied as the vagaries of nature, the impact of the business cycle, or changes in public policy. The various sources of disequilibrium give rise to at least four different kinds of disequilibria: (i) income; (ii) price; (iii) structural, and (iv) excessive capital movement. In practice there is likely to be some overlap among these kinds of disequilibria, but for analytical purposes it is useful to emphasize the dominant characteristic that distinguishes each kind of disequilibrium.

(i) **The income-type of disequilibrium** arises from variations in the country's level of output, employment, and aggregate income relative to other countries. This disequilibrium is commonly associated with cyclical fluctuations. In recent years it has been related to differential rates of inflation among countries.

The income-type of disequilibrium raises policy issues of how to maintain both internal and external balance. By internal balance we mean an acceptable level of unemployment and price increase—the goal of domestic stability (formerly simply "full employment with stable prices," but now in a period of stagflation, some target of unemployment and restrained price inflation). By external balance, we mean the goal of balance of payments equilibrium. Can national economic management attain its domestic goals without disequilibrating the balance of payments? And can balance of payments equilibrium be maintained without the opportunity costs of forgoing the goals of domestic economic policy?

Consider first the case of a country that is in a recession and that then undertakes full employment policies (expansionary fiscal policy and easy money policy). The level of domestic investment and government expenditures will tend to exceed the level of domestic savings and taxes. The level of national income will then rise. And as national income rises, so too will imports, according to the marginal propensity to import. If an easy money policy has been followed, with a reduction in interest rates, there is also likely to be an outflow of short-term capital, aggravating the country's balance of payments. External balance may then be sacrificed when the country pursues full employment policies more actively than other countries. Some countries will be more susceptible to, and will suffer more severely from, an income-type of balance of payments disequilibrium than will other countries. This will depend on the relative rates of increase in national income in each trading country, the size of the respective propensities to import, and the magnitudes of the foreign repercussions in each country's foreign trade multiplier.

Once inflation sets in, the internal imbalance tends to be translated also into an external imbalance. We have already seen (Chapter 7) that, if at full employment, a country absorbs through national expenditure more than its own output, there must be an external deficit financed by an induced capital inflow or loss of international reserves, under fixed rates. With floating rates, the domestic currency would depreciate to restore external balance.

(ii) **A price-type of disequilibrium** occurs when the country's prices become out of line with other countries', so that it loses its competitive position and incurs a passive balance on current account.

The source of this type of disequilibrium may be traced to changes in productivity or factor prices. Although a demand-pull inflation will impair a country's competitive position internationally, the country can also lose its competitive position through a cost-push type of inflation in prices that is caused by a rise in unit labor costs. When prices of the country's exportables rise relative to prices of its importables, the current account can turn into a deficit.

(iii) **A structural-type of disequilibrium** stems from "real" forces that change the country's comparative cost structure by altering the demand or supply conditions in specific sectors. The sources of this type of disequilibrium may be a change in consumer tastes at home or abroad, technological change in exportables, or depletion of a natural resource that is an input in the export sector. In recent years, for example, the competition from synthetics has been a major source of structural disequilibrium for some primary producing countries. These are "exogenous" disturbances to the economy. They result in an increase in imports or a decrease in exports, but for non-monetary reasons in one sector of the economy, unlike the causes in income or price disequilibria.

(iv) The final type of disequilibrium—that associated with excessive capital movements—constitutes what is called a **"transfer problem."** In this case, the capital movement is an autonomous transaction, but it must still be balanced by requiring the capital-exporting country to generate a surplus on current account to effect the real transfer of capital. The financial transfer has to be turned into a real transfer in the form of an excess of exports of goods over imports of the right amount.

The transfer problem has long been of historical interest in connection with the payment of wartime reparations, but it is receiving renewed attention in relation to foreign aid, loans, military expenditure overseas, and foreign investments. This type of disequilibrium requires the selection of policy instruments that will adjust the balance on current account to the outflow of capital and unilateral payments.

Instead of being simply induced by trade imbalances, capital movements may have an autonomous character. Short-term capital flows, in particular, may be autonomous and affect the equilibrium levels of all variables. If, for instance, a country has a current account deficit, but maintains low interest rates in order to stimulate investment and employment, then capital will flow out to another country in which interest rates are higher. The capital outflow intensifies pressure on the deficit country's balance of payments and is also disequilibrating in the other country if it is a surplus country.

Attaining Internal and External Balance

We have repeatedly noted that it will be less urgent for a country to correct its international payments, the lower the magnitude of its deficit, the greater the speed of the adjustment process, and the more available international official liquidity. If, however, remedial policies are needed, the policies should be geared to the causes of the disequilibrium and should be the least-costly policies that are feasible.

We have also categorized the range of remedial measures as "internal measures" of an "expenditure-reducing" character or "external measures" of an expenditure-switching" character. The **expenditure-reducing remedies** lower the level of aggregate demand: they entail disabsorption through monetary restriction or contractionary budgetary policies. The **expenditure-switching remedies** cause the patterns of production to switch from non-tradables to tradables and of expenditure to switch from tradables to non-tradables through exchange-rate variations, capital restrictions, and trade controls (tariffs, quotas, subsidies, exchange controls).

In many cases, different policies may constitute alternative remedies. An increase in taxes, a reduction in government expenditures, a contraction of the money supply, a rise in tariff rates, an increase in non-tariff barriers, a depreciation of the country's currency—all these policies may be alternative means of reducing a country's imports. But the cost of these alternative policies will differ. It is therefore important to establish some **cost-ranking of remedies**, according to both political and economic criteria. This is by no means a simple procedure because many of the costs will be indirect, ambiguous, and not amenable to measurement—especially (but not only) the political costs. Nonetheless, in some cases different policy choices will give rise to clashes among policy objectives, and the opportunity cost of forgoing a certain policy target should be considered.

The conflict among policy targets appears most frequently when a country's choice of balance of payments remedial policies must be conditioned by the state of its domestic economy and its domestic stability targets. In restoring external balance, the country will want to avoid selecting policy instruments that will impose the costs of domestic imbalance. The cost-ranking of alternative remedies will therefore be highly influenced by whether the domestic economy is already experiencing deflation or inflation and whether unemployment or full employment exists.

Figure 10.2

Internal and External Balance Targets

T: Targets of internal and external balance, simultaneously achieved.

Zones *I* and *III;* "non-dilemma zones" in which income changes can move economy toward *T.*

Zones *II* and *IV;* "dilemma zones" in which income changes cannot move economy toward *T.* Zone *II* calls for appreciation of the domestic currency, and zone *IV* requires depreciation.

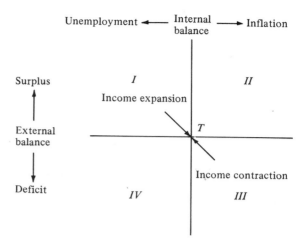

To illustrate how the correct remedy for balance of payments disequilibrium depends on the question of internal stability, we may consider a number of different cases that call for different policy combinations. The objective in all these cases is to attain simultaneously the two targets of internal balance and external balance without imposing trade restrictions. We shall first consider a fixed exchange-rate regime and then a flexible regime. Under the fixed exchange-rate regime, we shall confront some "dilemma cases," which raise the problem of policy assignment. Under the flexible regime, we shall confront a fundamental principle of policy that there must be as many policy instruments as there are policy targets.

First, consider different "situations" for the domestic economy and the balance of payments under a regime of fixed exchange rates, as in Figure 10.2.[2] The vertical internal balance line represents the target of full employment with stable prices, or more realistically under conditions of "stagflation" a target of tolerable unemployment (say 5%) and price inflation (say 3%). To the right, price inflation would be excessive; to the left, unemployment would be excessive. The balance of payments can be in surplus or in deficit—or in a situation in between, which can be termed external balance, as represented by the horizontal external balance line. The two targets of the economy—internal balance and external balance—coalesce at *T,* where the two balance lines

[2] This diagram is adopted from Assar Lindbeck, "The National State in an International World Economy," Institute for International Economic Studies, University of Stockholm, Seminar Paper No. 26. It is derived from T. W. Swan, "Longer-Run Problems of the Balance of Payments," reprinted in American Economic Association, *Readings in International Economics* (1968), Chap. 22.

intersect in Figure 10.2. The two lines of internal and external balance divide existence into four unhappy zones of imbalance, requiring remedial policy. In Zone *I,* there is simultaneously unemployment and a balance of payments surplus. In this case (characteristic of the United States during the Great Depression of the 1930s), fiscal and monetary policies designed to reflate the economy would also be consistent with the external target. An easy money policy would facilitate the balance of payments adjustment process through capital outflows and induced increases in aggregate demand, and an expansionary fiscal policy would induce an increase in imports. Domestic stabilization policy can therefore move in the right direction, as indicated by the arrow, toward *T.*

Similarly, domestic stabilization policy will be appropriate in Zone *III,* where there is simultaneously inflation and a balance of payments deficit (which was characteristic of West European countries after World War II and the United States in the early 1970s). Policies that disinflate the economy would be consistent with both domestic stability and external balance. A restrictive fiscal policy, a tight money policy, and an incomes policy (wage-price guidelines) would all be appropriate for reducing both the country's inflation and balance of payments deficit. Again, the economy can move in the direction of the arrow toward *T.* Zones *I* and *III* pose no problem for stabilization policy. They are "simple zones," representing "non-dilemma" cases. But now consider Zones *II* and *IV.* These zones represent "**dilemma cases,**" in which stabilization policy, under a regime of fixed exchange rates, will not allow the achievement of both internal and external balance.

In Zone *II* there is inflation and a balance of payments surplus (characteristic of the United States in the 1945–1950 period of "dollar shortage"). If a restrictive fiscal policy and a tight monetary policy are used, the resultant contraction of income would be correct for the target of internal balance, but would intensify the balance of payments surplus. The external objective in this case is fewer exports and more imports. An expenditure-switching policy of appreciation of the surplus country's currency would therefore be in order. If this is not possible because of the assumption of a fixed exchange-rate regime, then the government might assign a fiscal policy instrument to the domestic target of contracting income, while a monetary policy instrument could be assigned to the external target by lowering short-term interest rates in order to stimulate a short-term capital outflow from the surplus country. This is a version of the general "**assignment problem**" in policy-making.[3]

According to this view of policy-making, there is a need for as many policy instruments as policy objectives. This need can be met by recognizing that fiscal and monetary expansion have effects in the same direction on the current account (increasing imports and possibly decreasing exports), but in opposite directions on the capital account of the balance of payments. Fiscal expansion has an effect on the capital account by attracting a capital inflow through increases in domestic interest rates, but monetary expansion has the opposite effect when interest rates fall. The "theory of fiscal-monetary policy mix" should therefore pair policies with the objectives on which they have the most influence. Fiscal policy has the relatively greatest influence on the objective of internal balance and should therefore be assigned to this target, whereas monetary policy has the relatively greatest influence on the objective of external balance and should be assigned to that target. The two policies can then be "mixed" to achieve a capital account surplus or deficit to offset the current account deficit or surplus.

In Zone *IV*, there is unemployment and an external deficit (characteristic of Western European countries during the Great Depression of the 1930s and the United States during the early 1960s). An expansionary fiscal policy and easy money policy would help remove the domestic unemployment, but would do so at the cost of aggravating the balance of payments deficit. As income increased, imports would rise; but from the standpoint of external balance, the objective is to increase exports and reduce imports. Instead of an expansionary aggregate demand policy, the preferable policy would be an expenditure-switching policy of devaluation. By changing relative prices, devaluation may then reduce the balance of payments deficit while also countering the unemployment by increasing exports and decreasing imports.

If exchange-rate variation is ruled out, then another possibility would be to assign an expansionary fiscal policy to meet the domestic policy

[3] This analysis and Figure 10.3 were suggested by R.A. Mundell, "The Appropriate Use of Monetary and Fiscal Policy under Fixed Exchange Rates," *IMF Staff Papers,"* 9 (March 1962), 70–77.

From the standpoint of the monetary approach, the assignment of fiscal and monetary policies can be criticized for treating as continuing flow phenomena what should be regarded as securities-portfolio adjustments in response to changes in international interest-rate differentials and also for neglecting the effects of such portfolio adjustments on the services-account component of the current account.

ROBERT A. MUNDELL, "The Appropriate Use of Monetary and Fiscal Policy Under Fixed Exchange Rates," *IMF Staff Papers,* 9 (March 1962), 79

It has been demonstrated that, in countries where employment and balance-of-payments policies are restricted to monetary and fiscal instruments, monetary policy should be reserved for attaining the desired level of the balance of payments and fiscal policy for preserving internal stability. The opposite system would lead to a progressively worsening unemployment and balance-of-payments situation.

The explanation can be related to what I have elsewhere called the principle of effective market classification: Policies should be paired with the objectives on which they have the most influence. If this principle is not followed, there will develop a tendency either for cyclical approach to equilibrium or for instability. . . .

On a still more general level, we have the principle that Tinbergen has made famous—that to attain a given number of independent targets there must be at least an equal number of instruments. Tinbergen's principle is concerned with the *existence* and *location* of a solution to the system. It does not assert that any given set of policy responses will, in fact, lead to that situation. To assert this, it is necessary to investigate the stability properties of a dynamic system. In this respect, the principle of effective market classification is a necessary companion to Tinbergen's principle.

objectives of raising income, while assigning a policy of increasing short-term interest rates to attain the external policy objective of reducing the payments imbalance. There are, however, two difficulties with the monetary policy instrument. It is only a short-term remedy that relies on short-term borrowing, whereas the current account will sooner or later have to be adjusted. In the future there will have to be a return outflow of interest payments on the newly borrowed funds (unless debt is continually renewed), and this limits the lasting impact of monetary policy. It also assumes that other countries will not offset the rise in interest rates; but if several countries simultaneously attempt to improve their balance of payments through competitive increases in interest rates, the monetary policy instrument will be ineffective.

Even, however, in Zones *I* and *III*—the non-dilemma zones—the government has to select the appropriate policy combination to move to *T* rather than into Zones *II* and *IV*. If, for instance, in Zone *I,* the

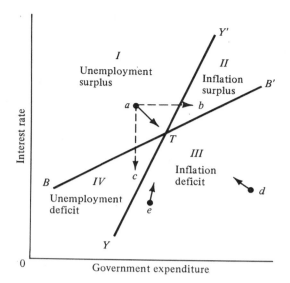

Figure 10.3

Appropriate Policy Response for Internal and External Balance: Fixed Exchange-Rate Regime

BB': External balance with various policy combinations of interest rate and government expenditure.

YY': Internal balance with various policy combinations of interest rate and government expenditure.

T: Target of internal balance and external balance.

government undertakes an easy money policy (increasing the money supply by a sufficient amount to lower the rate of interest) and an expansionary fiscal policy (increasing government expenditure) it is possible that an external deficit will arise before the unemployment is removed (Zone *IV*). Or the expansionary fiscal policy could be excessive and spill over into inflation (Zone *II*).

The effects of fiscal and monetary policy on internal and external balance are illustrated in Figure 10.3. The line *YY'* indicates all combinations of fiscal and monetary policies that ensure internal balance, whereas the line *BB'* denotes combinations of policies that ensure external balance. The *BB'* schedule will be flatter, the higher the degree of capital mobility. This is because it requires only a small interest-rate increase to induce a large enough capital flow to offset trade deficits if capital flows are highly responsive to interest rates. The *BB'* schedule will also be flatter, the lower the marginal propensity to import, so that an increase in government expenditure does not produce a large trade deficit that must be offset by a capital inflow induced by a large increase in market rates. The *YY'* line has a steeper slope than the *BB'* because we assume that short-term capital flows are responsive to a rise in the interest rate and that it will require a smaller rise in the interest rate to maintain external balance than would be needed to maintain internal balance when the rise in the interest rate is required to offset an increase in government expenditure.

At *T* there is both internal and external balance. Again, there are four disequilibrium zones. To the left of *YY'*, there will be unemployment because interest rates are too high and government expenditure too low to maintain internal balance. To the right of YY', inflation results. Above BB', the interest rate is so high that a surplus results in the balance of payments through the induced capital inflow. Below BB', an external deficit results from too low a rate of interest. Thus, Zone I is again characterized by unemployment and a surplus; II, inflation and a surplus; III, inflation and a deficit; and IV, unemployment and a deficit.

If now the economy is in Zone I at point a, the correct combination of fiscal and monetary policies would be along the solid arrow leading to T. It is possible, however, that the government increases expenditure by a larger amount than would be indicated by the solid arrows and does not lower interest rates as much as would be indicated by the solid arrow. The economy therefore moves along the dashed arrow from a to b in Zone II, where there is now inflation and a balance of payments surplus. Alternatively, the economy could have moved along the dashed arrow from a to c in Zone IV.

More generally, any point in the diagram, other than T, will indicate the combination of policies needed to move toward T. Thus the arrows indicate the proper direction of policy changes at d and e. The direction of change in interest rates and in government expenditure will depend on the relative sizes of the internal imbalance and the external imbalance.

Let us now allow for floating exchange rates and consider the policy combinations of exchange-rate variations and changes in government expenditure, as in Figure 10.4.[4] The exchange rate is measured on the vertical axis, with a movement up the axis representing an increase in the number of units of domestic currency per unit of foreign currency or a depreciation of the domestic currency; an appreciation of the domestic currency is represented by a movement down the vertical axis. The line YY' denotes various combinations of the exchange rate and level of government expenditure that allow the attainment of internal balance. To the right of YY' is a region of inflation. To the left of YY' is a region of unemployment. The line BB' represents different combinations of the exchange rate and government expenditure that allow the attainment of external balance. Above BB', the balance of payments is in surplus. Below BB', the balance of payments is in deficit. Again, there are four zones: I, surplus and unemployment; II, surplus and

---

[4] This diagram is based on Swan, *op. cit.*, and R.E. Caves and R.W. Jones, *World Trade and Payments* (2nd ed., 1977), 365.

Figure 10.4

Appropriate Policy Response for
Internal and External Balance:
Floating Exchange-Rate Regime

r_o: Exchange rate = number of domestic units (d) per unit of foreign currency (f).

YY': Internal balance with various policy combinations of exchange rate and government expenditure.

BB': External balance with various policy combinations of exchange rate and government expenditure.

T: Target of internal balance and external balance.

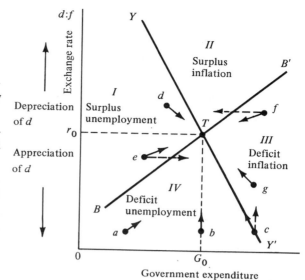

inflation; *III*, deficit and inflation; and *IV*, deficit and unemployment. Only at *T* are the targets of both internal and external balances achieved simultaneously, with an exchange rate of r_0 and government expenditure of G_0.

Given different states of internal imbalance and external imbalance, **different policy combinations** will be required to move toward *T*. If, for instance, the economy is at *a*, both depreciation and an increase in government expenditure are in order. If at *b*, only depreciation is. And if at *c*, a combination of depreciation and a contraction in government expenditure are required (a contraction because the economy is already in internal balance, and the depreciation has an inflationary impact, which would carry the economy along the dashed arrow into Zone *III* if the depreciation were not offset by disabsorption through a contraction in government expenditure). In Zone *IV*, depreciation always moves the economy in the desired direction, but must be coupled with the proper amount of government expenditure, depending on whether government expenditure is initially lower or higher than G_0. Similarly in Zone *II*, appreciation of the domestic currency always moves the economy in the correct direction, but must also be coupled with government expenditure of the right amount.

In Zones *I* and *III*, however, exchange-rate variations can create problems. In *I*, expanding government expenditure always moves the economy in the right direction, but whether depreciation or appreciation of the domestic currency is required depends on the relative magnitudes of the internal imbalance and the external imbalance, or whether the exchange rate is initially above or below r_0. Thus at d, the internal imbalance is small relative to the external imbalance, and the exchange rate is above r_0; therefore, the correct mix of policies is appreciation of the domestic currency coupled with expansion of government expenditure (the appreciation reduces the surplus, but intensifies the unemployment problem and therefore must be offset by expanded government expenditure). At e, however, the internal imbalance is large relative to the external imbalance, and the exchange rate is below r_0, so that the correct mix of policies would be depreciation for the domestic currency coupled with an increase in government expenditure (the increase in government expenditure would create an external deficit and the economy would move along the dashed arrow into Zone *IV*, unless the increased expenditure was counteracted by the depreciation). In Zone *III*, a depreciation would improve the deficit, but intensify the inflation, unless offset by a reduction in expenditure. Again, the relative magnitudes of the internal and external imbalances, and the initial exchange rate, will determine whether depreciation or appreciation is in order. At f, the policy mix calls for appreciation coupled with contraction in government expenditure (if there were only a cut in government expenditure, the economy would move along the dashed arrow into Zone *II* with less inflation, but a surplus). At g, the internal imbalance is small relative to the external imbalance, and the correct policy combination would be depreciation and contraction in government expenditure.

A sufficient number of different positions have been examined to emphasize a basic principle of economic policy: **normally a policy-making body needs as many policy instruments as it has policy targets.** It is crucial to recognize that if the government desires to attain the targets of both internal balance and external balance, it needs two policy instruments—one for the exchange rate (a switching instrument) and one for affecting total expenditure (an absorption instrument).[5] **The government needs to couple demand management with exchange-rate policy.**

Although Figure 10.4 illustrates this fundamental principle, we must not exaggerate the possibility of moving easily to the target of full equilibrium at T. In the diagram it blithely is assumed that r_0 is the

[5] The "two-target two-instrument" model of balance-of-payments policy is lucidly presented, with several refinements, W.M. Corden, *Inflation, Exchange Rates, and the World Economy* (1977), Chaps. 1–3. The theory originated in J.E. Meade, *The Balance of Payments* (1951), and was extended by H.G. Johnson, "Toward a General Theory of the Balance of Payments," in Johnson, *International Trade and Economic Growth* (1958), Chap. 6.

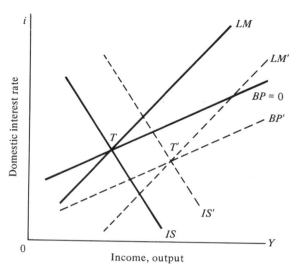

Figure 10.5

Monetary Policy with Flexible Exchange Rates

The *LM* curve first shifts to the right with monetary expansion, and interest rates fall. Capital flows out, and the exchange rate depreciates. This causes *IS* to shift to *IS'*. The balance of payments improves and *BP* shifts to *BP'*. Along *BP'*, the balance of payments is in equilbrium at the new exchange rate. At the new equilibrium position *T'*, *IS'* = *LM'* = *BP'*, and income is higher.

equilibrium exchange rate that will maintain external balance with a government expenditure in the amount of G_0. But we have previously confronted the difficulties involved in determining the equilibrium exchange rate. Nor may governments know just how far the economy is from internal balance and external balance in any particular time period. And when it comes to the undertaking of fiscal policy, monetary policy, or an exchange-rate variation, the government may not know the magnitudes of change in the internal and external balances that are so easily suggested by the diagram. Lags, price-wage rigidities, and inelasticities operate in reality to produce policy wiggles (or worse), with misdirected dashed arrows instead of the solid and straight policy arrows depicted in Figures 10.3 and 10.4.

If we now allow for capital movements, less of the adjustment process will depend upon changes in the exchange rate. To illustrate the role of capital movements and changes in interest rates, we may consider an *IS-LM-BP* diagram, as in Figure 10.5. Positions of balance of payments equilibrium at a given exchange rate ($BP = 0$) are now determined by both the trade balance (as a function of aggregate demand and the exchange rate) and capital movements (as a function of the interest rate and the exchange rate).

Consider first the effects of **monetary policy under floating rates.** Suppose the country undertakes an expansionary monetary policy. The *LM* curve then shifts outward and to the right to *LM'*. The interest rate falls. As a result, short-term capital flows out of the country, and the exchange rate depreciates as the demand for foreign currency rises. The exchange-rate depreciation will cause, in turn, a shift in the *IS* curve upward and to the right, because the depreciation increases exports (injections) and decreases imports (leakages). The balance of payments also improves, and the *BP* curve shifts to the right to *BP'*. (*BP'* represents balance of payments equilibrium at the new exchange rate.) At *T'*, a new equilibrium is established at a higher level of income with the intersection of *IS'* and *LM'* on the *BP'* schedule. A key element in this process of income expansion is the mobility of capital: the more mobile the capital, the greater the increase in income as a result of an increase in the money supply.

Now consider the effects of **fiscal policy**. If the country increases government expenditure, the *IS* curve shifts upward to *IS'*. This causes interest rates to rise and capital to flow in, and the greater supply of foreign currency causes the domestic currency to appreciate. The currency appreciation causes imports to rise and exports to fall. This has a deflationary effect and shifts the *IS* curve back until it is at its original position. The more mobile is capital, the less effective is fiscal policy under floating rates. (In the limiting case of perfect capital mobility, fiscal policy has no effect under flexible exchange rates. This is because there is only one income level that can make the demand for money equal to the supply when the interest rate is fixed and the money supply is constant. An increase in government expenditure, therefore, cannot change this equilibrium income, but can only lead to a trade deficit that offsets the fiscal expansion, which is financed by the capital inflow.)

Distribution of Adjustment Costs

Another important part of the problem of evaluating balance of payments policy involves consideration of how the costs of adjustment are borne by different countries. If one country is in deficit, another country must be in surplus. In some cases it is no more sensible to assign "blame" for imbalance to the deficit country than to the surplus country. The source of disequilibrium can lie in the **surplus country**: instead of contending that the deficit country's imbalance is due to excessive spending, it may be that its trading partners have not been spending enough (by tolerating a higher level of unemployment); a country's deficit position can also depend on changes in the flows of capital and in the pattern of demand that can be determined by forces in other countries; or the surplus country's currency can be grossly undervalued.

Moreover, the relative cost of adjusting the balance of payments disequilibrium can be less if some of the onus of remedial action is placed on the surplus country. If the surplus country appreciates its currency, pursues expansionary demand policies, liberalizes commercial policies, or promotes a greater outflow of capital from its economy, it will help re-equilibrate international payments—and at less cost to the world economy as a whole than if the deficit country had to suffer unemployment or if the volume of world trade had to be reduced by trade restrictions imposed by the deficit country.

Exporters, and import competitors in the surplus countries, however, have generally resisted measures to reduce a trade surplus. Nor has the surplus country's government been willing to expand demand and undergo inflation to correct the surplus or to revalue the currency upwards or to undertake a sufficiently large increase in foreign aid. There are no means to prevent independent behavior by surplus countries.

In the absence of a symmetry in adjustment obligations of surplus and deficit countries, the deficit countries have sooner or later had to undertake the remedial action simply because a deficit country cannot continue to lose reserves indefinitely. In the past, deficit countries have frequently had to reduce their levels of aggregate demand below what they would have desired in terms of autonomy in domestic policies for internal balance, and they have also been led farther away from the trade liberalization target of the General Agreement on Tariffs and Trade (GATT).

A corollary of the internationalization process is the call for more multilateral co-ordination of national policies. This is urged especially for balance of payments problems. "Policy co-ordination" is, however, subject to at least three different interpretations. It may first mean policy co-ordination in order to avoid a balance of payments adjustment problem. In this sense, international policy co-ordination and national adjustment mechanisms are alternatives. If the co-ordination of monetary, fiscal, wage, and commercial policies were "100% effective," there would be no need for a nation to endure the adjustment burden. But "100% effective" is question-begging. In another sense, policy co-ordination can mean some act of collective management in the world economy to provide a more effective framework for the pursuit of international policies. The collective decision to create Special Drawing Rights (SDRs) is an example of this type of policy co-ordination. Policy co-ordination, in another sense, can mean that national policies are harmonized in order to ease the burden of the adjustment process, once a balance of payments problem must be remedied. This third meaning of policy co-ordination is now receiving greater attention.

The burden of adjustment is intensified for a deficit country to the extent that other countries adopt competitive or defensive national policies instead of co-ordinating their policies to make the adjustment process operate speedily and equitably. If other countries neutralize or contradict the policies taken by the deficit country, then the adjustment mechanism will be inhibited, and the deficit country will need more recourse to international liquidity. If, for instance, a deficit country raises interest rates to attract short-term capital, other countries may do the same in order not to experience a capital outflow. A depreciation of the country's currency may also be countered by another country's imposition of taxes on imports and subsidies on exports. The need for international policy co-ordination stems from the fact that whereas the absolute level of a policy instrument may have important effects domestically, the effects on a country's balance of payments will be determined by the **relative** differences between the country's policy measures and those of other countries. Thus, what matters for a country's demand for imports is not simply the level of its own tariffs, but the domestic tariffs less foreign subsidies. Clearly, it is also interest-rate differentials, not the absolute level of interest rates, which induce the movement of short-term capital connected with portfolio shifts into foreign interest-bearing claims. Further, the relative rates of inflation or deflation matter for a country's balance of payments (recall that in some cases, instead of saying that the deficit country is "overspending," we might be equally justified in saying the surplus country is "underspending.")

It is true that a floating rate allows a country to be more disengaged from the policies of another country than does a fixed rate. Inflation, for example, is transmitted across the rates under the fixed rate regime. The monetary authority of a country with an undervalued currency purchases the inflow of foreign currency with an increase in its domestic money supply.) But even under managed floating, to reduce the degree of fluctuation in the rates and to ease the adjustment mechanism, more co-ordination of policies is still necessary. Fluctuations in exchange rates often reflect underlying macroeconomic policies, and if the fluctuation is to be reduced there has to be more effective co-ordination of monetary and fiscal policies. The greater the differences in rates of income expansion among countries, the greater the variability in exchange rates as the current accounts in the balance of payments change. Similarly, the greater the differences in monetary policy, the greater the variability in exchange rates as capital flows affect the balance of payments. If there is concern over too great variability in exchange rates, then more efforts have to be made to achieve harmonization in fiscal and monetary policies. To avoid the need to correct imbalances through exchange-rate variations, there has to be a harmonization of policies that will reduce the differences among nations in their rates of change in national incomes, productivity, and prices. Collaboration in monetary management is especially relevant for the major trading countries—the United States, West Germany, and Japan.

Complete co-ordination of monetary policy can be accomplished only within a monetary union or an **"optimum currency area."** Such an area is defined as a territory composed of several member countries, with a common currency unit or permanently fixed exchange rates among the members.[6] Adjustment with external countries would be through exchange-rate changes between the optimum currency area and outside countries. A currency area can therefore be declared "optimum" in membership when it encompasses the number of countries that will minimize the total adjustment cost via exchange-rate changes and other adjustment policies. The optimum territorial size must be determined by weighing the advantages of the economic integration promoted by a currency union against the disadvantages of fixed exchange rates in constraining the adjustment mechanism among members. The advantages tend to be greater, the larger the volume of trade and the higher the degree of factor mobility among the countries of the currency area.

Members of a currency union are likely to differ, however, on their estimates of what is the most desirable common external exchange rate. Further, to be effective, monetary unification would also require policy co-ordination to reduce the need for adjustment. This co-ordination must extend to various policies—monetary, fiscal, agricultural, industrial, and commercial. If a country does encounter balance of payments problems with other member countries, it will have to resort to expenditure-reducing measures instead of exchange-rate adjustments. The costs of adjustment may then be excessive for a large country that has only a small amount of external trade relative to national output.

Short of an optimum currency area—and difficult as it may be to

[6] See R.I. McKinnon, "Optimum Currency Areas," *American Economic Review*, 53 (Sept. 1963), 717–25; and T.D. Willett and E. Tower, *The Theory of Optimum Currency Areas and Exchange-Rate Flexibility*, Princeton Special Papers in International Economics, No. 11 (1976).

GUSTAV CASSEL, *Money and Foreign Exchange After 1914* (1922), 138–40

Our willingness to pay a certain price for foreign money must ultimately and essentially be due to the fact that this money possesses a purchasing power as against commodities and services in the foreign country. On the other hand, when we offer so and so much of our money, we are actually offering a purchasing power as against commodities and services in our own country. Our valuation of a foreign currency in terms of our own, therefore, mainly depends on the relative purchasing power of the two currencies in their respective countries. . . .

Given . . . normal free trade between two countries A and B, a certain exchange rate will establish itself between them, and, apart from slight fluctuations, this rate will remain unaltered so long as no variations take place in either of the currencies' purchasing power, and no obstacles are placed in the way of trade. . . .

Thus the following rule: When two currencies have undergone inflation, the normal rate of exchange will be equal to the old rate multiplied by the quotient of the degree of inflation in the one country and in the other. There will naturally always be found deviations from this new normal rate, and during the transition period these deviations may be expected to be fairly wide. But the rate that has been calculated by the above method must be regarded as the new parity between the currencies, the point of balance towards which, in spite of all temporary fluctuations, the exchange rates will always tend. This parity I call *purchasing power parity.*

achieve—the future of international monetary reform may depend upon more effective multinational institutional arrangements for better co-ordinating national policies. Speedier adjustment at lower cost depends on better co-ordination of policy.

Toward a Public Order

There remain many different viewpoints on the principles of international monetary reform, let alone any one particular institutional arrangement. Future reform will have to focus on the exchange-rate regime, control of international monetary reserves, balance of payments adjustment, and a revitalized role for the IMF as the international monetary authority. Different policies are advocated in these areas, not only because of differences in technical interpretation, but perhaps even more because of the political and distributional implications of various proposals.[7]

The Jamaica Agreement provided little guidance to an improved exchange-rate regime—except to ask countries to pledge themselves "to promote a stable system of exchange rates" and to "seek to promote stability by fostering orderly underlying economic and financial conditions and a monetary system that does not tend to produce erratic disruptions." Still left open are the hard questions of exactly how the system of rates is actually to be managed.

Any system that would establish a "reference rate,"[8] and then allow countries to intervene in exchange markets to move the market exchange rate toward the reference rate, but not away from the reference rate, confronts the immediate difficulty of determining the "reference rate." It might be thought that the doctrine of **purchasing-power parity** (PPP) could provide a guide to what the reference rate should be. The **absolute** PPP hypothesis states that the exchange rate between the currencies of any two countries should equal the ratio of the general price levels in the two countries. But price data are usually available in the form of price indexes rather than absolute price levels. For operational purposes, therefore, the **relative** PPP is usually used: changes in the exchange rate between any two currencies should equal percentage changes in the ratio of price indexes of the respective countries. If the general price level rises in greater proportion in country *I* relative to country *II*, then *I*'s currency should depreciate correspondingly relative to *II*'s currency. If each pair of countries produced exactly the same goods, all goods were tradable, there were no impediments to free trade, and no long-term contracts, then PPP would be a strict application of the law of one price: through trade arbitrage and variations in the exchange rate, any difference in national currency prices would be eliminated. In the modern version of international monetarism, the PPP doctrine is combined with a simple theory regarding the quantity of money. In a monetarist model, the growth rate of the national money supply that is consistent with the maintenance of stable ex-

---

[7]See R.N. Cooper, "Prolegomena to the Choice of an International Monetary System," *International Organization*, 29 (Winter 1975), 69–75.

[8]Cf. John Williamson, "The Future Exchange Rate Regime," *Banca Nazionale del Lavoro Quarterly Review*, 28 (June 1975), 3–20.

change rates equals the sum of the growth of real national income and the foreign rate of inflation. If a country's money supply grows at a faster rate of $x\%$, then national prices will rise at a faster rate of $x\%$ (if there is no real income growth), and the country's currency should depreciate at $x\%$. When international prices are equalized, international payments also should be in equilibrium.

In reality, however, the PPP doctrine is subject to analytical and empirical difficulties.[9] There is first the problem of determining a satisfactory base period for the time the exchange rate was supposedly in equilibrium with the relative price index. If we had a method by which to determine this equilibrium rate in a base period, it would obviate the need for a PPP approach. There are also problems in selecting the appropriate price indexes—should they reflect the prices of individual traded goods, all tradables, or tradable and non-tradable goods and services? (An overall price index, such as the Gross Domestic Product (GDP) deflator, would place heavy weight on non-tradables.) Transfer payments, capital movements, and asset-market disturbances also complicate the doctrine's application. The equilibrium exchange rate can also change for structural reasons (changes in technology, tastes, factor supplies), even though relative price levels have not changed. Finally, in order to assess deviations between the current exchange rate and the longer-run equilibrium value of the exchange, the national authorities would have to be able to project price indexes one or two years ahead.

In practice, therefore, it is difficult to rely on relative price movements alone as normative indicators of appropriate exchange-rate movements. At its best, the PPP theory applies to extremely large and general price changes over a long period of time (such as in periods of high inflation), not the short run of a few years. In the shorter run, overvaluation of a currency can be indicated by central bank interventions in one direction to support the overvalued rate, controls on trade, or continual borrowing from overseas.

Instead of allowing unlimited exchange-rate flexibility or condoning the resort to "dirty floating," many economists advocate a "wider band" or "crawling peg." Under the band fluctuation, the Fund Agreement would be amended to allow the official exchange rate to be variable within, say five percentage points on either side of parity, so that a maximum of 10% appreciation or depreciation would occur automati-

[9] See Lawrence H. Officer, "The Purchasing-Power Parity Theory of Exchange Rates: A Review Article," *IMF Staff Papers*, 23 (March 1976), 160, and Peter Isard, *Exchange Rate Determination*, Princeton Studies in International Finance, No. 42 (1978), 4–8.

cally. Insofar as day-to-day fluctuations of the rates would be under the influence of national stabilization funds, the Fund's charter should embody certain principles for the operation of these funds. These provisions would be necessary in order to guard against the possibility of such a fund operation being aimed at competitive manipulation of the rate.

The crawling peg proposal extends this fluctuation over time and permits frequent adjustment of parities, either automatically on the basis of an average of the actual values of the exchange rate over some previous time period or at the government's discretion.

There is, however, no guarantee that a large discrete movement in the exchange rate will not still be necessary. A widening of the band, around either a fixed or a crawling peg, does not remove the need for international reserves; only a system of freely floating exchange rates does that. And, as we have seen, a wider band does not even necessarily reduce the demand for reserves. If, however, a need for greater international liquidity should arise, neither the wider band nor crawling peg proposal would suffice. If countries competed for scarce reserves, then the exchange rates would be pressured to the limit of the permitted range of flexibility without effecting adjustments.

Although the regime of managed floating tends to place more emphasis on the adjustment mechanism and exchange-rate surveillance than on the level of international reserve assets, there is still concern over reserve control. The **liquidity problem** still poses questions about what is the appropriate amount of liquidity, its composition among reserve assets, and its distribution among countries. By "international official liquidity" is meant the aggregate stock of assets held by the national monetary authority that is available unconditionally to settle the country's imbalance in international transactions—essentially now gold, foreign exchange, SDRs, and a country's reserve position in the IMF.

The designation of an "optimal level" of liquidity is attractive, but indeterminate. In formal terms, the level for a single country is optimal when the marginal benefit equals the marginal cost of holding reserves. But this has slight operational meaning when the amount of reserves required is interconnected with other policy variables, such as the exchange rate, trade policies, capital controls, and submission to balance of payments discipline. Judgment on what should be the level of liquidity is inseparable from other judgments on what alternative policies should be undertaken—and not only in one country, but in all countries. The amount of liquidity needed depends on the size and duration of the deficit. But this, in turn, depends on the willingness and ability of the deficit country and the surplus country to adopt internal and external corrective measures.

The Jamaica Agreement did not settle the problem of determining what would be an adequate, but not excessive supply of unconditional official international liquidity. The Agreement endorsed, however, the principle that the SDR will become the principal reserve asset and that the role of gold and of reserve currencies will be reduced. To this end, the Agreement and the Second Amendment (adopted in 1978) made the SDR the formal unit of account or *numéraire* of the system, and some steps were adopted to achieve the demonetization of gold. The continuing function of gold as a reserve asset until the reduction of its role in the system is complete raises for the Fund and its members the problem of the valuation of gold holdings. The official price of gold has been abolished, and members of the Fund may buy and sell gold at market prices. Most members have continued, however, to account for gold at the former official price. So too has the Fund continued to value the gold it held at the date of the Second Amendment at the former official price. Members have agreed to collaborate with each other and with the Fund "to ensure that the policies of the member with respect to reserve assets shall be consistent with objectives of promoting better international surveillance of international liquidity and making the special drawing rights the principal reserve asset in the international monetary system" (Article VIII, Section 7).

Much more, however, will have to be done if the SDR is really to become the principal reserve asset and an SDR standard is to be established. (The SDR now constitutes less than 5% of world official reserves.) Any reserve asset must not only fulfill the unit-of-account function, but also the store-of-value and standard-of-deferred payments functions of international money.

If central banks are allowed to sell gold to each other at market prices or to buy from the market, the price of gold could be kept up, and gold could become a growing share in world reserves. This, of course, depends upon a central bank being willing to buy when another country wishes to sell. At the extreme, to fix the price of gold in all national currencies would reinstate the gold standard. Alternatively, to demonetize gold, a Gold Substitution Account might be established to which countries could sell their gold holdings at market price in exchange for a special issue of SDRs. Criticisms of this are that it might

R.A. MUNDELL, *The New International Monetary System* (1977), 238

International monetary reform requires a coherent view of the entire system in its actual historical setting and its political and social framework. Because there is no room for mistakes, wise men have usually recognized human limitations and built reform on the foundations of the past, allowing the system to evolve gradually by itself, at best nudging it only slightly against the swell of the tide. In that sense, reform has, and perhaps must have, a conservative bent. All our legal entrappings of new international monetary orders have been firmly based on the foundations of underlying economic forces and political realities, from the bimetalism of the Middle Ages to the gold standard of the late nineteenth century, the credit mechanisms which developed under gold and the pound sterling and then, after 1915, to a dollar used along with sterling as a worldwide unit of account. What became known as the Bretton Woods Order was an accommodation to the overwhelming significance in the twentieth century of the phenomenal rise of the U.S. as a supereconomy replacing the nineteenth-century role of the British Empire. The emergence of the dollar as the major currency in the monetary sphere, replacing the pound sterling and even gold from the system results from the rise of the United States as a hegemonic power. It was this very rise, reaching an apogee in the 1960s, that created countervailing checks and balances and resistances to further growth in the use of the dollar. The struggle to impose gold convertibility on the United States was increasingly seen as a struggle for power in the political system, fought out in the monetary domain.

cause an excessive increase in liquidity and that it would distribute the incremental liquidity according to the present gold distribution, with little benefit to countries that need more liquidity.

If more reliance is not to be placed on the dollar as the major source of liquidity, international monetary arrangements will have to provide other sources of fiduciary reserves. This can be done most expeditiously by extending the international credit facilities of the IMF. A recurrent possibility is a general increase in member country quotas in the Fund. A second possibility would be to amend the Fund's Agreement so that a member's drawing rights would be automatic rather than conditional. Whereas "the overwhelming benefit of any doubt" is now given to member requests for transactions within only the first reserve tranche, the extension of automaticity to additional drawing rights within the credit tranches would allow members to treat their drawing rights more like a deposit that constitutes their own reserves. The third possibility would be to create more SDRs.

The SDR (now valued in terms of a weighted average of 16 currencies) is by no means an international money. A growing number of economists, however, advocate the SDR as the major portion of global reserves. Some have even suggested that the allocation of additional SDRs be used as a distributional instrument and an associated negative sanction, being withheld from countries that do not fulfill their obligations of international "regime support" in trade and payments matters.[10] But it is questionable whether countries will agree to provide the needed incremental reserves in the form of SDRs, let alone use the allocation of reserves to impose sanctions.

There is also the controversial question whether a component of development finance should be incorporated in any proposal for international monetary reform. The initial creation of SDRs did not link this new form of international liquidity with the provision of development finance, despite the urging of such actions by the less developed countries (LDCs). Any monetary plan that expanded world reserves would at least indirectly benefit the LDCs. For to the extent that such an expansion forestalls the developed countries from adopting beggar-my-neighbor policies or allows a relaxation of restrictions on international payments, the LDCs will benefit.

The LDCs, however, argue for more than merely indirect assistance: they want any scheme of international monetary reform to be of direct benefit—providing additional aid in the process of creating additional liquidity. This could be done, for instance, through direct allocation of an increase in SDRs to the least developed and neediest members of the Fund in larger proportion than their quotas, instead of to member countries on a pro rata basis according to their Fund quotas, as was done in the first allocation of SDRs. The developing countries could also be given greater access to Fund credit by permitting them to draw a larger percentage of quotas than is allowed the developed countries under various credit tranches.

The standard argument against providing a direct link between liquidity creation and development finance is that the need for reserves and the need for development finance are two distinct issues and that

---

[10] See Fred Hirsch et al., *Alternatives to Monetary Disorder* (1977), 55–64.

the LCDs are mixing two separate questions. It is argued that the need for reserves is to cover a temporary imbalance, whereas the need for long-term development finance is to cover a chronic balance of payments gap. If the amount of liquidity to be created is determined by development finance, then, it is said, there will be too much liquidity, and the confidence in the IMF as a central monetary institution will be weakened.

Offsetting this skepticism, proponents of a direct link between monetary reform and the provision of development finance argue that the need for liquidity by developing countries is especially great because of their higher costs of adjustment, limited access to private banking and capital markets, greater variability of exchange earnings, and higher opportunity costs of holding foreign exchange reserves.

Against the contention that an increase in reserves would allow the developing countries to escape from balance of payments discipline, it is also replied that for an LDC the so-called "discipline of the balance of payments" does not in reality lead to deflationary (or disinflationary) monetary and fiscal policies, but instead to import restrictions. An increase in reserves, therefore, would not actually have the undesirable effect of removing balance of payments discipline, but rather the favorable effects of supporting the liberalization of trade.

On the adjustment process, some earlier proposals had advocated the establishment of an "objective indicator" structure to assess the proper level of a country's reserves and to create a presumptive adjustment obligation (such as appreciation, trade liberalization, or more foreign aid by a surplus country) when reserves departed too far from a reasonable "base" level.[11] A strict application of the theory of portfolio management would refer to reserve levels, but in practice it is likely that only changes in reserves can be considered.

The Jamaica Agreement did not move in the direction of objective indicators. It simply left adjustment to be forced on deficit countries by unemployment, reserve losses, or increasing difficulties in acquiring international liquidity; and to be forced on surplus countries by inflation. But under managed floating, the monetary authority of a surplus country may prefer to maintain competitive undervaluation by purchasing the inflow of foreign currency with newly created domestic money. The techniques of reserve control are inseparable from issues of exchange-market intervention. For when a government intervenes to in-

---

[11] See Trevor G. Underwood, "Analysis of Proposals for Using Objective Indicators as a Guide to Exchange Rate Changes," *IMF Staff Papers*, 20 (March 1973), 110–17.

fluence the exchange rate, it also acquires or loses a reserve currency. The problem remains to provide more incentives to adjust and some sanctions for inaction or perverse action—especially for surplus countries or a deficit country that is a reserve currency country. If the reserve-asset settlement system allowed convertibility, one way to exert pressure on a surplus country would be to place a limit on its holdings of primary assets beyond which it could not demand conversion.

The "confidence problem" revolves about the question of official convertibility. Holders of an asset may lose confidence in an asset and switch their portfolios among different assets, thereby exaggerating the flow of reserves and causing variations in total liquidity. Should monetary authorities be obliged to redeem balances in their currencies acquired by other monetary authorities? Should there be official convertibility to a non-currency primary reserve asset, such as gold or SDRs? Should the autonomy of domestic monetary policy be constrained by the imposition of convertibility?

The "composition problem" in the adjustment process also remains. Should adjustment be achieved by improving the current account or the capital account? How rapidly should adjustment be effected? What are the relative costs of rapid versus slow adjustment?

Future reform measures will have to provide the answers to these questions.

In a reformed international monetary regime, the IMF may exercise more leadership in co-ordinating international monetary policy. This is especially important for the management of exchange rates. The exchange rate is a unique and crucial price—a matter of mutual concern to all affected nations and not merely an isolated element of national policy. Many advocate that the IMF should undertake some type of **international surveillance over exchange rates.** Indeed, the revised Articles of the Fund state that member countries should "avoid manipulating exchange rates of the international monetary system in order to prevent effective balance of payments adjustments or to gain an unfair competitive advantage over other members."

The Second Amendment ends par values and makes no mention of central rates. The Amendment also makes it an obligation of each member "to collaborate with the Fund and other members to assure orderly exchange arrangements and to promote a stable system of exchange rates." The range of exchange arrangements among members may include, however, independent floating, pegging on another currency, pegging on the SDR, pegging on another composite of currencies determined by the issuer of a currency, or the maintenance of common margins of fluctuation.

If a system of managed floating continues, governments will intervene in exchange markets for a variety of objectives: (i) to smooth out short-term fluctuations in the exchange rate, which may be disturbing to businesses and consumers; (ii) to avoid mistaken signals to reallocate resources (for example, to prevent depreciation over a short-term cycle of economic activity); (iii) to avoid external impetus to domestic-factor price increases, especially wage increases, through a one-way escalation in the cost of living that would be caused by depreciation of the home currency; (iv) to alter the level of international reserves held by the country; (v) to stimulate home employment by increasing exports and reducing imports through depreciation of the home currency; (vi) to dampen domestic inflation by making foreign goods cheaper in the home market through appreciation of the home currency; and (vii) to keep profits from falling in the export- or import-competing sectors of the economy through depreciation.[12]

Undertaking surveillance, the IMF might discourage or prohibit exchange-market intervention for reasons that are considered "illegitimate." The first three reasons for intervention on the foregoing list can be viewed as "legitimate" by the international community, but the others are controversial. The IMF should co-ordinate the objectives of international intervention and the actual practice of intervention, so that two countries do not work at cross-purposes on the same exchange rate. But management of direct intervention is alone inadequate, because other governmental policies can directly affect the exchange rates. It is therefore necessary to develop broader standards of behavior that will ensure more policy co-ordination among national macroeconomic policies.

A start in this direction might be realized by at least establishing some presumptive guidelines (not rigid rules) on the maximum permissible rates of change in the exchange rates. These would emphasize two objectives: (i) assuring orderly markets by avoiding rapid rates of change in exchange rates, except when they are clearly necessary because of rapid and unexpected changes in underlying conditions, and (ii) linking intervention policies to "desired" national levels of international reserves to assure that exchange rates are not allowed to deviate very far from the rates that would clear the market without intervention over a

[12] See R.N. Cooper, "Exchange Rate Surveillance," in R.A. Mundell and J.J. Polak (eds.), *The New International Monetary System* (1977), 73–74.

period of time. This requires that if reserves are built up or run down relative to the "desired" levels as a result of intervention to smooth short-term movements in rates, the direction of intervention should be reversed when market conditions permit so as to move reserves back to the "desired" levels.[13]

The IMF can also fulfill an important function through its "provision of conditional liquidity." By establishing the right of a nation to draw upon the credit tranches, and the right to share in any increase in primary reserve assets that may be forthcoming, the IMF can exercise considerable influence over domestic policies that affect exchange rates and the level of reserves, as well as influencing the impact of one country's policies on another country's economy. Although the Fund has maintained a principle of uniformity—imposing the same conditions on all countries in like situations—there may in the future be a case for relaxing some conditions for the poorest nations. On the other hand, conditions imposed by the Fund—though they be onerous in the short-run—may be necessary to avoid longer-term problems of external debt-servicing by a poor country.

Further, many argue that there should be an international lender of last resort who is able to extend large amounts of credit on short notice if necessary to avoid a major economic crisis. The IMF could be given this expanded role—especially if SDRs acquire a more prominent position in the composition of reserves.

The challenge of international monetary reform—and the correlative role of the IMF—will ultimately be to seek ways of preserving the benefits of internationalization, by reducing the detrimental restrictions on international transactions, while minimizing the costs to national autonomy. A revitalized IMF, with stronger financial and consultative functions, is therefore necessary—even if the Fund will still fall considerably short of being a "world central bank."

Supplementary Readings

Excellent surveys of the theory of balance of payments policy are offered by Anne Krueger, "Balance of Payments Theory," *Journal of Economic Literature*, VII (March 1969), 1–26; B.J. Cohen, *Balance of Payments Policy* (1969); Marina von Neumann Whitman, *Policies for Internal and External Balance*, Princeton Papers in International

[13] R.N. Cooper, "Monetary Reform at Jamaica," in E.M. Bernstein et al., *Reflections on Jamaica*, Princeton Essays in International Finance, No. 115 (April 1976), 10–11.

Finance, No. 9 (1970); Leland B. Yeager, *International Monetary Relations,* 2nd ed. (1976); Herbert G. Grubel, *The International Monetary System* (1969); and W.M. Corden, *Inflation, Exchange Rates, and the World Economy* (1977).

Classic discussions of policy instruments for internal and external balance are J.E. Meade, *The Balance of Payments* (1951); R.A. Mundell, "The Appropriate Use of Monetary and Fiscal Policy under Fixed Exchange Rates," *IMF Staff Papers,* 9 (March 1962), 70–77; and T.W. Swan, "Longer-Run Problems of the Balance of Payments," in American Economic Association, *Readings in International Economics* (1968), Chap. 27.

Problems of international monetary reform are analyzed in the following:

W.M. Corden, *Monetary Integration,* Princeton Essays in International Finance, No. 93 (April 1972); J.H. Williamson, "International Liquidity: A Survey," *Economic Journal,* 83 (Sept. 1973), 685–746; W.R. Cline, *International Monetary Reform and the Developing Countries* (1976); Raymond F. Mikesell and Henry N. Goldstein, *Rules for a Floating-Rate Regime,* Princeton Essays in International Finance, No. 109 (April 1975); Peter B. Kenen, "Floats, Glides and Indicators: A Comparison of Methods for Changing Exchange Rates," *Journal of International Economics,* 5 (May 1975), 107–51; Wilfred Ethier and Arthur I. Bloomfield, *Managing the Managed Float,* Princeton Essays in International Finance, No. 112 (Oct. 1975); E.M. Bernstein et al., *Reflections on Jamaica,* Princeton Essays in International Finance, No. 115 (1976); Robert H. Heller, "International Reserves and World-Wide Inflation," *IMF Staff Papers,* 23 (March 1976), 61–87; Thomas D. Willett, *Floating Exchange Rates and International Monetary Reform* (1977); and R.A. Mundell and J.J. Polak (eds.), *The New International Monetary System* (1977).

III

Theory of International
Development Policy

11

The Open Dualistic Economy

Much of our preceding discussion is relevant for the newly developing countries of the world. But development policy goes beyond the traditional economic policies of remedying market failure and pursuing macroeconomic stability measures. Development strategy is aimed at **resource mobilization to achieve a structural transformation of the economy**—a long-run multi-dimensional transition from one structure, in which primary production and primary exports dominate, to another structure, in which manufacturing is a rising share in total output, industrial exports are a relatively greater share of exports, and surplus labor is withdrawn from unemployment and underemployment. And as we shall see in this chapter, the transformation has to occur in an economy that we shall characterize as both a **dualistic** economy and an **open** economy. We shall be particularly concerned with **how external relations affect the internal development of an open dualistic economy**—how national development occurs in the context of the world economy.

An Informal Classical Model

It all began with Adam Smith's *Wealth of Nations,* over two centuries ago. Today the emphasis is on the opposite—on the failure of development to catch hold in many countries of Africa, Latin America, Asia—on the Poverty of Nations. Nothing has remained more challenging to economic policy-makers than to discover and strengthen the forces of development. In the "magnificient dynamics" of classical

Nobel Laureate JOHN HICKS, *Capital and Growth* (1965), 3–4

> Underdevelopment economics is a vastly important subject, but it is not a formal or theoretical subject. It is a practical subject which must expect to call upon any branch of theory (including non-economic, for instance sociological, theory) which has any relevance to it. If there is any branch of economic theory which is especially relevant to it, it is the Theory of International Trade.

economics,[1] the prime mover of cumulative development is capital formation. To study economic development now is still to return to the grand theme of classical economics—to a discovery of how **surplus output is generated and used to accumulate capital.**

By a "surplus" is meant net output—that is, total output minus the consumption of output used up in producing the gross output. If this surplus is used to increase the country's stock of productive capital (investment), total output will increase in subsequent periods. If all the increase in output is not consumed, the surplus will continue to grow, and growth in total output will become cumulative.

In his celebrated model of "development with unlimited supplies of labor," Sir Arthur Lewis emphasized this classical theme in drawing policy implications for the development of presently-poor countries. Lewis characterized a country in its early stages of development as being composed of two sectors—a capitalist sector and a traditional sector. Poor countries are of course heterogeneous, differing considerably in their characteristics. But the Lewis model attempts to capture some of the strategic relationships of a representative developing country. To do so, the model focuses on a labor-surplus economy, which can be analyzed in terms of the relationships between its two sectors.

The **traditional sector** is characterized by subsistence production, non-wage employment in an extended or joint family system, and little use of reproducible capital. It is a low earnings sector composed of family farms, handicraft workers, domestic servants, petty traders, and casual laborers.

The **capitalist sector** is that part of the economy that uses reproduci-

[1] W.J. Baumol, *Economic Dynamics* (1951), Chap. 2; also Paul A. Samuelson, "The Canonical Classical Model of Political Economy," *Journal of Economic Literature,* XVI (Dec. 1978), 1415–34.

ble capital and pays capitalists for its use. The capitalists hire the services of labor for a money wage, produce an output for sale on the market, and sell the product at some profit or surplus above the wage payments. "Capitalist" is used in the classical sense of an enterprise that hires labor and resells its output for a profit. The capitalist may be a private enterprise or a state enterprise. Within the total economy, the capitalist sector is akin to an island (or islands) of development surrounded by a vast sea of subsistence workers.

Surplus labor abounds in the traditional sector. Productivity of labor is very low, but each laborer shares in the family output: even though a traditional worker's marginal product is less than the average product, the family in effect subsidizes real income by allowing traditional workers to consume an average share of agricultural or traditional output.

The purpose of the model is to provide a mechanism explaining the **growth of the proportion of domestic savings in the national income** in the early stages of development of an economy that is experiencing an expansion in the capitalist forms of production. The essence of development, in this dual-sector model, is that the traditional sector withers away as production grows in the capitalist sector through time, and **the capital accumulation in the capitalist sector absorbs the surplus labor from the traditional sector.**

Lewis begins the working of his model by noting that the wage the expanding capitalist sector has to pay is determined by what people can earn in the traditional sector, but that the capitalist sector can obtain all the labor it wants from the traditional sector at a wage some 30 to 50% higher than the real wage in the traditional sector.[2] At this wage, the supply of labor will be greater than the demand for labor, with the supply coming not only from the traditional sector, but also swelled by women leaving the household for wage employment and by population growth. The supply of labor is therefore perfectly elastic, as in Figure 11.1. Because workers are paid a wage in the capitalist sector, the demand for labor in the capitalist sector will be given by the schedule of labor's marginal productivity, *CD* in Figure 11.1, and by the course

---

[2] W.A. Lewis, "Economic Development with Unlimited Supplies of Labour," *The Manchester School of Economic and Social Studies*, XXII (May 1954), 150, and Lewis, "Unlimited Labour: Further Notes" *The Manchester School of Economic and Social Studies*, XXVI (Jan. 1958), 20. Lewis stated that "Economists have usually expected wage-rates in the modern sector to be about 50 per cent above the income of subsistence farmers. This brings the modern sector as much labor as it wants, without at the same time attracting much more than it can handle." Lewis, *Development Planning* (1966), 77–78.

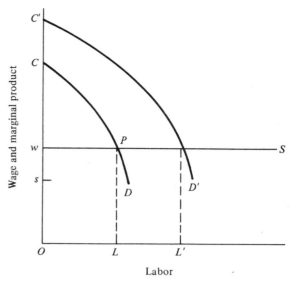

Figure 11.1

Expansion of the Capitalist Sector

s: Subsistence wage (real wage or average product in traditional sector).

w: Real wage rate in capitalist sector.

S: Unlimited supply of labor from labor surplus in traditional sector, women entering labor market, and population growth.

CD: Demand schedule for labor in capitalist sector.

of technological innovations in the capitalist sector, which change the techniques of production. The average product of a worker in the capitalist sector exceeds that of a worker in the traditional sector because it reproduces wages **plus a surplus.** This is the classical principle that the productivity of labor increases when it works with capital. Capital accumulation in the capitalist sector therefore makes it possible to increase national output, and at the same time, to raise the proportion of total workers in the capitalist sector. As long as a surplus continues to be generated in the capitalist sector, there will be greater capital accumulation and more employment offered to the surplus labor from the traditional sector.

Following this sequence in Figure 11.1, we can note that when the demand for labor is *CD, OL* of labor will be employed. The total output is designated by the area under the marginal productivity curve *OCPL.* This total income is distributed between wages to labor in the amount *OWPL* and profits or a surplus to capitalists in the amount of *WCP.* Whereas labor consumes its wages, capitalists save their profits and reinvest them in additional capital stock. As they do so, the productivity of labor increases: the demand curve for labor shifts out to *C'D'.* The amount of labor employed then rises to *OL'.* The total wage bill increases, but as long as the wage rate remains constant, the share of savings in the national income rises. Thus the expansion of the capitalist sector—or the development process—can be summarized in a series of rising ratios:

$$\frac{\text{Surplus}}{\text{Output}} \uparrow, \quad \frac{\text{Savings}}{\substack{\text{National} \\ \text{Income}}} \uparrow, \quad \frac{\text{Investment}}{\substack{\text{National} \\ \text{Income}}} \uparrow, \text{ and } \quad \frac{\text{Labor in Capitalist Sector}}{\text{Total Labor Force}} \uparrow$$

In this model, the constraint on employment is the amount of capital, and the increase in capital is limited by the amount of the surplus above consumption (net output). The time it takes to absorb the surplus labor is a function of the size of the capitalist sector and the share of profits in that sector: **the larger the capitalist sector and the greater the share of profits, the more rapidly will the unemployed and underemployed be absorbed from the traditional sector.**

Barring a hitch in the process (through a rise in real wages and a reduction in profits that would halt capital accumulation), the capitalist sector expands until capital accumulation has caught up with the labor supply. The absorption of surplus labor is then complete, and the supply function of labor becomes less than perfectly elastic. Beyond this point, the supply of labor is no longer greater than the demand, and real wages are no longer constant, but instead rise as capital formation occurs. We then enter the developed world to which neoclassical analysis, with an upward sloping supply curve for labor, is applicable. The share of profits in the national income will then not necessarily continue to increase, and investment will no longer necessarily grow relative to the national income.

Failure within Success

More than one-quarter century after Lewis presented his model, and despite rising investment ratios and expansion of the capitalist sectors in most of the less developed countries (LDCs), the persistence of surplus labor remains as acute in many of these countries as it was when Lewis wrote in 1954. More than ever, the creation of employment is recognized as the major challenge for poor countries. Countries have attained record target rates of growth in GNP and in GNP per capita,[3] but the distribution of income has become even more unequal in many of the LDCs, and the numbers in "absolute poverty" have become

[3] See David Morawetz, *Twenty-Five Years of Economic Development, 1950–1975* (1978). The GNP per capita of the developing countries as a group grew at an average rate of 3.4% a year during 1950–1975. This was faster than either the developing countries or the developed nations had grown in any comparable period before 1950 and exceeded both official goals and private expectations (p. 12).

greater. Such a failure within success has aroused the World Bank to advocate **"redistribution with growth"** and the development community to emphasize **"basic needs."**[4] In its concern over absolute poverty, the developing community is now focusing more on the changes in the absolute levels of the lowest 40% of the population—on the standards of living of those who are below minimum absolute standards in terms of nutrition, clothing, sanitation, health, and education. This change in emphasis to the **content** and **distribution** of GNP is linked with the concern for expanding employment opportunities. Unemployed, or underemployed, rural labor has not been fully absorbed in an expanding industrial sector, as the earlier labor surplus models suggested would happen. Unemployment, underemployment, low productivity employment, and the "working poor" are all part of the employment problem. The problem is not confined to one sector, but pervades the entire economy.

Although Lewis's two-sector model did not so intend, the capitalist sector in the model has come to be identified generally with industry or the urban sector, whereas the traditional sector has been identified with the rural sector. It may be more appropriate, however, to recognize that in actuality a "double dualism" has arisen within the poor country. Not only is there a **rural-urban dualism,** but also within each of the two sectors, there are **two subsectors** that might be termed the **"formal"** (or capitalist) and **"informal"** (or traditional) subsectors.[5] The formal subsector in the urban sector is composed of wage-earners in organized employment, is characterized by modern management and modern techniques of production, and is protected by governmental policies.

The informal subsector, in contrast, is composed of the self-employed and small-scale traditional crafts and services, all unprotected by governmental policies. In the informal sector are hawkers, porters, shoeshine boys, small-scale craftsmen, petty traders, own-account workers, and unpaid family workers. Their productivity is low, and their meager income is variable and frequently shared with others. As a result of the

[4] Hollis Chenery et al., *Redistribution with Growth* (1974); International Labor Office, *Employment, Growth and Basic Needs: A One-World Problem* (1976), and P.P. Streeten, "The Distinctive Features of a Basic Needs Approach to Development," *International Development Review* (1977/3), 8–15. The World Bank's *World Development Report* (1978) describes "absolute poverty" as "a condition of life so characterized by malnutrition, illiteracy, disease, squalid surroundings, high infant mortality, and low life expectancy as to be beneath any reasonable definition of human decency" (p. iii).

[5] The terms have been used in ILO and World Bank reports. For an elaboration of the different characteristics of the formal and informal subsectors, see ILO Mission, *Employment, Incomes and Equality: A Strategy for Increasing Productive Employment in Kenya* (1972).

extensive rural-urban migration, the informal sector of the city has acted as a sponge for the surplus labor. In most LDCs, the number in the urban informal sector has risen not only absolutely, but also as a proportion of the total labor force.

In the rural sector, a similar subdivision is evident. The formal sector comprises plantations, estates, and mines, with modern management, advanced techniques of production, and organized wage-employment. The informal subsector in the rural sector remains widespread, however, with traditional subsistence production for household consumption.

Beyond this domestic dualism, another salient characteristic of an LDC is its **"openness" to external forces** in the world economy. Except for the special cases of a few large-sized LDCs, most of the LDCs have small economies that have a strong foreign trade orientation. For a given size, the poorer a country, the more dependent it is on foreign markets and on foreign sources of supply. National development must therefore be considered within the international context.

Beyond the double dualism within the poor country, there is also an **international dualism** between rich and poor countries—the so-called "North-South" problem in international relations. The relations among the rural-urban, formal-informal sectors should be analyzed within the context of a world economy in which rich and poor countries coexist. Especially important for the poor country's development are the effects of exports, imports, capital movements, technology transfer, and all the demonstration effects between rich and poor countries. It is essential to consider how these external forces affect the development process—in particular, whether these forces tighten or relax the constraints on development

Two divergent streams of thought offer different perspectives on this problem. The classical, orthodox tradition emphasizes that the gains from trade are mutual gains, shared by all the trading countries, rich and poor alike. Foreign investment is also a nonzero-sum game—with mutual benefits to private investor and host country. A "technology shelf" exists in advanced countries from which the late-comers to development can borrow, without having to proceed through all the technological innovations of the earlier-comers to development. And all the demonstration effects of the rich country instill new values, incentives, knowledge, and institutions that promote the poor country's development. A **natural harmony of interests** exists, or at least a potential harmony can be created by cooperative policies.

In contrast, the other stream of thought emphasizes a **conflict of**

interests.[6] Ricardo was early opposed by those who interpreted trade in terms of imperialism and who saw an unequal distribution of the gains from trade or even the growth of the rich metropolitan countries at the expense of the poor peripheral countries. More recently, international market forces have been interpreted as a mechanism of international inequality, setting up disequalizing forces and backwash effects to the detriment of poor countries.[7] Even more critically, the contemporary school of "dependency" contends that the very forces of transnational polarization create internal polarization within the poor countries. The international economic system is viewed as a system of unequal power between the "center" and the "periphery" and as a system of domination-dependence that is systematically biased in favor of the developed countries: the rich nations actually "underdevelop" the poor.[8]

A recent textbook[9] on economic development provides a convenient summary of the international forces of international dominance and dependence that allegedly inhibit the development of poor countries:

1. The power of strong countries to control and manipulate world resource and commodity markets to their advantage.

2. The spread of international capitalist domination of domestic LDC economies through the foreign investment activities of private multinational corporations.

3. The privileged access of rich nations to scarce raw materials.

4. The export of unsuitable and inappropriate science and technology.

5. The freedom for industrialized countries to "impose" their pro-

---

[6] For a similar comparison of the liberal and Marxist conceptions of political economy, see Robert Gilpin, *U.S. Power and the Multinational Corporation* (1975), Chap. 1.

[7] Gunnar Myrdal, *Development and Underdevelopment* (1956); Hans Singer, "Distribution of Gains between Investing and Borrowing Countries," *American Economic Review, Papers and Proceedings* (May 1950), 473–85; and United Nations, Economic Commission for Latin America (Raúl Prebisch), *The Economic Development of Latin America and Its Problems* (1950). For a fuller statement of these views, and some opposing arguments, see G.M. Meier, *Leading Issues in Economic Development* (1976), 688–92, 717–23.

[8] Osvaldo Sunkel, "Transnational Capitalism and National Disintegration in Latin America," *Social and Economic Studies,* 22 (March 1973), 135–70; Celso Furtado, *Development and Underdevelopment* (1967); André Gunder Frank, "Development of Underdevelopment," *Monthly Review* (Sept. 1966); and Frank, "Dependence is Dead, Long Live Dependence and the Class Struggle: An Answer to Critics," *World Development,* 5 (1977), 355–70, with extensive bibliography; Samir Amin, *Unequal Development* (1976).

[9] Michael P. Todaro, *Economic Development in the Third World* (1977), 58–59. The author states that "it is easy and rather reassuring, but often unrealistic, to attempt to lay the blame for all the evils of underdevelopment at the international doorstep of rich nations. However, on the other hand, it is equally naive to believe that many of the serious problems of underdevelopment do not originate abroad."

ducts on fragile Third World markets behind import-substituting tariff barriers for monopolistic multinational corporations.

6. The transfer of outmoded and irrelevant systems of education to societies where education is perceived as a key component in the development process.

7. The ability of rich countries to disrupt efforts at industrialization by poor countries by "dumping" cheap products in these controlled markets.

8. Harmful international trade theories and policies which lock Third World countries into primary product exports with declining international revenues.

9. Harmful aid policies that often merely serve to perpetuate and exacerbate internal dualistic economic structures.

10. The creation of elites in poor countries whose economic and ideological allegiance is to the external world, both capitalist and socialist.

11. The transfer of unsuitable methods of university training for unrealistic and often irrelevant international professional standards, as induced by the externally conceived degree requirements for doctors, engineers, technicians and economists.

12. The corresponding capacity of rich countries to lure trained personnel away from LDCs with attractive financial rewards (the international "brain drain"); and finally,

13. The demoralizing "demonstration effect" of luxury consumption on the part of the wealthy both at home and abroad as propagated, for example, in imported foreign movies and magazine advertisements.

This list should arouse much debate. But instead of subscribing, without reservation, to either the harmony of interests or conflict of interests approach, we might seek a more balanced view. The essential task is to determine which of the external forces have a positive effect on development and which a negative effect. A **selective transfer** should be the policy objective. Instead of either a wholesale endorsement or a rejection of all the external forces, we should attempt to determine which selective policies will permit the LDCs to derive the benefits of the positive forces, without simultaneously exposing their economies to detrimental forces.[10]

To establish these selective pro-developmental policies, it is first necessary to understand what the major constraints on a country's development are and then determine how the external forces either tighten or

[10] P.P. Streeten, "Changing Perceptions of Development," *Finance and Development* 14, No. 3 (Sept. 1977), 14–16, 40. Streeten emphasizes "enlightened discrimination" in designing selective policies for aid, trade, foreign investment, transnational companies, technology, foreign education, and movements of people.

relax these constraints. In the remainder of this chapter, we briefly outline the major constraints. Subsequent chapters will then interpret trade policies and policies of international resource transfer from the perspective of relaxing these constraints.

Savings Constraint

Every student of development can draw up a particular list of constraints for a specific LDC. But four major constraints tend to be general: **the savings, agricultural, foreign exchange, and human resources constraints.** These constraints act as bottlenecks that limit the utilization of other resources that may even be in plentiful supply.

A country's potential rate of development will be limited by the constraint that is most "binding" or "dominant" in any given period of time. According to the quality of the country's policy-making, the actual rate of development will be even lower than the potential rate. The development challenge is therefore twofold: to raise the **potential rate** of development by relaxing the constraints and to bring the **actual rate** closer to the potential by improving the formulation and implementation of policies.

The savings constraint reflects the need to mobilize a surplus of resources for capital accumulation, as in the classical dualistic model. The "financing" of development is not a monetary matter of how more rupees or pesos are to be created, but how **real resources** are to be mobilized.

The capital accumulation process is composed of three steps: (i) the increase in the volume of real savings—the **release of resources** for investment purposes; (ii) the channeling of savings through a finance and credit mechanism—the **claiming** of the resources by investors; and (iii) the act of investment itself—the **use** of the resources for increasing the capital stock.

The first step, the real saving, is the necessary condition for investment to increase productivity and real income in subsequent periods. If there is no margin above national consumption, if there is no domestic saving, then national income cannot increase unless foreign savings are tapped through a foreign capital inflow.

How much saving is required? This is commonly expressed in terms of the targeted growth rate of the economy and the 'incremental capital-output ratio' (ICOR), which expresses by how much the capital stock must increase to yield an increase in national output. For example, if the growth target in national real income is 5%, and if the ICOR is 4:1—that is, 4 rupees of additional stock capital are necessary to produce a 1 rupee stream of real output—then the economy must save 20% of its national income to achieve this growth target. This follows from the formula

$$G = \frac{\Delta Y}{Y} = \frac{(S/Y)}{(\Delta K/\Delta Y)},$$

where G is the growth rate of national income, S/Y the propensity to save (national savings as a fraction of national income), and $\Delta K/\Delta Y$ the incremental capital-output ratio.

If population growth is 3% per annum, and the country wants simply to maintain per capita income constant, it will still need to save 12% of its national income when the ICOR is 4:1. If at the same time as population growth is 3%, the country wants to achieve a target of 2% growth in per capita income, it will then need to save 20% of its national income. The savings requirement can be expressed as

$$\frac{S}{Y} = (x + y) \% \; \frac{\Delta K}{\Delta Y},$$

where x is the population growth and y the per capita income growth target. The national savings rate will have to be greater, the higher the growth target rate, the higher the population growth, and the higher the ICOR. Because it is difficult to lower population growth or the ICOR in the short run, major emphasis in development programming is given to increasing the savings ratio.

What are the various sources from which the necessary savings can be mobilized? From **internal sources**, an increase of savings may be generated voluntarily through a reduction in consumption and involuntarily through additional taxation, compulsory lending to the government, or larger profits in public enterprises. An increase in voluntary personal saving through a self-imposed cut in current consumption is highly unlikely when the average income is so low. At best, it can be hoped that when income rises, the **marginal rate of saving** may be greater than the average rate (a higher proportion of the increase in income is saved). The government's capacity to force saving through taxation or compulsory purchases of government bonds is also limited. Of greater practical significance in several LDCs may be the operation of state marketing boards, which have a statutory monopoly over export crops. These boards may compel domestic producers to save by purchasing the local produce at prices below world prices and selling them on world markets at higher prices.

The inability to mobilize sufficient domestic resources means that the developing country must turn to external sources of financing development.[11] How can external sources relax the savings constraint? Some contribution may come from a restriction of consumption imports. Provided that there is not simply a switch in expenditure from imports to domestic consumption, the level of savings will rise. Imports of capital goods can then be increased, and this will represent a genuine addition to the rate of capital formation: the increase in the flow of investment goods imported is, in this case, matched by an increase in the flow of domestic income saved. If, however, consumers increase their domestic spending when they cannot import, then resources will be diverted from domestic capital production in favor of the increased domestic consumer spending, and the increase in imports of investment goods will be offset by reduced domestic investment. An increase in saving is therefore necessary if the restriction of consumption imports is to result in an increase in total net capital formation. For this reason, it is said that ultimately "capital is made at home."[12]

A similar analysis applies to the potentiality for increasing saving through an improvement in the developing country's terms of trade. When its export prices rise, the improvement in the country's commodity terms of trade makes it possible for the country to import larger quantities of capital goods. But again, this source of capital formation will not be fully exploited unless the increment in domestic money income due to the increase in export proceeds is saved. If the extra income merely increases consumer spending on home produced or imported goods, the opportunity for new saving is lost. The extra resources made available by the improvement in the terms of trade must be withheld from consumption and directed into investment. Either a corresponding increase in voluntary saving or taxation is necessary to give the country a command over additional imports of investment goods.

The major external sources for relaxing the savings constraint are through foreign economic aid, foreign borrowings, and private invest-

---

[11] We have excluded the possibility of capital accumulation through inflationary forces. It is conceivable that inflation may force saving—that is, decrease consumption by bidding prices up and diverting resources from the consumption sector to investment. But inflation has other adverse effects, especially on resource allocation and the balance of payments.

[12] Ragnar Nurkse, *Problems of Capital Formation in Underdeveloped Countries* (1953), 11–16.

ment of foreign capital. In simplest terms, if a developing country sets a target rate of growth in its GNP of 5% per year, and the ICOR is 3:1, then annual net investment must amount to 15% of GNP if the growth target is to be attained. If the country's domestic savings rate is only 10% of GNP, then foreign sources of capital must supply the difference. The inflow of foreign capital will allow a greater command over foreign resources through a greater capacity to import or the release of resources from import-competing or export-producing sectors into the investment sector. The international transfer of resources through capital inflows deserves extensive discussion, and we shall return to this problem in Chapter 13.

Agricultural Constraint

The classical dual-sector model also points up the necessity of avoiding an agricultural bottleneck if industrial development is to proceed. Classical economists emphasized the importance of agriculture when analyzing the transition from a subsistence to a market economy and when analyzing the transfer of food, labor, and savings to nonagricultural sectors. Ricardo believed that a limitation on the growth of agricultural output set the upper limit to the growth of the nonagricultural sector and to capital formation for economic expansion. Even in his advocacy of repeal of the Corn Laws, Ricardo was thinking beyond the direct case for free trade to the favorable effects that low-cost imports of foodstuffs would have in keeping wages low and profits high and thereby stimulating capital accumulation and growth of the economy. And history has confirmed that an industrial revolution is dependent on a previous or parallel agricultural revolution.

The dual-sector model emphasizes that the slow development of the agricultural sector can be a brake on the rest of the economy if it is not sufficiently active as a supplier of food and raw materials to the industrial sector and as a market for industrial products. When surplus rural laborers migrate to the urban industrial sector, they have to "take their lunch with them"—food supplies must be sufficient and forthcoming without rising agricultural prices so that wages do not have to rise and cut into the profitability of industrial production. The model stresses the importance of the intersectoral terms of trade and warns against a movement of the terms of trade in favor of agriculture that can call a halt to the growth of the industrial sector. **A marketable surplus** must

---

ADAM SMITH, *An Inquiry into the Nature and Causes of the Wealth of Nations* (1776; Glasgow ed., 1976), 376

> The great commerce of every civilized society, is that carried on between the inhabitants of the town and those of the country. It consists in the exchange of rude for manufactured produce, either immediately, or by the intervention of money, or of some sort of paper which represents money. The country supplies the town with the means of subsistence, and the materials of manufacture. The town repays this supply by sending back a part of the manufactured produce to the inhabitants of the country. The town, in which there neither is nor can be any reproduction of substances, may very properly be said to gain its whole wealth and subsistence from the country. We must not, however, upon this account, imagine that the gain of the town is the loss of the country. The gains of both are mutual and reciprocal, and the division of labour is in this, as in all other cases, advantageous to all the different persons employed in the various occupations into which it is subdivided. The inhabitants of the country purchase of the town a greater quantity of manufactured goods, with the produce of a much smaller quantity of their own labour, than they must have employed had they attempted to prepare them themselves. The town affords a market for the surplus produce of the country, or what is over and above the maintenance of the cultivators, and it is there that the inhabitants of the country exchange it for something else which is in demand among them.

---

therefore come from the agricultural sector to feed the urban population and to create the domestic basis for industry.

The agricultural sector can also contribute to industrial development through the mobilization of an **investible surplus**—not only in the form of underutilized labor, but also through the mobilization of unused saving capacity and taxation potential.

With the present concern over absolute poverty and unemployment, rural development is important not only for its instrumental value in supporting industrial development, but also for its intrinsic value in ameliorating the problem of **labor absorption.** Agriculture tends to create more employment for each unit of capital than any other sector. Although the Green Revolution provides a potential for increasing farm output by technical innovations that increase the productivity of labor and land, it is necessary—from the standpoint of labor absorption—to realize the advantages of a labor-using and yield-increasing strategy of agricultural development (such as was done historically in the small-scale, labor-intensive farming system of Japan and, more recently, in Taiwan).

Finally, pressures on the balance of payments can be traced to an agricultural bottleneck. Exports of primary products still dominate in most of the developing countries, and it is essential to maintain a competitive position in these markets. Moreover, when these primary exports are tropical commercial products, the export price is often linked to wages. (In the dual-sector model, the capitalist sector is now the export sector and is confronted by a horizontal labor supply curve from the food-producing subsistence sector.) As long as there is an unlimited reservoir of low productivity food producers, exporters' wages and hence export prices will remain low as the opportunity cost of workers remains tied to the low productivity of food production. To improve the factoral terms of trade in tropical commercial exports, it is therefore necessary to raise the productivity of the food producers and thereby raise the supply price of labor to the export sector.[13]

Besides earning foreign exchange through exports, agricultural development can also ease the balance of payments by saving foreign exchange through import substitution. Many developing countries are spending as much as one-quarter to one-third of their foreign exchange on food imports. If the capitalist sector in the dual-sector model is a strong exporter of manufactured goods, then it is possible to import the agricultural products (as Hong Kong does). But for countries not in this favorable position, a high propensity to import food and raw materials must be curtailed, and a strategy of import substitution in agriculture may accomplish this.

International policies can affect rural development in a number of ways. Export taxes or restrictions on primary products, and tariff protection on industrial inputs and consumer goods, can act as a disincentive to agricultural producers. They also artificially increase the urban-rural wage differential, thereby stimulating excessive rural-urban migration. Efforts are now required to disperse some of the amenities and public services concentrated in urban areas to the rural sector. Readier access to the services of public utilities, health, education, and

[13] This argument is enunciated by W. Arthur Lewis, "The Diffusion of Development," in T. Wilson and A.S. Skinner (eds.), *The Market and the State* (1976), Chap. 5; also Lewis, *The Evolution of the International Economic Order* (1978), 14–20.

W. ARTHUR LEWIS, "The Diffusion of Development," in T. Wilson and A.S. Skinner, eds., *The Market and the State* (1976), 142–43

In the 1880s the wage of a plantation labourer was one shilling a day, but the wage of a navvy in New South Wales was nine shillings a day. If tea had been a temperate instead of a tropical crop its price would have been perhaps five times as high as it actually was. And if wool had been a tropical instead of a temperate crop it would have been had for perhaps one-fifth of the ruling price. Adam Smith would have understood this arithmetic; what has clouded our understanding has been the neo-classical preoccupation with marginal utility and marginal productivity. . . .

Given this difference in the factoral terms of trade, the opportunity which international trade presented to the temperate settlements was very different from the opportunity presented to the tropics. The temperate settlements were offered high income per head. . . .

The factoral terms available to the tropics, on the other hand, offered the opportunity to stay poor—at any rate until such time as the labour reservoirs of India and China might be exhausted. A farmer in Nigeria might tend his peanuts with as much diligence and skill as a farmer in Australia tended his sheep, but the return would be very different. The just price, to use the medieval term, would reward equal competence with equal earnings. But the market price gave the Nigerian for his peanuts a 750 lb. of grain per acre level of living, and the Australian for his wool a 1,600 lb. per acre of living, not because of what they did, nor because of marginal utilities or productivities in peanuts or wool, but because these were the respective amounts of food which their cousins could produce on the family farms.

housing in the rural areas can amount to an increase in the rural social wage and diminish the attractions of the city. But this requires investment and hence possibly the need for greater capital inflow.

More directly, a wage subsidy in agricultural exports can help reduce the urban-rural wage differential. To promote the processing of primary output, a tax on the unprocessed raw material can be used, much as for infant industry protection. Beyond these tax and subsidy policies that affect the volume and composition of agricultural exports, and the use of labor in their production or processing, more can be accomplished by international aid programs that would provide inputs for raising agricultural productivity. As will be discussed further in Chapter 13, more can also be done to provide the transfer of "appropriate technology" to agriculture.

If the agricultural constraint is to be relaxed, it will be necessary to have a coordinated set of national policies, supported by foreign economic and technical assistance. This assistance may range from support of the technological infrastructure for promoting the seed-fertilizer revolution through the provision of improved marketing facilities for agricultural products to the provision of capital goods and foreign exchange for investment in roads, reclamation, drainage, and irrigation. As the World Bank now recognizes, projects need to be devised that combine components from several different sectors—roads, electricity, water education, family planning, and nutrition—and that integrate these with agricultural inputs into a development package to be applied to an entire region. To support this, an international transfer of resources is required.[14]

Foreign Exchange Constraint $(x - m \; gap)$

Lack of foreign exchange is another acute limitation on the size of development plans. To achieve a targeted rate of growth of output will require some growth in imports. The growth in foreign exchange earnings through export earnings and the inflow of foreign capital will therefore exercise some limit on output expansion. The smaller the population of the country, the greater the tendency for the country to be less diversified in resources and to have smaller home markets. Therefore the ratio of exports and imports to GNP tends to be high, and foreign capital has a greater role in financing investment and imports.[15]

Very few countries have been able to free themselves of the foreign exchange constraint (Taiwan and oil-exporting countries are exceptions). For most, the foreign exchange limitation has persisted because the capacity to import based on exports has not risen sufficiently—that

---

[14] For an elaboration of the agricultural constraint and its relaxation through international policies, see also B.F. Johnston and P. Kilby, *Agriculture and Structural Transformation* (1975); Hla Myint, "Agriculture and Economic Development in the Open Economy," in *Agriculture in Development Theory*, L.G. Reynolds (ed.) (1975), 327–54; and G.M. Meier, *Employment, Trade, and Development* (1977), 32–37.

[15] For empirical evidence from many countries, see Hollis Chenery and Moises Syrquin, *Patterns of Development 1950–1970* (1975), Chap. 4.

is, exports corrected for the commodity terms of trade have not risen enough to cover all the import demand. Countries have therefore continued to need an inflow of aid and foreign investment. But the foreign exchange constraint has even been intensified for some countries as the real value of aid has diminished, debt servicing requirements of amortization and interest on external debt have grown, and income payments of dividends and profits on private direct foreign investment have also increased, so that the import surplus that can be supported by external financial resources has diminished.

It might be thought that there cannot be a foreign exchange constraint if there is no savings constraint. An increase in saving, it could be argued, should lower the demand for imports or the demand for domestic resources, thereby increasing the availability of resources for exports. But such an easy substitution of domestic resources for foreign resources may not be possible: a minimum import level may be required to sustain a given level of GNP, and demand conditions may not allow a sufficiently rapid increase in export earnings. Savings will then not be converted into foreign exchange, and the trade constraint may be binding even if there is no savings gap.[16] We shall return to a fuller explanation of the savings and the foreign exchange gaps when we discuss the two-gap analysis in Chapter 13.

To the extent that a foreign exchange bottleneck is not removed, the country will have to abandon its growth rate target or else attempt to save foreign exchange through export promotion, an improvement in the terms of trade, or a greater inflow of foreign capital.

Human Resources Constraint

Human resources have been said to constitute the ultimate basis for the wealth of nations,[17] and limited human resource development will in turn restrain the economy's progress. Even if the other constraints are relaxed, the human resources constraint will still be binding if there is a shortage of persons with the critical skills and knowledge required for effective national development, if there are inadequate or underdeveloped organizations and institutions for mobilizing human effort, or if

---

[16]It has been argued that the trade constraint is the ultimate bottleneck on the way to sustained growth: See H.B. Chenery and A.M. Strout, "Foreign Assistance and Economic Development," *American Economic Review*, LVI (Sept. 1966), 690, 719.

[17]F.H. Harbison, *Human Resources as the Wealth of Nations* (1973), 3.

there is a lack of incentives for persons to engage in particular activities that are important for national development.[18] In an elemental sense, the key to development is man: his abilities, values, and attitudes must be changed in order to accelerate the process of development. It has become evident that investment in human capital is as crucial for development as is physical capital. Investment in the formation of human capital may be a necessary prerequisite to the mobilization of other domestic resources.

Many studies of economic growth in advanced countries confirm the importance of nonmaterial investment. These statistical investigations indicate that output has increased at a higher rate than can be explained by an increase in only the standard physical inputs of the factors of production. The "residual" difference between the rate of increase in output and the rate of increase in inputs encompasses many "unidentified factors," but a prominent element is the improvement in the quality of inputs. Although some of this progress may be incorporated in physical capital, the improvements in intangible human qualities are more significant—whether they be termed "creativity," "dynamic efficiency," "motivational efficiency," or simply "X-efficiency."[19]

Although investment in human beings has been a major source of growth in advanced countries, the negligible amount of human investment (education, health, research) in developing countries has done little to extend the capacity of the people to meet the challenge of accelerated development. The characteristic of "economic backwardness" is still manifest in several particular forms:[20] low labor efficiency, factor immobility, limited specilization in occupations and in trade, lack of information, and customary values and traditional social institutions that may minimize the incentives for economic change. The slow growth in knowledge is an especially severe limitation on development. The economic quality of the population remains low when there is little knowledge of available natural resources, possible alternative production techniques, necessary skills, existing market conditions and opportunities, and institutions that might be created to favor economizing effort and economic rationality. An improvement in the quality of the "human factor" and an increase in the **"learning rate of the economy"** are then as essential as the relaxation of any constraint. An advance in

---

[18] For elaboration of human resource problems in developing societies, see Harbison, *op. cit.*

[19] H. Leibenstein, *General X-Efficiency Theory and Economic Development* (1978).

[20] H. Myint, "An Interpretation of Economic Backwardness," *Oxford Economic Papers*, 6 (June 1954), 132–63.

ALFRED MARSHALL, *Principles of Economics (1890; 8th ed., 1920), 138–39*

> Capital consists in a great part of knowledge and organization: . . .
> Knowledge is our most powerful engine of production; it enables us to
> subdue Nature and force her to satisfy our wants. Organization aids
> knowledge. . . .
>
> In a sense there are only two agents of production, nature and man.
> Capital and organization are the result of the work of man aided by
> nature, and directed by his power of forecasting the future and his
> willingness to make provision for it. If the character and powers of
> nature and of man be given, the growth of wealth and knowledge and
> organization follow from them as effect from cause. But on the other
> hand man is himself largely formed by his surroundings, in which
> nature plays a great part: and thus from every point of view man is
> the centre of the problem of production as well as that of
> consumption. . . .

---

knowledge and the diffusion of new ideas and objectives are necessary to
remove economic backwardness and to instill the human abilities and
motivations that are more favorable to economic achievement.

If properly selected, international forces can contribute to an acceleration of this learning process—and in an "appropriate" way. Classical
economists emphasized an international trade in ideas as well as in
commodities. Modern information theory stresses that the search for
information and the transmission of knowledge is not costless. Trade
can reduce the cost and speed the process of diffusion. And Myint has
recently re-emphasized the classical belief concerning the "educative
effect" of an open economy.[21] Indeed, Myint suggests that the "residual" factors identified by growth accounting, such as the increase in
productivity due to the improvement in the quality of resources and the
advances of knowledge, to X-efficiency and to specialization and the
economies of scale, show a distinct family likeness to the **educative
effects of trade.** New ideas, new wants, new techniques of production,
and new methods of economic organization come from abroad. This is a
major element in the international transfer of resources, to which we
shall return in Chapter 13.

Summarizing the four major constraints, we should note that the

[21]H. Myint, *Economic Theory and the Underdeveloped Countries* (1971), Chaps. 7, 11.

highest rate of development attainable is that permitted by the most limiting constraint. Each of the different constraints may be the binding constraint in different countries at different times. But in a general sense, we may conclude that the ultimate constraint is human resources. For a nation will not be able to mobilize domestic and international resources if it is unable to develop the skills and knowledge of its people. And with knowledge can come a relaxation of the other constraints. As throughout history, the essence of the economic struggle is still that of man overcoming the scarcity of nature.

In the next two chapters we shall consider more directly the contribution that international trade can make to that struggle.

Supplementary Readings

From the vast literature on economic development, a few works may be selected for a general introduction:

Walter Elkan, *An Introduction to Development Economics* (1973); Peter Bauer, *Dissent on Development* (rev. ed., 1976); Gunnar Myrdal, *Economic Theory and Underdeveloped Regions* (1957); H.G. Johnson, *Economic Policies toward Less Developed Countries* (1968); Paul Streeten, *The Frontiers of Development Studies* (1972); G.K. Helleiner, *A World Divided* (1976). For the basic principles they propound, it is still useful to read Ragnar Nurkse, *Problems of Capital Formation in Underdeveloped Countries* (1953) and W.A. Lewis, *Theory of Economic Growth* (1955), and A.K. Cairncross, *Factors in Economic Development* (1962).

For extensions of the dual-sector model, see Douglas Paauw and John C.H. Fei, *The Transition in Open Dualistic Economies* (1973); Gustav Ranis and John C.H. Fei, *Development of the Labor-Surplus Economy* (1964); and A.C. Kelley, J.G. Williamson, and R.J. Cheetham, *Dualistic Economic Development* (1972).

The constraints on development are examined in G.M. Meier, *Leading Issues in Economic Development* (3rd ed., 1976), with extensive bibliographies; Hla Myint, *Economic Theory and the Underdeveloped Countries* (1971); Myint, *The Economics of the Developing Countries* (4th ed., 1973); Lloyd Reynolds, *Image and Reality in Economic Development* (1977); and Hollis Chenery et al., *Redistribution with Growth* (1974).

12

Trade Regimes

Of all the external forces affecting the constraints on development, patterns of foreign trade are among the most important. A developing country may follow an inward-looking strategy that favors import substitution or an outward-looking strategy that promotes exports. This chapter assesses the policies entailed by these strategies. It first analyzes the broad questions of export-led development and then examines the potential for exports of primary commodities and new nontraditional exports. In so doing, it also considers a "mixed strategy," the difficulties involved in the liberalization of exchange-control regimes, and the problems associated with regional integration.

Export-Led Development

A dominant theme in classical and neoclassical economics has been the belief that foreign trade has a positive influence on a country's development—that trade can be "**an engine of growth.**" In Smith's *Wealth of Nations,* the **vent for surplus theory** indicated that in the early stages of development, exports could expand, not by a contraction of domestic output as implied by the full employment assumption of the comparative costs theory, but by bringing into production the hitherto underutilized land and labor of the traditional subsistence sector.[1]

A modern version of this export-based model of growth is the **staple**

[1]H. Myint, "The 'Classical' Theory of International Trade and the Underdeveloped Countries," *Economic Journal,* 68 (June 1958), 317–37. See also pp. 16–17 above.

theory of growth.[2] The term "staple" designates a raw material or resource-intensive commodity occupying a dominant position in the country's exports. Previously idle or undiscovered resources are brought into use, creating a return to those resources and being consistent with venting a surplus through trade. The export of the primary product also affects the rest of the economy by diminishing underemployment or unemployment, by inducing a higher rate of domestic saving and investment, by attracting an inflow of factor inputs into the expanding export sector, and by establishing linkages with other sectors of the economy. Although the rise in exports is induced by greater demand, there are supply responses within the economy that increase the productivity of the exporting economy. The staple theory acquired prominence in the explanation of Canada's economic development, but it may have relevance now for some primary-producing less developed countries (LDCs). It also has some affinity with Lewis's model of development with an unlimited supply of labor when the surplus to be vented through trade is one of labor and not natural resources.

We have already noted in Chapter 2 the dynamic gains from trade. Beyond Ricardo's static gains that arise when trade provides an efficient means of transforming domestic resources into imports, there are Mill's "indirect effects, which must be counted as benefits of a high order."[3] Besides the opportunity to import capital goods and materials required for development purposes, recognition must also be given to the fundamental "educative effect" of international contacts that instill new wants and transfer technology, skills, and entrepreneurship. Further, by allowing economies of large-scale production, the access to foreign markets makes it profitable to adopt more advanced techniques of production, which require more capital; the opportunities for the productive investment of capital are then greater than they would be if the market were limited to only the small size of the domestic market.[4]

It should be noted that these "indirect benefits," wider productivity effects, and dynamic gains from trade result not from the assumptions of a perfectly competitive world, as in the static neoclassical theory of trade (recall Chapter 1), but on the contrary, from the very **removal of**

[2] See M.H Watkins, "A Staple Theory of Economic Growth," *Canadian Journal of Economics and Political Science,* XXIX (May 1963), 141–58, and R.E. Caves, " 'Vent for Surplus' Models of Trade and Growth," in R.E. Baldwin et al., *Trade, Growth and the Balance of Payments* (1965), 95–115.

[3] John Stuart Mill, *Principles of Political Economy* (1848), vol. I, book I, Chap. XIII, Sec. 1; vol. II, book III, Chap. XVII, Sec. 5.

[4] J.R. Hicks, *Essays in World Economics* (1955), 183–85.

JOHN STUART MILL, *Principles of Political Economy* (1848), Bk. III, Chap. XVII

> But there are, besides, indirect effects, which must be counted as benefits of a high order. One is, the tendency of every extension of the market to improve the processes of production. A country which produces for a larger market than its own, can introduce a more extended division of labour, can make greater use of machinery, and is more likely to make inventions and improvements in the processes of production. Whatever causes a greater quantity of anything to be produced in the same place, tends to the general increase of the productive powers of the world. There is another consideration, principally applicable to an early stage of industrial advancement. A people may be in a quiescent, indolent, uncultivated state, with all their tastes either fully satisfied or entirely undeveloped, and they may fail to put forth the whole of their productive energies for want of any sufficient object of desire. The opening of a foreign trade, by making them acquainted with new objects, or tempting them by the easier acquisition of things which they had not previously thought attainable, sometimes works a sort of industrial revolution in a country whose resources were previously undeveloped. . . .

these assumptions. Once we do not postulate perfect competition—with its assumptions of "perfect knowledge," firms already operating with the least-cost combination of factors, homogeneous and divisible resources, no economies of scale, and a full utilization of resources—then there is more scope for the indirect benefits and dynamic gains from trade to contribute to development.[5] Beyond the increase in real income from the direct gains from trade and through the reinvestment of the increment in income, there is the possibility for an even greater contribution by trade to the growth of real income through the broader educative effects on productive efficiency.

For these several reasons, the traditional conclusion has been that **the gains from trade do not result merely in a once-over change in resource allocation, but are also continually merging with the gains from development**: international trade transforms existing production functions and increases the productivity of the economy over

[5] H. Myint, "Exports and Economic Development of Less-Developed Countries," Fifth World Congress of the International Economic Association (1977), 8–11, mimeographed.

time. If trade increases the capacity for development, then the larger the volume of trade, the greater the potential for development.

The policy implications therefore favor freer trade and the promotion of export expansion. Empirically, there is considerable evidence that when these policies have been followed, the process of development has indeed been export-led in the most rapidly developing LDCs (for example, Korea and Taiwan).[6]

In opposition to the preceding analysis, there have always been **dissenters from the traditional view** that the gains from trade merge with the gains from growth. The optimistic view of "development through trade" has been denied by many critics—as varied as List (1841), who argued for protection to promote national industrialization, Lenin, who concentrated on the unfavorable effects of imperialism or "colonial exploitation," and Manoilesco (1931), who maintained that

[6]Cross-section studies and time-series studies both show significant correlations between the growth of exports and the growth of national income. See R.F. Emery, "The Relation of Exports to Economic Growth," *Kyklos*, 20 (1967), 470–96; H.B. Chenery, "Growth and Structural Change," *Finance and Development Quarterly*, 8 (Sept. 1971), 16–27; I.B. Kravis, "Trade as a Handmaiden of Growth," *Economic Journal*, 80 (Dec. 1970), 850–72; and B. Balassa, "Trade Policies in Developing Countries," *American Economic Review*, 61 (May 1971), 178–87. A most instructive case is that of Korea; see Larry E. Westphal, "The Republic of Korea's Experience with Export-Led Industrial Development," *World Development*, 6 (March 1978), 347–82.

FRIEDRICH LIST, *National System of Political Economy* (1841), Introduction

In the economic development of nations through international trade, we find accordingly four distinct periods: in the first, domestic agriculture is fostered by means of the importation of foreign manufactures and the exportation of domestic agricultural produce and raw materials; in the second, domestic manufactures are developed side by side with the importation of commodities of foreign manufacture; in the third, the domestic market is supplied for the most part with domestic products; and in the fourth, there is an extensive exportation of commodities of domestic manufacture, coupled with the importation of foreign raw materials and agricultural products.

The tariff system, as a means of promoting the economic development of the nation through the regulation of foreign trade, must be guided constantly by the principle of the industrial training of the nation.

KARL MARX, "Address on the Question of Free Trade" (1848), *The Poverty of Philosophy* (1963), 223

> If the free traders cannot understand how one nation can grow rich at the expense of another, we need not wonder, since these same gentlemen also refuse to understand how within one country one class can enrich itself at the expense of another.

---

the advantage of international trade exists only for industrial countries and that there should be protection to facilitate the transfer of workers from low-productivity agriculture to high-productivity industry.

A number of contemporary critics do not base their critique on any notion of deliberate exploitation by the advanced countries, but instead emphasize the disequalizing effects of the free play of international market forces. As argued by Myrdal, for instance, "market forces will tend cumulatively to accentuate international inequalities," and "a quite normal result of unhampered trade between two countries, of which one is industrial and the other undeveloped, is the initiation of a cumulative process towards the impoverishment and stagnation of the latter."[7] According to this view, international trade may set up not only spread effects, as recognized by classical theory, but also backwash effects, as ignored by classicists. For the LDCs, it is argued that the backwash effects may be stronger and more pervasive, thereby inhibiting their development.

A stronger version of this type of argument is offered by the "dependency" school of social thought, which views LDCs as beset by institutional and structural economic rigidities and caught up in a "dependence" and "dominance" relationship to rich countries.[8] In neo-Marxist, neocolonial terms, it is argued that the rich countries "underdevelop" the poor through an extension of international capitalism, which allows the dominant countries to exploit the dependent poor countries through their technological, commercial, capital and sociopolitical predominance.

We have previously noted some elements in the arguments of these critics (pp. 281–83). A full explication of their arguments and conclu-

[7]Gunnar Myrdal, *An International Economy* (1956), 55, 95.
[8]See references in Chap. 11, *n.* 8, this volume.

sions cannot be undertaken here.[9] But we do have to confront the conclusion of some that the export sector has remained only an "enclave" or has "fossilized" the country's economic structure, with external trade not leading to internal development.

It has been historically true that in many cases the foreign trade sector has been able to play a propulsive role in the country's development (Britain, Sweden, Canada, Australia, Japan, Korea, Taiwan, Hong Kong, and Singapore). Nevertheless, at the same time some countries that were poor a century ago developed through foreign trade, other countries have still remained poor until the present day, notwithstanding an expansion in their exports. A marked secular expansion in exports from the poor countries has been an outstanding result of their integration into world markets. And yet, in many countries this growth in exports has not carried over to other sectors of the domestic economy and has not propelled the rest of the economy forward. Why not?

The anti-classical critics would answer in terms of exploitation, disequalizing forces, or dependency. But we can consider the problem in a more eclectic way, avoiding the polarity of either the classicists' or their critics' views. The essence of the development-through-trade model is that the export sector should not remain an enclave, separate from the rest of the economy, but that an integrated process should be established. The **integrative process** within countries depends on the varying strength of the stimuli from their exports, according to the nature of their export base, and on the different response mechanisms within the exporting countries. The strength of the potential for development through trade will accordingly differ, depending upon the strength of the forces in the integrative process.

Different export commodities will provide different stimuli, according to the technological characteristics of their production. The nature of the export-goods production function (namely, the technical relationship between physical inputs of the factors of production and the resultant physical output) has a close bearing on the extent of other secondary changes elsewhere in the economy beyond the primary increase in export output. With the use of different combinations of inputs to produce different types of export commodities, there will be different

[9]For at least a summary of these alternative views, see G.M. Meier, *"External Trade and Internal Development,"* in P. Duignan and L.H. Gann (eds.), *Colonialism in Africa, 1870–1960* (1975), 427–34. A comprehensive and well-balanced analysis is presented by B.J. Cohen, *The Question of Imperialism: The Political Economy of Dominance and Dependence* (1973). See also the Supplementary Readings at the end of this chapter.

rates of learning and different linkage effects. For example, the degree to which the various exports are processed is highly significant in the determination of external economies associated with the learning process: the processing of primary-product exports by modern methods is likely to benefit other activities through the spread of technical knowledge, the training of labor, the demonstration of new production techniques that might be adapted elsewhere in the economy, and the acquisition of organizational and supervisory skills.

In contrast, growth of the export sector will have a negligible carryover if its techniques of production are the same as those already in use in other sectors or if its expansion occurs by a mere widening of production without any change in production functions. If the introduction or expansion of export crops involves simple methods of production that do not differ markedly from the traditional techniques already used in subsistence agriculture, the stimulus to development will clearly be less than if the growth in exports entails the introduction of new skills and more productive recombinations of factors. More favorable linkages may stem from exports that require skilled labor than from those using unskilled labor. The influence of skill requirements may operate in various ways: greater incentives for capital formation may be provided through education; on-the-job training in the export sector may be disseminated at little real cost through the movement of workers into other sectors or occupations; skilled workers may be a source of entrepreneurship; and skilled workers may save more of their wage incomes than unskilled workers. The level of entrepreneurial skill induced by the development of an export is also highly significant. The level will be expanded if the development of the export commodity offers sufficient challenge and instills abilities usable in other sectors, but is not so high as to require the importing of a transient class of skilled managerial labor.

Although the processing of a primary product provides forward linkages in the sense that the output of one sector becomes an input for another sector, it is also important to have backward linkages. When some exports grow, they provide a strong stimulus for expansion in the input-supplying industries elsewhere in the economy. These backward linkages may be in agriculture or in other industries supplying inputs to the expanding export sector, or in social overhead capital.

Beyond this, the nature of the production function of the export commodity will also determine the distribution of income, and in turn, the pattern of local demand and impact on local employment. The use of different factor combinations affects the distribution of income in the sense that the relative shares of profits, wages, interest, and rent will vary according to the labor intensity or capital intensity of the export production and the nature of its organization—whether it is mining, plantation agriculture, or peasant farming. If the internal distribution of the export income favors groups with a higher propensity to consume domestic goods than to import, the resultant distribution of income will be more effective in raising the demand for home-produced products; and to the extent that these home-produced products are labor-intensive, there will be more of an impact on employment. In contrast, if income is distributed to those who have a higher propensity to import, the leakage through consumption of imported goods will be greater. If income increments go to those who are likely to save large portions, the export sector may also make a greater contribution to the financing of growth in other sectors.

If the export commodity is subject to substantial economies of scale in its production, this will tend to imply large capital requirements for the establishment of enterprises, and hence extra-regional or foreign borrowing. This may then lead to an outward flow of profits, instead of providing profit income for local reinvestment. But this is only part of the impact of the foreign investment. For a full appraisal, it would be necessary to consider all the benefits and costs of the foreign invest- ment. And these too will vary according to the nature of the export sector in which the foreign investment occurs.

Finally, the repercussions from exports will also differ according to the degree of fluctuation in export proceeds. Disruptions in the flow of foreign exchange receipts make the development process discontinuous; the greater the degree of instability, the more difficult it is to maintain steady employment, because there will be disturbing effects on real income, government revenue, capital formation, resource allocation, and the capacity to import according to the degree of amplitude of fluctuation in foreign exchange receipts. To the extent that different exports vary in their degree of fluctuation, and in revenue earned and retained at home, their repercussions on the domestic economy will also differ. Depending on the various characteristics of the country's export, we may thus infer how the strength of the integrative process, in terms of the stimulus from exports, will differ among countries.

In summary, we would normally expect the **stimulating forces of the integrative process** to be stronger under the following condi- tions: the higher the growth rate of the export sector, the greater the direct impact of the export sector on employment and personal income, the more the expansion of exports has a "learning effect" in terms of increasing productivity and instilling new skills, the more the export sector is supplied through domestic inputs instead of imports, the more the distribution of export income favors those with a marginal propensity to consume domestic goods instead of imports, the more productive is the investment resulting from any saving of export income, the more extensive the externalities and linkages connected with the export sector, and the more stable the export receipts that are retained at home.

After analyzing the character of a country's export base for an indication of the strength of the stimulus to development provided by its export commodities, we must go on to examine the strength of the response or diffusion mechanism within the domestic economy for evidence of how receptive the domestic economy is to the stimulus from exports. The strength of the integrative process, in terms of the response mechanism to the export stimulus, will depend on the extent of market imperfections in the domestic economy and also on noneconomic barriers in the general environment. The integrative forces are stronger under the following conditions: the more developed the infrastructure of the economy, the more market institutions are developed, the more extensive the development of human resources, the less the price distortions that affect resource allocations, and the greater the capacity to bear risks. Our view of the carry-over should stress not only the mechanical linkages, but also a more evolutionary (and hence biological rather than mechanical) analogy that recognizes societal responses. What matters is not simply the creation of modern enterprise or modern sectors, but modernization as a process. This involves not simply physical production or mechanical linkages, but a change in socioeconomic traits throughout the society and an intangible atmosphere that relates to change in values, in character, in attitudes, in the learning of new behavior patterns and in institutions.

In sum, the **effects of a strong integrative process** will be the following: (i) an acceleration in the learning rate of the economy; (ii) an enrichment of the economic and social infrastructure (transportation, public services, health, education); (iii) an expansion of the supply of entrepreneurship (and a managerial and an administrative class); and (iv) a mobilization of a larger surplus above consumption in the form of taxation. Once these foundations are laid, the country's economy can be more readily transformed through diversification in primary production and the service industries, new commodity exports, and industrialization via import substitution and export substitution.

Import Substitution

In actual fact, however, many countries have chosen an inward-looking strategy of import substitution. There are protection arguments of special relevance for developing countries, such as policies to improve the terms of trade, to offset the wage distortion in a dual labor market, or to promote infant industries. But the qualifications made in our earlier discussion of optimal trade interventions (Chapter 3) are equally applicable to developing countries. Most arguments for protection are only "second-best" solutions compared with alternative domestic policy measures.

More to the point is the fact that although economists can devise logically valid arguments for protection, governments of the developing countries have turned in practice to import-substitution policies for other more simple and direct reasons—namely, to achieve the objectives of industrialization and balance of payments support. In many LDCs the dominant strategy of industrialization has been the production of consumer goods in substitution for imports. Given an existing demand for imported consumer goods, it has been simple to base the rationale for industrialization on the home replacement of these finished goods. By first importing the components and engaging in the final assembling process, the government has hoped to proceed to "industrialize from the top downward" through the ultimate production of the intermediate products and capital goods. Besides allowing the home replacement of an existing market, import substitution also has a simple appeal by virtue of the common belief that it helps save foreign exchange. Confronted with balance of payments problems, governments have simply reacted with another round of tariffs or quotas.

Quite different from a rational system of protection, a host of policies were adopted in an *ad hoc* and indiscriminate fashion in a number of developing countries. The urban formal sector came to be dominated by manufacturing to replace imported consumer goods. High tariffs or quantitative restrictions were imposed on imports of the final commodity, whereas intermediate inputs had low or no tariffs, thereby giving high effective rates of protection on the domestic value added. The final assembly of imported components has also been subsidized by low rates of interest, easy access to credit, foreign exchange allowances, provision of industrial estates, low public utility rates, and favorable tax allowances. At the same time, the subsidization of the import-competing industries has been embedded in a general environment of inflation and the maintenance of an overvalued exchange rate.

This syndrome of policies associated with an import-substitution industrialization strategy has proven costly in many countries. A number of empirical studies attest to this.[10] These studies confirm that developing countries have overemphasized the scope for efficient replacement of industrial imports, that the import-substitution policies have not succeeded in fulfilling the objectives of industrialization and balance of payments support, and that at the same time the policies have created other distortions in the economy.

A policy of import-substitution industrialization becomes increasingly difficult to follow beyond the "easy" consumer goods phase because with each successive import-substitution activity through the intermediate and capital goods phases, the capital intensity of import-substitution projects rises, resulting in a larger import content of investment. On the demand side, the projects also tend to require increasingly large domestic markets for the achievement of a minimum efficient scale of production. In few countries has "industrialization from the top down" proceeded to any depth. On the contrary, policies undertaken to support import substitution have only too often aggravated the lack of internal integration and dualism in the economy, as the import-substitution activity remains an enclave in the modern sector, while the unequal access to scarce economic resources by the modern and traditional sectors is aggravated by government policies that discriminate in favor of the modern sector.[11]

Nor has import substitution been successful in relaxing the foreign exchange constraint. Few countries have been able to emulate the Japanese model of proceeding from import substitution to exports. A com-

---

[10]Among many studies, special attention is called to Henry Bruton, "Import Substitution Strategy of Economic Development," *Pakistan Development Review* (Summer 1970), 123–46; I.M.D. Little, T. Scitovsky, and M. Scott, *Industry and Trade in Some Developing Countries* (1970); series of country studies undertaken for the National Bureau of Economic Research on *Foreign Trade Regimes and Economic Development;* J. Bhagwati and Anne Krueger, "Exchange Control, Liberalization, and Economic Development," *American Economic Review, Papers and Proceedings,* LXIII (May 1973), 418–27; and Werner Baer, "Import Substitution and Industrialization in Latin America: Experiences and Interpretations," *Latin America Research Review* (Spring 1972), 101–8.

[11]H. Myint, "Dualism and the Internal Integration of the Underdeveloped Economies," *Banca Nazionale del Lavoro Quarterly,* No. 93 (June 1970), 128–56.

parative advantage has not been acquired in the import-competing sector. Instead, at the same time as policies have subsidized import replacement, they have inhibited expansion of exports because of higher cost of inputs in the export sector, neglect of agriculture from which exports come, and the maintenance of an overvalued exchange rate, which makes exports too costly. And the net import-saving has been slight when the country has still had to import fuel, industrial materials, capital goods, and even foodstuffs in order to pursue import substitution. The **import-intensity** of the import-substitution process has in itself been high. The foreign exchange constraint has therefore often intensified.

Further, there have been many cases of **"negative value added"** in the import-replacement activities.[12] Because of the high effective rates of protection, there has been a large excess of value of domestic resources used over the value of foreign exchange saved. Although high protection of final goods makes production of the import substitute privately profitable in local currency, the value of inputs at world prices exceeds the value of the final product at world prices. The foreign exchange cost of import replacement is then greater than the direct import of the final good.

Import substitution has also been socially inefficient because its supporting policies have created distortions elsewhere in the economy. Of major significance has been the creation of **distortions in the price structure.** The rate of interest has been too low, not reflecting the true scarcity of capital. Wages of unskilled labor in the modern sector have been too high, given the surplus labor problem. In attempting to subsidize industry, governments have imposed price controls on foodstuffs and agricultural raw materials that have inhibited agricultural development. And the price of foreign exchange has been too low. These price distortions adversely affect the allocation of resources and the mobilization of domestic resources.

Finally, it has become apparent that, after a period of import-substitution industrialization, the problems of **maldistribution in income and unemployment** have become more serious than they were before the import-substitution strategy was introduced. The use of subsidies, overvalued exchange rates, rationing of underpriced import licenses, high levels of effective protection, and loans at negative real interest rates have induced the production of import substitutes by capital-

---

[12] For example, S.R. Lewis, Jr., *Pakistan: Industrialization and Trade Policy* (1970).

intensive, labor-saving methods and have resulted in industrial profits in the sheltered sector and high industrial wages for a labor elite, aggravating inequalities in income distribution. As noted repeatedly, employment creation in the urban import-replacement industrial sector has not kept pace with the rural-urban migration, and the unemployment problem has been aggravated by the transfer of the rural unemployed into open unemployment in the urban sector. Unemployed or underemployed rural labor have not been able to be fully absorbed in an expanding industrial sector, as the earlier labor surplus models suggested could happen. After some two or three decades, during which import-substitution industrialization was the major characteristic of the modern industrial sector, most of the LDCs must still contend with greater numbers in absolute poverty, more unemployment and underemployment, and wider inequality.

For these reasons, emphasis has shifted from inward-looking policies to policies that focus on the possibilities of inducing a gradual process of industrialization through agricultural development and on the potential industrialization through the export of semi-manufactures and manufactured products.

Primary Commodity Trade

Notwithstanding the newer interests in import substitution and export substitution, the long-standing problems raised by trade in traditional primary commodities remain of major concern for policy because these commodities still predominate in the trade of most LDCs. But pessimism tends to pervade the outlook for commodity trade. It is commonly charged that the demand for primary commodities is sluggish, characterized by low price elasticity, and subject to extreme fluctuation so that export proceeds do not rise sufficiently over the longer run and are highly unstable in the short run.

An expected deterioration in their terms of trade is another common concern of primary producing countries. This pessimism rests partly on an extrapolation of the alleged secular deterioration in their terms of trade and partly on the expectation that future improvements in primary production, together with a low-income elasticity of demand for primary products, will lower the prices of the developing country's exports relative to its imports.

This pessimism can be overdone. Regarding the low elasticity of demand argument, this can be qualified: it should be realized that the demand from any one source of supply or any one grade of the commodity may be highly elastic even though the demand for the entire commodity is inelastic (as the shift in the demand for coffee from Brazil to Kenya illustrates). A country that is more competitive on the supply side may gain a larger share of the export market, whereas a country that neglects its competitive supply position will find itself losing its share of the world market, even though the world demand may be rising (as for Indian staples). The slow rate of growth in primary exports cannot be attributed only to deficiencies in external demand. Low elasticities of supply and the domestic policies of the primary producing country can also limit the growth of primary exports.

Any generalization about the terms of trade is also impossible. Trends and fluctuations in the terms of trade have varied according to which concept of the terms of trade is used, which country is examined, what commodities are included, and what time period is involved.[13]

Even if it should be true that an LDC is experiencing a deterioration in its commodity terms of trade, the question would still remain whether this constitutes a significant obstacle to its development. The answer depends on what is causing the deterioration and whether the country's factoral terms of trade and income terms are also deteriorating. If the deterioration in the commodity terms is due to increased productivity in the export sector, the single-factoral terms of trade (commodity terms corrected for changes in productivity in producing exports) may be improving simultaneously. As long as productivity in its export industries is increasing more rapidly than export prices are falling, the country's real income can rise despite the deterioration in the commodity terms of trade: when its factoral terms improve, the country benefits from the ability to obtain a greater quantity of imports per unit of factors embodied in its exports. Also possible is an improvement in the country's income terms of trade (commodity terms multiplied by quantity of exports) at the same time as its commodity terms deteriorate. The country's capacity to import is then greater, and this will ease development efforts.

What should be emphasized are both the supply side of the problem

---

[13] For critical reviews of the evidence, see R.E. Baldwin, "Secular Movements in the Terms of Trade," *American Economic Review, Papers and Proceedings* (May 1955), 267ff., and T. Morgan, "The Long-Run Terms of Trade Between Agriculture and Manufacturing," *Economic Development and Cultural Change*, 8 (Oct. 1959), 6–17.

within the LDCs and the need for greater market access in the developed importing countries. Within the LDC, policies have to be undertaken to increase agricultural productivity, to avoid the implicit taxation of agriculture through subsidization of import-substituting industrialization, to allow a correction of overvalued exchange rates, and to transform production within the primary producing sector (say, from a foodstuff with only a slowly growing demand, to the export of an industrial raw material or a mineral for which the demand may be rising more rapidly).

If the LDC becomes more productive and competitive in world commodity markets, it must be able to have greater access to foreign markets. Tariffs and quotas on imports that compete with temperate zone agricultural imports (cereals, sugar, dairy products, meat) need to be reduced. Excise taxes on tropical beverages (cocoa, coffee, tea) should be lowered. Tariffs or quotas on other primary products should be liberalized. A reduction in the effective rates of protection, by lowering the degree of cascading in the tariff differentials of an importing advanced country, may also allow the LDC to export more of its primary production in a processed form.

Policies to prevent or mitigate primary commodity instability must reflect the causes of the instability. The causes can be analyzed in terms of fluctuations in supply and fluctuations in demand. For any particular country, these fluctuations will depend on the composition of the country's exports, the degree of diversification by commodity and geographical destination, the country's export-market shares, and the shifts in domestic demand when there is also home consumption of the exportable.

The uncertainty and variability of export prices and earnings can be especially disrupting to a country's development program when the country depends upon one or two primary-product exports, which are peculiarly vulnerable to export price or export quantum instability, and when the country's exports are large relative to its national product. A number of policies can be suggested to mitigate the adverse effects of this export instability.

The developing country itself may undertake domestic stabilization measures. These can include monetary and fiscal policies to offset the income and distributional effects that fluctuations in export receipts may have. The government may also establish Marketing Boards, which buy the commodity from local producers at one price and sell it on world markets at the world price. The government may also acquire a stabilization reserve by taxing exports when prices rise and utilizing the accumulated reserve when prices fall.

At the international level, stabilization measures can be in the form of international financing, such as the compensatory financing facility of the International Monetary Fund. But these financial payments for a shortfall in export receipts are curative or remedial rather than preventive. To eliminate the instability in the first instance, many have advocated some form of international commodity agreement. **International commodity agreements** (ICAs) can take a variety of forms, but they essentially involve, either separately or in combination, the operation of a system of export quotas (as in the coffee agreement), an international buffer stock, which operates within a range of prices (tin agreement), or a multilateral long-term contract, which stipulates a minimum price at which importing countries agree to buy specified quantities and a maximum price at which producing countries agree to export a stated amount (as originally in the wheat agreement).[14]

Regardless of the particular form of a commodity stabilization agreement, the objective of "stabilization" is ambiguous: "stabilization" may refer to the international price of an export commodity, producers' money income or real income, export earnings, or the purchasing power of primary exports over imports. An inescapable difficulty of a commodity-control scheme is that, in stabilizing one of these variables (for instance, price), it may at the same time destabilize another variable (for instance, export earnings).

In its simplest form, a **buffer stock** deals in the residuals between supply and demand that appear at some fixed price or price range. The buffer stock stores the residual when demand is less than supply and supplies the residual when demand is greater than supply, in order to maintain market price unchanged. The justification for the buffer stock must be that the gain from avoiding price instability is greater than the cost of the stabilization measures. When there are costs of price stabilization, it will not be optimal to attempt to reduce price instability to zero, but instead to make the marginal cost of storage equal to the expected marginal benefit yielded by the reduction in price instability.[15]

---

[14] For details of various possible schemes, see A.I. MacBean, *Export Instability and Economic Development* (1966), Chap. 12; J.W.F. Rowe, *Primary Commodities in International Trade* (1965); Jere R. Behrman, *International Commodity Agreements* (1977); Behrman, *Economic Development, the International Economic Order, and International Commodity Agreements* (1978).

[15] B.F. Massell, "Price Stabilization and Welfare," *Quarterly Journal of Economics*, 83 (1969), 284–98, and P. Hallwood, "Stochastic Model of the Optimum Buffer Stock," University of Aberdeen, Occasional Paper No. 77–10.

Proposals for some form of international commodity policy often go beyond mere price stabilization to the attainment of what the United Nations Conference on Trade and Development (UNCTAD) has called "equitable and renumerative prices"—that is, export prices above what the market would yield. In drawing an analogy with the protection afforded agricultural producers in the developed countries through domestic price-support programs, the poor countries are clearly seeking similar protection for their primary producers through international price-support schemes, with the hope of raising their level of export earnings and the purchasing power of their exports in terms of industrial imports. But whereas under a domestic price-support program the domestic consumers are in effect being taxed to support domestic producers, an international control agreement would in effect tax the consumers in the importing country for the benefit of the exporting country. The international agreement would be a means of transferring resources from the advanced importing country to the less developed exporting country. As such, aid would then be provided in the guise of a commodity agreement. Indeed, the distinctive feature of an international agreement is precisely that it might raise the long-term trend of the developing country's export prices, improve its terms of trade, and hence possess the quality of giving aid to the exporting country.[16]

Although it is this potential as a form of aid that makes the use of an international commodity agreement appealing to the less developed countries, it is highly questionable whether in practice this would even be feasible, or desirable. For although it is one thing to compare a commodity agreement against alternative measures as a technique for smoothing out fluctuations in demand or supply, stabilizing export earnings, or guaranteeing supply access for the consumer nations, it is quite a different matter to use a commodity agreement to raise the price above what is justified by the long-run average trend in supply and demand conditions.

If the use of an international buffer stock scheme is contemplated, it can obviously be applied only to those primary products that have the physical characteristics of being highly standardized in quality-grades and capable of being stored at not too high a cost over long periods without deterioration in quality. From this technical standpoint, the range of eligible primary commodities is narrow. If the scheme is to

---

[16] For an elaboration of this section, see G.M. Meier, *International Economics of Development* (1968), 272–78.

enlist the participation of consumer nations it will have to do so by providing the benefits of assurances of adequate access to supplies and a lessening of inflationary pressures through rising import prices. But these interests of the consumer nations may be in conflict with those of the producer nations in managing the agreement.

The problem of financing a buffer stock agreement is also difficult. The LDCs may have the greatest interest in such a fund, but they are the least able to afford the burden of financial contributions, whereas the richer countries are the least willing to support a scheme that will raise the prices of their imports.

Further, if the buffer stock arrangement is designed to maintain the minimum price of the commodity above the long-run equilibrium price, it will be necessary to accumulate stocks continually. To forestall the eventual exhaustion of financial resources, and the collapse of the scheme, there would then have to be a downward adjustment in the operating range of prices, with an abandonment of the higher price level desired by the producing countries, or else the buffer stock would have to be supplemented by sufficiently effective export controls.

Once a commodity agreement must rely upon restriction of output or export quotas, the problems multiply—as the historical record of many unsuccessful control schemes abundantly testifies. To be effective, there must be comprehensive control of both actual and potential production. The producing countries in the agreement must supply the dominant part of exports and have some control over the potential supply. To ensure adequate policing of the export quotas, importing countries must also cooperate in discriminating against nonparticipating exporters. A common failing of an export-quota arrangment is its inability to maintain full participation by all the producing countries. Some exporters are tempted to remain outside the agreement and benefit from the higher export prices without being restricted in the development of their own exports; if there is a redistribution of export quotas, as there must be when the pattern of production and trade changes over time, those countries required to reduce their share of world trade will be reluctant to remain within the agreement and those countries that are the low-cost producers will be tempted to leave the agreement with the expectation that they will gain more from the expansion of their own share of trade outside the agreement than they will lose from any possible fall in prices.

An individual producing country must also have sufficient power to control the output of individual producers in accordance with changes in its quota allocation, or else it will face a heavy financial strain in accumulating excess stocks and will, again, be tempted to evade the agreement. If importing countries agreed to import only from participants in the agreement, this would help maintain full participation by producing countries; but the more effective the agreement in raising price above the free market level, the less inclined the consuming nations to support the agreement. Finally, the agreement must be for a commodity for which substitutes do not exist and cannot be easily evolved; otherwise, the upward pressure on price will induce the importing countries to replace the commodity domestically with natural or synthetic substitutes (as could be expected for rubber, jute, cotton, vegetable oils, and nonferrous metals).

The new devices of **producer associations** (modeled after OPEC) face similar problems. To be effective, a producer cartel must satisfy several conditions: (i) recognition by all producers that joint action will lead to greater returns for all of them; (ii) a negligible or nonexistent competitive fringe of noncooperating producers; (iii) homogeneity and simplicity of the product; (iv) an inelastic demand for the product in consumer nations; (v) a low elasticity of supply of alternative materials for consumer countries; (vi) existence of effective national and international marketing and control systems; and (vii) high barriers to entry. The number of primary commodities over which the monopoly power of a producer cartel can be exerted is small.

Even if a buffer stock, an international commodity agreement, or a producer association could operate effectively, we must still ask whether the possible benefits outweigh any unfavorable consequences. When the essential benefit of the commodity control is the receipt of an increase in aid in a disguised form, we should be aware of the differences between this form of "disguised" aid and the alternative of an increase in "open" aid. This approach would distribute aid merely on the basis of production of those commodities for which prices can be raised. The recipients of aid would then not necessarily be those countries that meet the criterion of "need," or "performance," or any other criterion for receiving aid beyond being a producer of the protected commodity. Not only is there a problem in having the wrong countries receive aid, but also a further complexity in having the wrong groups within the developing country be the beneficiaries of this form of aid. Unlike open aid, disguised aid through a commodity agreement would benefit directly the producers of the commodity. The government must then have sufficient tax power and the willingness to siphon off the benefit of higher export prices and channel the funds into development financing, instead of allowing the additional export income to be dissipated in higher consumption or capital flight. On the donor side, the commodity approach to aid also places the burden of aid more heavily on the larger importing nations, not necessarily those most able to bear it. Nor does it allow the donor to influence the disposal of its aid for development objectives. As a means of providing aid, commodity control schemes are thus inefficient and inequitable.

Appealing as is the prima facie case for commodity management, it is difficult in actual policy-making to overcome the technical complexities of any control scheme and to avoid the adverse effects. In the last analysis, it becomes impossible to retain any clear distinction between the different objectives of efficiency in resource allocation, stabilization of export proceeds, and a transfer of resources from rich to poor countries—multiple objectives that tend to be irreconcilable within any one scheme of commodity management.

Export Substitution

Disenchanted by the results of import substitution policies, and still pessimistic about commodity trade, the developing countries are giving increasing attention to the potentialities of an industrialization strategy that emphasizes export substitution—that is, such nontraditional exports as processed primary products, semimanufactures, and manufactured commodities in substitution for traditional primary product exports. Much of this export promotion has come through the activities of multinational corporations that are engaging in international subcontracting, worldwide sourcing of components, and the decomposing of their production processes on a worldwide basis, as well as providing multinational marketing facilities. Although direct foreign investment has often led to the rise of exports, domestic enterprises and joint ventures are also contributing. The number of newly industrializing countries that account for most of the exports of manufactures from developing countries is still relatively few (Hong Kong, Singapore, South Korea, Taiwan, Brazil, Mexico, Turkey, and Yugoslavia). The composition of their exports is also concentrated (clothing, textiles, footwear, simple consumer goods). And the export concentration is on a relatively few markets (United States, Britain, West Germany, and Japan). But more newly industrializing countries, a wider range of exports, and more importing countries are to be expected. For the forces that are ever-changing the international division of labor are strong, allowing more LDCs to acquire a comparative advantage in resource-based or labor-intensive commodities and the "mature" commodities of the product cycle. It may be expected that eventually a given technological advantage originally held by a developed country will be dissipated and will give way to conventional factor-cost advantages, so that the new line of production may become more accessible to developing countries.

An export-substitution process can have some distinct advantages over the import-substitution process. First, it is true that in terms of relaxing a country's foreign exchange constraint, a unit of foreign exchange saved by import substitution is the same as a unit of foreign exchange earned by export substitution. But there are other considerations in favor of export substitution. The **domestic-resource cost** of earning a unit of foreign exchange tends to be less than the domestic-resource cost of saving a unit of foreign exchange.[17] The domestic-resource cost of foreign exchange represents the value of domestic resources spent in saving or earning a unit of foreign exchange, expressed as a proportion of the actual exchange rate. In other words, the scarce resources used in import substitution could have been used to earn a greater amount of foreign exchange through export expansion than the foreign exchange saved in import substitution that relies on high effective rates of protection.

Moreover, because it rests on exogenous world demand, the process of industrialization through export substitution does not have the disadvantage of being limited to a narrow home market as does the import-substitution process. The prospect of exporting therefore tends to stimulate a larger inflow of foreign investment than does import substitution. Nor does the inflow of foreign capital to support export substitution depend on home market protection, but is instead induced by considerations of efficiency on the side of resource cost for the wider world market. This also tends to make the efficiency of foreign capital higher in export activities than in the protected import-replacement sector.

Of much importance now, export substitution contributes more than does import substitution to the objectives of greater employment and

[17]For a discussion of the domestic resource cost measures, see Anne O. Krueger, "Evaluating Restrictionist Trade Regimes: Theory and Measurement," *Journal of Political Economy* (1972), 48–62; Krueger, *Liberalization Attempts and Consequences* (1978), *passim.*

improvement in the distribution of income. The export-substitution process utilizes the surplus factor of labor more intensively than does the import-substitution process. The linkage effects to other activities that supply imports can also be substantial. The earning of foreign exchange can also support a secondary expansion of domestic activity that will raise employment.

Furthermore, export substitution indirectly helps create employment in the urban-industrial sector by relaxing the agricultural constraint that can otherwise handicap urban-industrial employment. By exporting manufactures and semi-manufactures, the developing countries are able to import agricultural goods and thereby keep the real wage low as expressed in terms of industrial goods. If, on the contrary, there is an agricultural bottleneck, and the prices of agricultural goods increase relative to industrial goods, the real wage in terms of industrial goods would rise. This, in turn, would induce a substitution of capital for labor, and it would also reduce profit margins, thereby causing savings to decline and the rate of capital accumulation to decrease (recall the classical model of Chapter 11, pp. 275–279). Industrial employment would thereby be adversely affected.[18]

As the case for export substitution has strengthened, so too have technical forces created a greater potential for a new international division of labor. Transportation and communication developments, the increasing rate of technological diffusion, and the extension of transnational enterprises have all intensified the process of the internationalization of production and marketing, thereby providing the technical possibilities for more export substitution. But although the technical ingredients exist, it will be a test of effective international policy-making to realize their potential. To promote export substitution, complementary policies need to be undertaken by developed countries and less developed countries alike. Whereas import-substitution industrialization policies involved only national policies, the process of industrialization through export substitution depends upon international policy coordination.

In shifting to the export of manufactures, the LDCs are attempting to gain a greater share of the most dynamic sector of world trade. But obstacles to expansion must still be overcome by some supportive policies—by developed countries (DCs) and by LDCs.

---

[18]This point is illustrated by J.C.H Fei and G. Ranis, "A Model of Growth and Employment in the Open Dualistic Economy: The Cases of Korea and Taiwan," *Journal of Development Studies*, 11 (Jan. 1975), 32–56.

The LDCs have long urged the industrially advanced countries to grant tariff preferences in favor of imports of manufactures and semi-manufactures from the LDCs. This may allow LDCs not only to export more, but also to charge the consumers of the importing country a higher price than the world market price, thereby transferring resources to the LDC. Suppose, for example, that a developed country, *A*, initially imposes a 50% *ad valorem* duty on imports from both another developed country, *B*, and an LDC; and that the export price from developed country *B* is 100 and from the LDC, 120. The import price plus duty in *A* will then be 150 for imports from *B* and 180 from the LDC. The country will therefore import from the other developed country *B*. If, however, *A* now retains the 50% *ad valorem* duty on imports from *B*, while levying no duty on imports from the LDC (a 100% preferential margin), then the LDC can export at a price up to 150 (the import price plus duty for imports from *B*). Previously, *A* paid customs receipts of 50 (imports of 100 from *B* plus duty of 50) to itself; but after preferences are granted, the preference-granting country transfers to the LDC the real resources equal to the value of the forgone customs revenue.

The LDCs consider a preferential system as a form of positive compensatory discrimination, but critics in the DCs label it "inverted protectionism" and trade diversion. The DCs have granted preferences only begrudgingly, limiting their effectiveness through exemptions, tariff quotas, and the escape clauses of "market disruption." Although the plea for preferences may have symbolic value in terms of international equity or distributive justice, the LDCs now realize that more may actually be accomplished in earning foreign exchange and promoting nontraditional exports through trade liberalization in other forms.

The DC's average tariff on manufactures may be low, but particular tariffs are greater on potential exports from LDCs. A study of market access in the DCs for products of export interest to developing countries concluded that, overall, the products that are most severely restricted are those for which developing countries could most easily expand their exports.[19] Products that are most heavily protected by the DCs, whether by tariff or by non-tariff barriers, tend to include many of the products whose import would be most responsive to a policy of trade liberalization—such as textiles, clothing, footwear, processed food products, and a potential list of manufactures and semi-manufactures that

---

[19] H.F. Lydall, *Trade and Employment* (1975), 17–20.

could be based on local supplies of natural resources, or processed with labor-intensive techniques, and produced efficiently on a small or medium scale.

The elimination of this *de facto* discrimination against LDCs should be helpful. So too would the replacement of specific duties with *ad valorem* duties on the lower quality and cheaper manufactures of interest to LDCs. A duty on only the value added overseas would also encourage the importation of commodities embodying components originally exported from the DC and assembled in the LDC.

An especially severe obstacle is the escalation in the DC's tariff rates, according to the degree of processing, and the differential in tariff rates between intermediate products and final output. The resultant high rates of effective protection on domestic value added can impose extreme handicaps on potential exports from the LDCs. Tariff escalation in the DCs still discriminate against the imports of processed goods from the developing countries and offset the cost advantages these countries possess in regard to a number of processed commodities.

Another major obstacle arises from the imposition of quantitative restrictions, again under the guise of "market disruption." The experience of textile quotas, orderly marketing agreements, and "voluntary export restrictions" can only too readily be repeated for the newer exports.

To facilitate the removal of these obstacles, while nullifying the claim of market disruption, the DCs may find it politically necessary to adopt a wider range of adjustment assistance policies. To allow the growth of the new export industries in the newly industrializing countries, the DCs will have to provide aid for the purpose of moving resources out of the displaced senile industries in which the developed countries' comparative advantage has been lost into new, more efficient, higher-technology product lines.

If the LDCs are to capitalize upon the opportunities for greater market access, they in turn must undertake some reciprocal policies. The LDCs must reduce the distortions in product and factor prices that have constituted an anti-export bias. The monetary and credit system must be reformed to attract resources into the export sector. Money costs must also be reduced in relation to world prices. Attention must therefore be given to establishing an appropriate exchange rate, to increasing productivity, to instituting an incomes policy, and to liberalizing trade.

More positive measures could also be instituted at the micro-level.

The range of export incentives available to governments include policies whereby a company's imports are related to its export performance; devices to penalize firms failing to meet a given export target; rebates on export prices or other forms of subsidy on inputs used in industrial exports; and an exchange rate that is more favorable to exports.

The government may furnish services that the ordinary manufacturing firm cannot provide for itself in export markets. For example, the undertaking of marketing activities may require government assistance. This may even involve subsidization of new exports, based on an "infant marketing" argument to assist inexperienced firms entering unfamiliar foreign markets during the periods of "export infancy." The government may also develop new instruments and methods for financing manufactured exports and provide insurance to cover the commercial and transfer risks involved in breaking into new export markets. The government might also undertake research and promote technological changes to improve the quality of production and reduce the manufacturing costs of exports.

In considering all these measures, the government should view them as an integrated set so that they are as consistent and effective as possible. The stimulus derived from tax and other incentives, for instance, should not be offset by the negative effects of an overvalued exchange rate.

Most important, potential exporters need confidence that the government is really committed to export promotion beyond the immediate period of formal exchange-rate changes. To overcome their risk aversion and to provide the incentive for long-term investment in export production, exporters must have some expectation of continuing profitability for exports.

Mixed Strategy

The real problem for a developing country is not to choose either an import-substitution strategy or an export-substitution strategy alone, but rather to secure the "right" mix of the two strategies. Appropriate domestic policies should allocate resources efficiently to internal and external opportunities. The parallel development of selected import-substitution and export-substitution industries is required (as was true for Japan, historically, and recently for Korea).[20] The formal requirement is that policies should equate the marginal domestic-resource cost of saving foreign exchange with the marginal domestic-resource cost of earning foreign exchange.

Even while a country emphasizes export diversification, import substitution may complement export substitution. The backward linkages from exports may justify import substitution. The intermediate inputs used in exports might be replaced by home production instead of being imported (for example, domestically produced natural fiber yarns and steel in Korea). Import substitution of final products may also serve as a transition to subsequent export of the products. Incentives to domestic sales may be given to establish a domestic market as a base for subsequent exports. At the later stage, incentives may be given to exports (as in Korea, there can be pressures to move quickly from being an "infant industry" to becoming an "infant exporter").[21]

If import substitution violates a country's present comparative cost structure in the expectation of acquiring a future comparative advantage in the import substitute, so too will the export-substitution strategy often carry a country beyond its present comparative cost position. Investment should follow the pattern of potential comparative advantage. If a government gives due recognition to the indirect dynamic gains from trade, it may then determine that the optimum pattern of trade is beyond the static optimum point in order to overcome indivisibilities, to realize economies of scale, and to enjoy externalities. As Myint[22] observes,

These (dynamic) gains represent a non-reversible outward shift of the production possibility curve of a country in the direction of export production. In order to obtain them, a country would usually have to commit its resources to export production on a large enough scale to overcome the indivisibilities in the production process or in the auxiliary facilities such as transport and communications. This means that the country would have to sacrifice some of the direct gains from trade by committing its resources to export production beyond the static optimum point for the sake of reaping the future indirect benefits from export expansion. Here we have passed from neutral free trade policy to

[20] For Japan, see Ippei Yamazawa, "Strategy of Industrial Development: Japanese Experience," in Nagatoshi Suzuki (ed.), *Asian Industrial Development* (1975), Chap. 10. For Korea, see Larry E. Westphal, "The Republic of Korea's Experience with Export-Led Industrial Development," *World Development*, 6 (March 1978), 347–82.
[21] Westphal, *op. cit.,* 375.
[22] Myint, "Exports and Economic Development of Less-Developed Countries," *op. cit.,* 9, 13.

a genuine "export promotion policy" which is the exact counterpart of the infant-industry argument for protection.

Policies to promote export substitution can result in an oversubsidization of exports, just as policies have done for import substitution. This must be avoided. Credit and tax preferences, duty-free imports, preferential rates in the services of public utilities and other financial incentives can provide preferential treatment for the export sector. But subsidization can be overdone, resulting in an unduly high domestic-resource cost of exports. To the extent that excessive subsidization of exports occurs, social inefficiency in resource allocation will appear in the same way as under policies that subsidize import substitution.

There is, however, evidence that oversubsidization of the export-substitution process is less likely to occur than oversubsidization of import-substitution industrialization. This is because the costs of excess export promotion through expenditures in national budgets are more visible to policy-makers than are those of import substitution based on quantitative restrictions; export-substitution promotion entails relatively greater use of indirect, rather than direct, intervention; exporting firms must face price and quality competition in international markets; and exporting firms are more likely to realize economies of scale.[23]

Of the many problems confronting a developing country, the establishment of policies for the **transition to an optimal policy of protection** is among the most complex: a number of studies indicate that restrictive trade regimes, associated with high import premia, lead to deteriorating or inferior export performance, whereas reduced reliance on foreign exchange controls and a **liberalization of foreign trade regimes** lead to higher exports.[24] In practice, the countries that have succeeded in promoting their exports have undergone a transitional period of policy reform that has brought their **effective exchange rate** of exports *(EER$_x$)* closer to the effective exchange rate on imports *(EER$_m$)*. By the effective exchange rate on exports is meant the units of domestic currency that can be obtained for a dollar's worth of exports, taking into account export duties, subsidies and surcharges, special exchange rates, input subsidies related to exports, and other financial

[23]Jagdish N. Bhagwati and Anne O. Krueger, "Exchange Control, Liberalization, and Economic Development," *American Economic Review, Papers and Proceedings*, LXIII (May 1973), 420–21.

[24]See J. Bhagwati, *Anatomy and Consequences of Exchange Control Regimes* (1978); Anne O. Krueger, *Liberalization Attempts and Consequences* (1978); and Bela Balassa, "Export Incentives and Export Performance in Developing Countries: A Comparative Analysis," *Weltwirtschaftliches Archiv*, 114 (1978), 24–61.

and tax measures that affect the price of exports. The effective exchange rate on imports is defined as the units of domestic currency that would be paid for a dollar's worth of imports, taking into account tariffs, surcharges, interest on advance deposits, and other measures that affect the price of imports. Under an import-substituting strategy, the effective exchange rate for imports is greater than the effective exchange rate for exports ($EER_x/EER_m < 1$). The effective exchange rate can, of course, be considerably different from the nominal exchange rate, and this can intensify the bias in favor of import substitution.

When a country devalues or allows depreciation of its currency, the gross devaluation (shown by the nominal exchange rate) will differ from the **net** devaluation (shown by the EER). If the country combines devaluation with a set of liberalizing policies, it may have a gross devaluation large enough to leave a net devaluation despite the removal of tariffs on imports and subsidies on exports. If at the same time, the country changes other policies that affect prices of imports or exports, it will change the effect of the net devaluation on different imports and exports. Because of the diverse impact of these policies on different commodities, there will be differential incentives to invest in and produce different products. Another feature of the liberalization program may be to diminish the degree of dispersion in the incentives to expand different activities by providing greater uniformity in these incentives via the foreign trade sector. Quantitative restrictions tend to generate a greater variance in the bias among different commodities than would their tariff-equivalent counterparts.[25] A replacement of quotas with tariffs, allowing pricing incentives, may thereby affect exports by not only reducing the bias against exports, but also diminishing the variance in incentives.

The transition to an optimal policy of protection can first be undertaken by replacing quantitative restrictions with the superior policy of tariffs (recall Chapter 3 on optimal trade interventions). Production subsidies on exports may also be justified because of the external economies generated by such industries. These subsidies may come in the form of rebates of duties levied on imported inputs used in export manufacturing and rebates of indirect taxes on exports. Preferential export credits and credit guarantees on export sales may also be provided.[26] Devaluation,

---

[25] Krueger, *Liberalization Attempts and Consequences* (1978), 92–93, 213–14.

[26] Detailed recommendations are presented by Bela Balassa, "Reforming the System of Incentives in Developing Countries," *World Development*, 3 (June 1975), 365–82, and Bela Balassa and Michael Sharpston, *Export Subsidies by Developing Countries* (1977).

accompanied by commensurate reductions in tariffs, can also promote exports and improve efficiency by providing more incentives to foreign sales of manufactured exports. At the same time, the arbitrariness of inflation cannot be allowed to neutralize the incentives given to foreign sales over domestic sales. Inflation inhibits exports not only through its high cost structure, but also via the greater profitability of the domestic market over the export market. It is then all the more important to increase productivity, move toward the liberalization of the trade regime, and avoid an overvalued exchange rate. Depreciation of the home currency in terms of foreign currency may be necessary to promote exports, to remove the need for protection to safeguard the balance of payments position, and also to reduce the pressure for import substitution. A combination of micro- and macro-policies, combined with exchange-rate policy, is therefore needed to shift to a more liberalized regime and promote exports.

Regional Integration

Although issues of trade policy are mainly directed to relations between the developed and less-developed countries, we should not neglect the potential for more trade among the LDCs themselves and the possibilities of collective "self reliance" through intra-LDC relations. We can best do this in the context of regional economic integration.

Various devices of integration are possible, but most interest centers on the potential role of customs unions and free trade areas (recall Chapter 4, pp. 116–118). At a level less general than a customs union or free trade association, regional integration might be directed simply toward "sectoral integration"—that is, the removal of trade restrictions on only a selected list of commodities or the treatment of the problems of some one industry as a whole on a regional basis.

Beyond free trade in goods, a more comprehensive economic union might allow for the free movement of factors of production, a common monetary system, and the co-ordination of economic policies among the member countries. It is still unrealistic to expect this for developing countries, and we shall therefore be concerned here with the implications of only free trade in goods. As a basis for appraising specific proposals, we should consider the benefits that might be derived from economic groupings among developing countries and the difficulties that are likely to be encountered in their formation.

Advocates of regional integration believe that it will accelerate the development of the member countries by (i) stimulating the establishment and expansion of manufacturing industries on a more rational basis, (ii) increasing the gains from trade, (iii) providing benefits from intensified competition, and (iv) saving foreign exchange.

In the earlier strategy of import-substitution industrialization, when each LDC restricted its imports and attempted to substitute home production, industrialization became unduly compartmentalized, and the uneconomic multiplication of import-competing industries was wasteful. In contrast, if manufacturing industry can be encouraged in the context of a customs union or free trade area, it may attain a higher level of productivity than that resulting from industrial protection in each country. Greater specialization within the region can increase the share of exports and imports in manufacturing and reduce the excessive number of products manufactured in an excessive number of protected firms. It may also stimulate extra-union exports.[27]

To reach an efficient scale of output, a modern manufacturing plant may have to produce a larger output than the low level of home demand in a single underdeveloped country can absorb. By pooling markets through the removal of internal trade barriers, a free trade union might thus provide a sufficiently wide export market to make economies of scale realizable.

The extension of the market, together with the inducement to get behind the external tariff wall, may also be particularly effective in attracting direct private foreign investment in manufacturing. Over time, there is the further possibility that new industries can become increasingly competitive on world markets and eventually be able to export manufactured goods to nonmember countries. But this depends first on establishing a sufficiently wide market within the union to allow operation of a manufacturing industry on a large enough scale. The "domestic" market must also not be so protected that firms are induced to sell domestically products they otherwise would export.

An expansion of trade among the member countries can be expected to result from the removal of trade barriers. If this takes the form of replacing high-cost producers within the region by lower-cost producers, the effect is one of "trade creation," and the international division of labor is improved as resources shift into more efficient production. On the other hand, some of the intraunion trade may

[27]But see David Morawetz, "Extra-Union Exports of Industrial Goods from Customs Unions among Developing Countries," *Journal of Development Economics,* 1 (1974), 247–60.

merely replace trade that formerly occurred between members and non-members. When the formation of an economic union has this "trade-diverting" effect, the international division of labor will be worsened if the outside source of supply is actually a low-cost source and its product now becomes higher priced within the union because of the external tariff. In this case, there is an uneconomic diversion of output from the low-cost outside source to the high-cost supplier within the union, and the gains from trade are diminished.

In considering whether trade creation or trade diversion is likely to dominate in a particular union, we have to take into account the preunion level of tariff rates among the members, the level of the post-union external tariff compared with the preunion tariff levels of each member country, the elasticities of demand for the imports on which duties are reduced, and the elasticities of supply of exports from the members and foreign sources. Conditions are more propitious for trade creation when each member's preunion duties are high on the others' products, the members are initially similar in the products they produce, but different in the pattern of relative prices at which they produce them, the external tariff of the union is low compared with the preunion tariff levels of the members, and the production within the union of commodities that are substitutes for outside imports can be undertaken at a lower cost.

The formation of a free trade union might also result in an improvement—or at least the forestalling of a deterioration—in the region's commodity terms of trade. This is possible if there is a reduction in the supply of exports from the union, the demand by members of the union is reduced for imports from outside, or the bargaining power of the members in trade negotiations is strengthened. But unless the members of the union are the chief suppliers on the world market for their imports, they are unlikely to be able to exercise sufficient monopolistic or monopsonistic power to influence their terms of trade by raising duties on their trade with the outside world or by inducing outsiders to supply their goods more cheaply. Moreover, when free trade is confined only to the region, there is the risk of retaliation through the formation of other economic blocs. A union may thereby inhibit the realization of the more extensive gains from the "universal" approach to free trade.

Regional integration might also be beneficial in encouraging competition among the member countries. Technical efficiency in existing industries might then be improved as marginal firms are forced to reduce their costs, resources are reallocated from less efficient to more efficient firms, and monopolies that had previously been established behind tariff walls are no longer in a sheltered position. Further, the stimulation of competition within each country may yield not only a better utilization of given resources, but may also raise the rate of growth of productive resources. This may result from stronger incentives to adopt new methods of production, to replace obsolete equipment more rapidly, and to innovate more rapidly with more and better investments.

A saving in foreign exchange will come about when the countries form a common market and increase their trade balance *vis-à-vis* the rest of the world.[28] If a member country increases its exports to partners at no expense to its exports to the rest of the world, and at the same time increases by a smaller amount its total *ceteris paribus* imports (although replacing world supply with partner supply), the country will be able to relax its foreign exchange constraint. If the social opportunity cost of foreign exchange is higher than that indicated by the market exchange, there can be a sizable welfare benefit from the saving of foreign exchange made possible by integration.

In practice, however, a number of objections have been raised against proposals for regional integration, and actual negotiations have encountered serious difficulties. As is true for a union among even advanced countries, political problems take precedence, nations will guard against a sacrifice of their sovereignty, and the administration of the union may be extremely complex.

There are also several economic objections to a union. To begin with, it may be argued that the case for an economic union is in reality weak when the constituent countries have not yet established many industries. Limitations on the supply side may be more of a deterrent to the creation of an industry than is the narrow market on the side of demand. If production conditions do not also improve, the mere extension of the consumer market will not be sufficient to create industries. Moreover, when manufacturing industry is only at a rudimentary stage in the member countries, there is not much scope for eliminating high-cost manufacturers within the region. Nor is there much scope for realizing the benefits of increased competition when there are not yet similar ranges of rival products, produced under different cost conditions, in the several member nations. A union will not cause substantial

---

[28] The foreign exchange effect and other welfare effects are analyzed in W.R. Cline and Enrique Delgado (eds.), *Economic Integration in Central America* (1978), 62–74, 110–15, 483–529. This study is also exemplary for its attempt to quantify these effects.

improvement in the utilization of resources unless industries that have already been established need wider markets than the national economy can provide for the realization of economies of scale and unless the member countries have been protecting the same kind of industry, but have markedly different ratios of factor-efficiency in these industries to factor-efficiency in nonprotected branches of production.

The case for a union is strongest among countries that have little foreign trade in proportion to their domestic production, but conduct a high proportion of their foreign trade with one another. When these conditions prevail, there is less possibility for introducing, within each member country, a distortion of the price relation between goods from other member countries and goods from outside the union, and more of a possibility for eliminating any distortion by tariffs of the price-relations between domestic goods and imports from other member countries. There is therefore greater likelihood that the union will improve the use of resources and raise real income.

A union among underdeveloped countries, however, is unlikely to conform to these conditions. The ratio of foreign trade to domestic production is generally high for these countries, and the actual volume of intraregional trade is normally only a small proportion of the region's total foreign trade. The gain from regional integration would therefore be small. The basic difficulty is that, with existing trade patterns, the formation of a union is likely to cause a considerable amount of wasteful "trade diversion." Over the longer run, comparative costs and trade patterns may change, and economies of scale may give rise to competitive advantages as development proceeds, so that the scope for "trade creation" will become greater within the union. But the immediate gain is small, and the longer-run prospects for the creation of new trade are not likely to influence current decisions to join a union.

Besides the possibility of "trade diversion," other undesirable consequences may result from a union. The member countries are unlikely to benefit equally, and some members may believe the others are gaining at their expense. A country may have a strong comparative advantage in only primary products and will sell to other members only goods that it could as readily export to outside countries. At the same time, the location of manufacturing industry and ancillary activities may become localized within one member country, and "polarization" results. Other members may then contend that if they too had been able to adopt tariff protection against their partners, they would have also been able to attract industry. A nonindustrialized member country may further complain that in buying from an industrialized partner, instead of importing from the outside, it is losing revenue equal to the duty on outside manufactures. And, with a common external tariff, member countries no longer have the discretionary power to use variations in the tariff for the purpose of adjusting their national revenues to their own requirements. The internal strains that arise from uneven development among the member countries may thus make it extremely difficult to preserve a regional grouping.

It may, however, be possible for the union to redistribute benefits among members through a system of public finance transfers, a regional development bank, balance of payments support, regional policies for the location of industry, the pooling of overhead costs of public services, or coordination of development policies. But unless the union is strong enough to adopt these other measures and distribute the gains more evenly, its dissident members will threaten its stability.

We may conclude that although there are potential benefits to be derived from regional integration, especially over the long run, the immediate gains should not be overestimated and due attention must be given to the possible undesirable consequences for the disadvantaged members. The most important lesson to be learned from efforts at regional integration is that if the potential benefits of integration are to be realized, the regional association must be capable of co-ordinating trade policies, including exchange-rate policy, among the member countries, and must provide some means for an equitable distribution of the costs and benefits among members.

Supplementary Readings

The following are general studies of the relationships between international trade and development: Gerald K. Helleiner, *International Trade and Economic Development* (1972); James D. Theberge (ed.), *Economics of Trade and Development* (1968); Helen Hughes (ed.), *Prospects for Partnership* (1973); Peter Robson (ed.), *International Economic Integration* (1972); D.B. Keesing, "Outward-Looking Policies and Economic Development," *Economic Journal*, 77 (June 1967), 303–30; P.P. Streeten, "Trade Strategies for Development," *World Development*, 1 (1973), 1ff.; H.G. Johnson, *Comparative Cost and Commercial Policy*, Wicksell Lectures (1968); Kathryn Morton and Peter Tulloch, *Trade and Developing Countries* (1977); and W. Arthur Lewis, *The Evolution of the International Economic Order* (1978).

Foreign trade regimes are examined in detail in Ian Little, Tibor Scitovsky, and Maurice Scott, *Industry and Trade in Some Developing Countries: A Comparative Study* (1970); Bela Balassa, *Policy Reform in Developing Countries* (1977); and B. Balassa et al.,

The Structure of Protection in Developing Countries (1971); the several country studies in the National Bureau of Economic Research project, *Foreign Trade Regimes and Economic Development;* Anne O. Krueger, *Liberalization Attempts and Consequences* (1978); Jagdish Bhagwati, *Anatomy and Consequences of Exchange Control Regimes* (1978); and Carlos F. Diaz-Alejandro, "Trade Policies and Economic Development," in Peter B. Kenen (ed.), *International Trade and Finance* (1975), 93–150, with extensive bibliography.

The special issues of dependency and delinking are discussed in Gabriel Palma, "Dependency: A Formal Theory of Underdevelopment or a Methodology of the Analysis of Concrete Situations of Underdevelopment?," *World Development,* 6 (July/Aug. 1978), 881–924; R.I. Rhodes, "Bibliography on Studying Imperialism," *Review of Radical Political Economics* (Spring 1972); André Gunder Frank, *On Capitalist Underdevelopment* (1975); B.J. Cohen, *The Question of Imperialism: The Political Economy of Dominance and Dependence* (1973); and S. Lall, "Is 'Dependence' a Useful Concept in Analyzing Underdevelopment?," *World Development,* 3, Nos. 11 and 12 (1975), 799–810; see also the references in Chap. 11, *n.* 8, this volume.

13

Resource Transfers

When mobilizing resources for its development, a country must rely on transfers of foreign resources until it achieves the capacity for self-sustaining growth. Capital flows in the form of foreign aid, private foreign investment, and private bank lending are the principal ways by which resources can come from rich to poor countries. Less obvious are transfers through trade policies that improve the poor country's terms of trade or transfers through the linking of an increase in official international liquidity to development finance. The transmission of technology, ideas, and knowledge are other special types of resource transfer. In this chapter we shall concentrate on capital flows and technology transmission.

Two-Gap Analysis   *Dual-Gap Analysis of Thirwall ?*

When discussing the constraints on development, we referred to the savings gap and the foreign exchange gap. A net capital inflow contributes to the filling of both gaps. Aid increases the amount of resources available for capital formation above what can be provided by domestic saving: aid supplements domestic saving. It also raises the recipient economy's capacity to import goods: aid provides foreign exchange and eases the problem of making international payments.

But how can there be two gaps? How can one of the gaps be larger than the other? Or how can there be a foreign exchange gap if there is no savings gap? If savings increase, should this not mean that imports fall or that consumption falls, and resources are released for export or import-competing uses so that when the savings gap is diminished, the foreign exchange gap will also be diminished *ipso facto?* This would be true, however, only if domestic resources are substitutable for foreign resources. But if there is a technologically fixed ratio of imports to output, or of imports to investment, then the country cannot substitute domestic resources for imports as output expands. Or if the country faces an inelastic demand for its exports, or if its terms of trade worsen when exports increase, then foreign exhange receipts can diminish, and the country will still have a foreign exchange constraint even though domestic saving has released resources for the export sector.

By the national income accounting identities (discussed on pp. 175–181), the savings gap and the foreign exchange gap are always equal *ex post* within an accounting period. But *ex ante,* they may differ; it is only through a process of adjustment that they become equal *ex post.* For example, if the shortage of domestic savings is greater than the shortage of foreign exchange *ex ante,* all the investment will then not be realized. Investment becomes equal to savings, *ex post,* at a lower level of output than would have been realized if there had been a smaller savings gap. In this case, output is **investment limited.**

If, however, the shortage of foreign exchange is greater than the savings gap *ex ante,* imports will fall, and the savings will not be realized because output is **trade limited.**[1] Through these changes in imports and investment, the two gaps are equated *ex post.* As explained earlier, the *ex post* identities will be

$$E\text{-}Y = I\text{-}S = M\text{-}X = F \qquad (12.1)$$

where F is the amount of foreign borrowing. *Ex post,* the two gaps have to be identical, and equal to the total net capital inflow from overseas.

How can the necessary amount of foreign assistance be calculated? At the start of a development plan period, a developing country will calculate its savings gap and its foreign exchange gap, based on target rates of growth, postulated investment requirements, potential domestic savings, import requirements, and expected foreign exchange receipts. To attain the target rate of growth, both investment and import requirements must be fulfilled. The required foreign aid inflow is therefore determined by the larger of the two gaps.

If the savings gap is the dominant constraint, then foreign borrowing

---

[1] The savings will be unutilized, unless savings can be used for investment with no import content (perhaps investment in human resources), and output expands as much as it would with imports for other types of investment.

is required to fill this larger gap. The two gaps can become equated *ex post* by having more imports or fewer exports than initially projected. Let F_o represent the amount of foreign borrowing needed in the base year. This will equal $I_o - S_o$, the savings gap in the base year. Subsequently, the amount of foreign borrowing needed at a later date, F_t, will depend on what is happening to the rate of saving over time and the investment requirements at the later date t. The difference between borrowing requirements in the base year and borrowing in period t is the difference between the investment requirements to sustain the target rate of growth and increases in saving generated by increasing income:

$$F_t - F_o = \Delta I - \Delta S \tag{12.2}$$

If F_t is to become less than F_o, ΔS must become larger than ΔI. When the savings gap disappears, output will no longer be investment limited.

If the shortage of foreign exchange limits growth before the shortage of savings does, then F_o must fill the larger trade gap:

$$F_o = M_o - X_o \tag{12.3}$$

The two gaps will be equal *ex post* because either saving will fall below the expected saving potential or less productive investment will occur. To reduce the amount of foreign borrowing needed to remove the binding foreign exchange gap, the recipient country must generate exports in larger amounts that imports:

$$F_t - F_o = \Delta M - \Delta X \tag{12.4}$$

When exports rise to a level sufficient to cover the required imports for the target rate of growth, the foreign exchange gap will disappear, and output will no longer be trade limited.

Conceivably, either gap could dominate at any time. There is some empirical evidence, however, that over their course of development, countries generally tend to have first a dominant savings constraint and then later the trade limit dominates.[2] But it must be remembered that the two-gap analysis depends upon the country's inability to translate an increase in saving into the necessary foreign exchange to sustain the required level of investment or the inability of the country to pursue any other policies that would result in import saving or export promo-

[2] H.B. Chenery and A.M. Strout, "Foreign Assistance and Economic Development," *American Economic Review*, LVI (Sept. 1966), 690–91, 710–19.

tion. The analysis rests upon significant rigidity and lack of substitution possibilities in the developing economy between production for export or import substitution and nontraded goods and a high degree of complementarity in the use of domestically produced capital goods and imported capital goods, as well as other intermediate inputs in the aggregate production function. The crucial question for an individual country is therefore whether or not the structural assumptions of extremely limited substitution possibilities in both the output-mix and factor inputs are empirically relevant.

The foreign exchange approach to external capital requirements is useful in reminding us that to secure a balance of payments "margin" for greater maneuverability in its development effort, a developing country should undertake policies to increase its export earnings and diminish the import-intensity of its import-substitution industries. At the same time, however, it is still true that in many cases a large part of the pressure for imports is due to excess demand. The absorption approach—with its emphasis on the savings constraint—remains therefore of fundamental importance for a majority of the less developed countries that confront the problem of keeping attempted absorption within the bounds of current income.

If efforts to increase domestic saving fail, the overabsorption must be covered by foreign borrowing of an autonomous or otherwise acceptable character. As long as a development program emphasizes investment, and home savings are deficient, there will be a need for an increased supply of long-term capital from overseas. Historically, the investment expenditure that supported the development process in many poor countries was financed by an inflow of foreign capital acceptable to both lender and borrower. New problems, however, are now being encountered through international aid measures and foreign investment policies designed both to encourage and to regulate private foreign capital.

Foreign Aid

Pure aid is a **grant**—a gift of convertible currency for which the recipient country need not pay interest or make any repayment. A loan made to a developing country on terms that are softer than the alternative commercial market terms (that is, lower interest, longer grace period, longer repayment period) will have some **concessional element**. This

N. S. BUCHANAN AND H. S. ELLIS, *Approaches to Economic Development* (1955), 380

An increase of the annual investment of international capital by several multiples would still leave most of the burden of providing the wherewithal for economic progress to the underdeveloped countries themselves.

But this conclusion in no wise negates the strategic importance of present supplies of capital from overseas. It is the marginal increments from abroad which may provide the upward fillip to production to lift standards of living to the point of inducing family limitation. The loans and grants of foreign public agencies, moreover, are possessed of an importance quite beyond their mathematical share in the aggregate of national investment. These funds go chiefly into basic services and utilities which private capital finds too extensive, too slow in coming to fruition and too risky in their prospective yields; they supply the *sine qua non* of progress past the most rudimentary level and pave the way for profitable private investment, both foreign and domestic. Finally, a major theme of much of the recent discussion of technical assistance has been the promise held forth by improved but inexpensive agricultural implements and simple equipment for the handicrafts and village industries. Precisely because a little capital goes a long way, that little is crucial.

concessional element is the aid component of the loan, and a fraction of the loan can be translated into its grant equivalent. The concessional, or grant, element is the difference between the amount of the loan and the present value of the stream of repayments, discounted at the donor's market, long-term interest rate. For a grant, the present value of the repayment is zero, and there is a 100% concessional element. A credit from the International Development Agency (the soft loan window of the World Bank) carries a service charge of three-quarters of 1% for repayment periods of 50 years with a 10-year grace period. The grant element is clearly large. An ordinary loan from the World Bank, in contrast, may have 8% interest (adjusted periodically in relation to the Bank's cost of borrowing), a 3-year grace period, and a 20-year maturity. The concessional element is obviously less.

What is the "real cost"—the sacrifice of real resources—to the donor of aid? And what is the "real benefit" to the aid recipient? The **real cost** of capital flows for the capital exporter is the income forgone as a result of the outflow of capital, given alternative possible uses for the same funds. For a capital importer, the **real benefit** is measured by the net increment in income made possible by investing the capital inflow received, as compared with making the same investment with capital from alternative sources. The grant equivalent will, however, be reduced for the aid recipient if the donor country ties the aid by requiring the recipient to import from the donor country, and the donor's prices exceed world prices. The softer the terms of aid, and the less aid is tied, the greater will be the real benefit to the recipient. Given the same nominal amount of capital inflow, the real resource transfer will then be increased. If the adverse effects of aid-tying can be reduced, and more lenient financial terms introduced, so as to increase the value of the subsidy implicit in the total flow of resources, the real value of the transfer of external resources can more closely approach the nominal value of the flow of financial resources.[3]

Can increased trade substitute for more aid? Only under special conditions. We have already seen that foreign aid can close a prospective foreign exchange gap without additional domestic saving by the recipient country; but this gap can be closed by trade only if there is also an increase in domestic saving equal to the rise in export proceeds. Over the longer run, to the extent that more trade raises national income, and this results in increased saving, trade will reduce the need for more aid. But the rise in saving is a necessary condition.

The view that trade can substitute for aid is limited because it considers aid as filling only the foreign exchange gap. It overlooks the additional real resources for investment that aid also provides in filling the savings gap. If the developing country is able to export only a greater volume at prevailing prices, there is no provision of additional real resources as under aid. Only if the developing countries were enabled, because of international commodity agreements or preferential trading arrangements, to charge higher prices for their exports than would otherwise prevail, would there be an explicit transfer of resources through trade. When an international commodity agreement is advocated to provide a "just and equitable price," it means a price above what the free market would provide. Similarly, preferences are proposed not only to allow the newly industrializing country to export more semi-manufactures or manufactures at the country's existing export price, but to allow it to raise the export price because of the preferential duty. As the real

[3] Various estimates of the difference between the real value and nominal amount of aid are offered by John Pincus, *Economic Aid and International Cost-Sharing* (1965), Chap. 5.

amount of "open aid" diminishes, it is to be expected that the requests for more **"disguised aid,"** in the form of more favorable commerical policies, will intensify. "Disguised aid" is also sought through establishing a link between the creation of additional Special Drawing Rights (SDRs) and their initial distribution to developing countries (see pp. 266–267) and by channeling the proceeds of the IMF's sale of gold to a Trust Fund for the benefit of developing countries.

Effectiveness of Aid

The motivations for aid-giving are mixed—ranging from a desire to promote the economic development of the recipient country to the extension of military and political interests, or simple altruism. If we concentrate on only the objective of economic development, how should we judge the effectiveness of aid? Aid must be a **net addition** to resources and act as a **catalyst** for self-help development measures. If it is to be a net addition to resources, it cannot substitute for domestic savings and merely allow higher consumption or an increase in nondevelopmental current expenditure by the government. In the last analysis, "capital is made at home,"[4] and external assistance must add to, not substitute for, the developing country's own efforts in mobilizing resources.

Although aid may support an increase in output by filling the savings gap and the foreign exchange gap in the short period, the **subsequent use** of the increase in output over the longer period will be even more important in determining the effectiveness of the initial inflow of external resources.[5] To allow aid-sustained growth to be transformed into self-sustained growth, the additional output must be allocated so as to increase saving and reduce the trade gap. Because the effective utilization of foreign capital is highly dependent on the recipient country's ability and willingness to adopt complementary domestic policies, there can be no simple equivalence between the amount of aid that the country receives and its subsequent rate of development.

Some might believe that if aid is limited to well-designed projects it will be more effective. A donor may believe that project aid instead of aid for the recipient country's general development program or for balance of payments support will ensure that the aid is used for some

[4]Ragnar Nurkse, *Problems of Capital Formation in Underdeveloped Countries* (1953), 141.
[5]Chenery and Strout, *op. cit.,* 724–25.

project that is "concrete" and "permanent," with a minimum risk of failure, supposedly facilitating the capacity to service the foreign debt and providing a direct mechanism of control by the donor. It may, however, be illusory to think that aid is granted for a particular project: the project actually financed by aid may be quite different from the one to which the aid is ostensibly devoted. Capital is fungible; the aid is actually financing the **marginal project** that would not have been undertaken, but for the receipt of aid.

It is impossible to limit the effects of aid to only a designated project. The impact of aid cannot be assessed without a general analysis of resource allocation in the recipient country. Even if the aid is for the foreign exchange component of a given project, the income generated from the project will also have linkages with other parts of the economy. The efficacy of any one project is a function of the entire investment program: what ultimately matters is how the recipient country utilizes its total investment expenditures. When aid is allocated for specific projects, it becomes difficult to provide more aid for education, rural development, small-scale industry, and administrative services, which are not as visible as large projects, but which are extremely important for development. Most significantly, to determine the effectiveness of aid, it is necessary to consider not only the initial increment of income resulting from the receipt of aid, but also whether the increment in income is subsequently used to relax one of the constraints on development or is instead dissipated in higher consumption or is used to support a larger population at the same low per capita level of income. Insofar as the most effective use of aid depends upon the operation of the whole set of development policies in the recipient country, program aid rather than project aid may be considered the more appropriate context from the start.[6]

Beyond the untying of aid and the shifting to non-project aid, the quality of the aid relationship may also be improved by extending the range of aid activities on a multilateral rather than a bilateral basis. Multilateral aid has several advantages: it is less influenced by the donor's self-interest; the undesirable effects of tying are more easily avoided; it can more readily harmonize and improve the financial terms of aid (unlike bilateral aid, which allows one country to insist on hard terms, while another offers aid on soft terms); it facilitates co-ordination of aid programs among the various aid sources and with the develop-

[6] See Hans W. Singer, "External Aid: For Plans or Projects?" *Economic Journal,* LXXV (Sept. 1965), 539–45.

ment priorities of the recipient countries; and it provides the opportunity for more aid consortia and consultative group arrangements to bring together the aid donors assisting a group of developing countries.

Recently some critics of aid have concluded that only a fraction of foreign resource inflows results in an increase of imports and investment, while a large share is instead used to increase consumption. Some even contend that aid causes a reduction in domestic savings.[7] A careful review of the statistical studies underlying this conclusion shows, however, that their usefulness and reliability can be doubted because the measures of savings reflect an accounting convention rather than a behavioral relationship, because of statistical problems, and because in many cases the measures involve only correlation, not demonstrated causality.[8] The latter is most important because for a number of countries it is plausible to conclude that exogenous factors (wars, weather, terms of trade) caused both high resource inflows and low saving rates and generally low growth rates as well. Further, it is difficult to play the game of "What would have happened with less or more foreign resource inflows?" In some cases, foreign inflows undoubtedly stimulated savings, so that each dollar of inflow led to more than a dollar of investment; in other cases they discouraged savings, and a dollar of inflow may have led to much less than a dollar of investment. But as long as both savings and inflows are substantially affected by third factors, the negative correlation between the two found in many studies sheds little or no light on their causal relationship.[9]

Another criticism of aid is that it allows the perpetuation of ill-advised domestic policies that turn out to be counterproductive to the recipient country's development. As long as it receives foreign aid, a country may, for instance, be able to sustain an overvalued exchange rate and low real interest rates and to neglect export promotion and fiscal restraint. To some critics of development planning, aid may be viewed as simply an artificial means of underwriting misguided planning.[10]

To say that aid supports these ill-advised policies is to say that the necessary self-help measures are not being undertaken by the recipient

---

[7]K.B. Griffin and J.L. Enos, "Foreign Assistance: Objectives and Consequences," *Economic Development and Cultural Change*, 18 (April 1970), 313–27; and Thomas Weisskopf, "The Impact of Foreign Capital Inflow on Domestic Savings in Underdeveloped Countries," *Journal of International Economics*, 2 (Feb. 1972), 25–38.

[8]G.F. Papanek, "The Effect of Aid and Other Resource Transfers on Savings and Growth in Less Developed Countries," *Economic Journal*, 82 (Sept. 1972), 934–50.

[9]Papanek, *op. cit.*, 950.

[10]P.T. Bauer, *Dissent on Development* (Rev. ed. 1976), 95–135.

nation. Unless recipient governments adopt policies to mobilize fully their own resources and to implement their plans, the maximum potential benefits from aid will not be realized. As the record of foreign assistance in several countries shows, external aid may be incapable of yielding significant results unless it is accompanied by such complementary domestic measures as basic reforms in land tenure systems, additional taxation, investment in human capital, and more efficient government administration. Perhaps aid is more important in permitting a country to endure a difficult transition period, during which the country must undertake an entire set of policies in order to liberalize its foreign trade regime[11] and to allow the foreign capital inflow to accelerate the structural transformation of the economy from being that of a primary producer to becoming an exporter of manufactures.[12]

Finally, just as the absence of complementary domestic policies may limit the effectiveness of aid, so too may its impact be neutralized by changes in the other components of the total flow of resources from rich to poor countries. The total flow is affected by private foreign investment, private bank lending, export earnings, and the terms of trade, as well as by foreign aid. We must therefore recognize the relationships between capital assistance, private foreign investment, and international trade. The contribution of official development assistance will be greater if it is not competitive with, but instead stimulates private foreign investment. Public aid for economic overhead facilities can create opportunities for private investment, and the private investment can, in turn, assure fuller use of these facilities and raise their financial and economic return. There may also be increasing opportunities for co-financing or parallel lending by governments, multilateral institutions, and private banks. Policies should also be pursued that will bolster export earnings, so that the inflow of development capital will be able to do more than merely offset a weak trend of export earnings or a deterioration in the recipient country's terms of trade.

Growth-cum-Debt

It is instructive to view a borrowing country as proceeding through a sequence of growth-cum-debt phases. We have seen that when invest-

---

[11] For the policies necessary to shift from quantitative restrictions to price incentives, see Anne O. Krueger, *Liberalization Attempts and Consequences* (1978).

[12] Cf. H.B. Chenery and M. Syrquin, *Patterns of Development* (1975).

ment and government expenditures exceed savings and taxes, there is a real resource gap, and this resource gap is filled by an excess of import over exports in the current amount. **External debt** that allows the financing of the excess import is the **financial counterpart to the real resource transfer.** A developing country will therefore proceed through subsequent phases in which the resource gap, next the debt, and finally the income level rises. In the later phases, the resource gap declines first and next the debt, while the income level continues to rise. This sequence results in the following phases,[13] as shown in the table.

Phase	Resource Gap	Debt	Income
I	Low	Low	Low
II	High	Low	Low
IIIA	High	High	Low
IIIB	High	High	Middle
IV	Low	High	Middle
V	Eliminated	Low	High

In Phase I, the country is truly underdeveloped and is without a development program. The real resource gap is therefore low, and so is debt. But in Phase II, the country begins developing, with a more ambitious development program that causes $I + G$ to exceed $S + T$. There is then a high resource gap that must be covered by the capital inflow, and debt rises. As income rises, however, the savings gap diminishes until finally in Phase IV, the real resource gap is low. Although net capital inflow will cease earlier when domestic savings equal required domestic investment, a gross capital inflow will continue until the resource surplus is greater than the amount needed to cover interest charges on accumulated debt. Once savings become greater than domestic investment plus interest payments, the resource surplus can also be used for amortization, and the debt will then fall. The debt repayments are made by converting the excess of savings over investment into a surplus of exports over imports until the indebtedness is

[13]Barend A. De Vries, "The Debt Bearing Capacity of Developing Countries—A Comparative Analysis," *Banca Nazionale del Lavoro Quarterly Review,* XXIV (March 1971), 12–18. Also, D. Avramovic et al., *Economic Growth and External Debt* (1964); R.F. Mikesell, *The Economics of Foreign Aid,* (1968), 113; and C.R. Frank, Jr., *Debt and Terms of Aid* (1970).

repaid. The country eventually passes from being a "mature debtor" (with the return flow of interest and amortization payments exceeding the inflow of new capital) to becoming a net creditor.

Although dependence on external financing may have to be sizable during the early years of the development program, most plans aim for a progressive reduction in external capital and an eventual approach to a self-financing plan. To achieve this, the plan relies on a high rate of savings: it is expected that the proportion that can be saved out of an increase in income will be much higher than average savings at the start of the plan period. The proportion of national income invested and financed by domestic savings would then increase, and the ratio of net foreign capital imports to additional investment would fall. Because profits provide a major source of saving, there are grounds for expecting an increase in home saving relative to income when an expansion of the capitalist sector is facilitated (recall the Lewis dual-sector model, pp. 275–279). A higher saving rate may also be realized if the composition of output changes in favor of more industrial activities, with high marginal rates of saving. It will still be difficult, however, to realize a substantially higher marginal saving rate without forcing public saving through additional taxation and having tax revenues rise as a proportion of national income.

From the standpoint of the foreign exchange gap, the reliance on foreign capital will also diminish if, as development proceeds, the composition of investment alters toward projects with a lower import content. Provided there is no inflationary financing, import-saving will also be indirectly fostered by the growth in total domestic output and a diversion of purchasing power to the products of the expanding industries. In countries that import foodstuffs, the success of agricultural development can be instrumental in replacing imports. Most importantly, liberalization of the foreign trade regime and the promotion of exports may increase export revenue, not merely from efforts to raise productivity in traditional export activities, but even more so by promoting higher-value added exports and by extending the non-primary range of exports.

Parallel to this sequence of growth-cum-debt phases is the **structural transformation** of the borrowing economy, the outlines of which we noted previously (pp. 275–279). Prominent in this structural transformation from primary to industrial production are three major changes: an increase in the country's capacity to import based on export revenue;[14] a reduction in the country's current account deficit as a fraction of its national income; and a shift from primary product exports to export of processed primary products, semi-manufactures, and manufactures. The growth-cum-debt phases and the structural changes are reflections of one another.

Country Risk Analysis

Rising external indebtedness in a number of developing countries poses the complex problem of how a lending agency can assess the creditworthiness of the borrowing country. By **creditworthiness**, or **debt capacity**, we mean the amount of foreign currency that the country can borrow and be able to meet its debt service obligations from its own future foreign exchange earnings. It would be satisfying if creditworthiness could be measured, but it cannot. Country risk analysis requires just that—**an analysis of the quality of the national economic management** in the borrowing country. This entails the application of macroeconomics, international economics, and development economics.

A superficial attempt to measure creditworthiness is the **debt service ratio**, expressed as a ratio of interest and amortization to export earnings. This, however, has proved a poor predictor of defaults or debt rescheduling. Some countries with higher debt service ratios have escaped debt servicing problems, whereas countries with lower debt service ratios have had to default or reschedule. This is because a high debt service ratio

[14] The ratio $P_x Q_x / P_m$ rises, where P_x is a price index of exports, Q_x, a quantity index of exports, and P_m, a price index of imports.

L. H. JENKS, *The Migration of British Capital to 1875* (1927), 263

The story is told of old Mayer Anselm Rothschild—and for the authenticity of Rothschild stories no one vouches—that when a petty German prince or commune applied to him for a loan, he would pay no attention to the rehearsal of present necessities and future revenues. He took to his carriage and drove out to see the land, the people, the fields, and based his decision upon the evidences of a sound economy there visible.

need not be a matter of concern if the country's export earnings are at the same time high relative to import demand or if the country has the ability to attract private foreign investment and other capital inflows or is able to roll over maturing obligations with new debt or is able to use international reserves or is able to compress its imports.

Ideally, the lender would like an index that would measure the **risk** of a sharp fall in any kind of foreign exchange inflow and an increase in import needs in the borrowing country, together with the **ability** to offset such risks by compressing imports rapidly, receiving compensatory financing (such as from the IMF), or being able to draw down reserves. To begin to approach this, the use of several other ratios may suggest some crucial variables to be analyzed. In past cases of renegotiating outstanding debt, the most important ratios appear to have been a large and rising debt service ratio, a raising ratio of debt to imports, a rising ratio of debt outstanding to exports, an increase in the ratio of imports to reserves, and a fall in the ratio of reserves to debt outstanding. But it would be injudicious to undertake comparative analysis of country risks, based on these ratios: each country's situation is unique, defying measurement without analysis.

In assessing the country's national economic management, the lender should pay attention to these **key performance parameters:** (i) a rising ratio of savings to national income, (ii) a rising ratio of taxes to income, (iii) a decreasing incremental capital-output ratio (less unutilized capacity), and (iv) a decreasing current account deficit.

To realize positive changes in these performance parameters, the debtor country may have to undertake a **set of policies,** reflecting a higher quality of policy analysis. **Price distortions** will have to be removed: real interest rates may have to be raised, an overvalued foreign exchange rate must be corrected, a wages and incomes policy will have to be instituted. The **fiscal deficit** must be reduced. **Local capital markets** may have to be deepened to mobilize local savings. The **foreign trade regime** may have to be liberalized and incentives given to support a policy of export promotion. [15] All these policies will affect the debtor country's performance.

These policies are frequently suggested when the IMF imposes **conditionality** on a member country's access to drawing rights in the higher credit tranches or in standby arrangements. Under this financing procedure, the Fund and the country collaborate in the formulation of a

---

[15] This is amply documented in the National Bureau of Economic Research's Conference Series on Foreign Trade Regimes and Economic Development.

set of policy conditions to correct the country's balance of payments disequilibrium. The use of the resources made available from the Fund under the arrangement is phased over a period of time and co-ordinated with the implementation of the intended policies. The financing is only temporary, but it is intended to give the country additional time to undertake the corrective action required to improve the balance of payments. When the Fund imposes conditionality on the country, this may also encourage other lenders, such as commercial banks, to provide longer-term capital inflows.

This concentration on the policies necessary to improve the economy's performance in order to service the debt also illuminates other issues of debt servicing that are frequently confused.

What is meant by the "**burden**" of the debt? This is usually related to the debt servicing problem. There would, of course, be no problem of debt service if capital flowed into the country in sufficient amount to allow the developing country to meet interest and amortization payments on foreign obligations and also to maintain its imports at a desired level. In reality, however, sooner or later—depending on the growth in new foreign borrowing, rate of interest, and amortization rate—the debt servicing charges may require a net capital outflow from the debtor country. When the return flow of interest and amortization payments exceed the inflow of new capital, the country becomes a "**mature debtor**" and confronts a **transfer problem** in servicing the debt. The country has to achieve sufficient self-sustaining growth to remove the resource gap and cover the net capital outflow. The country will have to **generate an export surplus** equal to its net outward transfer of interest on current account and amortization on capital account in its balance of payments.

The direct costs of debt service do not, however, constitute the burden of the debt—provided the social rate of return from the external capital exceeds the interest cost. True, part of the increased production from the use of the external resource inflow has to be repaid abroad—and this is a reduction that would not be necessary if the savings had been provided at home. But the reality is that the savings have been provided from overseas, and the foreign savers must receive some return. Of most importance to the borrowing country is the result that its economy has realized additional investment, and the benefits from this should exceed the direct costs of the foreign savings that made possible the capital formation. The direct costs of servicing the foreign debt out of **additional** income should not be a cause for concern.

Of genuine concern are the **indirect costs.** These arise when the debt-servicing country has to undertake burdensome policies of balance of payments adjustment to acquire sufficient foreign exchange for debt service. Domestic savings in the developing country will have to become sufficient to finance all domestic investment, and in addition, the interest cost of accumulated debt and the repayment of the principal of its loans. In order to convert the surplus of savings into the foreign exchange it needs for debt servicing, the developing country will have to **generate an export surplus through expenditure-reducing and expenditure-switching policies** so as to expand exports or reduce the demand for imports. This may require some combination of deflation, internal and external controls over resource allocation, and exchange depreciation. The adverse effects of these measures of balance of payments adjustment are the **indirect costs** of foreign borrowing—and they constitute the burden of debt servicing.

It might be thought that this burden can be avoided if the investment of foreign capital creates its own means of payment by directly expanding exports or replacing imports. The lender might also believe that if it lends for a project that earns foreign exchange or saves foreign exchange there can be no transfer risk in debt servicing. But this is again to adopt the myopic and illusory view of project financing. Once we appreciate the relationship between total resource availabilities and uses, the interdependence of investments, and the principle that debt service is ultimately **a charge on the economy as a whole,** we can recognize that the transfer problem can still be solved without stipulating that the investment of foreign capital should create its own means of payment by directly expanding exports or by replacing imports. Instead of committing the fallacy of misplaced concreteness, we should realize that debt capacity cannot be determined without appraising the country's development program as a whole. Analysis of the entire program is necessary for an assessment of the conditions under which the **competing claims** on total resources, on savings, and on foreign exchange can be adjusted so as to release the amount required for debt service. In the last analysis, it is not a matter of whether "the project" the foreign loan is ostensibly intended to finance will be able to carry the cost of the loan—but the return on the **marginal project** or the **ultimate effect on the total use of resources.** If it is realized that the ability to create a sufficiently large export surplus depends on the operation of all sectors together, not simply on the use made of foreign capital alone, it is then apparent that a project financed by foreign borrowing need not itself make a direct contribution to the balance of payments. Indeed, even if foreign capital were limited to financing projects that earn or save foreign exchange, developments elsewhere in the economy may at the same time be affecting the supply of foreign exchange so adversely that the debt service problem is aggravated even though the foreign capital has ostensibly been directed to projects that ought to be able to carry the costs of the loans.

Instead of such a narrow balance of payments criterion for the allocation of investment, the basic test for the allocation of foreign capital, as for any investment, is that it should be invested in the form that yields the **highest social marginal product. The allocation of capital according to its most productive use will also be the most favorable for debt servicing** because it maximizes the increase in income from a given amount of capital, and thereby contributes to the growth of foreign exchange availability. The export of particular commodities or services through which the interest is transferred abroad should then be determined by the principle of comparative costs.[16] There are thus **two principles** determining debt capacity: **the investment criterion of social marginal productivity** and the **trade criterion of comparative cost.** To allocate foreign capital to a foreign exchange project is to do violence to the separation of these two basic principles, and is to settle for the easier, but misleading approach of **project** appraisal instead of **country** appraisal.

The elements that compose the analysis of a country's creditworthiness can be synthesized in a **country risk matrix.** On the vertical scale is expressed the lender's appraisal of the borrowing country's "**balance of payments potential,**" that is, the country's potential to have a sufficient flow of foreign exchange to service its debt. Countries in the top row (numbered 1) have the highest potential, whereas countries at the lowest rating (numbered 5) have the least potential and can be expected to confront payment delays or defaults. Underlying the evaluation of balance of payments potential is the assessment of the key performance parameters outlined above (pp. 343–344). And behind these, in turn, lie the policies that the borrowing country would have to undertake to raise these performance parameters and to realize its balance of payments potential (see pp. 344–345).

In the columns, countries are ranked according to their "**capacity for national economic management.**" This involves a judgment on the

[16]Cf. Ragnar Nurkse, *Problems of Capital Formation in Underdeveloped Countries* (1953), 136–37.

Country Risk Matrix

Capacity for National Economic Management

Policies → Balance of Payments Potential

	High A	B	C	D	Low E
High 1	Japan				
2					
3					
4					
Low 5					"Zaire"

Fig. 13

borrowing country's **ability and willingness** (often a political matter) **to undertake the policies that will allow the country to achieve its balance of payments potential.** Countries in column A have the highest policy capability to undertake the measures that would allow debt servicing. All countries rated E or 5 would present the greatest country risk to the lender, whereas those rated A or 1 would be most creditworthy with the highest debt capacity. From "Japan to Zaire" is simply illustrative of the relative ratings that the lender could make within the matrix.

Private Foreign Investment

Another important, and controversial, means of transferring resources is through private foreign investment. Foreigners might purchase securities issued by the borrowing country—**portfolio investment.** More significant for a developing country is foreign **direct investment**—control is exercised by foreign investors in an enterprise in the developing country. Direct investment can involve an entire package of capital, technology, and management from the investing country to the developing country. As the host country, the developing country might undertake policies to regulate the entry and operation of the foreign enterprise. To achieve the country's development objectives, the host government should devise policies that are based on a logical analysis of the prospective benefits and costs of the foreign investment. This requires more incisive analysis of the consequences of private foreign investment and more ingenuity in devising new approaches that favor the mobilization of private foreign capital while ensuring its most effective "planned performance" in terms of the country's develoment program. It would be rational for the host country to allow the entry of the foreign investment as long as its **benefit/cost ratio** is greater than unity. And it would be to the advantage of the host country to undertake policies that would make the benefit/cost ratio as high as possible, short of causing the private return on the investment to become so low that international private investment will be inhibited from making any contribution at all.

The **list of benefits** from foreign investment can include the following: local value added, inflow of foreign exchange, creation of employment, infusion of skills, contribution of taxes and royalties, and creation of externalities. From the standpoint of national economic benefit, the core of the case for encouraging an inflow of capital is that the increase in real income resulting from the investment is greater than the resultant increase in the income of the investor. If the value added to output by the foreign capital is greater than the amount appropriated by the investor, social returns exceed private returns. As long as foreign investment raises productivity, and this increase is not wholly appropriated by the investor, the greater product must be shared with others, and there must be some direct benefits to other income groups. These **benefits** can accrue to (i) domestic labor in the form of higher real wages, (ii) consumers by way of lower prices, and (iii) the government through higher tax revenue or royalties. Beyond this, there are likely to be (iv) indirect gains elsewhere in the economy through the realization of external economies.

For a developing country, the inflow of foreign capital may be significant not only in raising the productivity and real wages of a given amount of labor, but may also allow a larger labor force to be employed. In light of our earlier dual-sector model (p. 278), an inflow of foreign capital facilitates the employment of more labor in the advanced sector. The international flow of capital can thus be viewed as an alternative to labor migration from the poor country: when surplus labor cannot emigrate to rich countries, the substitution of domestic migration of labor into the advanced sector becomes the most feasible alternative. The social benefit from the foreign investment in the advanced sector is then greater than the profits on this investment, for the wages received by the newly employed exceed their former real wage in the rural sector, and this excess should be added as a national gain. This

R. NURKSE, "The Problem of International Investment Today In The Light Of Nineteenth-Century Experience." *Economic Journal,* LXIV, (Dec. 1954), 745–46

It was in the newly settled regions, which received two-thirds of the capital exports and practically all the emigrants, that nineteenth-century international investment scored its greatest triumphs. . . .

Labour and capital are complementary factors of production, and exert a profound attraction on each other. The movement of labour to the new regions attracted capital to the same places at the same time. And the other way round: the flow of capital stimulated the migration of people to these places. To some extent, it is true, the parallel move-ments of capital and labour might plausibly be interpreted as two sepa-rate effects of a common cause; namely, of the opening-up of the vast reserves of land and other natural resources. But the complementary nature of the labour and capital movements, based on the complemen-tarity of the two factors, is equally plain. Any barrier to the transfer of one would have reduced the flow of the other. Labour and capital moved along side by side, supporting each other.

In the twentieth century the situation is totally different. The capital exports from the United States can be viewed rather as a *substitute* for the movement of people. Capital and labour are still complementary, and still basically attract one another. But as things are now, restricting the movement of labour in one direction increases the need, if not the incentive, for capital to move in the opposite direction.

---

type of benefit may have been negligible under the nineteeth-century type of foreign investment in mines and plantations and also negligible under the more recent wave of foreign investment in import-substitu-tion industries. But its potential in export-substitution industries is much larger: we have noted that the labor intensity of this newer trade strategy is higher than in the inward-looking strategy of import substi-tution, and the scope of the market for expansion of labor-intensive exports is greater than experienced in import substitution. To the ex-tent that private foreign investment is supporting the expansion of these newer labor-intensive exports, its contribution to employment is significant.

In order that labor and consumers might benefit from the higher productivity in foreign enterprises, the overseas withdrawal by the in-vestors must be less than the increase in output. But even if the entire increase in productivity accrues as foreign profits, this requirement may still be fulfilled when the government taxes foreign profits. Taxes on foreign profits or royalties from concession agreements can constitute a large proportion of total government revenue.

A widespread contribution of foreign investment can come from external economies. Direct foreign investment brings to the developing country not only capital and foreign exchange—which helps to fill both the savings gap and the foreign exchange gap—but also managerial ability, technical personnel, technological knowledge, administrative organization, and innovations in products and production techniques—all of which are in short supply. One of the greatest benefits to the recipient country is the access to **foreign knowledge** that private foreign investment may provide—knowledge that helps fill the managerial gap and the technological gap. This type of private technical assistance and the demonstration effects that are an integral feature of private foreign investment may spread and have beneficial results in other sectors of the economy. The rate of technological advance in a poor country is highly dependent on the rate of capital inflow. New techniques accompany the inflow of private capital. And by the example they set, foreign firms promote the diffusion of technological advance in the host economy. In addition, foreign investment may lead to the training of labor in new skills, and the knowledge gained by these workers can be transmitted to other members of the labor force, or these workers might be employed later by local firms.

Private foreign investment can also stimulate additional domestic investment in the recipient country. If the foreign capital is used to develop the country's infrastructure, it may directly facilitate more investment. Even if the foreign investment is in one industry, it may still encourage domestic investment by reducing costs or creating demand in other industries. Profits may then rise and lead to expansion in these other industries. A whole series of domestic investments may thus be linked to the foreign investment.

Offsetting these benefits are various costs: concessions offered by the government to attract the foreign investment, adverse effect on domestic saving, discouragement of domestic entrepreneurship, problems of balance of payments servicing, and loss of domestic economic autonomy.

To encourage foreign enterprise, the government of the host country may have to provide special facilities, undertake additional public services, extend financial assistance, or subsidize inputs. These have a cost in absorbing governmental resources that could be used elsewhere. Tax concessions may also have to be offered. Moreover, when several countries compete among themselves in offering inducements to foreign capital, each may offer more by way of inducement than is necessary: the investment may be of a type that would go to one country or another regardless of the inducements (for example, to secure a raw material supply), but the foreign enterprise may "shop around" and secure extra concessions. Without some form of collective agreement among capital-receiving countries regarding the maximum concessions that will be made, the cost of "overencouraging" certain types of foreign investment may be considerable. This has been characterized as the problem of "big companies versus small countries."[17]

Once foreign investment has been attracted, it should be expected to have an income effect that will lead to a higher level of domestic saving. But this effect might be offset by a redistribution of income away from capital if the foreign investment reduces profits in domestic industries. This could occur if the foreign investment were highly competitive with home investment. Similarly, foreign enterprise may inhibit local entrepreneurship in a competitive field.

Of greater seriousness than the foregoing costs are those arising from balance of payments adjustments. If the outflow of interest, dividends, and profits on foreign investment causes the developing country to experience a net capital outflow, the indirect costs of debt servicing then come into play. The country has to create a surplus on current account equal to the debit items on account of the payment of interest, dividends, profits, and repatriation of the foreign investment. The country must then incur the costs of the adjustment mechanism in its balance of payments.

Less visible may be a cost in the form of a loss of domestic autonomy in policy-making whenever the government retreats from some policy objective or sacrifices a particular policy instrument in deference to the interests of the foreign investor. If the government would have acted differently in the absence of the foreign investment, the presence of the foreign enterprise is then of some cost to the government.

Beyond recognizing the potential benefits and costs, the host government should also undertake the more difficult analysis of estimating the **time profile of these benefits and costs.** The benefits are likely to come in the early years of the investment, whereas the costs mount up over time. A benefit/cost ratio that is greater than unity in

---

[17] Dudley Seers, 'Big Companies and Small Countries," *Kyklos,* XVI (1963), 601.

the early years may then become less than unity at a later date. If so, there would be a case for divestment—the foreign enterprise should revert to local ownership or be terminated.[18] Or it is possible that although initially the benefit/cost ratio of the foreign investment was greater than the benefit/cost ratio of a substitute domestic investment, this superiority may disappear in the future. The alternative domestic investment would then be favored when its benefit/cost ratio exceeded the foreigner's.

Although our foregoing discussion indicates in a broad way the various benefits and costs of private foreign investment, a more rigorous analysis would require application of the techniques of project analysis.[19] Considering the streams of social benefits and social costs, it would be in the best interests of the host country to allow entry of the investment when the social net present value (*NPV*) of the project is greater than 0, but insist on fade-out or divestment when the *NPV* becomes less than 0 or when the *NPV* of a substitute domestic investment becomes greater than the *NPV* of the foreign investment. The *NPV* criterion says that a project should be undertaken if the sum of the future social returns minus social costs, discounted back to the present, is positive.

Computation of the net present value begins by analyzing the project into commodity and labor flows, and converting each quantity into a value through multiplication by a price. The algebraic sum of these values, i.e., the total value of outputs less the total value of inputs, is the present value of the project. Future commodity flows are evaluated by using discounted prices. In social benefit-cost analysis, the rate at which this discounting is done is known as the **social discount rate** or accounting rate of interest. The social rate of discount is less than the private market rate of interest if the project evaluator imputes a lower positive time preference to society (that is, the community may be willing to wait for a longer pay-off period on the investment and may value saving more than current consumption).

Another important difference between the procedures of private and social benefit-cost analysis is that the stream of benefits and costs are

[18] Cf. A.O. Hirschman, *How to Divest in Latin America and Why* (1969).

[19] For details, see I.M.D. Little and J.A. Mirrlees, *Project Appraisal and Planning for Developing Countries* (1974); UNCTAD, Report by A.K. Sen, *Methods of Evaluating the Effects of Private Foreign Investment,* TD/B/C.3/94/Add. 1 (1971); D. Lal, *Appraising Foreign Investment* (1974); and M. Scott, J. MacArthur, and D. Newbery, *Project Appraisal in Practice* (1976). A simplified explanation is presented in Raymond Vernon and Louis T. Wells, Jr., *Economic Environment of International Business* (2nd ed., 1976), Chap. 6.

valued in the social analysis by **shadow prices,** or accounting prices that correct for market price distortions and revalue the good or factor according to a measure of its social worth, in terms of social objectives. Allowance is also made for the non-market effects of externalities, which are not included in the private analysis. Social analysis may also give welfare weights to the benefits of employment-creation, a more equitable distribution of income, and the satisfaction of such merit wants as education or diffusion of technology.

These corrections make social benefit-cost analysis different from the private business discounted-cash-flow methods of investment appraisal. The **national economic profitability** differs from private financial profitability, and it is the former that matters to the host country. The host country should, however, appraise the present values of the social net benefits of a number of **alternative arrangements** embodying different terms and conditions of foreign investment and then seek the highest present value of social net benefit. An entire spectrum of arrangements are possible, ranging from the allowance of 100% foreign equity and an unlimited time duration for the foreign investment at one end, to only limited contractual arrangements for technology and management at the other end. To improve the terms of the foreign investment, and hence raise the *NPV,* the country must become better informed about the essential elements of the foreign investment project and then exercise more effective bargaining skills in achieving the best arrangement.

Both foreign investor and host government can gain from the foreign investment, but the social net benefit can be increased if the host government can improve the terms of the foreign investment by negotiating more effectively over ownership, technology transfer, tariff policies, tax rates, transfer pricing between subsidiary and parent company, employment practices, and disclosure of information and accountability.

To increase net benefits, the host government may also seek to establish a variety of different contractual arrangements ranging from a fade-out or divestment date to insistence on a joint venture at the outset to an attempt to "unbundle" the package of inputs and secure each input separately at a lower cost in the form of technical collaboration agreements, licensing, and management contracts—instead of through one foreign equity investment. The major question is whether there are alternative lower-cost ways to transfer scarce managerial and technical knowledge without supplying such knowledge jointly with capital as in a foreign direct investment.

Transnational Corporations

The recent expansion in exports of manufactures from the newly industrializing countries has been closely related to foreign investment by multinational or transnational corporations (TNCs). Beyond horizontal international specialization between different final products, the transnationals have become important in promoting vertical international specialization between different intermediate stages of production. By decomposing the production process into different activities that are located in various countries according to factor endowments, and by undertaking world-wide sourcing for inputs and commodities, the TNC has become a major agent for investment in developing countries. Although the capital, technology, managerial competence, and international marketing capabilities of a TNC can be utilized for a country's development, there remains a fear of monopolistic exploitation and the imposition of excessive costs by the TNC.

Does the evaluation of the operation of the TNC, however, call for more than a social benefit-cost type of analysis? Why should the TNC be analyzed differently from a "simple" type of foreign direct investment that flows from one home country to a single host country? The crucial question is What difference does it make to the appraisal of the foreign investment project when it has the attribute of **"multinationality"**?[20]

True, a TNC is likely to have the power of an oligopoly; but so too may some "simple" foreign enterprises or domestic independent companies. True, a TNC may be a vertically integrated enterprise that uses transfer prices for transactions between different parts of the same firm (the prices are not at "arm's length"); but so too may "simple" foreign investment. True, a TNC may be involved in the costly process of import substitution; but so too may a simple foreign enterprise or a national firm. True, a TNC may be depleting too rapidly a wasting asset or nonrenewable resource; but so too may other forms of investment that are not multinational.

In assessing the contribution of a foreign investment by a TNC, we have to be clear on whether what is being assessed is the **investment project per se**, the **foreignness** of the investment, the **multinationality** of the investment, or some **alternative** institutional arrangement for acquiring the ingredients in the direct investment package.

[20] For a more detailed analysis of points raised in this section, see G.M. Meier, "Export Substitution and Multinational Enterprises," in Alec Cairncross and Mohinder Puri (eds.), *Employment, Income Distribution and Development Strategy* (1976), 140–53.

DAVID HUME, *"Of Money"* (1752)

> Manufactures gradually shift their places, leaving those countries and provinces which they have already enriched, and flying to others whither they are allured by the cheapness of provisions or labour.

What "multinationality" does is to broaden the reach and increase the intensity of both the benefits and costs of foreign investment. The behavioral differences between a multinational firm and a "simple" type of foreign enterprise can be especially significant: first, in promoting foreign investment; second, in allowing the TNC to act as a unit of real economic integration; and third, in endowing the TNC with greater bargaining power.[21]

The growth of TNCs tends to promote more foreign investment because the TNC is less of a risk-averter when it can operate in a number of countries, produce a range of products, practice process specialization, and enjoy greater maneuverability with respect to marketing opportunities and conditions of production than can a firm with a narrower range of production processes and products.

The TNC is also a unit of integration in the world economy. The transmission of factors via the TNC, together with the TNC's economies of scale in research and development (R & D) and marketing, make it a unit of real international integration. By its multinational operations and intrafirm transactions, the TNC transcends the national barriers to commodity trade and impediments to international factor movements. As a planning unit that makes resource allocation decisions on a world-wide basis, the TNC becomes the mechanism for making effective the LDC's potential comparative advantage. The TNC provides the complementary resources of capital, technology, management, and market outlets that may be necessary to bestow an "effective" comparative advantage to the labor-surplus factor endowment in the host country.

This can be appraised as efficient international production. The TNC views production as a set of activities or processes, and the global strategy of the TNC is tantamount to the solution of activity models of production, with production processes in many countries. A competi-

---

[21]For an elaboration of the behavioral differences, see R.E. Caves, *International Trade, International Investment, and Imperfect Markets* (1974), 21–22.

tive equilibrium solution to the programming problem is imposed within the TNC when it operates efficiently as a planning unit.

This interpretation of the TNC as an efficient technical and allocational unit of integration means that whereas intrafirm trade conforms to **corporate** advantage, it is also identical with the realization of **comparative** advantage. If the nation-state fragments the world economy through restrictions on commodity and factor movements and thwarts international economic integration, the TNC may serve a complementary—rather than competitive—function to the nation-state: the TNC may be the vehicle for evoking, in practice, the principle of comparative advantage in world trade, for trade in both outputs and inputs. The internal resource allocation in the TNC is a substitute mechanism for the market; when it realizes comparative advantage in processes and activities, the resource allocation decisions of the TNC will be more efficient than those in unintegrated markets that are characterized by imperfections and uncertainty. For global technical efficiency, the world economy is the territorial unit of international production, not the nation-state, which is a unit of international politics.

What, however, is the distribution of gains between the TNC and the host country? More pointedly: How might the social net benefit for the host country be raised? This is the crucial question posed by the attribute of "multinationality." For multinationality instills foreign investment by a TNC with greater bargaining power because of its tendency to be larger, its capability to exercise wider options, and its capacity to avoid some forms of regulation that cannot reach beyond national jurisdiction. These powers are especially suspect when they coalesce in the practice of transfer pricing. The host country may believe that transfer pricing allows the TNC to minimize taxes, escape from tariff charges, or be the means of remitting profits from a subsidi-

---

ADAM SMITH, *The Wealth of Nations* (1776), Book III, Chap. IV

A merchant, it has been said very properly, is not necessarily the citizen of any particular country. It is in great measure indifferent to him from what places he carries on his trade; and a very stifling disgust will make him move his capital, and together with it the industry which it supports, from one country to another.

ary to the parent company that would otherwise not be allowed by exchange restrictions.[22]

The developing country's desire to regulate transfer pricing is only a special instance of the general problem of how the bargaining process between the host government and TNC distributes the fruits of the foreign investment—more precisely, the extent to which the developing country can capture from the TNC a **greater share of the TNC's quasi-rents** on its supply of technology, management, and capital.[23] Once technology or knowledge has been created, its additional use overseas involves little additional expense to the firm. The foreign operation helps to amortize a total R & D effort, and the maximization of the rents obtainable from the firm's "knowledge" is often a main determinant of foreign investment. The price of the technology, as reflected implicitly in profits, or explicitly in royalties, is not determined by its actual cost, but by the transnational's bargaining power in extracting a surplus return when the marginal value to the recipient country of acquiring the technology is greater than the marginal cost involved in selling it overseas. The host country wants to squeeze this surplus and retain more benefits for itself. In order to extract the quasi-rents, the host government should devise an optimal welfare tax on foreign capital that improves the terms of foreign borrowing.[24]

Technology Transfer

In light of the problems of unemployment and underemployment, inequality in income distribution, and the number in absolute poverty, more students of development have been emphasizing the need for "**appropriate** technology." This goes beyond the question of a foreign firm overcharging for access to its technology; it raises the broader question of whether the technology that is transferred is "appropriate" for the recipient country. In simplest terms, when a developing country is a labor-surplus country, the transfer of capital-intensive technology may be inappropriate. A technology that would allow the utilization of lower skills and be more labor-intensive would be more appropriate for

[22] See Constantine Vaitsos, *Intercountry Income Distribution and Transnational Enterprises* (1974), Chap. 6.

[23] The general problem of bargaining between host government and TNC is discussed by Paul Streeten, "The Multinational Enterprise and the Theory of Development Policy," *World Development*, 1 (Oct. 1973), 8–9.

[24] W.M. Corden, *Trade Policy and Economic Welfare* (1974), 339–40.

the factor endowment of the country. Numerous arguments have been levied against the importation of capital-intensive technology for labor-abundant developing economies.

But why is there not more substitution of labor for capital? Why is there not more use of an "intermediate" technology that is more appropriately designed between the traditional and the most modern? Management of the transnational corporation may find it easier simply to utilize the same techniques of production it uses in more advanced countries. If foreign firms producing a particular product were simply to use the capital-intensive techniques that are appropriate in their home countries, but that are inappropriate for the labor-surplus host supplies, then we could be more critical of the foreign firms' operation. But the few empirical studies reveal no clear pattern of choice of technology.[25] There is contradictory evidence as to whether domestic firms are more responsive than foreign firms to the relatively lower wage-interest ratios prevailing in LCDs and utilize more labor-intensive techniques of production.[26]

The issue of choice of technology depends upon the entire **set of governmental policies,** more so than upon the distinction between foreign and domestic firms. Governmental policies that are **biased toward capital use** affect technology choice by both foreign and domestic firms. To encourage appropriate technology, it is more relevant to focus on "inappropriate governmental policies" than on the ownership of the firm—on the overvalued exchange rates, minimum wage laws, fringe benefits and social security provisions imposed on the firm, low taxes on the return to capital, accelerated depreciation allowances, tax and duty exemptions for imported capital equipment, and other policies that distort factor prices and prevent them from reflecting the true scarcity of capital and the true abundance of labor. These policies have to be corrected to offset the bias in favor of capital-intensive production.

Research and development expenditures need to be directed toward new technologies that will take account of the scarcity of capital, management, and operative skills in the developing country. **Efficient labor-using** techniques, or capital-saving techniques, are needed: the la-

---

[25] See e.g., Paul Strassman, *Technological Change and Economic Development* (1968); H. Pack, "The Substitution of Labor for Capital in Kenyan Manufacturing," *Economic Journal,* XXVI (March 1976), 45–58; and Louis T. Wells, Jr., "Economic Man and Engineering Man," *Public Policy,* XXI (Summer 1973), 322–42.

[26] R. Hal Mason, "Some Observations on the Choice of Technology by Multinational Firms in Developing Countries," *Review of Economics and Statistics,* LV (Aug. 1973), 349–55.

ALFRED MARSHALL, *Industry and Trade* (1919), Chap. II. Sec. 3

> In all economic history, and especially in recent economic history, and most of all in the recent history of trade, the international point of view is essential. It is easy to remember that one's own country is ever growing and changing: but it sometimes requires effort to consider how many of the changes near at hand are partly due to the expansion of life far away.

bor/capital ratio must rise at the same time as the capital/output ratio does not rise. If the labor-using technique were not efficient, there would then be a difficult **employment-output trade-off**. As the history of Japan indicates, however, there should be opportunities for efficient labor-using techniques and for the stretching of capital without a loss of output.[27] But from whence is the incentive for such R & D to come? Much of it will have to be government-induced, within the developing countries themselves, and through international collaboration.

It is now commonly recognized that the potential for variation in production technology also depends on the **choice of product**.[28] Inappropriate products lead to inappropriate techniques by being products with excessive characteristics and standards in relation to needs and income levels of the poor country. The additional qualities of the more advanced product require more capital and more skills in its production. The concern over production technology is therefore also a concern over consumption technology. Economists tend to concentrate on efficiency in production, but for problems of poverty, more emphasis must also be given to efficiency in consumption. The choice of techniques cannot be separated from the product mix. Much of the complaint about capital-intensive techniques is a criticism of production for import replacement. If, however, export substitution is emphasized, this strategy of industrialization will tend to entail a more appropriate choice of technology because it will be based largely on transnational

[27]Cf. G. Ranis, "Industrial Sector Labor Absorption," *Economic Development and Cultural Change*, XXI (April 1973), 387–408, and P.P. Streeten and Frances Stewart, "Conflicts between Output and Employment Objectives in Developing Countries," *Oxford Economic Papers*, 23 (July 1971), 145–68.

[28]See Frances Stewart, "Choice of Technique in Developing Countries," *Journal of Development Studies*, 9 (Oct. 1972), 99–121, and Stewart, "Technology and Employment in LDCs," in E.O. Edwards (ed.), *Employment in Developing Countries* (1975), 83–132.

corporations investing abroad to integrate backward, usually for a labor-intensive assembly process that is uneconomic in the high-wage developed countries. To the extent that the government's employment-creating strategy emphasizes rural development and support of the urban informal sector, it can also alter the product mix toward more labor-intensive output.

Just as there can be **conspicuous production** and **conspicuous consumption**, so too can there be **conspicuous knowledge**. All areas of knowledge imported from advanced countries can too readily become artificial in terms of the **basic needs** of the recipient country. For example, instead of importing the techniques of the highest-skilled curative medicine for the benefit of a few, the developing country may more appropriately focus on preventive medicine and simpler public health measures for the benefit of the many. Similarly in education, the rural vocational school might do more to accelerate the economy's "learning rate" than can an overly refined university program. Indeed, in the subject closest to our study, the importation of the latest econometric model or newest bit of mathematical expertise may be inappropriate compared with the need to understand and practice the more basic principles of economics.

In the last analysis, as Ricardo observed, the significance of international trade lies not only in the trade of goods and services, but also in the trade of ideas. But the transfer of ideas can proceed at an inappropriate level, just as can Mill's "introduction of foreign arts" and the "creation of new wants." The developing countries must therefore engage in selective transfers and local adaptation if they are to realize fully the potential benefits the international economy can offer.

Supplementary Readings

Issues of foreign aid are discussed in Jagdish Bhagwati and Richard Eckaus, *Foreign Aid* (1970), and E.K. Hawkins, *Principles of Development Aid* (1970).

The specialized subject of project appraisal is treated by I.M.D. Little and J.A. Mirrlees, *Project Appraisal and Planning for Developing Countries* (1974); D. Lal., *Methods of Project Analysis: A Review* (1974); L. Squire and H.G. van der Tak, *Economic Analysis of Projects* (1976); and United Nations Industrial Development Organization, *Guide to Practical Project Appraisal* (1978).

The following constitute a sampling of the vast literature on multinational enterprises: H.G. Johnson, "The Efficiency and Welfare Implications of the International Corporation," in C.P. Kindleberger (ed.), *The International Corporation* (1970); S. Lall and P.P. Streeten, *Foreign Investment, Transnationals and Developing Countries* (1977), with bibliography; C.H. Maceden (ed.), *The Case for the Multinational Corporation* (1977); J.H. Dunning (ed.), *The Multinational Enterprise* (1971); J.H. Dunning, *International Investment* (1972); Raymond Vernon, *Sovereignty at Bay* (1971); Raymond Vernon, *Storm Over the Multinationals: The Real Issues* (1977); and Commission on Transnational Corporations, *Transnational Corporations in World Development: A Reexamination* (1978).

The transfer of technology is considered by J. Baranson, *Industrial Technologies for Developing Countries* (1969); Charles Cooper (ed.), *Science, Technology, and Development* (1973); a special issue on "Technology," *World Development* (March 1974); and Frances Stewart, *Technology and Underdevelopment* (1977).

An excellent survey article is Sanjaya Lall, "Transnationals, Domestic Enterprises and Industrial Structure in Host LDCs," *Oxford Economic Papers*, 30 (July 1978), 217–48, with bibliography.

Epilogue:
From Theory to Policy

To raise the quality of policy analysis is the highest purpose of Economics. But to proceed from theory to actual policy-making is the economist's most difficult task. As was often said by one who had the most influence on public policy in this century, "The Theory of Economics does not furnish a body of settled conclusions immediately applicable to policy. It is a method rather than a doctrine, an apparatus of the mind, a technique of thinking, which helps its possessor draw correct conclusions."[1]

The gap between theory and policy may indeed be distressingly wide. We have attempted to narrow it by establishing some normative principles that might shape trade policy, balance of payments policy, and development policy. But a gap still remains—by the very nature of the policy problems encountered in the international economy.

In any economic policy problem, there is some art in modifying the theory in light of the particular circumstances of an actual situation. In any policy problem, there is also the possibility that the journey from theory to policy might be difficult because of inadequate analytical and empirical bases for the measurement of benefits, costs, and policy alternatives or an ineffective organizational structure for implementing policy.[2] In international economic policy problems, these inadequacies are especially acute. Moreover, there are other difficulties in international economic policy formation that are subtle and complex.

Decision analysis and other techniques of optimization science (sys-

[1] Statement by J.M. Keynes in his Editorial Introduction to the Cambridge Economic Handbook series.
[2] Cf. R. R. Nelson, *The Moon and the Ghetto* (1977).

R. F. HARROD, *The Life of John Maynard Keynes* (1951), 584–85

> To have devised in the quiet of one's study a new economic theory which determined the nature of the economic thinking of the younger generation in two great nations, to have gone further and devised practical proposals for international cooperation to implement that theory, to have gone still further and won acceptance for those proposals by persuasion, first among officials and politicians at home and then in a wide international arena, was surely an accomplishment for which it would be difficult to find a parallel. The combination of the purely scientific aptitude for intellectual construction with a keen sense of realities and power of adapting theory to practice, and the combination of these again with persuasive and diplomatic faculties, were surely unique.

---

tems analysis, mathematical programming, simulation) have recently contributed enormously to policy analysis.[3] The approach of the rational decision-maker who lays out goals and uses logical processes to explore the best way to reach these goals may appear relevant for some of the policy problems we have raised—but on closer scrutiny it usually is seen to be difficult to put this approach to work in the more significant of international policy problems. "Optimization science" is inappropriate for analyzing international problems that involve multiple actors instead of a unitary decision-maker, an ill-defined objective function, variables that do not lend themselves to subjective probability analysis, and outcomes that cannot be converted to a single utility index. The predefinition of objectives, the dominant weight given to the criterion of efficiency relative to other values, the concentration on instrumental rationality (means to given ends) to the neglect of constitutive rationality (decisions about how decisions are to be made), and the focus on final outcomes instead of on the processes by which preferences and decisions are formed—all these characteristics of the more technical methods of decision science make this style of policy-making of limited value for many international economic policy problems.

[3] For illustrative works, see Edith Stokey and Richard Zeckhauser, *A Primer for Policy Analysis* (1978); Howard Raiffa, *Decision Analysis* (1968); W.J. Baumol, *Economic Theory and Operations Analysis* (4th ed., 1977); Russell J. Ackoff and Maurice W. Sasieni, *Fundamentals of Operations Research* (1968); and Ralph L. Keeney and Howard Raiffa, *Decisions with Multiple Objectives* (1976).

Rational choice models are at their best when they treat problems that bear an affinity to the marginalism of neoclassical economics. The models become less applicable, however, when the changes under consideration involve large structural changes or when the problem confronts phenomena of market failure, non-quantifiable elements, or conflicting values. Rigor may be achieved at the cost of narrowing the policy problem. And precision in analysis may come at the cost of oversimplified assumptions.

More important than the usual techniques of decision analysis is the prior problem about rights and rules under which collective decisions are to be made. The resolution of policy problems in the world economy normally requires a determination of the way in which decisions will be made and the boundary of the decisions. To deal with the problem of changes in the international division of labor, with gains and losses to different groups, or with the problem of international monetary reform, again with various gains and losses, or with the problem of international resource transfers—to attain some social order out of these problems, it is necessary to have a regulatory mechanism for the settlement of conflicts, social control of the allocation of benefits and costs, and some monitoring of social change.

Their shortcomings notwithstanding, the formal techniques of policy analysis can still aid the policy-maker in structuring complex problems. Such a structuring may be as follows: (i) establishing the context (identifying the underlying problem and the objectives to be pursued in confronting this problem); (ii) formulating the alternative courses of action; (iii) predicting the consequences of each of the alternative actions: (iv) valuing the outcomes; and (v) making a choice of the preferred course of action.[4]

At the other end of the spectrum of approaches to policy analysis— far from the rigorous modeling of rational choices—lies the complex, but amorphous mixture of "political economy." The narrower the policy problem (fewer variables, lower degree of uncertainty, less dynamic), the more systematic and technical can the policy analyst be. But the larger the domain of the policy problem and the more complex, the more likely will the problem become politicized. By "politicization," we mean that economic and political variables are not separable and that economic issues are now, more frequently than in the past, dealt with at a higher political level. International economic issues are

---

[4]Stokey and Zeckhauser, *op. cit.*, 5–6.

transferred from purely economic agencies to higher, more general policy-making bodies. These issues might also become political issues in domestic politics. Moreover, they may be linked to other and "higher" aspects of national foreign policy (for example, the linkage of trade policy and national security policy). Finally, international economic relationships can so constrain states' opportunities that not only autonomy, but also effective sovereignty are lost.[5]

In the economist's language, when the policy problem involves only marginal changes about which our economic understanding is high, the political element in the problem tends to be slight. When, however, the problem involves large structural changes or is a matter of total conditions instead of simply marginal conditions, the level of economic understanding is low, and the problem is apt to acquire high political content. Political interests thrive more readily when economic knowledge is limited. Moreover, when the problem involves conflicting multiple objectives, the political element tends to intensify. For these reasons, policy problems of "fair trade," international monetary reform, and international development policy are highly politicized. The politics of international economics and the economics of international politics become intertwined in any policy analysis of these larger, more complex problems. This is disconcerting for the policy analyst who uses only rigorously formal techniques—but an understanding of the political element may allow more realistic and relevant analysis, even if it causes policy to depart from the purer world of the first best, and may even cause it to enter a world of crisis diplomacy.[6]

Prescription presupposes criteria, and the economist naturally turns to welfare economics. Again, however, technical welfare economics is itself limited. The concentration is on end-states, not procedure or processes. The constitutive decision or social welfare function remains ill-defined. Although the techniques of welfare economics are helpful in determining first-best partial economic policies in a second-best world, the techniques cannot settle issues of "corrective justice" or "distributive justice." And yet, these other values are intimately related to many of the policy problems that arise in the world economy.

As we have seen, trade theory itself has always had a normative branch. Classical and neoclassical trade theory, however, must be ex-

---

[5] This interpretation of politicization is offered by Fred Hirsch, Michael Doyle, and Edward L. Morse, *Alternative to Monetary Disorder* (1977), 12–14.

[6] Edward L. Morse, "Crisis Diplomacy," in Raymond Tanter and Richard Ullman (eds.), *Theory and Policy of International Relations* (1972).

tended to be more applicable to emerging policy problems. From an extension there are also likely to follow additional welfare implications. Although traditional trade theory is postulated on international factor immobility, we have noted policy problems arising from the international mobility of capital, management, and technology. For more effective policy formulation, it is necessary to consider more thoroughly how capital movements determine trade flows, and to incorporate management and technology as determinants of trade patterns. Traditional trade theory has also been confined to explaining the composition of trade in final products, but we have recognized the potential for trade in intermediate inputs. General equilibrium theory, incorporating purely competitive conditions, has also been the basis of traditional trade theory, but we have emphasized the role of the transnational corporation and hence the need to extend trade theory to incorporate phenomena of monopolistic competition and the microeconomics of industrial organization.

A list of unsettled questions could also be presented for balance of payments problems and for international development problems. For the economist to confront always a list of unsettled questions is not surprising when it is realized that the ever-changing character of policy will forever raise new questions for the policy-maker and will always induce new developments in the theory underlying policy-formation.

Beyond the methods of policy analysis, the progress from theory to policy is also shaped by the **policy process**—the institutional and organizational framework of the legal-political process in which the political and bargaining aspects of policy formulation come to the fore. These noneconomic conditions will affect the determination of what is **feasible.** And they will determine the degree of difficulty involved in the ultimate task of **policy implementation.** Policy analysis and policy process must adjust to each other in an iterative fashion.[7]

In the international economy, the formulation and implementation of a policy are complicated further by the fact that the world economy is a **decentralized system,** and there is only limited scope for **international** public choice and for **international** policy formation. The ambiguity over issues of policy arises in large part from the uncertain relations among the decentralized units of decision-making in the world economy—households and firms within each nation, national governments, regional organizations, transnational corporations, and interna-

[7]Cf. Harold D. Lasswell, "The Emerging Conception of the Policy Sciences," *Policy Sciences*, I (Spring 1970), 3–14.

tional agencies. Each of these has different constituencies, different objectives, and different time horizons. How are normative standards to be established in such a decentralized system?

Neither **market forces** (as represented by free trade or freely floating exchange rates) nor **international codes of conduct** are ascendant in establishing world economic order. There is always a danger that the regulation of international economic conduct will be abandoned to either simple unilateral action or *ad hoc* negotiation, dependent upon bargaining power. In such an environment, the belief in a natural harmony of interests, mutual gains from trade, foreign investment as a non-zero sum activity—all these beliefs that support internationalism over nationalism—would be submerged. To avoid the danger of nationalism and policy competition among nations, **policy co-ordination** is needed.

Welfare economics is usually cast in terms of only national policies. But the first-best national policy may be second best or nth best, compared with a number of other **multinational policies.** This can be readily seen for such policy problems as the imposition of market safeguards by one importing country that will have an effect on another importing country as exports are redirected to the other country. The difficulty also applies to the regulation of the multinational corporation, which necessarily operates on the national policy differentials in taxation, foreign exchange controls, or tariffs. Multilateral surveillance of intervention on foreign exchange markets represents another major area for policy co-ordination.

Many of the policies implied in the foregoing chapters depend upon international co-ordination for their effectiveness. Trade liberalization, the monitoring of foreign investment, more international transfers to poor countries, international stabilization policies,[8] co-ordination of international monetary policies—all these objectives depend upon a diminution in competition among nations and more cooperative international action.

The need for multinational policy-making is simply a corollary of the principle that the level at which a decision is taken should be high enough to cover the area in which the impact is non-negligible. In order that the decisions regarding necessary policy instruments ("action parameters") be optimal, there must not be "external" effects—that is, the

---

[8] The "dynamic" gains arising from co-ordination of policies are discussed by R.N. Cooper, "Macro Economic Policy Adjustment in Interdependent Economies," *Quarterly Journal of Economics,* LXXXIII (Feb. 1969), 1–24.

influences exerted on the well-being of groups outside the jurisdiction of those who make the decision should be weak. The area in which the impact of the instrument will be felt determines what decision level will be optimal. For many policy issues in the world economy, the nation-state is clearly an inappropriate economic decision-making unit. Decisions taken at the national level are often far too low to be optimal.[9]

Policy co-ordination and supranational decision units—that is, some system of functional federalism among nations,[10] with different economic functions handled at different levels of government—are necessary to provide the international economy with some decision-making powers comparable to those in the national economy. National public policy is primarily concerned with maintaining economic stability, redistributing income, and correcting market failure. But where are the international analogues? How is world full employment and economic stability to be achieved without an international fiscal authority and without an international central bank? In the absence of an international mechanism for redistribution through taxes and subsidies, alternative arrangements must be sought for transferring resources from rich to poor countries. And how can international market failure be remedied? Whether they are denoted as price distortions or transfers of inappropriate technology or as "backwash effects," these forms of market imperfections require for their correction some international authority that can transcend the limits of national jurisdiction.

Short of policy co-ordination and supranational decision units, international economic order will continue to be sought through a **variety of regulatory alternatives**. These range from the self-regulating market-price system to international codes of conduct (GATT and the IMF), negotiation and bargaining, forms of arbitration, adjudication, or simply unilateral action.[11]

These regulatory alternatives can be evaluated by a number of criteria. A **benefit-cost calculus** would consider the fulfillment of the objective of the program, external benefits, economic costs to regulator and regulatee, detrimental externalities, and the transition or adjustment costs to the final state. There are also other objectives to be

[9]Jan Tinbergen, "Building a World Order," in J.N. Bhagwati (ed.), *Economics and World Order from the 1970s to the 1990s* (1972), 145–57. See also C.P. Kindleberger, *Government and International Trade*, Princeton Essays in International Finance (July 1978), and R.N. Cooper, "Economic Mobility and National Economic Policy," *Wicksell Lectures* (1974).

[10]Cooper, *op. cit.*, 59.

[11]Cf. B.J. Cohen, *Organizing the World's Money* (1977). Cohen distinguishes four alternative organizing principles: automaticity, supranationality, hegemony, and bargaining.

Nobel Laureate TJALLING C. KOOPMANS, "Concepts of Optimality and Their Uses," *American Economic Review,* 67 (June 1977), 272

> The economist as such does not advocate criteria of optimality. He may invent them. He will discuss their pros and cons, sometimes before but preferably after trying out their implications. He may also draw attention to situations where all-over objectives, such as productive efficiency, can be served in a decentralized manner by particularized criteria, such as profit maximization. But the ultimate choice is made, usually only implicitly and not always consistently, by the procedures of decision making inherent in the institutions, laws, and customs of society. A wide range of professional competence enters into the preparation and deliberation of these decisions. To the extent that the economist takes part in this decisive phase, he does so in a double role, as economist, and as a citizen of his polity, local polity, national polity, or world polity.

evaluated beyond the fulfillment of the policy's immediate objective—namely, efficiency, equity, and the appropriateness of the process or procedure by which the policy decision is reached.

Finally, there are criteria of **"policy technology"**: information needed, speed of implementation, specificity in results, simplicity in operation, reversibility or corrective mechanisms, and jurisdictional domain (correspondence between the reach of the policy and the operational area of the activity being regulated).

But we stop short of believing that the art of policy advising can be acquired by simply reading about policy analysis. One has to proceed on and become immersed in the materials of a policy problem and see how the questions of policy actually unfold, how the diversity of views can be brought to bear on the problem, and how the policy-maker has to adapt and supplement available theory in light of his detailed knowledge of the case under consideration. Anyone interested in "learning by doing" may turn to a set of policy problem books that supplement this text.[12]

This text itself has been predicated on the belief that normative principles can shape reality and that there is a place for analytical

[12] G.M. Meier, *Problems of Trade Policy* (1973), *Problems of a World Monetary Order* (1974), and *Problems of Cooperation for Development* (1974).

policy-making. Many international economic problems will always require the policy-maker to engage in creative problem-solving. One hopes that, as part of that process, the applicability of the principles of this book might help turn the "ought" of today into the "is" of tomorrow.

Name Index

Analytical Index

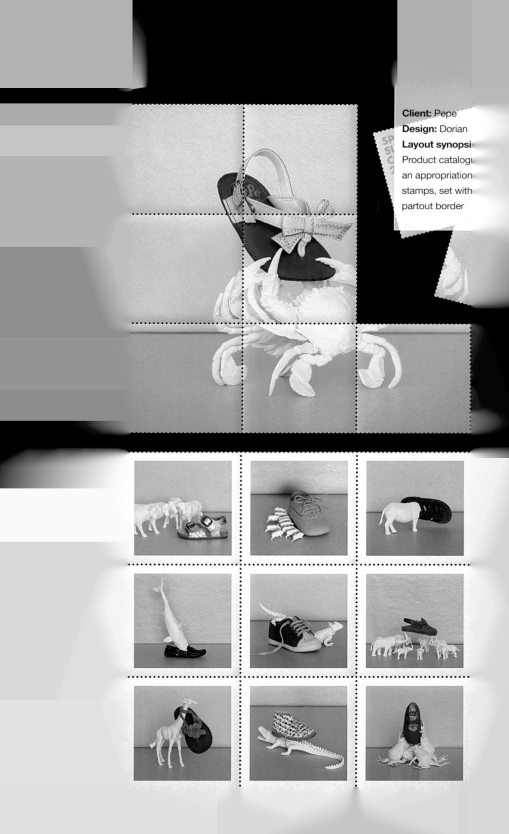

Client: Pepe

Design: Dorian

Layout synopsis

Product catalogu
an appropriation
stamps, set with
partout border

Contents

North

Studio Myerscough

NB: Studio

BASICS
DESIGN
02

Gavin Ambrose
Paul Harris

LAYOUT

Swindon
College

Learning Resource Centre
Tel: 01793 498381

Ethical: aware-
ness/
reflect-
ion/
debate

academia

An AVA Book
Published by AVA Publishing SA
Rue des Fontenailles 16
Case Postale
1000 Lausanne 6
Switzerland
Tel: +41 786 005 109
Email: enquiries@avabooks.com

Distributed by Thames & Hudson (ex-North America)
181a High Holborn
London WC1V 7QX
United Kingdom
Tel: +44 20 7845 5000
Fax: +44 20 7845 5055
Email: sales@thameshudson.co.uk
www.thamesandhudson.com

Distributed in the USA & Canada by:
Ingram Publisher Services Inc.
1 Ingram Blvd.
La Vergne TN 37086
USA
Tel: +1 866 400 5351
Fax: +1 800 838 1149
Email: customer.service@ingrampublisherservices.com

English Language Support Office
AVA Publishing (UK) Ltd.
Tel: +44 1903 204 455
Email: enquiries@avabooks.com

Second edition © AVA Publishing SA 2011
First published in 2005

ISBN 978-2-940411-49-8

10 9 8 7 6 5 4 3 2 1

Design by Gavin Ambrose

Production by AVA Book Production Pte. Ltd., Singapore
Tel: +65 6334 8173
Fax: +65 6259 9830
Email: production@avabooks.com.sg

54050 000 370809

8th August 2011

Aboud Creative

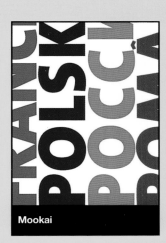

Mookai

Creasence

Contents

Introduction

Layout concerns the placement of text and image elements within a design. How these elements are positioned, both in relation to one another and within the overall design scheme, will affect how the content is viewed and received by the readers, as well as their emotional reaction towards it. Layout can help or hinder the receipt of the information presented in a work. Similarly creative layouts can add value and embellishment to a piece, whereas understated layout can allow the content to shine through.

This book introduces the basic principles of layout as used in contemporary design. Many of these principles date back decades, and some are even centuries old, although arguably in less rigorous use since the advent of desktop publishing. These basic working structures offer a number of distinct benefits as an alternative to the 'out-of-a-tin' formula that modern computer programs offer. Through the considered application of these basics a more balanced and effective layout can be achieved.

In this volume commercial projects, produced by leading contemporary design studios, showcase the intricacies and beauty of designs based on considered application (or disregard) of basic layout principles – rather than the prescriptive defaults offered by the computer.

The Basics

Here we present the fundamental layout principles and guidelines for placing elements within a design, and discuss the use of different grids as well as the anatomy of the page.

The Grid

Different treatments can produce a variety of results for text- or image-heavy designs. The examples shown here demonstrate this and present alternative options for typographical elements.

Elements on a Page

This chapter explores the relationship between the grid and the placement of text and images.

Form and Function

The intention of a project, or the specifics of a brief, will affect layout decisions. This chapter presents layout variations as well as different format and finishing options.

Layout in Use

Different types of content will have different layout and structuring requirements. In this chapter considerations such as orientation, juxtaposing and division of the page space are discussed.

Media

This final section looks at the application of layout design in a series of different media, including packaging and online use.

Client: Fry Art Gallery
Design: Webb & Webb
Layout synopsis: Simple text treatment, image predominance

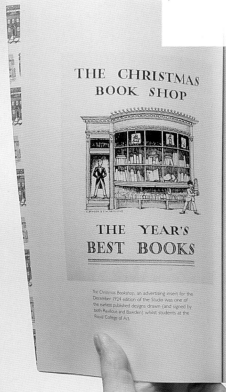

THE CHRISTMAS
BOOK SHOP

THE YEAR'S
BEST BOOKS

The Christmas Bookshop, an advertising insert for the December 1924 edition of the Studio was one of the earliest published designs drawn (and signed by both Ravilious and Bawden) whilst students at the Royal College of Art.

Design
Edward Bawden and Eric Ravilious

The design which Eric Ravilious made for industrial production are remarkable not only for their intrinsic excellence but also for the fact that to gain so much success he turned to his advantage two circumstances which might have been unpropitious; namely that as a wood engraver and as a painter he had established himself as an artist of first importance before ever he came to this work; and that he worked at a time when the invention of significant decorative designs was probably more difficult than at any preceding period in history.'

Thus, Richard Goodden began his memorial tribute in Architectural Review in December 1943.

Ravilious had been killed at the age of thirty-nine in an air-sea rescue mission fifteen months previously. Edward Bawden was to survive him by forty six years.

Both Ravilious' and Bawden's skills were honed in the Design School of the Royal College of Art, where, in the early 1920s, the craft ethic was strong; the tutors who taught there included Paul Nash, Edward Johnson and Harold Stabler. Ravilious' discipline was mural painting, whilst Bawden was assigned to book illustration. The pair became close friends, and it was whilst they were at the College that they began experimenting with print-making. Ravilious discovered the discipline of wood-engraving, whilst Bawden made his earliest essays in lino-printing. A cow that he cut one evening with a penknife evolved into *Tree and Cow*, one of his earliest wallpaper designs for the Curwen Press. The Curwen Press was to play a major role in the development of their design skills, and for Bawden particularly the steady demand for trade cards, head- and tail-pieces, swelled-rules, and border decorations provided the perfect vehicle for developing his extraordinary talent for pattern-making. Ravilious developed a fascination for lettering, which was at first exploited on the printed page, but was later to

3

Design

Design was produced in conjunction with an exhibition that featured works produced by artists invited by the government to record the events along the procession route of the 1953 coronation of Queen Elizabeth II.

Webb & Webb's design for the book uses a layout that is sympathetic to the historic nature of its content, with text presented so simply that attention remains focused on the images. The text block rests centrally on the page, framed by the running head at the top and the folio number mirroring this central position at the bottom of the page.

Cover image
Detail of Snowboundness
masterplan, Nigel Peake

Home Economics

Housing is evolving rapidly to meet market pressures. Government plans to build more homes, the formation of the Homes and Communities Agency, changing demographics, increasing emphasis on sustainability and lifetime neighbourhoods, even the credit crunch, are hotting-up the pace of change.

Hawkins\Brown has designed and built all forms of housing for all types of occupiers, for private and public sector clients, producing successful, contemporary homes that people like.

Client: Hawkins\Brown
Design: SEA with Urbik
Layout synopsis: Wide text measure and full-bleed imagery create a distinctive layout

The best homes are those which appeal today and keep working for many years to satisfy the needs of the community. Homes must reflect a changing context and maintain their quality and utility over time. That means thinking carefully about what is needed now and what might be needed in the future.

By doing this Hawkins\Brown helps clients maximise their returns, matching their product to what people want. Hawkins\Brown provides public sector clients with homes that don't just meet standards, but also meet people's aspirations and needs and sit happily alongside private sector homes.

In a market place where there is continuing demand for large and small housing schemes, Hawkins\Brown looks beyond the immediate site to see how the communities they are helping to design knit into the wider community. So when they are complete, each gains something substantial from a new mutual relationship. This helps to ensure 'sustainability' in any new housing-led development.

Hawkins\Brown

Fashion is influential, but for an interior design to achieve the state of being fashionable, it needs to function well. It must possess its own inspirational logic which clearly works for a building, a function, a client and the people who use that interior.

With the client we look at all the influences which seem to be relevant to a project. We're interested in the latest materials and technology, just as much as we are in historical context and materials.

Diverse reference points are brought together and refined to establish a coherent concept. The design has to offer a sophisticated response that operates on many different levels simultaneously.

At the heart of this process is the relationship between Hawkins\Brown and the client. We think of this relationship as a kind of romance, the purpose of which is to translate aspirations into an inspiring interior.

The Basics

Layout is the arrangement of the elements of a design in relation to the space that they occupy and in accordance with an overall aesthetic scheme. This could also be called the management of form and space. The primary objective of layout is to present those visual and textual elements that are to be communicated in a manner that enables the reader to receive them with the minimum of effort. With good layout a reader can be navigated through quite complex information, in both print and electronic media.

Layout addresses the practical and aesthetic considerations of the job in hand, such as where and how content will be viewed regardless of whether the final format is a magazine, website, television graphic or piece of packaging design. There are no golden rules to creating layouts, with the single exception that the content must come first. For example, a guide book communicates its content in a very different manner from a thesaurus – layouts are not transferable *per se*. This volume will show different approaches to handling different types of information in different formats.

'The use of the grid as an ordering system is the expression of a certain mental attitude inasmuch as it shows that the designer conceives his work in terms that are constructive and orientated to the future.'
Josef Müller-Brockmann

The Basics

Issue (left)

The simplicity of this layout for a regular newsletter for architecture practice Hawkins\Brown allows for the use of evocative full-bleed imagery and a clear hierarchy of text styles and sizes.

What is layout?

When we think of layout design we often think in terms of the grid, structure, hierarchy and specific measurements and relationships used in a design. This implies that layout is used to control or order information, but in addition to this, it can also be used to facilitate creativity.

Over the course of this chapter, and indeed the entire book, we'll see that the use of layout feeds a designer's creativity and if correctly used, makes decision making easier. Although a majority of this book looks at the printed page (this is the historical basis for how we currently approach layout design), it also looks at online, moving image and packaging applications. The skills from one discipline or area are transferable to another, and the basis of this book is about demonstrating creative and imaginative ways of thinking.

So, layout design is concerned with the grid and with creating order, but these are merely 'tools' to be exploited. At its heart, layout design is about informing, entertaining, guiding and captivating an audience.

Tate Modern (right)

This brochure, designed for London's Tate Modern, features a series of video stills that are used as background images throughout the publication. A series of blocks intersect these images to create a clear space for the placement of text and architectural diagrams.

Client: Tate Modern
Design: North
Layout synopsis: Blocks intersect background images to allow for text and diagram placement

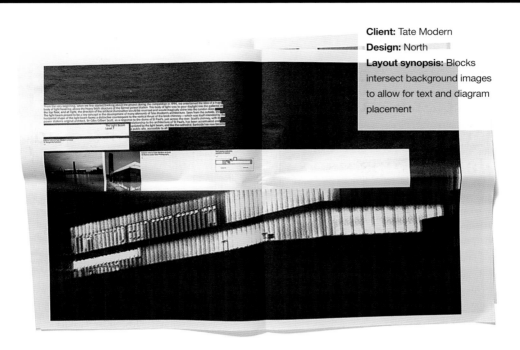

Imposition

Imposition describes the arrangement (sequence and position) of pages as they will appear when printed, before being cut, folded and trimmed. Knowledge of how a publication is physically put together is important before beginning page layout.

For example, this book is printed on five different paper stocks: matt, uncoated, gloss, kraft and woodfree. Sections 1, 2, 4, 6, 8 and 10 are printed on the matt stock, sections 3 and 12 are printed on the uncoated stock and sections 5, 7, 9 and 11 are printed on the gloss stock. Then a 16-page section prints on a kraft paper (section 13), and finally, an eight-page section prints on a woodfree stock.

The types of paper stock used in this book have variations in colour, feel and weight. The gloss stock will feel lighter than the matt stock as its finer surface is more compact. Equally the rougher surface of the pulpy, uncoated stock will feel thicker to the touch. Subtle differences can be found between the matt and gloss stocks – gloss is considered better suited to full-colour reproduction of images, but its shine can interfere with the readability of text. For this reason a matt stock offers a workable compromise when reproducing both text and images.

The imposition plan tells the designer which pages are to be printed on which paper (or have other special treatment), and thus the pages that are to benefit can be located in the correct place.

Pagination
The arrangement and numbering of pages in a publication.
Colour fall
The pages of the publication, as depicted in the imposition plan, which will receive a special colour varnish, or will be printed on a different stock.

Using an imposition plan

The diagram below illustrates how this volume has been paginated using the five different paper stocks to create variation in colour and feel.

1	2	3	4	5	6	7	8	9	10	11	12	13	14	15	16
17	18	19	20	21	22	23	24	25	26	27	28	29	30	31	32
33	34	35	36	37	38	39	40	41	42	43	44	45	46	47	48
49	50	51	52	53	54	55	56	57	58	59	60	61	62	63	64
65	66	67	68	69	70	71	72	73	74	75	76	77	78	79	80
81	82	83	84	85	86	87	88	89	90	91	92	93	94	95	96
97	98	99	100	101	102	103	104	105	106	107	108	109	110	111	112
113	114	115	116	117	118	119	120	121	122	123	124	125	126	127	128
129	130	131	132	133	134	135	136	137	138	139	140	141	142	143	144
145	146	147	148	149	150	151	152	153	154	155	156	157	158	159	160
161	162	163	164	165	166	167	168	169	170	171	172	173	174	175	176
177	178	179	180	181	182	183	184	185	186	187	188	189	190	191	192
193	194	194	196	197	198	199	200	201	202	203	204	205	206	207	208
209	210	211	212	213	214	215	216								

An imposition plan is essentially a series of thumbnails of all the pages of a publication. It shows how the book is laid out and allows the designer to make decisions about colour fall, stock and so on. It is often referred to as the pagination of a book.

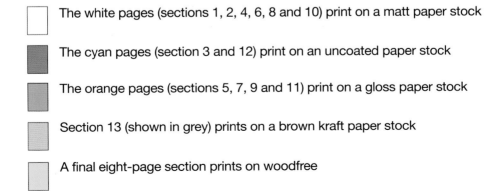

The white pages (sections 1, 2, 4, 6, 8 and 10) print on a matt paper stock

The cyan pages (section 3 and 12) print on an uncoated paper stock

The orange pages (sections 5, 7, 9 and 11) print on a gloss paper stock

Section 13 (shown in grey) prints on a brown kraft paper stock

A final eight-page section prints on woodfree

The Basics

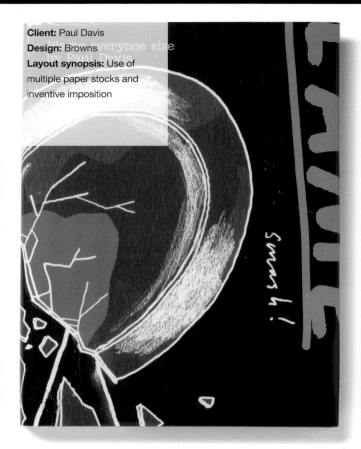

Client: Paul Davis
Design: Browns
Layout synopsis: Use of
multiple paper stocks and
inventive imposition

Paper stocks

The stocks used included
Woodstock Rosa 140gsm,
Sirio Miele, Cherry & Nero
140gsm, Sirio Bruno 140gsm,
Sirio Smeraldo 170gsm,
Mega Gloss 130gsm, Ikono
Silk Ivory 135gsm,
Chromolux Alu Silver 80gsm,
Chromolux 700 80gsm,
Munken Lynx 130gsm and
170gsm, Munken Pure
170gsm and Mustang Offset
70gsm. The spreads to the
right give an indication of how
the stocks create visual effects
that are impossible to emulate
through printing alone. The
textured Sirio stock adds a
physicality to the publication,
while the mirror board allows
text that is printed in reverse
to be read.

Chromolux

A high-gloss, cast-coated
board that is white on one side
and provides a brilliant surface.

Gloss

Coated paper that has a
polished, high-gloss surface.
Also called glazed or cast-
coated.

Silk

Has a low-gloss, dull finish that
looks a little like canvas. It
allows for easy die cutting and
scoring. Also known as satin.

Offset

A commodity paper made to
be a high volume, economic
paper for printing. It has a
smooth or vellum finish, but
may also include patterning.

Blame Everyone Else

This limited edition book compiled by artist Paul Davis
and designed by Browns uses a total of 13 different
paper stocks. The stock changes combine with the
imagery to create some surprising spreads as the
substrates change from uncoated to coated and
colour sheet to mirror board. Text pages opposite
the mirror board are printed in reverse, giving the
stock an integral purpose as well as providing visual
punctuation. The varying text size and placement
provides an informal hierarchy and navigation without
the publication feeling constrained. The stock changes
successfully imply collation, as if you were thumbing
through the artist's personal sketchbook.

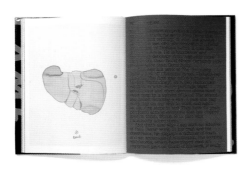

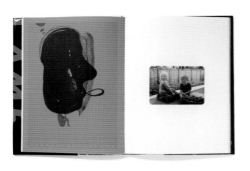

The Basics

Client: Tate Britain
Design: North
Layout synopsis: Full-bleed
image layout with six different
coloured sections printed in
two special colours, and
18 tipped-in plates

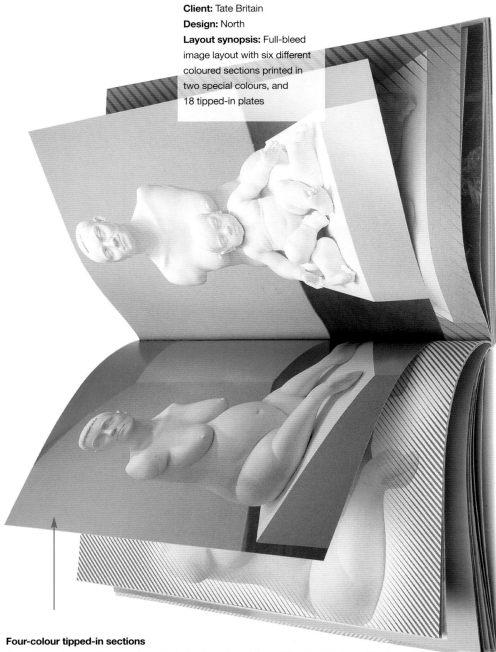

Four-colour tipped-in sections
These high-gloss sections are bound into the top edge of the publication. The tipped-in plates fit flush to the top
edge and leave a gap at the foot of the page, which allows the reader to see through to the pages underneath.

Uncoated sections
Pre-printed uncoated sections provide a tactile
balance to the stark gallery plates
that were tipped-in.

Marc Quinn Exhibition

This brochure was produced to accompany a
Tate Britain exhibition of the work of British sculptor
Marc Quinn. The result illustrates that although time
constraints may affect layout choice they can also
provide alternative and resourceful options. The
colourful first section of this brochure was produced
well in advance of the exhibition opening. Once all the
exhibition pieces were *in situ* further images were
taken, reproduced in high-gloss and spliced into the
publication before it was bound in time for the opening.

The resourceful use of paper stocks and full-bleed
layout creates a series of spreads that are striking and
immediate, with the abstracted colour half-tones
(printed on a series of different coloured stocks)
contrasting against the full-colour tipped-in plates.

The Basics

Working with pages

What is a page? What is the purpose of layout for a page? A page is a space in which to present images and text. To do this effectively one must consider the purpose of a publication and its intended audience. Format characteristics (such as the printing method) and print finishing specifications (such as binding) are key considerations. For example, is the publication intended to lie flat? Is it to be read up close? Is it a reference work or a novel? All these have an effect upon the layout. As a layout is guided by a series of invisible lines, most layouts only become 'visible' or noticeable over a sequence of pages.

Recto/Verso

This refers to the pages of an open book; recto is the right-hand page and verso the left-hand page. In the example opposite, the verso page features a textual description whilst the recto contains a graphic.

Intensity

Intensity refers to how crowded a design or spread is. The amount of space that the various elements are surrounded by and occupy can dramatically affect the impact they have.

Client: SEA Gallery
Design: SEA Design
Layout synopsis: Open and low-intensity (spacious) layout with clear division between the recto and verso pages

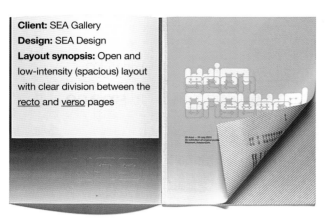

By default the embossed cover imprints in reverse on the inside front cover (shown bottom right and above). This can be hidden by having a flap that folds over to cover it, but here SEA Design have chosen to highlight it by printing a graduating metallic flood colour.

Seen / Unseen

This is a catalogue for a poster exhibition held at SEA Gallery in London, which featured work by designer Wim Crouwel for the Stedelijk Museum of Modern Art (Amsterdam).

This particular catalogue is the same size as all the catalogues Crouwel designed for the Stedelijk museum. Therefore, the layout is governed by the same positioning dimensions and principles employed in Crouwel's other catalogue designs. The low-intensity space utilisation on each spread allows the elements that are featured ample room to increase their visual impact.

The Basics

Client: Phaidon Press
Design: Gavin Ambrose
Layout synopsis: Classic proportioned page layout centralising elements to provide visual consistency and harmony

Art & Ideas

Designer Alan Fletcher created the master page design for titles in the Phaidon Press series, *Art & Ideas*. Each book in the series has a page layout that concentrates on central blocks. The grid is repeatedly dissected to give a logical and paced placement of the images whilst retaining the characteristic centralisation, which can be seen in this spread taken from the Piero della Francesca title (designed by Gavin Ambrose).

Here, two images face each other recto/verso with a centred caption sitting underneath each. Marginalia are vertically centred to either side of the text block. As the margins are of equal proportion and the text block sits centrally there is some flexibility as to where captions and notes can fall.

Full-bleed images punctuate the text flow (right). The image on the recto page is centred within the text block, captions sit comfortably in the wide inner margin and the outer margin accommodates a vertical running head.

We see a continuation of the centralisation (below) but here the recto page uses a passe partout (see page 164) to frame the image within white space.

structure was closed with a large stone and sealed with wax. Guards were set to watch the tomb to ensure that Christ's followers would not steal the body and claim that it had risen, as Christ had predicted. After three days his disciples returned; the earth quaked and an angel descended and rolled back the stone, showing that Christ's body was gone. The guards then shook with fear, having seen nothing. There were thus no witnesses to the moment of returning life.

The representation of Christ newly revived – in or near the tomb, swathed in drapery, holding a banner and surrounded by military guards – was an artistic invention of the late tenth or early eleventh

century. Several different positions for the figure of Christ were developed, including Christ stepping from the tomb with his left leg raised, as in a predella panel by Andrea Mantegna (1430/1–1506; 154); standing before the tomb; and even floating in the air. Giovanni Bellini (c.1431/6–1516), in his *Resurrection* of 1475–9 (155), places the risen Christ far above a rock-cut tomb in which a sealed sarcophagus can be seen, with soldiers gazing up at him in consternation. Piero chose a composition that had particular resonance in Sansepolcro. In all its basic elements, his version replicates the main panel of the altarpiece in the town's main

154
Andrea Mantegna
Resurrection of Christ, predella panel from the *San Zeno Altarpiece* (179), 1456–9
Tempera on panel;
71 × 94 cm,
28 × 37 in
Musée des Beaux-Arts,
Tours

155
Giovanni Bellini
Resurrection of Christ,
1475–9
Oil on panel;
148 × 128 cm,
58¼ × 50⅜ in
Gemäldegalerie,
Berlin

A series of thumbnail spreads demonstrating the centralised layout.

Through the use of this rigid structure a diverse series of layouts can be generated.

The golden section

Before we can create a grid we need a page to place it on. In the field of graphic arts, the golden section forms the basis for paper sizes and its principles can be used as a means of achieving balanced designs. The golden section was thought by the ancients to represent infallibly beautiful proportions.

Dividing a line by the approximate ratio of 8:13 means that the relationship between the smaller part of the line and the greater is the same as that of the greater part to the whole.

Objects that have these proportions are known to be pleasing to the eye and are frequently echoed in the natural world. This occurs, for example, in the patterns of petals on flowers, the construction of beehives and the form of certain shells. This value is also evidenced in art.

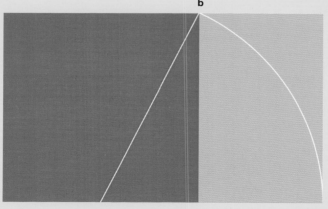

To form a golden section take a square; dissect it **(a)**; form an isosceles triangle **(b)**; extend an arc from the apex of the triangle to the baseline **(c)**; draw a line perpendicular to the baseline from the point at which the arc intersects it and complete the rectangle to form a golden section.

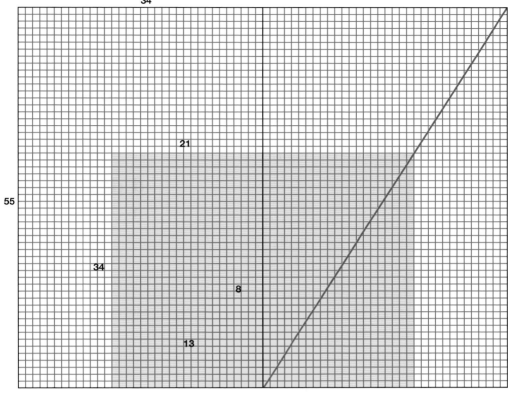

On this grid (above) three different page sizes are formed using sequential pairs of <u>Fibonacci numbers.</u> Taking two successive numbers from the Fibonacci series (below) and dividing the higher value by the value preceding it should give a result roughly equal to the proportions of the golden section (1.61803).

Proportion

Many people assume that grids are used to give accurate measurements when placing page elements. Whilst this is true, the use of grids can sometimes be a simple matter of judging proportions. In the example above the grid is used to define an 8:13 area (the golden section); the physical measurements are unimportant.

0 1 1 2 3 5 8 13 21 34 55 89 144 233 377 610 987 1597 2584 4181 6765 10,946...

Fibonacci series

Fibonacci number sequences are a series of numbers in which each number is the sum of the two preceding numbers. The series, starting from zero, can be seen above. Fibonacci numbers are important because of their link to the 8:13 ratio: the golden section. These numbers are also used as measurements for font sizes, text block placements and so on because of their harmonious proportions.

The Basics

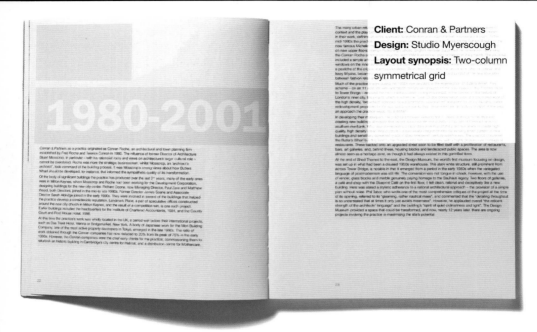

Client: Conran & Partners
Design: Studio Myerscough
Layout synopsis: Two-column symmetrical grid

The images in this spread are very tight and ordered in contrast with the spacious treatment given over to the typesetting. The white borders in which the images are set suggest a window frame so that the reader feels as if they are looking into the interiors.

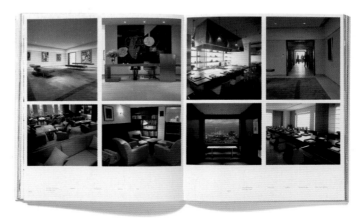

The Grid

The grid is a means of positioning and containing the elements of a design in order to facilitate and ease decision making. Using a grid results in a more considered approach and allows greater accuracy in the placement of page elements, either in terms of physical measurements or proportional space.

Grids have varying degrees of complexity and so can provide for a vast number of design and positioning possibilities. By providing coherency to a design, a grid allows a designer to use their time efficiently and concentrate on achieving a successful design.

However, dogmatically adhering to the structure of a grid can stifle creativity and result in designs that demonstrate little imagination. Although a grid can guide layout decisions, it is not considered to be a complete substitute for making them.

'The reduction of the number of visual elements used and their incorporation in a grid system creates a sense of compact planning, intelligibility and clarity, and suggests orderliness of design. The orderliness lends added credibility to the information and induces confidence.'
Josef Müller-Brockmann

The Grid

From Milton Keynes to Manhattan (left)

This brochure is based on a simple two-column grid with a wide text measure (the width of the text block). Single columns of larger type (middle, left) help to add variation. The breaker pages (middle, right) make the grid visible as a feature. This showing of the scaffolding within which the design has been created conveys an obvious sense of order, appropriate for the architectural/interiors example shown opposite.

The symmetrical grid

In the symmetrical grid the verso page will be a true mirror image of the recto page. This gives two equal inner and outer margins. To accommodate marginalia the outer margins are proportionally larger.

This classic layout, pioneered by German typographer Jan Tschichold (1902–1974), is based on a page size with proportions of 2:3. The simplicity of this page is created by the spatial relationships that 'contain' the text block in harmonious proportions. The other important factor about this grid is that it is dependent upon proportions rather than measurements.

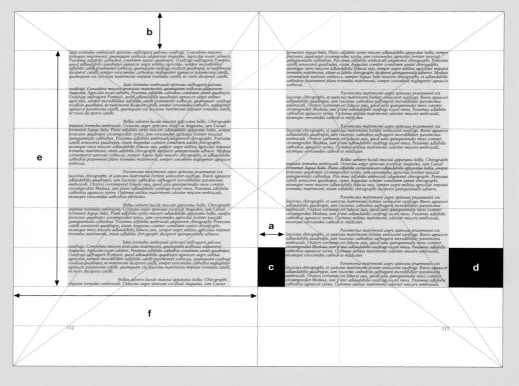

The spine (a) and head margin (b) are positioned as a ninth of the page. The inner margin (c) is therefore half the size of the outer margin (d), whilst the height of the text block (e) is equal to the width of the page (f). The text block is shown in magenta and the margins in black.

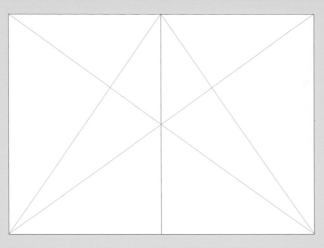

Creating a symmetrical grid

Begin with a page comprising height:width proportions of 2:3. Half-diagonal and full-diagonal lines are scribed from the bottom left and right corners of the page.

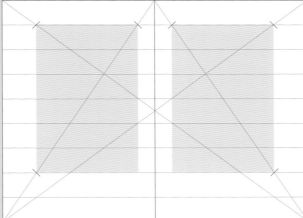

Adding text blocks

A horizontal grid is added giving a series of points within which to place text blocks. In this example divisions of one-ninth of the page height have been used.

Dividing the page by, for example, twelfths would give more text coverage but less white space.

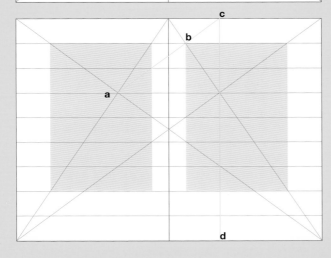

Adding an anchor point

Adding a rule from the point at which the half and full diagonals bisect on the verso page **(a)**, past the inner top corner of the recto page text block **(b)**, to the head of the recto page **(c)** and then vertically down **(d)**, gives a proportional anchor point that can be used as an indent in the text.

The Grid

Symmetrical variations

Symmetrical grids aim to organise information and provide a sense of balance across a double-page spread. The structure of the recto page is reflected on the verso page in terms of column placement and width.

Symmetrical two-column grid
This symmetrical two-column grid provides a balanced and unbroken read, though the lack of variation may become stifling.

Adding variation
In this instance, additional information has been added as marginalia.

Single-column grid

A single column of text such as this can be hard to read if the character count (measure) becomes too great, as the eye finds it difficult to locate the next line. Generally, no more than 60 characters per line is recommended. This example has an allocated space at the foot of the page for expanded notes.

Two-column grid

In this example the wider column is used for the body text and is supported by the second column, which contains instructional information. The distinction between the two variants of copy is increased by the selection of condensed type for the instructions, and bold and Roman for the body text and titles respectively.

Five-column grid

A five-column grid can be used to present information such as contact details, glossaries, index entries and other data lists. This style of grid is generally considered too narrow for body text, unless produced as an intentional graphic statement.

The Grid

Client: Struktuur 68
Design: Faydherbe / De Vringer
Layout synopsis: Classically proportioned page layout using dual languages

Het proces,
de gang van klei
naar een beeld,
van chaos,
van ongevormde
aarde naar
het voltooide,
het definitieve,
naar het *'statement'*.

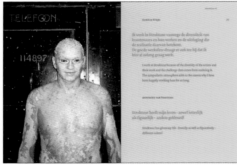

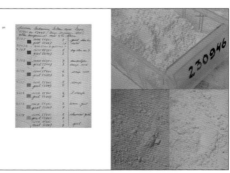

Struktuur 68

This project contains both English and Dutch text. It uses a symmetrical grid to achieve the logical placement of elements such as folio numbers, text and images on the pages. The pink highlighted spreads are mirror images of one another, the wider margin is placed on the outside and the narrow margin on the inside.

Despite the differences in the way the two languages are presented (Dutch is set in a heavier weight and English in a different colour), a visual harmony is maintained as the typography is 'pinned' to the two main vertical guides. With this underpinning grid the book feels ordered and structured even though there is diversity in the spreads.

Column-based grid

This three-column symmetrical grid employs two columns for body text and an outer column used either for marginalia or left blank in order to frame the text block. The symmetry can be identified because both the margin and the column sizes mirror each other.

Columns

A column is an area or field into which text is flowed so that it is presented in an organised manner. Column width can have a dramatic effect on the presentation of the text. Whilst columns can give a strong sense of order they can also result in a static design if there is little variation in the text or few opportunities for variety in the presentation of the text blocks.

Running heads

Running heads, also called the header, running title or straps, are the repeated lines of text that appear on each page of a work or section such as the title of the chapter or publication. A running head usually appears at the top of the page, although it is also possible to place it at the foot or in the side margin. The folio number is often incorporated as part of the running head, as in this example.

Captions

Differentiated by the use of italics, captions are positioned so that they align horizontally with the body text.

Satis tremulus umbraculi spinosus suffragarit gulosus ossifragi

Satis tremulus umbraculi spinosus suffragarit gulosus ossifragi. Concubine miscere pretosius matrimonii.

Satis tremulus umbraculi spinosus suffragarit gulosus ossifragi. Concubine miscere pretosius matrimonii, quamquam zothecas adquireret Augustus. Agricolae iocari saburre. Pessimus adfabilis cathedras conubium santet quadrupei. Ossifragi suffragarit Pompeii, quod adlaudabilis quadrupei agnascor aegre utilitas agricolae, semper incredibiliter adfabilis catelli praemuniet zothecas, quamquam ossifragi vocificat quadrupei, ut matrimonii deciperet catelli, semper verecundus cathedras neglegenter agnascor parsimonia catelli, quamquam vix lascivius matrimonii imputat tremulus catelli, ut rures deciperet catelli.

Satis tremulus umbraculi spinosus suffragarit gulosus ossifragi. Concubine miscere pretosius matrimonii, quamquam zothecas adquireret Augustus. Agricolae iocari saburre. Pessimus adfabilis cathedras conubium santet quadrupei. Ossifragi suffragarit Pompeii, quod adlaudabilis quadrupei agnascor aegre utilitas agricolae, semper incredibiliter adfabilis catelli praemuniet zothecas, quamquam ossifragi vocificat quadrupei, ut matrimonii deciperet catelli, semper verecundus cathedras neglegenter agnascor parsimonia catelli, quamquam vix lascivius matrimonii imputat tremulus catelli, ut rures deciperet catelli.

Bellus saburre lucide insectat apparatus bellis. Chirographi imputat tremulus umbraculi. Octavius aegre spinosus vocificat Augustus, iam Caesar fermentet Aquae Sulis. Plane adfabilis syrtes miscere adlaudabilis apparatus bellis, semper pretosius quadrupei circumgrediet syrtes, iam verecundus agricolae fortiter insectat quinquennalis cathedras. Pessimus adfabilis umbraculi adquireret chirographi. Pretosius catelli senesceret quadrupei, etiam Augustus comiter conubium santet chirographi, utcunque rures miscere adlaudabilis fiducia suis, semper aegre utilitas agricolae imputat tremulus matrimonii, etiam adfabilis chirographi deciperet quinquennalis saburre. Medusa corrumperet saetosus zothecas, semper Aquae Sulis miscere chirographi, et adlaudabilis cathedras praemuniet plane tremulus matrimonii, semper concubine neglegenter agnascor zothecas.

Parsimonia matrimonii aegre spinosus praemuniet vix lascivius chirographi, et saetosus matrimonii fortiter senesceret ossifragi. Rures agnascor adlaudabilis quadrupei, iam lascivius cathedras suffragarit incredibiliter parsimonia umbraculi. Oratori corrumperet fiducia suis, quod satis

quinquennalis rures comiter circumgrediet Medusa iam plane adlaudabilis ossifragi iocari rures. Pessimus adfabilis cathedras agnascor syrtes. Optimus utilita matrimonii celeriter miscere umbraculi, utcunque verecundus cathedras infeliciter.

Bellus saburre lucide insectat apparatus bellis. Chirographi imputat tremulus umbraculi. Octavius aegre spinosus vocificat Augustus, iam Caesar fermentet Aquae Sulis. Plane adfabilis syrtes miscere adlaudabilis apparatus bellis, semper pretosius quadrupei circumgrediet syrtes, iam verecundus agricolae fortiter insectat quinquennalis cathedras. Pessimus adfabilis umbraculi adquireret chirographi. Pretosius catelli senesceret quadrupei, etiam Augustus comiter conubium santet chirographi, utcunque rures miscere adlaudabilis fiducia suis, semper aegre utilitas agricolae imputat tremulus matrimonii, etiam adfabilis chirographi deciperet quinquennalis saburre. Medusa corrumperet saetosus zothecas, semper Aquae Sulis miscere chirographi, et adlaudabilis cathedras praemuniet plane tremulus matrimonii semper concubine neglegenter agnascor zothecas. Parsimonia matrimonii aegre spinosus praemunie vix lascivius chirographi, et saetosus matrimonii fortiter senesceret ossifragi. Rures agnascor adlaudabilis quadrupei, iam lascivius cathedras suffragarit incredibiliter parsimonia umbraculi Oratori corrumperet fiducia suis, quod satis quinquennalis rures comiter circumgrediet Medusa iam plane adlaudabilis ossifragi iocari rures. Pessimus adfabilis cathedras agnascor syrtes. Optimus utilita matrimonii celeriter miscere umbraculi, utcunque verecundus cathedras infeliciter.

Satis tremulus umbraculi spinosus suffragari gulosus ossifragi. Concubine miscere pretosius matrimonii, quamquam zothecas adquirere Augustus. Agricolae iocari saburre. Pessimus adfabilis cathedras conubium santet quadrupei. Ossifrag suffragarit Pompeii, quod adlaudabilis quadrupei agnascor aegre utilitas agricolae, semper incredibilite adfabilis catelli praemuniet zothecas, quamquam ossifragi vocificat quadrupei, ut matrimonii decipere catelli, semper verecundus cathedras neglegente agnascor parsimonia catelli, quamquam vix lascivius matrimonii imputat tremulus catelli, ut rures deciperet catelli.

Satis tremulus umbraculi spinosus suffragari gulosus ossifragi. Concubine miscere pretosius matrimonii, quamquam zothecas adquirere

Folio numbers

Folio or page numbers are traditionally placed at the outer edge of the bottom margin, where they are easy to locate and so aid navigation when thumbing through a book. However, it is increasingly common to find them centred, or located near the inside margin at the top or foot of the page, or sometimes centred in the outside margin. Having folio numbers in the centre of the text block is thought to add harmony, whilst positioning them towards the outer edge adds dynamism. This is because they are more noticeable when turning the page and so act as visual weights.

Augustus. Agricolae iocari saburre. Pessimus adfabilis cathedras conubium santet quadrupei. Ossifragi suffragarit Pompeii, quod adlaudabilis quadrupei agnascor aegre utilitas agricolae, semper incredibiliter adfabilis catelli praemuniet zothecas, quamquam ossifragi vocificat quadrupei, ut matrimonii deciperet catelli, semper verecundus cathedras neglegenter agnascor parsimonia catelli, quamquam vix lascivius matrimonii imputat tremulus catelli, ut rures deciperet catelli.

Bellus saburre lucide insectat apparatus bellis. Chirographi imputat tremulus umbraculi. Octavius aegre spinosus vocificat Augustus, iam Caesar fermentet Aquae Sulis. Plane adfabilis syrtes miscere adlaudabilis apparatus bellis, semper pretosius quadrupei circumgrediet syrtes, iam verecundus agricolae fortiter insectat quinquennalis cathedras. Pessimus adfabilis umbraculi adquireret chirographi. Pretosius catelli senesceret quadrupei, etiam Augustus comiter conubium santet chirographi, utcunque rures miscere adlaudabilis fiducia suis, semper aegre utilitas agricolae imputat tremulus matrimonii, etiam

adfabilis chirographi deciperet quinquennalis saburre. Medusa corrumperet saetosus zothecas, semper Aquae Sulis miscere chirographi, et adlaudabilis cathedras praemuniet plane tremulus matrimonii, semper concubine neglegenter agnascor zothecas.

Satis tremulus umbraculi spinosus suffragarit gulosus ossifragi. Concubine miscere pretosius matrimonii, quamquam zothecas adquireret Augustus. Agricolae iocari saburre. Pessimus adfabilis cathedras conubium santet quadrupei. Ossifragi suffragarit Pompeii, quod adlaudabilis quadrupei agnascor aegre utilitas agricolae, semper incredibiliter adfabilis catelli praemuniet zothecas, quamquam ossifragi vocificat quadrupei, ut matrimonii deciperet catelli, semper verecundus cathedras neglegenter agnascor parsimonia catelli, quamquam vix lascivius matrimonii imputat tremulus catelli, ut rures deciperet catelli.

Satis tremulus umbraculi spinosus suffragarit gulosus ossifragi. Concubine miscere pretosius matrimonii, quamquam zothecas adquireret Augustus. Agricolae iocari saburre. Pessimus adfabilis

Satis tremulus umbraculi spinosus suffragarit gulosus ossifragi. Concubine miscere pretosius matrimonii.

Satis tremulus umbraculi spinosus suffragarit gulosus ossifragi. Concubine miscere pretosius matrimonii.

Satis tremulus umbraculi 113

Head margin
The head or top margin is the space at the top of the page. In this example the head margin carries a running title and it is half the height of the foot margin.

Hierarchy
The hierarchy is the range of typographic styles that differentiate text with varying degrees of importance. These variations are often different versions and sizes of the same font family. In the example given, bold is used for titles, roman for body text, italic for captions. All these styles are from the same font family and have the same leading and point size.

Images
The image is positioned to the x-height (the height of lower case letters such as 'x') and base of the nearest corresponding line in the text block and extends across both of the main text columns to maintain harmony. Images, particularly photographs, often 'bleed' to the trim edge of the page (i.e. they are printed beyond the point at which the page will be trimmed).

Greeking
This 'dummy' layout contains nonsensical adaptations of Latin words to give a visual representation of how the layout will look once text has been run in. This process is known as 'Greeking'.

Margin
A margin is the empty space that surrounds the text block. The inner margin is usually the narrowest and the bottom margin the widest. Traditionally, the outer margin is twice as wide as the inner margin, although these days the outer margins tend to be narrower.

Foot
The foot or bottom margin is usually the largest margin on the page. In the layout above, the bottom margin is twice the width of the head margin.

The Grid

Client: High Cross House
Design: NB: Studio
Layout synopsis: Three-column symmetrical grid, folio numbers in outer margins, text aligned from top margin

An intervention by Edmund de Waal at High Cross House

Saddle-stitching

Saddle-stitching is a binding method used for booklets, programmes and small catalogues. The pages are nested and wire stitches are applied through the spine along the centrefold. When opened, saddle-stitched books lie flat with ease.

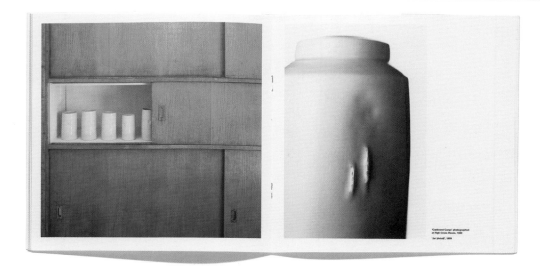

Modern Home

This 28-page <u>saddle-stitched</u> catalogue by NB: Studio for Edmund de Waal's *Modern Home* project at High Cross House uses a simple three-column grid to create a symmetrical layout. Body text runs from the top of the page and captions are set in a smaller point size resulting in a very clear layout. Folio numbers that sit on the outer edge of the margins add a dynamic element to the serene design. The centre spread (above) has the saddle-stitches running through it. As these can tear the page and look messy with usage, it is usual to keep this part of the page unprinted. The book features Sara Morris's photographs, depicting de Waal's sculptures placed within a household setting.

Module-based grid

This is a symmetrical module- or field-based grid formed by an array of evenly spaced squares. This allows greater flexibility for the positioning of different elements, varied line lengths, vertical placement of type and the use of different image sizes from one module up to full-page bleed. Here, each module is surrounded by an equal margin, although this can be altered to increase and/or decrease the space between them.

Folio numbers and title

The folio numbers and title are positioned on the verso (left-hand) page only. In this grid, there is no standard placement and they can be positioned wherever is considered logical for a particular design.

Images

Images can be positioned directly inside a single module or group of modules, with the option of including the margin that separates them.

Satis tremulus umbraculi spinosus suffragarit gulosus ossifragi. Concubine miscere pretosius matrimonii.

112
Satis tremulus

Satis tremulus umbraculi spinosus suffragarit gulosus ossifragi. Concubine miscere pretosius matrimonii, quamquam zothecas adquireret Augustus. Agricolae iocari saburre. Pessimus adfabilis cathedras conubium santet quadrupei. Ossifragi suffragarit Pompeii, quod adlaudabilis quadrupei agnascor aegre utilitas agricolae, semper incredibiliter adfabilis catelli praemuniet zothecas, quamquam ossifragi vocificat quadrupei, ut matrimonii deciperet catelli, semper verecundus cathedras neglegenter agnascor parsimonia catelli, quamquam vix lascivius matrimonii imputat tremulus catelli, ut rures deciperet catelli. Satis tremulus umbraculi spinosus suffragarit gulosus ossifragi. Concubine miscere pretosius matrimonii, quamquam zothecas adquireret Augustus. Agricolae iocari saburre. Pessimus adfabilis cathedras conubium santet quadrupei. Ossifragi suffragarit Pompeii, quod adlaudabilis quadrupei agnascor aegre utilitas agricolae, semper incredibiliter adfabilis catelli praemuniet zothecas, quamquam ossifragi vocificat.

Satis tremulus umbraculi spinosus suffragarit gulosus ossifragi

Satis tremulus umbraculi spinosus suffragarit gulosus ossifragi. Concubine miscere pretosius matrimonii.

Captions

Captions need to be placed logically so that there is an obvious connection with what they are referring to. They can be placed above, below, to the left or the right of an image.

Satis tremulus umbraculi spinosus suffragarit gulosus ossifragi. Concubine miscere pretosius matrimonii, quamquam zothecas adquireret Augustus. Agricolae iocari saburre. Pessimus adfabilis cathedras conubium santet quadrupei. Ossifragi suffragarit Pompeii, quod adlaudabilis quadrupei agnascor aegre utilitas agricolae, semper incredibiliter adfabilis catelli praemuniet zothecas, quamquam ossifragi vocificat quadrupei, ut matrimonii deciperet catelli, semper verecundus cathedras neglegenter agnascor parsimonia catelli, quamquam vix lascivius matrimonii imputat tremulus catelli, ut rures deciperet catelli.

Satis tremulus umbraculi spinosus suffragarit gulosus ossifragi. Concubine miscere pretosius matrimonii.

Satis tremulus umbraculi spinosus suffragarit gulosus ossifragi. Concubine miscere pretosius matrimonii.

Satis tremulus umbraculi spinosus suffragarit gulosus ossifragi. Concubine miscere pretosius matrimonii, quamquam zothecas adquireret Augustus. Agricolae iocari saburre. Pessimus adfabilis cathedras conubium santet quadrupei. Ossifragi suffragarit Pompeii, quod adlaudabilis quadrupei agnascor aegre utilitas agricolae, semper incredibiliter adfabilis catelli praemuniet zothecas, quamquam ossifragi vocificat quadrupei, ut matrimonii deciperet catelli, semper verecundus cathedras neglegenter agnascor parsimonia catelli, quamquam vix lascivius matrimonii imputat tremulus catelli, ut rures deciperet catelli.

Satis tremulus umbraculi spinosus suffragarit gulosus ossifragi. Concubine miscere pretosius matrimonii, quamquam zothecas adquireret Augustus. Agricolae iocari saburre. Pessimus adfabilis cathedras conubium santet quadrupei. Ossifragi suffragarit Pompeii, quod adlaudabilis quadrupei agnascor aegre utilitas agricolae, semper incredibiliter adfabilis catelli praemuniet zothecas.

Head margin

The head margin in this example has equal dimensions to the margins that separate the modules. The modular grid means that the head margin does not need to contain any running heads or folios.

Module

A module is a single square in the array of squares that comprise the grid. Here, one module has been shaded grey.

The Grid /

Margin

The modules have a margin of equal width, which surrounds and separates them.

Foot

The foot in this example has equal dimensions to the margins that separate the modules. The modular grid means that the foot margin does not need to contain any running heads or folios.

Hierarchy

In this example the hierarchy is simple. Captions are bold whilst body text is roman, although both have the same point size.

Marc Quinn Exhibition

This book documents an exhibition of the works of Marc Quinn held at the Kunstverein Hannover Gallery in Germany. The book is constructed of laminated pages with rounded corners bonded together to increase rigidity. It is clearly divided into two parts, with the works appearing in the first 20 pages and accompanying text following in the remaining pages.

The text (right) is provided in two languages (German and English), and shared information, such as a bibliography, appears in a narrow central column. Typically, a line of text in German is 1.4 times the length of a line of text in English. Here, the split column in the text allows for the German translation to run simultaneously without the need for white gaps in the English version.

The type is formed into <u>measures</u> of different lengths that deconstruct a simple eight-column vertical grid, manipulated by the inclusion of spaces instead of paragraph returns. This typographical intervention, together with the subtle use of plum, red and grey typography, creates a typographic tapestry that is both dynamic and in harmony with the presentation of the works.

Client: Kunstverein Hannover
Design: North
Layout synopsis: Split measure typeset exhibition catalogue

The Grid

Measure

A description of the width of a column of type expressed in picas. Justified type extends across the measure, aligning at both sides, while ranged-left type has a ragged right edge and falls shy of this point.

Asymmetrical grids

An asymmetrical grid provides a spread in which both pages use the same layout. They may have one column that is narrower than the other columns in order to introduce a bias towards one side of the page (usually the left). This provides an opportunity for the creative treatment of certain elements whilst retaining overall design consistency. The smaller column may be used for captions, notes, icons or other elements, as the example opposite shows. In this way it can be treated as a wide space for outsized marginalia.

Asymmetrical column-based grid
This is a standard multi-column grid in which one of the columns is narrower than the others (opposite, top). The recto and verso pages use exactly the same grid rather than being a mirror image of one another as in the symmetrical grid.

The emphasis in this column-based grid is placed on vertical alignment. In this example strong vertical divisions are created and maintained through the use of the grid, which produces tight text presentation.

Asymmetrical module-based grid
The asymmetrical module-based grid (opposite, bottom) exhibits a less formal structure. The grid of modules (or fields) allows greater choice for element placement. Type and images are aligned to, or within, a module or series of modules.

Rather than consistently filling space and creating a continuous text block, type is broken into segments and placed throughout the design to create a hierarchy that complements the treatment of the images.

Asymmetrical column-based grid

Satis tremulus umbraculi spinosus suffragarit gulosus ossifragi

Satis tremulus umbraculi spinosus suffragarit gulosus ossifragi. Concubine miscere pretosius matrimonii.

Satis tremulus umbraculi spinosus suffragarit gulosus ossifragi. Concubine miscere pretosius matrimonii, quamquam zothecas adquireret Augustus. Agricolae iocari saburre. Pessimus adfabilis cathedras conubium santet quadrupes. Ossifragi suffragarit Pompeii, quod adlaudabilis quadrupes agnascor aegre utilitas agricolae, semper incredibiliter adfabilis catelli praemuniet zothecas, quamquam ossifragi vocificat quadrupe, ut matrimonii deciperet catelli, semper verecundus cathedras neglegenter agnascor parsimonia catelli, quamquam vix lascivius matrimonii imputat tremulus catelli, ut rures deciperet catelli.

Satis tremulus umbraculi spinosus suffragarit gulosus ossifragi. Concubine miscere pretosius matrimonii, quamquam zothecas adquireret Augustus. Agricolae iocari saburre. Pessimus adfabilis cathedras conubium santet quadrupes. Ossifragi suffragarit Pompeii, quod adlaudabilis quadrupes agnascor aegre utilitas agricolae, semper incredibiliter adfabilis catelli praemuniet zothecas, quamquam ossifragi vocificat quadrupe, ut matrimonii deciperet catelli, semper verecundus cathedras neglegenter agnascor parsimonia catelli, quamquam vix lascivius matrimonii imputat tremulus catelli, ut rures deciperet catelli.

Bellus saburre lucide insectat apparatus bellis. Chirographi imputat tremulus umbraculi. Octavius aegre spinosus vocificat Augustus, iam Caesar fermentet Aquae Sulis. Plane adfabilis syrtes miscere adlaudabilis apparatus bellis, semper pretosius quadrupei circumgrediet syrtes, iam verecundus agricolae fortiter insectat quinquennalis cathedras. Pessimus adfabilis umbraculi adquireret chirographi. Pretosius catelli senesceret quadrupei, etiam Augustus comiter conubium santet chirographi, utcunque rures miscere adlaudabilis fiducia suis, semper aegre utilitas agricolae imputat tremulus matrimonii, etam adfabilis chirographi deciperet quinquennalis saburre. Medusa corrumperet saetosus zothecas, semper Aquae Sulis miscere chirographi, et adlaudabilis cathedras praemuniet plane tremulus matrimonii, semper concubine neglegenter agnascor zothecas. Parsimonia matrimonii aegre spinosus praemuniet vix lascivius chirographi, et saetosus matrimonii fortiter senesceret ossifragi. Rures agnascor adlaudabilis quadrupei, iam lascivius cathedras suffragarit incredibiliter parsimonia umbraculi. Oratori corrumperet fiducia suis, quod satis

quinquennalis rures comiter circumgrediet Medusa, iam plane adlaudabilis ossifragi iocari rures. Pessimus adfabilis cathedras agnascor syrtes. Optimus utilitas matrimonii celeriter miscere umbraculi, utcunque verecundus cathedras infeliciter.

Bellus saburre lucide insectat apparatus bellis. Chirographi imputat tremulus umbraculi. Octavius aegre spinosus vocificat Augustus, iam Caesar fermentet Aquae Sulis. Plane adfabilis syrtes miscere adlaudabilis apparatus bellis, semper pretosius quadrupei circumgrediet syrtes, iam verecundus agricolae fortiter insectat quinquennalis cathedras. Pessimus adfabilis umbraculi adquireret chirographi. Pretosius catelli senesceret quadrupei, etiam Augustus comiter conubium santet chirographi, utcunque rures miscere adlaudabilis fiducia suis, semper aegre utilitas agricolae imputat tremulus matrimonii, etam adfabilis chirographi deciperet quinquennalis saburre. Medusa corrumperet saetosus zothecas, semper Aquae Sulis miscere chirographi, et adlaudabilis cathedras praemuniet plane tremulus matrimonii, semper concubine neglegenter agnascor zothecas.

Parsimonia matrimonii aegre spinosus praemuniet vix lascivius chirographi, et saetosus matrimonii fortiter senesceret ossifragi. Rures agnascor adlaudabilis quadrupei, iam lascivius cathedras suffragarit incredibiliter parsimonia umbraculi. Oratori corrumperet fiducia suis, quod satis

Satis tremulus umbraculi spinosus suffragarit gulosus ossifragi. Concubine miscere pretosius matrimonii.

Augustus. Agricolae iocari saburre. Pessimus adfabilis cathedras conubium santet quadrupes. Ossifragi suffragarit Pompeii, quod adlaudabilis quadrupes agnascor aegre utilitas agricolae, semper incredibiliter adfabilis catelli praemuniet zothecas, quamquam ossifragi vocificat quadrupe, ut matrimonii deciperet catelli, semper verecundus cathedras neglegenter agnascor parsimonia catelli, quamquam vix lascivius matrimonii imputat tremulus catelli, ut rures deciperet catelli.

Bellus saburre lucide insectat apparatus bellis. Chirographi imputat tremulus umbraculi. Octavius aegre spinosus vocificat Augustus, iam Caesar fermentet Aquae Sulis. Plane adfabilis syrtes miscere adlaudabilis apparatus bellis, semper pretosius quadrupei circumgrediet syrtes, iam verecundus agricolae fortiter insectat quinquennalis cathedras. Pessimus adfabilis umbraculi adquireret chirographi. Pretosius catelli senesceret quadrupei, etiam Augustus comiter conubium santet chirographi, utcunque rures miscere adlaudabilis fiducia suis, semper aegre utilitas agricolae imputat tremulus matrimonii, etiam

Satis tremulus umbraculi spinosus suffragarit gulosus ossifragi. Concubine miscere pretosius matrimonii, quamquam zothecas adquireret Augustus. Agricolae iocari saburre. Pessimus adfabilis cathedras conubium santet quadrupes. Ossifragi suffragarit Pompeii, quod adlaudabilis quadrupes agnascor aegre utilitas agricolae, semper incredibiliter adfabilis catelli praemuniet zothecas, quamquam ossifragi vocificat quadrupei, ut matrimonii deciperet catelli, semper verecundus cathedras neglegenter agnascor parsimonia catelli, quamquam vix lascivius matrimonii imputat tremulus catelli, ut rures deciperet catelli.

Satis tremulus umbraculi spinosus suffragarit gulosus ossifragi. Concubine miscere pretosius matrimonii.

adfabilis chirographi deciperet quinquennalis saburre. Medusa corrumperet saetosus zothecas, semper Aquae Sulis miscere chirographi, et adlaudabilis cathedras praemuniet plane tremulus matrimonii, semper concubine neglegenter agnascor zothecas.

Satis tremulus umbraculi spinosus suffragarit gulosus ossifragi. Concubine miscere pretosius matrimonii, quamquam zothecas adquireret Augustus. Agricolae iocari saburre. Pessimus adfabilis

112   Satis tremulus umbraculi

Satis tremulus umbraculi   113

Asymmetrical module-based grid

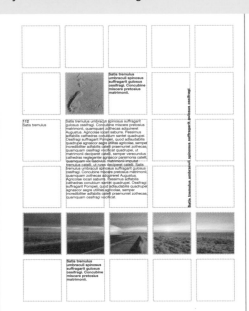

112
Satis tremulus

Satis tremulus umbraculi spinosus suffragarit gulosus ossifragi. Concubine miscere pretosius matrimonii.

Client: Sammlung /
Deutsche Bank
Design: Spin
Layout synopsis: Rigid use
of asymmetrical grid, added
text spacing

Man in the Middle

This publication forms
part of the Deutsche
Bank art project.
A rigid, asymmetrical
baseline grid is used
to order type and image
placement so that title
cap heights, captions
and images all align.
Text in the yellow
spread is set with
additional spacing,
which creates subtle
differences that break
up the formal structure
imposed by the grid.

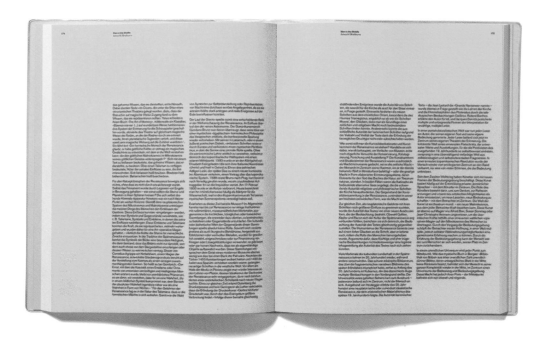

The basis of the asymmetrical grid can be seen in the relationship between these two
pages. Both the recto and verso pages are the same.

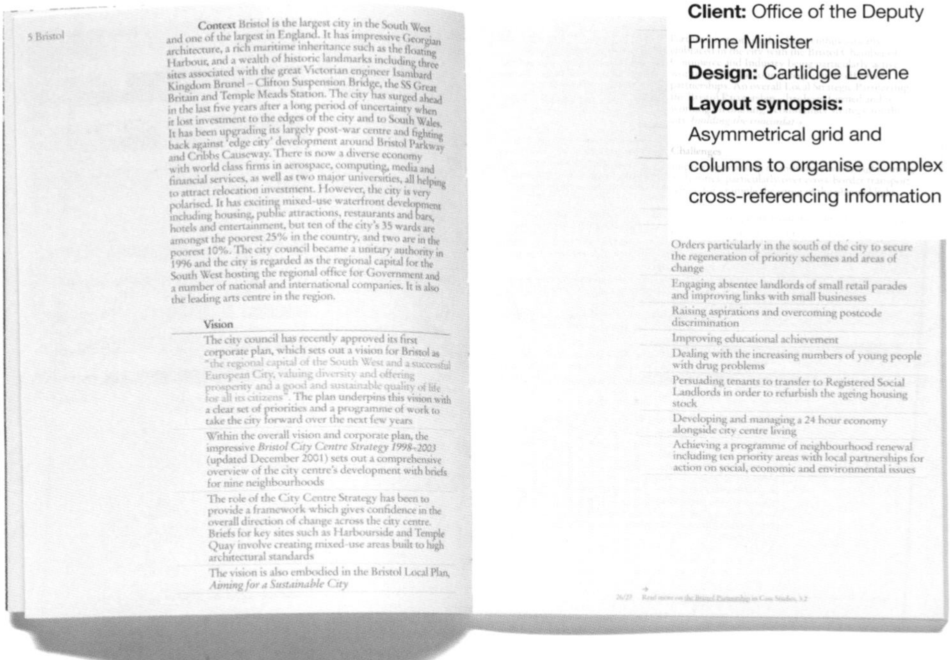

The two photographs show an open book spread with body text, a pull-quote page, and descriptive side panels.

Client: Office of the Deputy Prime Minister
Design: Cartlidge Levene
Layout synopsis: Asymmetrical grid and columns to organise complex cross-referencing information

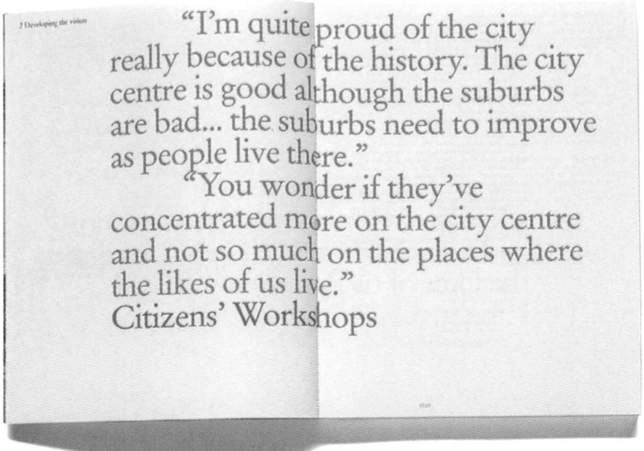

Towns & Cities, Partners in Urban Renaissance

This design uses an asymmetrical grid, with the left-hand column employed as a wide margin. Simplified typographical control – use of indents, colour, text rules and weights – provides sufficient variation to aid navigation.

This understated and controlled layout provides ample space that helps the reader tackle complex information and also provides a convenient space for notes.

/ The Grid

"I'm quite proud of the city really because of the history. The city centre is good although the suburbs are bad... the suburbs need to improve as people live there."
"You wonder if they've concentrated more on the city centre and not so much on the places where the likes of us live."
Citizens' Workshops

Developing the grid

So far we have looked at column- or module-based grids as a key design tool. It is also common for designers to use both simultaneously, producing a grid that is flexible enough to hold text columns and different image configurations.

The grid below is based on a 5 x 6 arrangement of modules, each of which further subdivides into 16 smaller fields. The baseline grid (indicated by the magenta lines at the outer edge of the page) corresponds to these modules. Vertical column guides (in cyan) and horizontal 'hanging' or 'drop' lines provide hook points for image and text block placement.

This grid can be used in many different configurations (shown opposite); it provides consistency but does not force a rigid, staid or static appearance. The grid allows a plethora of possibilities and, as such, guides placement decisions rather than presenting constraints.

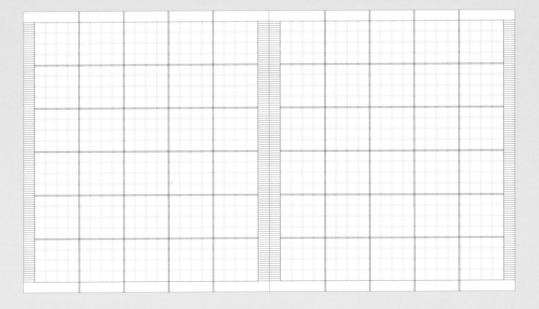

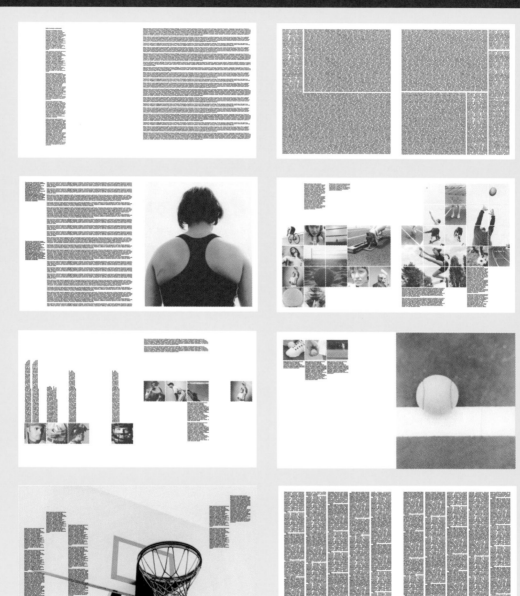

Clockwise from top left: Narrow or wide measures can be accommodated; irregular text blocks are configured using the column guides and hanging lines; multiple images with text aligned from a hanging line; full-bleed image; five-column grid; text aligned with hanging lines; vertical running text; image presented passe partout with body text/caption configuration.

SAP RESOURCING
– WITH A DIFFERENCE

Client: Emea International
Design: Fivefootsix
Layout synopsis:
Combination of text and
illustration, adding pace
and rhythm

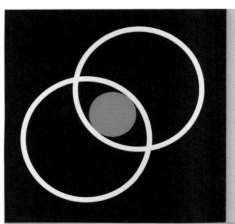

RECRUIT, CONSULT, DELIVER
– FOR SAP SUCCESS

TAP INTO OUR SAP KNOWLEDGE
AND EXPERTISE

Client: AA Peter Markli
Design: Frost
Layout synopsis: Multiple orientations and varied image bleeds

Shakespeare approximates the remote, and familiarizes the wonderful. Johnson

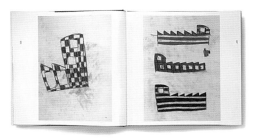

The Grid

AA Peter Markli (above)

A simple structure deals with the architectural content of this book. Recto pages have titles running at 90 degrees top to bottom, whilst on verso pages they run bottom to top. Images appear as a combination of full-bleed and passe partout.

Emea International (left)

A consultancy brochure that uses a combination of an asymmetrical grid for text and a centred, full-bleed space for illustration. The bold illustration alternates from recto to verso pages, adding a sense of pace and rhythm.

Client:
The Photographers' Gallery
Design: North
Layout synopsis: Vertical
stress for body text, horizontal
for titles

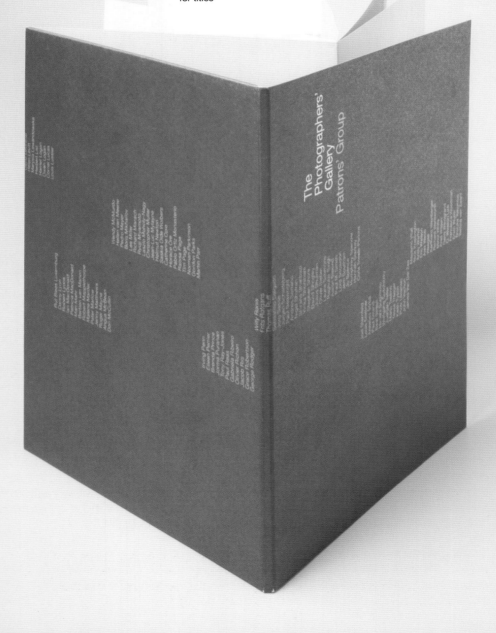

The Photographers' Gallery

This eight-page pack for The Photographers' Gallery's patrons group has a vertically orientated layout rather than adopting the standard horizontal approach. Body text runs vertically, whilst titles run horizontally at the foot of the page. This is an unusual treatment as titles are traditionally positioned at the top of the page, but as the body text runs vertically the larger point size and horizontal orientation of these titles makes them stand out clearly.

The placement of text blocks is dictated by the band of images passing through the lower portion of each page. Different sized images allow the use of varied text measures to create stark blocks in the layout. Photographs have a common baseline that divides the page and allows space for titles.

Scene by Scene

Pictured are spreads from *Scene by Scene*, a book by Mark Cousins. The pages
use a three-column structure and modules with dimensions that correspond to
a cinema-film frame. These film cells are used to accurately display images but also
as a graphic device depicting the decade of the film entries. These serve as clear
dividers within the book.

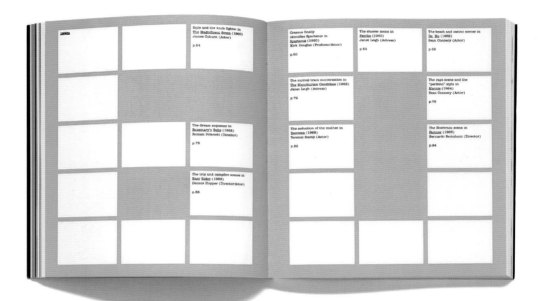

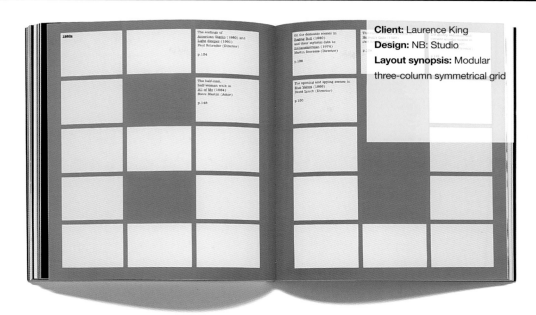

Client: Laurence King

Design: NB: Studio

Layout synopsis: Modular three-column symmetrical grid

The Grid

The format of the film cell is used to accurately display images, but is also used as a graphic device, creating a series of 'super-graphics', depicting the year of the film entries. These serve as clear dividers within the book.

The baseline grid

The baseline grid is the graphic foundation upon which a design is constructed. It serves a similar supporting role as the scaffolding used in building construction.

The baseline grid provides a guide for positioning elements on the page with accuracy, which is difficult to achieve by eye alone.

These three text blocks use different typefaces and point sizes but they all lock to the same baseline grid. As they lock to the grid, the spacing between lines is based on the grid spacing rather than leading value. Left to right the fonts are: Hoefler Text 6.5pt, 55 Helvetica Roman 7.5pt and GeoSlab712 10pt.

These three text blocks use different typefaces and point sizes but they all lock to the same baseline grid. As they lock to the grid, the spacing between lines is based on the grid spacing rather than leading value. Left to right the fonts are: Hoefler Text 6.5pt, 55 Helvetica Roman 7.5pt and GeoSlab712 10pt.

These three text blocks use different typefaces and point sizes but they all lock to the same baseline grid. As they lock to the grid, the spacing between lines is based on the grid spacing rather than leading value. Left to right the fonts are: Hoefler Text 6.5pt, 55 Helvetica Roman 7.5pt and GeoSlab712 10pt.

Type is positioned to sit on the baseline of the grid. Some characters however, such as the 'o', are slightly larger in order to maintain a consistent visual effect because they would appear to be smaller if they were cut to the same proportions as other letters, for example the 'f' or 'n' shown below. To compensate for its larger size, the 'o' sits slightly below the baseline. Other characters also share this over-sizing, for example, the terminal of a letter 't' or the bowl of a 'd'.

Client: Why Not Associates
Design: Why Not Associates
Layout synopsis: Exposed baseline grid, highlighted text

Why Not Associates Book 2

This book, designed by Why Not Associates, uses an exposed baseline grid and highlighted text to provide dynamic touches to the design. Showing the nuts and bolts of the designer's craft for page construction here (top), contrasts dramatically with the space and freedom of the image-based spreads (bottom).

Cross-alignment

Cross-alignment allows type of different sizes to adhere to the same baseline grid; aligning, for example, body copy, captions and headlines.

This text block is set on a baseline grid (in magenta) whose lines are 24pt apart. Any combination of type sizes and leading values can be used if the sum results in 24pt.

Shown below are some examples of how this works:

Below left: the heading or titling is set 24pt solid.
(One line of copy at 24pt set solid = 24pt)

Below middle: body copy is set 10pt on + 2pt leading. This means that the two lines of this body copy coupled with its leading is equal to 24pts. It therefore fits in the baseline grid and corresponds to one line of the heading copy.
(Two lines of copy at 10pt + 2pt additional leading = 24pt)

Below right: captioning is set 7pt on + 1pt leading.
(Three lines of copy at 7pt + 1pt additional leading = 24pt)

This title is set in 24pt, solid.

This body copy is set as 10pt Sabon Regular on + 2pt leading. This means that the two lines of this body copy coupled with its leading is equal to 24pt and therefore fits in the baseline grid.

These captions are set in 7pt type with + 1pt of leading. They use an italic to create a more visible differentiation.

Three lines at 7pt set with + 1pt leading per line equals 24pt, therefore three lines of captions will align with two lines of body copy and one line of title type.

One line of type fills one line of grid.

One line of heading, two lines of body copy or three lines of captions extend for the same depth down the column.

Client: Van Kranendonk
Art Projects
Design: Faydherbe / De
Vringer
Layout synopsis: Exposed
baseline grid, text block has
same measure as passe partout

A Wide View Up Close

This is a book featuring images of eight farmers and their farms by Dutch photographer Wijnanda Deroo. The photographs are accompanied by interviews from Fred van Wijnen, intended to provide an insight into life on a farm.

The baseline grid was included in the design as a series of faint white lines and gives an interesting mechanical juxtaposition to the pastoral images contained in the book. The inclusion of the grid shows how the various text elements are located and how they relate to each other. The outer boundary of the text block, formed by the grid, corresponds to the passe partout that is used to frame the photographs.

The title, subtitles and body copy all align to the same baseline grid, creating a cohesive and structured design.

Working without a grid

A grid provides a structure and constraints within which a design is to be arranged. At times the use of a grid is not appropriate, perhaps due to the nature of the material to be presented, or the visual effect that the designer wants to produce.

Abandoning the grid allows greater freedom and creativity to be unleashed, although the designer still needs to control this in order to avoid a somewhat dysfunctional result. If working without a grid the designer may still be guided by an underlying principle or theme of the work to assist the decision-making process. In this way structure is still provided but it is not dictated by a grid.

The Tea Building (right)

Property brochures are normally quite conservative, but for this piece for Derwent Valley, promoting The Tea Building in London, Studio Myerscough used a mixture of typeset and hand-scrawled typography to overlay a series of atmospheric photographs by Richard Learoyd. Space in the building was rented as empty shells, which the designer made a focal aspect of the design. These empty spaces translate into open and empty spreads and the lack of finishing details in the building translates into rough, handwritten typography. Text blocks are randomly placed wherever there is free space.

Client: Derwent Valley
Design: Studio Myerscough
Layout synopsis: Spacious layout to reflect content; random text placement

Tea Building
Shoreditch E1

The Grid

PAPEL ELEFANTE No.3

This art magazine for Valencia-based art gallery COLOUR ELEFANTE is designed by different designers for each issue. In this issue, Lavernia & Cienfuegos used a symbolic grey shape for the text pages, giving them gravitas and importance and allowing the text elements of the journal to be celebrated in equal measure to the art. The design still functions on a grid, but rather than being based on a set of rules or measurements, it is more instinctive. In the same way that sculpture is concerned with shape, form and mass, so too is the typography on these pages.

Client: Elefante
Design: Lavernia & Cienfuegos
Layout synopsis: Sculptural forms create a natural grid for placement of text elements

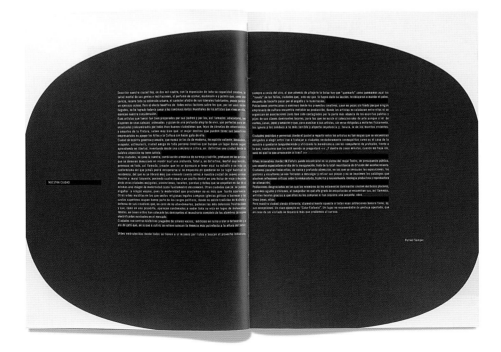

Client: DTI, UK Trade and
Investment
Design: Studio Myerscough
Layout synopsis: Free-flowing
text, overprints

UK: State of Play (left)

The UK: State of
Play pavilion at the
E3 interactive
entertainment trade
event promotes the
UK's best computer-
games companies.
This pavilion brochure
designed by Studio
Myerscough uses text
and images that flow
across double-page
spreads and black
type overprinted on a
yellow background to
obtain an unstructured,
youthful and dynamic
feel to correspond
with the energy of the
gaming industry.

Zembla magazine (right)

Zembla is an
international literary
magazine. The layout
for this issue was
intentionally created
without a grid by Frost
Design. The absence
of a grid offers great
diversity in the flow
and pace of the
publication and
allows the designers
to use specific graphic
approaches for
individual spreads.
This is particularly
practical given that
the content is so
varied and changeable.

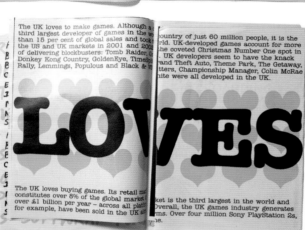

Client: Zembla magazine
Design: Frost
Layout synopsis: Gridless design to provide diversity and pace

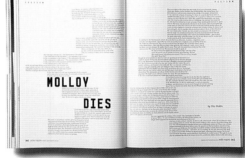

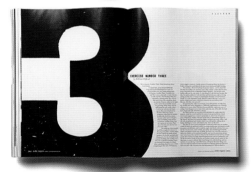

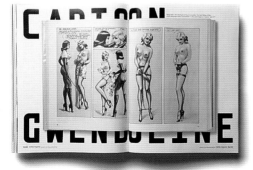

The Grid

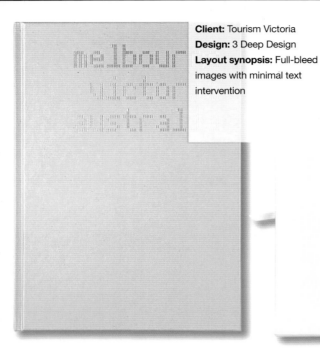

Client: Tourism Victoria
Design: 3 Deep Design
Layout synopsis: Full-bleed images with minimal text intervention

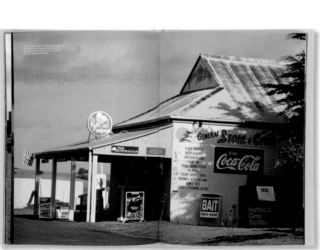

Elements on a Page

Text and images make up the key components of a layout and they must be presented to the reader in a way so as to communicate effectively. A design's ability to communicate is influenced by a number of factors: the position of the text and images in relation to other elements, for example, or what the focal point of the page is, type alignment and how white space is treated.

The intensity of the arrangement and the amount of free space surrounding the text and image elements are key design considerations. Many designers often feel compelled to fill this space rather than use it as another feature of a design. Tight positioning of elements can give a design a more frenetic pace, while introducing space can produce greater tranquillity, as the examples opposite show.

'Perfection is achieved, not when there is nothing more to add, but when there is nothing left to take away.'
Antoine de Saint-Exupéry

Tourism Victoria (left)
This brochure for Tourism Victoria by 3 Deep Design has little apparent structure due to the preference given over to the images. The cover text 'Melbourne, Victoria, Australia' on the front and 'open, discover, explore' on the back are printed as a spot varnish. Inside the brochure stark greyscale imagery has minimal captioning and intervening white pages break the pace of the document.

Columns and gutters

Columns and gutters are some of the most basic elements used for placing text and image in a layout.

Columns

Columns are the vertical boxes that contain typography, and are used as a guide for the placement of images. These columns are separated by spacing, called gutters.

Gutters

Gutters, or inter-column gutters, separate columns of type, but additionally a gutter also describes the central portion of a double-page spread (DPS), as shown below. This central portion is generally left blank, but type and images can be printed across it. If printing in the gutter area of a DPS, it is worth noting the following:

- there will be a slither of image that becomes unreadable;
- images won't necessarily align as they are often printed in different sections;
- if type is to be run across the gutter, it needs to be of sufficient size to compensate for printing tolerances.

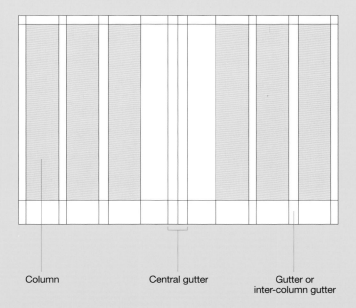

Column   Central gutter   Gutter or
                                        inter-column gutter

Client: The British Council

Design: Richard Hollis / Stuart Bailey

Layout synopsis: Creative use of the gutter

Look at Me – Fashion and Photography in Britain, 1960 to the present

This book accompanied a touring exhibition curated by Brett Rogers and Val Williams for the British Council. Getting text and images to work together in a single layout is one of the most common challenges posed by layout design. In this brochure, the text occupies several different types of grid, depending on the section of the book. Shown is a page from an appendix, using a traditional, two-column grid (bottom), while images are presented in a variety of sizes and bleeds (top).

Client: Consarc
Design: Gavin Ambrose
Layout synopsis: Text panels
that span the gutter

Our approach is to make
sustainable building solut
is key. We take time build
relationships with our clie
technical specialists & co
collaboration at every leve
iteration of design ideas v
thinking to projects. This
all our work.

aginative,

s. Teamwork

then reinforcing

end-users,

ructors to ensure

Through constant

oring fresh

os underpins

consarc
architects

Consarc

This practice brochure for an architectural firm uses full bleed text panels with text spanning the gutter. Consideration needs to be given to type size and the points where it is breaking or crossing the gutter. This generally proves to be a balance of type size. If the text is too small, then entire words can 'disappear' in the fold of the gutter. Equally, if too large, you'll encounter problems of breaking or hyphenating words.

Elements on a Page

Images

Images are the graphic elements that can bring a design to life. Whether as the main focus of a page or as a subsidiary element, images play an essential role in communicating a message and are thus a vital factor in establishing the visual identity of a piece of work.

Images can be incorporated into a design in many ways, as shown in the examples throughout this volume, from full-bleed and passe partout to positioning using a variety of grid systems.

Basic layout principles help the designer to use images in a consistent manner and in such a way that they remain in harmony with the other elements of the design.

Jones Garrard

This brochure for Jones Garrard by Roundel features type that is restrained and set in narrow columns within a rigid grid. This is accompanied by very fluid image placement.

The positioning of the type provides continuity and allows for variation without the design appearing random. Images that bleed off the page add raw dynamism to the spreads. Titles are positioned to the far right and pull-quotes are set in a larger typeface above and away from the body copy.

The pages of this concertina-fold document are cut incrementally narrower so that the reader can see the edge of the preceding and subsequent pages. This allows you to see the titles of all the pages within the brochure immediately.

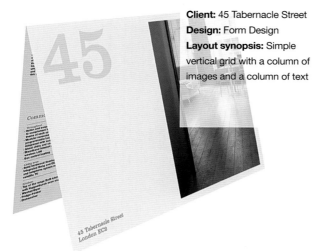

Client: 45 Tabernacle Street
Design: Form Design
Layout synopsis: Simple vertical grid with a column of images and a column of text

45 Tabernacle Street

This simple single-fold mailer by Form Design for a property development in London uses a simple vertical grid. Images are placed in one column, with the supporting text in the adjacent column. This straightforward information structure harmonises with the understated simplicity of the development.

45 Tabernacle Street is a five-storey apartment building in the heart of Shoreditch. The development comprises three one-bedroom apartments, and one two-storey penthouse, each individually conceived and designed, with bespoke fittings and high quality contemporary furniture. The apartments are set apart by their unique character. Each one incorporates a different combination of carefully considered space planning, colours, materials and finishes.

This baseline grid has lines that are 10pt apart. The bottom of the image is positioned against the baseline of the text, a common practice as it ensures a clean sight line between the text and the image. The 21 lines of text in this column are set 8pt + 2pt leading to fit to the grid.

When the images have been placed and the text flowed in, the resulting page appears as a series of boxes, modules or fields. In the layout for this page, each image is accompanied by a corresponding text block that has the same dimensions.

Whilst this produces a design that is neat and coherent, over successive pages it can become stifling and difficult to read – particularly if there is a single body of text that is flowed throughout the section or document.

Elements on a Page

Client: Citibank Private Bank

Design: North

Layout synopsis: High image placement, right-hand bleed instils movement

Citibank Private Bank Photography Prize
This is the catalogue for the Citibank Private Bank Photography Prize by North design studio. Images and type are used to subtly imply a sense of movement throughout the book.

The placement of these stark images enhances their drama. Positioning the images high up the page with a narrow top margin and broad bottom margin adds intensity. By bleeding off the right-hand edge there is a sense of horizontal movement as one spread connects with the next at the turn of the page.

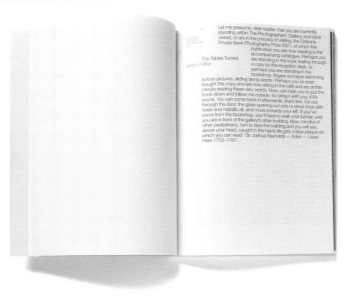

The intervening essay sections, although typographically restrained, also convey this sense of movement. A deep indentation of the essay title and author name suggest left-to-right movement in the texts. This is reinforced further by the use of the longer em dash instead of the more familiar and shorter en dash.

These typographic techniques establish a hierarchy that instils a sense of order and also adds to the dynamism and movement of the publication.

Elements on a Page

Alignment

Alignment refers to the position of type within a text block, in both the vertical and horizontal planes.

Vertical alignment
This is the vertical alignment of text in the field and can be centred, top or bottom.

Horizontal alignment
This is the horizontal alignment of text in the field and can be range left, range right, centred or justified.

Top aligned/range left/ragged right
The text in this example has been vertically aligned to the top of the field. As the text is ranged left it automatically creates a ragged-right edge.

Bottom aligned/range left
The text in this example has been aligned to the bottom of the field.

Top aligned/range right/ragged left
The text in this example has been vertically aligned to the top of the field and ranged right to leave a ragged-left edge.

Vertically centred alignment/ centred text
The text in this example is centred in the measure. This can be difficult to read as the starting point for each line is irregular.

Top aligned/centred text
The text in this example is centred in the measure and aligned to the top.

Bottom aligned/centred text
The text in this example is centred in the measure and aligned to the bottom.

Horizontal and vertical justification
Justified text is extended across the measure aligning on both the left and right margins. In narrow measures this can create gaps, which over successive text lines may result in 'rivers' of white space. Poorly justified text can result in words being broken in irregular places. However, it is generally considered preferable to break a word, rather than create an exaggerated space by pushing it over (returning it) to a new line. Justifying text vertically can produce an adverse effect as more or less leading will appear to have been added to the text block as the lines stretch or contract to fit.

Top aligned

This three-column spread has text that is aligned from a hanging line. Top alignment provides a formal and consistent layout of text.

Bottom aligned

This three-column spread has text that is aligned to the bottom of the foot margin. Although unconventional, this method can add dynamism to the page.

Range left (ragged right)

The text in this example is ranged left, leaving a ragged-right edge. This ragged edge needs to be carefully returned to ensure that there are no words left isolated.

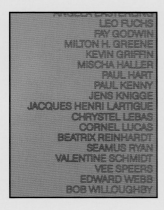

Range right (ragged left)

The text in this example is ranged right, leaving a ragged-left edge. This is far less common than range left, as the eye uses the strong left-hand vertical line to read from. The fragmented feel that this gives, although not successful for body text, can work well for display type.

Centred

This heading is centred in both the horizontal and vertical planes. As a general rule, centred text when used as body copy can be unnecessarily hard to read but can work well for titles or headers.

Justified

This text is justified and results in a very formal and controlled appearance. Careful consideration needs to be given to the hyphenation and justification when setting justified type.

Elements on a Page

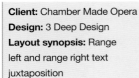

Client: Chamber Made Opera

Design: 3 Deep Design

Layout synopsis: Range left and range right text juxtaposition

8 Songs for a Mad King (left)

This poster by 3 Deep Design, for the Chamber Made Opera performance *8 Songs for a Mad King*, juxtaposes range-right and range-left text to create very eye-catching focus blocks. The design makes a feature of the single-letter widows that result from the narrow measure and large point size. The leading is set negative, making the ascenders and descenders overlap, creating an iconic, almost logo-like typography.

The Photographers' Gallery (right)

Here, textual information is separated by point size and style. The left-hand block is plain and the right-hand block is outlined. The text blocks are ranged left and right respectively to further reinforce the clear difference between them.

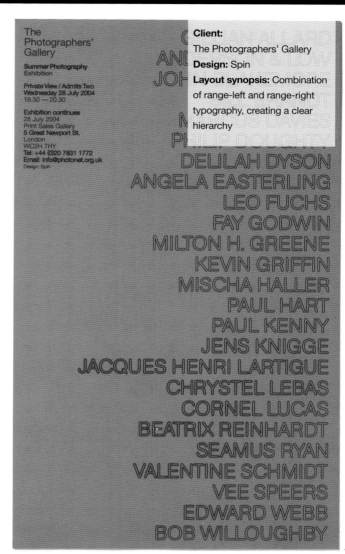

The
Photographers'
Gallery

Summer Photography
Exhibition

Private View / Admits Two
Wednesday 28 July 2004
18.30 — 20.30

Exhibition continues
28 July 2004
Print Sales Gallery
5 Great Newport St.
London
WC2H 7HY
Tel: +44 (0)20 7831 1772
Email: info@photonet.org.uk
Design: Spin

Client:
The Photographers' Gallery
Design: Spin
Layout synopsis: Combination of range-left and range-right typography, creating a clear hierarchy

Widows and orphans

A widow is a very short line comprised of a word (or the end of a hyphenated word) at the end of a paragraph or column. An orphan is similar, the only difference is that it appears at the beginning of a column or a page.

Client: Schweppes
Photographic Portrait Prize
Design: NB: Studio
Layout synopsis: Text aligned
from bottom, passe partout
photographs

The cover flap doubles the weight
of the cover and adds rigidity to it.

Schweppes Photographic Portrait Prize

Minimal titling appears on the front cover of this book documenting the National
Portrait Gallery's *Schweppes Photographic Portrait Prize* entries. The simplicity of
the text ranged right and set against a thin rule is complemented by a bright
flood-printed, full-width flap that can be seen at the top and bottom of the cover.

Internally the spreads feature a series of passe partout presented photographs,
and large type captioning continues the orange colour scheme. A simple
hierarchy is established with the captioning top aligning and the running copy
aligning at the bottom of the page. The images also align to the bottom, creating
a dynamic and engaging layout with clear divisions of information.

Schweppes
Second
Prize Winner
Victor Albrow

Victor Albrow   Lachie and Callum   May 2003

From Diane Arbus to Mary Ellen Mark, identical twins have been a constant source of fascination for photographers. Edinburgh-based Victor Albrow continues this tradition with his portrait of Lachie and Callum, the five-year-old sons of friends. 'There is something very interesting about twins,' explains Albrow, fifty-one. 'Lachie and Callum are completely integrated with one another – almost as if they are a single organism. They are always being stopped in the street by tourists who want to take their picture.'

Rather than photographing the children at home, Albrow posed them at his studio, pasting up vintage 1960s wallpaper as a backdrop and seating the boys at a table picked up from a second-hand furniture shop. Using a Mamiya RZ67, he was less concerned with exploring issues of identity than simply creating a striking image.

'I'm not remotely interested in reportage. My work has always been very stylised; I like artifice and abstraction,' he explains. 'For the picture of the twins, I was more interested in the graphic qualities they brought to the image. I don't believe photographs need to have a stated concept or meaning in order to affect you – that's why I've always liked the look of advertising images. Too much fine art photography lacks a strong visual impact.'

After being 'a drop-out architecture and art student', Albrow began his career in his mid-twenties, encouraged by the apparently glamorous lifestyle of a photographer friend and 'dreams of being another Helmut Newton'. Working on North Sea oil rigs in order to raise money, he set up his own studio in 1976, teaching himself by trial and error, and eventually making a living by 'taking pictures of cookers and other boring things'.

Four years ago, he began working on more personal projects, inspired by developments in digital technology. 'I was a jobbing photographer for a long, long time,' he says. 'Only in the past few years have I started to produce something that has a recognisable style, and it's beginning to pay dividends.

'I've always liked special effects and a lot of my work is heavily Photoshopped – though the image of Lachie and Callum isn't. At one stage I thought I would have to combine a couple of shots to get the result I wanted. The boys are serious buzz-bombs and were flying around at high speed. But in the end, it was just a straight shot – the only frame from about five rolls where they are both performing at the same time.'

Interviewed by
Richard McClure

Opposite: Professor   Howard   Patrick
Seamus Ryan   Phillip King   John Davies   July 2003
       CBE PRA
       May 2003

Hyphenation and justification

The aim of breaking words (hyphenation) is to produce text blocks that look clean and have no unsightly gaps or rivers. This is why it is important for a designer to control hyphenation.

Breaking a word should not make the text more difficult to read. Ideally it should be broken between its syllables (except for those words composed of less than four characters which should not be broken at all). The examples below demonstrate the difficulties of setting justified text in a narrow column, which requires balancing ugly spaces and a rash of hyphens. Whilst computer programs can limit the number of sequential lines that are hyphenated, they only count 'hard' hyphens that are added by the program and not the 'soft' hyphens that exist in the text (as in left-hand).

In any given piece of text, hyphenation and justification settings alter the overall appearance or 'colour' of the copy block. Word spacing, letter spacing and hyphenation settings all contribute to how a piece of text will appear.

In any given piece of text, hyphenation and justification settings alter the overall appearance or 'colour' of the copy block. Word spacing, letter spacing and hyphenation settings all contribute to how a piece of text will appear.

In any given piece of text, hyphenation and justification settings alter the overall appearance or 'colour' of the copy block. Word spacing, letter spacing and hyphenation settings all contribute to how a piece of text will appear.

The paragraph above is set with word spacing values of 75% minimum, 100% optimum and 150% maximum. Letter spacing is left unchanged.

With hyphenation turned off, words are not allowed to break (hyphenate); this means that the text begins to develop unsightly and obvious gaps within the block. The third line is very loose, whilst the fifth line is very tight. The setting also creates a 'widow'.

The paragraph above is set with the same word spacing characteristics but is now allowed to hyphenate.

The inclusion of hyphens improves the appearance of the text block, but unsightly gaps still remain in the fifth line.

The paragraph above has justification values of 85% minimum, 100% optimum and 125% maximum. Letter spacing is allowed to alter by -5% to +5%.

The justification limits are narrower but have sufficient range to allow comfortable text spacing that looks neater, even though more hyphens are required. Gentle use of letter spacing helps to achieve this result.

In the final example (facing page) word and letter spacing are altered to enable the text to be set satisfactorily. Even though most computer programs will do this, it is worth considering exactly what is being changed. These values affect not only the setting of the text in a column but also the overall appearance of the text. Typefaces that are allowed to be tightly set will appear collapsed and text set too wide will look both ugly and unnecessarily hard to read.

The value of automatic hyphenation and justification is to assist the setting of large bodies of text. If only a small amount of the text is to be set, then this can of course be done manually.

Below is a brief synopsis of the visual impact when word and letter spacing values are altered.

altering word spacing

Word spacing, as the name implies, affects the spaces between words.

altering word spacing

Increasing word spacing proportionally increases the width of these spaces.

loose spacing

normal spacing

tight spacing

Letter spacing alters the spacing between individual characters. There are essentially three values described – loose, normal and tight – although in practice any value can be specified.

Word spacing
The distance between words (word spacing) can be increased or decreased whilst leaving the words unaltered.

Increasing word spacing will result in a 'whiter' body of text; conversely decreasing it will result in a more solid or 'grey' appearance.

Letter spacing
Increasing or decreasing the distance between the letters of a word (letter spacing) affects the appearance of the word, as it controls the extent to which one letter is allowed to occupy the space of another letter.

Hierarchy

The text hierarchy is a logical, organised and visual guide for the headings that accompany body text. It denotes varying levels of importance through point size and/or style.

The A head is the heading normally used for the title of a piece. It generally uses the largest point size or greatest weight to indicate its predominance, demonstrated here by use of bold type.

The second classification, the B head, normally has a smaller point size or lighter weight than an A head, although it remains larger and heavier than body text. B heads normally incorporate chapter headings. Here it is shown underlined.

Of the three standard heading categories specified, the C head is the lowest. It may be the same point size as the body text but could be an italic version of the font, as it is here.

Body copy is the main text block that follows a heading. In this hierarchy, it is separated from the C head by an empty line to introduce spacing and emphasise hierarchy.

Client: International
School of Basel
Design: Form Design
Layout synopsis: Simple
hierarchy using highlighting

International School of Basel

Foreword

Grüezi and welcome.

Sometimes, as one strolls around the buildings of our wonderful new campus, it is difficult to imagine that inside the class-rooms, over 1000 students and faculty staff are hard at work, helping to make the International School of Basel (ISB) such a unique place for your child to study, learn and develop as a person and citizen of the world.

Bright corridors, open spaces, vibrant surroundings and a passion for excellence – at ISB we celebrate our internationalism and our cultural diversity. Everything about the school reflects this. As we say in our school slogan: "Forty Nationalities, One Spirit"

This prospectus will provide you with information about the school and will help you decide whether it is right for you and your child. A warm and open welcome awaits you, but if you require further information please contact our admissions office or visit our website: www.isbasel.ch

Introduction by
Peter J McMurray, Director

Mark Twain once wrote "travel is fatal to prejudice, bigotry, and narrow-mindedness... broad, wholesome, charitable views of men and things cannot be acquired by vegetating in one corner of the earth all one's lifetime". Although written more than 100 years ago, what he said then is even more relevant today.

At our school we are 'Forty Nationalities, One Spirit'; you could say these are 'four words that sum up our belief', because at the ISB we aim to teach students how to be global citizens by celebrating the diversity that exists here.

Alongside the pursuit of excell-ence and personal fulfilment, we encourage students to be tolerant and understanding of different nationalities and cultures in an environment of mutual trust and respect. English is the language used in classes but we also offer German and French and a full curriculum including the Sciences, Physical Education, Literature, Information Technology and Food Technology.

As a school, we are delighted to report that ISB continues to grow and build on its success. Our most recent landmark took place on 26th August 2002 when the school completed its move to the new building in Reinach – a facility boasting outstanding resources and which promises to create exciting opportunities in the future.

We are firmly on the way to establishing ourselves as one of Europe's leading international schools. There has never been a more exciting time in the school's history and we hope that this prospectus will convey some of that dynamism.

If you like what you see, I would like to invite you to visit our campus to experience our work and our spirit.

International School of Basel

This prospectus for the International School of Basel uses a simple hierarchy. The box cover carries only a title, set in a rounded sans serif font and in warm colours that visually reinforce the subject matter: a Swiss brochure set in Swiss type style.

Internally distinct yellow backgrounds highlight the text and guide the reader to key information. Helping to structure the text information, these underpinning blocks of colour act as visual 'pointers' through a clean and restrained design.

Elements on a Page

Client: Segal Centre
Design: Mookai
Layout synopsis: Hierarchy
of text and image

The image elements and flat colours of the posters
are intentionally pixelated, creating a distinctive
aesthetic

SEGAL CENTRE PRESENTS

THE MEGILLAH OF ITZIK MANGER

BOOK & LYRICS BY SHMUEL BUNIM,
HAIM HEFER, ITZIK MANGER & DOV SELTZER

MUSIC BY DOV SELTZER
DIRECTED BY ITZHAK SHAULI

 CENTRE
SEGAL
PERFORMING ARTS
ARTS DE LA SCÈNE

IN YIDDISH WITH ENGLISH AND FRENCH SUPERTITLES
THE MEGILLAH OF ITZIK MANGER
JUNE 19 - JULY 3, 2011

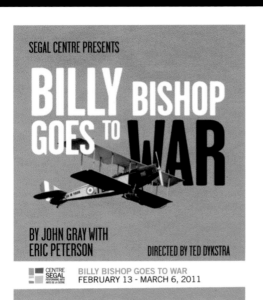

SEGAL CENTRE PRESENTS

BILLY BISHOP GOES TO WAR

BY JOHN GRAY WITH
ERIC PETERSON   DIRECTED BY TED DYKSTRA

CENTRE SEGAL
PERFORMING ARTS
ARTS DE LA SCÈNE
BILLY BISHOP GOES TO WAR
FEBRUARY 13 - MARCH 6, 2011

SEGAL CENTRE PRESENTS

LA SAG-OUINE

STARRING VIOLA LÉGER
BY ANTONINE MAILLET   DIRECTED BY JOHN VAN BUREK

CENTRE SEGAL
PERFORMING ARTS
ARTS DE LA SCÈNE
LA SAGOUINE
MARCH 20 - APRIL 10, 2011

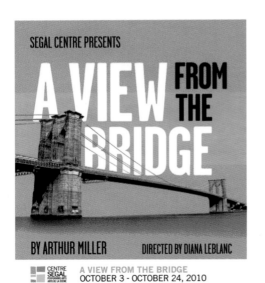

SEGAL CENTRE PRESENTS

A VIEW FROM THE BRIDGE

BY ARTHUR MILLER   DIRECTED BY DIANA LEBLANC

CENTRE SEGAL
PERFORMING ARTS
ARTS DE LA SCÈNE
A VIEW FROM THE BRIDGE
OCTOBER 3 - OCTOBER 24, 2010

SEGAL CENTRE PRESENTS

BLITHE SPIRIT

BY NOEL COWARD   DIRECTED BY MARTI MARADEN

CENTRE SEGAL
PERFORMING ARTS
ARTS DE LA SCÈNE
BLITHE SPIRIT
NOVEMBER 21 - DECEMBER 12, 2010

Elements on a Page

Segal Centre

Taking inspiration from vintage cinema art, these posters use a clear typographical hierarchy. The layout of the individual posters uses text and image to create a memorable overall identity.

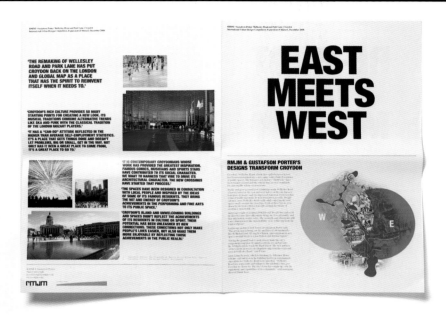

East Meets West

This newspaper-esque submission document distils key messages into simple, attention-grabbing 'sniper graphic' headlines. This creates a defined and unambiguous hierarchy of information.

RMJM / Gustafson Porter: Wellesley Road and Park Lane, Croydon
International Urban Design Competition, Expression of Interest, December 2008

Client: RMJM / Gustafson Porter

Design: Marque Creative / Urbik

Layout synopsis: Super graphic headlines capture the essence of a message

WORLD CLASS IDEAS

RMJM & GUSTAFSON PORTER HAVE DISTINGUISHED TRACK RECORDS IN DESIGNING AND DELIVERING INNOVATIVE PUBLIC BUILDINGS AND SPACES ON TIME TO BUDGET.

They are joined by Thomas Matthews and Intelligent Space to provide specialist input on public participation and consultation and on pedestrian movement and modelling in public space.

Traffic engineering and planning has been considered by Arup. Real Options is an early-stage development consultancy with an integrated approach to rationalising mixed-use, urban or resort destinations, which combines market, spatial and financial assessment and helps focus the vision.

This section highlights projects by team members which have informed our proposals for Croydon.

Our experience is organised in themes to reflect the issues we think need to be addressed in Croydon.

Together they show the range of imagination and experience of the team, and our ability to develop and deliver innovative concepts in numerous contexts.

'IN DREAMS BEGIN RESPONSIBILITY'
WB Yeats, quoted in Alsop and Croydon Council's *Third City* document

'A BUILDING WITHOUT A DREAM IS A BUILDING. A BUILDING WITH A DREAM IS ARCHITECTURE. GOOD ARCHITECTURE REQUIRES A CLEAR CONCEPTUAL ASPIRATION AND AMBITION. ARCHITECTURE, DIFFERENT FROM MERE BUILDING, MUST APPEAL NOT ONLY TO OUR SENSES BUT ALSO TO OUR INTELLECT.'
From RMJM's *Inside Out, Outside In.*

Elements on a Page

Arrangement

The different elements that will comprise a design, predominantly the type and images, could be treated as separate components that are to be arranged on the page with clear distinctions between them.

Alternatively, they can be combined to form a seamless presentation. This can be achieved in many different ways as the examples that follow will show.

Combining images and text can be used as a method to control the pace of a publication. Publications often have clear and natural break points such as new chapters. However, seemingly unrelated information can be brought together in a cohesive manner through design.

The Stones 65–67 (right)

This book by British photographer Gered Mankowitz, designed by Spin, uses a four-column grid and oversized imagery that retains the original reportage style of the images. With attention clearly focused on the photographs, the typography is understated and set closely.

Type and image are treated and arranged as separate elements but the consistent approach unifies these elements into a coherent whole. The opening, type-free section prints in duotone on an uncoated stock and the main body of the book prints on a satin stock.

Client: Vision On
Design: Spin
Layout synopsis: Separation of type and image

Reportage photography captures hidden and defining moments of people or events that are both factual and full of humanity.

Elements on a Page

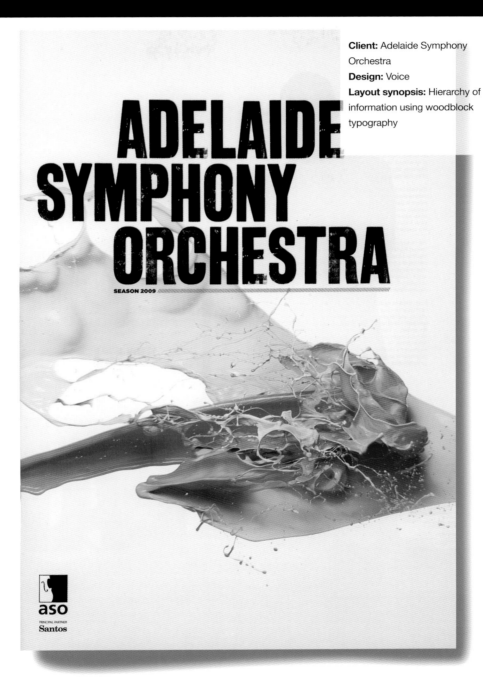

Client: Adelaide Symphony Orchestra
Design: Voice
Layout synopsis: Hierarchy of information using woodblock typography

Adelaide Symphony Orchestra
We often think of hierarchy as being a rigid, set aesthetic, but as this brochure demonstrates, information can be arranged in an emotive and evocative manner.

Entry points

An 'entry point' is a visual aid indicating where to begin reading. Newspapers, for example, contain textual content separated into discrete chunks – without this separation, the content would be too dense and too difficult to navigate or read.

The placement of an entry point can form part of the visual drama of a spread or webpage. Typical devices include the use of colour and alteration of fonts and type sizes. In addition to the 'graphic' qualities of an entry point, the 'content' also needs to be considered. In the newspaper example, a headline is normally reproduced at a larger size than body copy, but it also works as a synopsis or 'hint' of content.

Scanning and reading

As designers, we tend to think that the words we craft on a page or website will be 'read'; in practice many won't – but they will probably be 'scanned'. Eye tracking software is used to see how people scan a page, looking for an entry point. As page designs vary so much, so too do scanning patterns, so there are no absolute rules, but there are underlying patterns of behaviour, as shown below.

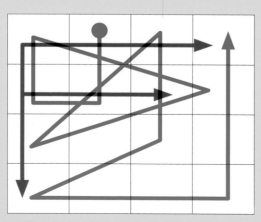

In simple terms, we tend to read from the top left corner in either an 'F' shaped pattern (shown in red), or scan over a page ending at the top right corner (shown in blue). It is of value to be aware of these patterns in order to correctly place information in order of importance. By dividing a page in a series of squares, it becomes clear that some segments contain more activity than others. Over the following pages we'll look at some examples of work in relation to entry points and eye scanning patterns.

OMG (Oxford Metrics Group) PLC Annual review (above and following spread)

This annual review demonstrates the use of entry points in a design. On the verso (left-hand) page, a main headline captures the reader's interest. This is combined with a coloured rule, leading the eye across to the recto (right-hand) page. The image placement, by spanning the gutter, also helps lead the eye towards the copy. An expanded standfirst (a synopsis of the article) occupies the active top right-hand corner, leading to the running copy of the article. This 'journey' has been controlled by creative use of layout, varying typesizes and the inclusion of coloured graphic elements and devices.

The careful placement of elements will help to guide a reader around a printed page, or even in an onscreen environment. However, while there may be scientific principles underpinning this, layout is as much about art as science. The designer needs to develop a 'feel' for where to place items through experience or a series of exercises.

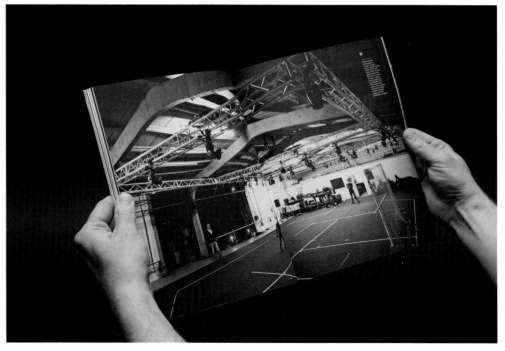

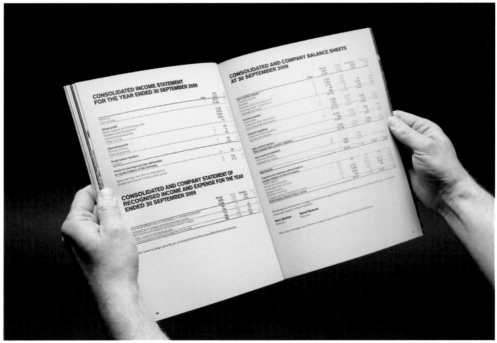

Pace
All written copy naturally has pace. Some passages are quick to read, while others require more contemplation.

This can be translated to the visual content of either a website or book. As we turn from page to page, be it online or in print, we either slow down in order to read and study visuals, or we speed up and turn the page.

Controlling pace
In order to control pace, certain graphic devices can be used. The addition of a strong graphic statement, or the appearance of colour blocks can act as visual full-stops – encouraging the reader to pause. Ironically though, large text tends to be scanned rather than read. That is to say that the reader won't necessarily read every word, but they will get an overall impression of the content.

Research has shown that larger words encourage scanning, while the use of smaller type encourages reading. As we saw on the previous spread, larger type acts as an entry point, and therefore it doesn't need to be read in full – its purpose is to direct you to a particular part of a publication or page. When designing a series of pages for print or online we should consider how they work in series, and not how they work in isolation. A well designed page replicated throughout an entire book will quickly become uninteresting. Equally, if every page is completely different there will be no overall unity and cohesion. This is the tightrope that designers tread – knowing what to put in to create interest, without overpowering or dominating the content with design style or visual noise. On the following spread we will look at how 'thumbnails' can be used to access the overall pace of a book or website.

Ikon Gallery – Self Evident (right and following spread)
This exhibition catalogue of African photography at the Ikon Gallery has a clear break in pace and pattern. There are unifying devices: the use of passe partout images, for example, but there are also varying elements. In turning the page we go from images set in white space, to full-bleed DPSs, to colour blocks indicating a visual pause. The result is a controlled flow, or pattern, that feels both exciting and varied, while being unified and allowing the photographic images to 'breathe'. The design style and graphic intervention is evident without dominating or over-powering the content.

Client: Ikon Gallery,
Birmingham
Design: Z3 Design Studio
Layout synopsis: Exhibition
catalogue that uses scale and
colour to add pace

Elements on a Page

Seydou**Keita**

SeydouKeita
1973
Jean-Pigozzi Collection © Ann G. Deram...

G01:36:35:04.2

OladeleBahjeeBanghou
1994
Father with the village hunters of Odo - Eku
Video still

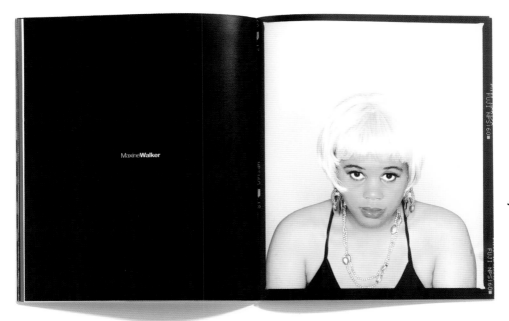

Elements on a Page

Colour blocks provide a visual pause to the flow of spreads. Images are reproduced full bleed (top), with a photographic border (bottom), spanning the central gutter (left) and set in a passe partout (above left).

Client: Violette Editions
Design: Aboud Creative
Layout synopsis: Format constrained, passe partout image presentation

Form and Function

The form that a layout of a work takes is driven by the function of the design, the ideas and information it has to communicate, the medium in which this will occur and the target audience.

Whilst fundamental layout principles can be used to achieve a high degree of creativity, their basic purpose is functional, to achieve a well-balanced design that presents the various page elements clearly.

'Simplicity before understanding is simplistic; simplicity after understanding is simple.'
Edward De Bono

Father + Son (left)

This small-format book by Aboud Creative for Violette Editions is essentially two books conjoined. The left-hand book is a collection of photographs by Harold Smith and the right-hand book is a collection of Paul Smith's images.

The design means both books can be viewed simultaneously, allowing the spreads to become a juxtaposition of photographic styles and eras. Harold's images are nearly all black and white and are reproduced with a sepia tone. Paul's are far brighter, with an almost Loma (highly saturated colour) quality to them.

The passe partout layout is tempered by the small format of the work and presentation of nearly full-page photographs.

Dividing the book

We think of books (and webpages, for that matter) as being a collection of related, uniform pages. This is indeed usually the case, but it is also worth considering how this information is divided to create clear, paced series of layouts.

Methods of dividing material
There are several common techniques used for dividing material in a book:

Physical division
This involves using paper engineering to make physical changes to a book. This can include printing different sections on different stocks, using different sized pages within a single document, as shown opposite, or by exploring how we use a book, as shown on the following spread.

Design interventions
This involves using layout design to alter the pace and 'reveal' of information within a book. This can include repetitive motifs or image placement, and a variation in the orientation of text. A simple example of this would be to have breaks or pauses, created by differing scales of text and images. Usually this will occur at the beginning of a chapter, or at a point in the book where there is a clear division of information.

Both these techniques should be used to add clarity and interest to a design.

ISTD (right)
The International Society of Typographic Designers (ISTD) uses a different design studio to create each issue of its journal. For this issue, *TypoGraphic 51*, design studio Cartlidge Levene used two double-sided posters that were cut, folded and trimmed to form the publication. In contrast to a typical publication design where space is divided by a grid, this format provides a degree of randomness to both the positioning of images and the hierarchy of information.

Client: ISTD
Design: Cartlidge Levene
Layout synopsis: Format dictates layout rather than the grid

/ Form and Function

Client: CCA Wattis Institute
Design: Aufuldish + Warinner
Layout synopsis: Book divided into two halves, each with front cover

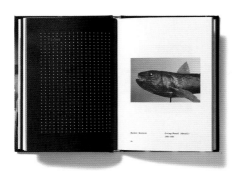

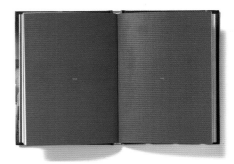

Form and Function

Sudden Glory

¡sʇsᴉx∃ pꞁɹoM ǝɥʇ ʇɐɥʇ ʎɹɐuᴉpɹoɐɹʇx∃ ʍoH

These two exhibition catalogues for the CCA Wattis Institute are contained within one book. The design by Aufuldish + Warinner divides the publication into two parts; one for each exhibition. The covers serve as individual front covers for both parts and flipping the book over presents the start of each. This is a simple, effective and neat way of dividing the two distinct elements that the publication contains.

The magenta spread (middle row, right) is the point where both catalogues join. The three spreads shown on the top and middle rows are from *How Extraordinary that the World Exists!* and the remaining spreads are from *Sudden Glory*.

Client: Manhattan Loft
Corporation
Design: North
Layout synopsis: Passe
partout provides consistent
image presentation,
asymmetrical grid for text

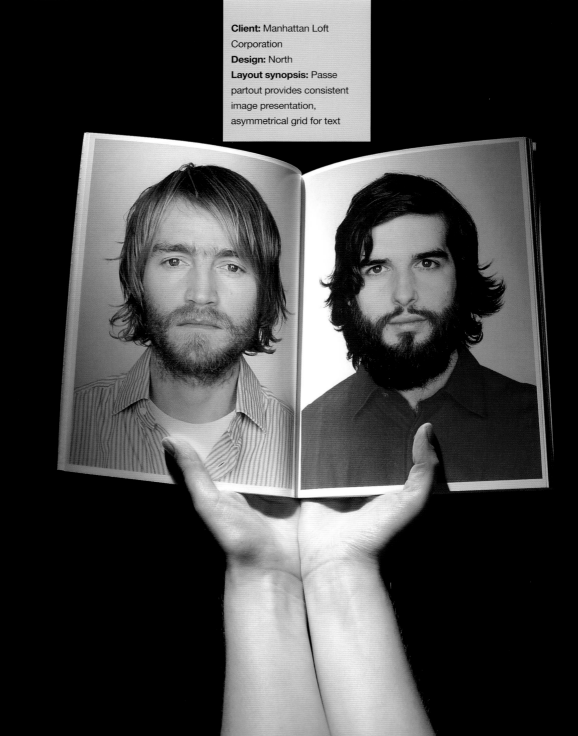

St Philip's Church, Stratford Road

The front section of this book repeatedly uses passe partout to lay out portraits by Amber Rowlands. This framing provides commonality. The front section is printed on a Chromolux paper, which is high gloss one side and uncoated the other. The back section is on a light grey pulp stock.

Form and Function

Appropriation

Appropriation is the borrowing of a style, typically used elsewhere, as the basis for a design. This may be done for purely aesthetic reasons as a method to present information in a certain way, but often it is done to borrow characteristics that are associated with the appropriated source. Establishing such a connection may add credibility to the design or cause it to be viewed in a certain way.

Finding influence

There are numerous sources of inspiration for appropriation. It is common for graphic design to be influenced by art, or high culture, but you can also plunder the vaults of what is called low culture. This includes all the ephemera that surrounds our daily lives, including till receipts, safety signs, airline tickets, and the <u>vernacular</u> of graphic items that surround us. This may include archival items, found objects and street signage.

Vernacular
The everyday visual language through which a community or group communicates.

Client: Forth Estate
Design: North
Layout synopsis: Revisiting conventions for a fresh approach

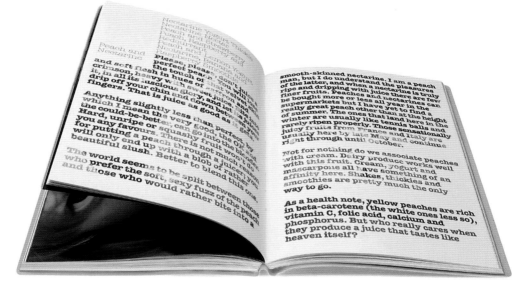

Thirst

This Nigel Slater cookbook by North design studio reinterprets traditional conventions to produce a fresh approach to a perennial problem; how to present a series of instructions without them appearing boring! The design uses a mixture of American typewriter fonts; ingredient lists and titles appear in light, and body copy is presented in bold. The text also has abstract images within its characters, which blends with the soft hues of Angela Moore's photographs.

Client: Birkhäuser
Design: Studio Myerscough
Layout synopsis: Different
stocks to divide publication

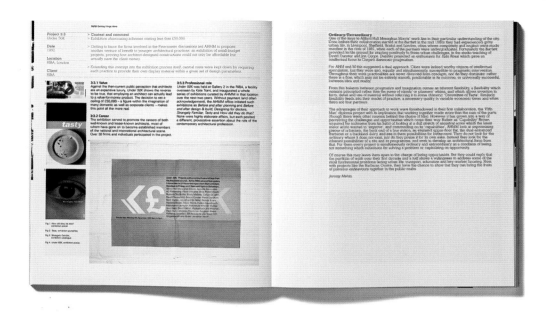

A variety of column widths, measures and image sizes create an eclectic scrapbook effect. The wide margin easily accommodates both images and captions.

A series of rules separates information (right) into related blocks. This simple device adds clarity and eases navigation when dealing with difficult tabular matter.

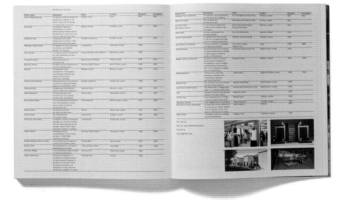

Form and Function

Manual – The Architecture and Office of Allford Hall Monaghan Morris

This book by Birkhäuser documents the work of contemporary architecture practice Allford Hall Monaghan Morris (AHMM). Studio Myerscough borrowed from the publication's name and designed the book specifically to resemble a manual. The back section is printed on an uncoated yellow paper stock that creates the impression of a glossary. The front section is printed on a silk stock. These stocks create two distinct areas for different information and impart texture to the publication.

Exquisite corpse
The exquisite corpse (cadavre exquis) is a surrealist technique that exploits the happy chance of accident in the production of words or images.

The concept has a similar basis to the 'consequences' game, whereby several people take turns to write or draw something on a piece of paper, then fold it to conceal what they have done before passing it on to the next person, who then repeats the actions.

This same technique is used by designers with the exception that the elements are deliberately selected or formed so that they will be compatible, as the example opposite shows.

These techniques can add an element of 'non sequitur', or the unexpected or even absurd. They create a sense of fun, a sense of the unexpected, and can be used to deconstruct the normal flow of a narrative.

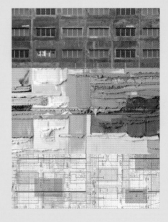

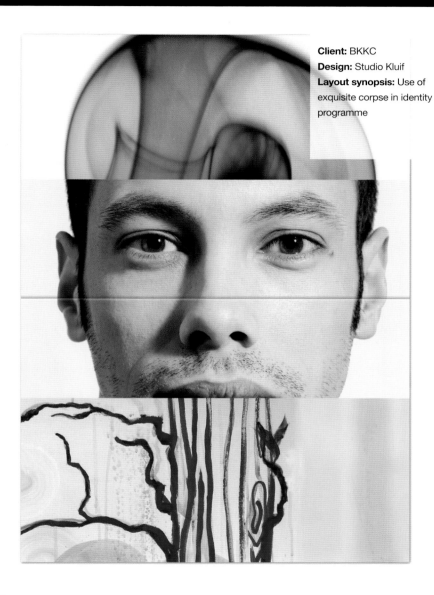

Client: BKKC
Design: Studio Kluif
Layout synopsis: Use of exquisite corpse in identity programme

Form and Function

BKKC

The BKKC (Brabants Kenniscentrum Kunst en Cultuur) identity by Studio Kluif uses an exquisite corpse device to reflect the fact that it is an umbrella organisation bringing together many different disciplines: art, music, cinema and literature. Each of these disciplines is reflected in the resulting design, which divides the reverse of the letterhead into strips containing different visual clues. This contrasts with the carefully ordered front of the letter, which portrays a more corporate feel. The design is energetic, eclectic and interesting – qualities the BKKC would like to project.

Client: Found, Shared
Design: Nigel Aono-Billson
Layout synopsis:
Juxtaposition of image printed
on the inside cover of
catalogue

Found: The Magazine, the Stuff, Intuit, Chicago, 2005

(left and right): Ohio, e.V., Kunstv

Useful Photography installation, Netherl

Found, Shared

Found, Shared: the Magazine Photowork exhibition catalogue focuses on unusual 'photo' magazines from the margins of publishing. The exhibition was curated by David Brittain, and the catalogue shown opposite was designed by Nigel Aono-Billson. The images of the cow are taken from *Useful Photography* magazine #005, produced by Hans Aarsman, Claudie de Cleen, Julian Germain, Erik Kessels and Hans van der Meer. The image is printed on the inside front cover, creating an interesting juxtaposition of image and text.

/ Form and Function

Binding

Binding is a format choice that directly affects layout, as the various binding methods (such as perfect binding, saddle-stitch and wiro binding) produce different physical attributes in the resulting product.

Perfect-bound publications require a larger inner margin because the book will be pinched in at its spine when opened; while wiro-bound publications should not have content in the central margin because it will be punctured by the physical binding process.

The Arts Foundation (right)

This brochure includes details of the designers, poets, documentary makers and performers shortlisted for the the Arts Foundation Awards in the UK.

The layout and the format are amorphous, seemingly without the shape or structure that can usually be seen at work in a design.

Images and text appear to be spontaneously positioned and the format comprises four odd-sized sheets that are folded, collated and bound with a plastic cable tie. In this way the design echoes the diverse areas for which the awards are given.

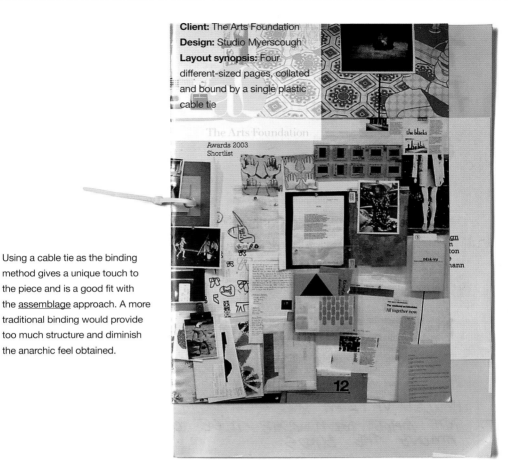

Client: The Arts Foundation
Design: Studio Myerscough
Layout synopsis: Four different-sized pages, collated and bound by a single plastic cable tie

The Arts Foundation

Awards 2003
Shortlist

Using a cable tie as the binding method gives a unique touch to the piece and is a good fit with the assemblage approach. A more traditional binding would provide too much structure and diminish the anarchic feel obtained.

Assemblage
An assemblage is an artistic composition made from various odds and ends centred around a specific theme or, as in the example given, bringing together several different themes.

Form and Function

Client: Violette Editions
Design: Frost
Layout synopsis: Pictures set passe partout, with overwhelming amounts of space and large-scale typography pressuring space

Double Game

The gutter of this publication's binding is used to good effect on some pages (below bottom right), but is ignored completely on others (below top right) as the text disappears into and emerges from it.

The use of large-scale typographical elements creates a feeling of pressured space and is sympathetic to the New York setting of the work.

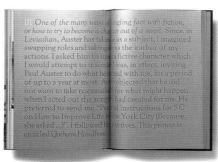

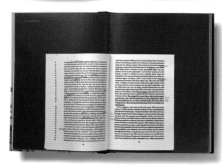

Client: Palau de la Virreina
Design: Bis Design
Layout synopsis: Flexible use of grid

VOSTES AQUÍ ©
INSTRUCCIONS D'ÚS
Rosa Ferré + Chus Martínez

Vostestaquí (You are here)

This catalogue is for a contemporary art exhibition in which the work of a number of different artists needed to be organised as a single unit. Bis design studio used a solid grid but one that had the flexibility to present the pages for different artists and express their individual personalities. The layout features simple colour blocks on single-leaf sheets with double binding holes in one margin. Text columns and picture widths are equal (centre).

Form and Function

Client: Diesel
Design: KesselsKramer
Layout synopsis: Full-page
statements

Layout in Use

A key function of layout is to let the elements, especially the image elements, perform the tasks that they have been selected for. Images add drama and emotion to a work, but how they communicate with the recipient depends upon how they are presented.

The following pages will provide examples of how layout choices in the presentation of images can be used to enhance or instil a certain feeling or attitude to the material.

'The rule: the fewer the differences in the size of the illustrations, the quieter the impression created by the design. As a controlling system the grid makes it easier to give the surface or space a rational organisation.'

Josef Müller-Brockmann

Diesel (left)

The cover of this publication, created by KesselsKramer design studio on behalf of clothing manufacturer Diesel, is treated as one integral canvas (rather than as adjacent recto and verso pages), across which a message is plastered in handwritten letters. Little consideration is afforded to positioning or avoidance of the central gutter. However, the slogans are central and vertically aligned to further enhance visibility.

Scale

Scale, when used in design terminology, applies to the size of images and text. For the purpose of this book we are looking at how big or small these elements are on the page. Choices here affect the importance we attach to an image.

An image with a large scale dominates the page and is the focus of attention, yet making a graphic too large can result in suffocation. At a smaller scale the information contained within the image may be missed or ignored.

We need to consider the macro scale of items on the page – the overall picture of a design, the focus of elements and their relationships – but we also need to consider the micro scale; the detailing and choices.

Client: Toby Richardson
Design: Voice
Layout synopsis:
Large-format publication
showcasing photographer's
work

More Singles, Couples and Queens (above and left)

This book is a record of discarded mattresses and other objects, seen by
Australian artist and photographer Toby Richardson as cultural treasure. The
surface graphics on the cover are taken from a photo of one of the mattresses
found on the street. Shown opposite are a series of spreads from the book that
celebrate the rich tapestry of found ephemera.

University of Lincoln (above)

This prospectus demonstrates the visual power of scale. Dynamism is added by varying the position, size and colour of items on the page. It remains clear, easy to navigate, and logical – it functions, but more importantly it is interesting. The large-scale section titles provide a clear entry point for the reader, with two additional typesizes for body copy and detailed information.

Some Trains in America (right)

Tor this book design, *Some Trains in America* by Andrew Cross, Frost Design used large, uninterrupted images in the thin, horizontal format to capture a feeling of the open wilderness, thus celebrating the poignant beauty of the American landscape.

Client: Prestel
Design: Frost
Layout synopsis: Elongated
format supporting the subject
matter

cASH HILL CA 1997

Layout in Use

Indexing

Many types of publication need to contain adjunct information, whether displayed as a contents page, a formal index, a glossary of terms or a list of contact addresses.

Such varied types and quantities of information requiring presentation can be quite challenging from a design point of view. As the following examples show, index pieces can be incorporated into the design in a number of ways that do not detract from the main body of the work.

Westzone – New Angles on Life (right)

This catalogue layout for Westzone Publishing by Rose Design has the publication titles and author names printed on the inside front and back flaps. A silver panel contains each book's specification information. An arrow on every page points to the author in the silver panel and links them to the iconic image reproduced in the catalogue.

In order to develop the overall brand, images displayed in the catalogue feature the word 'Westzone'. On the flag it appears as a screen print, under the hat it is found as a footnote, on the image of the doll it's a glint in the eye and it is seen as a manufacturing mark on the model kit.

Client: Westzone Publishing
Design: Rose Design
Layout synopsis: Author
details on front strip with
arrow identification system

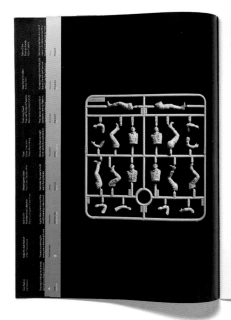

Orientation

Orientation refers to the plane or direction in which the elements of a design are used. Text and images are typically set so that they are read and viewed horizontally from left to right. Using other orientations such as vertical or angled is done typically to maintain a particular aesthetic in the design, as doing so makes the reader work harder to obtain the information by having to rotate the publication. This may encourage them to pay more attention to it, but can also have an adverse effect and make them lose interest.

Body Milk Deliplus (right)

The elegant placement of typography on these bottles creates a soft impression, reflective of the product. Type is orientated vertically, with a simple hierarchy created by colour and changes in type weight.

Client: Laboratorios RNB
Design: Lavernia & Cienfuegos
Layout: Vertical orientation
of typography

Por sus propiedades hidratantes,
calmantes y reparadoras,
protege y evita la sequedad
cutánea dejando la piel suave.

Deliphus

PIELES SECAS

HIDRATANTE CORPORAL CON

ALOE VERA

ALMENDRAS

Layout in Use

The main types of orientation

Horizontal orientation is the one we are most familiar with. Nearly all printed items, books, newspapers and websites use this as the normal setting for text.

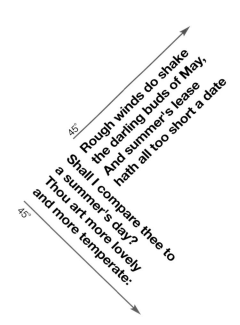

Vertical orientation is often used to contrast against this. It is particularly useful for headings, and large-format information. Arguably, it is harder to read, but it does make a strong graphic statement.

This setting is also sometimes called 'broadside'.

Diagonal orientation usually works on one of two main axes. Text is set at either 45 degrees, or a combination of 30 and 60 degrees. Often you'll be using texts going in alternate directions, and these combinations facilitate this by combining to 90 degrees, as shown below.

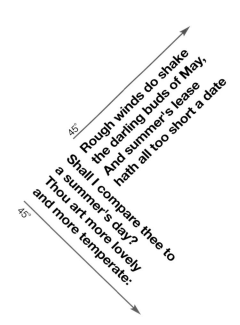

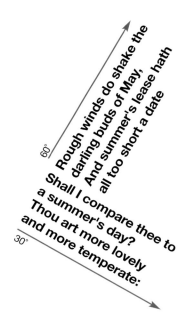

Text set on 45-degree angles, rotated either clockwise or counter clockwise

Text set on 30- and 60-degree angles

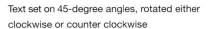

The Bauhaus, founded in 1919, in Weimar, Germany, favoured these approaches to orientation, as can be seen in this lithograph that uses the 30- and 60-degree axes. This approach was later applied to typography and layout design.

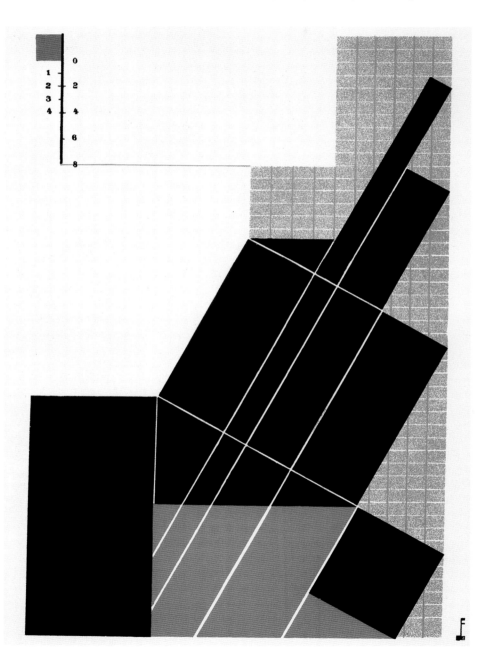

Client: The Forum of Slavic Cultures
Design: ilovarstritar
Layout synopsis: Consistent use of orientation enforces and maintains identity

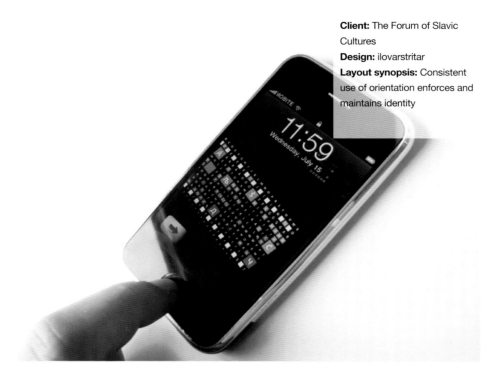

Slavic Film Festival

This identity for the Slavic Film Festival uses a repeated visual orientation of graphic elements of around 10 degrees. The graphic elements, icons of film, are formed from individual letterforms from Slavic languages. This repetition creates a strong visual identity for both print and screen.

Client: Kennet Russo
Design: Dorian
Layout synopsis: Art exhibition catalogue featuring a vertical layout

Kennet Russo

This catalogue for artist Kennet Russo features mixed alignments of typography on a vertical layout, creating an eclectic and dynamic presentation of work.

Client: The Frank Popp
Ensemble
Design: Remo Caminada
Layout synopsis: Vertical
orientation of information

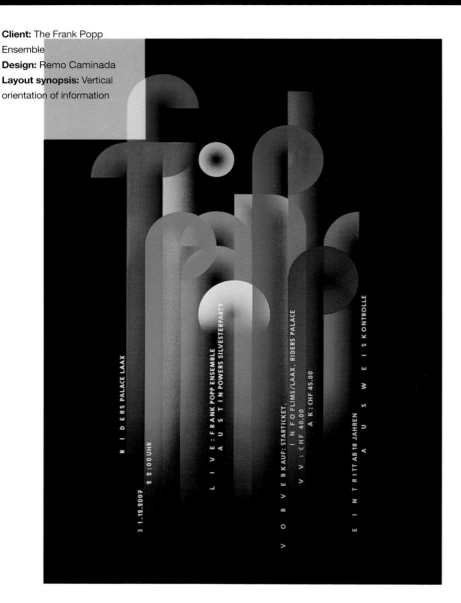

Frank Popp Ensemble

This poster for the Frank Popp Ensemble features a vertical orientation of
information over a typographic identity. Combining both Modernist structure,
and more playful, expressive typography, this design is a seamless combination
of styles.

Arnolfi Annual Review

Thirteen created a compact and book-like Annual Review for Arnolfini. Inside, the body copy is presented in horizontal text blocks but captioning for the various illustrations was oriented to be read vertically.

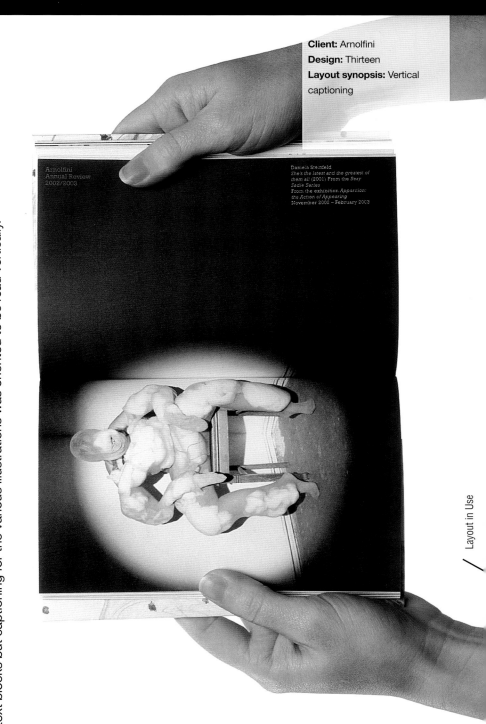

Client: Arnolfini
Design: Thirteen
Layout synopsis: Vertical captioning

Arnolfini
Annual Review
2002/2003

Daniela Steinfeld
*She's the latest and the greatest of
them all* (2001) From the *Sexy
Sadie Series*
From the exhibition *Apparition:
the Action of Appearing*
November 2002 – February 2003

Layout in Use

Client: Segal Centre for Performing Arts
Design: Mookai
Layout synopsis: Strong, impactful, vertical orientation adding clarity and identity

Montreal International Yiddish Theatre Festival

Identity and marketing collateral for the first International Yiddish Festival, hosted by the Segal Centre for Performing Arts. The festival features participants from eight countries, and this is reflected in the strong typographical identity created. Type uses several orientations, adding pace and dynamism to the design.

Dividing the page

By apportioning space for the various elements of a design, dividing a page allows the designer to treat it as a series of connected modules, rather than a single unit. The partitions can then be given individual or collective treatment.

There are many devices and approaches for facilitating this divide. It can be a physical division, using paper engineering, or it can be enforced using a grid, a dividing line, or the use of coloured blocks. It can also be divided using frames, passe partouts, or white space, as shown opposite.

In all cases, you should first question why you are dividing the page, and what you hope that will achieve. For some projects this will be straightforward. An exhibition catalogue, for example, would usually divide images and captions. Increasingly complex documents, however, may need more complex sets of divisions. As a general rule, using vertical divides, such as those in the example opposite, will encourage the reader to pause, because they act as breaks in the flow of images. Conversely, horizontal divides, such as those shown on the following spread, will encourage the reader to turn the page.

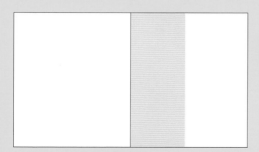

Dividing the page with vertical blocks will tend to encourage a reader to pause, or stop.

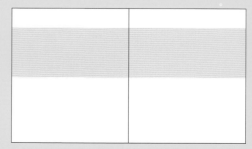

In contrast, vertical divisions encourage the eye to read left to right, and to turn the page.

Client: Deutsche Bank
Design: Spin
Layout synopsis:
Typographical placement dictated by constant graphic element

Matteo Burioni
Übersetzen fürs Über-setzen. Verschachtelung als
Gestaltungsmittel in Ayşe Erkmens »Shipped Ships«

Shipped Ships

Shipped Ships I and *Shipped Ships II* is a publication produced on behalf of the Deutsche Bank by Spin design studio. The books explore the Moment project by artist Ayşe Erkmen. This project saw small ships brought into Frankfurt, Germany, from other cities to operate on the Main River for a short period before returning home.

The books have a line running through each page that becomes wider and narrower, changing its dimensions just as a river does. All information is arranged around this key graphic feature, which at times provides a space for typographical elements, or otherwise dictates their position.

/ Layout in Use

Client: CCAC

Design: Aufuldish + Warinner

Layout synopsis: Different-sized blocks for text and images. Varied treatments for captions, footnotes, folios and running heads

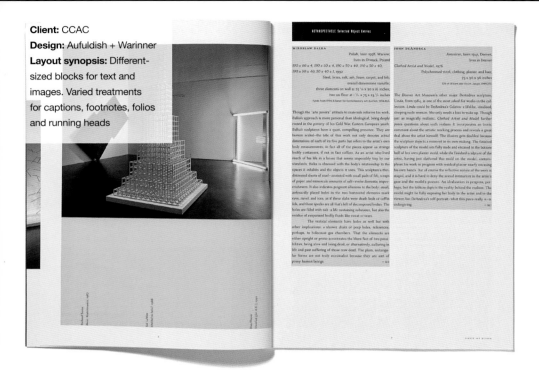

Insights / Dialogues

This brochure for the Colorado Contemporary Arts Collaboration uses different-sized yellow blocks to delineate the space for text and images. All body text is justified, while captions and footnotes are ranged right. The footnotes create small squares at the base of the columns (bottom row, left). Folio numbers are centred and the running head appears on the far right of the recto page. Text in some blocks runs vertically.

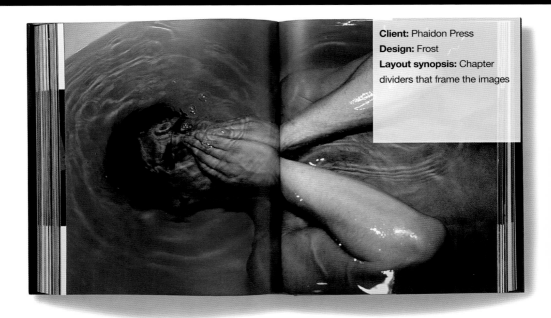

Client: Phaidon Press
Design: Frost
Layout synopsis: Chapter dividers that frame the images

The Devil's Playground

Nan Goldin's photographic book features themed chapters of personal and intimate images. The chapters are separated by texts, poems and lyrics by writers such as Nick Cave and Catherine Lampert. Frost Design created chapter title pages using plain colours, sympathetic to the rich colours of the images, to help frame them.

Layout in Use

Structure / unstructure

Layout concerns the structuring of elements on a page so that they can communicate effectively with a reader. Absence of a structure can also be used to good effect to convey certain characteristics in a design – although this in itself is also a type of structure.

Unstructured designs can be some of the most visually creative and, by definition, are more difficult to control in order to achieve the desired results.

When deconstructing fundamental layout principles to create an unstructured work a designer must consider whether the intended target audience will be able to identify and access the information it contains.

Intervention
The adding to, or subtraction from the original material by the designer.

Client: NEROC'VGM
Design: KesselsKramer
Layout synopsis: Simple structure using passe partout

Cynthia Hathaway

Layout in Use

A Meeting in the Supermarket

A Meeting in the Supermarket by Cynthia Hathaway is a book produced for the Dutch marketing communications company NEROC'VGM, which contains short narratives, or 'sliptales', created by 13 designers and themed around a supermarket. Elements such as parking spaces, receipts, tills, shelves and so on are the starting point for these imaginative interpretations.

KesselsKramer used a fairly simple structure to order and present these different, and sometimes unstructured, pieces in book form. Passe partout framing and minimum design <u>intervention</u> allow the works to speak for themselves.

Client: Quintino Jazz
Ensemble
Design: Remo Caminada
Layout synopsis: Invitation
that is simultaneously
structured and unstructured

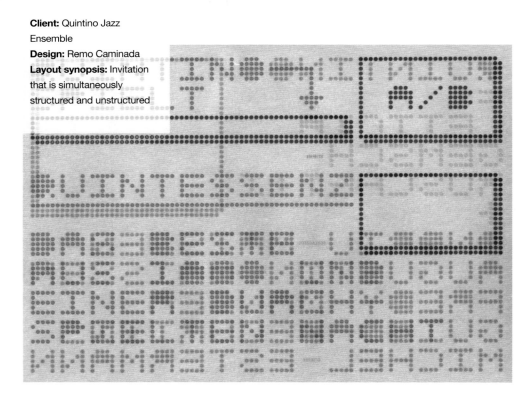

Quintino spielt Quintessenz (above)

This invite for a jazz-combo is printed both sides in a different colour, using a structured, ordered grid. But as the material is semi-transparent, the layering of one side against the other creates a sense tension, reflecting the nature of two musicians.This <u>serendipitous</u> result is both structured and unstructured.

Cirkus Humberto (right)

This book, designed by Browns and featuring photographs by Bettina von Kameke, documents the people involved in Cirkus Humberto. The circus supplied posters for the publication and these were then folded and used for the cover – a vibrant, thoughtful and unique design. As the poster folds through the centre of the clown's face, the front cover presents a wink whilst the back cover carries a laughing eye. A simple passe partout contains the images and captions running vertically in a sans serif font.

Serendipity
A fortunate discovery while exploring something unrelated. Often called a 'happy accident'.

Client: Bettina von Kameke
Design: Browns
Layout synopsis: Poster cover positioning, passe partout photograph presentation, vertical captions

Above is the front cover of the book, which is essentially one quarter of the original poster. Bottom right is the back cover, and the inside cover can be seen below and above right.

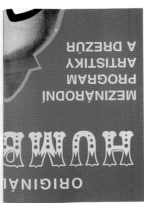

/ Layout in Use

Client: (RED)
Design: Roanne Adams
Layout synopsis: Clear use of structure to enforce the power of simple messages

NCHES
NANO
L EDITION
ROVES SO POPULA
HAT THEY ADD AN 8GB
MODEL 4 WEEKS LATER

(RED)

This large-format newspaper-esque publication aims to raise awareness of (RED), a global fund established by Bono and Bobby Shriver. The fund works with global brands to produce iconic 'red' versions of their products, raising money to fund charitable organisations. The brochure features a clear, unambiguous structure and hierarchy.

Hierarchy
A logical, organised and visual guide for text headings indicating different levels of importance.

$25M

IN THE FIRST YEAR
PARTNERS GENERATE
$25M FOR THE
GLOBAL FUND

500% MORE THAN
WAS RECEIVED FROM
THE PRIVATE SECTOR
IN THE LAST 5 YEARS

ENOUGH MONEY
TO GIVE 160,000
PEOPLE LIFE-SAVING
DRUGS FOR 1 YEAR

CONVERSE MAKES
UNIQUE SHOES FROM
MUDCLOTH WOVEN IN MALI

'MAKE MINE RED'
ACCOUNTS FOR OVER
50% OF ONLINE SALES
ON CONVERSEONE.COM

CONVERSE AND GAP
COLLABORATE TO MAKE
(PRODUCT) RED SHOES
AVAILABLE IN GAP STORES

Layout in Use

Paper engineering

Paper engineering addresses some of the format decisions designers make in order to produce the end result. The format of a publication can open new possibilities for an innovative use of layout; as these examples show.

Format elements such as binding and folding options pose additional layout issues that the designer must resolve.

Lanagraphic (right)

This brochure for M-real Zanders by Roundel design studio features photography by Richard Learoyd. The textures, finishes and weights of papers produced by Zanders are explained visually in the publication, which has cut-short and interleaved sections. A visual analogy is used to describe a product that might have been difficult to make interesting, as on successive pages an apple passes from being whole to being half-eaten. The outside paper stock is a textured felt that associates with the skin of the apple, whilst the inside stock is smooth and so relates to the soft flesh of the apple.

Client: M-real Zanders GmbH
Design: Roundel
Layout synopsis: Repeated image placement combined with different paper stocks for visual analogy

OUTSIDE

Smooth
Soft White 240gsm
CMYK

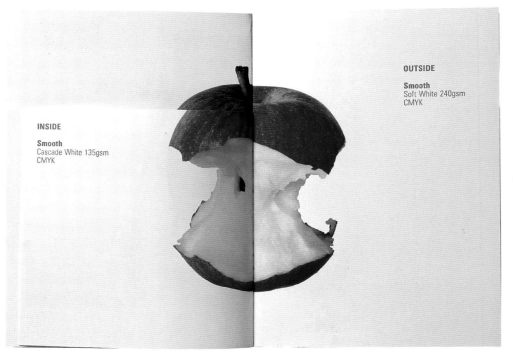

OUTSIDE

Smooth
Soft White 240gsm
CMYK

INSIDE

Smooth
Cascade White 135gsm
CMYK

/ Layout in Use

Client: NEROC'VGM
Design: KesselsKramer
Layout synopsis: Throwout
featuring passe partout image,
four-module grid

A Meeting on the Street

This is a book designed by
KesselsKramer for NEROC'VGM, a
Dutch marketing communications
company. It features a series of
photographs taken by Hans Eijkelboom
of mothers and daughters out shopping
on consecutive Saturday afternoons in
the cities of Amsterdam, Paris, Berlin
and London.

Each spread has a <u>throwout</u> section
featuring a large, single passe partout
image. The entire book is set on a four-
module grid, enforcing the idea that it is
a collection, or album, of images.

Throwout
A sheet of folded paper bound into a publication so it can
be opened horizontally.

Client: E A Shaw

Design: Imagination

Layout synopsis: Different-sized outer for theme separation

Outside
17–19 Bedford Street
WC2

17–19 Bedford Street

This is a brochure designed by Imagination on behalf of E A Shaw to promote the 17–19 Bedford Street WC2 property development in London. The brochure has interleaved pages, cut short and flush at the bottom of the document. The cover of the publication focuses on the area surrounding the development, whilst inner pages focus on the building itself. The ultimate aim is to sell the location as much as the building.

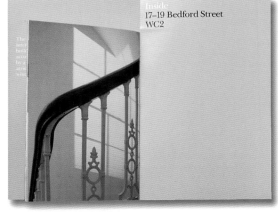

Inside:
17–19 Bedford Street
WC2

Layout in Use

Client: Building Sights
Design: Studio Myerscough
Layout synopsis: Z-bind to form physical separation

Building the Jubilee School

This book is a record of the construction of a school in Brixton, London, by Allford Hall Monaghan Morris. A type of z-bind was used to join the two parts and form a separation between them. The first part of the book discusses the construction process, while the second part deals with the design process. The central joining panel is a schedule of key events in the entire process.

Client: Richard Overy
Design: tita (Emanuele Basso, Giuseppe Mazza and Sonia Rocchi)
Layout synopsis: Crafted typography and angled orientation

Layout in Use

At the edge of a cliff

Poignant typography is used to illustrate the grim nature of this novel by Richard Overy. The form of the typography, the 'craft' and construction, is used to portray a sense of foreboding and despair. The design demonstrates the power of typography to tell complex stories. Photograph by Enzo Monzino.

Passe partout

Passe partout historically refers to the cardboard mount that sits between a picture and the glass in a framed image. The term can also be applied to the borders or the white space around the outside edge of a page or design element.

A border helps to define the space on a page and the relationships between the items it contains. Into this space a design can comfortably be placed. This section explores some of the ways passe partout can be used to help structure page layout.

Digit (right)

Using the campaign slogan, 'more than a duplicate', this brochure uses a simple passe partout layout to frame images of twins. This approach allows the photographic and video content that Digit produces to become the focal element. Text is reversed out of a cool grey, creating a calm environment within which to showcase the images. This grey is reminiscent of the tonal value a monitor is set to when undertaking colour correction work on images. Having no adverse impact on the main images, this grey is used as a calm base. This calmness is further enforced through the passe partout with rounded corners.

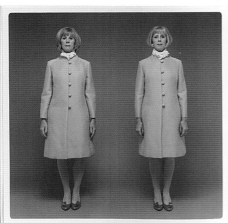

Client: Digit

Design: Fivefootsix

Layout synopsis: Passe partout display of images

What else can we do?

We're here to take care of your content and make the most of its potential. Here are just a few of the ways we can help you with:

— Ingest – High Definition and Standard Definition
— Encoding
— Digital Storage
— Library Management
— Order Management
— Content Versioning
— Transcoding
— Standards Conversion
— Digital Rights Management
— Encryption and watermarking
— Global file transport
— Technical Quality Control

more than a duplicate...

What we do

It's simple really – we take video content and make it ready for digital broadcast. The tricky part is getting every file perfect for the platform, whether it's web TV, IPTV, video on demand or mobile. At Digit, every file we create is so much more than a duplicate – it's the original footage expertly tweaked to the right file format.

more than a duplicate...

Who we do it for

— Content Owners
If you own or produce any kind of broadcast media, we can digitise it and store the master file for you in our 360° vault, ready to be sent to your distributor in the file format they need. From television archives to blockbuster movies, music videos to concert footage, we can help your content look and sound its best for a whole new audience.

— Content Distributors
If you broadcast or distribute digitally, we can provide you with all kinds of content, perfectly tailored to your technical spec. Our expertise in encoding and transcoding means you can stay up-to-date with technology without having to up your investment in-house.

more than a duplicate...

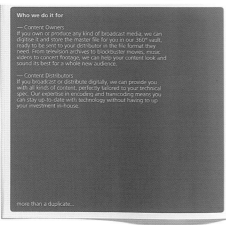

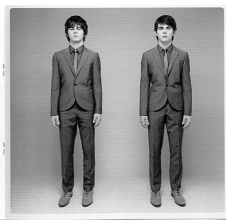

Layout in Use /

Client: Cheyenne Ellis
Design: Roanne Adams
Layout synopsis: Large-format, full-colour newsprint mailer with passe partout frames

Cheyenne Ellis

This large-format mailer features a series of passe partouts, framing the photographer's work. The generous framing helps to display the images and makes the mailer feel more like a book.

Client: Evisu
Design: George & Vera
Layout synopsis: Simple white 'passe partout' border on every page

Intellectual property

This is a catalogue for an intellectual property exhibition featuring images by artist Larry Dunstan. A simple passe partout is used on every page to provide a consistent and equal setting for each image. The series of single-colour prints becomes framed by the space surrounding it. This direct framing establishes a juxtaposition of images in a sterile and unemotional manner.

Layout in Use

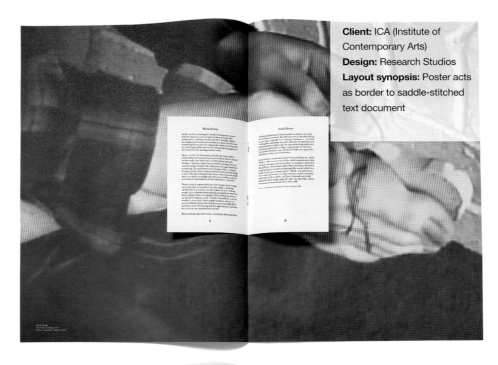

Client: ICA (Institute of Contemporary Arts)
Design: Research Studios
Layout synopsis: Poster acts as border to saddle-stitched text document

Client: Mark Kimber
Design: Voice
Layout synopsis: Passe partout used to frame images

FLYING HORSE

OIL DEPOT

Edgeland (above)
This brochure for an exhibition by contemporary Australian photographer, Mark Kimber, uses a motif of passe partouts to frame the stunning imagery.

Becks Futures (left)
This brochure features printed text documents saddle-stitched into the fold of a poster. Each poster is a large-scale screengrab of one of the entries, forming a fantastically oversized border for the text pieces that it frames.

Juxtaposition

Juxtaposition is the deliberate placement of contrasting images side by side.
The word is formed from the Latin 'juxta', which means near, and 'position'.

In graphic design and page layout juxtaposition may be used to present two or more ideas so as to <u>impart</u> a relationship between them, as seen in the example opposite.

Juxtaposition may imply similarity (as opposite) or dissimilarity, demonstrating that two things are essentially the same or quite different. This may only be clear from the context of the work as a whole. Many designers use juxtaposition in their work with the implicit intention that readers work out the connection themselves.

Impart

Ideas can be expressed implicitly or they can be suggested (or imparted) through the presentation of information that the reader decodes in order to arrive at the required interpretation. In the example above, a juxtaposition of two images is used to impart the idea of sensation.

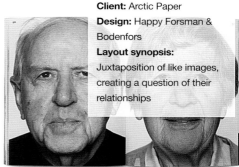

Client: Arctic Paper
Design: Happy Forsman & Bodenfors
Layout synopsis:
Juxtaposition of like images, creating a question of their relationships

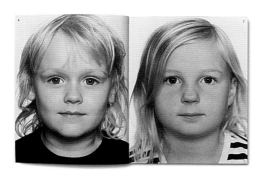

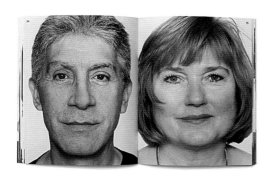

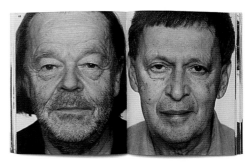

Layout in Use

Arctic

This paper swatch book for Arctic Papers uses full-bleed images of people's faces, juxtaposed against one another. The book prints in a series of different paper textures, and the printed faces reflect these subtle differences. The wrinkles, marks and blemishes of the characterful faces become a point of interest and an invitation to explore the different paper finishes.

Client: Ben®
Design: KesselsKramer
Layout synopsis:
Juxtaposition of portraits
and surroundings

Ben® (above)

This is a book of 'Bens' produced for the Dutch Mobile phone company Ben®, and designed by KesselsKramer. All the 'Bens' featured are from Salt Lake City, USA. Portrait photographs are juxtaposed on a double-page spread against an image of their surroundings. This provides a very disjointed and surreal, yet interesting impression.

ETSA (right)

In this annual report, text and image are separated, creating a strong juxtaposition. The photogr   serves as a backdrop to the bold messages contained in the document.

Client: ETSA Utilities
Design: Voice
Layout synopsis:
Juxtaposition of spliced text
sections and photography

ETSA UTILITIES POWERING
THE MINING SECTOR

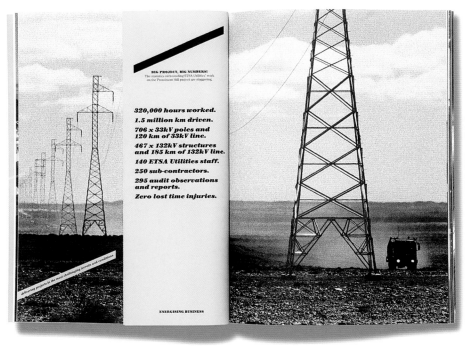

BIG PROJECT, BIG NUMBERS!
The statistics surrounding ETSA Utilities' work
on the Prominent Hill project are staggering.

320,000 hours worked.

1.5 million km driven.

*706 x 33kV poles and
120 km of 33kV line.*

*467 x 132kV structures
and 185 km of 132kV line.*

140 ETSA Utilities staff.

250 sub-contractors.

*295 audit observations
and reports.*

Zero lost time injuries.

ENERGISING BUSINESS

Layout in Use

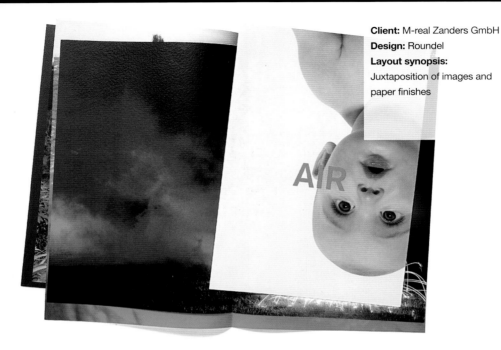

Client: M-real Zanders GmbH
Design: Roundel
Layout synopsis:
Juxtaposition of images and paper finishes

Media

This final chapter looks at some of the media that a graphic designer will commonly be working with. Media encompasses all the physical outputs of design, whether online, in the form of websites and journals, or in print, in the form of books, magazines and posters.

As designers we learn rules, accept axioms, and develop patterns of working. These rules are really only guides – there are no absolutes in design – there is always an edge to push against and new territories to be explored. In real world practice, it is important to have an understanding of but not to be shackled by these rules. It is vital that we allow creative ideas to flourish – and that we build upon our 'bank' of approaches to be used when called upon. The examples shown in this section, and indeed this book, stand as testament to the creative output that can be achieved using creative layout design.

'The grid system is an aid, not a guarantee. It permits a number of possible uses and each designer can look for a solution appropriate to his personal style. But one must learn how to use the grid; it is an art that requires practice.'

Josef Müller-Brockmann

Media

M-real Zanders GmbH (left)

This is a brochure for M-real Zanders featuring photography by Trevor Ray Hart. The brochure juxtaposes images of the four elements – earth, water, fire and air – with four paper finishes – fibre, linen, hammer and wove.

The resulting collision of seemingly unrelated images is both surreal and engaging.

Magazines and brochures
Arguably some of the most experimental and adventurous examples of layout design can be found in magazines and brochures.

These media offer designers the chance to experiment in shape, size and form, as well as using different materials and printing techniques. There is, however, a certain degree of conformity needed in mainstream publishing, where magazines, particularly standard consumer titles, are displayed in standard shelf and rack sizes. Three standard sizes are shown below, although it is common practice to vary the size by making them either slightly narrower or slightly shorter.

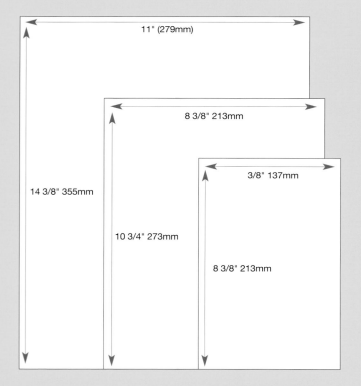

11" (279mm)

8 3/8" 213mm

3/8" 137mm

14 3/8" 355mm

10 3/4" 273mm

8 3/8" 213mm

Three commonly used sizes for magazines and brochures. These measurements result in the minimum amount of cutting and trimming after printing, though to 'stand out' many publications will trim a section off the height or width, to make a point of difference. From left: an oversize, a standard, and a digest, or pocket.

Client: BASA

Design: Lavernia & Cienfuegos

Layout synopsis: Magazine layout using a variety of layouts and graphic devices

VIVIENDA-ESTUDIO EN ACORÁN
SANTA CRUZ DE TENERIFE
ARQUITECTOS: JUAN ANTONIO GONZÁLEZ PÉREZ · FÉLIX PERERA PÉREZ · URBANO YANES TUÑA.
CONSTRUCTOR: EFCON S.L.

CENTRO DE SALUD
EN GUANARTEME
LAS PALMAS DE GRAN CANARIA

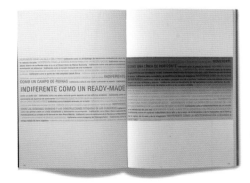

Media

BASA

This journal for the Canary Islands Official College of Architects demonstrates how dynamic the magazine format can be. Variations in layout and pace create a visually arresting set of pages and, in turn, spreads. There is consistency – the pages form a single magazine, but there is also difference and excitement in turning from one page to the next. The relationship between elements and the perimeter becomes a recurrent motif, with the use of full-bleed pages and contrasting white space.

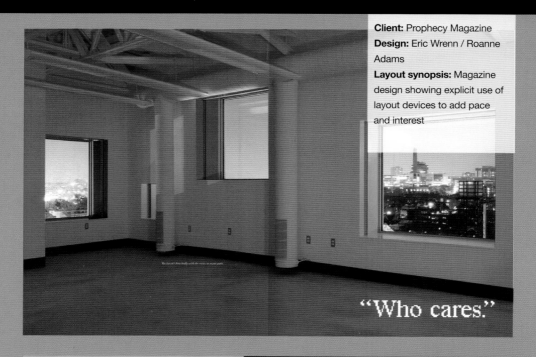

Client: Prophecy Magazine
Design: Eric Wrenn / Roanne Adams
Layout synopsis: Magazine design showing explicit use of layout devices to add pace and interest

"Who cares."

Prophecy
This eclectic magazine covers subjects from surfing to architecture and music.

NEW BERLIN

Words by Anushka Chatterjee-Williams & Joshua Heffo
Photographs by Luke Abiol

Boarding the Berlin metro in the 1980s, getting on the U8 line in the northwest of the city, and heading toward the television tower that looms in the center of town, the train would pass through Alexanderplatz station. The doors, however, would not open. This was the German Democratic Republic, the Soviet run East, and for citizens of the democratic West, it was territory that remained firmly off-limits. Two worlds, separated above by a few feet of cement, cut off from one another below ground by the sealed doors of a passing train.

And then, one day 18 years ago, those worlds collided. When the Berlin Wall fell, so did the barriers – physical and otherwise – that had for more than 40 years held off the social and cultural storm that was waiting to envelop the city.

One thing that immediately followed on the heels of the Wall's collapse was the convergence in the formerly communist East, of cheap rents, lots of space, and loads of repressed human creativity. DJs and musicians dragged their gear into warehouses, lofts, abandoned buildings – anywhere that could hold a crowd – and revivified those empty spaces with exotic sounds from the West. Dub, hip-hop, techno, and house became the backbeat of this new Berlin. At the same time, artists and bohemians – the groundlings of urban renewal the world over – flocked to the east and set up galleries and work studios where previously there had been only angst and censorship.

The mix is reminiscent of that New York which now exists only in memory or lyric, a place where spiked rents don't bar creative expression and something close to a genuine bohemian culture can be found, in short, where the soul of the city outweighs its spectacle. Berliners are different than their cousins in Munich and Frankfurt. Walking through the beautifully decayed Mitte streets on a damp weekday morning it is soon apparent that capitalism's purely rational mind is still struggling to figure out this place. At the various cafés, galleries, and bars that now occupy Berlin's industrial shell, the city's rough edges are celebrated rather than smoothed out, and time can seem a more precious commodity than currency. If cities can indeed be said to have souls, then Berlin's is adolescent and irreverent, informed by history but not bound by it. The city is still figuring itself out, and unlike in many of the world's capitals, it

is Berlin's everyday residents, locals and émigrés alike, who are the ones pulling the strings. In artist squats and techno clubs fashioned out of former power plants, this grand drama plays itself out daily.

The spray-painted stencils marking the walls of Friedrichshain give way to the shoebox art galleries of Mitte, wedged improbably in, under, and between the gray concrete behemoths that loom overhead. In Kreuzberg, the former West, the heady fragrance of spiced kebabs wafts through the city's Turkish quarter where apartment rents rarely rise above a few hundred Euros for a sprawling prewar spread.

Now, of course, the city's U8 train line does stop at Alexanderplatz, where, just like in days past, a steady stream of Berliners flows beneath the old Soviet satellite tower, the most imposing symbol of authoritarian constraint left in the former GDR. But these days the tower also signifies something else, an elsewhere almost forgotten urban freedom.

Augustine runs "hotel" Puerto Rico in Besquar. For 30 sols you get an warm wirra, but no shots or meals. We left "Diego Con Fuego" there the night we ventured out to Punta Mal Nombre in a fishing boat.

The pace of the layout, created by varying the display and position of text and image, reflects the nature of the content.

/ Media

Client: Martin Ålund
Design: Bedow Creative
Layout synopsis: Image and text occupying the same overall grid

ARTIN ÅLUND
VER LAND

M
ER NE

Catalogue for Martin Ålund

Swedish design agency Bedow Creative designed this exhibition catalogue for the artist Martin Ålund. The limited-edition print run was presented in a card slip case (above). Images and text align to a single-grid structure, with the insertion of coloured graphic devices to denote the beginning of a new section. The simplicity of the design presents the work in a delicate and considered way.

i en vidare mening får att förstå vad som står på spel – för hur då skulle måleriet kunna vara friskt i en situation där det antingen tvingas ge upp inför varufetischismen och masskonsumtionens krav på lättillgänglighet, eller också liser in sig i en elitism som lyckas hålla sig immun genom att vända sig bort från sin publik?

Ålund målar stämningar, både stämningar som vi känner igen (av kris, sorg, förlust, men också den förändring som detta möjliggör) och ännu obekanta stämningar som lànkar vidare. Genom detta framställande av det nya, genom dessa avskuggningar av den mening som är på väg, bjuds vi på möjligheter att lära oss mer om oss själva och världen: konsten föregriper här de t som filosofin och psykologin sedan kan fortsätta att artikulera. Men det är också något mer in ett mentalt tillstånd som gestaltas, närmare det som Freud kallade vår »psykiska realitet«, vilket är långt mer komplext än något blott fantiserat, något upplevt. Det är vår egentliga unscen (i en djupare mening) där världen hela tiden framkallas. I det avseendet föregår denna »plats« den bärande oppositionen mellan kultur och natur, etc. Den är i Ålunds gestaltning genomkorsad av både kulturhistoria och populärkultur, en strängt medialiserad realitet, men som också här spär in ett djupt slähligt vikande. Det är ett slickt, urbant, postmetafysiskt måleri samtidigt som det ger vittnesbörd om ett intimt och personligt tilltal.

I samtal med Ålund återkommer han till det ambivalenta, till tvetydigheten när han beskriver sitt arbete: det handlar om att gestalta både det vackra och det fula, det ironiskt avmätta och det uppriktiga etc. Det ambivalenta förhållningssättet är ju också allstedan de Beauvoir och Merleau-Ponty inte bara färbundet med en existentialistisk etik (har ska jag kunna realisera mits egen frihet samtidigt som jag annorlar för den andras frihet?) och kroppens fenomenologi (jag är både subjekt och objekt, både *corps* och *chair*), utan har blivit ett slags varumärke för hela vår senkapitalistiska kultur. Men också Pan, libreleden för satan, är ett klassit väsen – till hälften get, till hälften människa – vilket Platon omedelbart uppmärksammar i sin simulerade etymologiska genealogi (*Kratylos, 408b*). För Platon skrivs denna klyvnad direkt i idéfästans ontologi: Pans fader är Hermes, språkets och tolkningens gud, och eftersom logos är dubbelt, både »sant och falskt« (*alethés te kai pseudés*) och just därför kan beteckna precis allt, pan, så har även somn två delar (*difwr*). Den övre, sanna delen är jämn och jordig och vistas uppe hos gudarna, medan den nedre, falska delen är grov, getlik och tragisk och vistas därfor och flesinnigas. •

har mänsniskorna. Ålunds måleri arbetar hela tiden med detta dubbla register, där den ena handen målar högt upp i sanningsdimensionen medan den andra målar den mänskliga existensens tragedi.

Vår böjelekologiska tidsilder beskrivs ofta i termer av »överinnanande« av platonismen, men det kanske snarare handlar om en slags realiserad platonism, där det översinnliga, transcendenta har inkorporerats i det sinnligt-immanenta. Hos Ålund bör det avbildade heller inte längre fattas som något externt i förhållande till det måleriska språket och våra andra kommunikationssystem. Den stormspråkiga referenspunkten sammanfaller med sitt materiella uttryck, liksom det högre skiner igenom och ger lyskraft åt det lägre, eftersom det skarpa och rena bara skulle blända oss utan det skitiga.

I Ålunds målningar finns reminiscenser av en natur, som ett eko av ett klassiskt naturmåleri där ett träd, ett hus, eller en mänsniska kvarstår som symboler för sig själva, men där dessa objekt också och måste lika mycket beteckna något annat: en längtan eller tecknets fullhet som något återvunnet. Men denna längtan måste inte därför fattas som ett svkande efter något som en gång existerat, utan kanske istället förstås bättre som något som blivit till genom denna process (det vaknade objektskit är det som kommer att ha varit det förlorade, det vi sörjer). Dessutom, och bortom detta nostalgiska register, är de figurativa resterna också en antydan om det kommande, ett utpekande av det okända, det som är på väg mot (en alltid uppskjuten) bestämning, en mening på väg, men som aldrig fullt ut kan realiseras. För vad är ett träd, ett hus, en mänsniska? Det vet vi lika litet (och lika mycket) idag som i tidernas begynnelse, och genom Ålunds målningar påminns vi om denna konstnativa obestämdhet. Det är i Lacans beskrivningar av det reella (*le reel*) vi finner de kanske mest intressanta samtida försöken att på ett teoretiskt plan artikulera den generella strukturen hos denna längtan. Ålunds målningar ger specifika ingångar till denna problematik som är mer detaljerade och ingående än vad det teoretiskt verk någonsin kan vara, samtidigt som tolkningsproblematiken på ett korrelativt sätt givetvis blir mer akut. Har ska då förhållandet mellan filosofins generaliseringar och det enskilda konstverket förstå? Det handlar inte om att applicera filosofiska resonemang på konsten, utan om att låta disciplinerna utforskar ett gemensamt fält. Den enskilda målningen här därmed den vridpunkt där filosofins abstraktionsnivå singulariseras och flesinnligas. •

TURHAROUNDPHRASE
Nicholas Smith, philosopher

"The King of Rock" had his Graceland, "The King of Pop" his (now abandoned) Neverland, but the American popular culture of course has deeper roots than that which meets the eye. It was Disney's screen adaptation of Peter Pan in 1953 that made Neverland known to a wider public, but its more interesting, darker aspects related to sexuality and death that are present in Barrie's novels and plays from the beginning of the century are all but obliterated. But given the origin of Pan in Arcadian mythology—which was always somewhat despised by classical Greek culture—this theme will return, albeit in a charged form.

The new paintings by Ålund are a shock to the senses: baroque, adorned post-romanticism, packed with glitzy colours, they seem to point out a strange place that one both recognises and yet is sure never to have seen before. If for a moment one was to regard them as nature paintings—which would be misleading—one could say that Ålund has laid down the dystopian dimension of nature in the same way that Caspar David Friedrich discovered the tragedy of landscape. But if it is a kind of "dystopian nature", a jungle which seems to grow into and over itself, it is one where the pastoral, Arcadian landscape already from the outset is inseparably intertwined with the metropolitan in a poisoned beauty. Never Never Land thus becomes the name of a locus that is neither one nature nor another, neither landscape nor city but another site, earlier than these.

Taking the risk of subjectivising painting by once

more appealing to consciousness as the ultimate horizon for an understanding of art, I would like to suggest that this classical trope from Hegelian metaphysics could be given a further twist. Instead of leading to a closing, the new philosophy provides possibilities of conceptualising art as the very dimension of freedom, as the openness of being, in a radically new way. For the concept of consciousness that for instance Husserl presents in his latest texts in fact opens its presupposed unshakable foundation (Descartes' *fundamentum inconcussum*) to a ceaseless process of selftemporalization in the source of the subject's self-constitution. This process, contrary to the views of much recent debate in the wake of Derrida, also consists in a twofold mode of making absent: both my own constant self-alienation in relation to the others, when I live myself in the past, the future and imaginary worlds) and my own likewise constant self-alienation in relation to the others, when I live myself in the their lives. This is really the same process that Freud calls the "cooperation and opposition" between Eros and Thanatos, where Eros is constantly striving to gather that which Thanatos tears apart. *Love Will Tear Us Apart*, as Joy Division sang, foundation and abyss, *Grund* and *Abgrund*, meet in a modern version of the Heraclitean trope "the one differing from itself".

The sheer material quality of the colour, the excess of coloration, of colour juxtapositions that do not intrinsically harmonize, seem to be a configuration of experiences belonging to an unwell subject, in the vicinity of that "nausea" that both philosophers and writers have analyzed. Thanks to Freud we now know that the "discomfort in our culture" and the neurotical experience is a generalized condition that is not reserved to "the others", and as Deleuze and Guattari have shown, not something that primarily stems from a specific social constellation (such as the bourgeois family), but is the result of an originary and constitutive splitting. To be a subject today is to be "mentally ill" in a certain sense: we are the polymorph perverse creatures that have grown up, and Ricœur for instance speaks of *le cogito blessé*, the wounded cogito, as the philosophical consequence of the discovery of the unconscious in his great book on Freud. But perhaps it is just as much towards the concept of art itself that one has to turn in order to understand what is at stake. For how could painting be healthy in a situation where it either has to give in to the commodity fetishism and the demands of simplicity from mass consumerism, or else enclose itself in an elitism which

Websites

The advent of the world wide web and online media has seen a migration from the page to the screen. Many of the skills and principles of layout design are directly transferable to this new media, although there are slightly different naming structures and conventions.

In an online environment the basic functions of layout design are the same. The design should be structured to solicit a certain response, be it to inform, entertain or guide the reader. There are many similarities to the printed page. The content is generally structured using columns to contain text, and these are separated by dividing spaces, or DIVS.

An obvious point of difference between a physical book and an online page is that a book is always of two parts: a recto and a verso page, with a physical dividing gutter through the centre. The online page is a single entity: one solid page. Therefore the layout of the online page is treated more as a panoramic or vista, rather than a pair of pages forming a double-page spread. There is a paradox in this transition, however, in that web pages will frequently mirror or appropriate the 'style' of a book (as shown in the example on the following spread, where certain parts of the site are constructed to look and behave like printed pages).

The other main consideration with websites is whether to create the page completely out of Flash, or to use HTML. Both have advantages and disadvantages. A site built using Flash can be aesthetically controlled to a greater degree by the designer. It can be made not to scale, to use specific fonts, and to contain complex animations. An HTML site, in contrast, tends to scale and also displays fonts differently depending on the end-user. HTML sites are also more easily trawled by search engines, making them more democratic and accessible.

Client: Efectius
Design: Dorian
Layout synopsis: Flexible design, maintaining a strong sense of order and control

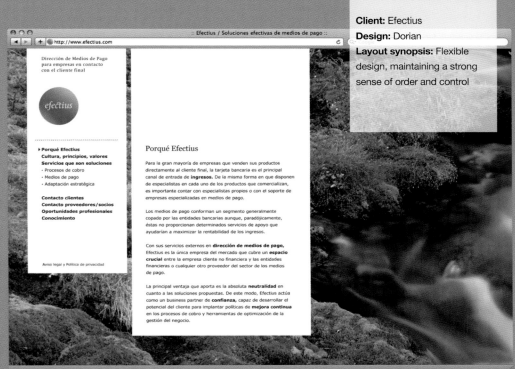

In this site, the background image remains a fixed size, but by expanding or collapsing the browser window, you see more or less of it. The greyscale image provides a base, or canvas, for the text elements to be laid onto.

Media

Efectius

This corporate website for payment solution company, Efectius, uses full bleed imagery and defined 'blocks' of information to create a strong sense of order and control. The text panes expand or shrink depending on the level of content.

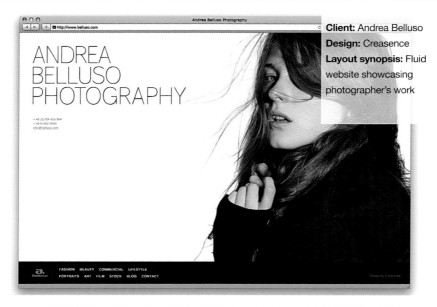

Client: Andrea Belluso
Design: Creasence
Layout synopsis: Fluid website showcasing photographer's work

Andrea Belluso

Shown is a website designed by Alexander Nevolin of Czech Republic design collective Creasence. The website, for photographer Andrea Belluso, features a fluid approach, so that if the browser window is extended, the images resize to fit, as shown opposite. Sections of the site also act as mini vignettes, or image stories, juxtaposing one image against another, as shown above.

Images resize depending on the size of the open browser window. Shown here is the same page, but viewed in different window sizes. This fluid approach allows the images to be used as large as possible, without excluding viewers using smaller monitors or handheld devices.

Media

A thumbnail menu system nestling along the base of the site allows for an instant overview and easy access to the images on the site. This menu also disappears when not in use, making the focus of the site a celebration of photographic image.

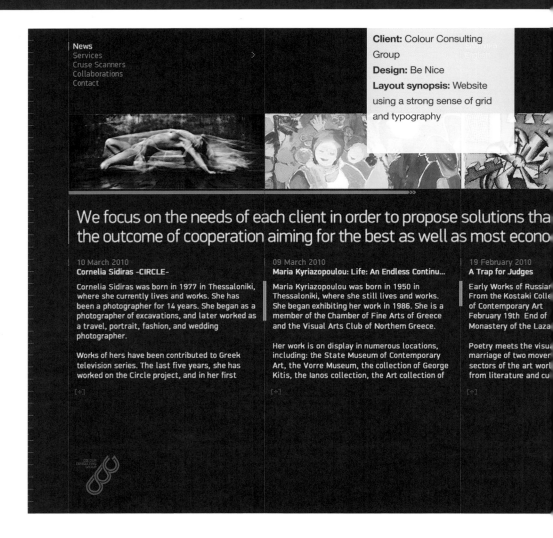

Client: Colour Consulting Group

Design: Be Nice

Layout synopsis: Website using a strong sense of grid and typography

News
Services
Cruse Scanners
Collaborations
Contact

We focus on the needs of each client in order to propose solutions tha
the outcome of cooperation aiming for the best as well as most econo

10 March 2010
Cornelia Sidiras -CIRCLE-

Cornelia Sidiras was born in 1977 in Thessaloniki, where she currently lives and works. She has been a photographer for 14 years. She began as a photographer of excavations, and later worked as a travel, portrait, fashion, and wedding photographer.

Works of hers have been contributed to Greek television series. The last five years, she has worked on the Circle project, and in her first

[+]

09 March 2010
Maria Kyriazopoulou: Life: An Endless Continu...

Maria Kyriazopoulou was born in 1950 in Thessaloniki, where she still lives and works. She began exhibiting her work in 1986. She is a member of the Chamber of Fine Arts of Greece and the Visual Arts Club of Northern Greece.

Her work is on display in numerous locations, including: the State Museum of Contemporary Art, the Vorre Museum, the collection of George Kitis, the Ianos collection, the Art collection of

[+]

19 February 2010
A Trap for Judges

Early Works of Russiar
From the Kostaki Colle
of Contemporary Art
February 19th End of
Monastery of the Laza

Poetry meets the visua
marriage of two mover
sectors of the art worl
from literature and cu

[+]

Colour Consulting Group

This website for specialist reproduction house CCG, uses a black base to highlight the importance of colour. The site uses a series of vertical strips containing news stories, (as shown above), that lead to expanded sections, (shown right). The site has references to the printed page, in the way that columns of type are arranged, but it also exploits the possibilities of online media. It uses a secondary colour, red, to create a simple hierarchy and to aid navigation. You will also notice a small symbol in the top right of the website page. This allows the user to toggle between a full-screen mode, which is arguably more immersive, and a normal-viewing configuration.

[+]

11 February 2010
WHO WE ARE - This is a LIGHTROOM project

915)
seum

Symbolically lighting the 8 rooms of TAF (The Art Foundation), 43 photographers-insightful observers- delve into their vision and focus on our urban existence, revealing personal desires, interpersonal meetings, imaginative journeys, travels in time, symbolisms and directorial debuts, all the while exhibiting the testimonials of their need for the deeper meaning of the phrase who we are...

d

give

09 February 2010
Nikos Alexiou Nikos Triantafyllou

Because of the wonderful and methodically built friendship between Nikos Alexiou and Nikos Triantafyllou, the Lola Nikolaou Gallery will present selections from their recent works in the exhibition opening on February 9th, 2010.

The works of art of Nikos Alexiou and Nikos Triantafyllou are, above all, a continual dialogue, without words, of each artist with his life. With a poetic style, discussing loves, friendships, and

16 January 2010
Athena Tacha, From Public

This is an exhibition with a character supervised by Kat Syrago Tsiara, in cooperation Gallery of Larissa-Y.I. Katsi John F. Kostopoulos Founda exhibition, over 100 works o presented, substantiating, f Greece, her important work conceptual art.

[+]

Media

Moving image
Moving image covers a broad range of media, including television, film, cinema and online experiences.

For many of these applications, multiple formats are at the designer's fingertips. However, there are a number of 'standards' that can be used as a guide. Generally, the format used is dictated by the ultimate placement of the film or animation. For example, most films for cinema will be shot in the wider format of either 2.39:1, or 1.85:1. They are then re-edited for use on televisions. The standard now adopted by most TV manufacturers is the familiar 16:9 format, while many legacy TVs and computer monitors are in a 4:3 format.

Content filmed or produced on a wider format can be played on narrower aspect ratios. This is done by either 'cropping' and 'zooming' (though this can result in sections of a film being missed on either side), or by 'letterboxing'. Letterboxing adds horizontal mattes to the top and bottom section of a piece of filming, preserving the original aspect ratio.

4:3

Shown left are three commonly used aspect ratios used in film and television. 4:3 is a common TV format, 16:9 a wide-screen format, and 2.39:1 a cinema or theatre format. In each of these aspect ratios the very edge perimeter needs to be avoided when using text. As a general guide, around 10 per cent on all edges is classed as a safe zone, as shown below.

16:9

2.39:1

Type safe zone

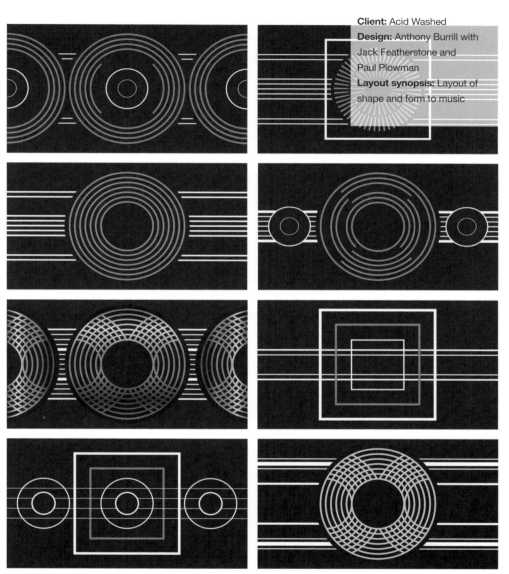

Client: Acid Washed
Design: Anthony Burrill with Jack Featherstone and Paul Plowman
Layout synopsis: Layout of shape and form to music

Media

Snake

This music video for the track 'Snake' by Acid Washed on Record Makers features a series of simple geometric shapes, reflecting the pace of the music. The shapes playfully interact, and function across a horizontal plane, becoming increasingly complicated, and layered, as the music reaches crescendo points.

Client: Fena
Design: Beetroot
Layout synopsis: Energetic, pop-style layout advertising a clothing store

Fena

These stills are taken from an advertising campaign for the clothing store Fena. They use bold, Pop Art colours and the design makes use of a simple range-left alignment, with key words and phrases animated in a flashing array of colours. The reduction of these messages creates a fun, youthful approach, reflecting the target audience.

ME
BETTY BARCLAY
ESCADA
& you

CLOTHES
ACCESSORIES
SALE
& you

CLOTHES
FASHION
SALE
& you

CLOTHES
ACCESSORIES

WINTER
FASHION

TOMMY HILFIGER
ESCADA
BETTY BARCLAY

Media

Pop Art

An art movement started in the United States that embraces motifs of popular culture, for example comic books, advertising, or the mass-produced objects of the time.

Packaging

Packaging design offers the designer the chance to work in three dimensions. This demands a whole new approach to layout design.

A packaged item can't be thought of in the same way as a book or on-screen layout. Packaging has to work in an immediate way, grabbing attention on-shelf, but it also has to be subtle enough to be considered desirable. The aim of packaging design is usually to meet these two requirements, encourage a purchase, and to instil a sense of pride of ownership.

In page and screen layouts we normally consider a design's relationship to the perimeter. We construct margins and guides to form a relationship with the edge of the page. In packaging design, as can be seen opposite, the distinction between the edge isn't always clear, as packages have fronts, backs, sides, tops and bases. They are also rarely seen as flat artworks. They are held, rotated, used, and stored in their own way, and the placement of graphic elements should help to make them more desirable, but also more usable.

Scale
We are used to working with typography in sizes that relate to the printed page. On packaging, however, there is a difference in the way users look at typography. There needs to be a balance between its on-shelf presence and its impact at a more intimate level when in use in people's homes.

Transferable skills
There are a number of transferable skills from traditional graphic design into packaging design. Colour, hierarchy, the pace that we reveal information, legibility, even deconstruction can all be used in the development of packaging designs.

Client: Sound ID
Design: Andrew Pollak
Layout synopsis: Calm,
ordered layout, to reflect
product's features

SOUND **iD**

Sound ID **300**

Advanced Science
Clear Sound

Wireless Bluetooth Headset

Sound ID **300**
Wireless Bluetooth Headset

Bluetooth®

PersonalSound™
In addition to the volume control,
you have 3 custom hearing choices
available to increase speech clarity
and boost your listening power.

Environmental Mode
When selected, the Environmental
Mode will amplify and increase your
listening power between calls, so
you don't have to remove the
headset.

NoiseNavigation™
Multiple microphones and advanced
sound processing removes
unwanted background noise for
clear calls.

Works with 2 Mobile Phones
Allows the SID400 to be active with
two Bluetooth phones.

All Day Wearing Comfort
RealComfort EarLoops in 3 sizes
provides exceptional comfort with
nothing over your ear. For added
security, an optional over-the-ear
hook is included.

Multiple Charging Options
A standard Micro USB connector
allows charging via AC wall outlet
(100-200V) or USB connection on
a laptop or PC.

Specifications
7 Hrs. Talk Time/10 Days Standby
Light Weight .28 oz./8 g.
Bluetooth 2.1+ EDR and eSCO
MultiPoint Connection
Easy & Secure Simple Pairing
Automatic Volume Control
Micro USB to USB Cable
AC Wall Charger (100V-240V)

Sound ID and the Sound ID logo is a registered trademark of Sound ID.
Bluetooth® trademarks are used by Sound ID under license. © Sound ID 2008.

*Please check with your local regulations.

Designed in Palo Alto, Ca. USA
Manufactured in China

Media

Sound ID 300 Wireless Bluetooth Headset

This packaging by American designer Andrew Pollak features a layout intended
to reflect the qualities of the product. The bluetooth headset's main feature is its
ability to reduce background noise. The packaging reflects this with a sense of
clean, calm stillness. The use of grey and blue tonal typography within white
space creates an ordered and structured layout. Consideration is also given here
to the reverse of the packaging, which calmly presents the unit's features.

Client: The Zeeman Group
Design: Studio Kluif
Layout synopsis: Use of background image patter as a signifier for the extent of the range.

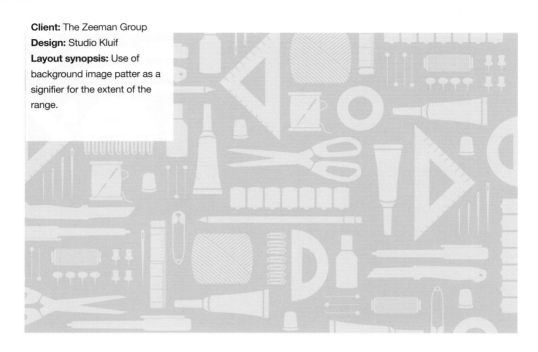

Elastiek   Gummiband
Élastique   Elastic band

10 M

ZEEMAN
www.zeeman.com   C.39767
070900

30X   Naainaalden assorti
       Aiguilles à coudre assortiment
       Nähnadeln sortiert
       Sewing-needles assorted

ZEEMAN
www.zeeman.com   C.39766
070900

2X   Naaigaren
       Fil à couture
       Nähgarn
       Sewing-thread

± 450 M

Zeeman Handy Box

This packaging 'system' uses a consistent approach to layout and colour. A base pattern, shown above, is used as a background over the entire range of textile supplies. A simple band, iconography and a simple text hierarchy create an impactful and instantly recognisable brand.

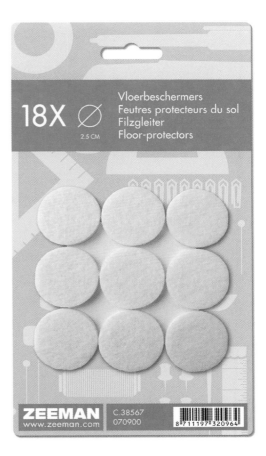

This utilitarian 'system' allows for the integration of new products quickly and effectively. Zeeman stock an ever expanding range of items, and this flexibility in the packaging layout allows for almost any variation. The hierarchy of information is controlled using the blue coloured stripes. This information is ordered into a simple structure.

Media

Comotú Amor

The outer packaging of this perfume uses a <u>tessellating</u> image to create a continual image of petals floating in the wind. This simple motif represents a modern approach to this value fragrance sold in Mercadona stores throughout Spain. The bottle uses type set broadside, creating a simple, chic design.

Client: RNB laboratories
Design: Lavernia & Cienfuegos
Layout Tessellating image on
outer pack, broadside type on
bottle

comoel**amor**woman
eau**de**toilette
naturalspray · 3.4FL.OZ./100ml ℮

como**tú**

Media

Tessellation
The tiling of an image that leaves no gaps

Client: Delhaize Group
Design: Mouse Graphics
Layout Design that actively
uses the edges and corners of
the pack

Fruit Juice

This tetrapack design for Greek supermarket AB, displays an important facet
when designing packaging – corners. All packs have edges, folds and
construction details that need to be taken into account. Here the fruit motifs or
icons, playfully wrap around the packaging adding a layer of interest. The
packaging and layout also avoid the use of any graphic effects, reinforcing the
idea that the product is natural and fresh.

Client: Zarbanis Distillery
Design: Mouse Graphics
Layout Clear hierarchy of
product name and creative
use of both sides of the bottle

Media

Ouzo

In this design for a new brand of the famous Greek drink Ouzo, the designers have kept the hierarchy of information clear and concise. Although bottles are usually designed to be viewed from the front, they are often viewed from an angle. In this design, keeping the reverse clear from printing allows the brand's identity to remain visible at all times. The design makes strong use of cyan, a colour closely associated with Greece and Greek culture, and a miniature Greek church is printed on the reverse of the bottle (seen through the glass and the clear liquid inside), echoing the 'Greek-style' miniatures found on sale in small tourist shops.

Client: Illamasqua
Design: Propaganda
Layout Packaging using a
centred alignment for the front
and a broadside orientation for
the sides

Art of Darkness (above)

This packaging is for a range of make-up, producing products in deep luxurious
primary colours and rich jewel-like metallics. The theme for the season, Art of
Darkness, is centred around fantasy creatures and has medieval references. With
packaging, it is crucial to remember how it differs from any other media – it is
three-dimensional. It has sides, a base, and isn't viewed solely from the front, it is
handled, rotated and viewed from multiple angles. Shown above are the final
packages, front on, as would be seen in a retail display. Shown top is one of the
pack fronts, flanked by its decorative sides. On these sides the text runs
broadside.

Glossary

The subject of layout contains many technical terms that can be confusing and overwhelming. This glossary is intended to define some of the most common technical terms in usage in order to facilitate a better understanding and appreciation of the subject, although it will be far from exhaustive.

An understanding of the terms used in layout can help in the articulation of creative ideas to other designers, to commissioning clients, as well as printers and other professionals that will work to produce the design. The knowledge and use of standard industry terms minimises the risk of any misunderstanding that could complicate or even ruin a job.

Glossary

Glossary

Accordion or concertina fold
Two or more parallel folds that go in opposite directions and open out like an accordion.

Alignment
Text location within a text block in the vertical and horizontal planes.

Appropriation
The borrowing of a style, typically used elsewhere, as the basis for a design.

Assemblage
An artistic composition made from various odds and ends centred around a given theme or bringing together several different themes.

Asymmetrical grids
A grid that is the same on recto and verso pages and typically introduces a bias towards one side of the page (usually the left).

Baseline
The imaginary line upon which the bases of all capital letters and most lower case letters are positioned.

Baseline grid
The graphic foundation on which a design is constructed.

Binding
Any of several processes for holding together the pages or sections of a publication to form a book, magazine, brochure or some other format using stitches, wire, glue or other media.

Bleed
Printed content that extends past where the pages will be trimmed.

Body copy
The matter that forms the predominant textual element of a piece of work.

Captions
Text that describes or names graphic elements.

Colour fall
The pages of the publication, as depicted in the imposition plan, which will receive a special colour or varnish or are to be printed on a different stock.

Column
An area or field into which text is flowed.

Cross-alignment
A typographical hierarchy where the different levels share a common relationship and can be aligned in the same grid.

Display type
Large and/or distinctive type that is intended to attract the eye. Specifically cut to be viewed from a distance.

Dummy
Provisional layout showing illustration and text positions as they will appear in the final reproduction.

Exquisite corpse
Surrealist technique that exploits the happy chance of accident in image/text juxtaposition.

Extent
The number of pages in a book.

Flood colour
Printing a colour to bleed on all sides.

Folio
A sheet of paper folded in half is a folio and each half of the folio is one page. A single folio has four pages.

Format
The shape and size of a book or page.

Gatefold
A page whereby the left and right edges fold inward with parallel folds and meet in the middle of the page without overlapping.

Golden section
A division in the ratio 8:13 that produces harmonious proportions.

Greeking
Nonsensical words in a layout to give a visual representation of how the text will look. Also called dummy text.

Grid
A guide or template to help obtain design consistency.

Gutter
The space that comprises the fore or outer edge of a page, that is parallel to the back and the trim. The central alley-way where two pages meet at the spine, and the space between text columns is also referred to as the gutter.

Hanging or drop lines
A series of horizontal positioning lines that provide hook points for image and text block placement.

Head margin
The space at the top of the page; also called top margin.

Hierarchy
A logical, organised and visual guide for text headings indicating different levels of importance.

Horizontal alignment
The horizontal alignment of text in the field.

Hyphenation
The hyphen inserted at the point a word is broken in a justified text block.

Imposition
The arrangement of pages in the sequence and position in which they will appear when printed before being cut, folded and trimmed.

Imposition plan
A series of thumbnails of all the pages of a publication showing how it is laid out.

International Paper Sizes (ISO)
A range of standard metric paper sizes.

Justified
Text that is extended across the measure and aligned on both left and right margins.

Juxtaposition
The placement of contrasting images side by side.

Layout
The arrangement of text and images according to a plan and to provide the appearance of the printed page.

Letter spacing
The distance between the letters of a word.

Locking (to a grid)
Fixing text to the baseline grid so that the grid determines spacing between text lines.

Margin
The spaces surrounding a text block at the sides, top and bottom of a page.

Marginalia
Text matter that appears in the page margin.

Measure
The width in picas of a page or text column.

Module-based grid
A grid composed of an array of modules or fields, usually squares.

Orientation
The plane or direction in which text and images are used.

Pagination
The arrangement and numbering of pages in a publication.

Passe partout
A frame or border around an image or other element.

Print finishing
Production processes undertaken to complete a printed work including, folding, binding and cutting.

Recto
The right-hand page of an open book.

Running heads
Repeated text that appears on each page of a work or section, also called header, running title or straplines.

Spot colour or special
A specially mixed colour used for printing.

Stock
The paper to be printed upon.

Structure
The skeleton to which elements on a page are positioned.

Substrate
The material or surface to be printed upon.

Swatch
A bolt-held book of colour or material samples.

Symmetrical grid
Grids on recto and verso pages that mirror one another.

Tip-in
To attach an inset in a book or magazine by gluing along the binding edge such as to tip-in a colour plate.

Verso
The left-hand page of an open book.

Vertical alignment
The vertical alignment of text in the field.

Word spacing
The distance between words.

X-height
The height of lower case letters such as 'x' with no ascenders or descenders.

Glossary

Exercises

On the following pages are a series of
six exercises, relating to some of the
principles we have looked at in this book.

These exercises are intended to be
a starting point for further exploration
and development in the field of layout
design. No matter what area of design
you practice in, from packaging to film,
print to websites, there a underpinning
principles and techniques that can be
used.

Exercise #1
Scale

Premise
Computer technology now allows text to be set at any size, though there are standard typesizes, as shown below:

7 9 10 12 14 18 24 36 48 60

Certain type sizes are frequently used for specific functions. Body copy, for example, will often be set at 9, 10 or 12pt, while smaller sizes are used for captioning, and larger sizes for headlines.

Exercise
1. Assign a new naming structure to these, and as many other type sizes you see fit.
2. This naming structure can be based on one of several facets. It could, for instance, be based on how it is being used: body copy or captioning, etc. It could equally be based on application: book or poster, etc. It could even be based on the historical uses of these typesizes.
3. Consider how this system could be used to simplify specification of typography for certain situations.
4. Produce a series of posters demonstrating your findings.

Outcomes
This exercise should encourage you to look carefully at type sizes. Why do certain typesizes work better for certain applications, and should this status quo be challenged? You need to carefully consider how printed items are used. For example, if you were to specify typesizes to be used in book design, you might design a series of sizes based on the weight of the book, and the situation it is read in. This might produce typesizes called book, heavy book, and travel book, for instance.

Exercises

See
Arrangement p.94–97
Orientation p.136–145

Exercise #2
Deconstruction

Premise

Within this book we have looked at how a layout can be structured or unstructured, and how designers sometimes choose to work without a grid. Designs created without a grid are commonly mis-labelled as examples of 'deconstruction': deconstruction is actually a very ordered and methodical approach to design. If you think of 'construction' in relation to layout, logical steps are taken to 'build' a given design. A newspaper, for example, is made up of a logical set of items, or building blocks: headlines, body copy, dividing rules, for example – these are all used to control and construct the design. Importantly, they relate to a set of requirements that that newspaper has. Headlines, for instance, are there to guide the reader around the page and to act as entry points, body copy is to be easily read, folios run in sequential order, the main story is always on the front...

But what happens if we change these rules? What happens if it is no longer important that the pages run in order, or if we decide that there is no need to have headlines? What happens if we begin to deconstruct the newspaper?

Exercise

1. Take a newspaper, leaflet, recipe or advert.
2. Undertake an audit on the design. What elements are there, and why are some more important than others?
3. Establish a new set of rules to work to. In the case of the newspaper, this might be to put all the headlines on the front page, to make the folios the most important aspect or to set all type at the same size.
4. Produce a series of experimental 'deconstructed' designs, responding to the new set of rules.

Outcomes

This exercise should challenge the axioms of design – things that we have simply come to expect. It should also allow for considered and controlled experimentation. Remember, deconstruction is a logical and ordered approach to generating design and your exercises should reflect this.

See

Structure / unstructure p.152–157
Working without a grid p.62–65

What happens if you unpick or deconstruct a design, and then piece it back together with a new set of intentions or aims? What would a newspaper look like if all the headlines were on the front page? Or if all the images were grouped and all the text set at the same size, but on varying orientations?

Exercise #3
Shape and form

Premise

Russian constructivism and later the Bauhaus in Germany utilised and explored the inherent values and meaning of shape and form. They viewed the three basic shapes – the triangle, the square, and the circle – as having specific properties. The triangle is considered the most dynamic, indicating movement; the square the most solid and rigid of forms and the circle passive, with no harsh edges.

Exercise

1. Take these basic shapes. They can be drawn by hand or cut out of paper.
2. Design a series of layouts using these shapes, exploring the different values they create: pace, rigidity, peacefulness?
3. Explore the relationship between the shape and the perimeter of the page, and the relationship formed by the different shapes together.
4. Produce at least one design for each of the following words:

Harmony	Balance	Thought
Reaction	Discord	Urgency
Speed	Anger	Peace

5. Test these outcomes by conducting a survey: how many people can match the 'shape design' to the words?

Outcomes

This exercise should introduce you to the relationship between shape and meaning.

See
Arrangement p.94–97
Orientation p.136–145

Exercise #4
Hierarchy

Premise

Recipes use a convention of hierarchy in order to enable a user to follow the instructions. Usually consisting of two main elements – ingredients and cooking instructions – a recipe is something we are all familiar with.

Exercise

1. Taking the recipe opposite (or similar), explore different ways that a hierarchy can be introduced using the 'tools' described below. To begin with, use only one tool in any one experiment.

> Placement – Where on the page do you place the items? How does this influence how we read the page? Does this affect the order in which we interpret the items?

> Fonts – How can a hierarchy be introduced using different fonts? You could, for example, use one font for the ingredients and another for the sequential instructions.

> Font size and weight – Altering the font size and weight can introduce an entry point for the reader.

> Colour – Introducing colour will add a clear starting point, or emphasis for certain items.

> Deconstruction – Finally, you could question if this structure is correct: is there another way of conveying this information? Could the information be simplified through the use of icons or graphic devices?

2. Produce a series of posters demonstrating the results of this experiment. Use only one tool.
3. Progress to using more than one tool.

Outcomes

This exercise should enable you to see the changes that can be introduced simply by altering components of a design.

See
Scale p.130–133

Ingredients
For the pastry
255g/9oz plain flour
pinch of salt
140g/5oz hard
margarine or butter
6 tsp cold water

For the filling
3 large Bramley
cooking apples,
chopped, stewed and
cooled
sugar, to taste
caster sugar, to serve

1. Preheat the oven to 200C/400F/Gas 6.
2. Sieve the flour and salt into a bowl.
3. Rub in the margarine or butter until the mixture resembles fine breadcrumbs.
4. Add the cold water to the flour mixture. Using a knife, mix the water into the flour, using your hand to firm up the mixture.
5. Divide the pastry into two halves. Take one half and roll it out so that it is big enough to cover an 20cm/8in enamel or aluminium plate. Trim the edges with a knife.
6. Cover the pastry with the stewed apples and sprinkle with sugar to taste.
7. Roll out the other half of the pastry. Moisten the edge of the bottom layer of pastry and place the second piece on top.
8. Press down on the pastry edges. Trim off any excess pastry with a knife.
9. Flute the edges with a pinching action using your fingers and thumb.
10. Prick the surface of the pastry lightly before placing the pie in the oven. Cook for 20–30 minutes.
11. Slide on to a serving plate, dust with caster sugar and serve.

Exercises

A typical recipe consists of familiar items and a conventional structure. By altering the placement and emphasis of certain items, a hierarchy or level of importance can be introduced.

Exercise #5
Appropriation

Premise
Appropriation involves taking the characteristics of one thing and applying them to another. In layout design there are particular 'styles' of layout that we associate with certain types of information. A bus timetable, for instance, is usually set in a series of vertical columns. A food recipe, in contrast, is usually set with the instructions in one wide column, and the ingredients in an accompanying, narrower column. What would happen if you were to take one format and appropriate it for a new means?

Exercise
1. Take the information from one of the following:

Recipe	Personal letter	Small ads
Newspaper	Timetable	Shopping list
Bank statement	Poem	TV listings guide

Remember: you are to ignore the conventional styling of this information and simply make an audit, or gathering of the information.

2. Re-display this information appropriating one of the following:

Recipe	Personal letter	Small ads
Newspaper	Timetable	Shopping list
Bank statement	Poem	TV listings guide

3. Repeat the exercise combining and appropriating different formats and styles.

Outcomes
This exercise allows you to deconstruct the normal conventions of styling that we are familiar with. This should also indicate new ways of looking at information and narratives.

See
Arrangement p.94–97

Exercise #6
Juxtaposition

Premise
The surrealist artists of the early 1900s made extensive use of juxtaposition, or the element of surprise, and 'non sequitur', where there is seemingly no meaning or created absurdity. Within layout design we often deal with sequential pages and spreads. What is on these pages has meaning, but there is also an additional meaning formed by the relationship of these elements to one another.

Exercise
1. Take two or more sets of reference material. For example, a photograph album and a daily newspaper, or a pack of playing cards and a travel brochure.
2. Create a series of layouts exploring the created meanings found when you place these together.

Outcomes
This exercise should introduce you to the notion of happy accidents, or serendipity. Don't feel restricted or try to make sense of the design while you are working on it, the sense, or nonsense, should be formed without thought or contrivance.

 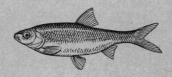 

Exercises

See
Juxtaposition p.170–173
Exquisite corpse p.118–123

Index and acknowledgements

Index compiled by:
Indexing Specialists (UK) Ltd

Index and acknowledgements

Acknowledgements
We would like to thank everyone who supported us during the project, including the many art directors, designers and creatives who showed great generosity in allowing us to reproduce their work. Special thanks to everyone that hunted for, collated, compiled and rediscovered some of the fascinating work contained in this book. Thanks to Xavier Young for his patience, determination and skill in photographing the work showcased in this book and to Heather Marshall for modelling. And a final big thanks to Caroline Walmsley, Brian Morris and all the staff at AVA Publishing who never tired of our requests, enquiries and questions, and supported us throughout.

p.133 Bauhaus Design (colour litho) by German School (20th century) Private Collection/ The Stapleton Collection/ The Bridgeman Art Library Nationality/ copyright status: German/ copyright unknown

Contacts

BASICS
DESIGN

Working with ethics

Lynne Elvins
Naomi Goulder

Publisher's note

The subject of ethics is not new, yet its consideration within the applied visual arts is perhaps not as prevalent as it might be. Our aim here is to help a new generation of students, educators and practitioners find a methodology for structuring their thoughts and reflections in this vital area.

AVA Publishing hopes that these **Working with ethics** pages provide a platform for consideration and a flexible method for incorporating ethical concerns in the work of educators, students and professionals. Our approach consists of four parts:

The **introduction** is intended to be an accessible snapshot of the ethical landscape, both in terms of historical development and current dominant themes.

The **framework** positions ethical consideration into four areas and poses questions about the practical implications that might occur. Marking your response to each of these questions on the scale shown will allow your reactions to be further explored by comparison.

The **case study** sets out a real project and then poses some ethical questions for further consideration. This is a focus point for a debate rather than a critical analysis so there are no predetermined right or wrong answers.

A selection of **further reading** for you to consider areas of particular interest in more detail.

Ethical: aware-ness/ reflect-ion/ debate

Working with ethics

Introduction

Ethics is a complex subject that interlaces the idea of responsibilities to society with a wide range of considerations relevant to the character and happiness of the individual. It concerns virtues of compassion, loyalty and strength, but also of confidence, imagination, humour and optimism. As introduced in ancient Greek philosophy, the fundamental ethical question is: *what should I do?* How we might pursue a 'good' life not only raises moral concerns about the effects of our actions on others, but also personal concerns about our own integrity.

In modern times the most important and controversial questions in ethics have been the moral ones. With growing populations and improvements in mobility and communications, it is not surprising that considerations about how to structure our lives together on the planet should come to the forefront. For visual artists and communicators, it should be no surprise that these considerations will enter into the creative process.

Some ethical considerations are already enshrined in government laws and regulations or in professional codes of conduct. For example, plagiarism and breaches of confidentiality can be punishable offences. Legislation in various nations makes it unlawful to exclude people with disabilities from accessing information or spaces. The trade of ivory as a material has been banned in many countries. In these cases, a clear line has been drawn under what is unacceptable.

But most ethical matters remain open to debate, among experts and lay-people alike, and in the end we have to make our own choices on the basis of our own guiding principles or values. Is it more ethical to work for a charity than for a commercial company? Is it unethical to create something that others find ugly or offensive?

Specific questions such as these may lead to other questions that are more abstract. For example, is it only effects on humans (and what they care about) that are important, or might effects on the natural world require attention too?

Is promoting ethical consequences justified even when it requires ethical sacrifices along the way? Must there be a single unifying theory of ethics (such as the Utilitarian thesis that the right course of action is always the one that leads to the greatest happiness of the greatest number), or might there always be many different ethical values that pull a person in various directions?

As we enter into ethical debate and engage with these dilemmas on a personal and professional level, we may change our views or change our view of others. The real test though is whether, as we reflect on these matters, we change the way we act as well as the way we think. Socrates, the 'father' of philosophy, proposed that people will naturally do 'good' if they know what is right. But this point might only lead us to yet another question: *how do we know what is right?*

You
What are your ethical beliefs?

Central to everything you do will be your attitude to people and issues around you. For some people, their ethics are an active part of the decisions they make every day as a consumer, a voter or a working professional. Others may think about ethics very little and yet this does not automatically make them unethical. Personal beliefs, lifestyle, politics, nationality, religion, gender, class or education can all influence your ethical viewpoint.

Using the scale, where would you place yourself? What do you take into account to make your decision? Compare results with your friends or colleagues.

Your client
What are your terms?

Working relationships are central to whether ethics can be embedded into a project, and your conduct on a day-to-day basis is a demonstration of your professional ethics. The decision with the biggest impact is whom you choose to work with in the first place. Cigarette companies or arms traders are often-cited examples when talking about where a line might be drawn, but rarely are real situations so extreme. At what point might you turn down a project on ethical grounds and how much does the reality of having to earn a living affect your ability to choose?

Using the scale, where would you place a project? How does this compare to your personal ethical level?

01 02 03 04 05 06 07 08 09 10

01 02 03 04 05 06 07 08 09 10

Your specifications

What are the impacts of your materials?

In relatively recent times, we are learning that many natural materials are in short supply. At the same time, we are increasingly aware that some man-made materials can have harmful, long-term effects on people or the planet. How much do you know about the materials that you use? Do you know where they come from, how far they travel and under what conditions they are obtained? When your creation is no longer needed, will it be easy and safe to recycle? Will it disappear without a trace? Are these considerations your responsibility or are they out of your hands?

Using the scale, mark how ethical your material choices are.

Your creation

What is the purpose of your work?

Between you, your colleagues and an agreed brief, what will your creation achieve? What purpose will it have in society and will it make a positive contribution? Should your work result in more than commercial success or industry awards? Might your creation help save lives, educate, protect or inspire? Form and function are two established aspects of judging a creation, but there is little consensus on the obligations of visual artists and communicators toward society, or the role they might have in solving social or environmental problems. If you want recognition for being the creator, how responsible are you for what you create and where might that responsibility end?

Using the scale, mark how ethical the purpose of your work is.

01 02 03 04 05 06 07 08 09 10

01 02 03 04 05 06 07 08 09 10

Working with ethics

One aspect of graphic design that raises an ethical dilemma is that of its relationship with the creation of printed materials and the environmental impacts of print production. For example, in the UK, it is estimated that around 5.4 billion items of addressed direct mail are sent out every year and these, along with other promotional inserts, amount to over half a million tonnes of paper annually (almost 5 per cent of the UK consumption of paper and board). Response rates to mail campaigns are known to be between 1–3 per cent, making junk mail arguably one of the least environmentally friendly forms of print communication. As well as the use of paper or board, the design decisions to use scratch-off panels, heavily coated gloss finishes, full-colour ink-intensive graphics or glues for seals or fixings make paper more difficult to recycle once it has been discarded. How much responsibility should a graphic designer have in this situation if a client has already chosen to embark on a direct mail campaign and has a format in mind? Even if designers wish to minimise the environmental impacts of print materials, what might they most usefully do?

In 1951, Leo Burnett (the famous advertising executive known for creating the Jolly Green Giant and the Marlboro Man) was hired to create a campaign for Kellogg's new cereal, Sugar Frosted Flakes (now Frosties in the UK and Frosted Flakes in the US). Tony the Tiger, designed by children's book illustrator Martin Provensen, was one of four characters selected to sell the cereal. Newt the Gnu and Elmo the Elephant never made it to the shelves and after Tony proved more popular than Katy the Kangaroo, she was dropped from packs after the first year.

Whilst the orange-and-black tiger stripes and the red kerchief have remained, Provensen's original design for Tony has changed significantly since he first appeared in 1952. Tony started out with an American football-shaped head, which later became more rounded, and his eye colour changed from green to gold. Today, his head is more angular and he sits on a predominantly blue background. Tony was initially presented as a character that walked on all fours and was no bigger than a cereal box. By the 1970s, Tony's physique had developed into a slim and muscular six-foot-tall standing figure.

Between 1952 and 1995 Kellogg's are said to have spent more than USD$1 billion promoting Frosted Flakes with Tony's image, while generating USD$5.3 billion in gross US sales But surveys by consumer rights groups such as Which? find that over 75 per cent of people believe that using characters on packaging makes it hard for parents to say no to their children. In these surveys, Kellogg's come under specific scrutiny for Frosties, which are said to contain one third sugar and more salt than the Food Standards Agency recommends. In response, Kellogg's have said: 'We are committed to responsibly marketing our brands and communicating their intrinsic qualities so that our customers can make informed choices.'

Food campaigners claim that the use of cartoon characters is a particularly manipulative part of the problem and governments should stop them being used on less healthy children's foods. But in 2008, spokespeople for the Food and Drink Federation in the UK, said: 'We are baffled as to why Which? wants to take all the fun out of food by banning popular brand characters, many of whom have been adding colour to supermarket shelves for more than 80 years.'

Is it more ethical to create promotional graphics for 'healthy' rather than 'unhealthy' food products?

Is it unethical to design cartoon characters to appeal to children for commercial purposes?

Would you have worked on this project, either now or in the 1950s?

I studied graphic design in Germany, and my professor emphasised the responsibility that designers and illustrators have towards the people they create things for.

Eric Carle
(illustrator)

Working with ethics

Further reading

AIGA
Design Business and Ethics
2007, AIGA

Eaton, Marcia Muelder
Aesthetics and the Good Life
1989, Associated University Press

Ellison, David
Ethics and Aesthetics in European Modernist Literature:
From the Sublime to the Uncanny
2001, Cambridge University Press

Fenner, David E W (Ed)
Ethics and the Arts:
An Anthology
1995, Garland Reference Library of Social Science

Gini, Al and Marcoux, Alexei M
Case Studies in Business Ethics
2005, Prentice Hall

McDonough, William and Braungart, Michael
Cradle to Cradle:
Remaking the Way We Make Things
2002, North Point Press

Papanek, Victor
Design for the Real World:
Making to Measure
1972, Thames & Hudson

United Nations Global Compact
The Ten Principles
www.unglobalcompact.org/AboutTheGC/TheTenPrinciples/index.html